The Complete Guide to Macro and Close-Up Photography

Cyrill Harnischmacher

The Complete Guide to
Macro and Close-Up
Photography

rockynook

The Complete Guide to Macro and Close-Up Photography
Cyrill Harnischmacher

Project editor: Maggie Yates
Project manager: Lisa Brazieal
Marketing: Jessica Tiernan
Copyeditor: Stephanie Pascal
Translator: David Schlesinger
Layout and type: Cyrill Harnischmacher
Cover design: Helmut Krause, www.exclam.de
Indexer: Cyrill Harnischmacher

ISBN: 978-1-68198-052-2
1st Edition 2016 (3rd printing)
© 2016 Cyrill Harnischmacher
All images © Cyrill Harnischmacher, unless otherwise noted

Rocky Nook, Inc.
1010 B Street, Suite 350
San Rafael, CA 94901 USA

www.rockynook.com
info@rockynook.com
(415) 747-8756

Distributed in the UK and Europe by Publishers Group UK
Distributed in the U.S. and all other territories by Publishers Group West

Library of Congress Control Number: 2015958928

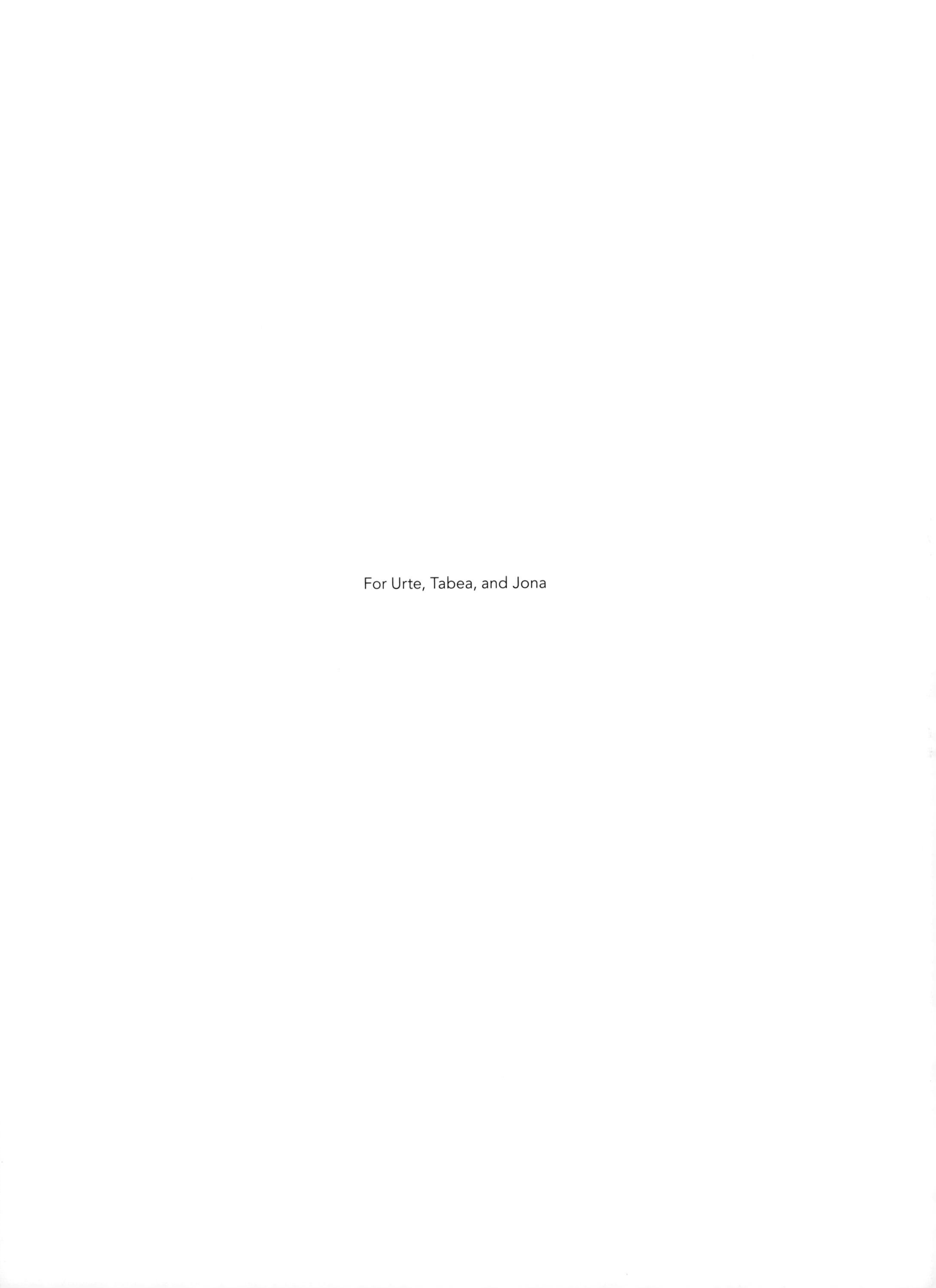
For Urte, Tabea, and Jona

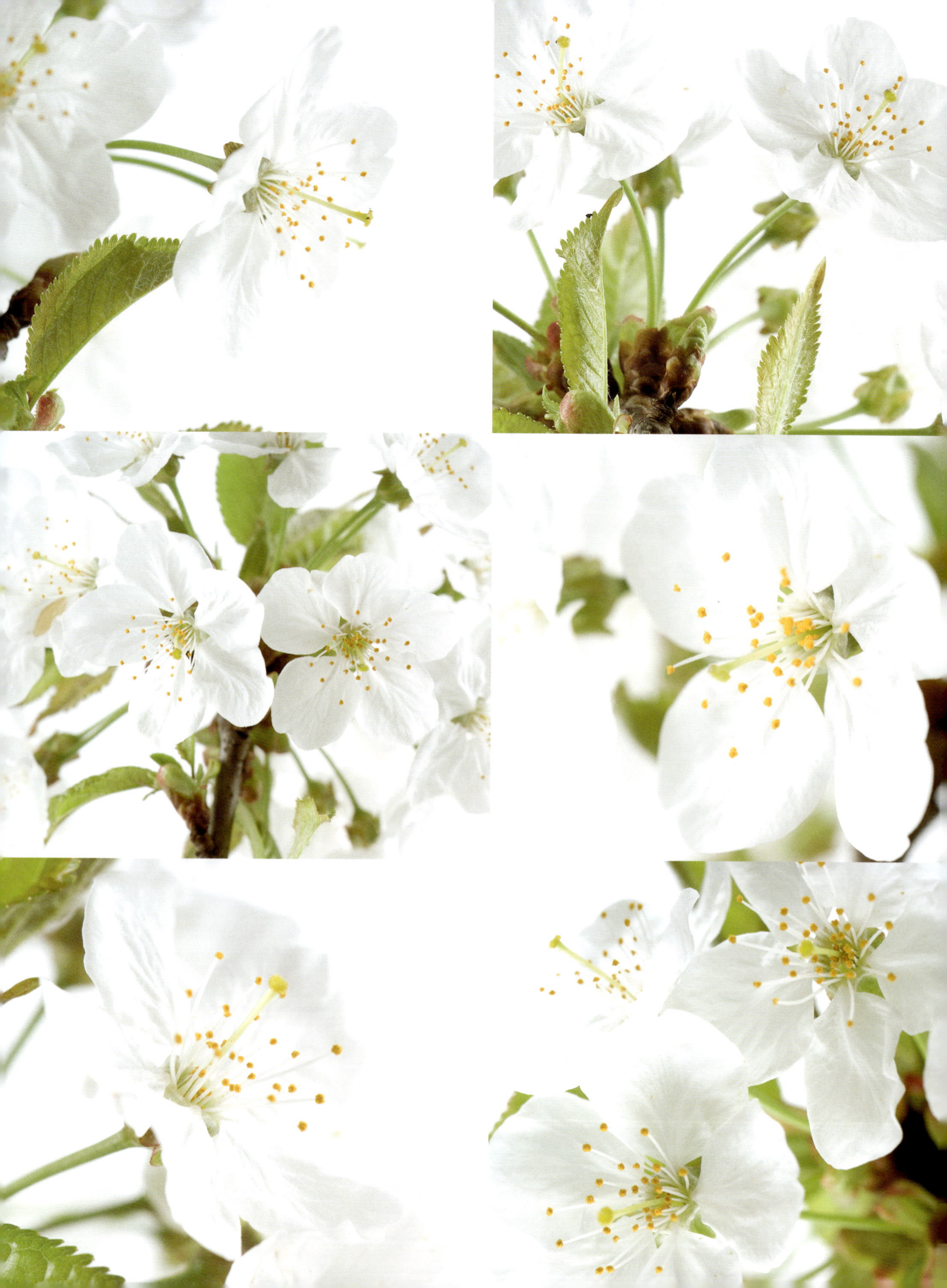

In Japan, cherry blossom festivals are a centuries-long tradition that marks the beginning of spring. The flower of the cherry tree has become a symbol both for pristine beauty and for the transience of time.

These concepts are of central importance to macro photography. With the end of the cold season comes the return of life and movement to the natural world: insects take to the skies, and the first plants begin to bloom.

The quest for that perfect moment when the subject, your perspective, and the light come together in perfect harmony is what photographers live for. A camera and a lens are tools to document these fleeting moments for ourselves and for others. And with macro photography in particular, the technical details are of great concern. But even so, they are simply a means to the end of being able to capture and express your ideas in your pictures. Nevertheless, they are tools that we can't do without, and the more technical know-how you possess, the easier it will be to translate into images what moves you about noteworthy passing subjects in the natural world.

Precisely this mixture of mastery and intuition is what makes photography so exciting. The craft combines the appeal of clearing technical hurdles, the challenge of waiting for the perfect light, and the will to never to accept a compromise that results in an image inferior to your own expectations.

Despite all of the technical knowledge about the craft that I need in order to reach my photographic goals, there is one thing I never want to do without: allowing myself to be carried across a blossom-strewn meadow through a sea of subjects while shooting on instinct—not searching for the perfect moment, but allowing the moment to absorb me completely.

Cyrill Harnischmacher

2016

Table of Contents

Table of Contents

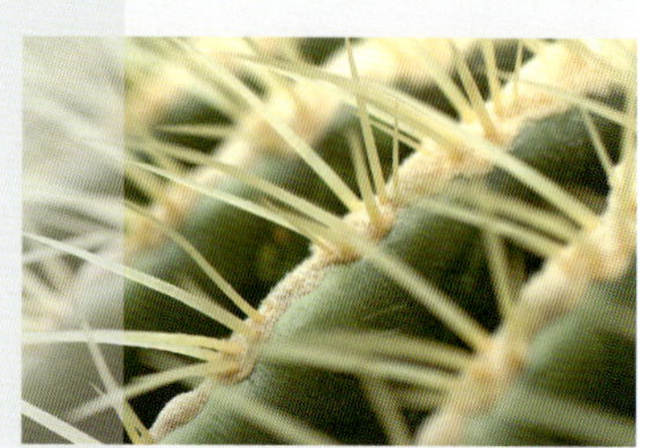

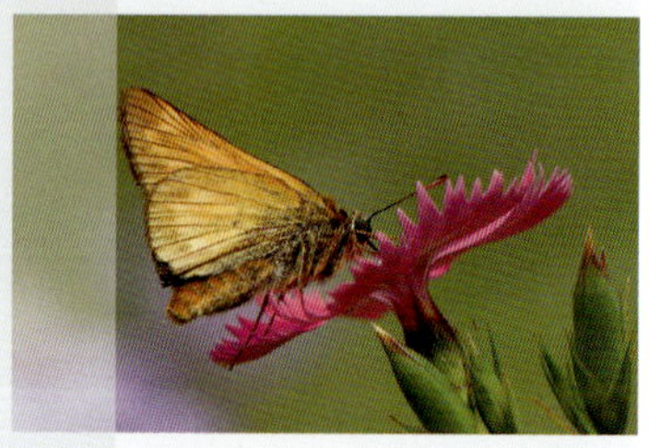

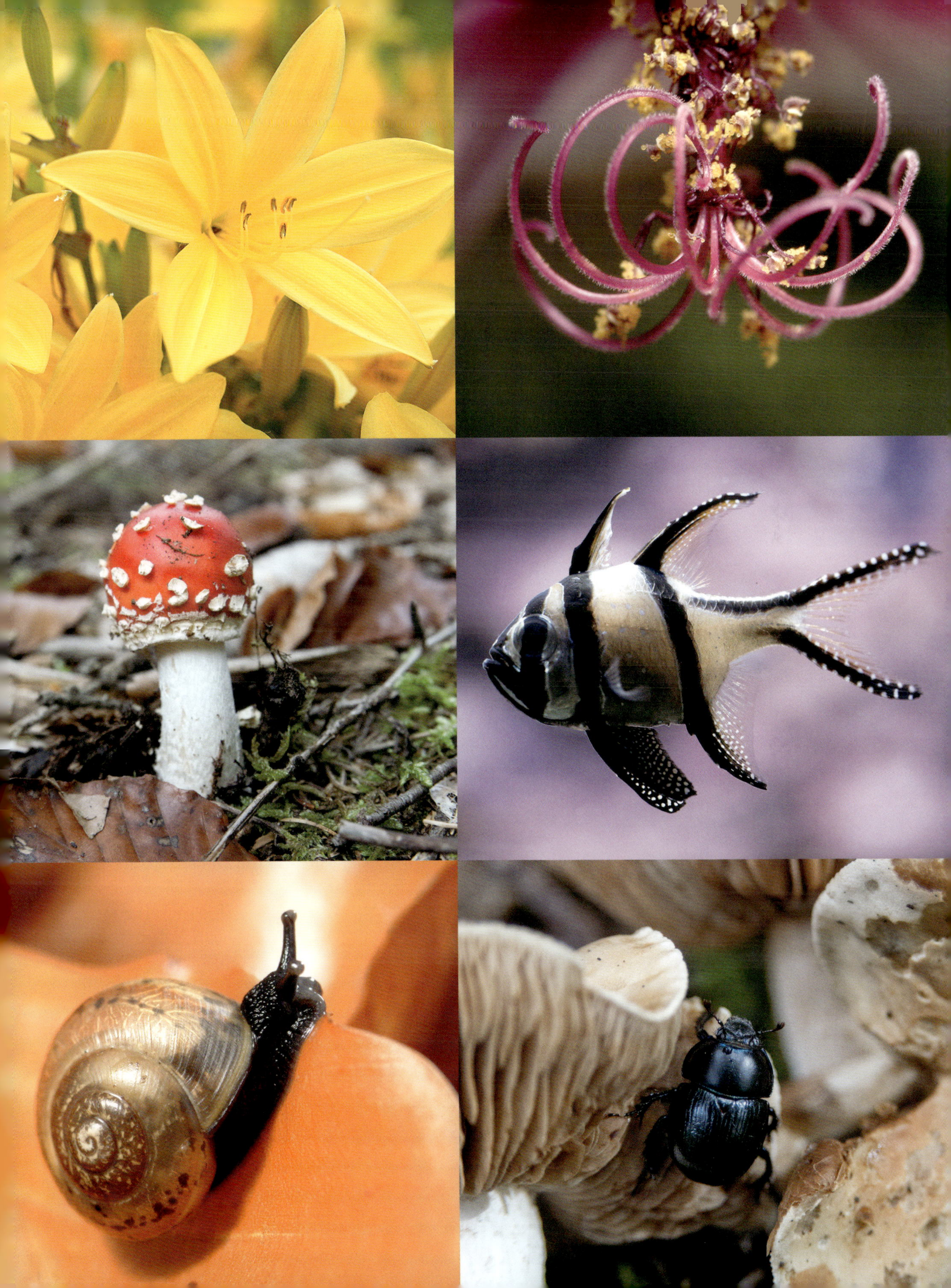

The Fascination of Macro Photography

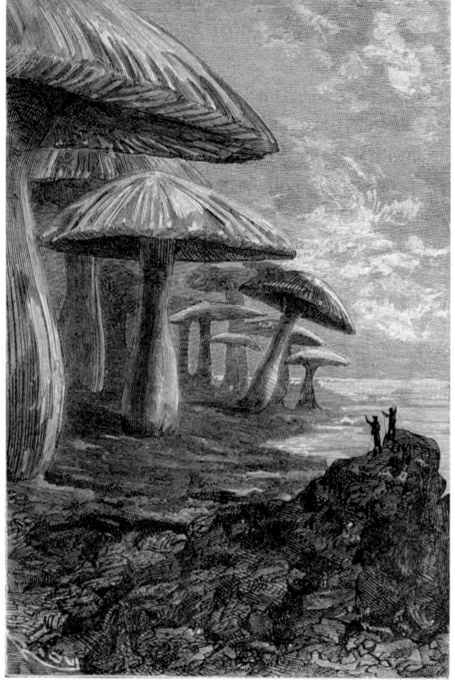

An illustration of a colossal mushroom forest for Jules Verne's novel Journey to the Center of the Earth *by the French artist Édouard Riou*
Image: Public domain

Most of you will know the science fiction novel *Journey to the Center of the Earth* by Jules Verne. I cherished it when I was a child and dreamed of undertaking similar adventures of my own to come face to face with strange animals and to discover objects that people didn't even know existed. Instead of climbing into the crater of the island volcano Snæfellsjökull as the heroes in the book did, however, I eventually picked up a camera and a macro lens to explore hidden worlds in more familiar environs. Macro and close-up photography enable us to discover things that escape our normal powers of perception. We can see parallels to the larger world we inhabit in the smaller and tiniest details around us.

Shapes, Substances, and Structures

The discoveries made while researching the world of the miniscule have had—and continue to have—an influence on our lives that is hard to overstate. Many of the structures around us simply would not exist without being able to see what microscopes and macro photography can make visible. The natural world is the inspiration for a vast number of human architectural and engineering feats.

One branch of science that concerns itself principally with applying the technical lessons of nature to manmade inventions is bionics. Scientists engineer materials, for example, that mimic the characteristics of natural substances. A spider's silk has a tensile strength that far surpasses the most modern high-tech materials. Snail shells and bee honeycombs reveal how to optimize space in a room while using a minimal number of building materials.

The intricate structures of a leaf reveal an astoundingly simple and elegant system for delivering nutrients across the whole of its area; the surface of a shark's skin shows us how to build ship hulls to minimize the water's resistance.

There are also elements in our everyday lives that contain biotechnology—things we may not even be consciously aware of. Velcro, for example, the lotus effect, or self-cleaning surfaces; the roofs of modern industrial buildings, aircraft wings, even data networks; or, of course, the optical elements of a camera lens—all these things have their prototypes in nature.

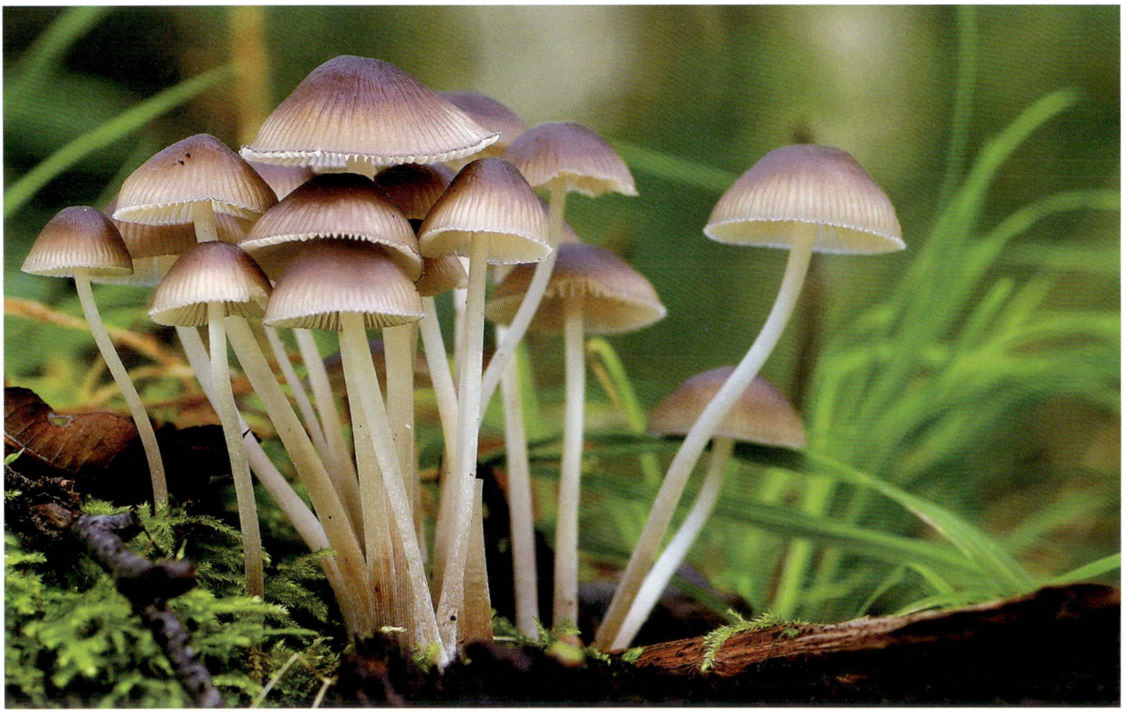

A tiny mushroom grove
Photo: Stefan Dittmann

Nature's shapes are as diverse as they are elegant, which for me is a huge reason why I took up this journey in the microcosms to begin with. Time and time again the same principles of design will come into focus under a macro lens in wildly different settings—symmetries, spiral formations, infinitely repeating patterns, for example.

Even though nature never operates as a designer exclusively to make something look a certain way without also fulfilling various purposeful functions, its creations nevertheless amount to a breathtaking beauty that offers a boundless source of inspiration for me as a graphic artist.

Images for the following two pages:

Top left: Maple seed
f/26, 1/200 s, ISO 100, 60mm, studio flash system

Bottom left: The wings of a housefly
f/22, 1/200 s, ISO 100, 90mm macro lens bellows, system flash unit with softbox

Top right: The arm of a squid
f/9.5, 1/60 s, ISO 200, 50mm, system flash unit with softbox

Bottom right: Fern frond
f/5.6, 1/90 s, ISO 200, 90mm, natural light

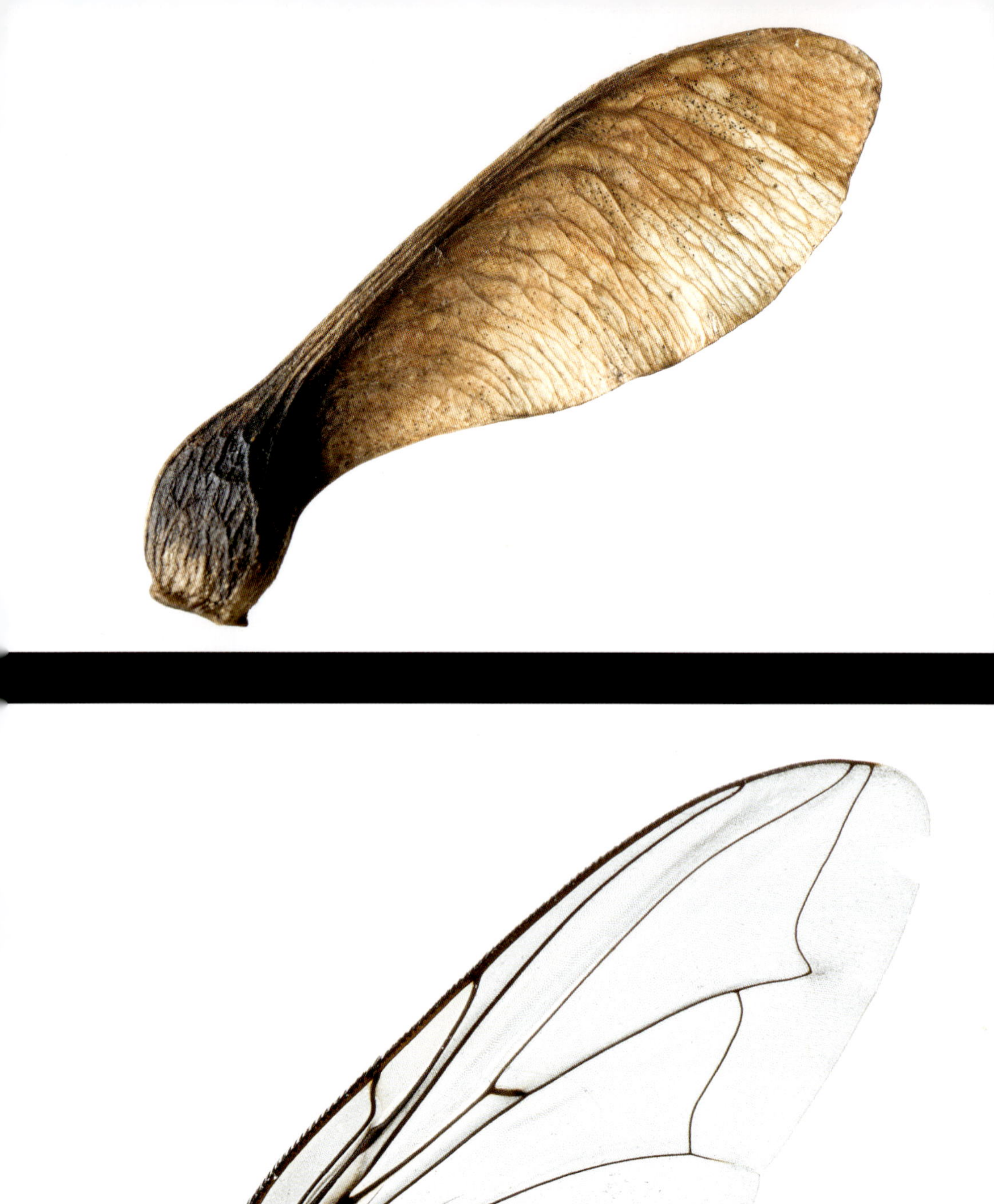

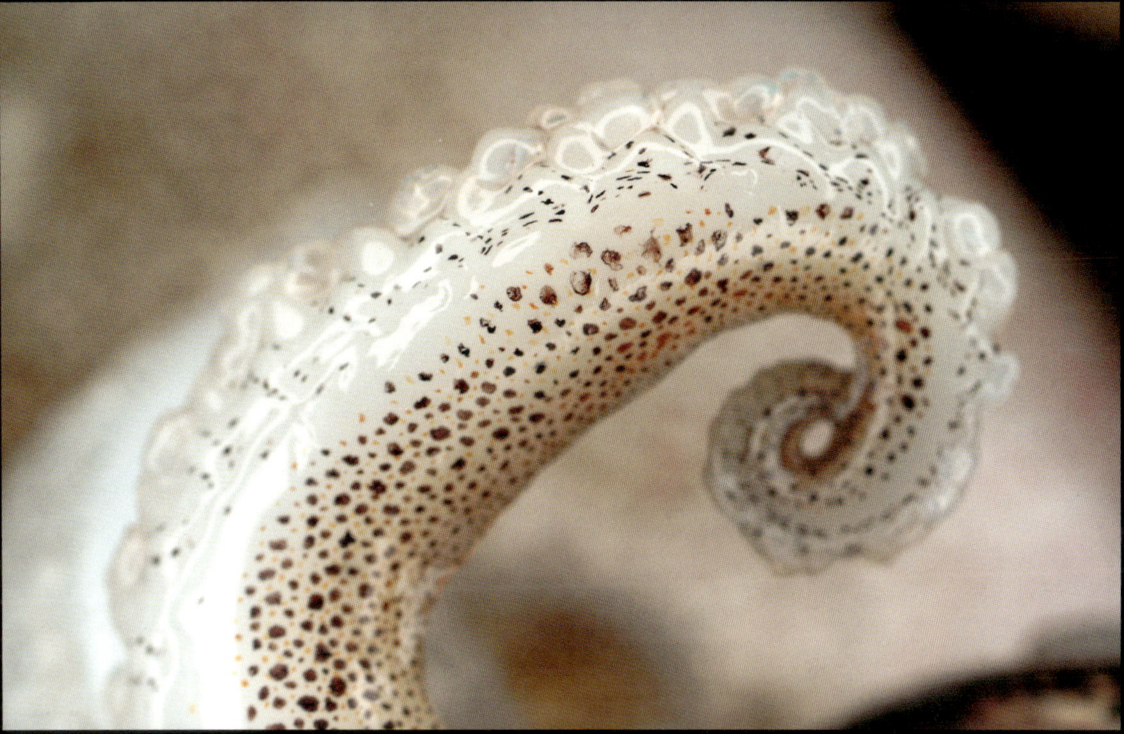

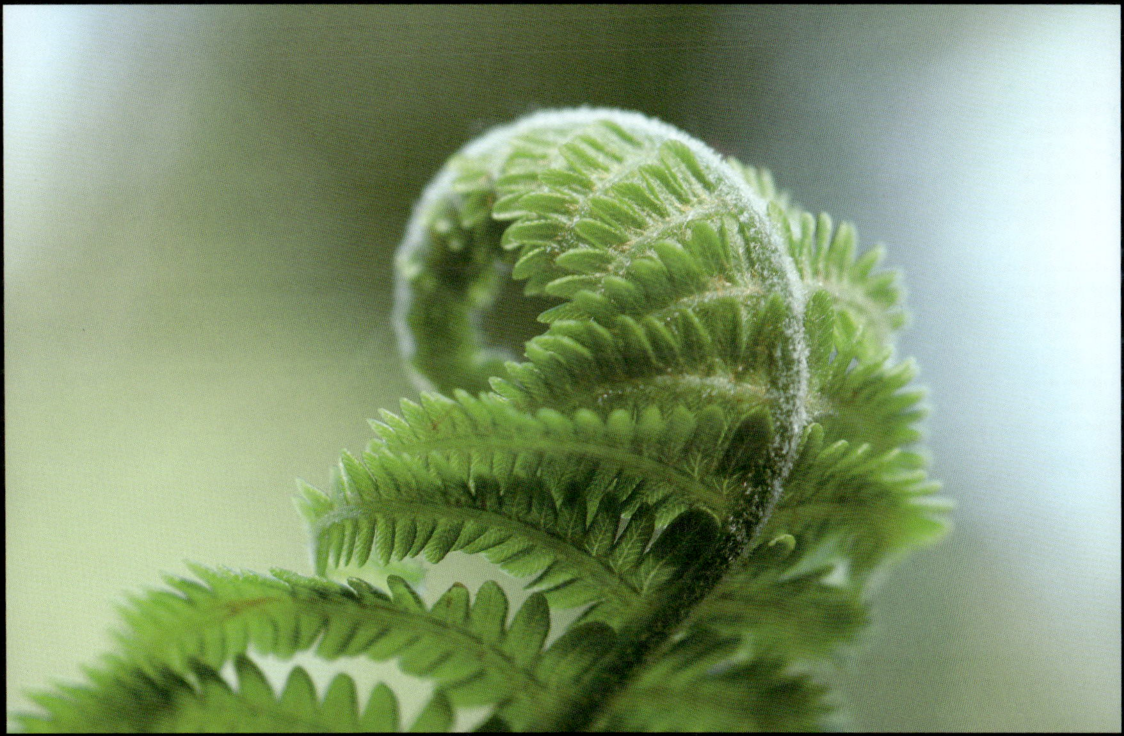

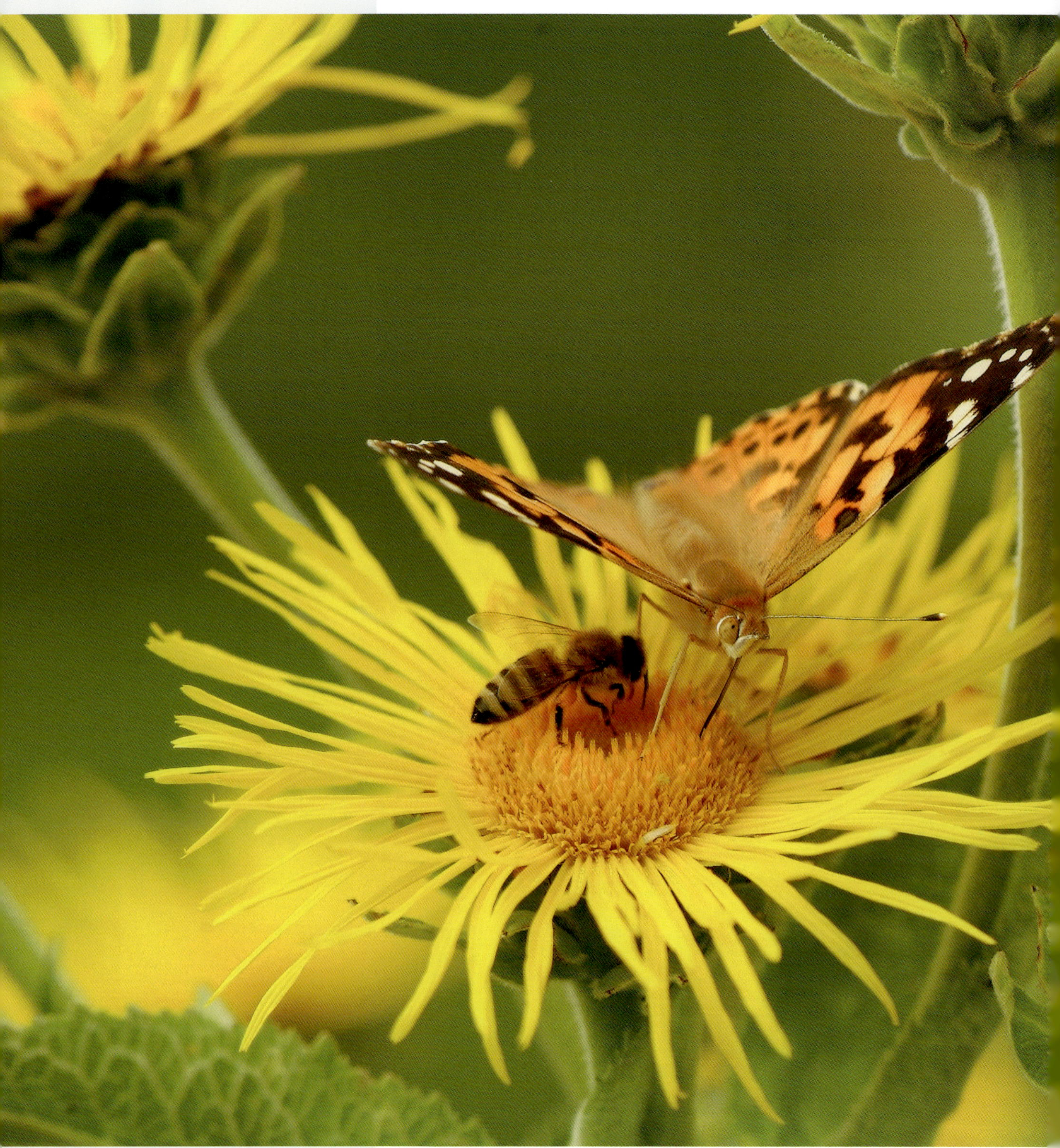

The Basics

Diverse factors attract photographers to macro photography. They range from simply wanting to create attractive images to having a scientific interest in creating art.

What remains the same no matter what your motivation, however, are the optical fundamentals. These basics, once mastered, are the key to success. The goal of knowing these principles is not to create technically perfect images, but to discover the boundaries and limits of the craft so that you can use them purposefully when composing your own pictures.

Curiosity was the main reason I took an interest in macro photography. I wanted to discover the world that surrounds us, but remains hidden to the naked eye. To put it differently, I wanted a glimpse into a world that exists in parallel to the world we know. And, of course, accompanying this wish is the desire to portray my discoveries in a manner as aesthetically pleasing as possible.

A bee and a small tortoiseshell
f/4.8, 1/500 s, ISO 400, 150mm

The Basics in Theoretical Terms

To move beyond needing to rely on dumb luck to achieve noteworthy images, it is necessary to become familiar with several basic principles. Gaining this knowledge will inform your ability to compose and design images. Let's start by looking at a few of the terms that will come up repeatedly when discussing macro photography.

Magnification

Magnification describes the relationship of the actual size of a physical object to the size of its reproduction on the exposure medium. A magnification factor of 1:1 is achieved when an object is reproduced at its actual size on a camera's film or image sensor. In other words, 1cm in nature corresponds exactly to 1cm on the exposure medium, independent of the sensor size. With a magnification factor of 2:1, the object appears twice as large as its actual size, meaning a length of 0.5cm would be captured as 1cm. I would also add here that magnification is dependent on the lens's focal length and the focusing distance.

Sensor Format

Smaller sensor formats, such as the 1/2.5" sensors that are often found in digital compact cameras, produce a larger depth of field than the larger sensors found in digital single-lens reflex cameras or 35mm film cameras.

This phenomenon results from the fact that different sensor formats will produce varying factors of magnification when you depict an object at the full sensor size. The depth of field varies based on the magnification factor. Depicting a beetle that is 36mm long full frame on a sensor that is 18mm wide would require a magnification factor of 1:2. With an f-stop of f/8, this situation would result in a depth of field of 2.4mm. Depicting the same beetle full frame on a full-format sensor (36mm) would require a magnification factor of 1:1 and would feature a shallower depth of field. Again, with an f-stop of f/8, the depth of field shrinks to 0.96mm. This means that a digital single-lens reflex camera with a large sensor is not always the optimal tool for the job; in some cases, a small compact camera might be the right choice.

The magnification factor does not depend on the sensor format

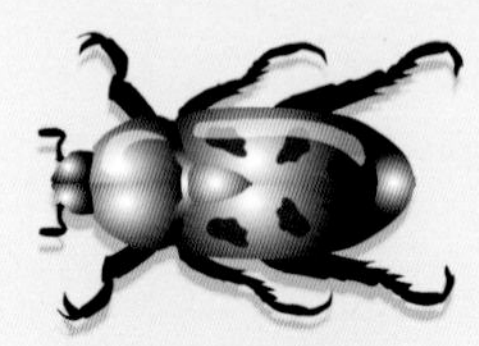

An object's actual size

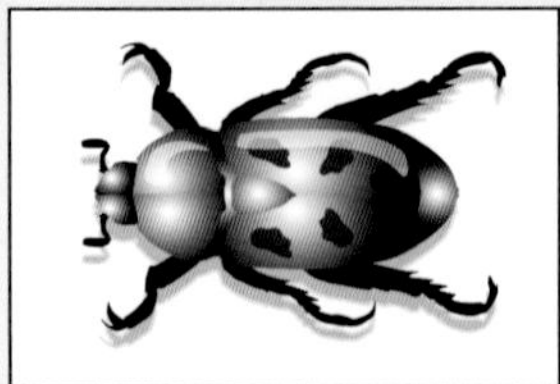

A magnification of 1:1 on a full-format sensor

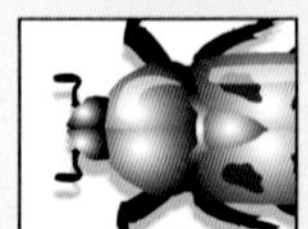

A magnification of 1:1 on a 3/4" sensor

Circle of Confusion

If an object is portrayed sharply, all of the points on the subject that lie exactly on the focal plane will also appear as points on the sensor. All of the other points on the subject will not be rendered as perfect points, but rather as soft disks, the so-called circle of confusion. Our powers of vision, however, perceive these disks effectively as points up to a certain threshold without registering any blur. If the circle-of-confusion diameter limit goes beyond this threshold of our perception, we start to notice blur. The maximum circle-of-confusion diameter is dependent on the sensor format.

Bokeh

The shape of the circle of confusion has no influence on the depth of field of an image, but it does affect the overall look and feel of a picture. Its shape is determined by the shape of the aperture opening and the number of aperture blades used to dilate and constrict the opening area. Constructions with six or eight blades are common. Sometimes the circle of confusion is round, which can be ideal, as is the case with many with mirror telephoto lenses. Preferences about this particular visual characteristic, which is called bokeh, are highly subjective. A camera's bokeh influences how a photo looks in areas that transition from sharpness to blur. Many people also consider bokeh a measuring stick for the reproduction quality of a lens.

Optimal Aperture and Diffraction Blur

Macro photographers are often forced to stop down the aperture to high f-stops because depth of field can become compressed down to millimeters or less with increasing degrees of magnification. Up to a certain point, this method makes a lot of sense, but moving beyond a range referred to as the optimal aperture, however, reduces image sharpness due to the increasing quantity of light diffracted at the aperture blades.

This softening effect is called diffraction blur. It also occurs at low f-stops, but the effect is not noticeable, because a significant percentage of the light is able to pass straight through the larger aperture opening.

As a baseline, you can treat an aperture of f/22 as the optimal limit when shooting with a magnification factor of 1:1. In practice, however, it would be unusual to use this aperture setting because it would necessitate such a slow shutter speed. Things start to look different as we move into more extreme macro perspectives. At a magnification of 2:1, f/16 is the optimal limit; at 5:1, it's already down to f/5.6. Needing to work with such strict aperture limits is problematic, especially with macro photography. Fortunately, there are a few tricks

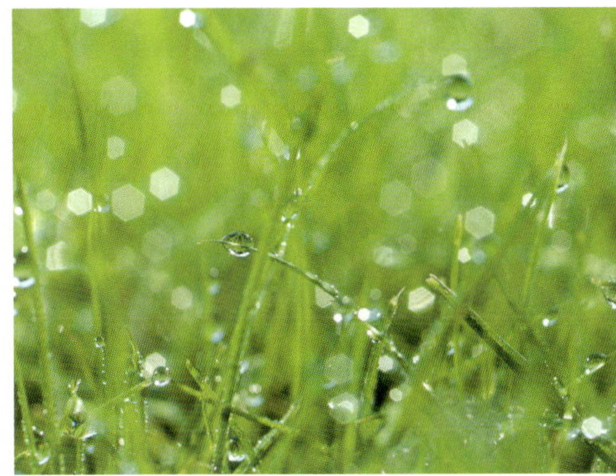

The shape of the bokeh depends on the number of aperture blades and the structure of the iris. This image reveals the effect of a six-bladed aperture.

The wider the aperture opening, the shallower the perceptible depth of field as determined by the size of the circle of confusion

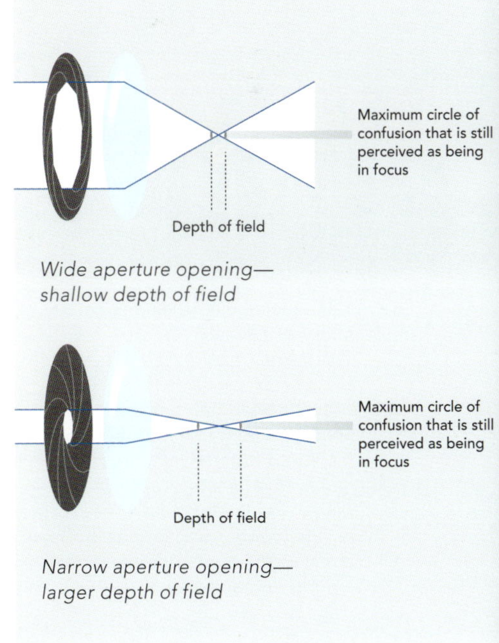

Wide aperture opening— shallow depth of field

Narrow aperture opening— larger depth of field

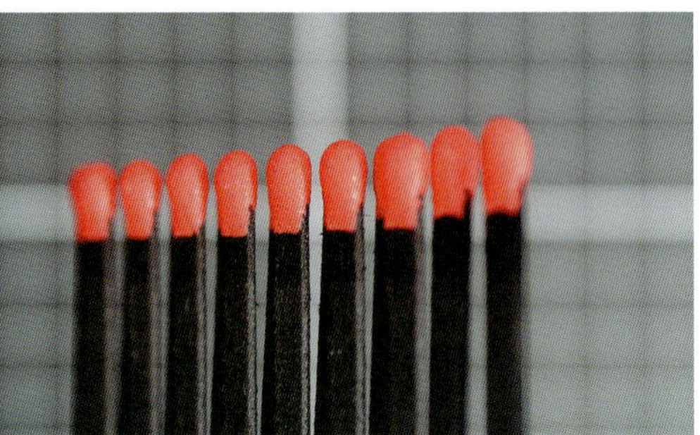

50mm macro lens, magnification factor of 1:3, f/5.6

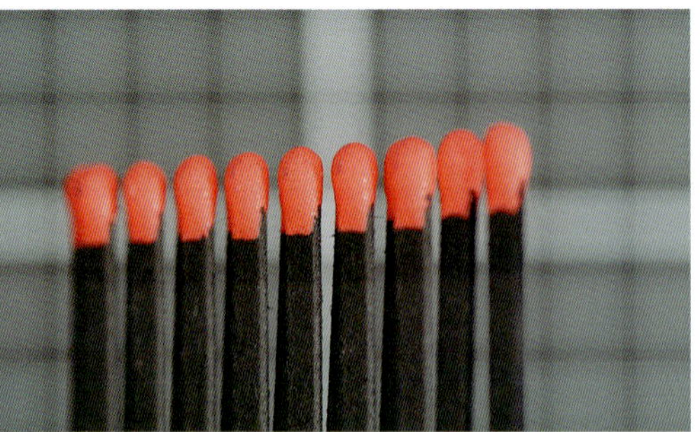

105mm macro lens, magnification factor of 1:3, f/5.6

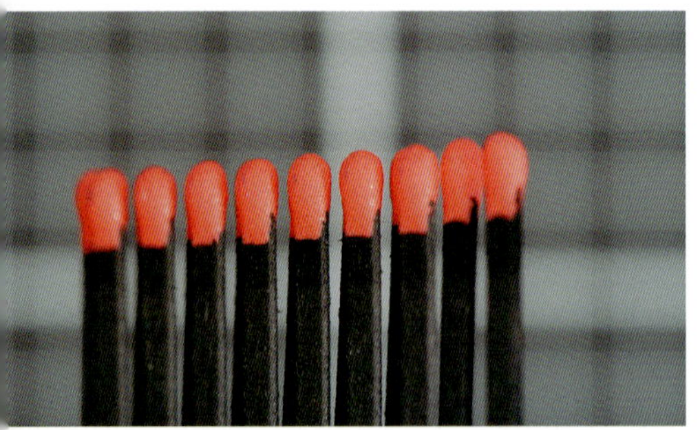

150mm macro lens, magnification factor of 1:3, f/5.6
The depth of field in all three images is the same, because the influence of the focal length on the depth of field is offset by varying shooting distances with the magnification factor held constant in the macro range. The background is less visible for the longer focal lengths, however, because the angle of view demands a tighter perspective.

and methods that help to circumnavigate this issue, including focus stacking, which involves compositing a photo out of individual pictures with different focus settings to create an image that is in focus throughout the image area.

Depth of Field in Macro Photography

Aperture influences much more than shutter speed; in combination with the magnification factor, aperture determines how much of an image's subject will appear within the depth of field or how much of the subject will appear acceptably sharp to the human eye (circle of confusion).

Composing an image with a large depth of field necessitates the use of a small aperture opening (a high f-stop); conversely, a shallow depth of field requires the use of a wide aperture opening (a low f-stop). Both sharpness and blur are powerful effects for composing images, and many DSLRs accordingly offer a depth-of-field preview function that allows you to inspect your effective depth of field at various aperture settings.

In most cases, a lens's focal length also influences the depth of field because magnification is partly a function of focal length. Wide-angle lenses generally offer a larger depth of field than telephoto lenses.

However, altering the focal length affects depth of field only when the shooting distance is kept constant. If the aperture and magnification factor remain constant, which is often the case with macro photography because magnification is of such importance, then the focal length won't influence the depth of field.

If you want to shoot the same subject with a different focal length, but want it depicted at the same size, you'll have to alter your shooting standpoint. Doing so completely cancels out the influence of focal length in the macro range.

In contrast, a constant shooting distance with different focal lengths will feature different depths of field as well as a different image area and level of magnification. In other words, a different image area will be represented, and the subject will appear larger or smaller on the sensor depending on the focal length.

Aperture, Shutter Speed, and ISO

Successive f-stops are related to one another by a factor of approximately 1.41. Starting with f/2.8, the next step is f/4, then f/5.6, f/8, and so on. Reducing the aperture by a full stop equates to halving the quantity of light that can enter the camera during the same window of time. In other words, if you reduce the aperture by one full stop, you'll need a slower shutter speed (twice as slow) to allow enough light to pass through the smaller aperture area to obtain the same exposure.

Things get more complicated with macro photography, because the farther you journey into the world of the tiny, the greater the loss of light you will encounter. This effect is readily observed if you set your camera in aperture-priority mode and attempt to focus on an object with a constant aperture at varying shooting distances. The automatically determined shutter speed will vary, becoming longer the closer you approach to your object. The very tight depths of field involved with macro photography always require stopping down to some degree, which means that the loss of light necessitates longer shutter speeds to compensate. And this, in turn, means that it is impossible to capture images free from camera shake while shooting freehand.

To bring the shutter speeds back into the manageable range, you'll need to alter the lighting conditions to make things brighter. Reflectors are one key tool for this task, but other sources of light such as flash units and LED lamps also have their place.

Yet another option is increasing the light sensitivity by boosting the ISO value. The drawback of this method is that increased light sensitivity comes with a decrease in image quality. High ISO settings lead to images with a grainy appearance showing more visible image noise. Many contemporary DSLRs, however, especially those with full-format sensors, allow photographers to shoot with ISO speeds that were simply unfathomable even a few years ago. Modern cameras, depending on the model, can produce nearly noiseless images at ISO 800 or ISO 1600. In addition to increased image resolution, the advances in image quality at high ISO settings are one of the most important recent advances in camera technology with respect to macro photography.

Another option, of course, is to work with a tripod or with a camera or lens that features image stabilizers and to shoot with slower shutter speeds. Both of these options require a stationary subject, however; otherwise you run the risk of unwanted motion blur ruining your shots.

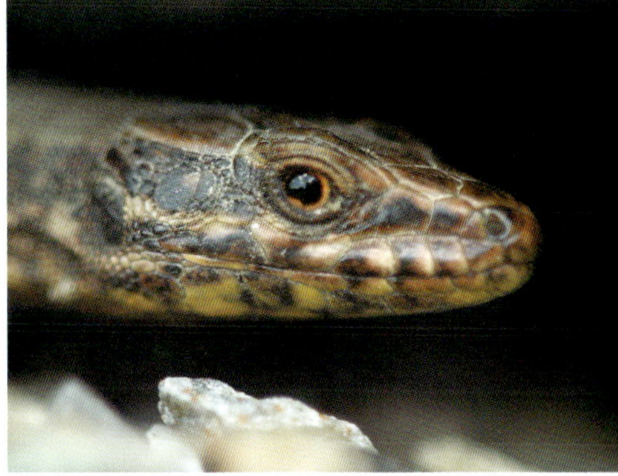

f/5.6, 1/250 s at 300mm

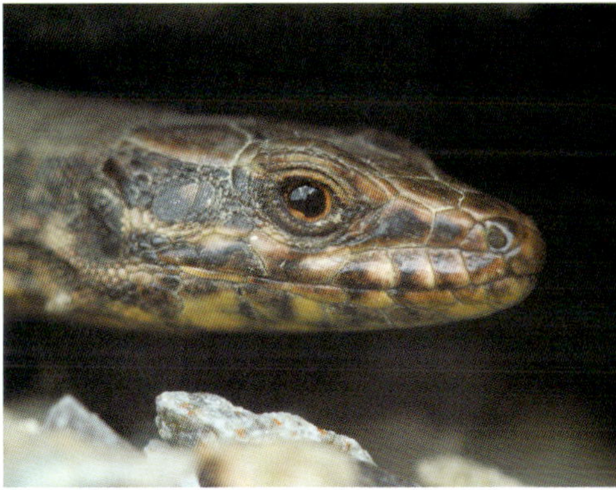

f/9.5, 1/90 s at 300mm

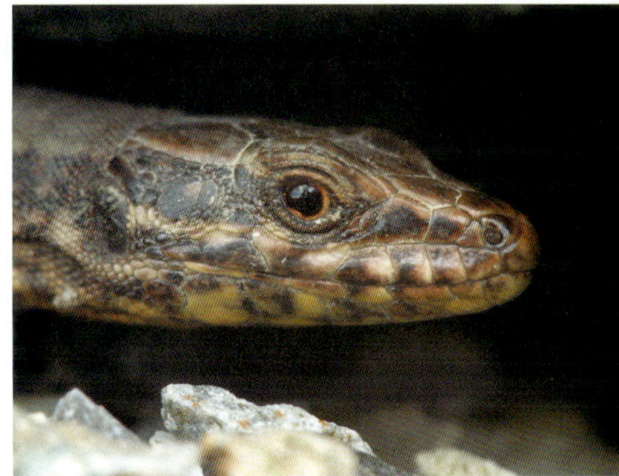

f/19, 1/15 s at 300mm
Stopping down the aperture dramatically increases the depth of field, but it also slows down the shutter speed significantly

The Basics in Numbers

The theoretical principles of macro photography naturally affect the practical side of actually taking pictures. These concepts come into play as soon as you consider which camera to purchase and remain relevant as long as you're composing pictures thoughtfully.

But don't worry: there's never going to be a time when you're called on to photograph a subject with a specific magnification factor. With depth of field, however, knowing some technical specifications can have interesting benefits.

For the most part, photographers use their instincts to shoot while paying attention to the composition of the photo, the lighting conditions, and the flight zone of the subject at hand. But that is exactly the reason why it's necessary to become familiar with some of the fundamental rules of macro photography. You want them to become second nature so you can focus your attention on making the right decisions in the heat of the moment.

This advice doesn't mean that beginners shouldn't spontaneously shoot pictures based on a gut feeling. Photography should always be fun, and accidentally successful images often provide a good lesson in figuring out why certain things work well. Afterward, you can inspect the EXIF data to figure out what settings the camera used to create an interesting look, and then you can replicate these settings in the future.

You'll find various formulas and tables on the following pages. The information presented here has value from a standpoint of the theories of photography, but it also will help inform you of practical skills. The data reveal that all of the various factors are interconnected and represent individual facets of a much larger whole.

Online Calculators and Apps

If you're averse to using a calculator to compute one of the figures you may need in your practice, you'll find plenty of strong alternatives on the Internet and in the app store. The links below are examples of apps and websites that perform these calculations.
http://www.cambridgeincolour.com/tutorials/dof-calculator.htm
http://dofsimulator.net/en/
https://itunes.apple.com/us/app/depth-of-field-calculator/ id356339910?mt=8

Calculating the Magnification Factor

The magnification factor of an image can be calculated with the following formula:

$$\beta = \frac{I}{O}$$

Magnification factor (β) = Image size : Object size

Image size describes the size of the object as it is depicted on the image sensor or film, and *object size* refers to the actual dimensions of the subject being photographed. Consider an example in which a beetle that is 12.5cm long is photographed full frame with a camera that has a sensor 25mm wide. The magnification factor is 2:1 (25 : 12.5 = 2). You can use this information to draw conclusions about the expected depth of field or the optimal aperture to be used (see table).

Determining the Overall Output of Multiple Flashes

If you wanted to use multiple flash sources to extend the depth of field, for example, you can calculate the overall flash output of all of the units.

$$\text{Overall output} = \sqrt{GN1^2 + GN2^2 + GN3^2\ldots}$$

Example: Instead of using a single, small flash with a guide number of 12 and ISO 100 and a 35mm focal length, you want to use four identical flash units simultaneously, or, in the case of a long exposure, fire them four times from the same direction.

$$\text{Overall output} = \sqrt{12^2 + 12^2 + 12^2 + 12^2}$$

The overall output accordingly equals 24. That seems like a significant increase in the flash output, but it's a gain of only two stops when it comes to the exposure—approximately moving from f/8 to f/16. The improvement to the depth of field is in turn dependent on the magnification.

Optimal Aperture as a Function of Magnification	
Magnification Factor	Optimal Aperture
1:2	f/32
1:1	f/22
2:1	f/16
3:1	f/11
4:1	f/8
5:1	f/5.6

Stopping down beyond the optimal aperture will result in a loss of sharpness resulting from diffraction blur caused by light reflecting off the aperture blades

The Relationship of Aperture, Shutter Speed, ISO, and Lighting

Photographers enjoy a great deal of creative freedom to alter the appearance of images by modulating shutter speed, aperture, and ISO speed. There are times, though, when it's desirable or necessary to fix one or more of these settings at a specific point. You may need to keep the shutter speed as fast as possible, for example, to avoid motion blur while also stopping the aperture down to increase the depth of field. The table below reveals how these key variables of aperture, shutter speed, and ISO interact, or in other words, what compromises you might need to make in order to make the exposure work for a specific shot.

Aperture, Shutter Speed, and ISO at a Fixed Exposure

Aperture	f/2.8	f/4	f/5.6	f/8	f/11
ISO 1,600	1/8,000 s	1/4,000 s	1/2,000 s	1/1,000 s	1/500 s
ISO 800	1/4,000 s	1/2,000 s	1/1,000 s	1/500 s	1/250 s
ISO 400	1/2,000 s	1/1,000 s	1/500 s	1/250 s	1/125 s
ISO 200	1/1,000 s	1/500 s	1/250 s	1/125 s	1/60 s
ISO 100	1/500 s	1/250 s	1/125 s	1/60 s	1/30 s

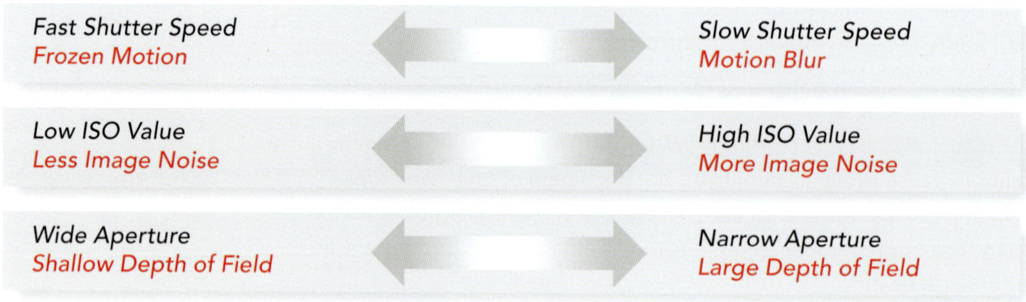

Example: Assume that you're working in a situation where your shooting distance and the focal length of your lens necessitate that you use a shutter speed of 1/500 s in order to capture a quickly moving object in focus and that you need to use an aperture of f/11 to have your desired depth of field. If the internal exposure meter leads the camera to select ISO 100 and f/4 at a fixed shutter speed of 1/500 s, then you'll need to increase the ISO by the equivalent of three exposure values (EVs) to ISO 800 so that you can keep the exposure constant and stop down the aperture three EVs to f/11.

Undertaking this shift will likely incur an increase in image noise. If you're not willing to accept the diminished image quality as a consequence, then you'll need to alter the lighting of the scene, perhaps with the use of flash.

Depth of Field for Various Shooting Distances, Focal Lengths, and Factors of Magnification

In the macro range, it's possible to achieve the same depth of field at various focal lengths and with a constant aperture if you adjust your shooting distance so the image frame remains unchanged. If you change your focal length without adjusting your shooting distance, you'll end up with an altered image frame, magnification factor, and depth of field.

Comparing Focal Length, Depth of Field, and Shooting Distance (values rounded)

Focal Length	Aperture	Depth of Field	Shooting Distance	Magnification Factor	Image Frame
150mm	8	5.8mm	80cm	1:3	10.8 x 7.2cm
100mm	8	5.8mm	53cm	1:3	10.8 x 7.2cm
50mm	8	5.8mm	27cm	1:3	10.8 x 7.2cm
150mm	8	1.0mm	60cm	1:1	3.6 x 2.4cm
100mm	8	8.3mm	60cm	1:4	13.3 x 8.8cm
50mm	8	51mm	60cm	1:10	36 x 24cm

Depth of Field Measurements for Full-Format DSLRs (values rounded)

Magnification Factor	f/2.8	f/4	f/8	f/16	f/22
1:4	3.7mm	5.3mm	10.7mm	21.3mm	29.4mm
1:3	2.3mm	3.3mm	6.5mm	13.0mm	17.9mm
1:2	1.1mm	1.6mm	3.2mm	6.4mm	8.8mm
1:1	0.4mm	0.5mm	1.1mm	2.1mm	2.9mm
2:1	0.1mm	0.2mm	0.4mm	0.8mm	1.1mm
4:1	0.06mm	0.08mm	0.2mm	0.3mm	0.5mm

As the magnification factor increases, the depth of field shrinks down to values as small as fractions of a millimeter. When these situations arise, you'll need to use special techniques such as focus stacking to achieve thorough sharpness across your image. You'll find instructions for this method later on in this book.

The Deepest Depths

Just how far can you go into the world of macro photography? What results will you be able to achieve with different pieces of equipment?

With a macro lens and a DSLR you will be able to take high-quality photos at a magnification factor of 1:1 without needing any additional equipment. You can actually focus macro lenses on infinity, and they serve perfectly well for taking pictures of more conventional subjects such as landscapes. Creating high-quality images with macro lenses at a magnification greater than 1:1 requires the use of specialty equipment with a DSLR.

Most compact and bridge cameras come equipped with a macro function, but the effectiveness of their macro mode is highly variable from model to model, so it's possible only to give a vague point of reference for what they can accomplish. In general, you'll be working with a magnification factor between 1:3 and 1:2. Depending on the camera, however, there are also ways to achieve a magnification of 1:1—more on that later.

As you'll be able to tell readily from the example photos here, the depth of field diminishes markedly as the magnification factor increases. Yet another challenge when using various lengths of lenses in combination with a macro bellows is lighting. With this setup, your lens ends up being so close to your subject that ensuring a satisfactory lighting situation can be problematic.

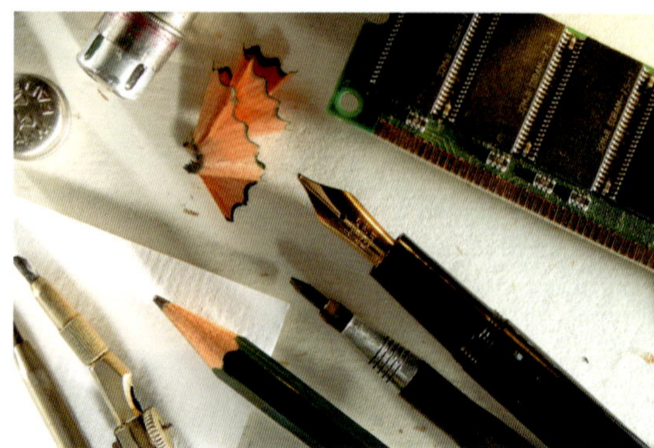

Standard zoom lens with a macro setting at 70mm. Attainable magnification levels vary on a lens-by-lens basis depending on minimum focus or macro functionality.

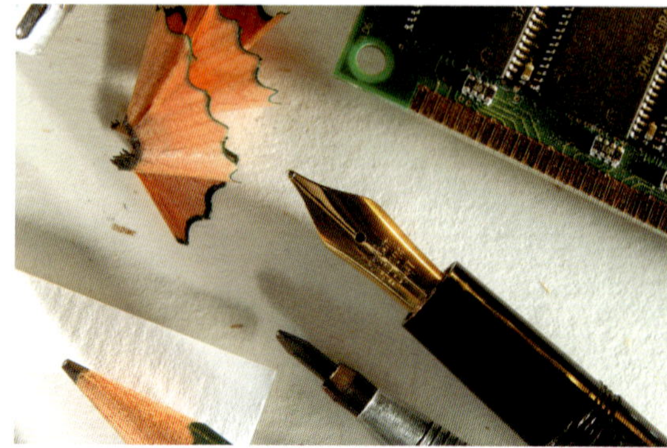

Standard zoom lens with macro setting at 70mm with a +2 diopter close-up lens. Close-up lenses are a cost-effective way to journey somewhat farther into the macro world.

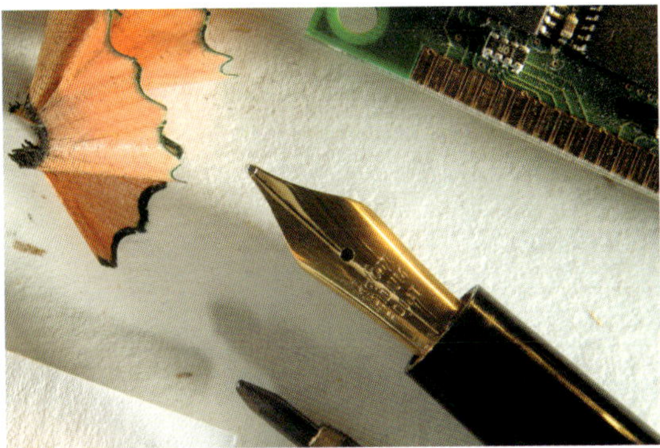

50mm lens with 12mm extension tube. The background is still sharp here with the aperture at f/16. Many compact cameras are not capable of closer macro pictures than this sample photo.

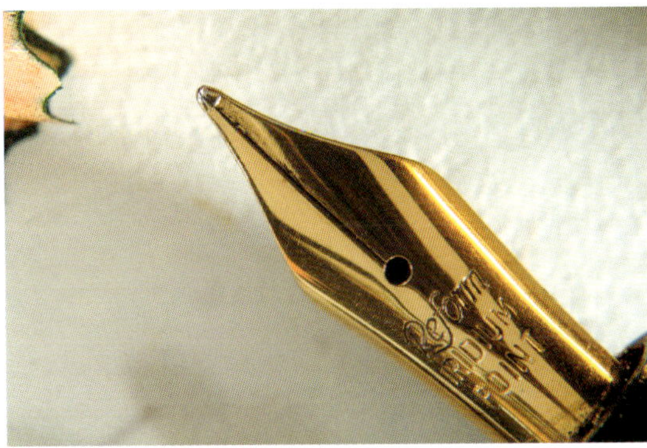

Standard zoom lens with macro setting at 70mm with a +10 diopter close-up lens. This image was still shot at f/16, but the depth of field decreases dramatically as the magnification level increases.

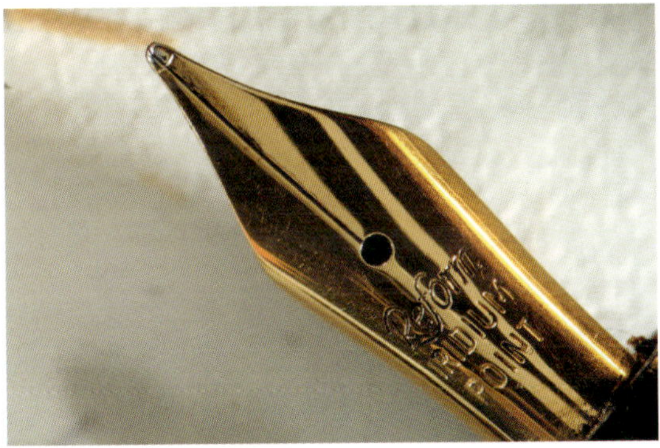

The magnification level here is 1:1, achieved in this case by using a true macro lens with a focal length of 105mm

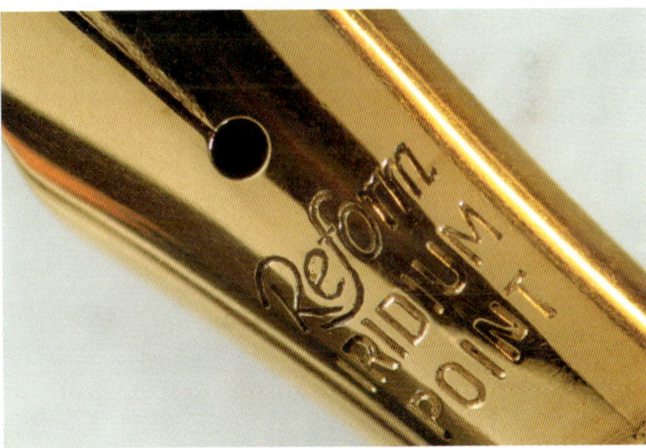

Using a 2x converter with a 50mm macro lens produces a focal length of 100mm with a magnification of 2:1

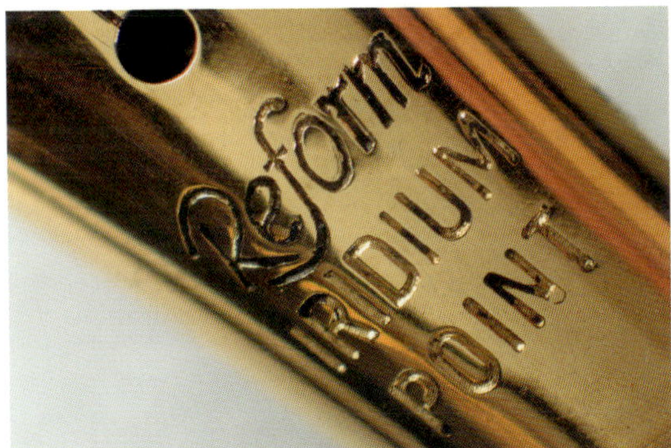

A 90mm macro lens with a bellows that has a maximum extension of 150mm brings us in to a magnification factor of 2.7:1

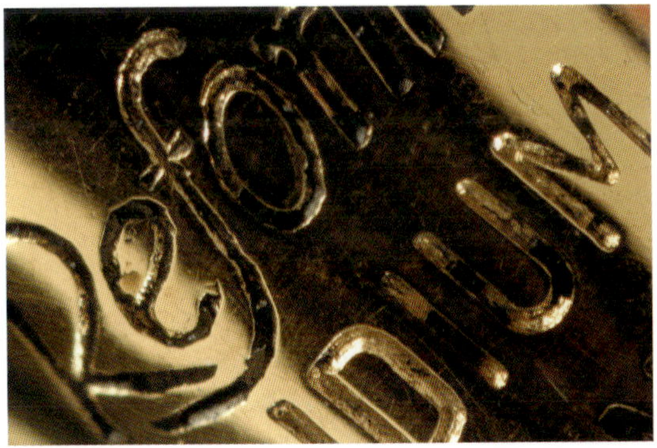

Here we have the result of reverse mounting a 25mm lens with a bellows at its maximum extension. The magnification level is 5:1, which is the upper limit for most normal macro photographers—higher levels of magnification require special microscopic lenses.

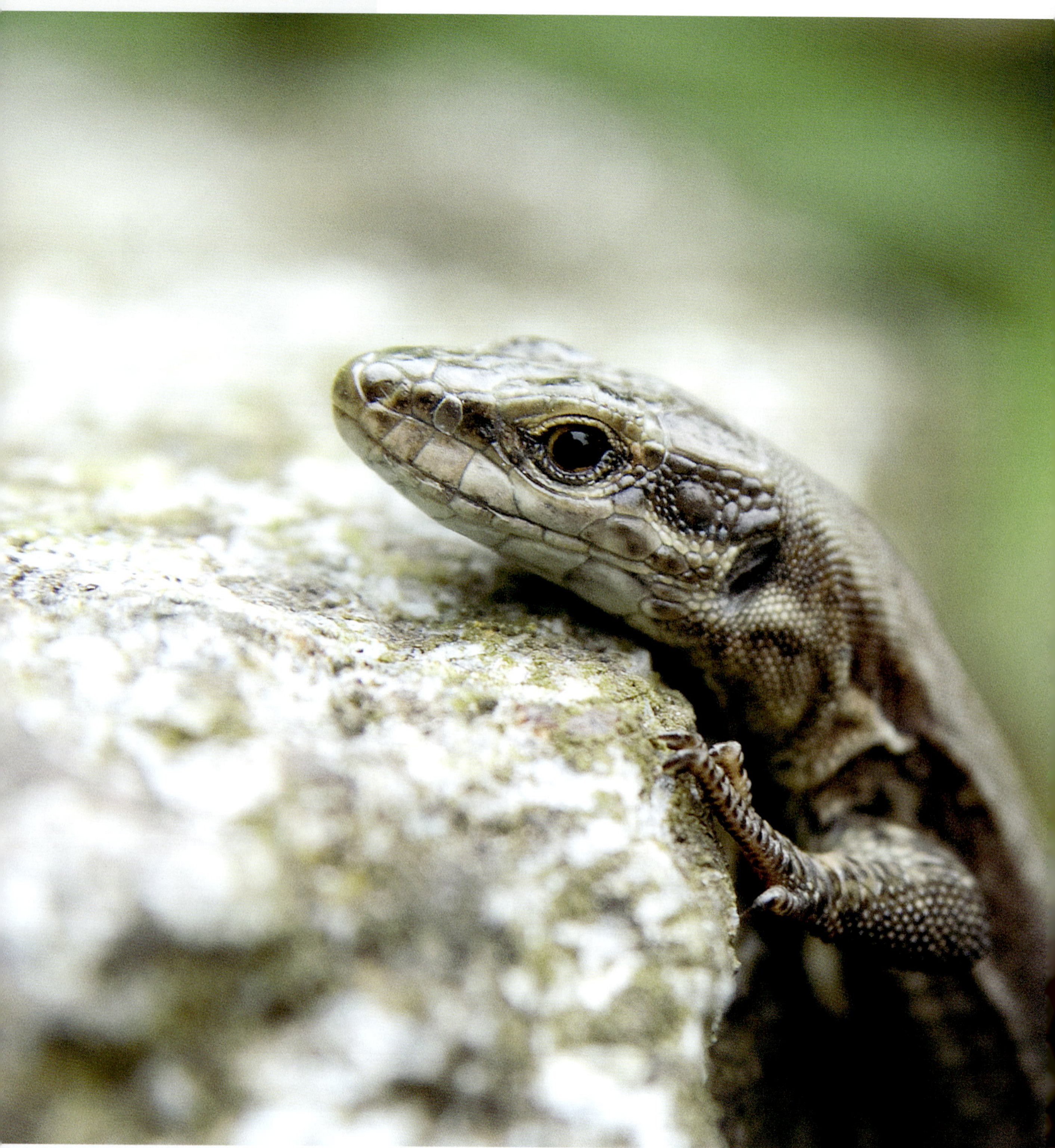

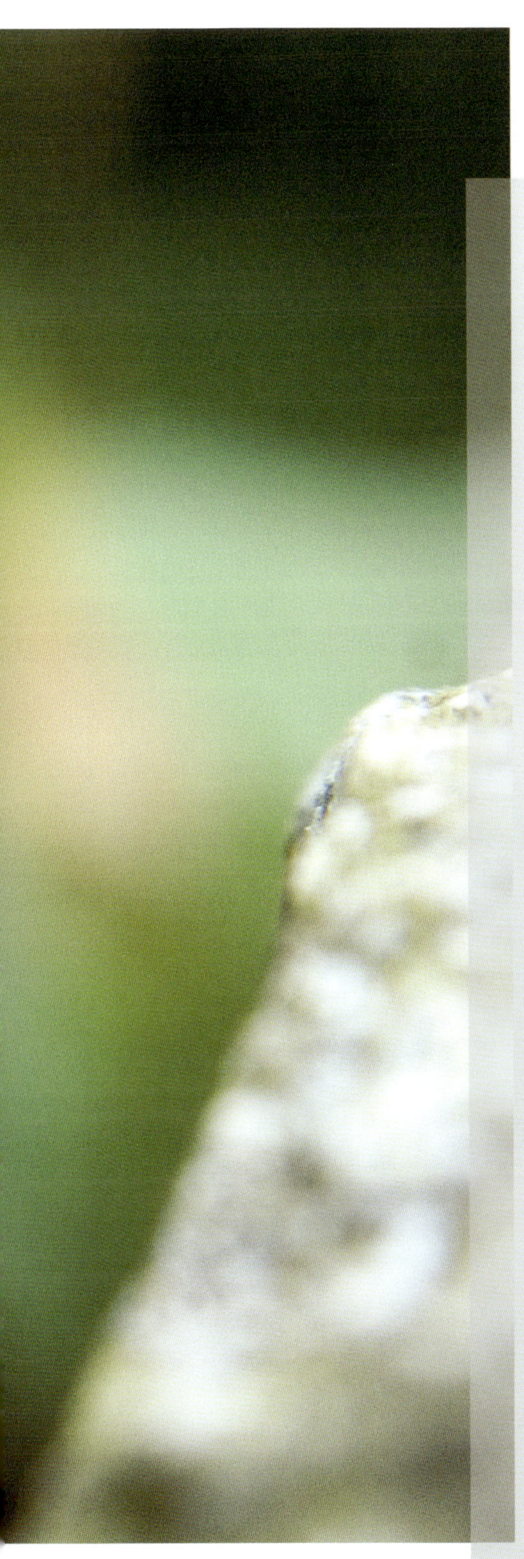

Equipment

What's the overall best camera on the market for taking macro photographs? What about the best available macro lens? There isn't a clear answer to these questions, because the demands for shooting macro subjects are as diverse as the subjects them-selves. Personal preferences also factor in here, so if you ask two photographers, you'll likely get two different answers.

I have a few favorite lenses. One of them is the AF Nikkor 28–105mm 1:3.5–4.5 D, which I used to shoot the lizard on these pages. This lens has been around for a while, but it offers a magnification of 1:2 from 50mm to 105mm and good sharpness performance.

For close-up and macro shots in the studio, I prefer the 60mm Micro Nikkor from Nikon. It offers excellent results for a variety of variables: shooting distance, sharpness, magnification, and bokeh. It's a true standout.

When I'm out in the field, I usually opt for a Sigma 180mm telephoto macro. Used in tandem with a fitting teleconverter, this lens lets me photograph subjects that are even farther away.

On the whole, my gear bag tends to be relatively empty. I prefer having the ability to move unbur-dened while I'm working and to maximize my at-tention on what I'm taking pictures of. Fortunately, I don't live with the fear of missing a particular subject because I don't have the right lens on hand at the time.

Lizard on a garden wall
f/7, 1/160 s, ISO 400, 60mm

Cameras for Macro Photography

Aside from resolution, cost, and minimum focal distance, there are a variety of personal preferences that influence which camera to purchase. In other words, the camera and the photographer need to be a good match. Even ergonomics influence the quality of your images in a not insubstantial way. If control buttons and dials are too small and poorly arranged, or if a manual mode is only accessible by navigating through layers of submenus, then you're likely to get frustrated while shooting and have less success in composing and designing your images. You should definitely spend some time holding a camera model in your hands and testing it out at a retail store, friend's house, or trade show before purchasing it.

If you already own a camera, then you have a valuable point of reference for how deeply you're able to dive into the macro world and what else you might need to get to your desired depths.

Smartphones and Tablet PCs with Integrated Cameras

Even as the resolution of cameras built into cell phones improves with each model, these cameras are still not practical for macro photography. The same goes for the various tablets on the market. Nevertheless, you can find special macro attachments that will improve your ability to shoot in the close-up range with these devices. The power of these tools is limited. They might, for example, be suitable for a snapshot of the decoration on your ice cream sundae.

Pros:
• Always on hand

Cons:
• Many limitations for use in the macro range

Summary:
Smartphones and tablets are not designed for macro use, but don't discount their utility completely because their technical capabilities are rapidly advancing.

Compact Cameras

Digital compact cameras can be found in any price class: from simple entry-level devices up to prestigious lifestyle cameras with retro styling. After you get up to 12 megapixels, you don't need to worry much about image quality as long as the lighting conditions are sufficient. If you're shooting in dim light, though, all bets are off because many compacts have fairly poor noise performance even at ISO 400.

Most common compact cameras on the market feature a macro mode, and they usually clearly indicate the minimum focusing distance. The indication that you can shoot in "macro up to 1cm" sounds seductive at first, but that limit is almost always available only when shooting with wide-angle focal lengths. In general, the maximum magnification you're likely to obtain is 1:2. Setting up lighting can be tricky when using compact cameras for macro imaging at such a close shooting distance, because you'll be blocking your own light.

Most compact cameras come equipped with a monitor that is between 2.5 and 3.5 inches (6.3cm and 8.9cm)—distances that refer to the diagonal length of the screen. If the display pivots and turns, then you'll be able to shoot subjects from ground level—from a worm's-eye view.

The monitor is your only option for inspecting and controlling your photo, which means that your ability to compose your photo is limited to some degree by the lighting conditions. You have less control over your picture in very bright conditions. One way to address this concern is to build a simple shade screen out of cardboard to make the monitor more visible.

The process of focusing manually with these cameras is often a weak point because it involves the use of a rocker switch. Fine-tuning the focus via this type of control is difficult and means your ability to set the sharpness accurately is limited.

Pros:
• Compact and easy to handle

Cons:
• Working in macro mode is inconvenient
• Not conducive to enhancing performance with add-ons

Summary:
Without question, compact cameras are fantastic for many uses; but because of various limitations, they are better suited to close-up photography than macro work. For pictures of large flowers, mushrooms, and the like, they range from good to very good depending on the model.

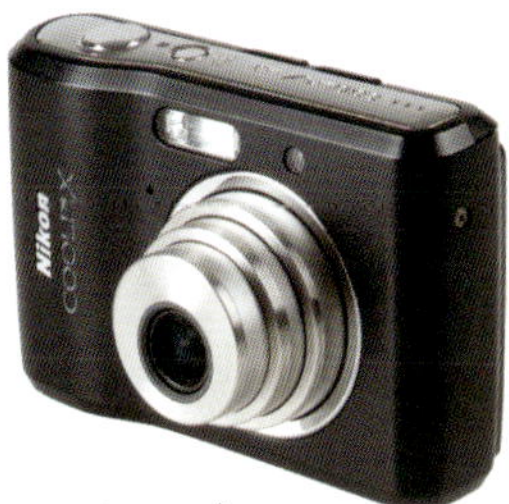

Compact cameras range in quality from affordable beginner models...

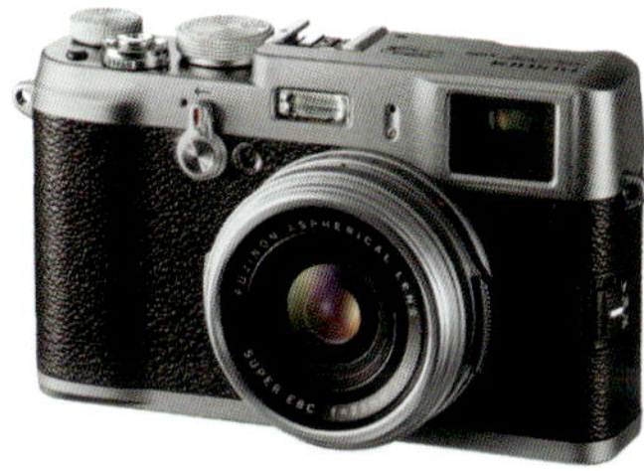

...up to highly respected premium compacts with fixed prime lenses
Photo: Fujifilm

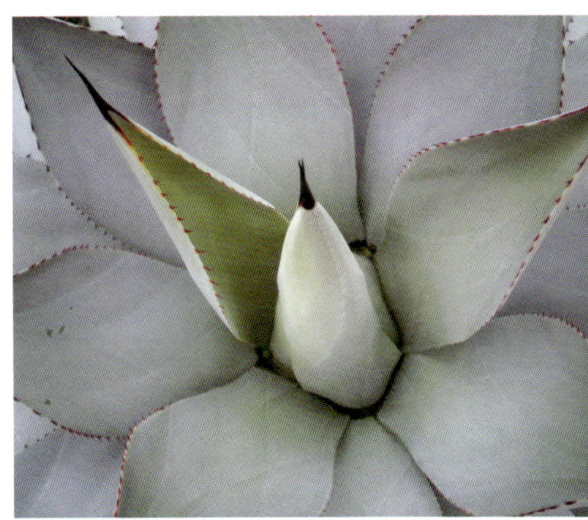

Compact cameras are well suited for close-up photography, but true macro photography is beyond their practical scope

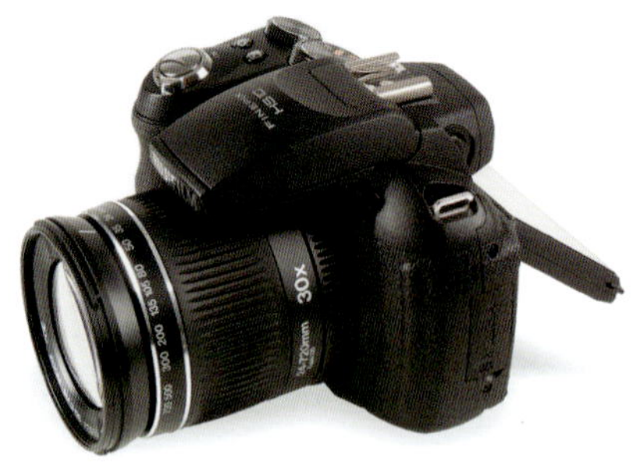

Bridge cameras typically offer a respectable macro mode. Users who want to up their magnification will need to look to close-up filters

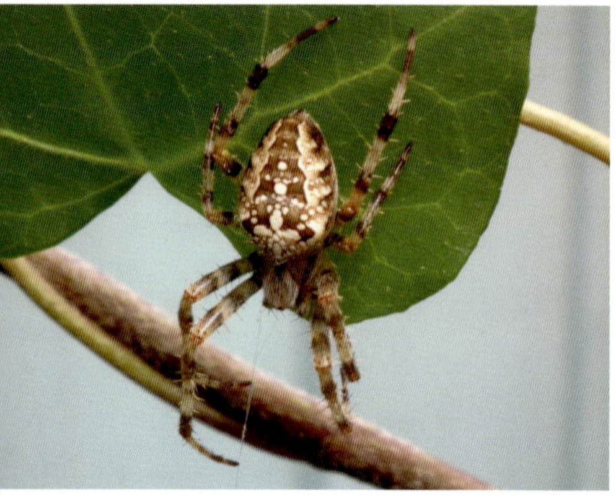

A garden spider, displayed here at the maximum magnification of a Fujifilm FinePix HS10 bridge camera in super macro mode

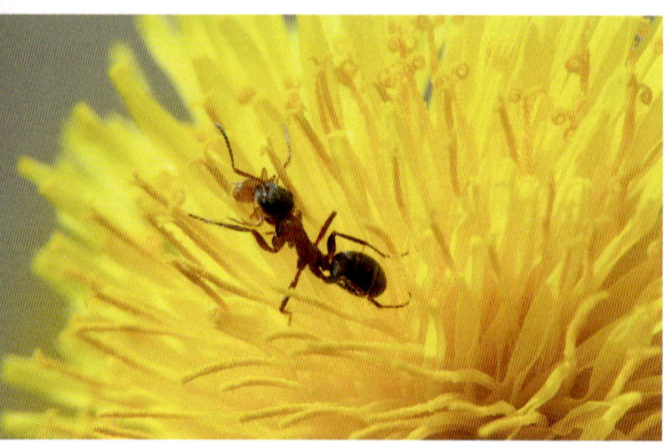

Ant on a dandelion. Using a +1 diopter close-up lens brings you a bit closer to the macro range.

Bridge Cameras

These cameras actually serve as a happy, all-in-one solution for macro photography. Their method of operation is very similar to DSLRs, which is one reason they are becoming more popular. Their reputation is also owed to their extensive features, which often include a foldable viewfinder, an expansive zoom range, image stabilizers, and a great deal more at a price that, in many cases, wouldn't even purchase a single macro lens.

Without using any accessory equipment, you can typically achieve a magnification factor between 1:4 and 1:2 with cameras in this class. When equipped with image stabilization and an impressive zoom lens, these cameras are well suited for photographing insects comparable to the size of a butterfly. If you want to extend your macro capabilities with these cameras, you'll need to use close-up lenses, also known as *diopters*, since these cameras typically don't feature interchangeable lenses. By using close-up filters, you can generally achieve magnification levels of 1:1 and sometimes even higher. Using a reverse setting with a coupling ring, the fixed wide-angle or normal lens of a bridge camera can realize magnification levels of 2:1 and beyond.

If you decide to purchase one of these cameras, you should pay close attention to the minimum focus distance as well as how easy it is to use the manual focus. In general, a focusing ring is both easier to use and more precise than a rocker switch. Also check for the ability to attach flash units. A simple shoe mount will do the trick; with this, you will be able to install an adapter enabling the use of remote flash units.

Pros:
- Large zoom range
- Articulated display screen
- Usually feature integrated image stabilizers

Cons:
- Digital viewfinder
- Operation specific to macro functions is sometimes ungainly
- Shutter lag

Summary:
Because of their large zoom range and their image stabilization technology, bridge cameras are ideal for taking pictures of large insects such as dragonflies and butterflies.

Mirrorless System Cameras

Although the flexibility afforded by DSLRs has not fully been replicated for mirrorless system cameras, this status of things is largely owing to the fact that this class of camera has been on the market for a relatively short period of time, and the diversity of third-party lenses and accessories has yet to thrive.

The primary advantages of these cameras with regard to macro photography are their modest weight and their relatively compact dimensions. Photographers using these cameras will be able to use proper macro lenses, and they won't have to worry about a mirror that has to swing out of the way for the sensor to capture an image (a motion that causes vibrations that can compromise image quality).

Photographers who are fond of electronic support will find plenty of tools at their fingertips: QR code and Wi-Fi functionality, superimposed guidelines to assist with image composition, electronic viewfinder magnification for macro exposures, rich video functionality, integrated image stabilization, and much more.

The image quality attainable with these cameras and their integrated Micro Four Thirds or APS-C sensors ranges from very good to excellent. You won't replicate what a full-format camera can achieve, but they are on par with half-frame DSLRs.

Pros:
- Interchangeable lenses
- Lighter in weight than DSLRs
- Articulated display screens
- Often include image stabilization
- No vibrations caused by a swinging mirror

Cons:
- Digital viewfinder
- Relatively limited selection of accessories from third-party manufacturers

Summary:
Situated between bridge cameras and DSLRs, system cameras score high marks in many areas and should be treated as a serious option for macro photographers.

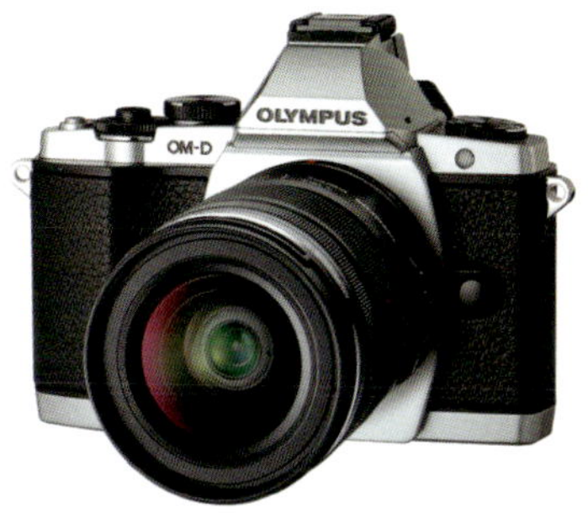

The best of both worlds. Mirrorless system cameras bring together a number of the advantages of various camera systems.
Photo: Olympus

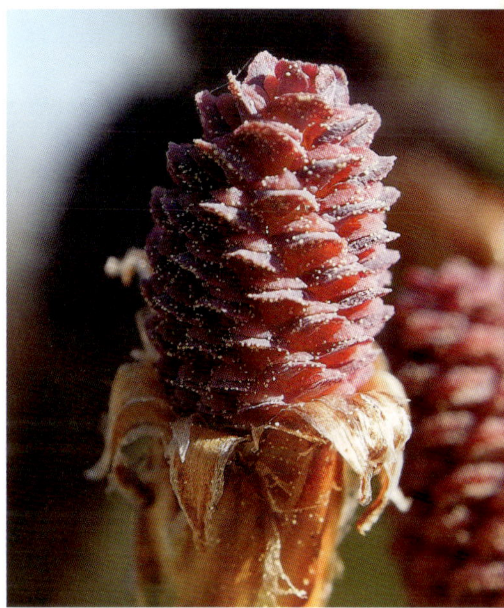

Thanks to ability to swap out lenses, mirrorless system cameras can reach well into the macro range
Photo: Olympus

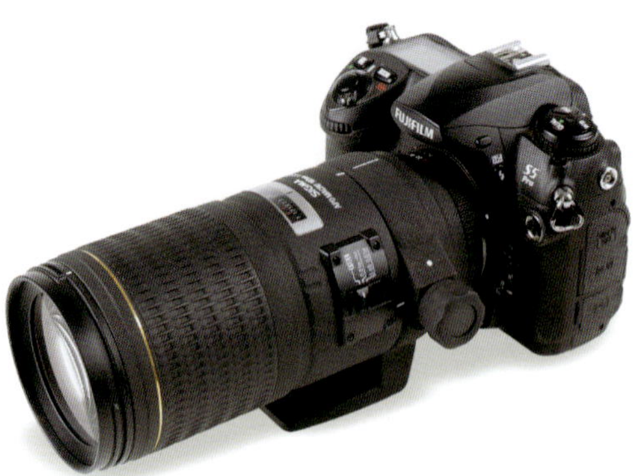

Fujifilm FinePix S5 Pro with Sigma 180mm 1:3.5 D APO macro. The crop factor with this setup makes it seem as though the focal length extends by a factor of 1.5 from 180mm to 270mm.

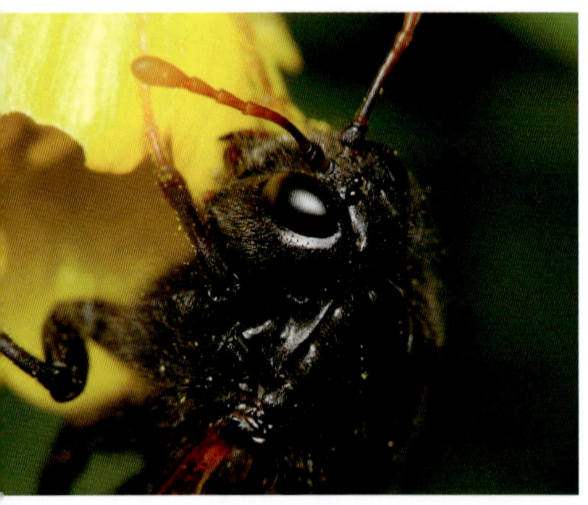

Bee. Thanks to the crop factor, even medium telephoto lenses are powerful enough to keep you beyond the flight zone of shy animals.

DSLRs with Half-Frame Sensors

No other camera system offers as many diverse possibilities for macro photography as DSLRs. Anyone who has rigorous demands for image quality, operation, add-ons, and levels of magnification cannot ignore this camera class. There is a seemingly endless range of solutions available for practically any photographic situation even for the specific purpose of macro photography—starting with macro lenses all the way to sophisticated flash control options. The price of this flexibility is the need to acquire and carry every piece of additional accessory equipment—whether lenses, angle viewfinder, or bellows.

Half-frame sensors are somewhat smaller than the traditional 35mm format, offering what at first appears to be a 1.5x or 1.6x focal length extension. In reality, this effect is called a crop factor. The smaller sensor captures a tighter angle of view, which seems to produce a telephoto effect. For example, a 150mm lens used with a DX or APS-C format sensor will have the same telephoto effect as a 225mm lens on a 35mm or full-frame digital camera. Crop factors don't influence the achievable level of magnification at all.

The resolution of modern DSLRs leaves nothing to be desired, giving photographers ample opportunity to enlarge image details at excellent levels of quality. These cameras feature noise performance at high ISO values that is good enough to produce acceptable results even in poor lighting conditions.

One downside to this type of camera is their susceptibility to having dust settle on the sensor as a result of their open internal construction. Swapping out a lens in spring when pollen levels are high can lead to an unfortunate blemish on the delicate image sensor.

Pros:
- Many options for expansions and add-ons
- Simple, intuitive operation
- High resolution
- Optical viewfinder

Cons:
- Sensor is not protected against dust

Summary:
If you are serious about becoming a macro photographer, then you can't do without a DSLR.

DSLRs with Full-Frame Sensors

Many of the characteristics and descriptions about half-frame DSLRs apply to full-frame DSLRs as well. One big difference is noise behavior, however; the larger pixels on the sensor enable dramatically improved noise performance. The high resolutions offered by these cameras mean enlarging details is easy. Another advantage is that lenses can be used at their actual focal length—something many photographers are used to from the days of film. A wide-angle lens will stay a wide-angle lens; a 100mm focal length will remain a 100mm focal length.

Many full-frame cameras allow you to shoot using a reduced format, should you want to, which means you can replicate the crop factor of 1.5 or 1.6; you'll just need to accept a loss of resolution to do so. You could effectively achieve the same result by altering your image area accordingly, but the plus side of diminishing the sensor format is that it will be easier to use lenses designed for smaller formats.

The high standards for the resolving power of the lens necessitated by the powerful sensor is not really a concern, because macro lenses are built to high optical standards. The larger image sensor significantly improves the noise performance at high ISO values. Rather than using artificial lighting to brighten up a dark scene, you can instead boost the sensitivity up to ISO 1600 or 3200. This benefit is hugely useful when shooting in some places where flash is not permitted, such as zoos. Even sensitivities of ISO 6400 and up are at your disposal, but visible noise starts to become more of an issue.

Pros:
- Very high resolution
- Image quality at high ISO values
- Lenses operate at the same effective focal length as on 35mm film cameras

Cons:
- Not very cheap
- Can be heavy and large

Summary:
If you want to get the absolute most out of your camera and you want to take your macro photography to the next level, you should look into the full-frame cameras currently available from the leading manufacturers.

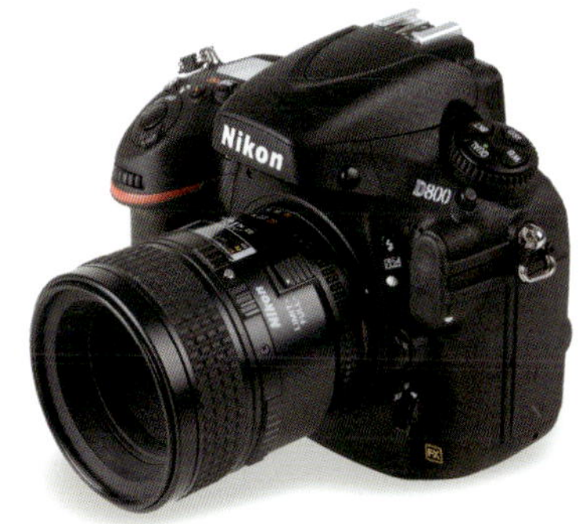

Nikon D800 with AF Micro-Nikkor 60mm 1:2.8 D. When using full-frame cameras with very high resolution, you should use lenses that have the highest possible imaging performance.

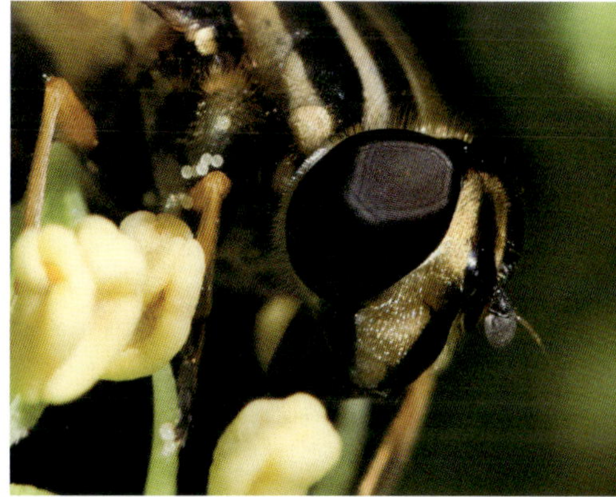

Even at ISO 6400 you will be able to achieve excellent images with minimal noise. D800, detail enlargement.

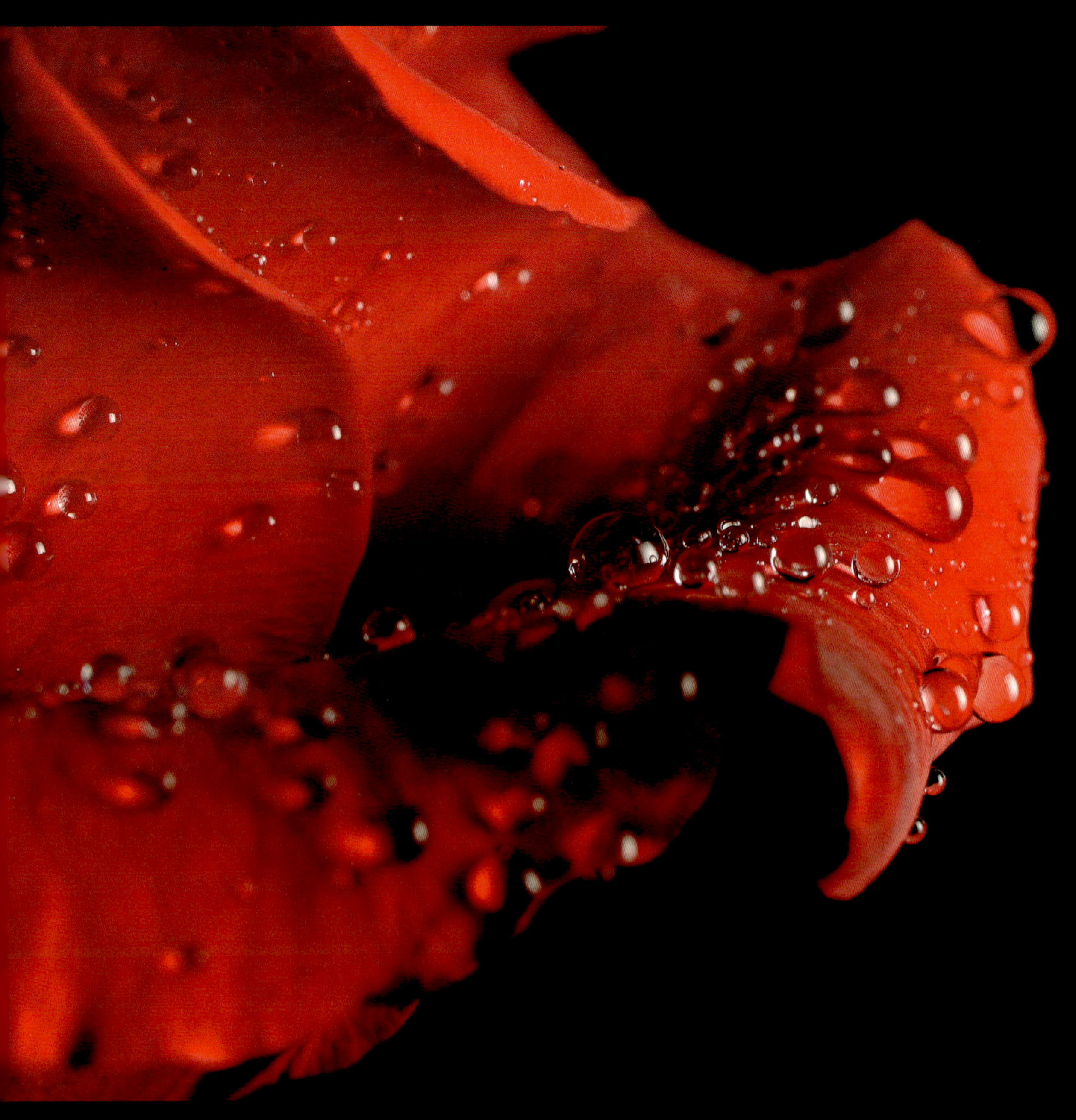

Water drops on a rose petal
f/13, 1/125 s, ISO 100, 50mm, system flash
unit with softbox

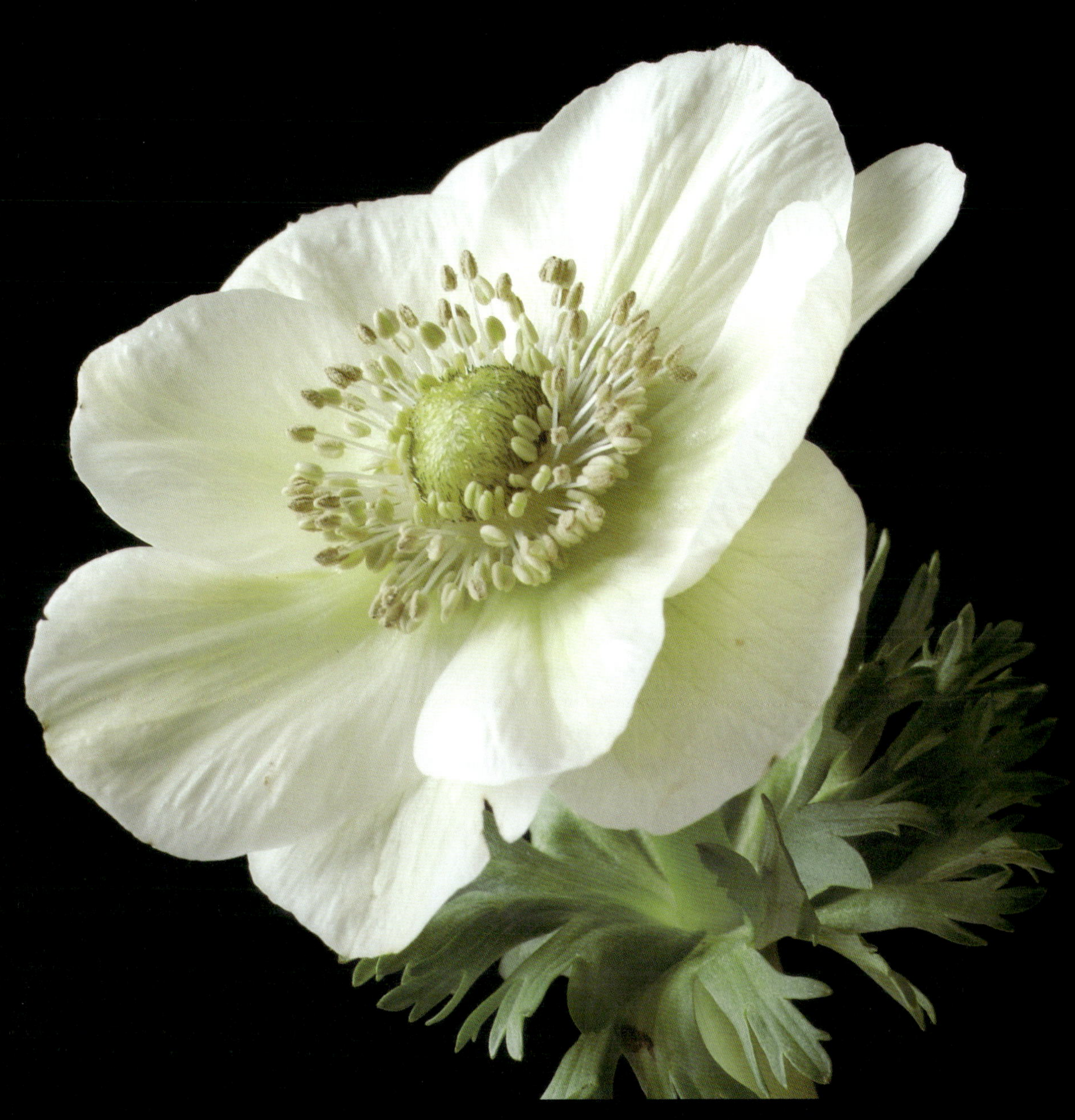

Anemone on a black background
f/13, 1/125 s, ISO 100, 50mm, studio flash unit

Standard Lenses

Zoom Lenses

Most people who purchase their first DSLR also acquire a zoom lens. In general, these lenses offer a range of focal lengths from a moderate wide angle to a relatively short telephoto angle of view, and they often feature a macro function.

The term *macro* in this context is somewhat inaccurate; it would be better to say that these lenses feature a favorable minimum focusing distance. With common magnification levels up to 1:3, or even 1:2 for some models, it is possible to capture a variety of subjects full frame, such as butterflies, flower blossoms, mushrooms, and the like. Because most zoom lenses aren't particularly fast and their macro functionality often necessitates that the focus is in the telephoto position, you'll frequently encounter situations where it won't be possible to shoot freehand.

Extension tubes and close-up lenses both offer methods for enhancing macro capabilities, but note that the image quality you're able to attain is highly dependent on the main lens as well as the optical quality of the close-up filter in use.

There aren't any true macro zooms. The one exception is the AF Micro-Nikkor 70–180mm 1:4.5–5.6 D ED, which offers a magnification of up to 1:1.32. But you'll find this lens only on the secondhand market, where it often is still quite expensive.

Fixed-Focal-Length Lenses without Macro Functionality

The story with fixed-focal-length, or prime, lenses is similar; your max attainable magnification is around 1:3. The advantage of prime lenses, however, is they tend to be much faster than zoom lenses, which means they'll pair better with teleconverter and extension tubes.

If you're not starting with a prime lens to begin with as you start on your macro quest, it probably makes the most sense for your next purchase to be a true macro lens. If you're on a budget, you might consider looking for an old 90mm or 100mm macro lens on the used market. You sometimes can find models with a magnification factor of 1:2, which also offer utility as modest portrait lenses.

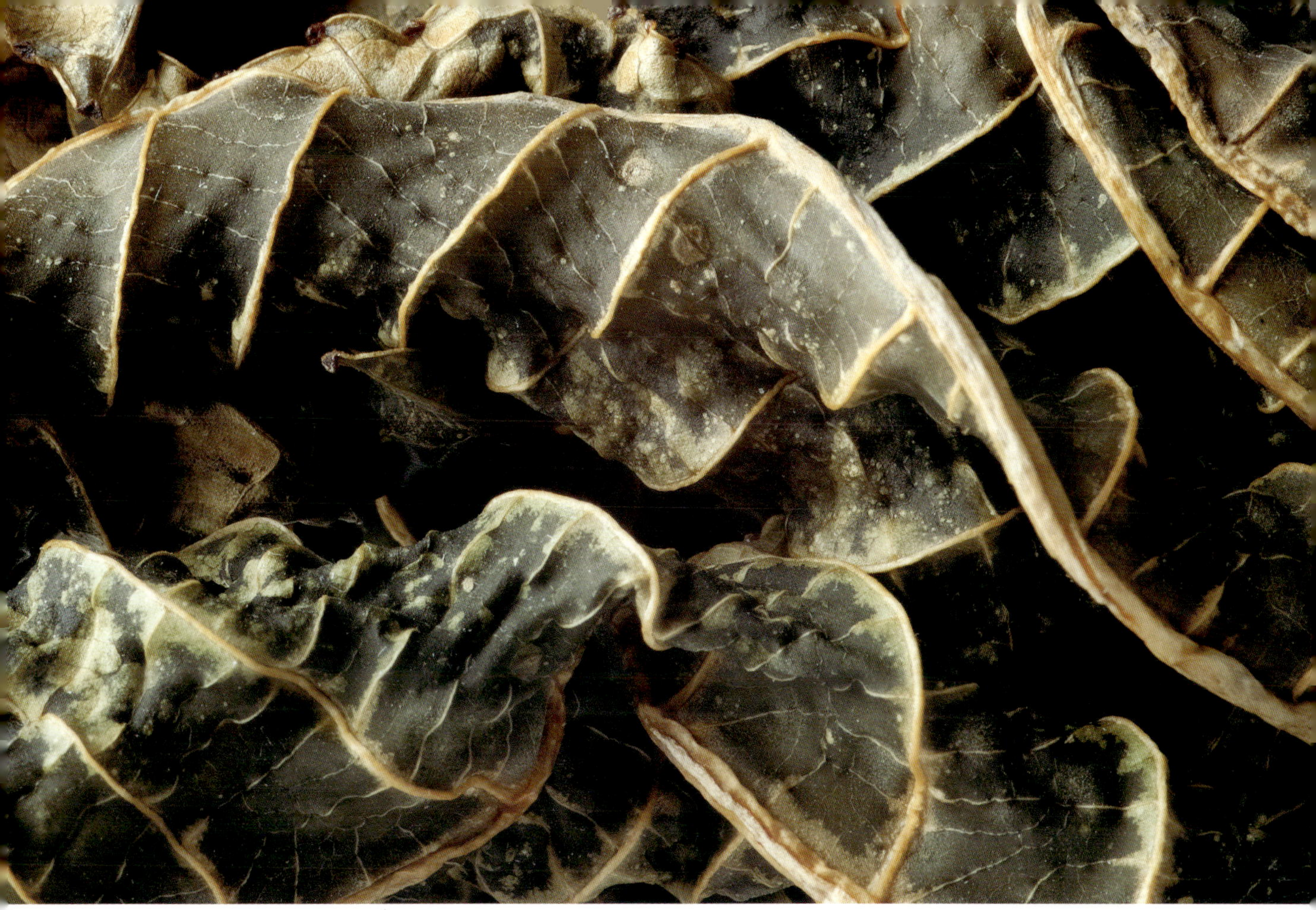

Detail image of a dried leaf
Magnification 1:2, f/22, 1/125 s, ISO
100, AF Nikkor 28–105mm 1:3.5–4.5 D
at 90mm, studio flash unit with softbox

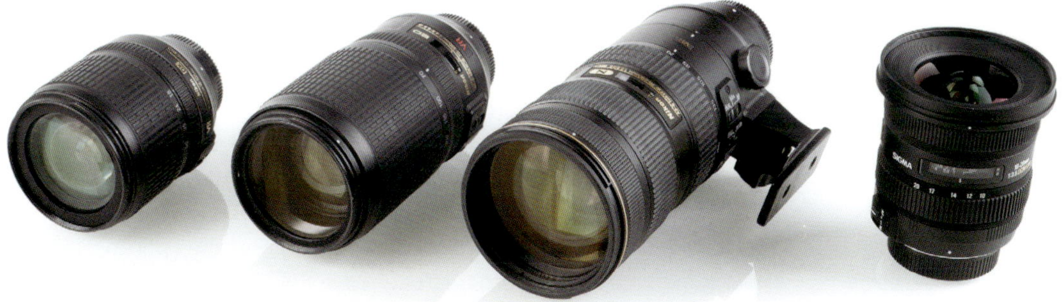

Zoom lenses offer limited functionality for macro photography. In most
cases, the magnification level ends
up being approximately 1:3.

Macro Lenses

People coming to macro photography for the first time often have to decide what focal length to purchase for their first macro lens. Ideally, the lens would be well suited for shooting a plethora of subjects from plants and insects in the wild to any possible studio subject. Unfortunately, a macro lens that is ideal for every possible subject doesn't really exist. Macro lenses have a fixed focal length, which means that different lenses need to be used for different applications.

A quality macro lens is a lifetime investment. It will allow you to capture photos focused from infinity down to a magnification of 1:1 without any additional equipment. Which focal length you decide to pursue depends wholly on your primary needs and intentions.

Nearly all macro lenses offer a maximum aperture of f/2.8, enabling photographers to shoot freehand even in difficult lighting. But you'll get the best image quality if you stop down the aperture a few stops, which is also important for macro work to ensure that your depth of field is sufficiently large.

Macro Lenses: Under 50mm

Macro lenses with focal lengths in this range tend to be designed for use with smaller sensors such as the APS-C or DX sensors or those adhering to the Micro Four Thirds standard. When used with these sensors, they effectively replicate the classic macro lens with a 50mm normal focal length. They are rarely intended to be used with full-frame cameras, although there are some wide-angle lenses designed for full-frame use that offer a magnification of up to 1:2. These products allow you to include some of the surrounding elements of your subject in your images.

Macro Lenses: From 50mm to 60mm

Focal lengths in the 50mm to 60mm range are ideal for reprography uses because they provide essentially distortion-free results. They also are great for macro uses, though, when you're working with a decent shooting distance, as is often the case when photographing plants or details of larger structures in the studio.

Macro Lenses: From 90mm to 105mm

Lenses with focal lengths ranging from 90mm to 105mm are useful for a variety of shooting situations. Because they allow a larger

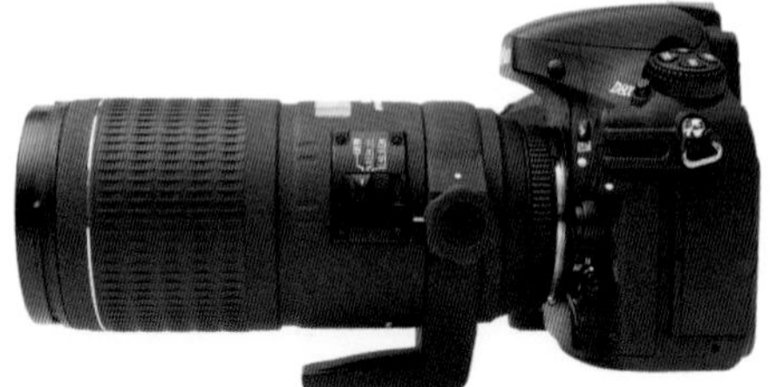

For lenses with internal focusing, the length of the lens remains the same for all focus settings

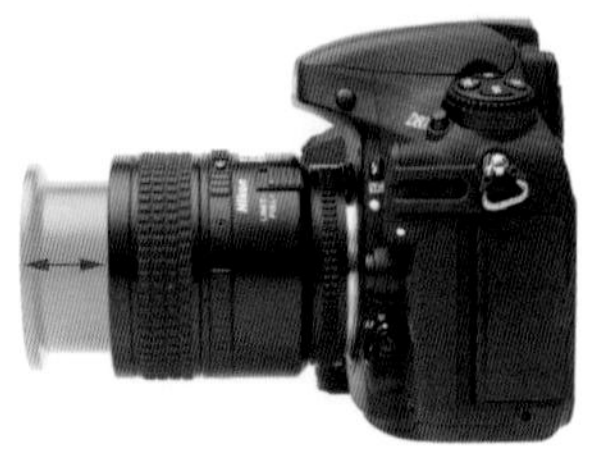

For lenses with external focusing, the length of the lens varies depending on the focus setting

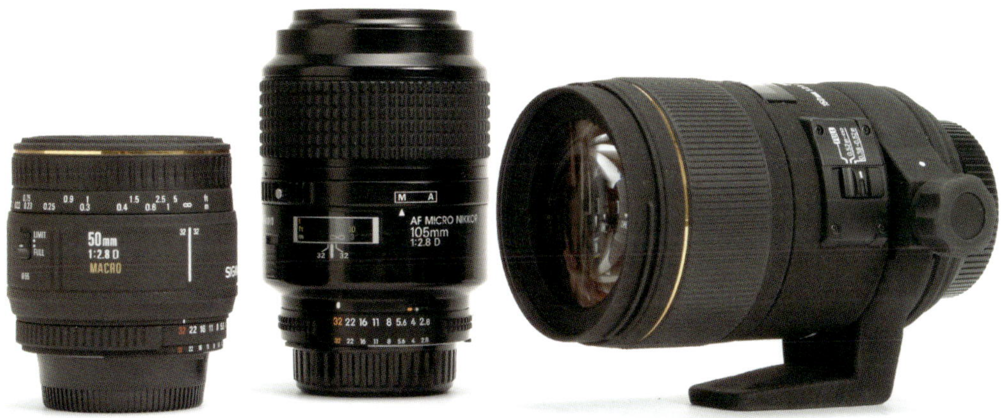

The most common focal lengths for macro lenses are 50mm, 100mm, 150mm, and 180mm

shooting distance, it's easier to cater the lighting to suit your subject. As long as the aperture isn't radically stopped down, these lenses also allow for freehand shooting. Some manufacturers have even started including image stabilization for models in this range.

Macro Lenses: 150mm and up

Telephoto macro lenses in the 150mm to 200mm range are ideal for photographing insects such as dragonflies and butterflies. The shooting distance of around 30cm from the front lens is large enough that you'll stay safely out of the flight zone for most insects, assuming you're not unduly loud or aggressive in your pursuit of your subject. If you need more distance, you can always use a teleconverter, as well.

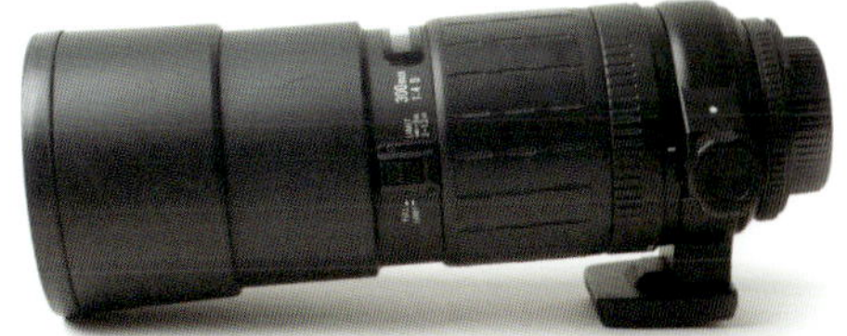

The Sigma 4/300 telephoto macro lens works well for photographing butterflies and dragonflies

Macro Lenses: 300mm and up

Lenses in this category have functionally disappeared from the market. If you search used equipment listings, you'll be able to find examples such as the Sigma 4/300mm and the Sigma 5.6/400mm. Both achieve a magnification of approximately 1:3. For this reason, their macro applications are minimal. They are more likely to help serve your efforts photographing butterflies, birds, and dragonflies.

Canon Extreme Macro Lenses

Canon offers an alternative to bellows attachments in the form of the Canon MP-E 65mm 1:2.8 1–5x macro lens. This ultra–macro lens works exclusively with Canon cameras and offers magnification powers ranging from 1:1 to 5:1. Accordingly, it offers the opportunity to dive very deeply into the macro world with the highest level of reproduction quality.

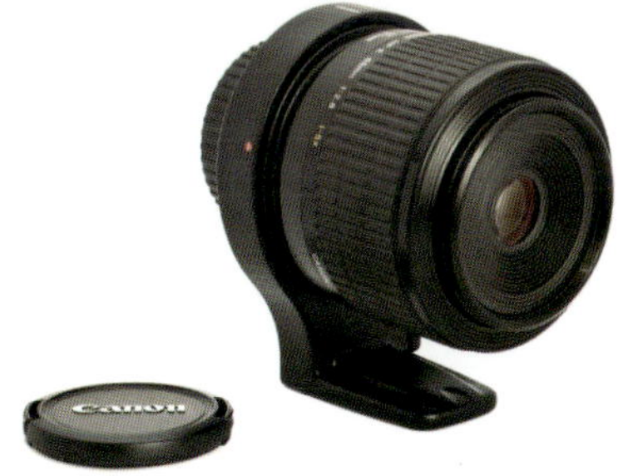

The Canon MP-E 65mm offers a magnification factor up to 5:1

Close-Up Lenses

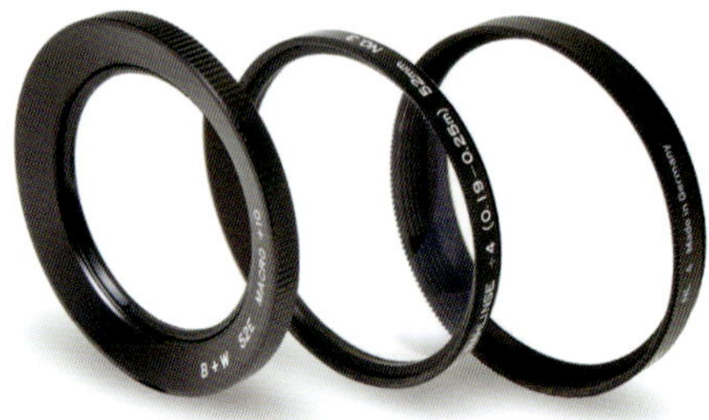

Close-up lenses are a viable option when you want to step into the world of macro photography without a great deal of effort or cost up front

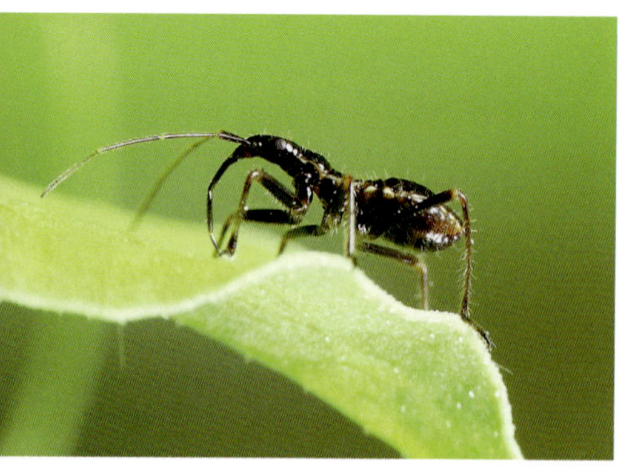

A close-up lens with a power of +2 diopters allows you to get significantly closer to your subject than the basic macro setting on a bridge camera would
Minolta Dimage, f/9, 1/640 s, ISO 100, 50mm

Close-Up Lenses

Close-up lenses are by far the most affordable entry ticket to the world of macro photography. They can be screwed directly into the filter threads at the end of a lens. By shortening the focal length of the lens, they reduce the minimum focusing distance for the lens, allowing for larger reproductions of subjects on the image sensor or film surface.

The image quality attained when using these lenses is dependent both on the optical quality of the main lens itself and the attachments. To obtain the highest imaging performance possible, you should stop the lens down at least three aperture stops.

The best results are obtained when pairing achromatic close-up lenses with high-quality prime lenses. More basic lenses may save you some money at the register, but they'll also result in clear distortions and blurring around the image borders. For these reasons, these lenses are not ideal for reprographic purposes.

The strength of a close-up lens is measured in diopters, and its magnification potential is always dependent on the lens to which it is attached. The properties of the camera lens are the basis to which the value of the close-up lens is added. A strength of +1 diopter is a modest increase, while +10 is a very significant increase.

Close-up lenses have the added advantage that they don't affect the speed of the lens or the brightness of the viewfinder image. They are light, simple to work with, and have a place in every gear bag. For starters, I recommend purchasing a close-up lens with a power of +2 diopters. Next I would go for one with a strength of +4 diopters. Close-up lenses—and their optical effects—can be combined or used simultaneously, so this combination offers plenty of versatility—but you will have to do with a loss in image quality.

These types of add-on lenses are especially practical if your camera has a fixed lens. One key prerequisite, of course, is that your lens needs to have filter threads, a trait that is all but universal for bridge cameras. Compact cameras often feature an optional adapter tube for this specific purpose.

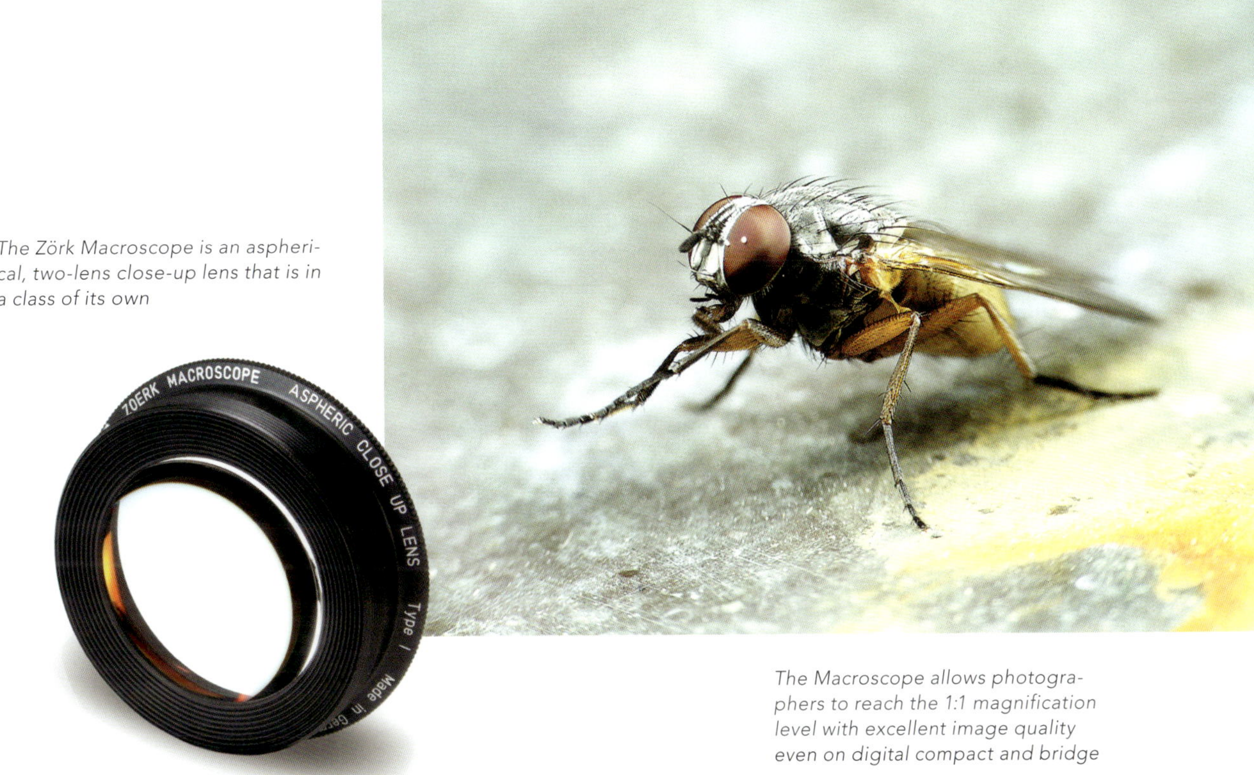

The Zörk Macroscope is an aspherical, two-lens close-up lens that is in a class of its own

The Macroscope allows photographers to reach the 1:1 magnification level with excellent image quality even on digital compact and bridge cameras

Zörk Macroscope

The Zörk Macroscope is a top-class aspherical, two-lens close-up lens with a power of +12 diopters. Its optical quality is vastly superior to most traditional close-up filters, but it still works in combination with the main camera lens, whose quality still factors into the equation. When coupled with an 80mm lens, the Zörk Macroscope can produce a magnification of 1:1—at a shooting distance of around 6cm to 9cm. That distance will encroach on the flight zone of many animals, but it is large enough to adjust the lighting specifically based on the needs of your subjects. In the wide-angle range, however, vignetting effects can crop up from time to time. As with other close-up filters, the Zörk Macroscope attaches directly to the lens filter threads. Its best application is with zoom lenses, but it also can be paired well with true macro lenses to produce magnification levels far beyond 1:1. Attaching this tool to a bridge camera that has image stabilization makes for a powerful and compact all-around macro solution for shooting on the go.

Teleconverters and Extension Tubes

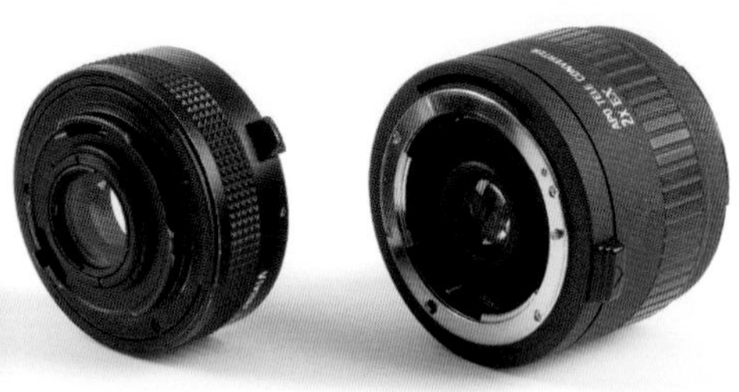

Teleconverters, which increase the focal length of the lens by a specific factor, can be found with conversion factors of 1.4x, 1.5x, or 2x

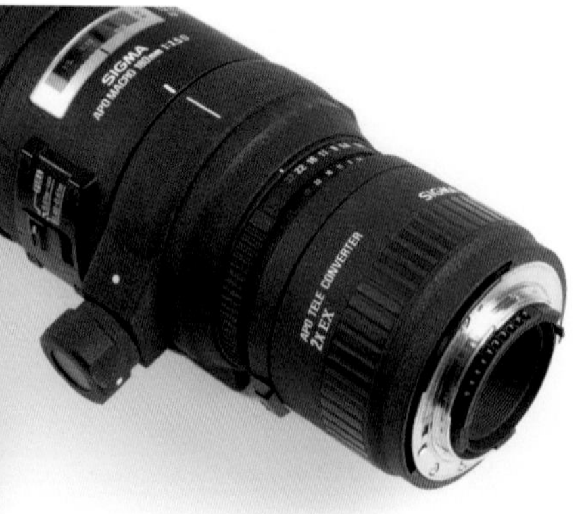

Some manufacturers design teleconverters to pair with specific lenses. Doing so allows engineers to design the converters in a way to work perfectly with the individual lens and to maximize the attainable image quality of the system.

Buying a new lens isn't always an option, and it's an expense that may not make sense if you suspect you will use it only infrequently. For photographers in this position, teleconverters and extension tubes offer a practical solution. They can enhance the shooting applications for a lens so that it can effectively be used as a macro lens.

Teleconverters

Teleconverters are composed of an optical system that alters the focal length of a lens by a specific factor. For macro photography applications, this means that if you keep the shooting distance constant, then the reproduced image of the subject on the image sensor will be increased by the factor of the converter. In other words, the shooting distance is altered accordingly when the magnification level is kept constant. For example, a system comprising a 50mm macro lens with a magnification of 1:1 paired with a 2x converter would effectively operate as a 100mm macro lens at 2:1. Shooting at a magnification of 1:1 would double the shooting distance. Teleconverters are accordingly cost-effective alternatives to significantly more expensive telephoto macros.

One downside of converters is that they affect the speed of the lens they're paired with, so it's best not to use them with particularly slow lenses. You'll have to accept a loss of light on the order of two stops with a 2x converter and around one stop with a 1.5x converter. The viewfinder image will also be darker by the same factor.

Some converters are engineered to pair with specific lenses, and these systems tend to produce excellent image quality. Unlike with extension tubes, converters will allow you to still focus the lens at infinity.

Extension Tubes

Extension tubes are hollow devices without any optical elements that are installed between the camera and the lens. Their purpose is to increase the extension of the lens—to move the front lens farther away from the image sensor.

Getting into the macro range with extension tubes is possible only by combining different lenses, which can be ungainly to achieve while working. Extending a 50mm normal lens by 50mm produces a magnification of 1:1. The attainable image quality will be highly dependent on the lens. Using an extension tube in tandem with a macro lens or a wide-angle lens can produce great results with magnifications beyond 1:1—but the distance between the lens and the subject will be quite small.

For the pictures of the peacock feather below, the subject's distance from the front lens when using a 13mm extension tube was about 50mm. But with the 31mm extension, the shooting distance dropped to only 10mm. At such a small distance, it's a real challenge to manage lighting well.

If you do opt for going the extension tube route, look for models capable of automatically relaying information from the camera to the lens.

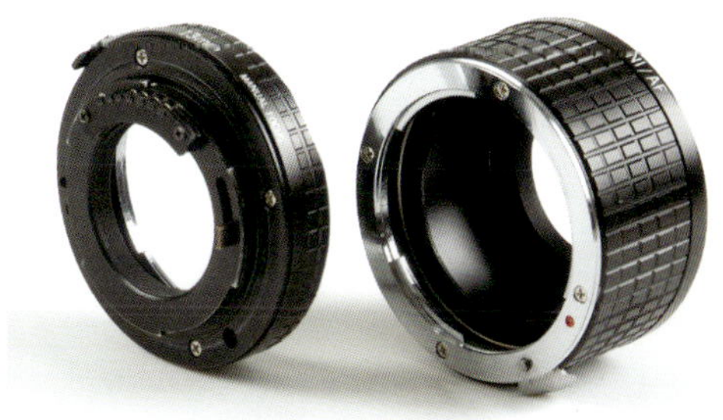

Extension tubes increase a lens's extension. They are available in fixed sizes of 13mm, 21mm, and 31mm.

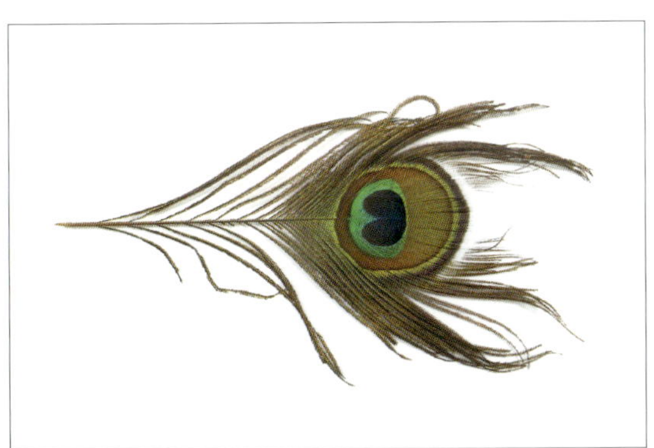

A 24mm lens by itself doesn't have a minimum focusing distance conducive to macro imaging

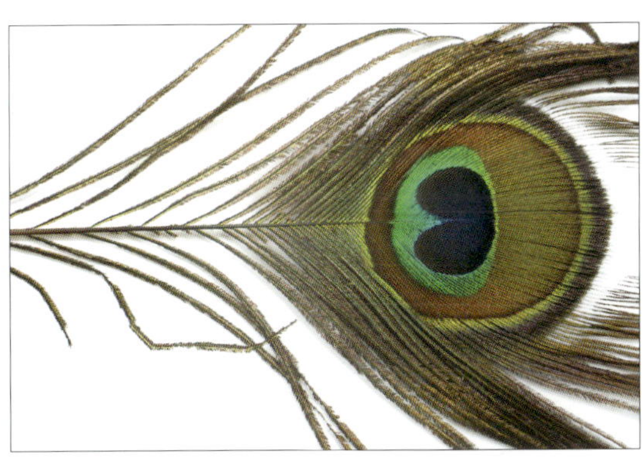

It's possible to get much closer to the feather when using this lens in combination with a 2x teleconverter

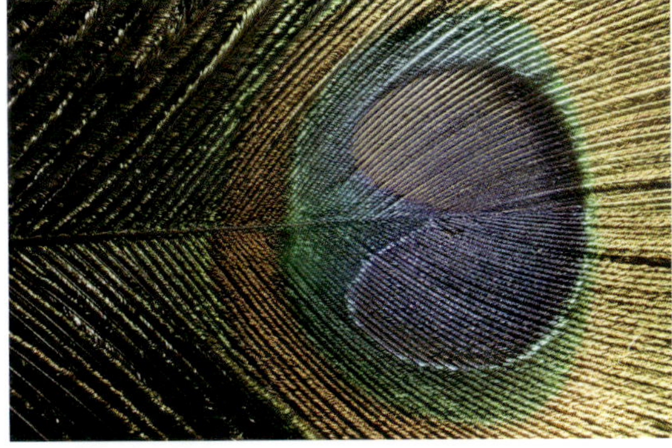

Using a 13mm extension tube in combination with the 24mm wide-angle lens almost produces a magnification of 1:1

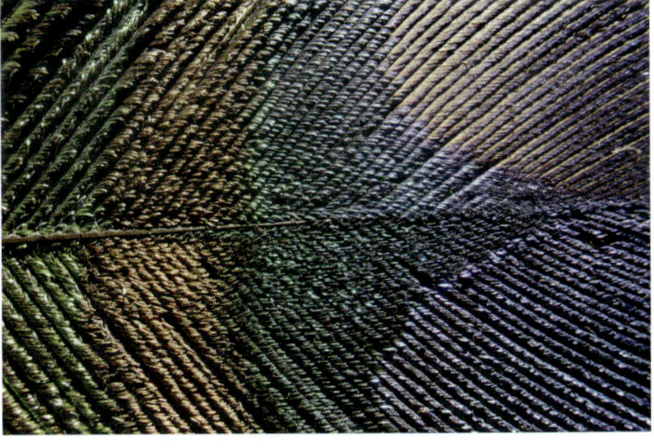

And when paired with a 31mm extension tube, the lens is able to supersede the 1:1 threshold significantly

Reversing Rings and Coupling Rings

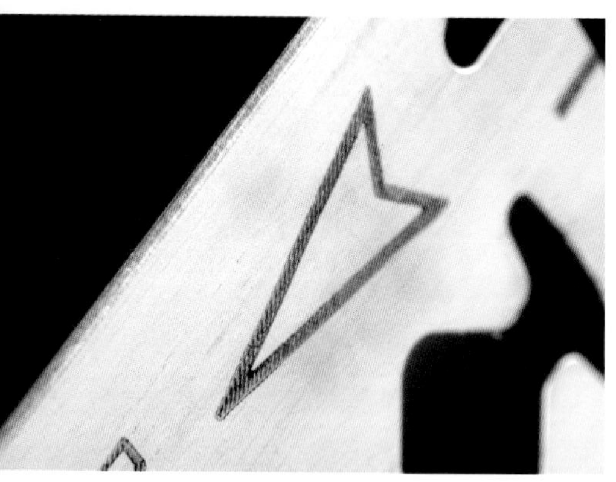

Detail of a razor blade. Reversed 24mm wide-angle lens at f/22. The depth of field is reduced to a few scant millimeters.

Reversing Rings

A reversing ring allows you to attach a lens to your camera body backward—in a reversed position. A reversed 35mm lens is capable of producing a magnification factor of around 1:1, and a 20mm lens, can shoot upward of 3:1.

On one side of a reversing ring, you'll find the bayonet mount required to attach to the camera body, and on the other side, you'll find threads that can be screwed onto the front of the lens where filters would normally be attached. Reversing a lens means you'll have to do without the electronic communication between the camera and lens that controls aperture and other settings automatically. This loss of functionality makes things somewhat more difficult: even though you'll be able to focus with an open aperture, you'll have to stop the aperture down manually when you're ready to capture your image. Doing so darkens the display image accordingly. An additional challenge stems from the sensitivity of the focus point, which shifts with the slightest movement of the camera. Using a very stable tripod in combination with a focusing rail is a way to overcome this particular obstacle.

When installing a lens in reverse, it doesn't have to make use of the camera manufacturer's proprietary bayonet mount, which means you can use any lens you wish for the purpose. The only requirement is that it must have fitting threads to attach to the reversing mount. But there are even thread adapters on the market, should you want to use a lens that doesn't fit on its own for whatever reason.

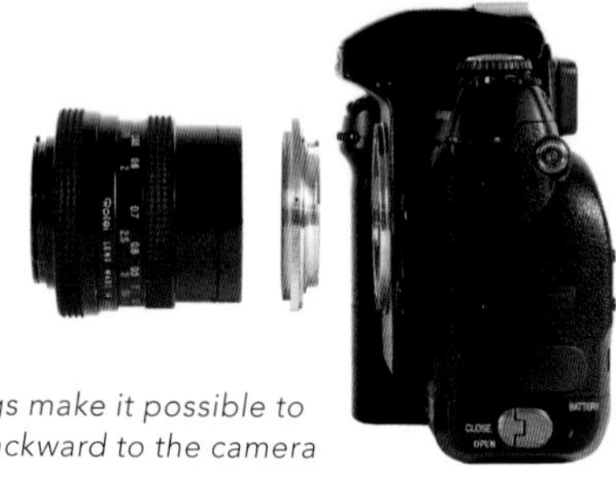

Reversing rings make it possible to affix lenses backward to the camera body

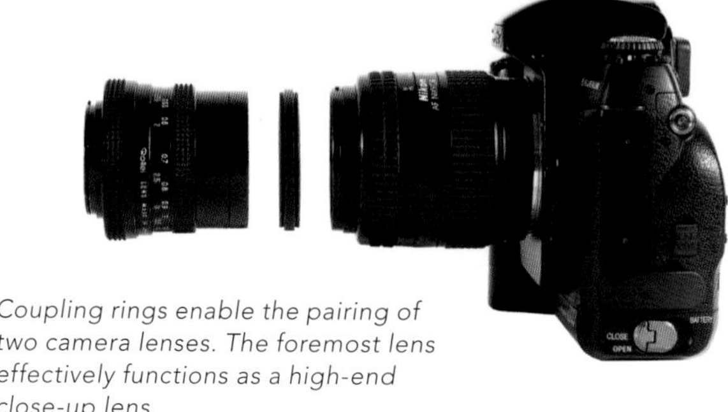

Coupling rings enable the pairing of two camera lenses. The foremost lens effectively functions as a high-end close-up lens.

Managing light for your exposures can be a bit finicky when shooting with a reverse-mounted lens. The shooting distance will be dramatically reduced, so depending on the focal length you're using, you may have only a few centimeters between the end of your lens and the subject, which makes it difficult to set up lamps to illuminate your subject in a desirable way. Further complicating the matter is the fact that reverse-mounted lenses are particularly sensitive to stray light, and there likely won't be room for a lens hood of any kind.

Canon EOS photographers have an interesting solution in the form of the Novoflex reverse adapter. This delightful tool comprises a cable and a second attachment ring that enables the communication of various information from the lens to the reversed lens. When using this device, you'll still be able to focus with an open aperture and a bright viewfinder image, because the aperture will automatically adjust when the shutter button is pressed.

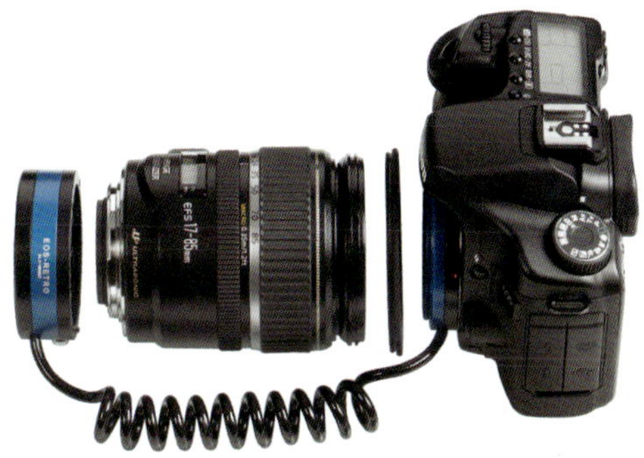

The Novoflex reverse adapter for Canon cameras and lenses relays all of the relevant exposure details from the camera to the lens—even if the lens is reverse installed
Photo: Novoflex

Coupling Rings

Coupling rings allow a second camera lens to function essentially as a high-end close-up lens attached to the primary lens. The ring has male threads on either side so the lenses can be attached front to front. It's ideal to use a wide-angle lens as the add-on, but regular lenses with wide openings will also work. If the attachment lens is too small, then you will lose some of the image area or your images will suffer from significant vignetting.

When exposing your image, set the aperture for the reversed lens so it is wide open. Other than that, you can shoot normally, because the main lens is affixed to the camera as it normally would be.

You can also use coupling rings to reverse a second lens with compact and bridge cameras as long as they possess threads of the right diameter.

The foremost reversed lens mounts via threads as opposed to a specialized bayonet mount, which means you can use any inexpensive lens from a secondhand shop or Internet auction to do the job. This method offers a very affordable entry point for very powerful macro capabilities.

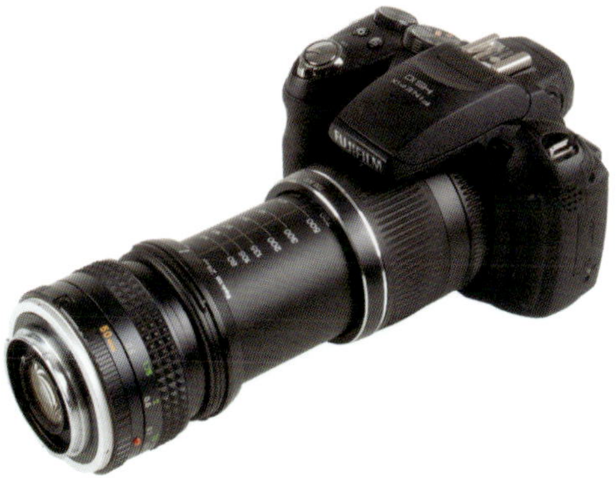

Fujifilm FinePix HS10 bridge camera with the 1:1.7, 50mm Minolta MF lens installed in reverse...

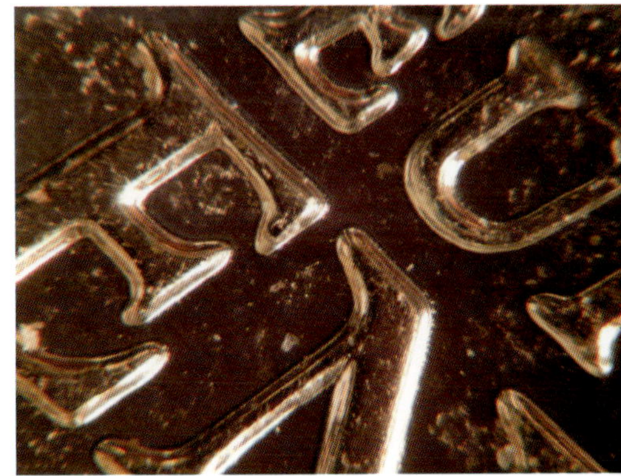

...and the result of this setup: a detail from a one-cent coin

Bellows

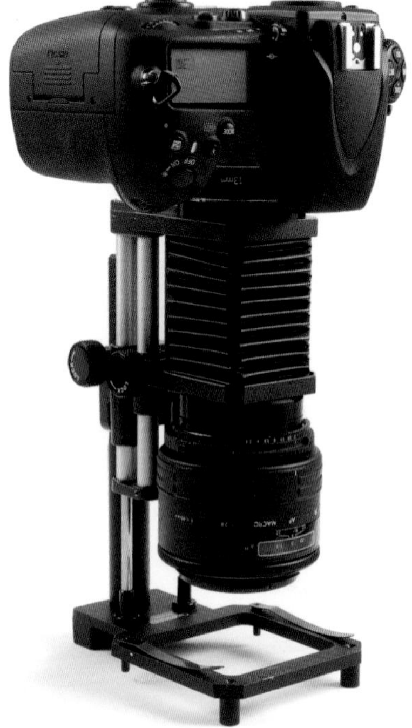

Bellows extensions enable magnification levels well beyond the 1:1 threshold. This illustration shows an older model with a small shooting stand that also doubles as a slide copier.

In simple terms, a bellows is a variable extension tube. A *bellows* increases the extension of a lens—not in defined steps, but in a gradual manner as controlled by a rack-and-pinion adjustment system. Aside from the special lens heads designed specifically for use with bellows units, macro lenses with a focal length range of 60mm to 100mm are also very functional, because they will give you enough room between your lens and your subject to manage the light effectively. The bellows unit I use is an old 90mm Sigma APO Macro that is capable of producing a magnification of only 1:2. I like it, however, because it's relatively compact and leaves a good bit of distance in front of my subject.

One potential drawback of using bellows extensions—in particular with DSLRs—is the dust that tends to settle in their folds. It's important to use a dust-removing tool every time before you attach the device to your camera body.

Some bellows models relay the exposure data, including the automatic aperture, which means you can focus your image with an open aperture and a bright viewfinder image. On the camera side, it's a real advantage if the camera can meter the exposure with manual lenses. It's not strictly necessary, however, because you'll need to use additional lighting in most cases with a bellows lens on account of the extreme levels of magnification produced and the subsequent need to stop the aperture down significantly to extend the depth of field as much as possible.

It's possible to use normal and wide-angle lenses in reverse positioning, which means, depending on the extension offered by the bellows and the lens in use, you can produce magnification levels upward of 6:1.

Slide-copying adapters are one interesting tool for use with bellows as they can be used as small photography tables. Paired with the bellows unit, they create a very stable setup that minimizes the risk of camera shake.

Ring lights and twin-flash units or LED lamps are highly useful with bellows devices, because they don't take up much space and offer good lighting for the likely tight conditions in front of your lens.

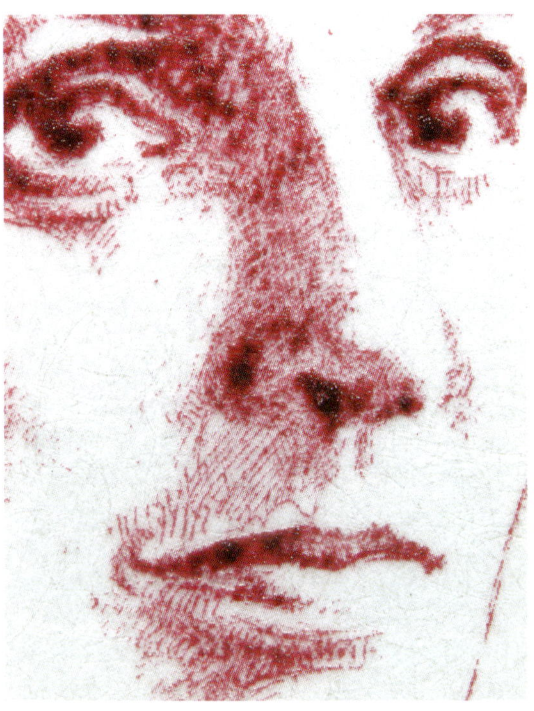

Detail of a stamp shot with a 90mm macro lens and a ring flash on a bellows

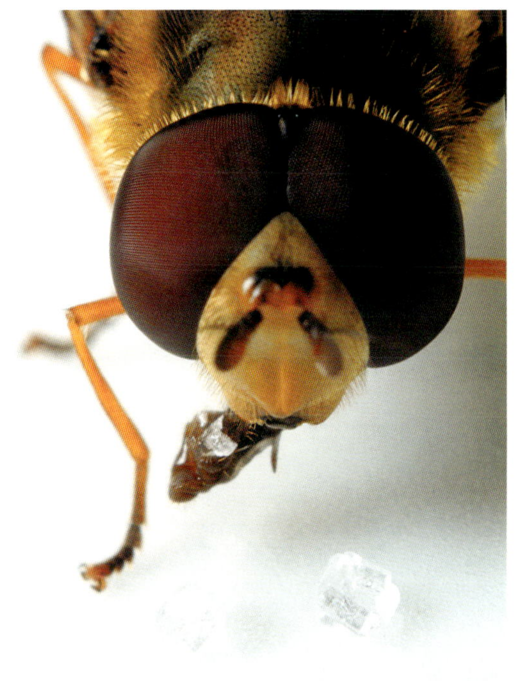

A fly snacks on sugar. A reversed 50mm normal lens on a bellows and a small flash (GN22) used manually with a softbox.

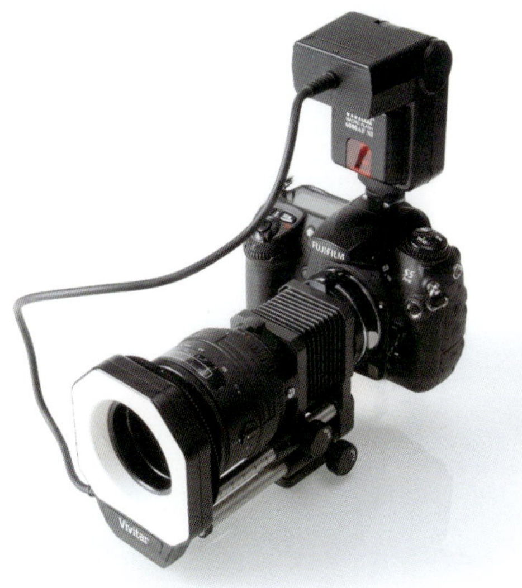

Ring flash units are especially practical and effective when shooting with a bellows attachment

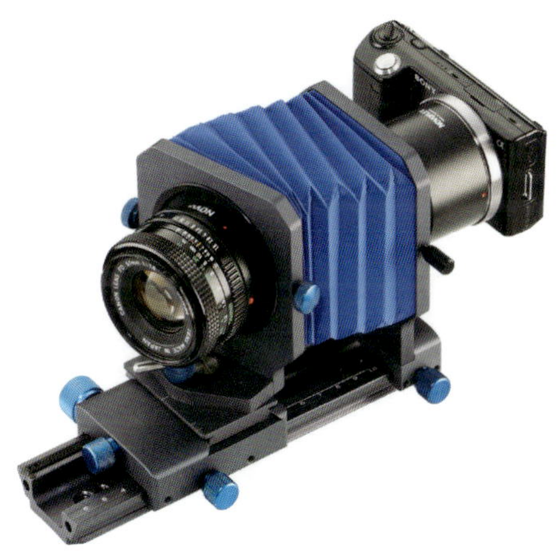

The newest generation of bellows units offers tilt-shift swiveling as well as adapters for a wide variety of cameras and lenses
Photo: Novoflex

Altering Depth of Field

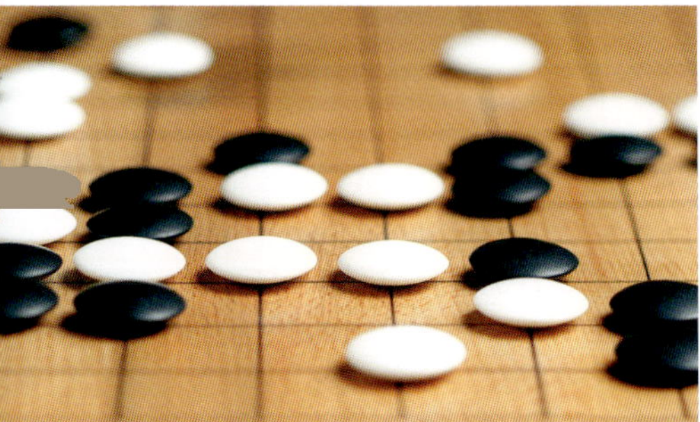

With an aperture of f/4.5 and a normal orientation, the depth of field appears very tight

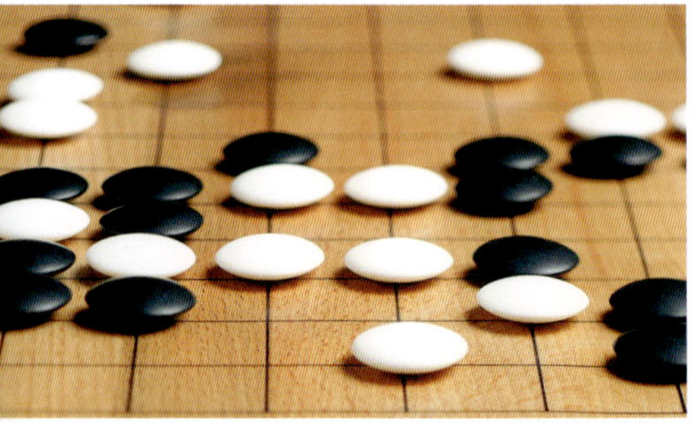

Tipping the lens vertically noticeably extends the depth of field without needing to alter the aperture

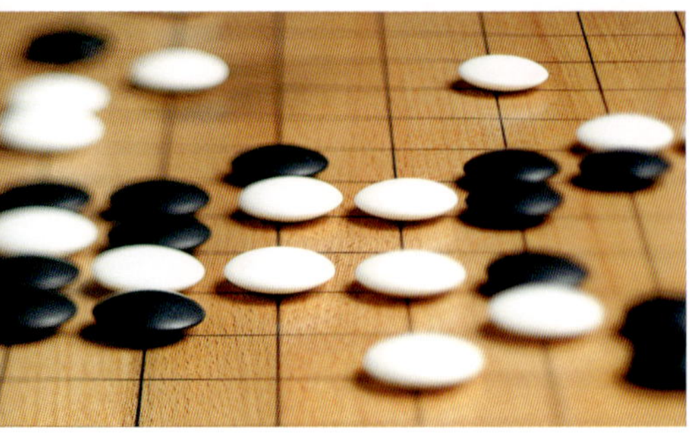

Pivoting the lens laterally shifts the alignment of the depth of field

With conventional cameras, the focal plane is always parallel to the plane of the film or image sensor. The depth of field extends forward and backward from that plane. To increase the depth of field, it's necessary to stop down the aperture.

Pivoting the lens can shift the focal plane, causing areas that previously were beyond the depth of field to now be positioned within it. This method of altering the orientation of the depth of field, referred to as the *Scheimpflug principle*, allows for very brief exposure times because the lens doesn't need to be stopped down to increase the depth of field. Tilting the lens doesn't extend the depth of field; it is still defined by the aperture setting. But the shifted lens realigns the focal plane, allowing more critical elements of your photo to appear in focus. This effect makes it seem to viewers that the depth of field is larger. Photographers can use this method to compose their images purposefully; you might, for example, redirect the focal plane so the entire length of a pen lying on a diagonal appears sharp or so that only certain elements appear sharp. Adjusting your position or the focal length of the lens to increase the depth of field unavoidably leads to a smaller magnification factor, which is not a viable option. When using a special bellows lens with an additional shift function, you can also correct certain perspective distortions, similar to removing converging vertical lines in architectural photos.

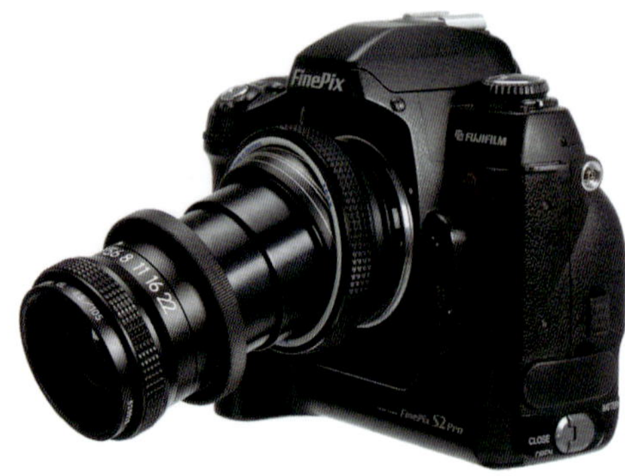

The Zörk Multi Focus System offers a high degree of flexibility with focusing and generally enables photographers to shoot freehand

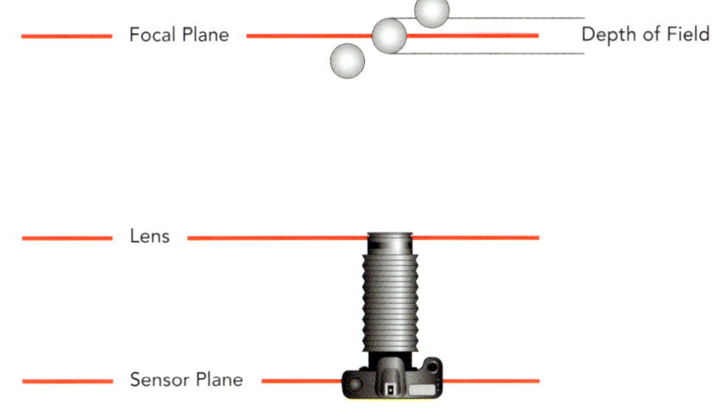

The focal plane lies parallel to the lens and the film/sensor plane. This orientation makes the depth of field extend from front to back. A larger depth of field can be achieved by stopping down the aperture.

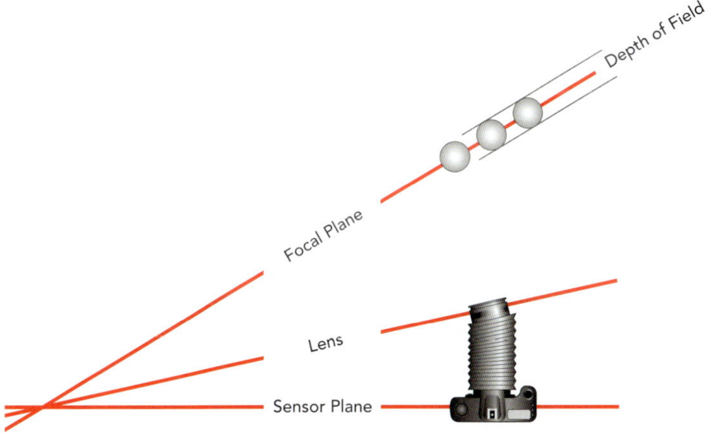

Turning the lens also causes a shift in the orientation of the focal plane, and in this illustration, the shift means that all of the key elements of the subject now fall within the depth of field. The size of the depth of field remains unchanged, but its orientation with respect to the camera and subject is altered. Stopping down will still increase the depth of field.

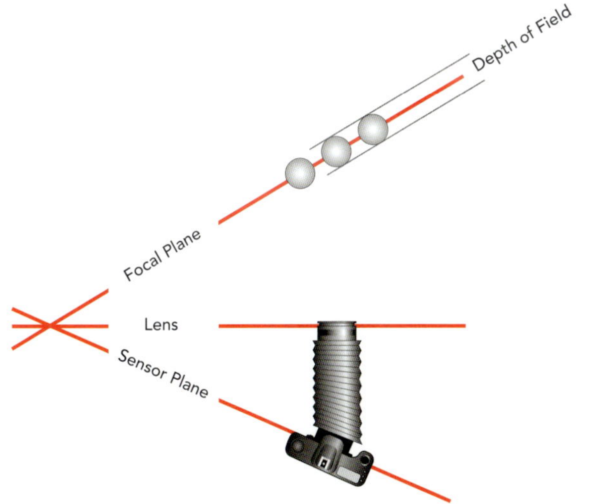

View cameras allow for the film or sensor plane to be shifted, and some modern bellows attachments enable this functionality for current DSLRs, too

Lighting for Close-Up and Macro Photography

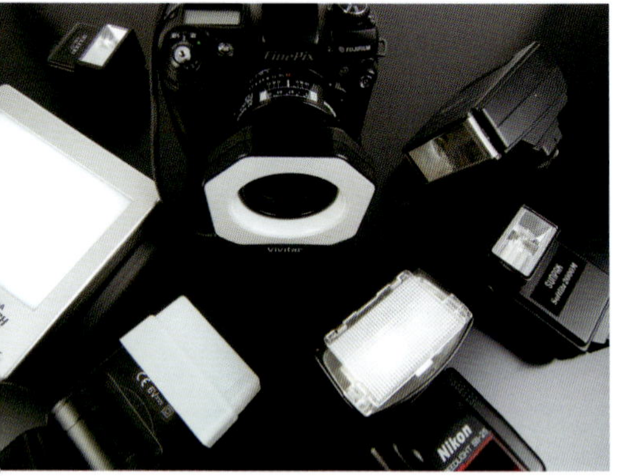

Flash units can be found in any number of shapes and sizes. They offer the most universal solution for macro photography lighting situations.

Light makes the picture. That saying might be a bit simplistic, but it gets to the heart of the question: what sort of lighting source should you use for your macro photographs?

For the most part, all of the sources of light discussed here can be divided into two categories: flash and continuous lighting.

The big advantage of continuous lighting is that you can watch through your viewfinder in real time to evaluate the result of every minor adjustment to the lighting setup. This particular benefit may appeal to beginning photographers in particular, because it makes the process of managing light much less abstract than it is when using flash lighting.

The advantages of flash units, however, are their compact size, impressive power output, and battery-powered operation. They're also very popular and widespread. The number of photographer households without at least one system flash unit is probably tremendously low.

Yet another key plus for flash units is their exceptionally fast flash duration, which, depending on the model, can be as brief as 1/12,000 second. This feature allows photographers to freeze movements like falling droplets or flying insects in place. To achieve the same effect with continuous lighting would require a vast amount of light. If you're curious why that is, flip ahead to the chapter on high-speed photography.

System Flash Units

The power outputs offered by system flash units are wholly sufficient for macro photography uses. They are compact and offer much more flexibility of use compared to larger studio units, and because they are not reliant on a power outlet, you can also take them out into the wild for on-site shooting adventures.

Working with flash units tends to be a bit abstract, because you won't be able to judge how effectively they are set up until you see the results in your first exposure. But with practice you will quickly figure out how to better approach even complicated lighting situations with flash.

The flash2softbox system further makes system flash units practical. This system allows you to adapt any light-shaping device designed for professional flash units for use with your camera. System

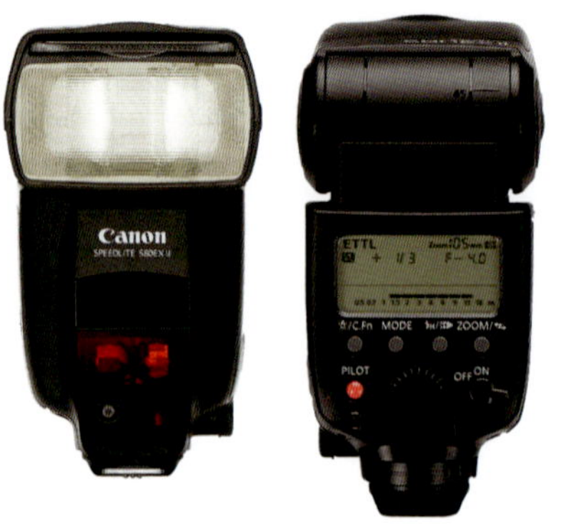

*Modern system flash units are designed to communicate seamlessly with the camera and with each other
Photos: Canon*

flash units are traditionally mounted to a shoe mount on the camera body, but they can also be removed and positioned remotely. In this case, flash control is communicated via a cable, or wirelessly via infrared or radio signals.

Ring and Twin Flashes

The ring and twin flash units on the market range from simple models with a fixed output to TTL-regulated models to high-end options featuring multiple flash tubes that can be individually regulated via wireless communication from a central, master device such as the Nikon Macro Flash Kit R1C1/R1.

Basic ring flashes tend to produce somewhat flat results because they emit uniform light from the front of the lens; they don't accentuate specific parts of the image through intriguing light and shadow play. One option for trying to improve this result is to use tape to cover up half of a ring flash with a piece of grey translucent material. Units that allow you to modulate individual areas of a ring flash tend to produce significantly better images.

Twin flashes have two—sometimes more—flash heads that can be controlled separately; they're functionally comparable to a mini photo studio. One option with a three-unit model, for example, is to set one flash up to serve as background lighting, one to serve as the key light, and one to provide accent lighting—the classic setup for studio lighting.

Ring Flash Adapters for System Flashes

This lighting solution features a device comprising reflectors and diffusers to transform the light produced from a system flash into a ring flash. The advantage of this method is that all of the TTL functionalities of the flash will still work. The disadvantage is that you'll lose two to three stops of lighting—but that loss shouldn't be an insurmountable obstacle if your system flash is of adequate strength.

Studio Flash Units

Studio flash systems are more powerful and diverse than system flashes and the like. They typically offer 100 watts or more and are available in every price class imaginable. Macro photography doesn't require a tremendous amount of light—an entire room doesn't need to be illuminated—so a small entry-level studio flash device would be more than enough. All the main brands offer an overwhelming variety of light-shaping tools that can handle any of your needs. The size of these devices, however, tends to be on the large size for use with macro photography.

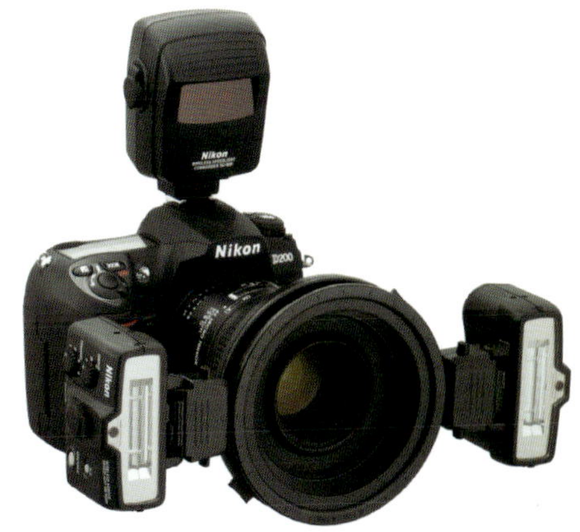

*The Nikon Macro Flash Kit R1C1 is a wireless flash system comprising one central control unit and two small flash heads with a guide number of 10. The central control unit also allows you to incorporate additional flash units to extend the creative possibilities of your lighting.
Photo: Nikon*

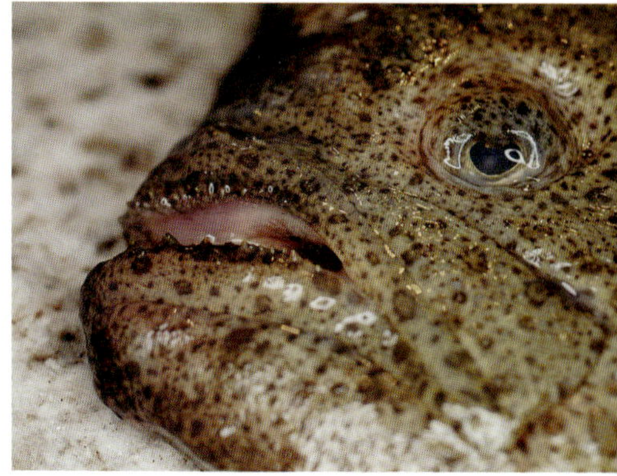

Ring flashes produce circular reflections on shiny surfaces—which can be creatively used to create appealing results

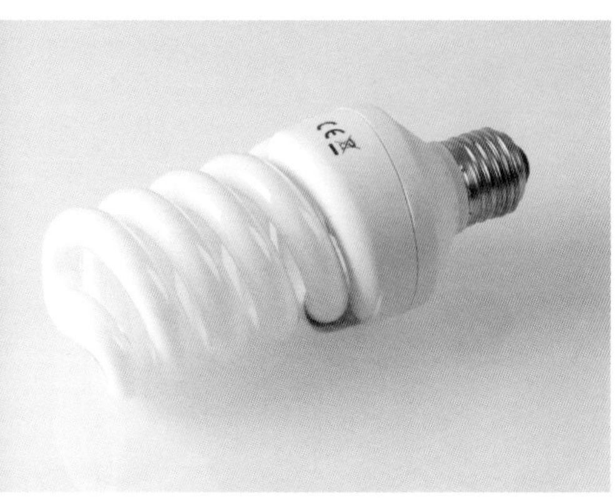

Daylight lamps can be used in any normal bulb socket, making them a practical choice for photographers who are just getting started collecting lighting devices for a studio

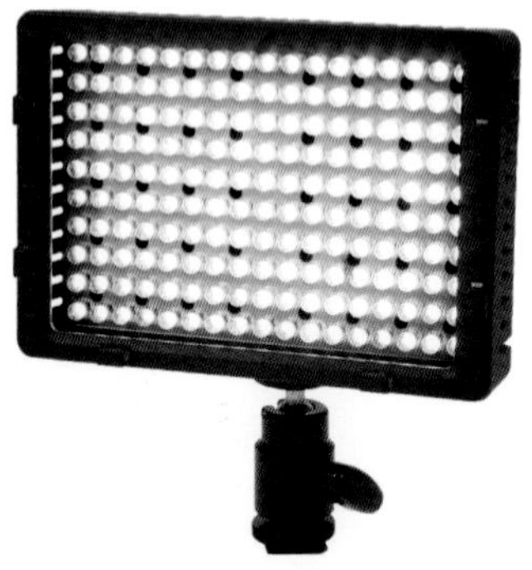

LED area light
Photo: Dörr

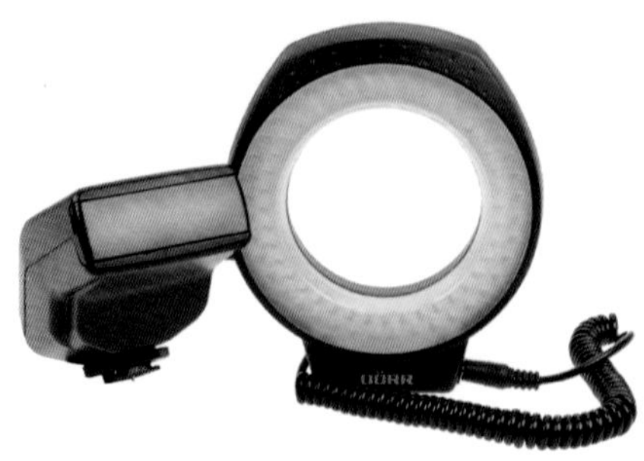

LED ring light
Photo: Dörr

Incandescent Bulbs

Traditional light bulbs unfortunately convert a significant amount of the energy they draw into heat, which is why they are disappearing from the market. The light spectrum emitted from these bulbs is very even, and the temperature of the light they produce tends to range between 2,000 Kelvin and 2,700 Kelvin, which amounts to a yellow-orange light. These lights are not ideal for macro photography because of the warmth they produce.

Low-Energy Light Bulbs

The successors to the incandescent bulb offer the same luminosity but at a significantly reduced consumption of energy. These bulbs are not ideal for photographic purposes, however, because the light they produce is entirely lacking in some areas of the light spectrum.

Halogen Lamps

Halogen bulbs produce light between 3,000 Kelvin and 3,200 Kelvin, which is somewhat whiter than traditional incandescent bulbs. They're much more compact than common light bulbs, but conversion filters are generally required when using them for photographic lighting—heat generation is also a problem with them.

Daylight Lamps

Daylight lamps are effectively constructed in the same way as low-energy bulbs, but they put out a spectrum of light that mimics natural lighting. This quality makes them ideal candidates for supplementing shots involving natural daylight with additional light.

The availability of light-shaping devices for daylight lamps leaves something to be desired, but it's relatively easy to improvise solutions by building a diffuser out of translucent film, for example, because daylight lamps produce a very minimal amount of heat.

LED Lights

LED lights are small and bright and use minimal amounts of electricity—ideal characteristics for macro photography in the studio. You'll find a wide array of inexpensive LED bulbs in hardware and electronics stores, but even though they may be tempting, they aren't very suitable for macro photography applications because they don't offer a continuous spectrum of light. Using them means many colors won't reproduce well.

The LED lights that are specially designed for use with photography are significantly more expensive, but they emit the full spectrum of light. They're available as surface, ring, and spot lights, and they are very practical for illuminating small subjects. As your subjects start to increase in size, however, as may be the case with some tabletop photography applications, LED lamps tend to reach their limit. As with all continuous lighting options, LEDs aren't ideal for freezing movement; flash options simply can't be outdone for this purpose. LEDs are especially useful for brightening up poorly lit subject areas. Just as with ring flash units, the more flexibility for modulating the way LED bulbs emit their light, the better you will be able to design the light and shadow play to appear attractive.

Fluorescent Lights

Common fluorescent lights are not ideal for photography. First, the light they emit is not composed of a continuous spectrum of light. Second, when used during daylight, the mixed lighting situation results in a green cast that is difficult to correct. More appropriate are fluorescent tubes optimized for photography. They are usually offered as surface lights, and they're similar to the fluorescent tubes used in lightboxes and in viewing booths used to proof printed colors against originals.

When using these types of lights for photography, it's necessary to use models that include an electronic ballast to prevent flickering that can appear distracting at some shutter speeds. These types of lamps are intended for use when color reproduction is of the utmost importance.

Lightboxes for Transmitted Lighting

Lightboxes are widely used in the graphic arts industry. They generally emit a color of light comparable to natural daylight—around 5,000 Kelvin. If you use lightboxes for transmitted light, be sure that the fill lighting that you will likely need from above is the same kind of light to avoid color distortions resulting from mixed light.

Light Guides

Light guides are transparent glass fibers that you can use to direct pointed light at a subject. In principle, you can use light guides with all sources of light, but the most well-known use for these tools is for microscopy with a cool light source. The glass fibers are generally flexible goosenecks that often feature a focusing lens on the outlet end.

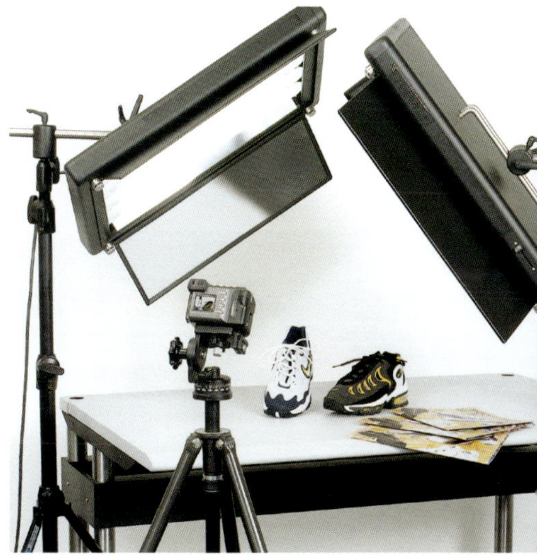

*Special surface lights with photo-optimized fluorescent tubes are ideal for color-critical situations
Photo: Just-Normlicht*

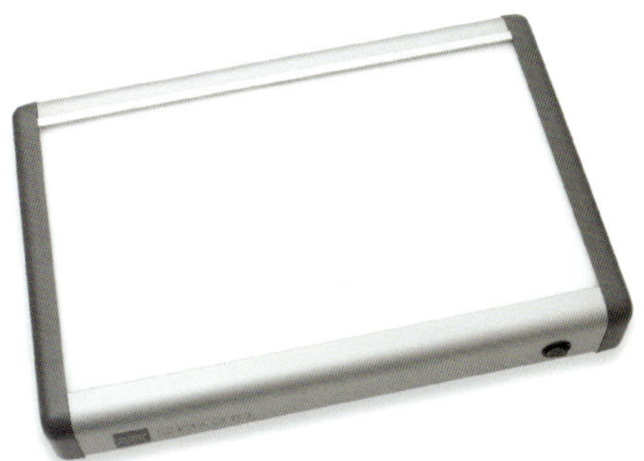

Lightboxes with standardized light sources are designed for shooting with transmitted lighting, but they can also function as surface lights

Colors of Light and Color Reproduction

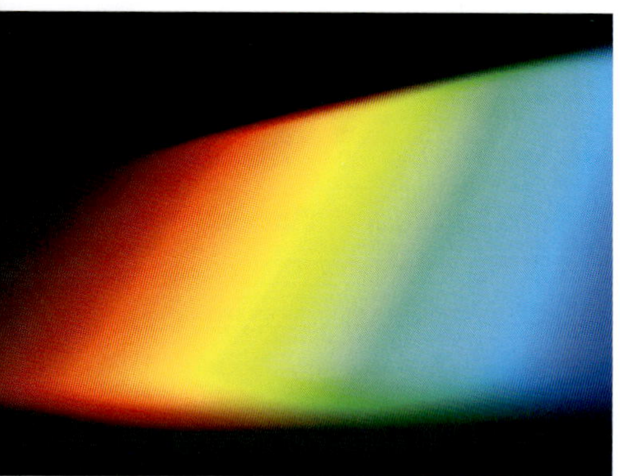

Directing white daylight through a prism produces the spectrum of colors

"Why is it necessary for lighting to fulfill certain requirements? Why can't I use any old light for my photographs? All types of light make things brighter, right?" These questions and ones similar to them often come up in conversations about lighting macro photographs.

To answer these questions, we need to back up a little and go over some fundamental concepts first.

The Spectrum of Light

The spectrum of visible light is a small fraction of the much larger spectrum of electromagnetic radiation, which includes everything from gamma rays, X-rays, and UV and infrared radiation; even radar and radio waves. The span of this spectrum that is relevant to photography (in other words, the span of energy that an image sensor can capture and process into a photograph) roughly corresponds to what the human eye is capable of perceiving. A sensor is actually capable of detecting some infrared and UV light, but upstream filters in the camera remove these types of radiation because they can have undesirable effects on the reproduction of colors in the visible spectrum.

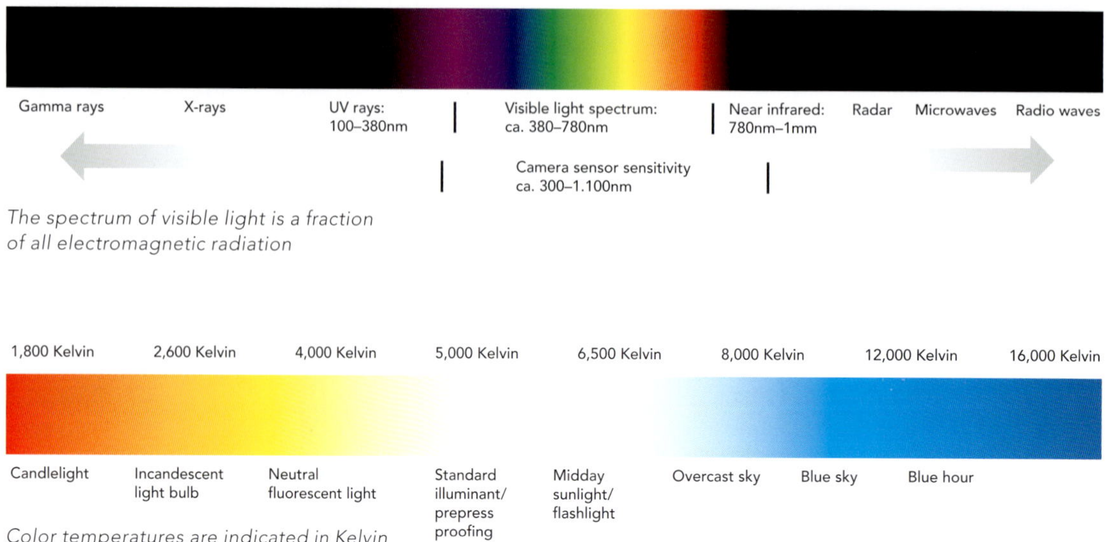

The spectrum of visible light is a fraction of all electromagnetic radiation

Color temperatures are indicated in Kelvin

Color Temperature

Color temperature, measured in Kelvin, is a critical concept for photography. Different color temperatures correspond to different colors of light on the spectrum. For example, the light from the sun in the middle of the day is usually between 5,500 Kelvin and 5,800 Kelvin, a color temperature we perceive as white. In contrast, an incandescent bulb produces a yellowish light of around 2,800 Kelvin, and a cloudy sky produces a bluish light with a temperature of about 7,500 Kelvin. Light emitted from a flash unit is typically around 5,500 Kelvin and accordingly exhibits a similar quality to normal, white daylight.

A camera's white balance can be programmed to correspond to the temperature of the lighting for individual exposures. You can adjust the white balance by choosing a predefined setting from a list such as "incandescent light," "overcast sky," and so on, or you can manually set the white balance by running a quick test using a neutral grey card.

Mixed Light

Photographs featuring multiple sources that emit light of varying temperatures may display color casts of varying prominence. The appearance of this situation will be familiar to you from pictures of houses with interior incandescent lighting shot during the blue hour. If the camera's white balance is based on the natural light, then the house's interior light will appear yellow. If the white balance is alternatively based on the light bulbs, then the indoor lighting will appear normal but the twilight outdoors will look very blue in contrast. It's not possible to correct mixed lighting situations with an individual white balance setting or the use of conversion filters. Unfortunately, you'll need to employ a compromise for the white balance or make use of the effect creatively.

Color Reproduction

Daylight—as emitted from the sun—provides a continuous spectrum of light. This quality means that sunlight represents colors correctly. When sources of light lack certain areas of the spectrum, as is the case with common low-energy bulbs and LEDs, then a subject's colors will not be reproduced faithfully in a photograph. In other words, light sources offering an incomplete spectrum of light will reflect an accordingly incomplete spectrum of color, which makes a faithful color reproduction of all colors impossible.

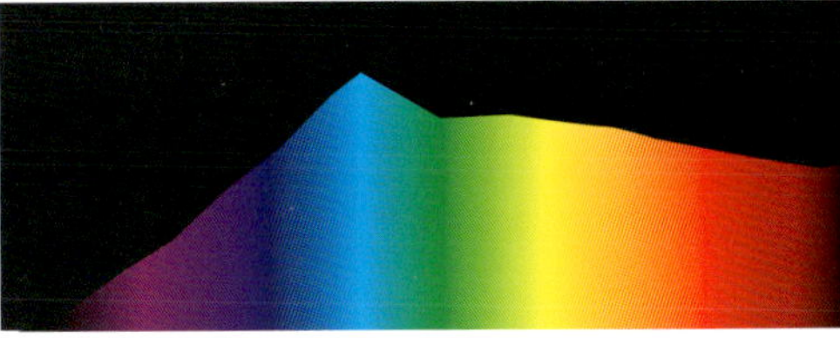

The light spectrum of daylight
Color temperature: ca. 5,500 Kelvin,
R_a index: 100
All colors are present and more or
less evenly distributed

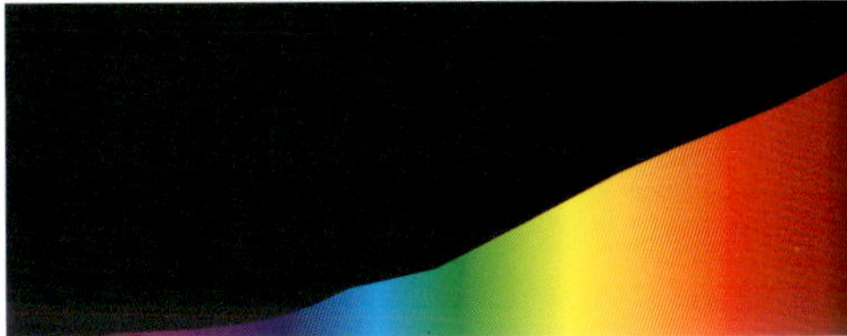

The light spectrum of an incandescent light bulb
Color temperature: ca. 2,800 Kelvin,
R_a index: 100
All colors are present, but the red and yellow components are much more prevalent

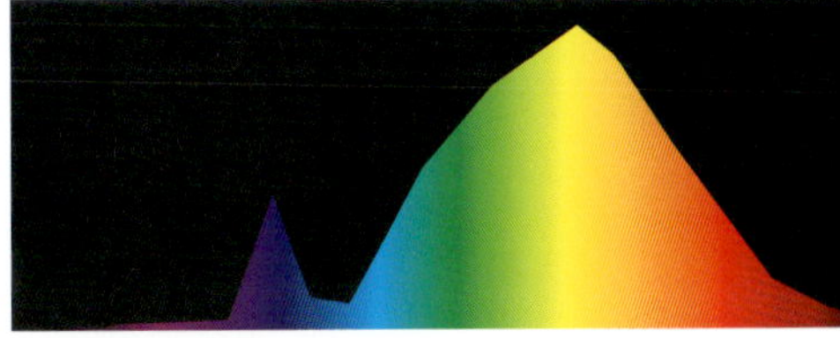

The light spectrum of LEDs
Color temperature: ca. 3,800 Kelvin,
R_a index: 90
The color components are unevenly distributed

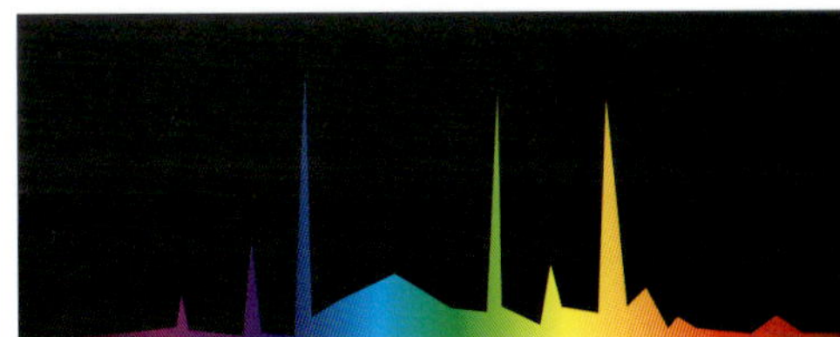

The light spectrum of low-energy light bulbs
Color temperature: ca. 4,500 Kelvin,
R_a index: 80
Some color components are almost entirely missing, and it is not possible to achieve faithful color rendering

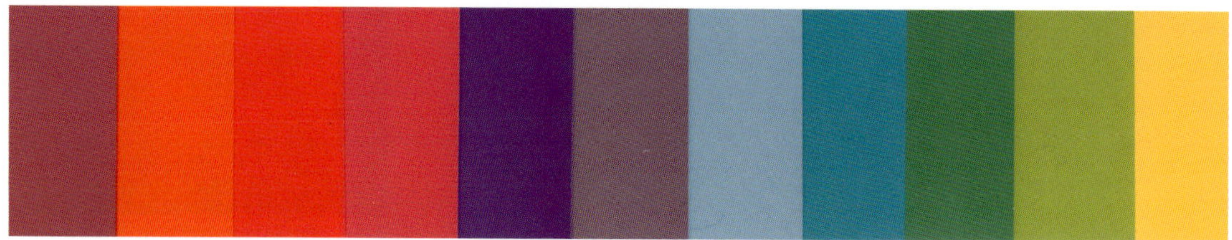

Color cards exposed in daylight. Custom white balance based on a standardized grey card. All of the colors—even the ones very similar to one another—are clearly distinguishable.

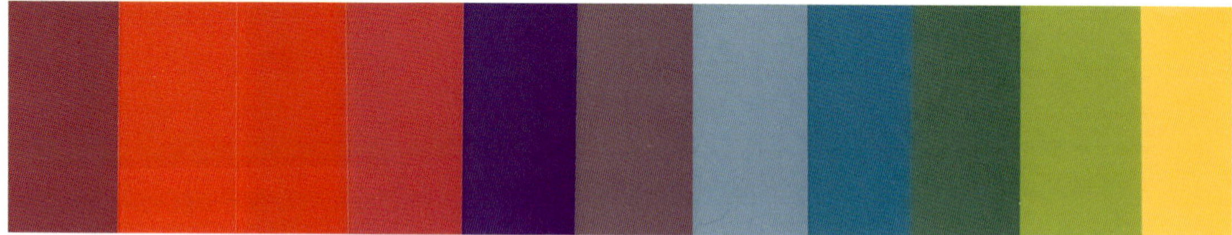

Color cards exposed in the light from a low-energy light bulb. Custom white balance based on a standardized grey card. Some of the red tones are barely distinguishable, and turquoise, violet, and dark green are slightly off. The other colors reproduce nearly identically to those exposed in natural daylight.

The ability of a source of light to correctly reflect a color is measured with the color rendering index R_a. Light sources intended for photography should have a value of at least 95 R_a. Lights with an index of 90 R_a and lower are generally not suitable and should definitely not be used when accurate color reproduction is critical.

Using Additional Lights

As you can tell, not all light is equal. When you need to use a supplemental source of light for shooting a macro photograph, try to use something that is as close in color temperature to the main light source as possible. If you're considering purchasing a continuous lighting device, pay careful attention to the maximum color rendering index score of your options, especially with fluorescent and LED lights.

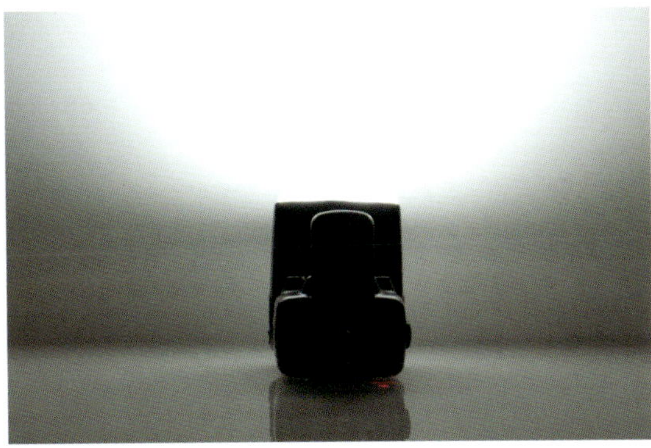

System flash units are designed to mimic daylight. This illustration displays hardly any color casts. White balance set at 5,600 Kelvin.

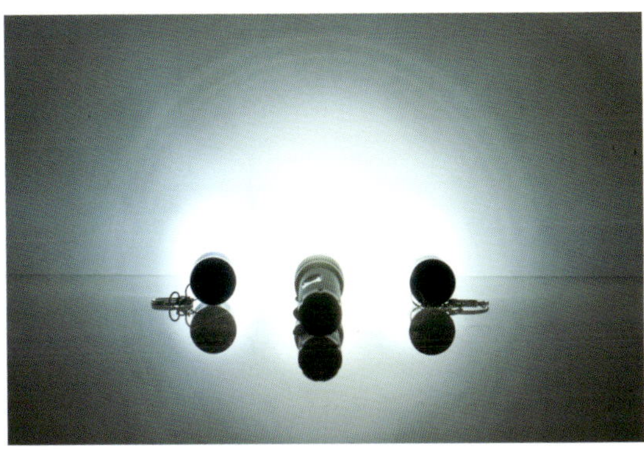

LED lights. The light emitted from normal white LEDs has a very cold appearance, producing a definite blue cast. White balance set at 5,600 Kelvin.

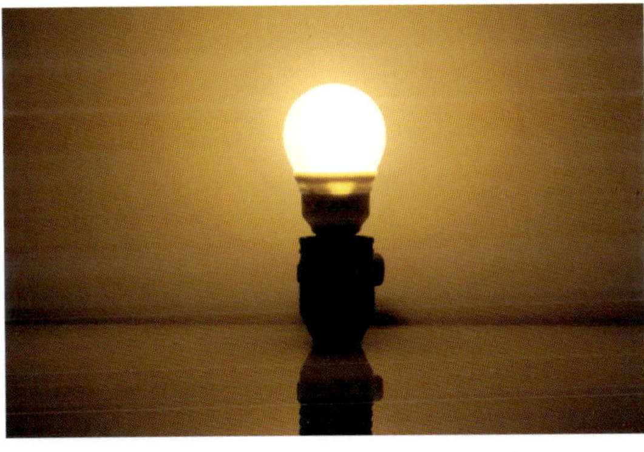

Warm light from a low-energy bulb. Here the light is very yellow and more suitable for creating a cozy ambiance as opposed to photographic uses. White balance set at 5,600 Kelvin.

At roughly 2,800 Kelvin, this 60-watt incandescent bulb produces the warmest color temperature of the lot. Its light is nearly orange. White balance set at 5,600 Kelvin.

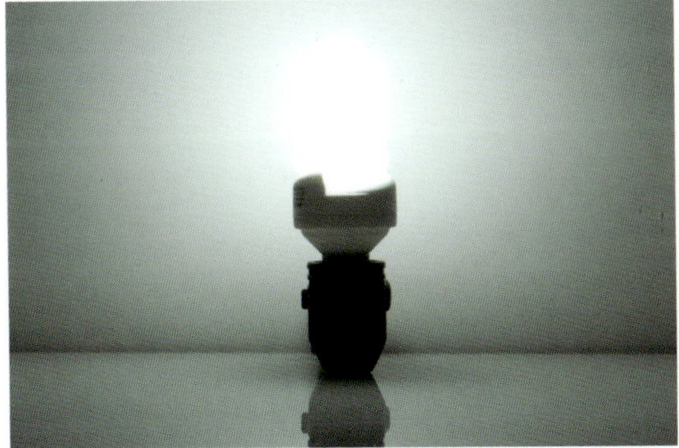

Photography daylight rated at 5,000 Kelvin. The difference of 600 Kelvin reveals a slight color cast. White balance set at 5,600 Kelvin.

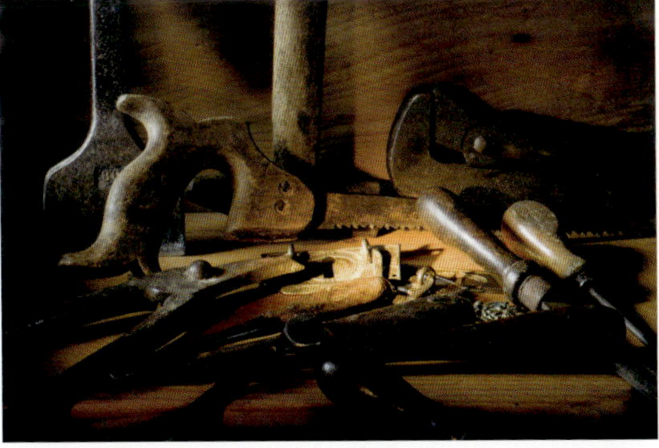

Mixed lighting can be used creatively, as is the case here where a golden accent light is featured. The white balance here was set to Daylight, and a flashlight producing light around 2,700 Kelvin was used for a spotlight treatment.

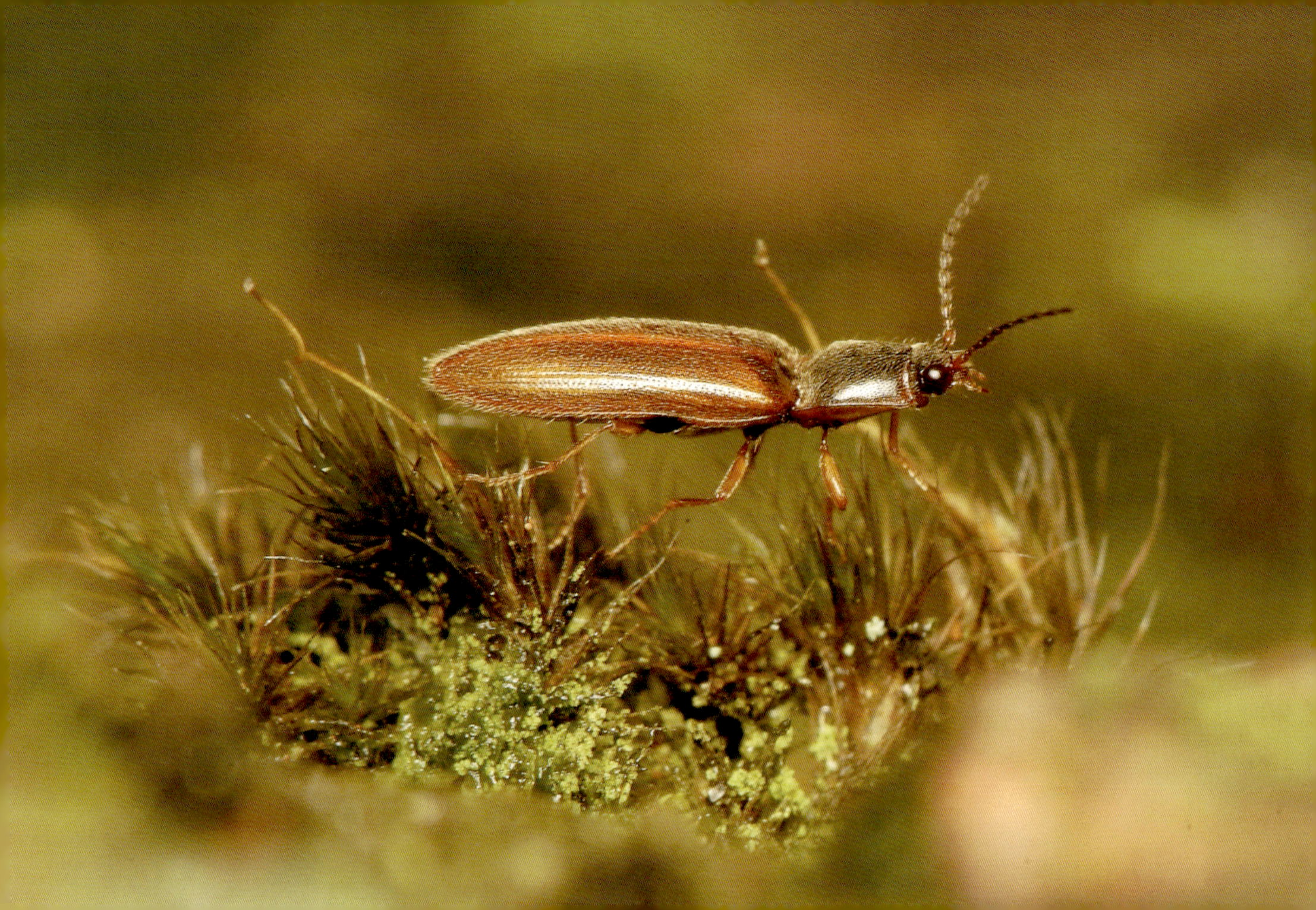

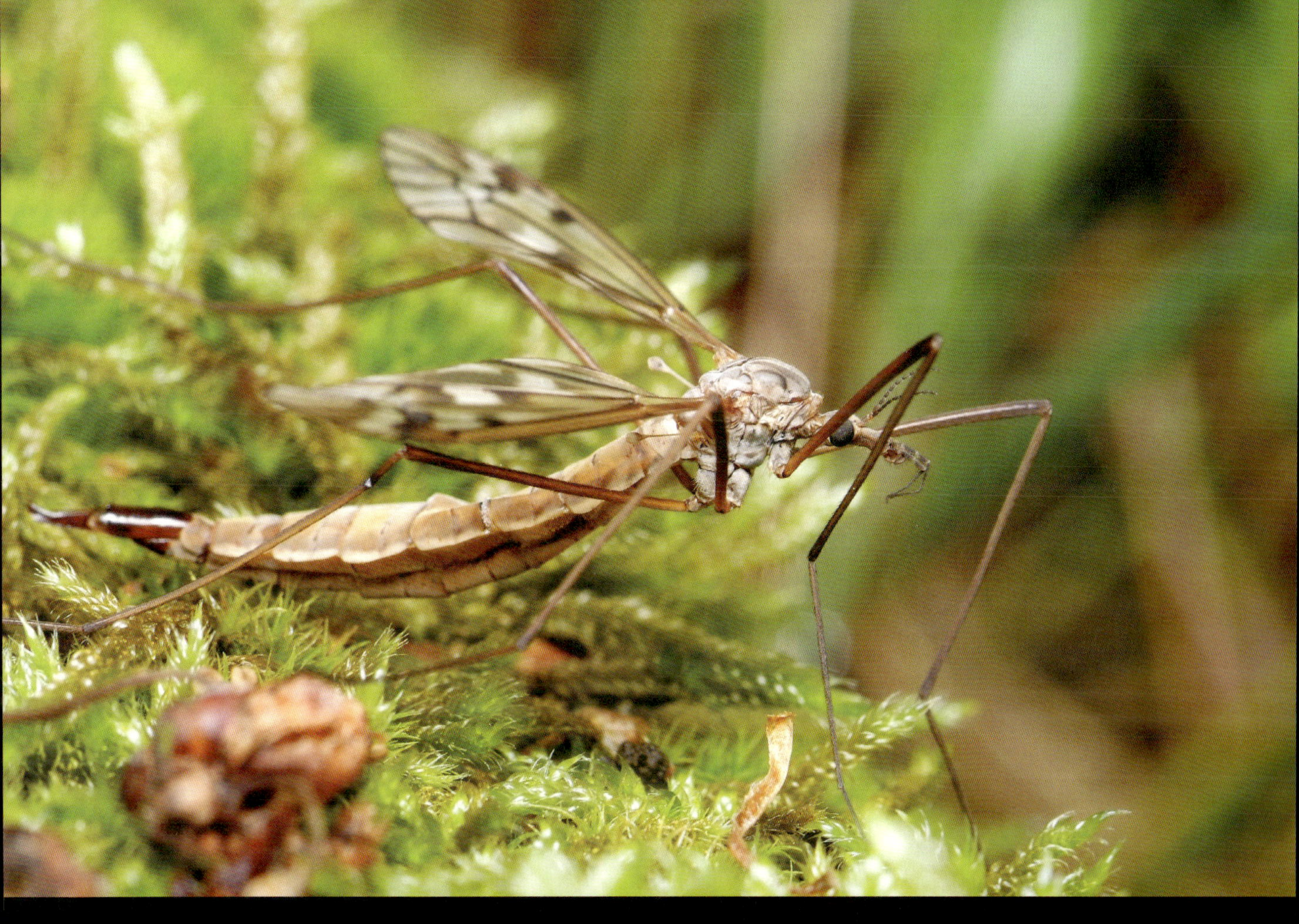

Crane fly on a cushion of moss
f/9.5, 1/60 s, ISO 400, 105mm, separated system
flash with a softbox

Shutter Release Accessories

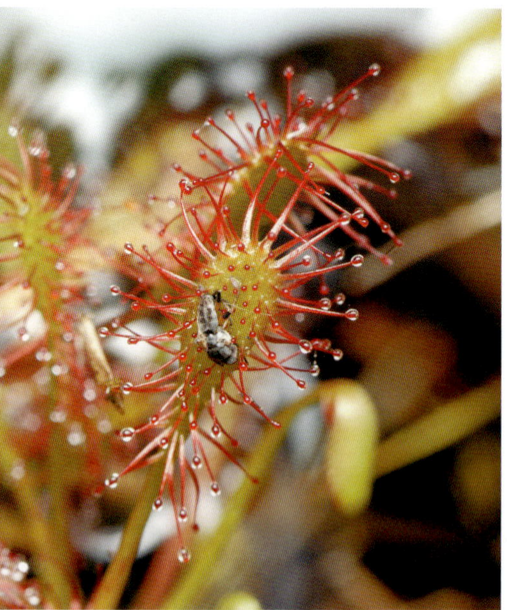

A right-angle mirror is a helpful tool for photographing subjects that may otherwise be difficult to approach

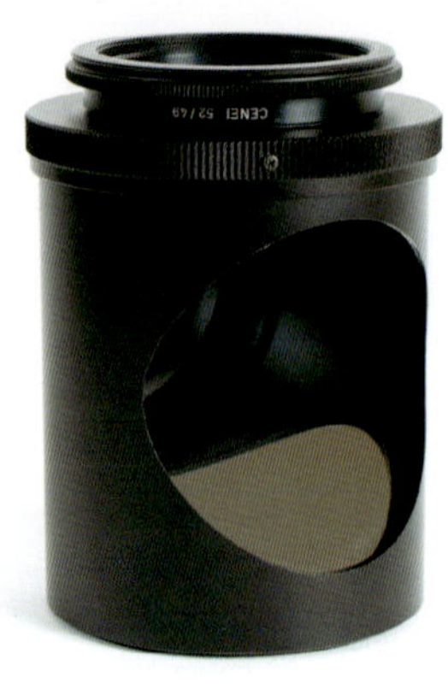

Aside from the classic optical and mechanical accessories that have traditionally been available to photographers, electronic devices are gaining more and more usefulness. It is even possible to adjust and control your camera via a smartphone. The potential for new inventions is still enormous, but there are already enough tools on the market to facilitate images that previously would have required exorbitantly expensive equipment.

Right-Angle Mirror

A right-angle mirror offers welcome flexibility for shooting situations when your subject is difficult to access or, for example, if you don't want to disturb the surroundings of a plant. This device is made out of a metal tube with two openings containing a mirror at a 45° angle that reflects the incident light. The tool makes it easier to photograph objects that may be accessible only from above or from the side, but it also helps when there isn't enough room for the photographer and the camera to maneuver as necessary to get the shot; for instance, if your subject is positioned in a hollow tree hole. Right-angle mirrors are attached to the end of the lens via the filter threads and an adapter. Accordingly, it makes sense to use a lens whose front element doesn't turn when focusing.

Angle Viewfinders

Angle viewfinders have gone out of fashion a bit, in part because newer camera models frequently come equipped with display screens that can be flipped, turned, and folded and that can display a live image. In other words, modern cameras have all the functionality of an angle viewfinder built in. Nonetheless, there are still situations when an angle viewfinder can be of real use. These tools are attached to the viewfinder window and reflect the viewfinder image at 90° so you can compose and shoot your images from unusual perspectives. The most versatile models also include a 2x magnification, depict a true-sided image, and are fully rotatable for 360°.

LCD Glare Shield

Because bright light makes it difficult to make out detail on the camera's monitor, a foldable glare shield made out of plastic or black cardboard can prove to be a useful accessory. Any number of versions are available on the market for specific camera models, but if you're in a pinch without a shield, a little bit of improvisation can go a long way. Using the lens hood, for example, to shade the screen is often highly effective.

Wired Remote Shutter Release

Photographers need a remote trigger of some kind to be able to avoid any unwanted vibrations, like the blur caused by camera shake that results from physically pressing the shutter release button on the camera. Photography stores offer simple solutions for this purpose that are quite affordable. You should look for models that not only allow you to release the camera's shutter but also enable you to create long-exposure pictures. More-advanced solutions feature integrated timers for time-lapse or delayed shooting. The wired remote release models that used to be very common are largely incompatible with modern camera models because manufacturers have done away with the requisite threads on the camera's shutter button.

Wireless Remote Shutter Release

Infrared triggers communicate the shutter release signal wirelessly, but they require a visual direct line with the camera. And in some bright lighting situations, they sometimes malfunction.

Radio-controlled remote-release models allow photographers to be much farther removed from the camera, which is especially practical when photographing animals. You can, for example, set up your camera near a feeding site, focus your shot in advance, and then release the shutter from a safe distance. Combo radio release solutions that can trigger either the camera or a flash unit are especially practical.

Remote Shutter Release with Display

Some remote control devices relay the live image from the camera. This functionality allows you to control the camera's settings while being physically separated from it. This option is particularly useful when you're photographing a subject that you shouldn't disturb, such as a reflective surface.

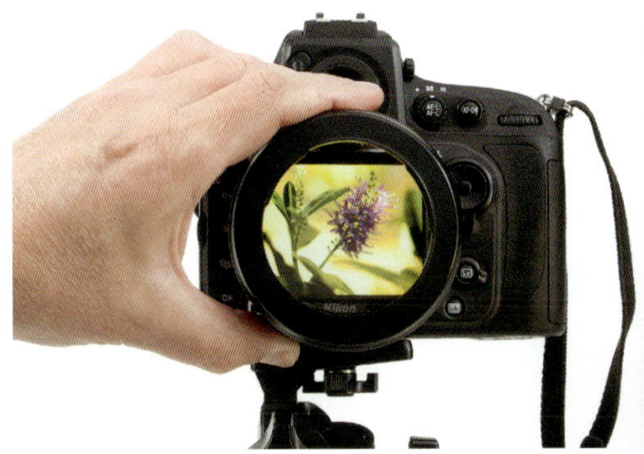

A lens hood will serve as an improvisational shade for your camera display in a pinch

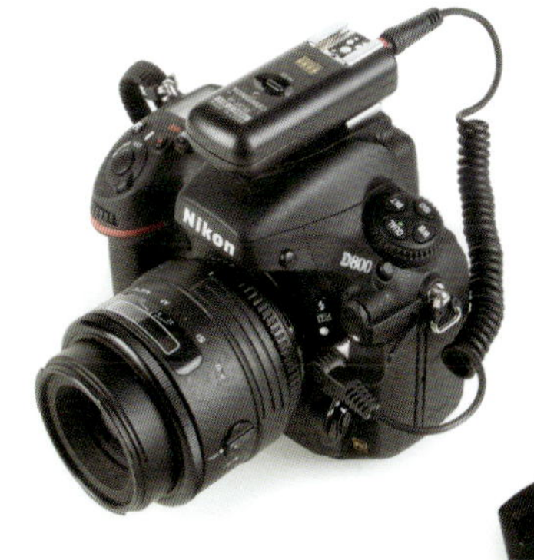

Radio remote shutter release triggers allow you to control your camera from substantial distances

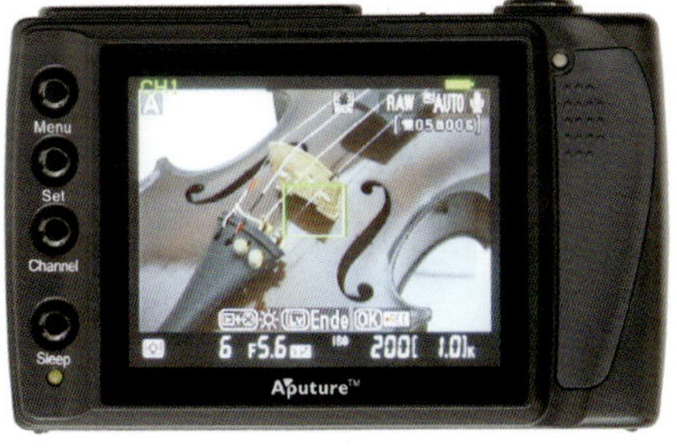

Many radio shutter triggers are also capable of transmitting the camera's live image substantial distances, including into neighboring rooms

Remote Control via Smartphone or Tablet

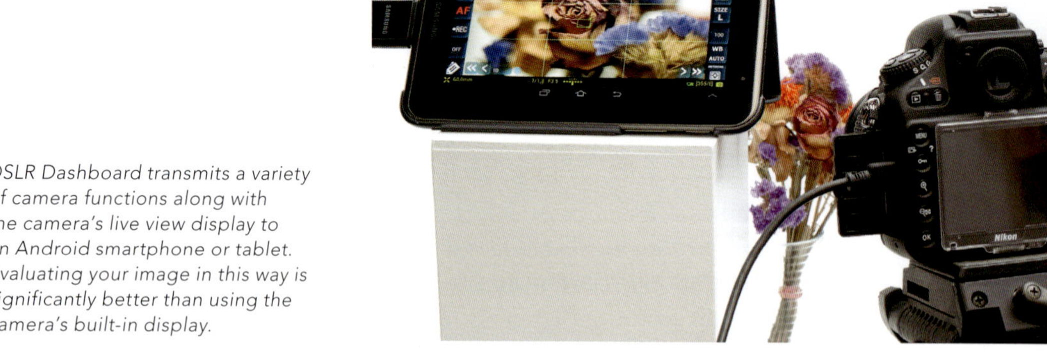

DSLR Dashboard transmits a variety of camera functions along with the camera's live view display to an Android smartphone or tablet. Evaluating your image in this way is significantly better than using the camera's built-in display.

More and more camera manufacturers, as well as third-party software developers, are creating applications that enable photographers to control their cameras with a smartphone or tablet. The range of functionality supported on these applications varies significantly. At the modest end of the spectrum, these programs may simply allow you to release the shutter remotely. At the advanced end, you effectively have complete control of your camera, including access to the live image and playback of captured images on your device. Some apps additionally offer time-lapse shooting; self-timers; long-exposure shooting; automatic shutter release triggered by noise, vibration, or movement; and much more. These devices also vary in how they communicate with cameras, either relying on a wired connection or a wireless one using infrared, Bluetooth, or Wi-Fi technology.

The days when you would need to set up an additional notebook computer to establish a network for the camera and the smartphone are not entirely behind us. The market of apps is growing steadily, and new updates continue to expand what exactly each can offer, so the information here is in no way a comprehensive list. Treat the apps listed on the next page as a starting point for your own research, and as you learn about the different programs out there, pay special attention to their compatibility with your own smartphone or device. The costs you may incur to run these programs range from a few dollars for a necessary cable to two-digit amounts for a dongle, and up to several hundred dollars for specialized equipment.

CamRanger | This app enables the wireless shutter release of Nikon and Canon cameras with the required hardware. For iOS and Android; free.

DSLR.Bot | Infrared shutter release for many DSLR cameras with infrared sensors. A separate infrared transmitter is required. Only for iOS; not free.

DSLR Camera Control iR | Infrared shutter release for nearly all DSLR cameras with infrared sensors; separate iRed transmitter required. Only for iOS; free.

DSLR Controller | Wired or Wi-Fi remote control functionality for Canon EOS cameras. Special cables and additional hardware are required. Live image transmission. Only for Android; not free.

DSLR Dashboard | Wired or Wi-Fi remote control. Special cables are required. DSLR Dashboard supports Nikon's WU-1a and WU-1b adapters. Live image transmission. Only for Android; free, but the handbook is available only as a for-purchase e-book.

IguanaLapse Pro | Wireless control of DSLRs with special hardware required. Only for iOS; not free.

Nikon Wireless Mobile Utility | Remote shutter release and data transmission for many contemporary Nikon Cameras via Wi-Fi and Nikon's WU-1a and WU-1b adapters. For iOS and Android; free.

WeyeFeye | Wireless control of DSLR cameras with the required hardware. Transmission of live view. For iOS and Android; free.

DSLR Remote | If you're interested in a do-it-yourself option for building some hardware to enable remote control options for your camera, check out DSLR Remote from Dirk Meuser. You can use infrared, Bluetooth, or a traditional cable to trigger DSLRs, but special hardware is required. Instructions for assembling them and a list of compatible smartphones can be found on the developer's website: *http://bitshift.bplaced.net/en/dslr-remote.htm*. Only for Android; free.

Remotely controlling your camera via a smartphone opens a variety of creative possibilities. One of the most exciting apps for macro applications specifically is Triggertrap, which I'll discuss in detail on the next pages.

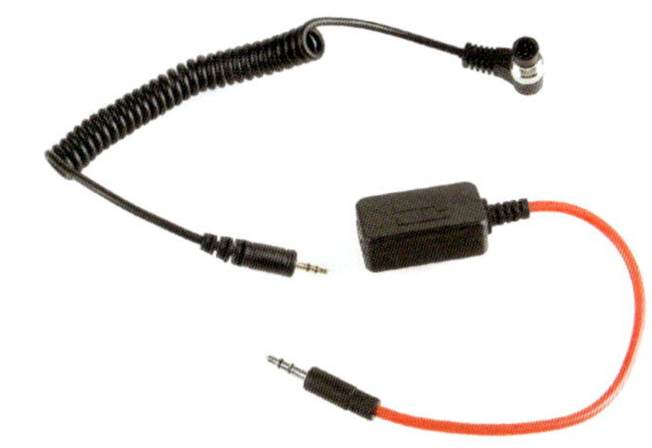

A shutter-release cable and the right dongle make for a simple and reliable way to control your camera remotely

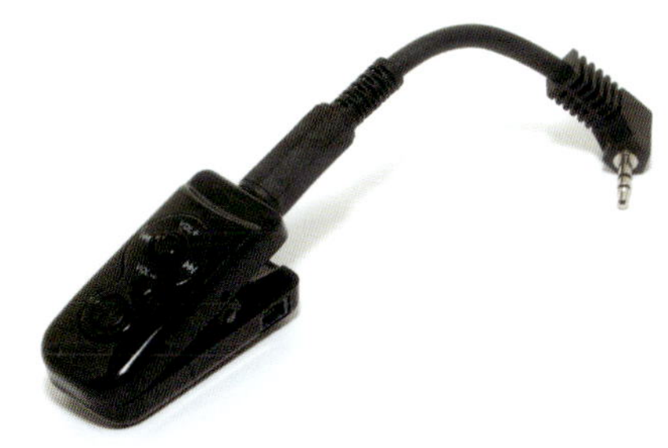

It's relatively easy to build a Bluetooth remote trigger yourself using a headset and a simple remote-release cable. See the DSLR Remote section for the URL that provides instructions. Photo: Dirk Meuser

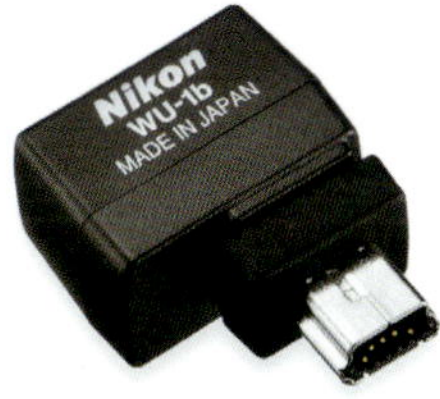

The Nikon WU-1a and WU-1b adapters make it possible to control many cameras wirelessly via the right app on your smartphone or tablet Photo: Nikon

Remote Control with Triggertrap

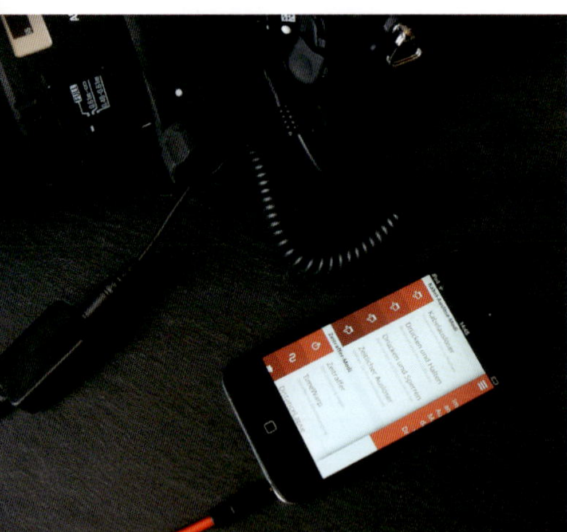

The connection between the camera and the mobile device running Triggertrap is outfitted with a camera-specific remote trigger cable and a hardware dongle. You can find more information on the web at www.triggertrap.com.

One app that is definitely worth purchasing if you have a mobile device is Triggertrap, which includes features for high-speed photography as well as time-lapse and stop-motion exposures. Provided you have a smartphone, tablet PC, iPad, or iPod touch to begin with, you'll be able to pull together a complete remote control system for a DSLR with the purchase of a simple remote trigger device. The complete system comprises a hardware dongle that connects to the mobile device on one end and the camera on the other via a special adapter designed for your camera and the free Triggertrap application.

The dongle and the remote control cable will set you back around $40, and the app can be downloaded for free from whichever app store you use. You can also test out the range of options before purchasing the dongle and cable by using the app with the built-in camera of your smartphone. This method worked very well for me using an iPod touch 4.

The range of functions for the Android app is somewhat more modest than the iOS version. The design of the app is also different. The interface of the Android version is more technical and oriented for photographers, but the iOS version is more stylistic and streamlined, which goes well with its straightforward operation. The following trigger modes are available:

Cable Release | Various exposure options ranging from manually releasing the shutter to being able to keep the camera's shutter open until the trigger is released.

Time-Lapse Modes | Here you can define the intervals between your exposures.

TimeWarp | This mode allows you to define a specific number of exposures for a period of time, the frequency of which can be increased or decreased.

DistanceLapse | This mode syncs with a smartphone's GPS system; it captures an image every time that a defined distance has been traveled.

Star Trail | Create multiple exposures with fixed durations.

Motion Sensor | Take pictures triggered by motion; ideal for photographing animals, such as insects during the start or landing of their flight.

Sound Sensor | Exposure triggered by any noise that is louder than the minimum volume threshold.

Vibration Sensor | This mode triggers an exposure when the smartphone detects any shaking.

Peekaboo | This mode uses facial recognition to trigger an exposure.

LE HDR | Create HDR time-lapse sequences with customizable shooting durations and light values.

Wi-Fi Master/Slave | Send a wireless shutter-release signal from a master mobile device to a slave mobile device.

The noise-triggered shutter release is particularly appealing to me, but it is practical only in relatively quiet areas and should be activated right before you want to collect your desired image. Otherwise, you'll end up with a bunch of images of yourself as you set up your shot.

The Wi-Fi Master/Slave mode also can work with multiple devices, so that one central smartphone can trigger multiple cameras simultaneously. Facial recognition triggering isn't entirely useful for macro purposes, but it is fun to play with.

With the right mounts, you can affix the slave mobile device to a flash bracket next to the camera or even attach it to the camera's shoe mount. Version 2.0 of the mobile app also allows users to control up to two flash units with a separate adapter.

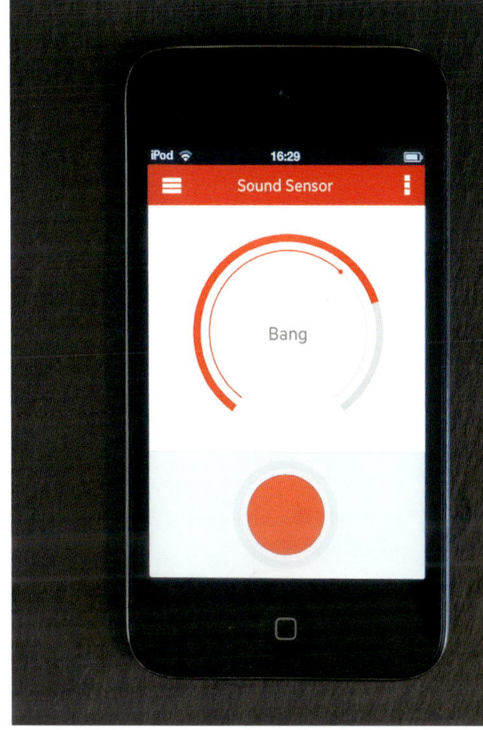

Triggertrap's sound sensor mode can capture interesting pictures of bursting balloons or objects falling to the ground—but only in relatively quiet circumstances

Optical Filters

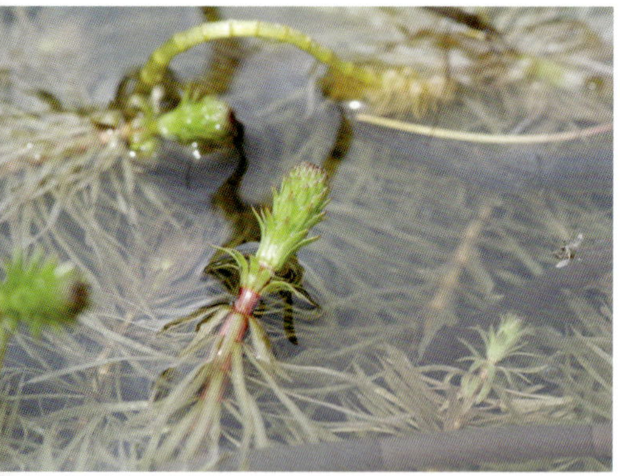

Without using a polarizer filter, the sky's reflection is clearly visible in the surface of the water

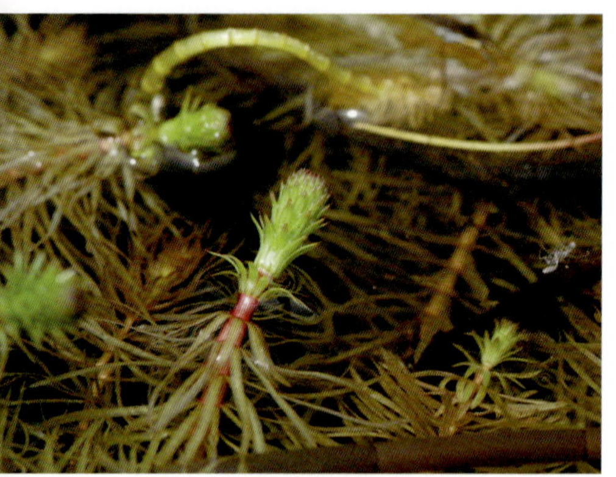

The polarizer filter eliminates the reflections on the water's surface, allowing viewers to see the underwater parts of the plants much more clearly

Even in the digital era of photography, filters have not become obsolete. Sure, some types are less valuable because their effects can be introduced digitally in an image-editing program, but some filters still are worth using.

UV Filters
These filters absorb UV light, allowing for more brilliant images with clearer colors. They're also often used as a measure of protection for the lens.

Skylight Filters
These filters have a slight red tint and help to achieve natural-looking colors for outdoor images. They reduce blue casts and can serve as a good shield for your lens.

Polarizer Filters
This type of filter can be rotated to increase or decrease its effect of tempering reflections off of water, glass, or plastic surfaces. Polarizer filters also make the blue of the sky appear more intense, causing clouds to take on something of a plastic appearance. Some cameras require the use of a costlier circular polarizing filter, rather than the inexpensive linear polarizers, to ensure that the autofocus and exposure metering systems work properly.

Warm-Tone Filter
Exhibiting a light orange coloring, these filters are ideal for portraiture because they cause skin tones to appear more natural.

Grey Filters
Shooting flowing water, such as a waterfall, with a slow shutter speed creates a fluid, dreamlike appearance. Neutral grey filters allow you to achieve this effect even in bright conditions without suffering a loss in color quality. They're also useful in bright conditions when you want to use a wide aperture to create a shallow depth of field.

Graduated Filters

Graduated filters darken specific areas of an image as opposed to the entire image area. Their main use is when shooting with a very bright sky; they allow landscape photographers to expose the scene in the foreground of their images properly without having to over-expose the sky. Colored graduated filters might allow you to make a normal landscape image appear as though it were shot during sunset. Tobacco graduated filters are particularly popular—they seem to always be used in photographs of golf courses in particular.

Effect Filters

Blur, rainbow, color effect, prism, or star filters add specific effects to photographs. You can also achieve creative results by making filters yourself. For instance, smear some Vaseline on a UV filter, or scuff up a CD jewel case with sandpaper, or use colorful pieces of glass to alter your subject's appearance.

Conversion Filters

Conversion filters were used in the days of film photography in situations when your lighting and your film weren't well matched—you might, for example, have had daylight film in your camera and have been shooting in neon or incandescent lighting. Because digital technology makes it so easy to recalibrate the white balance for every exposure, using conversion lenses in front of your lens is no longer required. But you can use these filters to alter the light emitted from an artificial light source. You can filter halogen light, for example, so it won't create a color cast when daylight is also illuminating your subject.

The red, green, and yellow filters that are used in black-and-white photography create images with more pronounced contrast by filtering out specific components of the ambient light.

Infrared Filters

Digital technology has made infrared photography much easier. These filters block out visible light, leaving only near infrared wavelengths to reach the image sensor. Green, sunlit leaves appear nearly white, and blue skies look dark. Infrared shooting typically requires very slow shutter speeds and not all cameras are suited for creating these images.

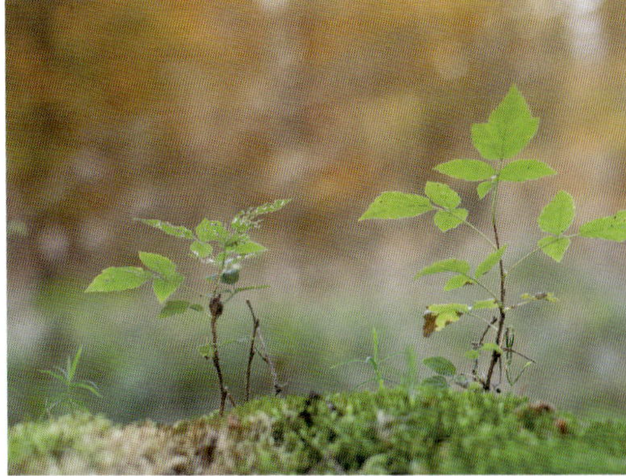

Tobacco graduated filters create a reddish-brown gradient

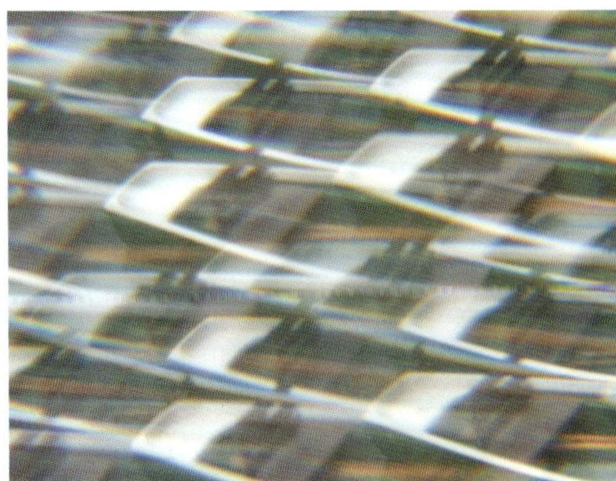

Prism filters multiply individual sections of an image

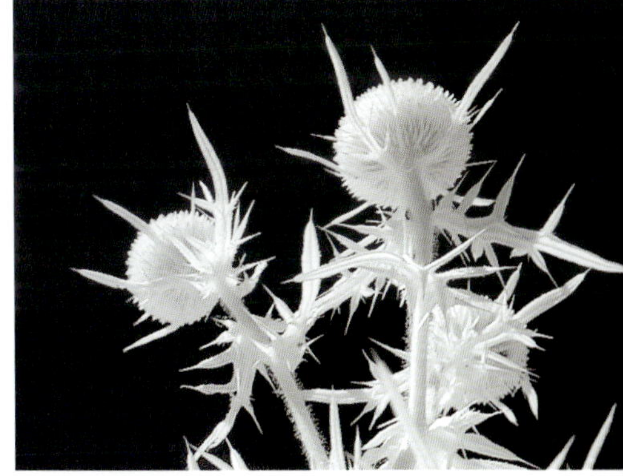

Infrared filters allow only near infrared light to reach the sensor

Tripods and Mounts

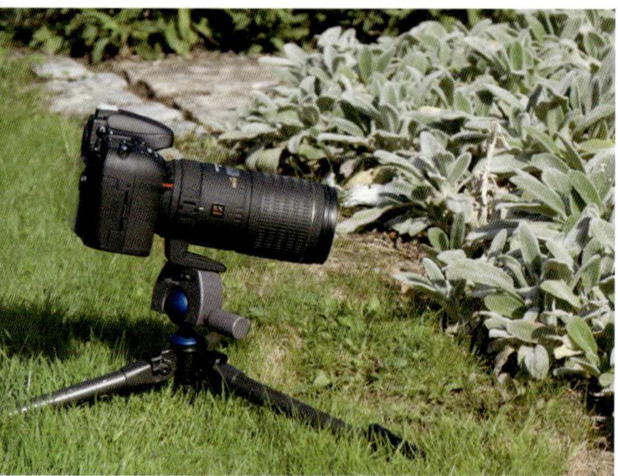

For shooting near the ground, you'll want a tripod whose legs can be angled horizontally. If you want to use an even lower perspective, you might consider using a beanbag as an alternative camera stand.

There is an overwhelming number of camera stands on the market. Trying to find the perfect tripod for all shooting situations is a fool's errand because you'll end up with something that isn't stable enough for work in the studio or portable enough to carry when shooting on location. Accordingly, you'll want to have two camera stands at your disposal.

Tripods for Outdoors

What makes a tripod ideal for outdoor use? For me, it's very important for a tripod to be light enough to carry easily and very easy to set up. These qualities mean that I'll be more likely to bring it with me on outings and use it regularly. If a tripod is too heavy or too ungainly to assemble—perhaps both hands are needed to secure any clasps while setting it up—it's more likely to be left in a closet at home. You also want your tripod to have legs that can be angled in a full horizontal position and to have a center column that can be either partially or fully removed so you can easily shoot at ground level. Furthermore, your tripod should be no longer than your equipment bag when fully collapsed. That way you can use a few belts to secure it to your pack when you don't need it, enabling you to hold your camera with both hands.

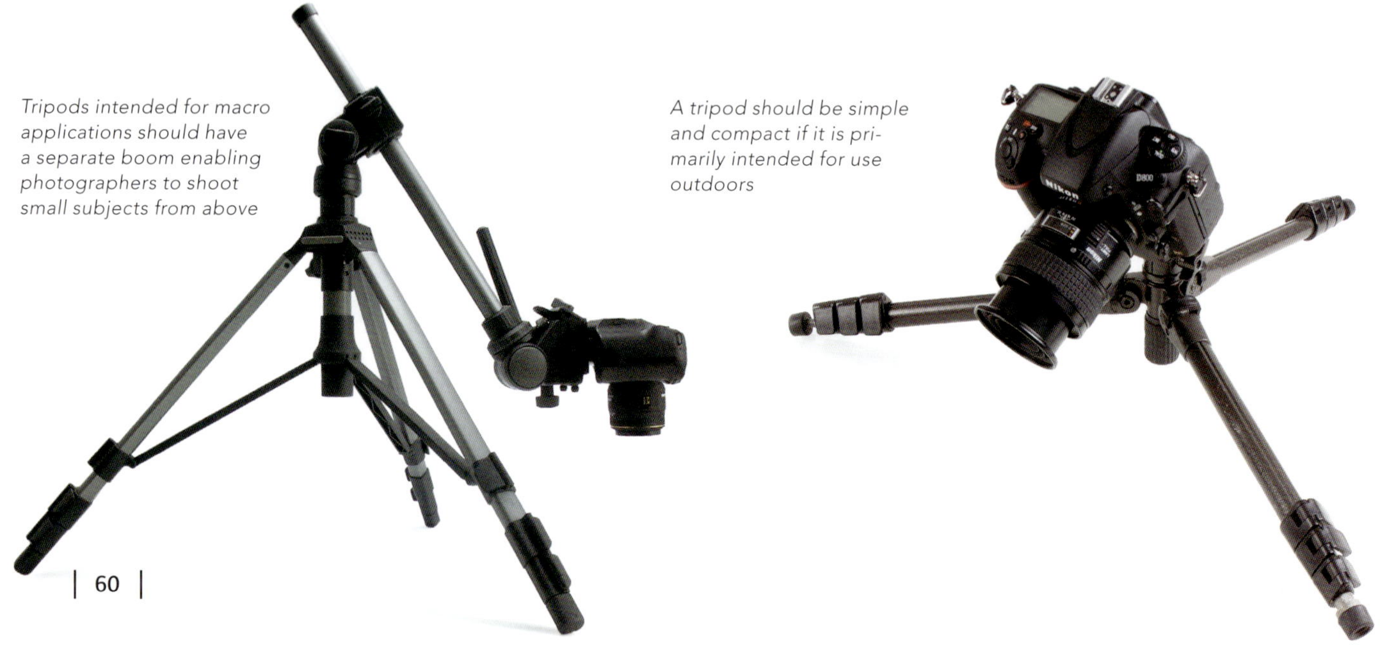

Tripods intended for macro applications should have a separate boom enabling photographers to shoot small subjects from above

A tripod should be simple and compact if it is primarily intended for use outdoors

Tripods for Studios

Weight isn't a key variable for tripods intended for use in the studio. What is important is the flexibility with which you can position your camera with respect to your subject. You want to be able to shoot from in front of, next to, behind, and over your subject. The stability of the main camera boom is critical. A tripod should be constructed so that even when the arm is fully extended and supporting a camera of moderate weight, the leverage won't cause the stand to adjust or fall.

Table Tripods

A small table tripod is a practical purchase both for outdoor shooting and studio work. These stands allow you to get very close to your subject, which is particularly beneficial when shooting with short focal lengths. Because these devices have fairly short legs, you'll want to be careful that heavy cameras don't cause them to fall over. Some models feature a center column that can be removed so you can insert a monopod. This alternative construction won't stand securely by itself, but it endows the monopod with a great deal more stability—a good compromise when you don't have a lot of room in your gear bag.

Pan/Tilt Heads

Pan/tilt heads are common in video applications. They are not as compact as ball heads, but they offer a bit more precise control for photographers. Some high-end models feature geared rotation adjustments, which enable very fine movements using gear mechanisms for all axes. Because these devices are very heavy, they are mostly practical if you'll be primarily working in a studio.

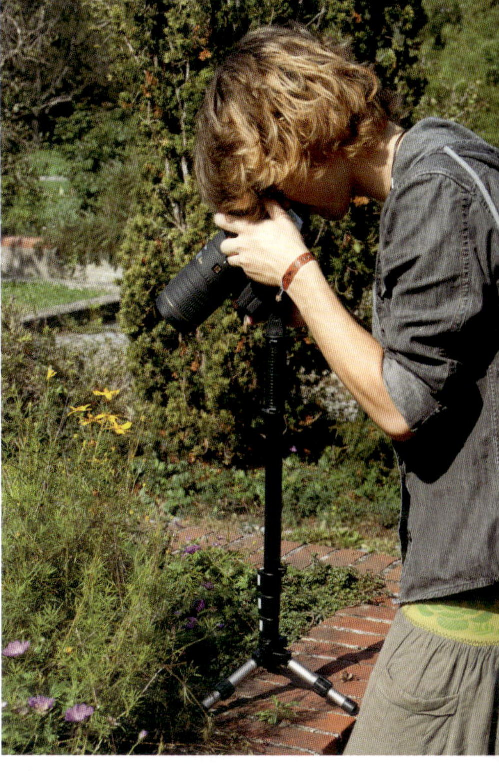

Combining a monopod with a small table tripod is an effective way to add a great deal more stability without adding much more weight to your gear

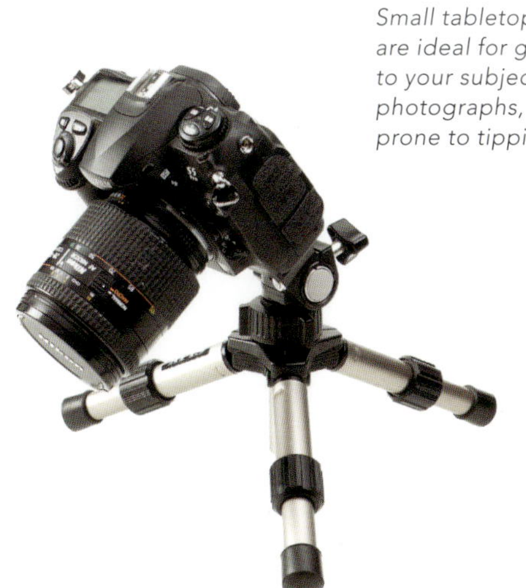

Small tabletop tripods are ideal for getting close to your subject for macro photographs, but they are prone to tipping over

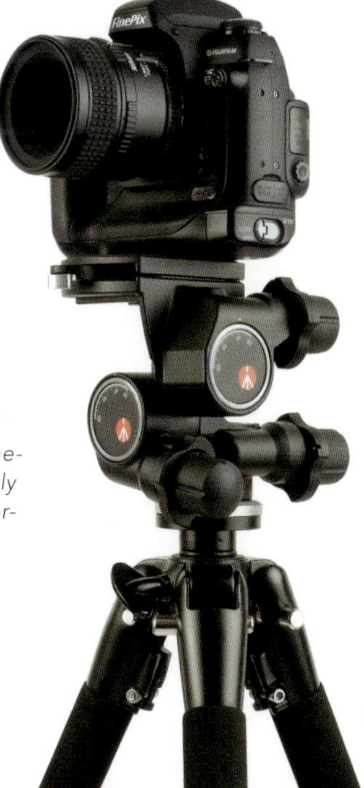

Geared pan/tilt heads enable highly precise fine-tuning, but they're usually too heavy to serve as portable camera stands

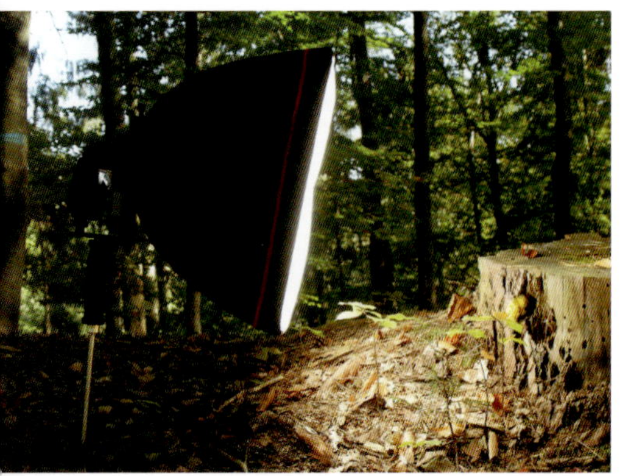

A stake driven into the soft forest earth supports a system flash unit equipped with a flash2softbox adapter

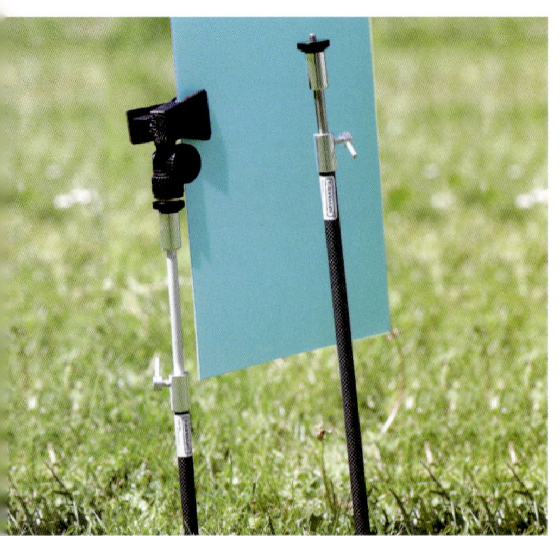

Height-adjustable stakes designed for photographic purposes can be found in two sizes from www.fotonovum.de Photo: Markus Gläßel

Photography stakes are ideal for positioning flash units and other accessories when working in the field

Ball Heads

Ball head tripod mounts come in a variety of sizes and designs. The key advantage of this type of tripod head is the ease and speed with which you can reposition your camera as needed. Before purchasing a ball head, you should test it out with your camera and lens combination to ensure that the stand head will hold its place and not lose its positioning under the weight. Smaller ball heads sometimes have trouble adequately supporting the weight of a camera and its lens. If the ball head you're testing loses its position, try moving up to a larger model. Some ball heads on the market feature horizontal adjustment in the form of a panoramic plate. An integrated quick-release plate is a nice feature for ball-head mounts, but it's best if it can be retrofitted. That way if you decide to switch to a different ball-head mount or panoramic mount in the future, you'll be able to continue using the retrofitted quick-release system.

Focusing Rails

If you're shooting with a tripod, focusing rails can be extremely helpful to get your focusing just right. Instead of adjusting your lens to position the focal plane where you want it on your subject, you can use focusing rails to physically shift the entire camera with a high degree of precision. If you use two focusing rails set up at right angles to one another, you'll create a cross rail that allows you to shift your camera from side to side as well as from front to back.

Panoramic Tripod Plates

The best way to pan your camera horizontally is with a panoramic plate. The device should feature a bubble level, a focusing scale, and the ability to lock the settings in place. There are two ways to use panoramic heads: on top of or below the ball head. Positioning the plate on top of the ball head makes sense when you want to pan

Focusing rails make it easier to adjust the positioning of the focal plane precisely, especially when shooting with a large magnification

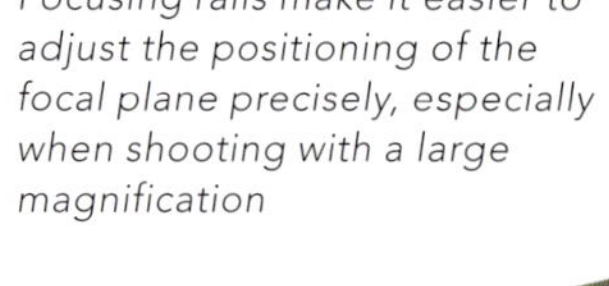

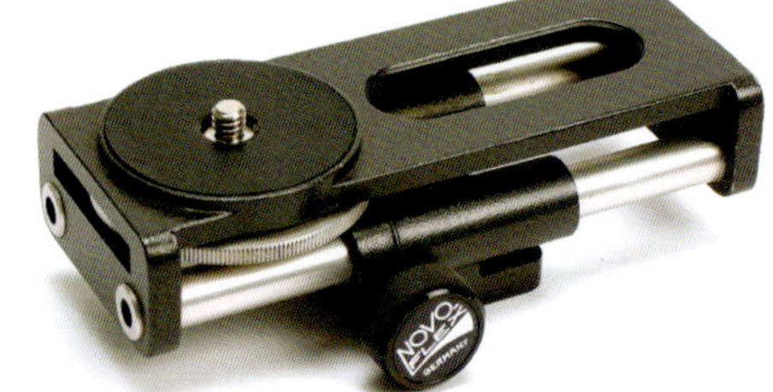

the camera in a fixed horizontal motion. The ball head allows you to turn the camera without needing to adjust the tripod. The second method—below the ball head—requires that the tripod be aligned horizontally, but the camera can be pivoted with a downward perspective, for example.

Spikes and Rods

Some manufacturers offer long metal rods that have a mount with traditional tripod threads on one end and a spike on the other end that can be driven into soft ground. Even though cameras can be used on these stands in a pinch, they are much more suited to support flash heads and reflectors.

Flexible Stands

Camera stands such as the Novoflex Minipod or the Gorillapod from Joby are particularly useful when shooting at ground level. You can manipulate the legs of these devices individually—a trait that makes it much easier to position your camera on unlevel ground. The Gorillapod can also be outfitted with spikes to ensure a stable positioning on sand, dirt, or snow.

Clamps with Tripod Threads

Clamps equipped with standard tripod threads make it possible to position flash heads and other pieces of equipment in highly custom and creative ways. When paired with a ball-head mount, you'll have an even greater flexibility for setting up your shots. These tools won't support large, heavy cameras, but they can easily hold up a compact camera next to a bird's nest, for example. With the aid of a remote trigger, you can then capture a shot of a bird in its nest without disturbing it.

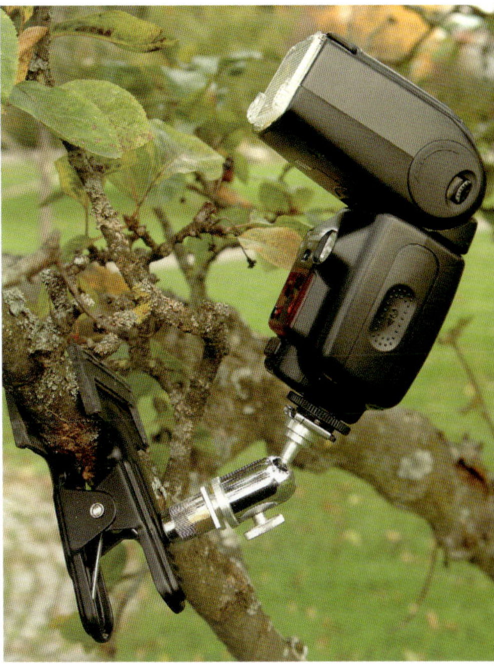

Special claps outfitted with tripod threads and tilt heads allow photographers to position flash units in practically any position imaginable

The Gorillapod is a flexible tripod that can also be outfitted with spiked feet
Photo: Joby

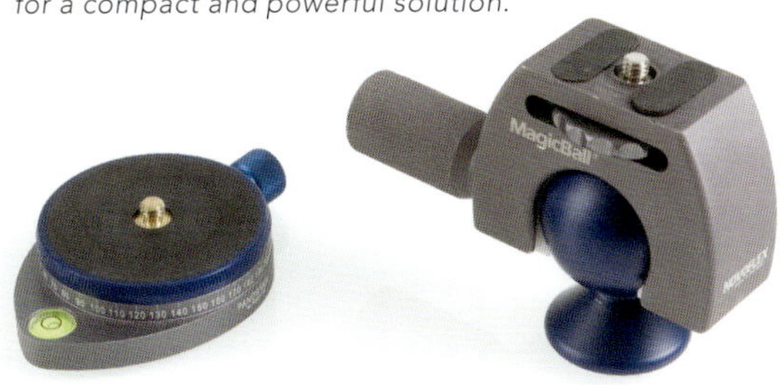

Ball heads make it very easy to position your camera quickly for the subject at hand. When paired with a panoramic plate for horizontal panning they make for a compact and powerful solution.

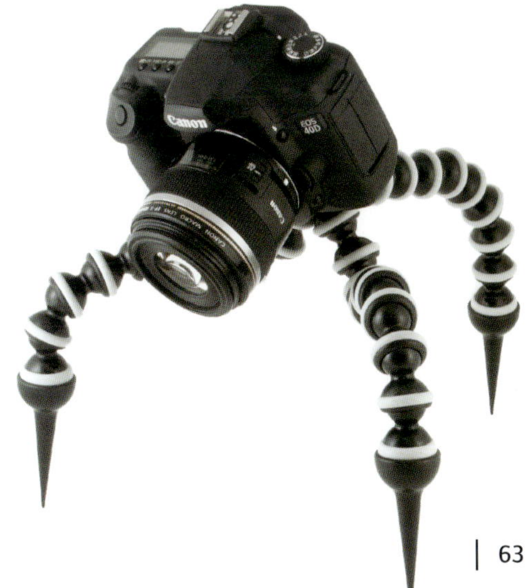

Transportation and Safety

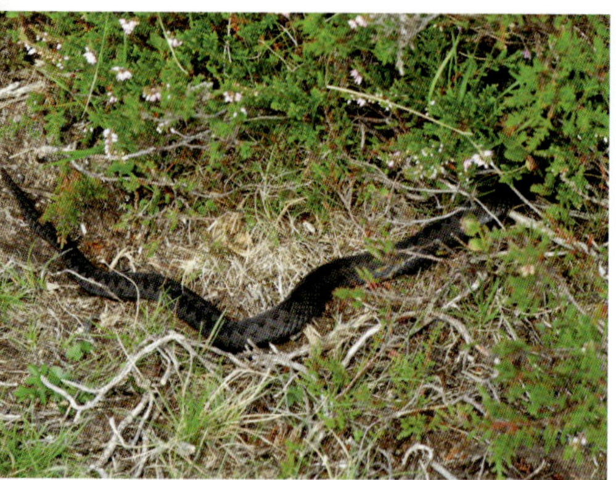

Even parts of the world where you might not expect to come across dangerous species have their own cast of poisonous creatures, such as this European adder
Photo: Rudolf Krahm

Safety

The main security issue to consider is your personal safety, which involves protecting yourself against accidents and illnesses. If you plan to spend time hiking through forests and fields for your photography, you should take precautions against ticks at a minimum, and you probably should consult your doctor, too. He or she can make recommendations about immunizations and provide advice about assembling a first-aid kit. Always keep medicine for treating insect bites on hand because even stealthy, well-meaning interactions with bees and wasps can go wrong.

If you're headed to an exotic destination, you should also educate yourself about poisonous animals and plants that you may encounter. Taking pictures in the wild may mean you'll be visiting the homes of poisonous snakes and insects. Reading up on their behavior and characteristics can't hurt.

What preventative measures to take will naturally depend on the location of your adventure. Consulting others who have been there is always a good idea. Inform yourself about any widespread illnesses enough in advance of your trip so that you can get any vaccines you may need or want. The Centers for Disease Control and Prevention is a good resource for getting started.

Equipment

The security of your equipment is also a key concern. Theft and negligence are both worth considering and planning for.

Photographers who shoot with expensive DSLRs and lenses should take out insurance on their gear because general travel insurance may not cover it in certain cases. In order to react quickly to theft, take and print pictures of your important pieces of equipment at home, and write the serial numbers on the back of the printouts.

If you want to protect your gear from pickpockets while being out and about, consider buying a special camera security belt, which comes lined with a steel cable that can't be easily cut with a robber's knife.

If you use a backpack for your gear, always double-check that you have fully closed the zipper before putting your bag back onto your back.

File Security

Photographers who are shooting for any extended amount of time should make plans for backing up their image files. The photography market offers any number of devices to solve this problem, from portable external hard drives to battery-powered CD burners. Laptops are also practical tools for this purpose. Whatever technology you use, duplication is the name of the game. Don't make the mistake of transferring your files to a storage device and then deleting the files from your memory card. Doing so only perpetuates the problem.

Backing data up to the cloud is one option, but it may become impractical if you're working with large amounts of data. When you factor in roaming charges that you'll likely encounter if traveling abroad, the cloud can end up being a costly endeavor.

Another option for travelers who are not too far off the beaten path is jumping into a photo shop or drugstore to have files duplicated onto CDs or DVDs. You can then mail one copy of the files to your home address and store another somewhere in your luggage separate from your camera and memory cards. Some cameras even have the option of writing image files to multiple storage devices—an SD card and a compact flash card, for example. If this option is available to you, then you may not need to pursue other means of file redundancy.

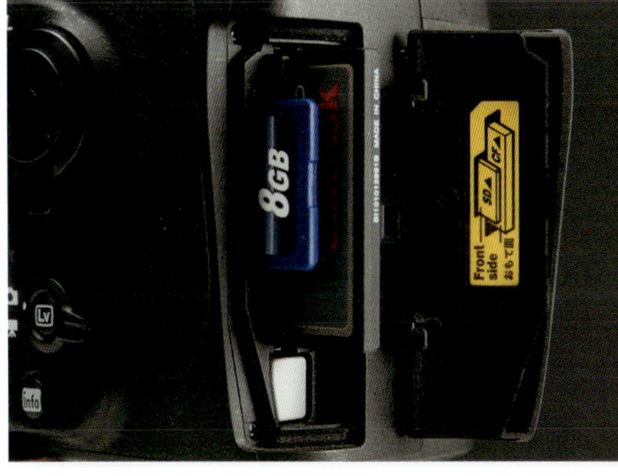

Writing files to multiple memory cards simultaneously is one option for file security, but this function is only available with more expensive cameras

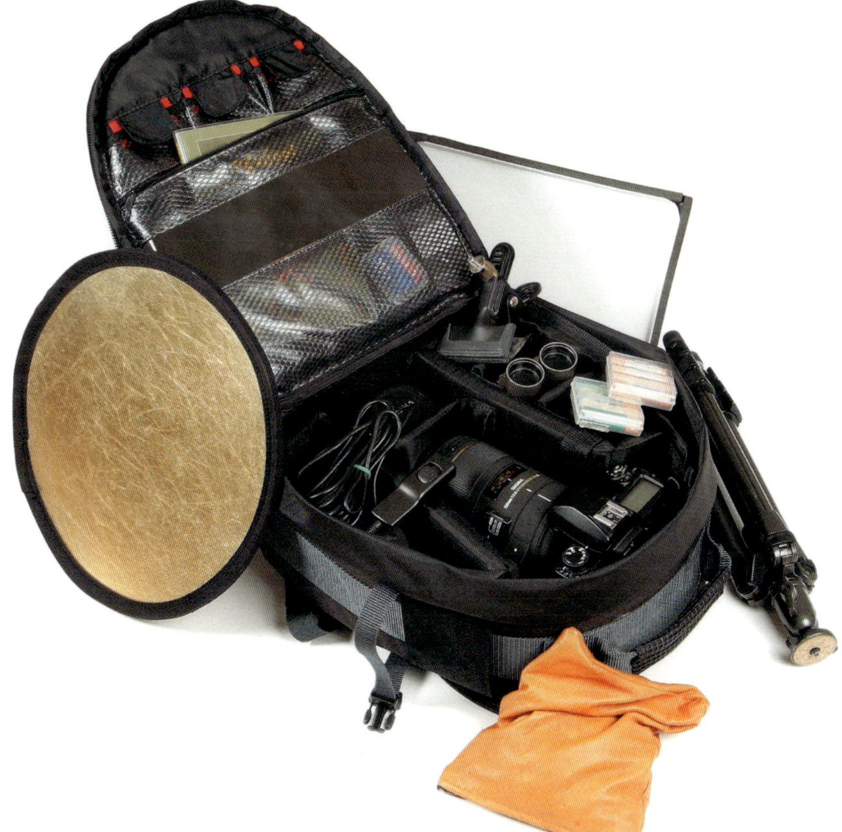

Even relatively modest collections of gear can be very costly, making camera insurance a worthwhile investment

Additional Macro Accessories

Sometimes you need an extra hand to hold your camera and flash, to position a reflector, and to focus your shot. The tools below will help with those situations, but their general usefulness is hard to overstate.

Reflectors | Large, flat objects made out of white cardboard or covered with silver or gold foil. They brighten up dark areas of an image.

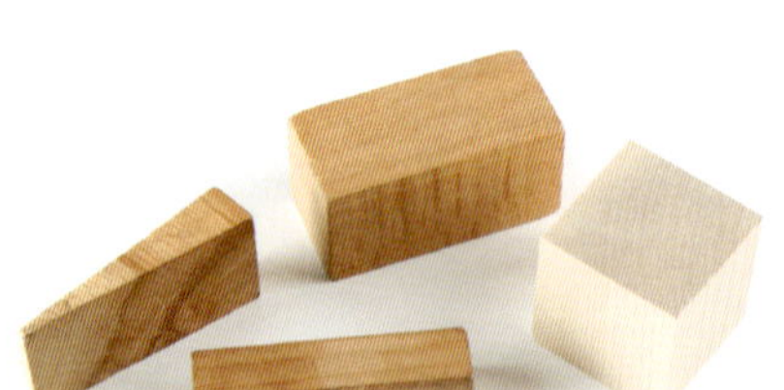

Toy Blocks | Objects of varying size that are handy for propping up elements in your subject.

Cleaning Blower | Although these tools are designed for keeping your image sensor free from deposits of dust, they're also well suited for tidying up your subject.

Flash Tilt Heads | Devices installed between the flash mount and the flash itself. They allow for angling your flash forward so you can illuminate your subject from above when shooting at close range.

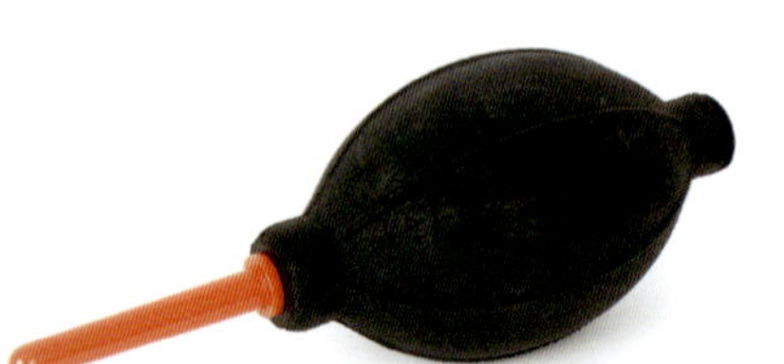

Flash Rails | Flash mounts that make it possible to position your flash away from your camera, thereby making it easier to manage shadows in your photos.

Helping "Third Hand" Tool | A small stand with multiple clamps capable of holding up small objects. Some such tools feature a magnifying glass as well.

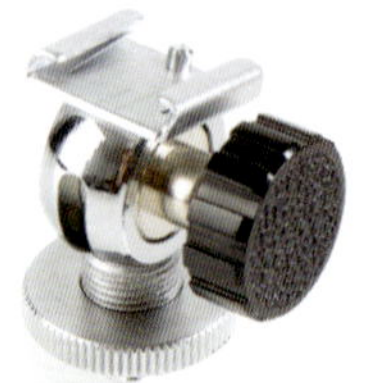

Translucent Color Sheets | Colorful sheets of foil or film that can be positioned in front of a flash for interesting effects of color.

Neutral Grey Cards | Cards with a grey surface designed to reflect a standardized value of light: 18 percent. They help in obtain the proper white balance for a given shot.

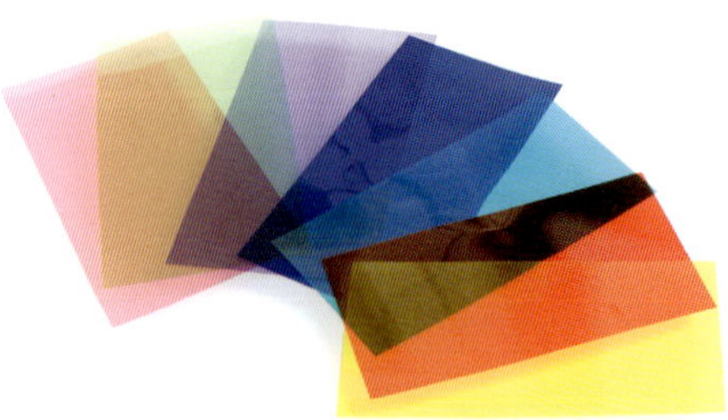

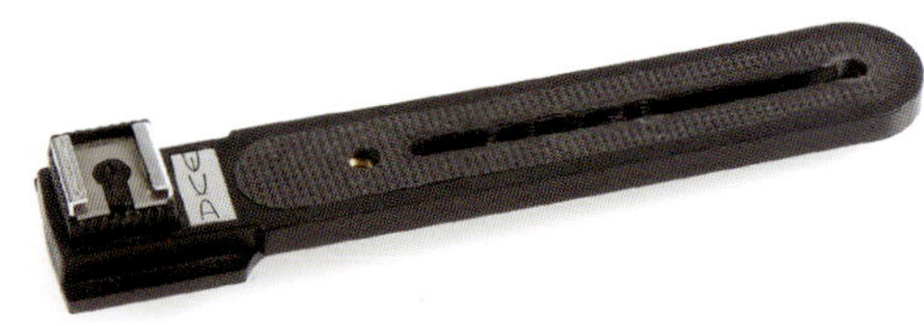

Hot Glue Gun | Hot glue dries quickly and can easily be removed from smooth surfaces. A very practical tool for quick fixes.

Cardboard | Different colors have different uses: white is good for reflecting light or brightening images, black for darkening, and various colors produce colorful effects (as backdrops, etc.).

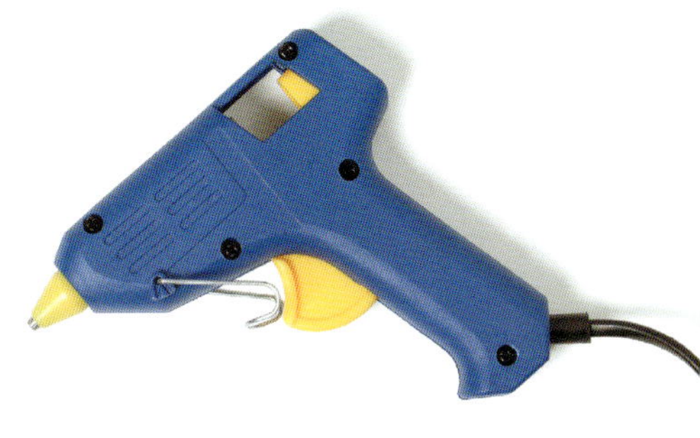

Clamps and Clips | Versatile tools for securing equipment and holding up background elements and decoration. They come in a variety of sizes, and some even feature tripod threads for holding flash units.

Adhesive Tape | An absolute must-have for securing everything imaginable for macro photographers. Tape that can be easily removed is also useful for marking off specific locations on your shooting table.

Modeling Clay | Very useful for fixing parts of your subject in place when shooting in the studio.

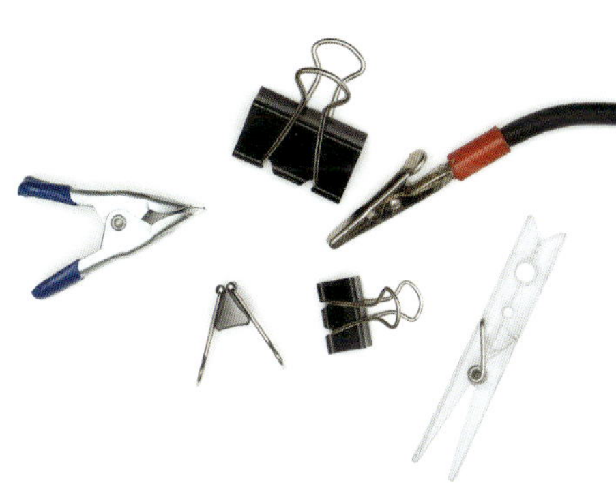

Magnets | Magnets offer an effective and invisible way to secure objects in place. Neodymium magnets are particularly strong and work through even thick materials. Magnets are particularly useful when you've lined the top of your shooting table with a magnetic material.

Sponge Rubber | A substance especially good for supporting delicate objects. It can be carefully cut and sculpted with a sharp knife.

Nylon Twine | If you need to hang objects or decorations from the ceiling, a thin nylon twine, such as fishing line, is your best bet because it won't be conspicuous in your images.

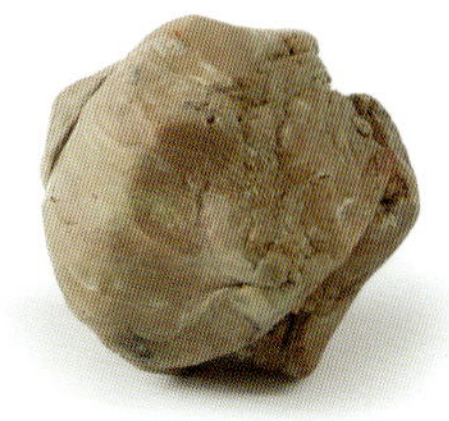

Brushes | A fine watercolor brush is an effective device for removing dust from your subject.

Tweezers | For positioning or removing tiny elements from your tabletop pictures.

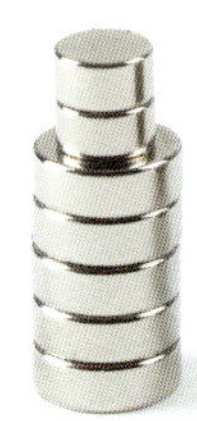

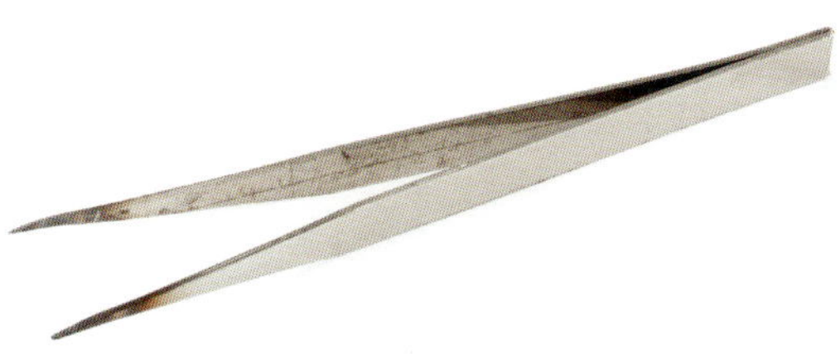

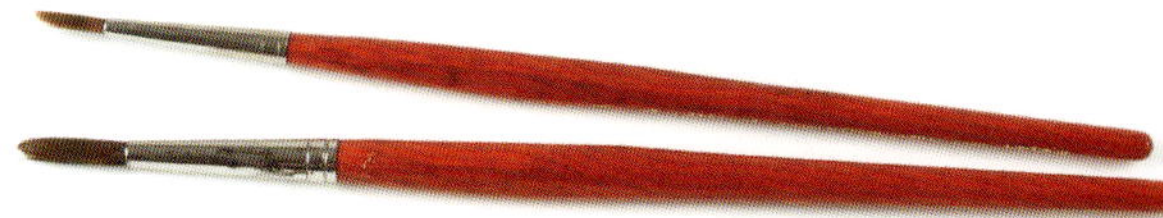

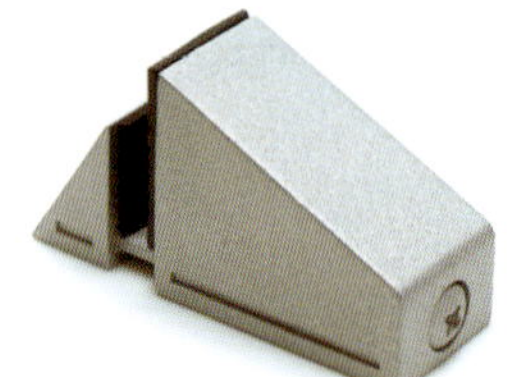

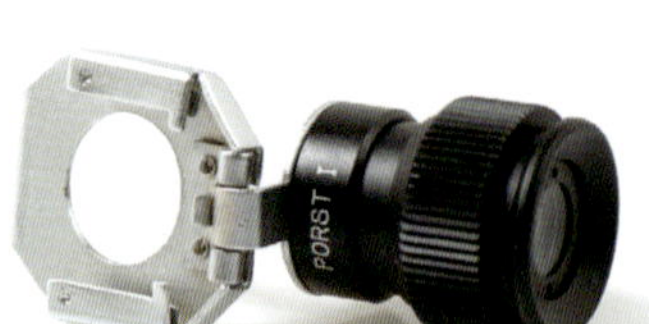

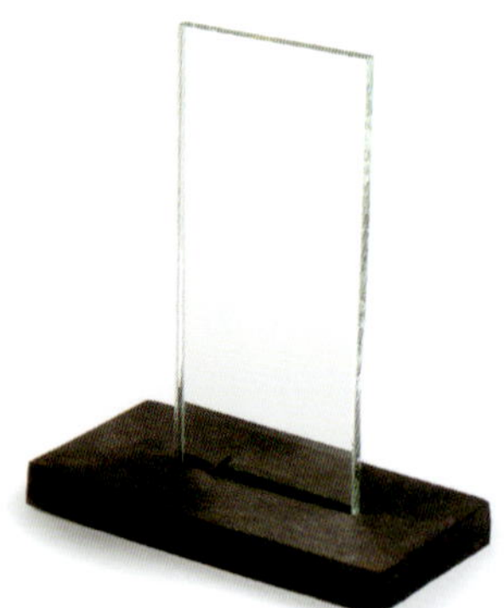

Bookshelf Brackets | Although they're intended to secure bookshelves to the wall, these brackets make excellent stands for reflectors, mirrors, and the like.

Slave Flash Units | These auxiliary flash units can be wirelessly triggered to fire by the pulse of light from the main flash. They can be used to create interesting effects or simply to brighten areas of your image, such as the backdrop. Slave flash trigger adapters make it possible to retrofit your regular flash heads to work as slave flash units.

Mirrors | Small mirrors let you direct light to shine exactly where you want it to. You can cut mirrors with glass cutters, but you can also simply use broken mirror pieces. Sponge rubber is a good material for supporting mirrors, as is modeling clay. Smooth off rough edges of mirrors using sandpaper.

Pushpins | Great little devices for pinning parts of your subject in place.

Viewfinder Magnifiers | Placing a magnifying glass over the viewfinder window enlarges the viewfinder image, making it easier to focus precisely.

Flashlights | The ideal tool for light-painting techniques and for illuminating targeted areas in your pictures. When using them for fill lighting, use models that have the same kind of light bulb as your main light sources to avoid color casts.

Q-tips | Q-tips are great for cleaning tough-to-reach parts of your subject, but they also come in handy when cleaning your camera body. When cleaning your image sensor, however, you'll want to use specialized equipment designed for that purpose.

Atomizer | A sprayer or atomizer is useful when you want to place water droplets on specific parts of your subject or if you want to emulate the look and feel of dew or rain. Small perfume bottles that you can find in a drugstore do the job nicely.

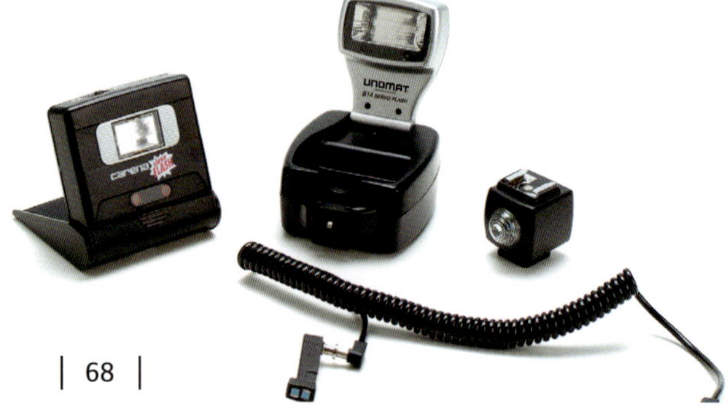

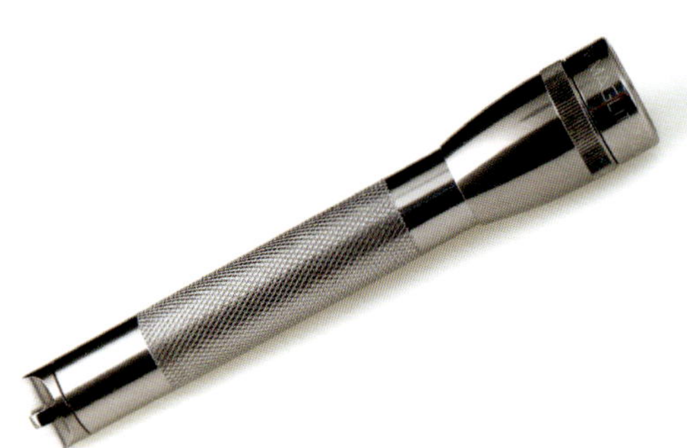

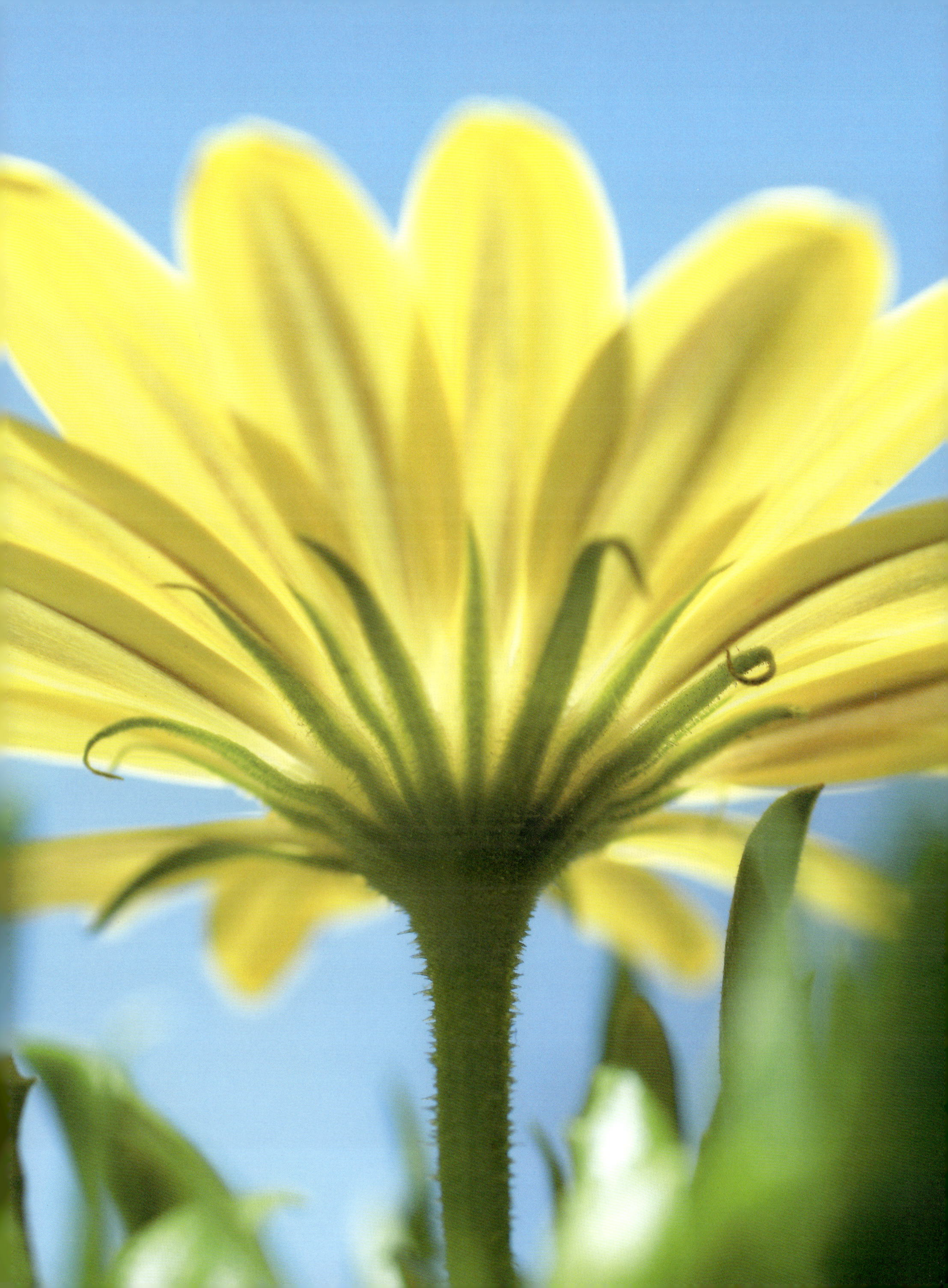

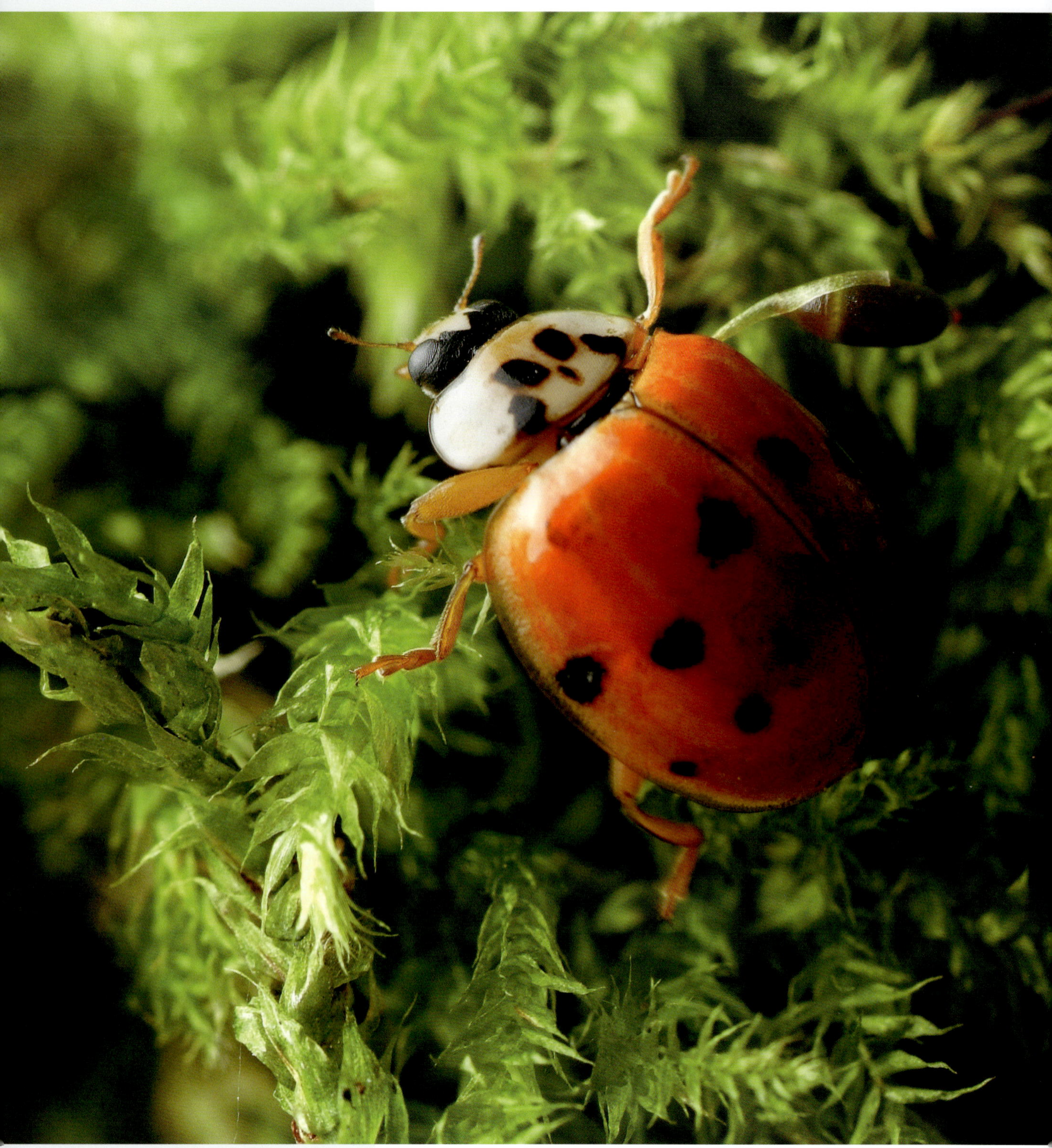

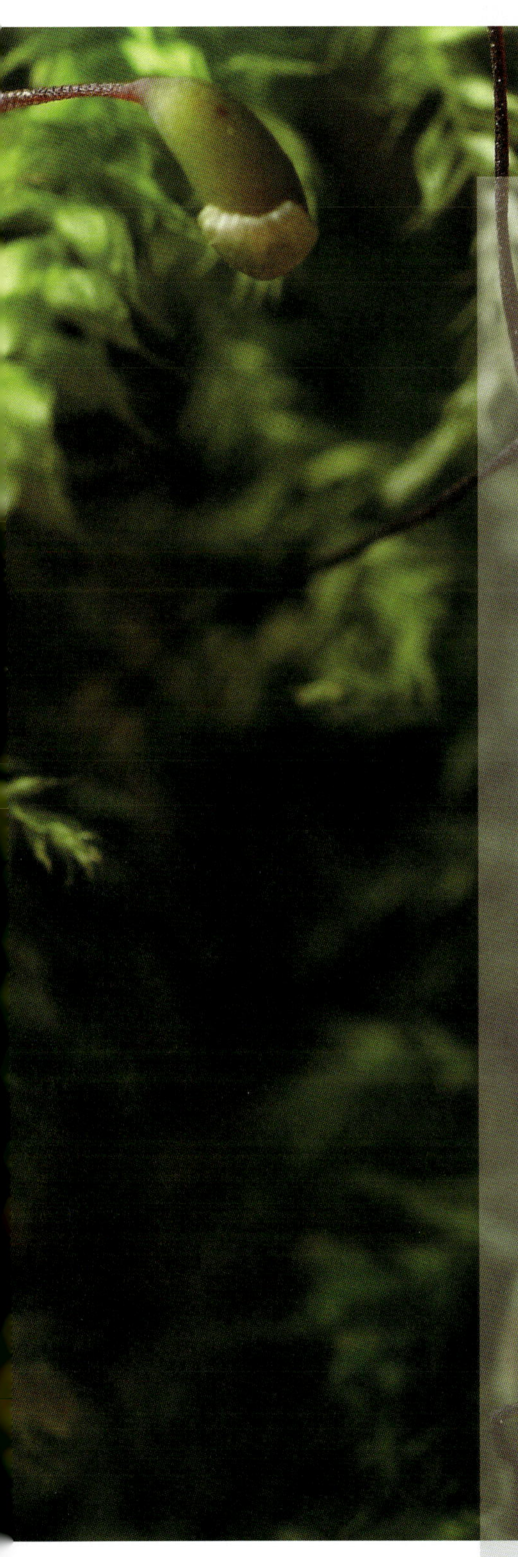

Shooting Techniques

This ladybug dropped in unannounced while I was working in the studio shooting some plants. I already had my tripod and lights set up, so I placed the bug on a piece of moss and took a series of pictures. After a while it spread its wings and disappeared.

Coincidences like this one are more of an exception than a rule. In most cases, capturing a photo requires careful planning or at least a fair amount of preparations.

Forethought is required not only when selecting your subject, but also when choosing your exposure techniques. Some of the decisions are somewhat technical, but many come down to intuition. As with so many things in life, photography is less about what you do than about how you do it. Figuring out the right settings to approach the task at hand—and having the patience to allow the subject to come to you—are often the keys to success.

Ladybug on moss
f/11, 1/125 s, ISO 200, 50mm, flash with softbox

Strategies for Dealing with Blur

Macro photographs feature depths of field that are especially shallow, which means that focusing precisely and minimizing camera shake are of paramount concern. Even when exercising extreme caution, blur can still ruin your images—sometimes it arises due to technical limitations, but often it is because certain errors made their way into your exposure techniques. When this is the case, go over your process for exposing your images and more times than not, you'll find a way to improve your process in a way that you previously hadn't considered.

Camera Shake

The cause of images ruined by camera shake is a shutter speed setting that is too slow. In this case, the solution is very straightforward: choose a faster shutter speed. A good general rule for selecting a shutter speed is that the inverse of the shutter speed should not be shorter than the focal length of the lens. When shooting with a 50mm lens, for example, you have a good chance of getting sharp pictures if you use a shutter speed of 1/60 s or faster. If you're shooting with a DSLR, you also have to consider any focal length extension factor. In these cases, it's generally wise to choose the next fastest shutter speed; so with the 50mm lens just discussed, you'd want a shutter speed of 1/90 s or 1/125 s.

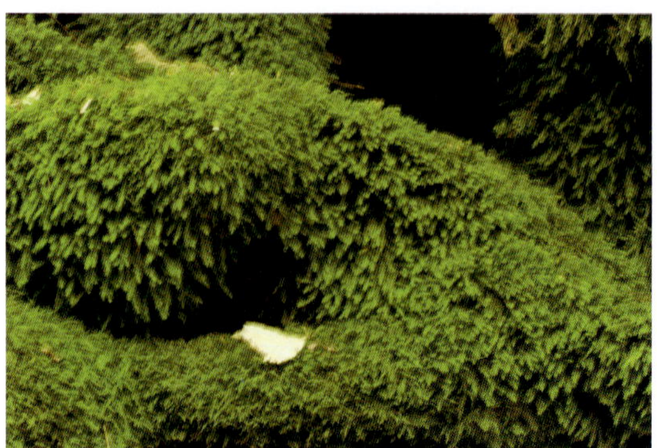

This photo turned out blurry despite using a tripod. With a shutter speed of 1.3 s, the vibrations caused by pressing the shutter release are significant enough to be problematic.

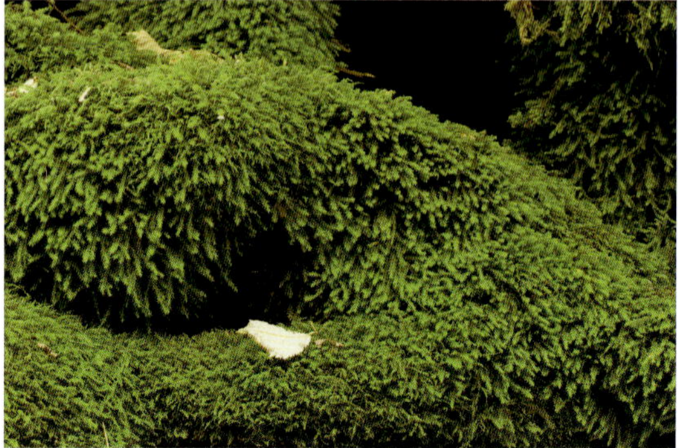

Using the self-timer gives the camera enough time to stabilize from the vibrations caused by pressing the shutter button before the exposure occurs. Both images: f/9, 1.3 s, ISO 100 180mm

Enlarging the Aperture

Opting for a large aperture opening leads to an increased shutter speed. A shutter speed of 1/60 s at f/10, for example, has an equal exposure to a shutter speed of 1/125 s at f/6.3 and 1/250 s at f/4.5. You pay for this increase in shutter speed with a reduced depth of field, which isn't always an acceptable trade-off.

Tripods

A tripod can help if you're trying to avoid altering the aperture. Using a tripod limits how spontaneous you can be, so don't use the largest model on the market. Instead bring a compact one with you and use it only when circumstances demand it.

A tripod is not a cure-all antidote for camera shake issues, however: how you trigger the shutter release also comes into play. Even photos shot when using a tripod may end up with blur. One cause of camera shake with DSLR cameras is the resulting vibrations that occur as the mirror swings up to allow light to reach the image sensor. Some cameras have a mirror lockup option that eliminates this problem, but in most cases you'll want to employ a remote shutter release system to get around the problem when working with a tripod. An infrared trigger is ideal, but wired systems also do the job. If no such option is available, use the camera's self-timer.

When shooting with a magnification greater than 1:1, you probably don't want to rely on focusing using the lens anymore. Instead, you'll be able to make subtler adjustments if you mount your camera to focusing rails.

High ISO Values

Upping the sensitivity setting is another way to get shorter shutter speeds. Even just a few years ago, this tip wouldn't have been advisable, because higher ISO values led to increased image noise. Today, however, many DLSRs are capable of producing clear images at ISO 1600 and higher. Bridge cameras and compact cameras have also made progress with respect to noise performance, offering good image quality at ISO 400. Much beyond that limit, however, and reproduction in the details tends to suffer.

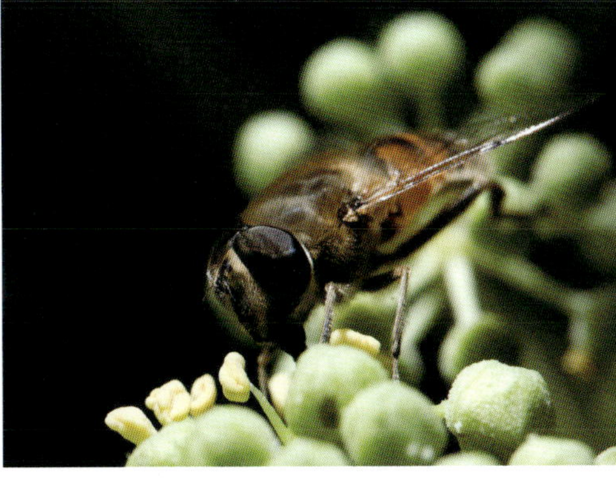

Modern cameras have dramatically better image noise performance than their predecessors—even at high ISO values. This improvement means you can increase shutter speeds when using a small aperture opening and still be able to shoot freehand.
Nikon D800, f/13, 1/2,000 s, ISO 6400, 180mm

Remote shutter release options prevent camera shake from occurring as a result of physically touching the camera body

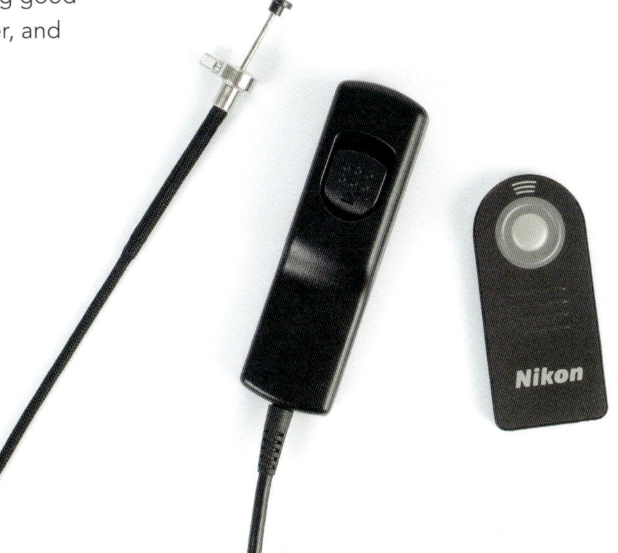

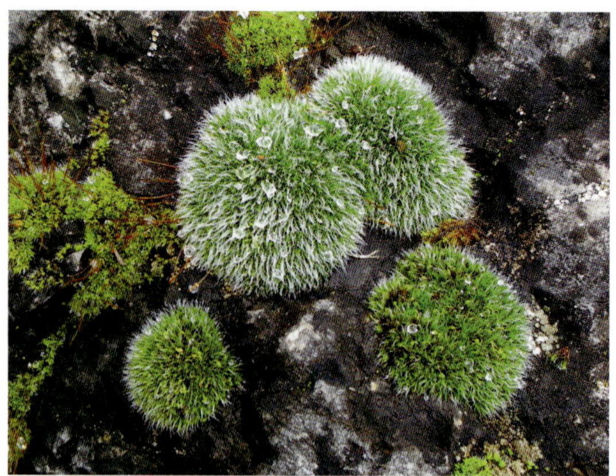

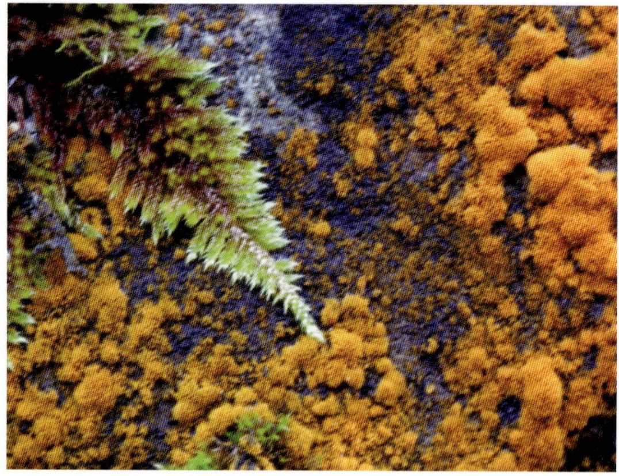

Thanks to image stabilizers, it's still possible to achieve sharp images while shooting handheld at 1/20 s
Fuji HS10, f/4, 1/20 s, ISO 100, 14.6mm

At an exposure time of 1/6 s, however, we've reached the limits of the stabilization technology and visible blur resulting from camera shake is creeping into the image
Fuji HS10, f/4, 1/6 s, ISO 100, 17.5mm

Image Stabilizers

Camera manufacturers offer two different types of technology to compensate for camera shake. The goal of both methods is to counteract the movements caused by camera shake to produce sharp images even with slower shutter speeds. The first method is a stabilization system built into the lens itself, which causes elements of the lens system to move. The second method is built into the camera and causes the position of the sensor to adjust. That's it for the theory of these methods. In practice, image stabilizers are a tremendous help when it comes to shooting freehand in poor lighting conditions.

The general effectiveness of these systems depends largely on the conditions you're shooting in. Even though image stabilizers allow for relatively sharp images with longer exposure times, they won't stop moving objects from creating motion blur in your pictures.

Some people claim that when shooting from a tripod with image stabilizers activated the ultrasonic motors will introduce slight touches of blur. But there are special image stabilizer modes that can be activated to prevent this when using a tripod.

Mirror Lockup

Many DSLR cameras models allow photographers to lock the mirror up in advance of actually exposing an image. This feature enables you to eliminate the possibility that the mirror's swinging motion could cause the camera to shake and introduce unwanted blur into your pictures. When using this feature, it goes without saying that you should also be using a remote trigger system. And this method is viable only when you're shooting perfectly stationary subjects, because as soon as you lock the mirror up, your viewfinder will go black and you won't be able to react to any changes in your subject. If you're taking pictures of plants on a windy day or animals on the prowl, this option won't be practical.

Altering the Light

Sometimes a small reflector can create a big impact. Using a small piece of white cardboard or a foldable reflector is often an effortless way to brighten up a subject. You can similarly use an LED lamp or a flashlight, although in this case, you need to consider any mixed lighting situations that would lead to unwanted color casts.

Creating fill flash with the camera's built-in flash is another way to get sharper images. But the increased sharpness here is not owed to a faster shutter speed but to the ultra-brief pulse duration of the flash itself.

Motion Blur

If a subject moves during the exposure window, the image sensor won't capture it sharply. The longer the exposure window, the more conspicuous this movement will appear in the final image. You have a few options at your disposal if you want to increase your shutter speed:

• Alter the lighting by using a reflector
• Increase the lighting by using fill flash, for example
• Open up the aperture
• Use a higher ISO value

A makeshift windscreen is yet another viable option for countering motion blur if you're trying to get grass or similar subjects to stand still. No such luck if you're photographing a moving animal. If it's impossible to eradicate motion blur entirely from your images, you might consider deliberately featuring it as a conscious design element in your photo. In many cases, thoughtfully included elements of blur can give pictures more life than the same subject captured perfectly still.

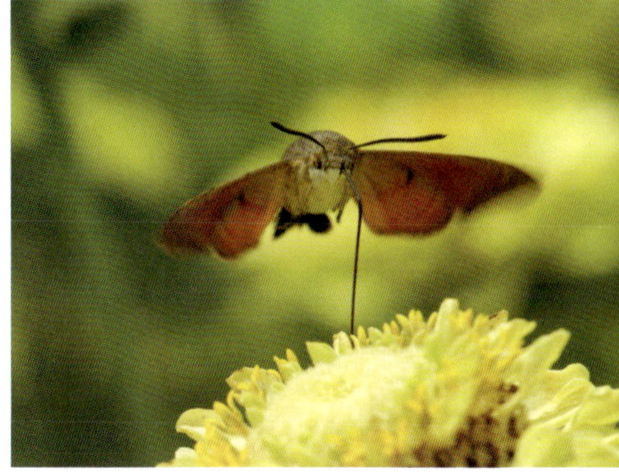

A hummingbird hawk-moth on a blossom. To attempt to capture its wings sharply, I bumped up the sensitivity to ISO 1600, which allowed me to shoot at 1/1,500 s. But even that shutter speed was too slow and yielded visible motion blur in my photo.

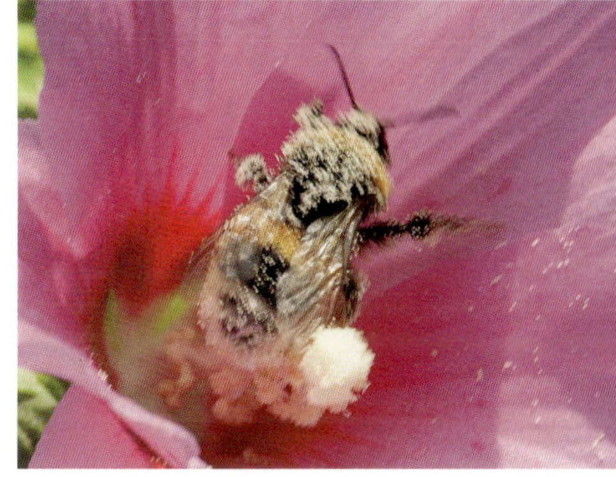

An exposure window lasting 1/60 s was too long for this heavily loaded bumblebee. I should have opened up the aperture so I could have used a faster shutter speed. f/13, 1/60 s, ISO 400, 150mm

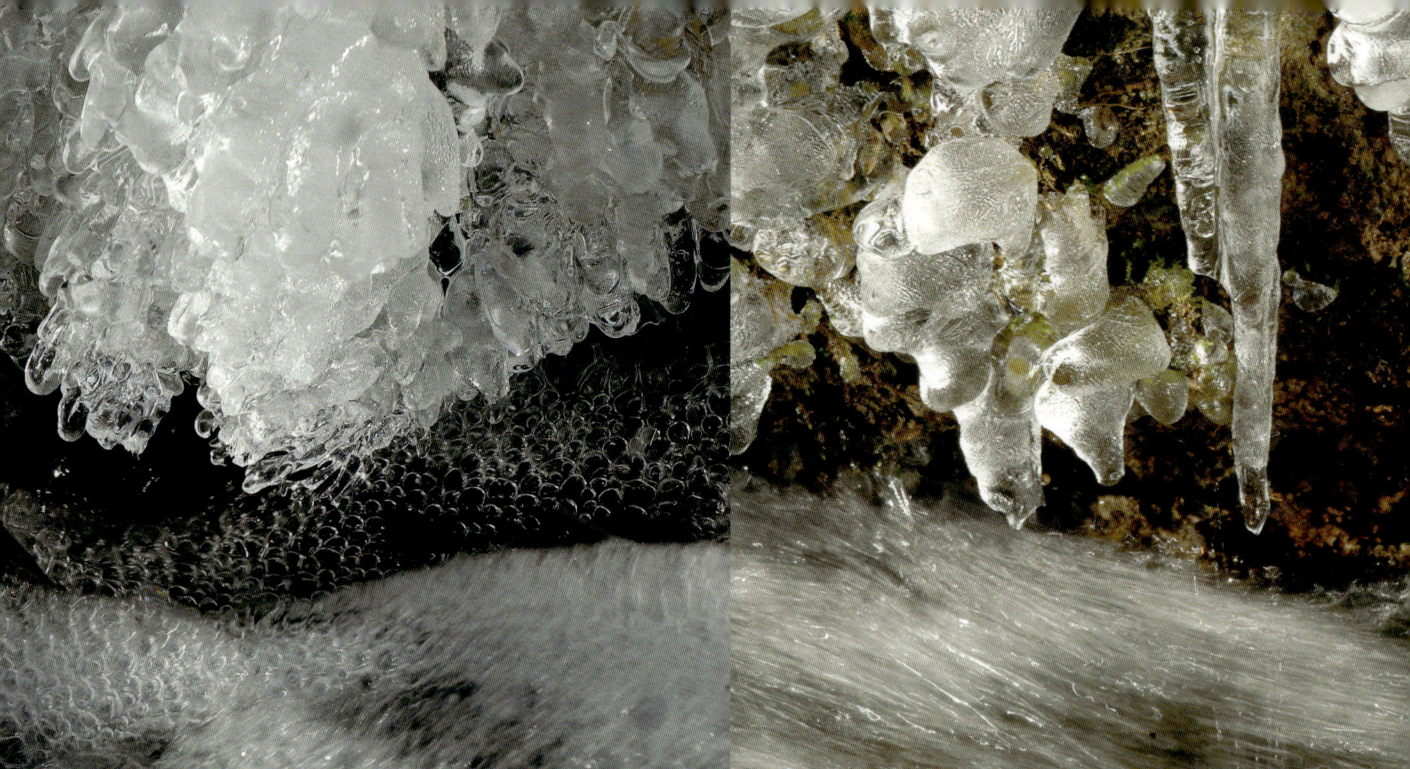

At 1/180 s you can still make out individual bubbles of air in the quickly moving water. Some areas of the water's surface, however, already exhibit significant blur. f/9.5, 1/180 s, ISO 200, 150mm, tripod

The flow of the stream is much more visible with the shutter speed slowed down to 1/45 s f/16, 1/45 s, ISO 200, 150mm, tripod

Using Motion Blur Creatively

Images that artfully feature both motion blur and sharpness simultaneously are often especially appealing, as this series of close-up photos of an iced-over stream shows. Just how much blur factors into such an image is dependent on the shutter speed. To ensure that some areas appear sufficiently sharp, it's often necessary to use a tripod to stave off any unwanted camera shake from causing blur to appear throughout the image area. Another factor for the degree of blur in these images is the speed of the object in motion, which for our example here is the rate at which the stream is flowing. The shooting distance is also relevant, however, because the relative speed of your subject will increase the closer you are to it. For this stream, which was moving relatively briskly, even a quick shutter speed of 1/180 s ended up with some blurry areas on the water's surface while other areas were sharply in focus. Slowing the shutter speed down to 1/45 s makes the motion blur even more conspicuous, and at 1/10 s, the surface of the water is reduced to a soft, milky current.

Subjects with a slower velocity will require slower shutter speeds. Lazy waves moving around a stone on the beach, for example, may require shutter speeds up to several seconds to achieve your

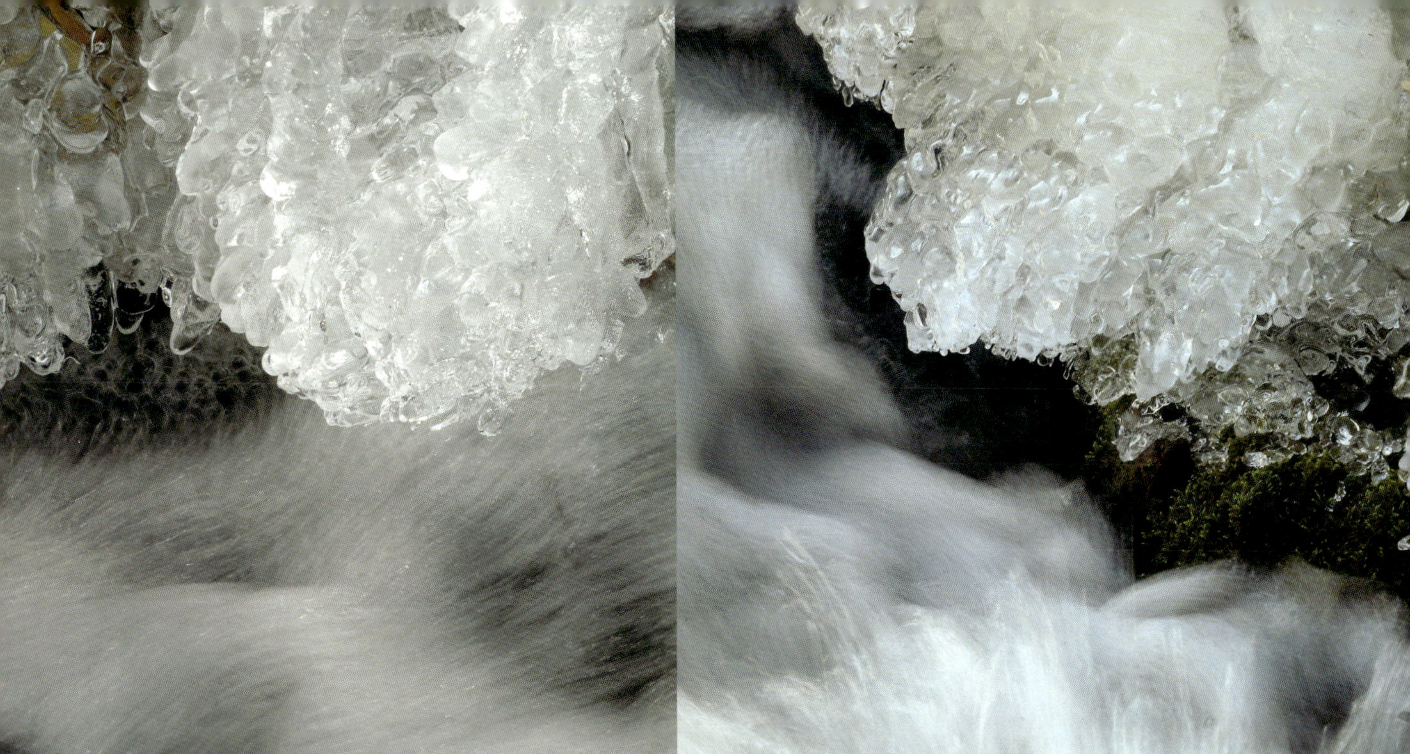

At 1/30 s, the motion of the water is even more blurry, appearing very milky in some areas while still exhibiting some static detail in areas where the water is moving a bit slower
f/22, 1/30 s, ISO 200, 150mm, tripod

Slowing the shutter speed to 1/10 s effaces nearly all of the detail from the water's surface. The soft, milk-like stream contrasts dramatically with the sharp ice structures on the bank of the creek.
f/22, 1/10 s, ISO 200, 150mm, tripod

desired effect. Another dynamic way to incorporate both motion and stillness in your images is to use a pulse of light from a flash to freeze objects in place during a longer exposure window as you might do when photographing a leaf falling to the ground from a tree branch. This technique can be carried out in two ways, depending on your desired intentions: syncing the flash with the shutter's first curtain or with the rear curtain.

First Curtain Sync

With this technique, the flash fires at the start of the exposure window. If we think about the example of a falling leaf, this method would produce an image with a sharp representation of the leaf at the beginning of its downward fall and a blurred trail of its form extending toward the ground below along its path of travel.

Rear Curtain Sync

Syncing the flash with the rear shutter curtain means the flash will fire at the end of the exposure window, immediately before the shutter closes. The result here will be a blurred streak of motion leading down to an image of the leaf closer to the ground frozen sharply in place by the brief pulse of light.

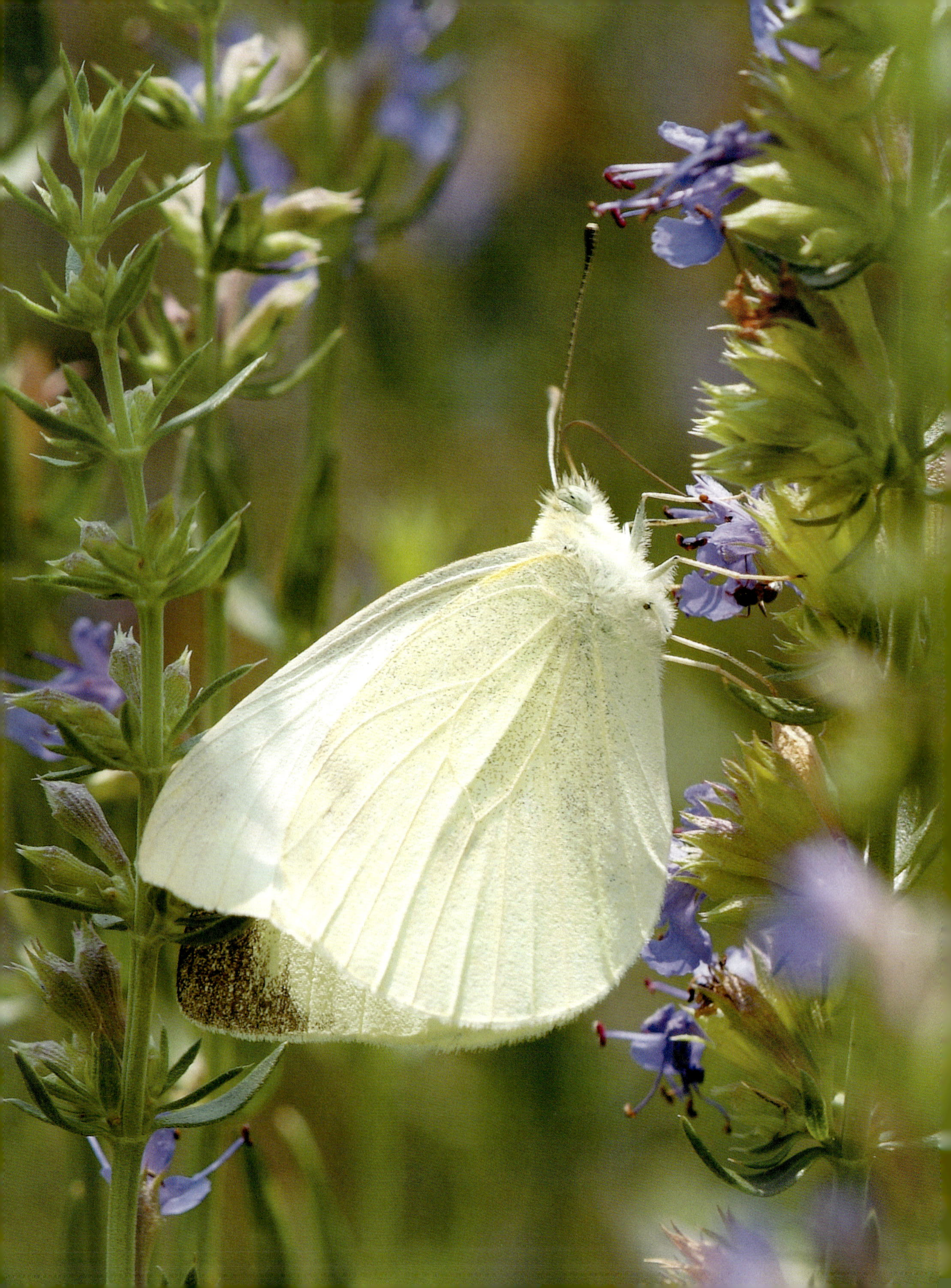

Focusing Problems When Using a Tripod—Equipment Error

Although it's quite uncommon, one cause of focusing error is rooted in the technology of your lens. The technical terms used to describe this issue are back focusing and front focusing. These terms describe what happens when a lens errantly focuses in front of or behind the targeted point as determined by the autofocus system or by manually focusing. It is relatively easy to test whether one of your lenses has this particular issue by shooting a series of photos of a ruler on a table.

To carry out this test, shoot a number of photos focusing on different hash marks on the rule—for example, at 10cm, 20cm, 30cm, and 40cm. It goes without saying that you'll want to use the sturdiest tripod you have as well as a remote shutter release system when taking these shots. After collecting your images, examine the results on a monitor. If the focal plane is exactly where it should be for all of your shots, then everything is in order. If not, run the test again to eliminate any chance of error in your process and to confirm your results.

If your second test confirms that there is a back or front focusing problem, you may be able to make the necessary micro adjustments with your camera's internal programming, depending on your camera model. If you don't have this option available, contact your lens and camera manufacturer to see if the autofocus can be readjusted. Fortunately, this type of error is very rare.

Focusing Problems When Using a Tripod—User Error

Another potential cause of focusing error when working with a tripod is an unsound process or workflow, or in other words, an element of human error.

When looking through the viewfinder of the camera when it's mounted on a tripod, many photographers instinctively press their forehead against the camera. Others firmly grasp the camera to offer added stability when adjusting the focus manually. Both of these behaviors can cause the position of the camera to shift slightly. As soon as you remove your eye from the viewfinder, the camera may spring back to its original position before you actually expose your image. In some cases, even this tiny shift is enough to throw the focus off slightly.

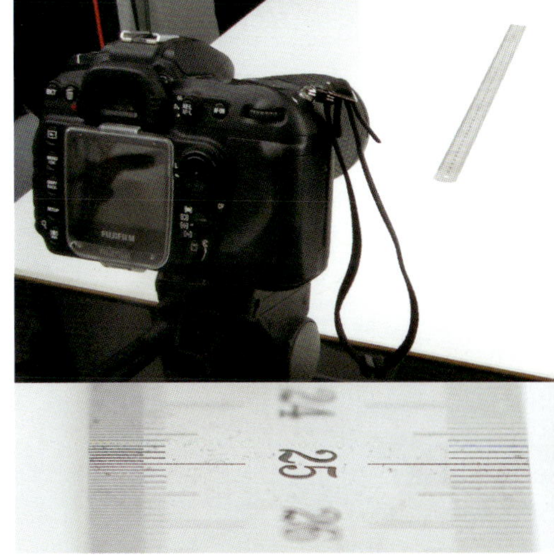

Photograph a ruler—ideally one with hash marks down to the 0.5mm level—using a tripod to test the focusing precision of your equipment. The focus of your resulting test images should be exactly where you intended it to be when looking through the camera's viewfinder.

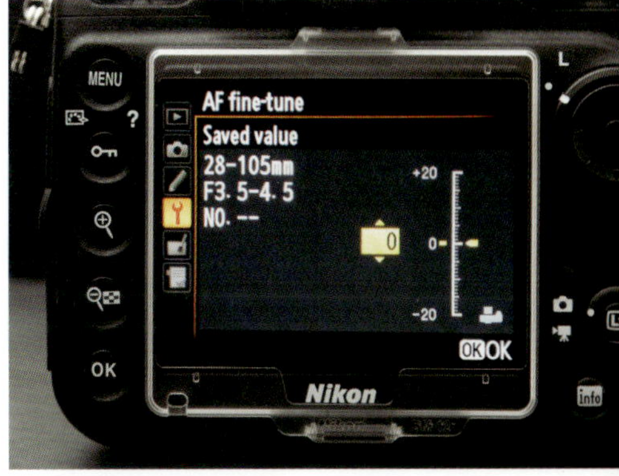

Some camera models, such as the Nikon D800, allow users to fine-tune the autofocus

Opposite page: Cabbage butterfly
f/8, 1/180 s, ISO 200, 150mm

Holding a Camera Properly

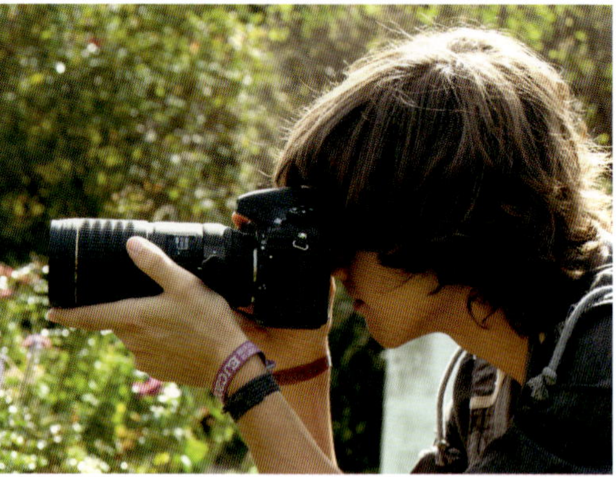

Use your hand as a prop beneath the center of gravity for your camera and lens—especially when shooting with slow shutter speeds

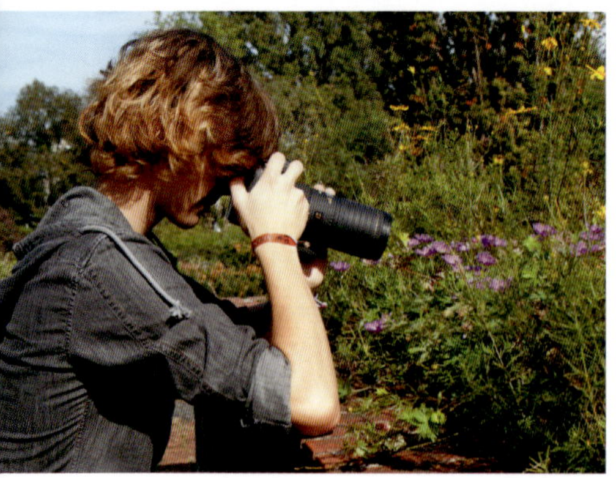

Leaning your elbows against a wall effectively creates a sturdy tripod with your rigid torso

Using the proper technique while taking pictures can save you critical tenths of a second. The methods described here may seem somewhat banal, but my personal experience has shown that the right posture, breathing technique, and so on can be that little something extra to help achieve quality images free from camera shake.

Holding the Camera

The way you hold your camera makes a big difference in whether you will be able to take sharp pictures, especially at slower shutter speeds. Always position your second hand—the one that is not positioned to press the shutter release button—underneath the lens to support the weight of the camera as opposed to on the camera body itself.

Autofocus or Manual Focus

In most cases photographers rely on the precision of the autofocus system to position the focal plane in exactly the right spot. The farther you move in toward your subject, however, the more difficulty the autofocus system will have in accomplishing this feat. There are multiple reasons for this, starting with the fact that the focus range often becomes so miniscule that even tiny camera movements force the camera to readjust the focus. Furthermore, macro subjects such as insects looking for food on a flower blossom or busy bees and butterflies, tend to move themselves. When they do, the autofocus needs to readjust, often settling on elements farther away such as a flower's petals. And with some camera settings (focus priority), you won't even be able to capture any image until the autofocus system gives you the green light. Gusts of wind are another source of movement that can shift delicate elements of a subject mere millimeters beyond the depth of field. All of these challenges generally mean that manual focusing is the way to go when shooting in the macro range.

The first step in focusing manually is to adjust the focus approximately at first and then to become more precise in your adjustments as you place your eye up to the viewfinder. If the focus is positioned on your desired target, fire away. It's actually much easier to react quickly to your subject's movements using this technique than it is to rely on the most modern of autofocus systems.

Breathing Techniques

Breathing naturally causes the body to move, but your brain naturally filters this detail away from your everyday consciousness. If you mindfully take a deep breath in and out, however, you'll see how much your body moves—action that can lead to blur in your images if you're not careful.

Movements related to breathing can be thought about in a wave-like motion. The peaks and valleys of this wave are when you transition between inhalation and exhalation, and those times are the stillest moments of the breathing cycle. Shooting your images during these critical times maximizes your chances of holding your camera as steady as possible.

The Natural Tripod

Whenever possible, lean your elbows up against something stable while shooting. Your arms and torso will effectively form an organic tripod that will allow you to use slower shutter speeds.

Improvisation

On some days, you're overcome by a desire to head out into the forest unencumbered and to simply walk around without having to carry a bunch of gear, so you leave your tripod at home. Without fail, these are the days when you'll come across something that can't be sharply photographed without a stand. Sure you can bump up the ISO value and open the aperture to get a faster shutter speed, but sometimes those measures aren't enough. In these moments, one option is to rummage around in the underbrush for a branch with a fork in it. If you carry a pocketknife, you can quickly trim the branch down to the necessary length, and in no time you'll have an improvised tool that can lend a surprising amount of stability to your shot.

Holding Your Position

Proper shooting technique goes a long way in making your photography more stable and in allowing you to shoot handheld for longer shutter speeds.

Good technique starts with holding your camera in place for longer than you may initially think necessary. Beginner photographers in particular have a tendency to assume that as soon as the shutter button is pressed, there's no harm in moving the camera. That logic would hold true if shutter lag weren't a natural part of working with digital cameras. Moving your camera too quickly after a shot can sometimes mean that you're actually moving it before the exposure window is completely finished. Forcing yourself to hold your camera still for an extra moment or two is a simple but effective way to

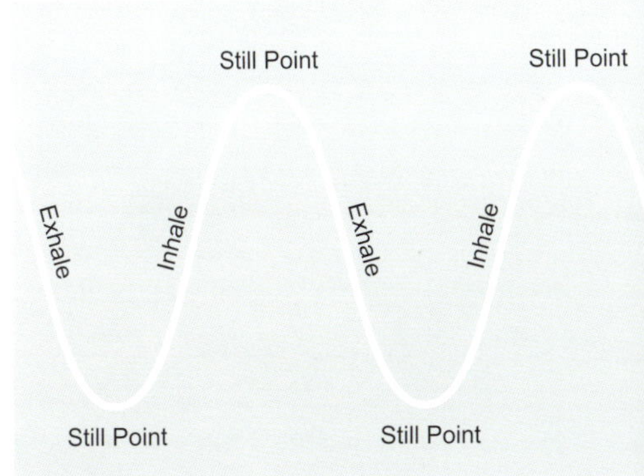

Inhaling and exhaling naturally causes the body to move. At the upper and lower transition points of this cycle, this movement is at its most minimal.

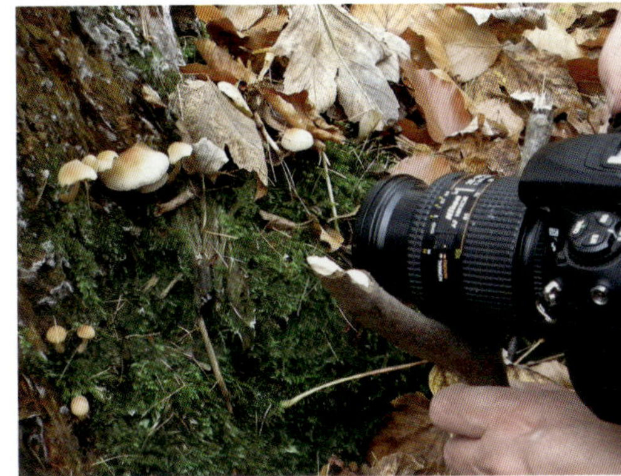

The fork of a tree branch can be used as a makeshift monopod. Using this method is a great option if you've left your tripod at home.

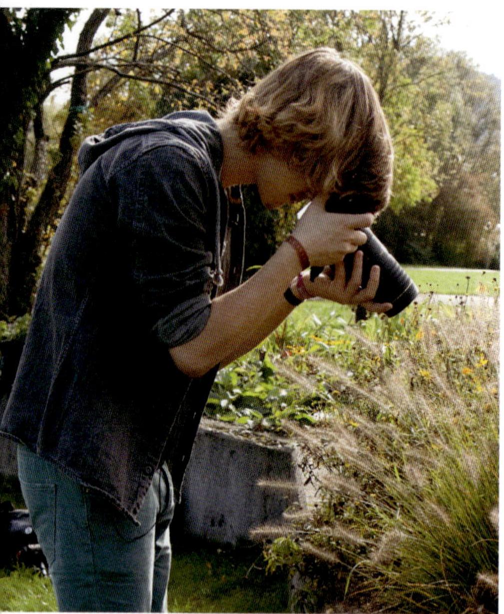

It's difficult to hold a camera steadily while leaning forward.

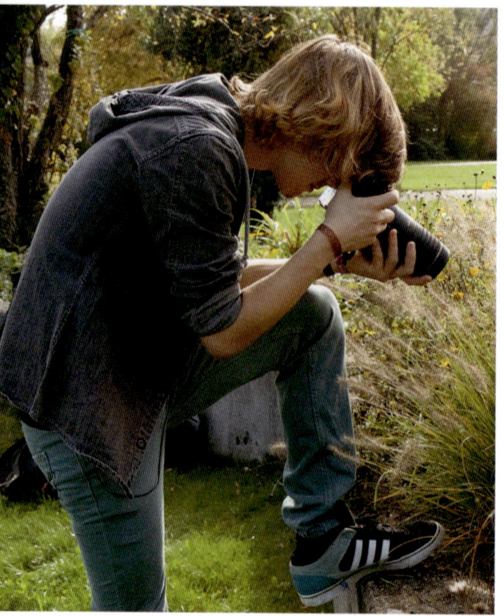

If it's possible to lift your leg, place your foot on something sturdy, and then brace yourself against your knee; you'll end up with a much more stable shot

increase your yield of photos that are free from the ruinous effects of camera shake.

Staying Calm

Approaching any task with a measure of calm generally helps to improve your chances of success. Taking pictures under stress or pressures of time is a good way to compromise the quality of your macro photographs. Hurried movements and internal agitation will lead only to images marred by unwanted blur and frustration over missing out on desirable opportunities. Take a seat in a peaceful meadow for a couple of minutes before starting your work, look around, and relax for a bit. Then you're likely to have a steadier hand when you pick up your camera and get to work.

Seat Cushions

A stable stance leads to stable exposures. Unfortunately, macro photography often requires that we get closer to our subjects by quickly dropping down to the ground in a crouch that better resembles a balancing act than a stable base for taking a picture. The reason for resorting to an unstable squat usually stems from a desire to keep our clothes from getting dirty. One solution to this problem is to wear the right clothes for the job; another is to bring a seat cushion or some other similar material that you can sit or kneel on. Properly sitting or kneeling on this material will give you a much sturdier stance.

Finding Support

Support your camera on stable objects whenever possible. Walls, branches, or even your own knees often make for a practical brace. Lay a soft towel or cloth over whatever you end up using if you're concerned about getting scratches on the bottom of your camera.

Beanbags

Beanbags are a truly versatile tool for macro photographers. A small leather sack filled with beans is a fantastic way to protect your camera body from rough surfaces as well as to hold your camera in a desired position. The Do It Yourself chapter at the end of this book has simple instructions for making a beanbag of your own.

Exploiting Depth of Field

In some instances, your entire subject won't appear in focus even though you've stopped down the aperture to increase the depth of field significantly. One potential cause of this problem is positioning the focal plane on the closest detail of your subject. Doing so

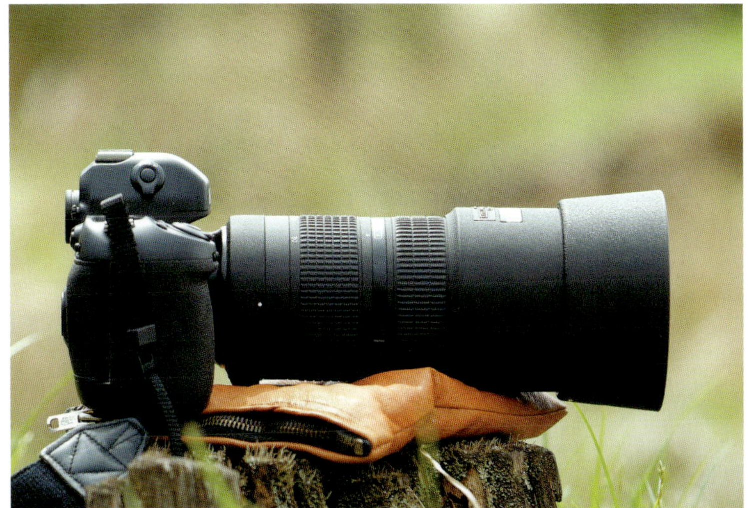

A small leather bag filled with dried beans is surprisingly effective and useful for holding your camera in place. Such a tool is also very easy to put together on your own.

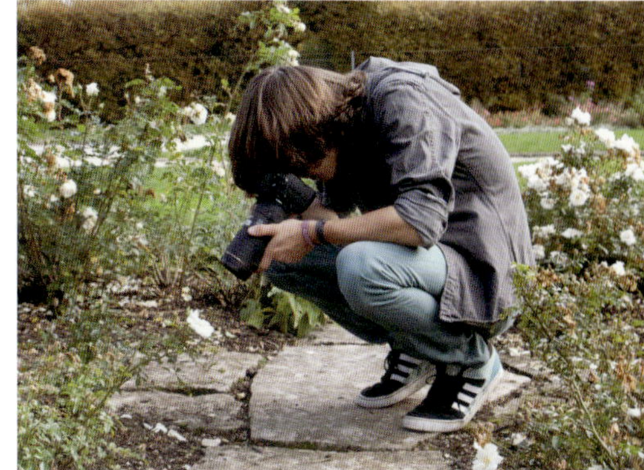

In this stance, the photographer's entire body weight is supported by two small points of contact with the ground—not a stable stance

means that the back half of the depth of field is used effectively to include subject details just past the focal plane. But the front half of the depth of field will be positioned in front of your subject. If you accordingly push the focal plane back to a more central element of your subject, you'll be able to exploit the full range of the depth of field effectively.

Approaching Flight Zones

Bad posture may increase the likelihood of unwanted blur in your photos, but so will hectic movements. Always approach your subject slowly and fluidly when trying to take photographs of small animals such as lizards and insects. Animals often won't perceive you as a threat—up to a point, of course—if you are careful with your movements. Inadvertently casting a shadow on these animals can also cause them to bolt. If you move in slow motion, you'll be amazed at how closely you can approach some animals. Using the longest possible focal length is also a key to success.

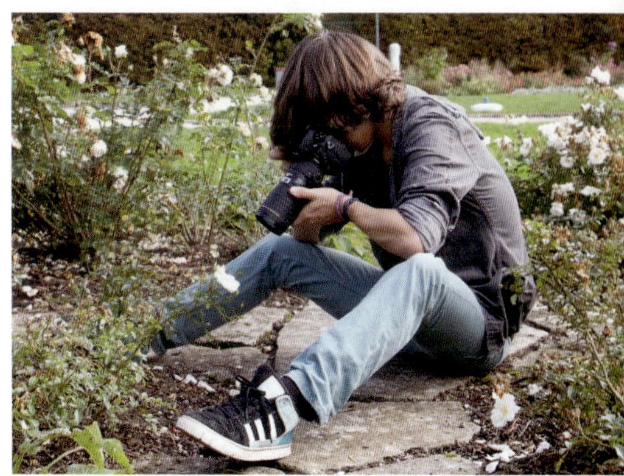

In this alternative position, the camera's shooting height is the same, but now the photographer's stance is much more secure. He is able to use his legs to support his elbows because he is sitting down, resulting in a very steady posture.

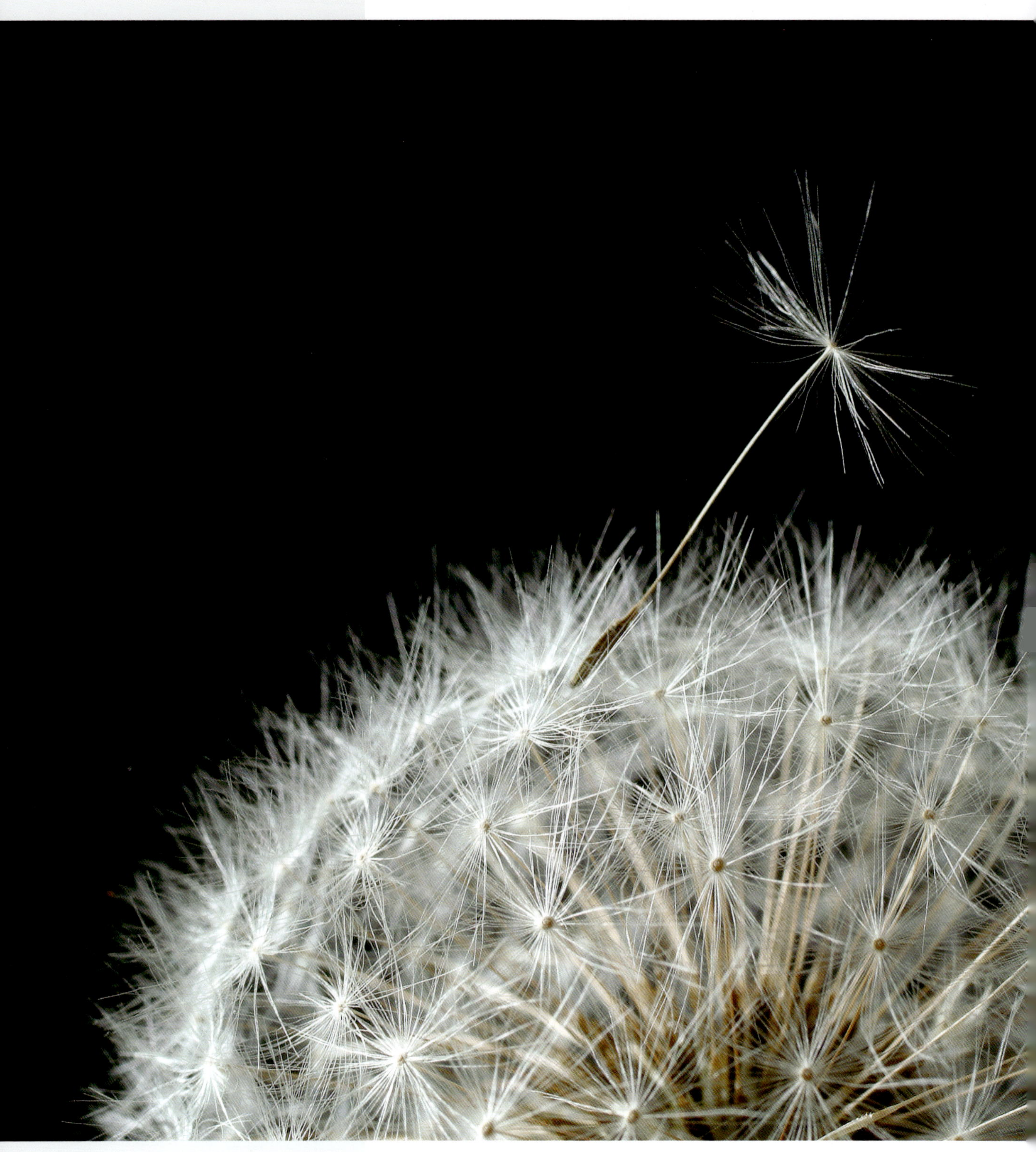

Macro Photography in the Studio

Shooting under controlled and reproducible circumstances is possible only in the studio. When I'm working indoors, my objective and style are completely different from what they are when I'm shooting outdoors. With the ability to control my surroundings completely, I aim to highlight the shape of an object and to use light to tease out its beauty. In a word, design is everything. For me, this goal is best achieved by entirely manual methods, which allow me to customize lighting, shutter speed, and aperture to achieve my targeted results.

Taking pictures in the studio is somewhat abstract and takes some practice. In many cases, the way an object looks on the shooting table will differ dramatically from how it appears in a photograph. Even a little practice, though, goes a long way in building up expertise about how to get the results you want. The lessons you learn by working in the studio will prove valuable for shooting outdoor as well. If you need to use fill flash, for example, studio experience will help you quickly determine the proper amount of flash to employ.

Dandelion
f/11, 1/125 s, ISO 200, 50mm, system flash with softbox

Studio Light

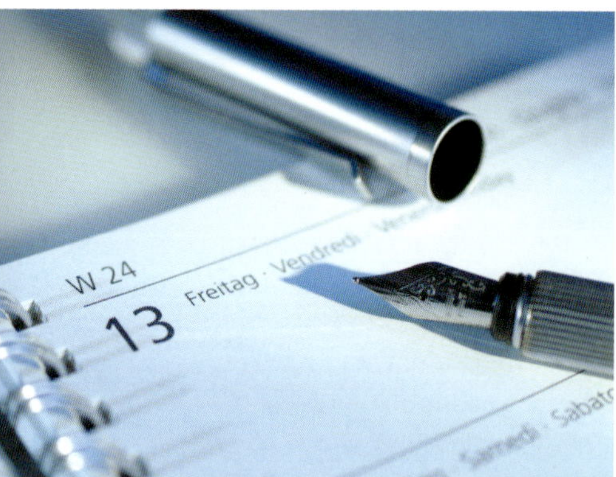

Close-up and macro photography have relatively modest lighting demands, which make system flash units a practical and affordable lighting solution

The quality of daylight and the prevailing weather conditions do not have influence on the work you do in the studio. You are entirely in charge of the lighting conditions as the photographer, which means the entire process for approaching your photographs is somewhat different. When shooting out of doors, you can blame a photo that falls flat on circumstances out of your hands—not so when working in the studio, because the quality of the lighting is entirely based on your setup. In theory, there is no unachievable lighting condition in the studio.

Reproducible Lighting

The big advantage of studio lighting is that you can re-create exact lighting situations for subsequent use. It behooves you to master certain standard setups that you will use time and time again. If you have these particular configurations down, you'll be able to expend much more effort and thought on your specific subjects rather than on the basics of creating desirable lighting. Adding in a few reflectors or auxiliary flash units to these basic designs allows you to develop even more complex lighting situations.

In the examples that follow, I have used system flash lighting exclusively rather than proper studio lighting. My goal was to make the configurations approachable for people new to macro photography, but all of these setups would work with continuous studio lighting as well.

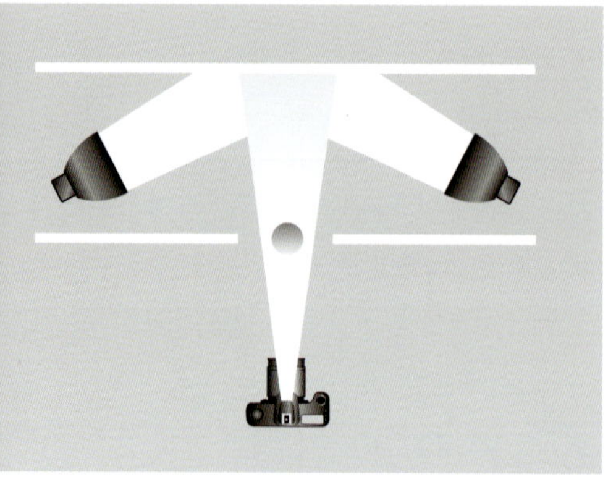

A completely white backdrop requires a lighting setup specially designed for the purpose. Fill lighting is often required to rescue the main subject from falling into darkness.

Pure White Background

One effective method for isolating an object against a white background is to light up the background so it is effectively overexposed. To employ this method, you'll want to light the background separately from your main subject. Using two flash heads set up with small softboxes is a good way to get an even lighting. Fill flash for the subject is often required to prevent it from appearing as a silhouette void of detail—this setup is effectively a classic backlit situation. When using this method, set up white cardboard pieces on either side of the subject so they are just beyond the image area to prevent stray light. If you're using flash units without softboxes, you can bounce the flash off these shields, using them as reflectors to better effect an even lighting across the entire background.

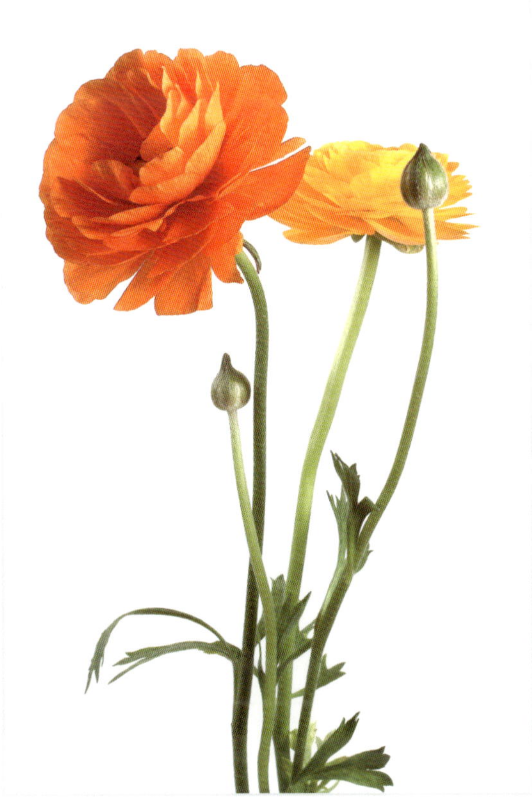

A pure white backdrop requires a separate source of light
f/13, 1/125 s, ISO 200, 50mm, system flash unit with softbox

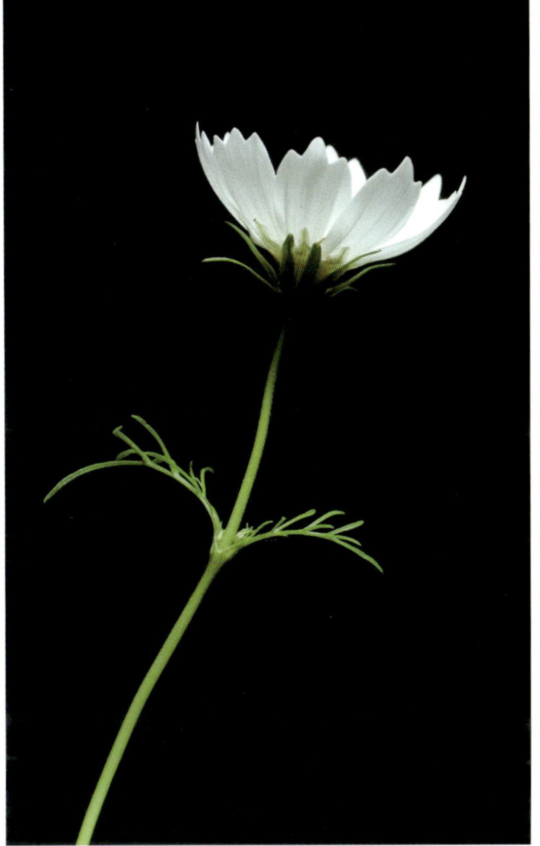

A pure black backdrop requires that stray light be
shielded and that the subject be sufficiently far away
f/13, 1/125 s, ISO 200, 50mm, studio flash unit with
softbox

A light tent is yet another option for creating a white background.
If using this method, you'll still want to use separate lighting for the
background. The farther back in the light tent that you position your
subject, the more it will be illuminated from the side by the reflective walls, which, in extreme cases, will lead to an image with weak
contrast. Positioning your subject closer will ensure that the reflected
light has a less significant influence on the subject.

Pure Black Background

When trying to create a pure black background, you have to take
care to ensure that no light reaches the background. Set up a couple
black pieces of cardboard as light shields, and make sure that the
distance between your subject and the background is as large as
possible. Set up your flash heads so that they strike your subject at
a very flat angle. You want your backdrop material to be particularly
absorbent for light. Velvet is an ideal choice—or any other specialized materials designed specifically for this purpose from photography shops.

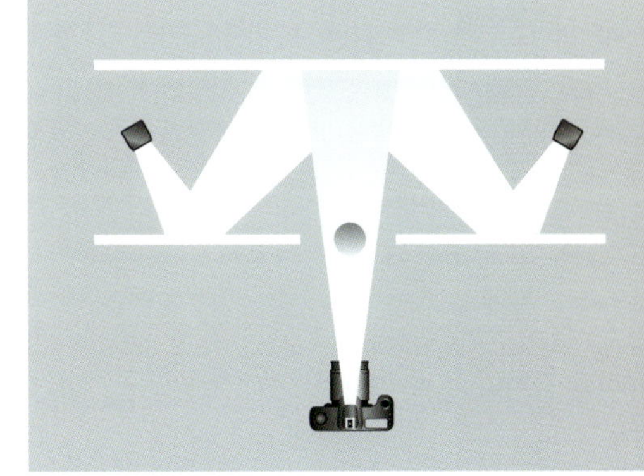

Using the backlight shields as reflec-
tors is an effective way to produce an
even lighting on the backdrop with
indirect lighting

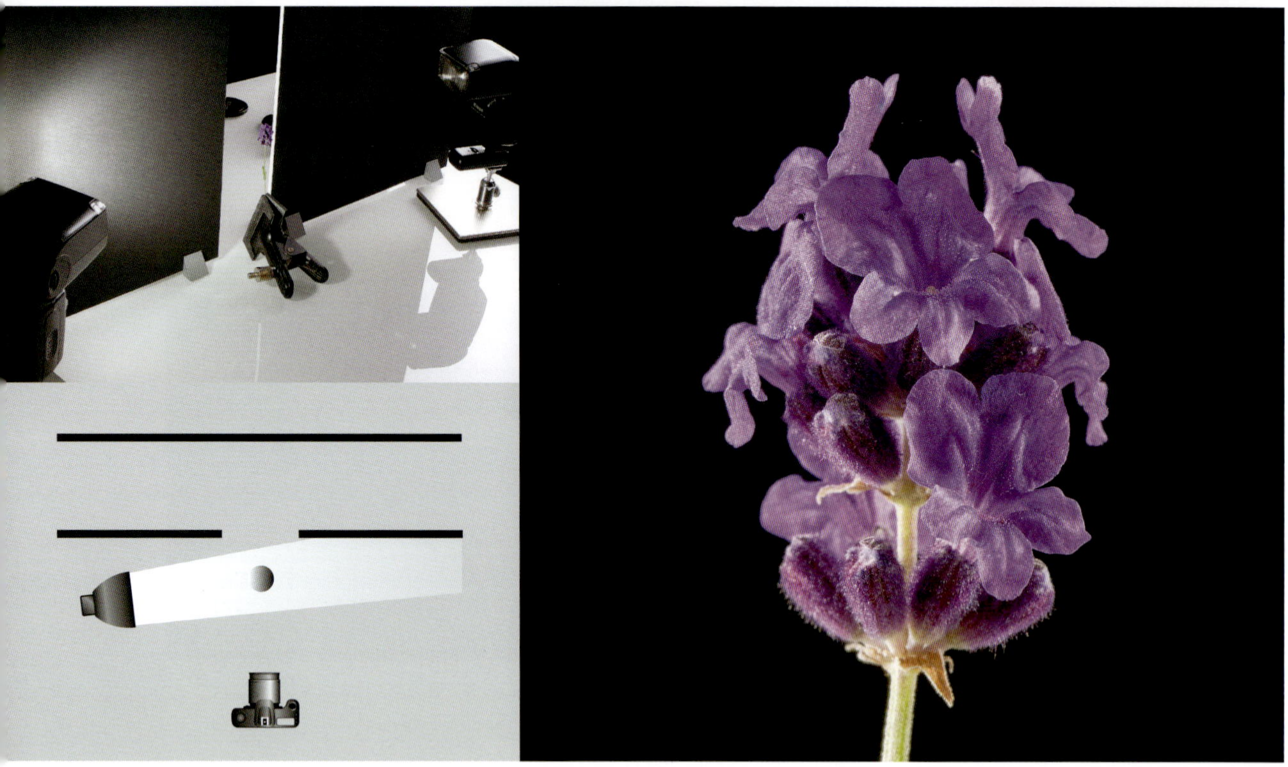

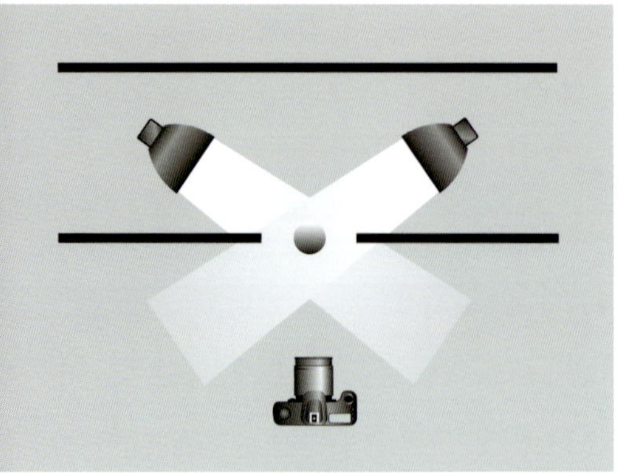

Black cardboard used as shades prevents light from the flash from reaching the backdrop. The graphic on the left shows the setup; the image on the right shows the result.

When trying to achieve a black background with backlighting, shades prevent flash light from striking the lens directly

Black Background with Backlighting

This lighting situation is very similar to that for a pure black background, except the main subject is lit from behind in this case. You'll still want to use two pieces of black cardboard on either side of the image to prevent light from reaching the backdrop. A third flash with a reduced output may be necessary for brightening your subject if it gets a little dark. This technique is particularly effective for plants, which exhibit delicate structures around their edges such as thorns, bristles, and the like. When illuminated from behind, these subjects radiate, giving the subject a warm aura. Flowers with thin petals and other semitransparent elements are also very attractive when styled in this way.

Transmitted Light

Translucent objects often reveal unfamiliar detail when illuminated with transmitted light. Glass marbles are ideal candidates for this treatment, but so are orange slices, colorful lollipops, gummy bears, and much more. When placed on a glass pane or a slide viewer and illuminated from behind, these objects take on brilliant colors. Many subjects will require some additional lighting from the front to retain detail in the areas that are less translucent. Your results will be best if you can achieve an even lighting on the subject's back side, which isn't an issue if you're using a slide viewer. But if you're using a flash head for light, use a softbox or a diffuser and position the flash as far away as possible or bounce its light off a reflector. Using consistent temperatures of light for both sides of your subject will prevent unattractive casts of color from occurring in your images. When shooting a subject with reflective surfaces, the front light plays a key role in the size and shape of the resulting reflections in your image.

Reproductions

Although reproduction photography may seem pretty straightforward at first glance, this type of work requires excellent lighting, staging, and lens quality. A camera angle that is even slightly off kilter can lead to visible distortions in your images—using a high-end, stable camera stand is all but necessary. Your lens will also need to support nearly distortion-free image reproduction. Unfortunately, zoom lenses generally aren't up to the task, because they exhibit pillow or barrel distortion at nearly all focal lengths. If you're shooting with a DSLR, you'll accordingly want to consider using a fixed-length lens—for example, a 50mm macro or normal model. Digital compact and bridge cameras are generally not well suited for photography when exact reproduction is called for.

   Strive for a uniform lighting free from shadows by setting up two lamps or flash units at an equal distance from the subject and angled at 45°. If your subject doesn't lay perfectly flat, lay a glass plate over it to avoid unwanted reflections. For your exposure, choose a small aperture to attain a large depth of field, and release the shutter using a remote trigger system or the camera's self-timer.

Mixing Light

One creative way to make use of the different color temperatures of flash units and other forms of artificial light is to simulate the warm evening light of the setting sun. Flashlights are ideal for this purpose because their light can be focused in a small area. To use this method, you'll need a darkened room to limit the influence of ambient light and a stable tripod for your camera. Select a narrow aperture and a shutter speed of a few seconds. Take a few test shots to determine how much exposure time you need to achieve your desired lighting effect. For the image on the next page, two seconds at f/22 was already long enough to bathe the coffee beans in a nice warm glow of golden light. To create this picture, the camera flash unit served to establish the baseline lighting. Bouncing the flash off a white reflector or using a softbox in this situation is helpful, because

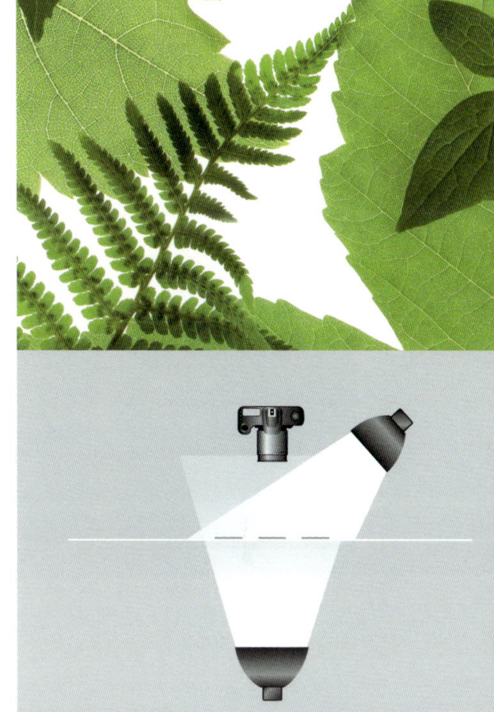

Transmitted light brings details and textures into view that otherwise are not readily visible

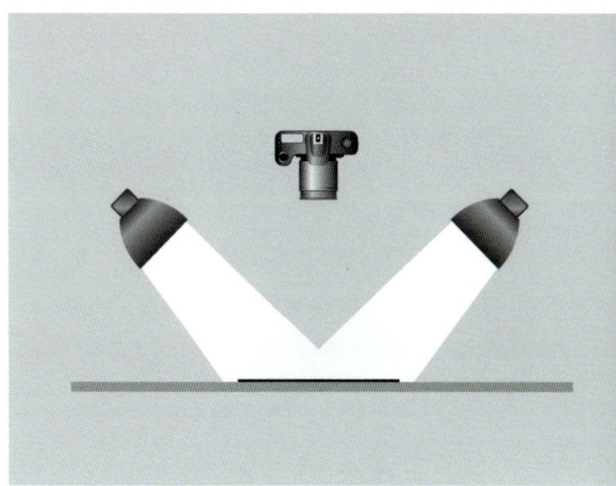

A symmetrical setup is essential for creating the uniform lighting that is needed for reproduction photography

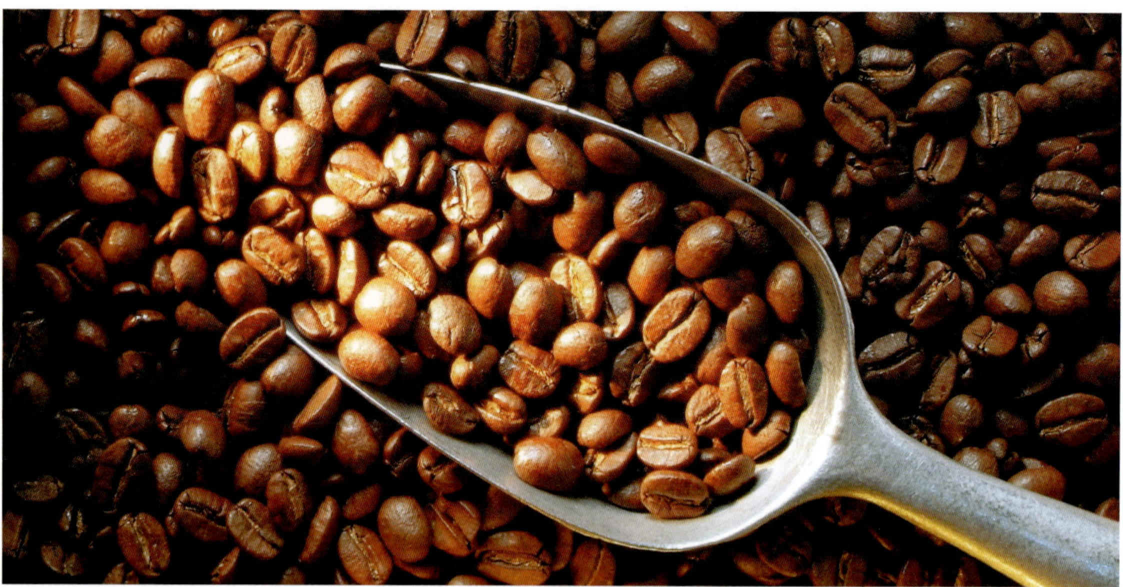

Mixed lighting comprising natural daylight (creating neutral colors) and the incandescent light from a conventional flashlight (creating an orange accent)

these light-shaping tools soften the shadows and prevent the baseline light from competing with the accent lighting from the flashlight. You can further refine your lighting by altering the flash unit's output or adjusting the shutter speed. Alternatively, you can manually fire the flash unit one or more times during the exposure window.

Colorful Light

Colorful lighting in the studio can be put to creative uses. One particularly engaging look is to incorporate a combination of multiple colors of harshly directed side lighting from different angles. With this setup, the shadows take on the color of the light opposite them. The transparent colorful films that you need to effect this look can be purchased at photography stores, but you can also find them at retail locations that provide presentation equipment. You can use the variety of colors available on the market to create yet others by overlapping them in front of your light source or by setting them side by side.

In addition to coloring your lighting, these translucent sheets can also be used to filter your lens. Depending on how intense the color of the filter is, your resulting images will appear subtly colorized to heavily dyed. You can even create various gradient filters by holding these color films partially over the front of your lens. The filters will be outside of the focus range for the lens, so the image will reveal gradual gradients of color rather than distinct or abrupt separating transitions of color.

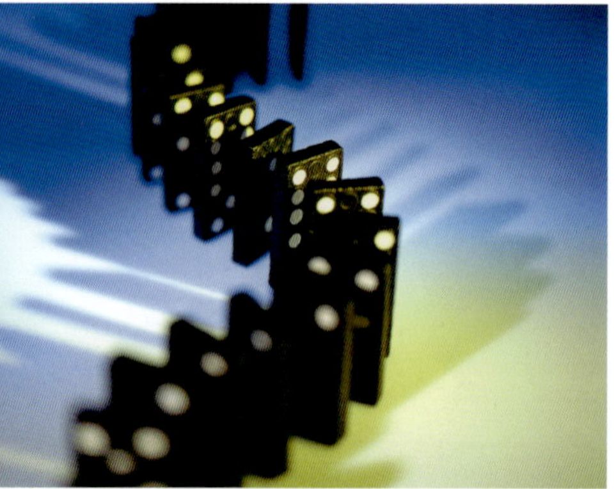

Colorful lighting opens the door to a wide range of creative effects. Here you can see the interesting results of using multiple sources of directed side lighting.

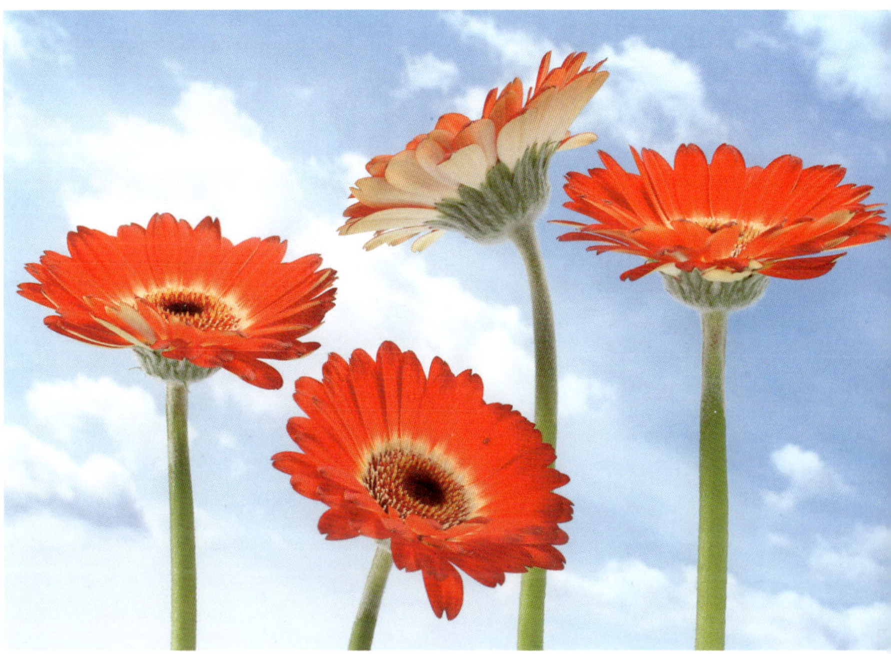

This arrangement of gerberas was photographed in a studio despite clues to the contrary
f/13, 1/125 s, ISO 100, 50mm, studio flash unit, two flash heads with softboxes

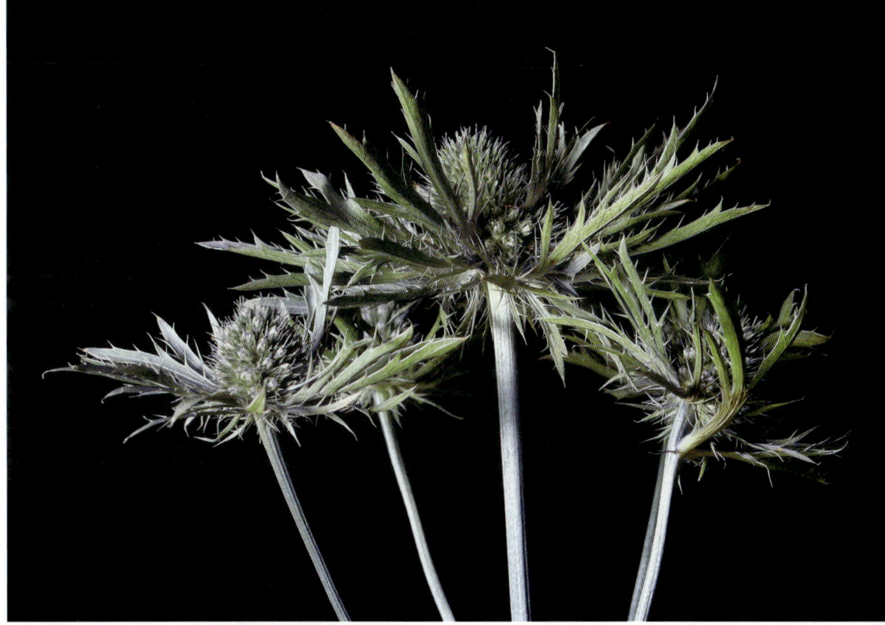

A black background causes the colors of even relatively nondescript objects to shine. Side lighting has a tendency to give subjects a plastic appearance.
f/9.5, 1/125 s, ISO 200, 60mm, studio flash unit with softbox

Lighting Compared

Macro photographers have similar options for shaping light available to them as professional product photographers, but in most cases the devices are much smaller. System flash units are particularly practical for macro studio photography for this reason. But LED bulbs and daylight lamps also have a place in a macro photographer's lighting arsenal.

The images in the following series were all shot with a distance of 40cm separating the light source and the subject. The light was set up at 90° to the subject and to prevent excessively dark shadows, I placed a white reflector at 15cm on the opposite side of the subject. Note that the ring flash was mounted on the camera for that image, of course. The piece of the circuit board helping to illustrate this lighting comparison is approximately 4cm by 6cm.

Think of these example photos as a starting point for what you can effect in terms of different types of light. In reality, you can experiment with multiple sources of light, different lighting angles or distances, alternate light-shaping tools, and so on to create an endless variety of additional lighting conditions.

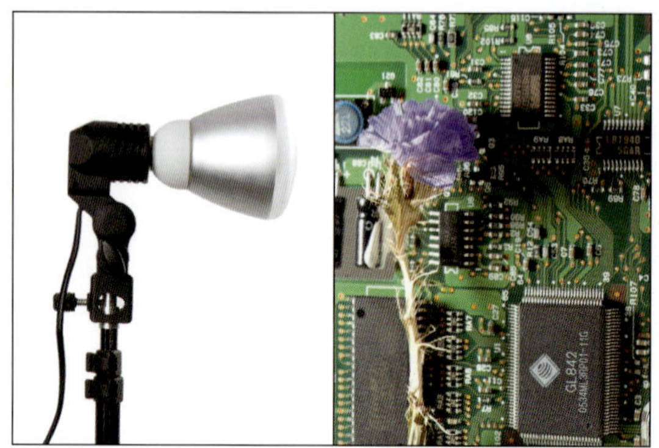

Daylight lamp: Soft, but directional shadows. The purple tones in the flower blossom are rendered differently from the photo using light from a flash unit.

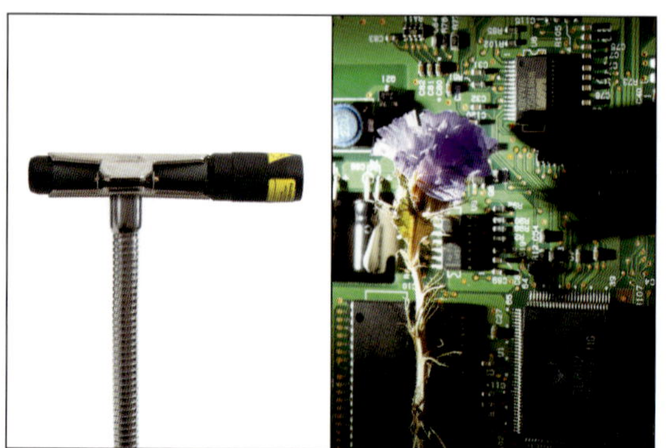

LED flash light: A spotlight effect with very dark shadows; the color reproduction leaves something to be desired.

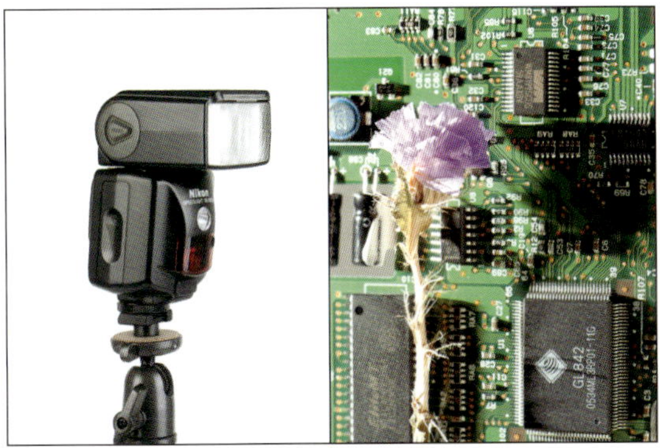

System flash unit, direct: distinct shadows and some overexposure in the image highlights

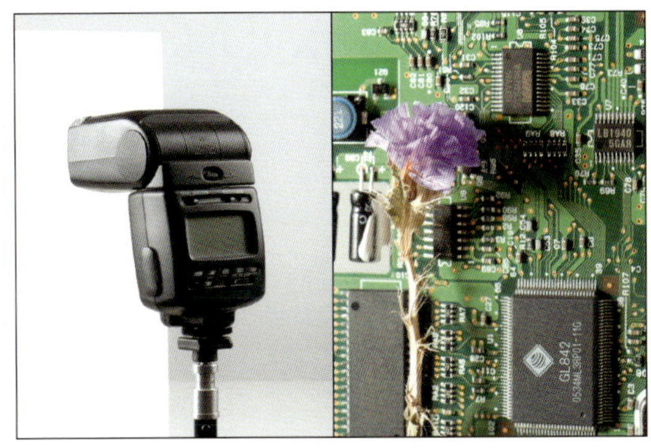

System flash unit, indirect (bounced off a white reflector): soft shadows and vivid color

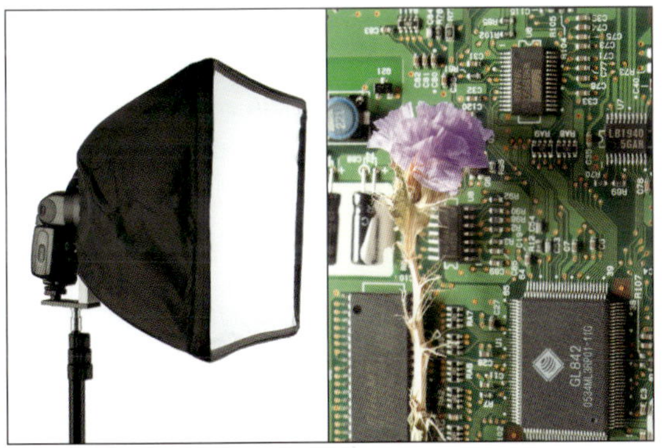

System flash unit with 30cm x 30cm softbox: significantly softer shadows than those created by direct flash lighting

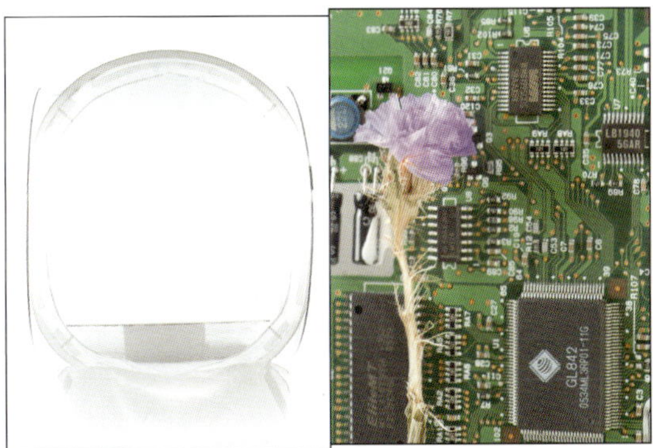

System flash with light tent: completely free of shadows, but the light is very flat and the colors lack sharpness

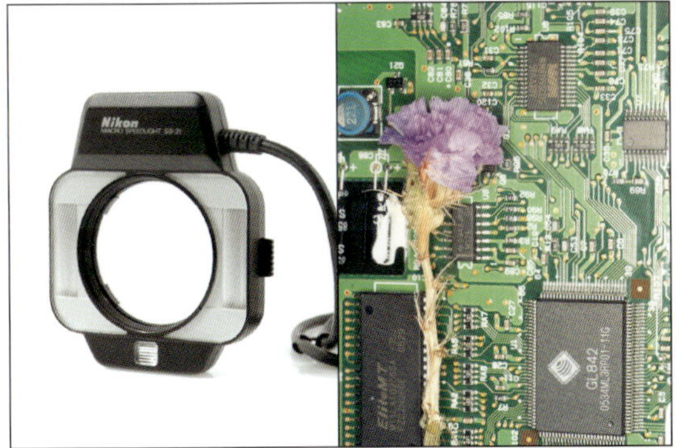

Ring flash: no shadows, but the light reflects off some of the shiny parts of the circuit board

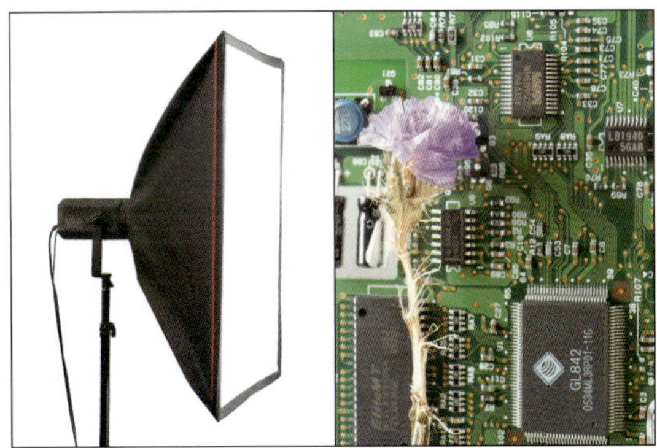

Studio flash unit with 70cm x 100cm softbox: optimal color reproduction, very soft shadows

Building a Small Macro Studio

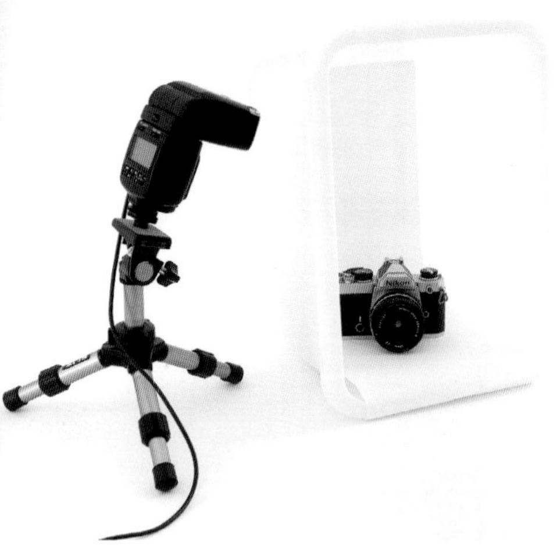

A translucent plastic container can easily be used to improvise a small light tent. A simple sheet of white paper will serve well as an infinity cove here.

Fortunately, macro photography concerns itself with the world of the miniscule, so the demands for equipment and studio space are more modest than what would be required to assemble a studio for portraiture or product photography. Nevertheless, even macro photographers require a fair amount of space to set up shop.

Start Small

If you're just getting started with macro photography, there's no need to go overboard with acquiring new equipment: an organized table, a white sheet of paper to serve as an infinity cove, and a system flash unit are all you need. This minimalist configuration gives you enough flexibility to create a wide variety of images. Only when you're ready to start experimenting with lighting, backgrounds, and capturing subject movements will you run up against the limitations of this modest equipment setup.

Space Considerations

Deciding how much room you'll need for your close-up and macro studio is not entirely straightforward. The first thing to consider is the size of the objects that you wish to photograph. For a full bouquet of flowers, you may need a shooting table that's 90cm by 90cm, but if an individual flower petal is in line with your interests, then something smaller will do the job. In general, I would recommend a shooting table of at least 50cm by 50cm even if your subjects will ultimately end up being only a few centimeters or millimeters large.

In addition to the size of your subject, you also have to consider the other elements that will be positioned on your shooting table, including any lighting instruments. Your shooting table should be wide enough to accommodate lamps and flash units.

The Right Space

A room with walls painted white is ideal for setting up a macro studio. White walls make it possible to bounce flash off of them to create indirect lighting when necessary. If the walls or ceiling in your macro studio are painted a different color or are exposed wood, then using them as reflectors will create casts of color in your images. It's also a huge advantage to be able to completely darken your macro studio room if necessary. This option makes it possible

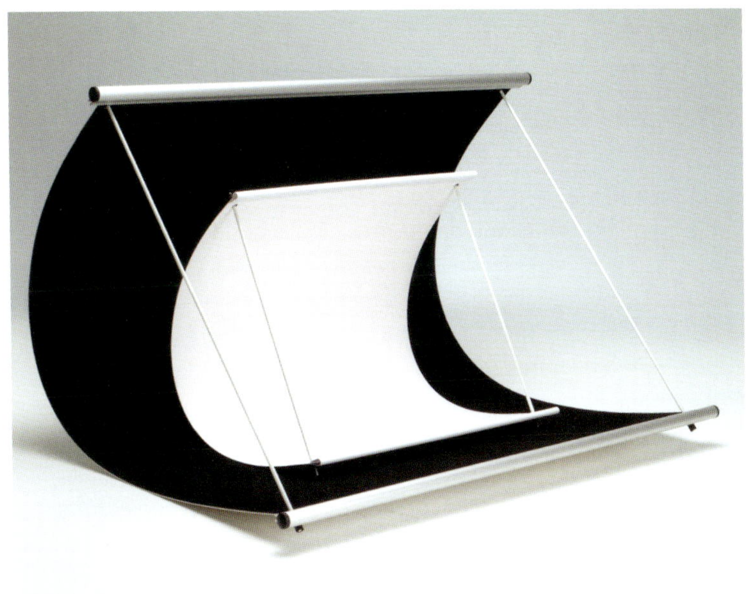

Infinity coves help create a seamless transition from the ground to the background. You can build them yourself with a bit of crafty ambition. The rods visible in this illustration serve to alter the curvature of the cove and to hold the materials in place.

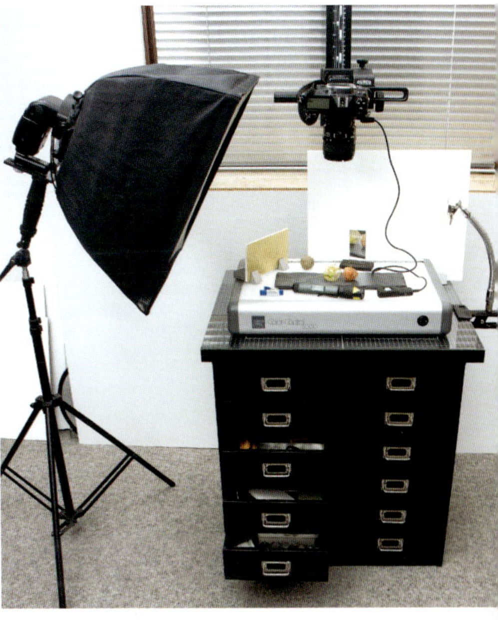

It doesn't take much room to construct a small photo studio for macro photography. The drawers in these cabinets supporting a repro stand setup serve to house every imaginable tool that a macro photographer would need: reflectors, clamps, mirrors, flashlights, and so on. A system flash filtered through a softbox produces even, soft light. Images lit with transmitted light can be realized with a lightbox.

to shoot with very slow shutter speeds, such as those required for light-painting photographers, at any time of day.

Organization Is the Key to Success

The smaller your studio is, the more critical it is that every object and tool has its proper home. A well-organized studio will allow you work efficiently; the frustration that arises when searching for an elusive tool amid a cluttered studio will not help your photography.

Macro photography requires the frequent use of a variety of tools for holding things in place. Macro photographers often need to locate supports, reflectors, flash accessories, filter foils, decorative material, and much more. One of the shooting tables that I have set up in my macro studio features a reprography stand on top of two metal cabinets with a number of drawers. The storage below the shooting table lets me stow away all of the various equipment while still keeping them close at hand for easy access.

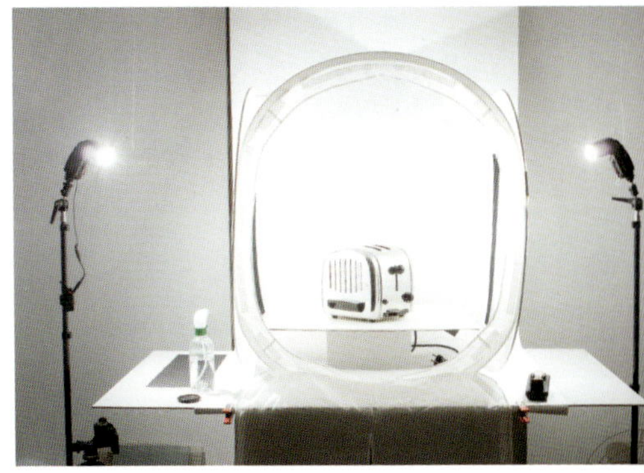

If you want the flexibility of occasionally photographing larger subjects, a collapsible light tent is the way to go. You can fit an entire flower bouquet in one with no trouble—even if your intention is to capture individual blossoms.

Bringing Nature Indoors

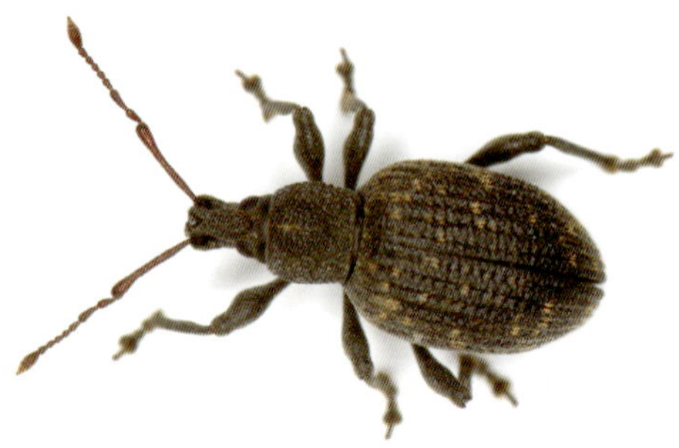

Weevil. Photographed in a studio with a white background. The image feels neutral and clinical.

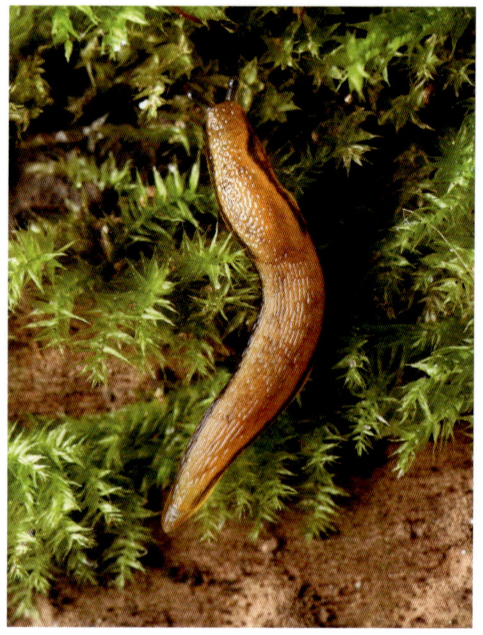

Snail on a bed of moss. This photo was also shot in a studio, despite its natural appearance. The setting was staged to mirror the animal's natural habitat.

Photographing plants and animals indoors is not necessarily any easier than working outside. On one hand, you have greater control over the circumstances and easy access to more lighting if you need it, but on the other hand, it can be challenging to create images that appear natural. Photos shot in a studio often have a fake or staged feel to them. If your intention is to create an image that looks as though it were shot in a studio, this challenge isn't a problem, but if your intention is to create something that looks as authentic as possible, then you'll need to spend a lot of effort creating natural lighting and surroundings. For starters, images should be illuminated with only one key light source to mimic natural lighting situations, where the sun is the only source of light. You can employ other light sources for fill lighting, if necessary, but they shouldn't ever compete with the main light source.

Simulating Various Kinds of Daylight

The quality of natural light varies widely based on the time of day and other conditions. Filters and light-shaping tools can be employed to mimic these different qualities of natural light.

Here are a few examples:

- *High Noon*
  Flash positioned from above to function as a point light without any shaping tools.

- *Late Afternoon*
  Beauty dish set at 45°—a moderate yellow filter of the flash may also help.

- *The Golden, Evening Hour*
  Flash modified by an orange filter, a beauty dish, and a honeycomb filter at an angle of 85°. An alternative option is using a traditional incandescent bulb with the white balance set for natural daylight.

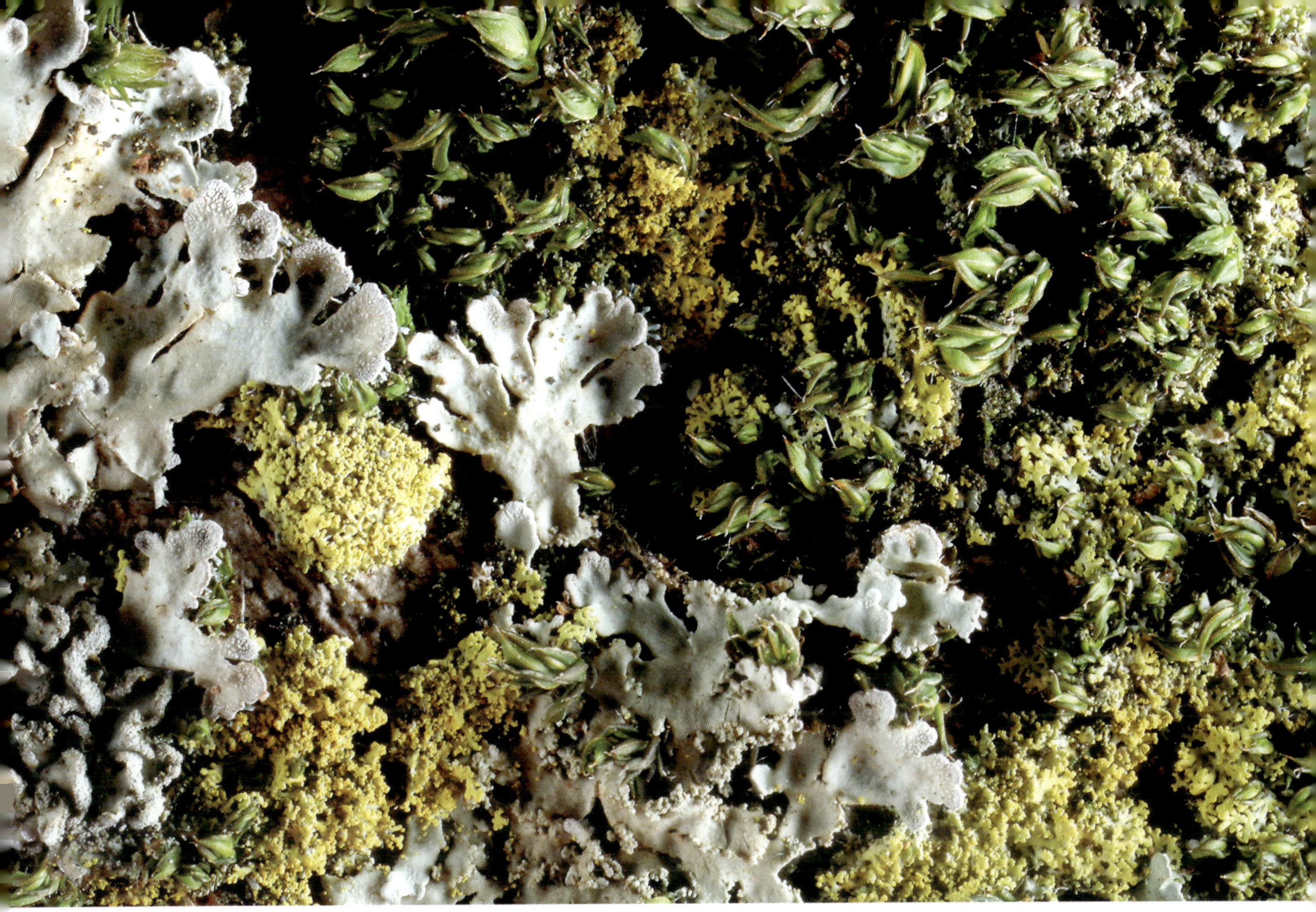

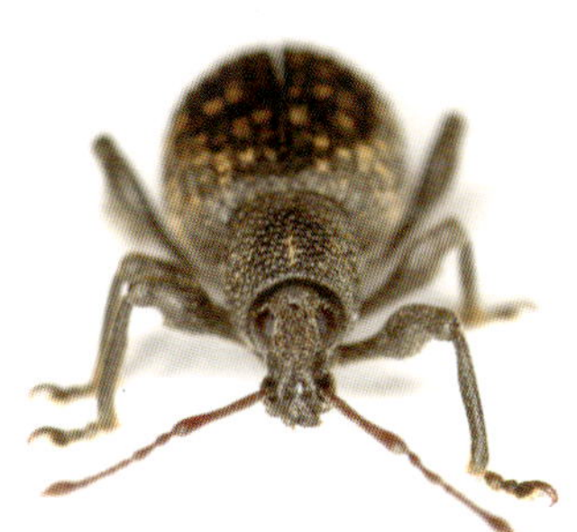

- *Twilight, or the Blue Hour*
  Flash filtered through blue foil and reflected off a white wall. Adjusting how much of the flash is covered with the transparent blue filter will alter the appearance of the light. If you don't have any material to function as a filter handy, set the white balance to tungsten light.

- *Overcast Sky*
  Flash equipped with a large softbox, or bounced off of a white ceiling.

- *A Foggy Day*
  Light tent with the flash positioned based on where you want the position of the sun to appear. To give the results an even more realistic appearance, use an image-editing program to desaturate the colors somewhat.

Achieving desired lighting is easier in the studio when photographic immobile subjects, such as this collection of lichen from a tree trunk
f/22, 1/125 s, ISO 200, 50mm, system flash unit with softbox

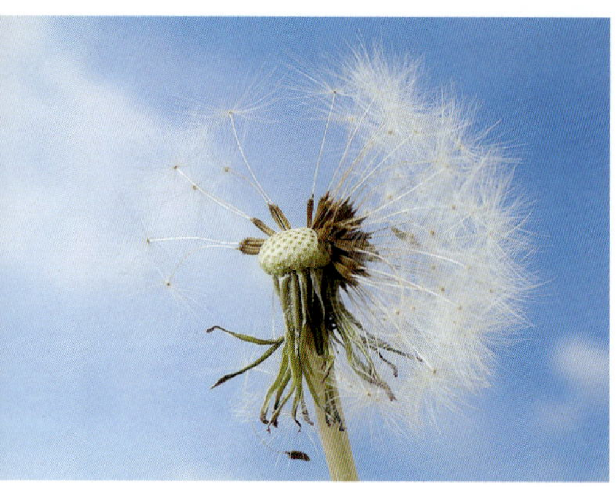

The sky in the background is actually a photographic print of the sky made on matte paper and affixed to a piece of stable cardboard. To prevent betraying shadows from appearing on the background, illuminate the background with a separate source of light.

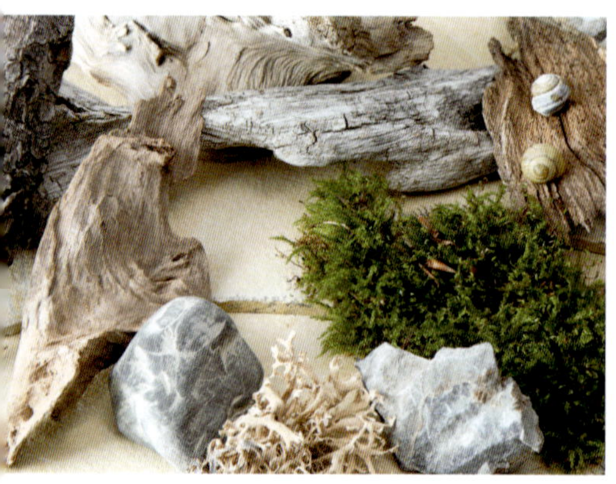

A large and diverse store of background elements and decorations is essential for creating realistic natural scenes in the studio

Decorative Material and Backgrounds

Backdrops and decorations are a critical component to creating natural-looking macro photographs in the studio. Having a stockpile of props makes the job all the easier: varieties of moss, bark, wood, stones, sand, and the like should be easily accessible to stage a realistic scene. A spray bottle filled with water can also go a long way in simulating raindrops and reviving moss to look fresh and healthy.

Other materials, such as twigs, grasses, and rocks, are key for building textured compositions. For example, you might build a background out of a large piece of wood, a few leaves, or a piece of colored cardboard that goes with your subject. If you position these objects a bit farther away from your subject, they'll appear blurred, which can elevate the authenticity of their appearance.

One common mistake when staging natural macro scenes is to fail to build a dense enough background or ground layer. Nothing ruins an image's authenticity faster than a visible part of the shooting table. The same goes for cords, pins, or adhesive tapes used to hold the scene together. Use care to keep these elements well hidden.

Animals in the Studio

Photographing live insects or small animals is never easy. Beetles, caterpillars, and even snails are relatively cooperative, but other animals are a challenge because of their propensity to move. In many cases, it's simply easer to work outdoors in nature. Never resort to using cold sprays or other tools for immobilizing animals.

The use of flash lighting when photographing insects is always hotly debated. As is often the case, what matters is how you go about doing it. In my opinion, it's best to position your flash as far away from your living subject as possible, and when possible to use a softbox or indirect lighting via a reflector for aesthetic reasons. Softer shadows tend to produce an image that feels more relaxed than harsh, direct lighting.

I photographed the ladybug on the opposite page at ISO 200, f/11, and 1/125 s while using a system flash unit hooked up to a softbox. The light source was about a meter away from the subject, producing an intensity of light similar to what you would find on an average day outside with a cloudy sky. Accordingly, this amount of light won't cause any harm to your subjects.

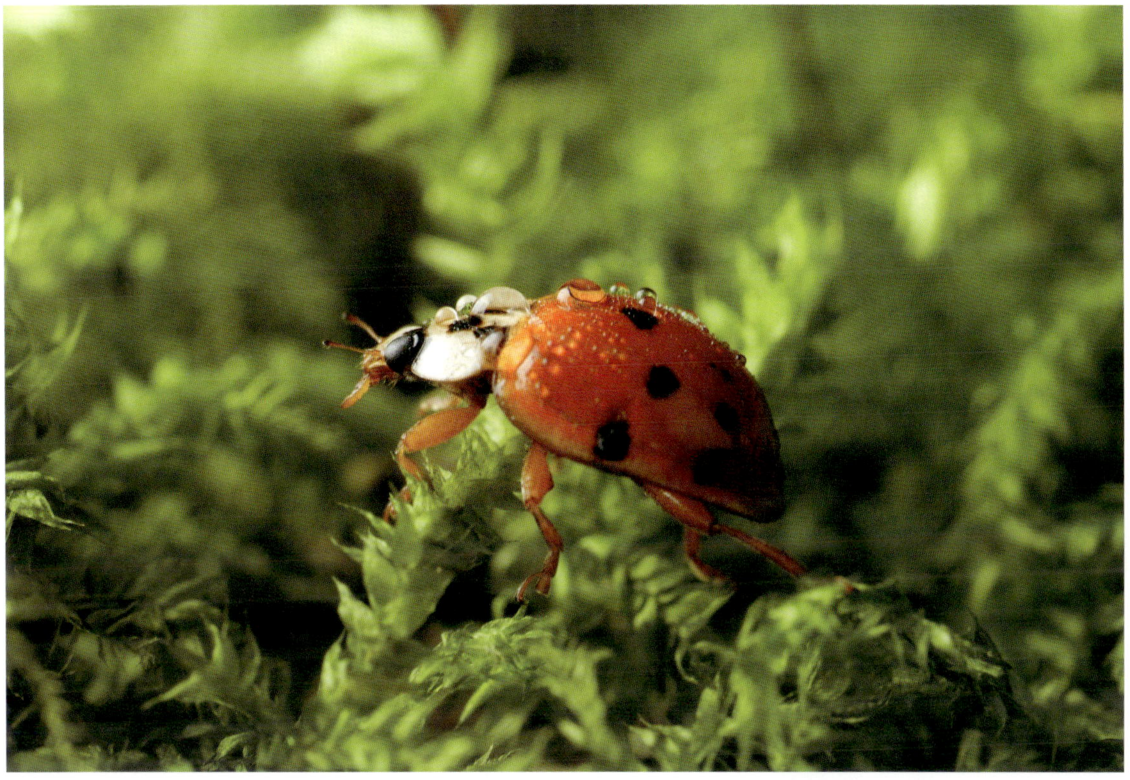

Ladybug on moss
f/11, 1/125 s, ISO 200, 50mm, system
flash with softbox

Plants in the Studio

Photographing plants and mushrooms in the studio is no problem.
Working in a studio means you have all of the creative control you
could wish for. To prevent plants from wilting for longer shoots,
include some dirt when you dig up the roots so you can keep them
adequately moist. A spray bottle comes in handy for this purpose, too.

Conservation

Rare plants and animals that are protected by ordinances should
never be picked, dug up, or removed from their native environs for
the purpose of photographing them in the studio. If you're not sure
about a specific species, err on the side of caution and photograph
the subject in its natural setting.

The Glowing Snail Shell

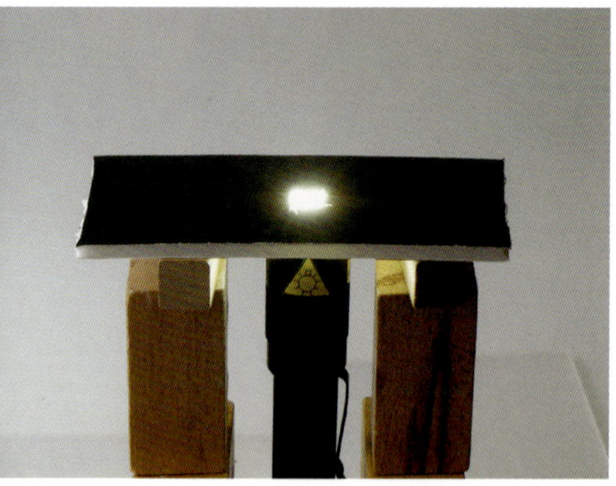

The shot's setup is very simple: an LED flashlight shines directly through a hole in a piece of cardboard

Macro photographers walk about with eyes peeled for a subject that will yield an exceptional image. I came up with a glowing golden snail shell lit from within, resting on a bed of moss.

The Setup

Lighting my subject in the way that I wanted did not require all that much effort. I rested a sturdy piece of cardboard horizontally atop pieces of lumber. This structure served as scaffolding under which I could position an LED flashlight. I used a sharp knife to cut a hole in the cardboard equal in size to the snail shell and lined up the light directly below it. I also arranged the bed of moss to ensure that the shell would be adequately bright. Finally, I arranged the moss and the shell on the cardboard for my shot.

The Shot

The first task was to figure out the ideal shutter speed for the shell. The LED light is bright, but the shell itself absorbs a lot of light, and I had the camera stopped down to f/16, which slowed the shutter speed down to several seconds. The simplest method is to put the camera in aperture priority and to use the internal exposure meter to produce the baseline starting point for the shutter speed.

Then I switched the camera to manual exposure mode while retaining the shutter speed setting and took a few test shots with various aperture settings. The goal was to find the right exposure settings to slightly underexpose the shell.

To capture my actual final image, I set up a studio flash unit with a softbox to produce some soft fill lighting from above. I started with a relatively weak output (around 1/16 of the max power) and gradually increased the brightness until I attained my desired exposure.

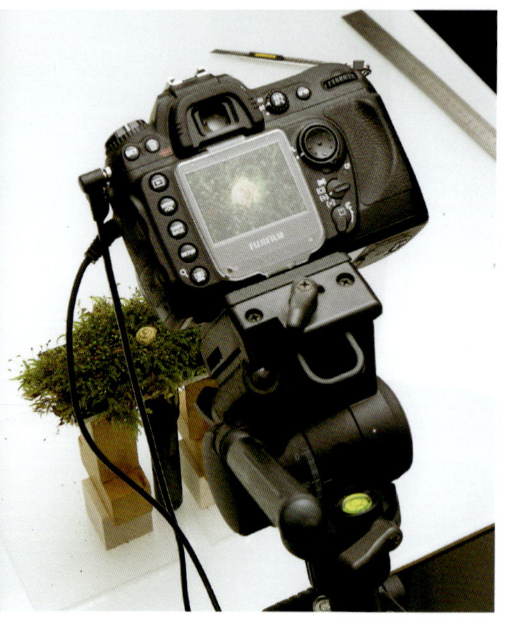

The moss and the snail shell were positioned on the cardboard, and a tripod was used because of the slow shutter speed that was required

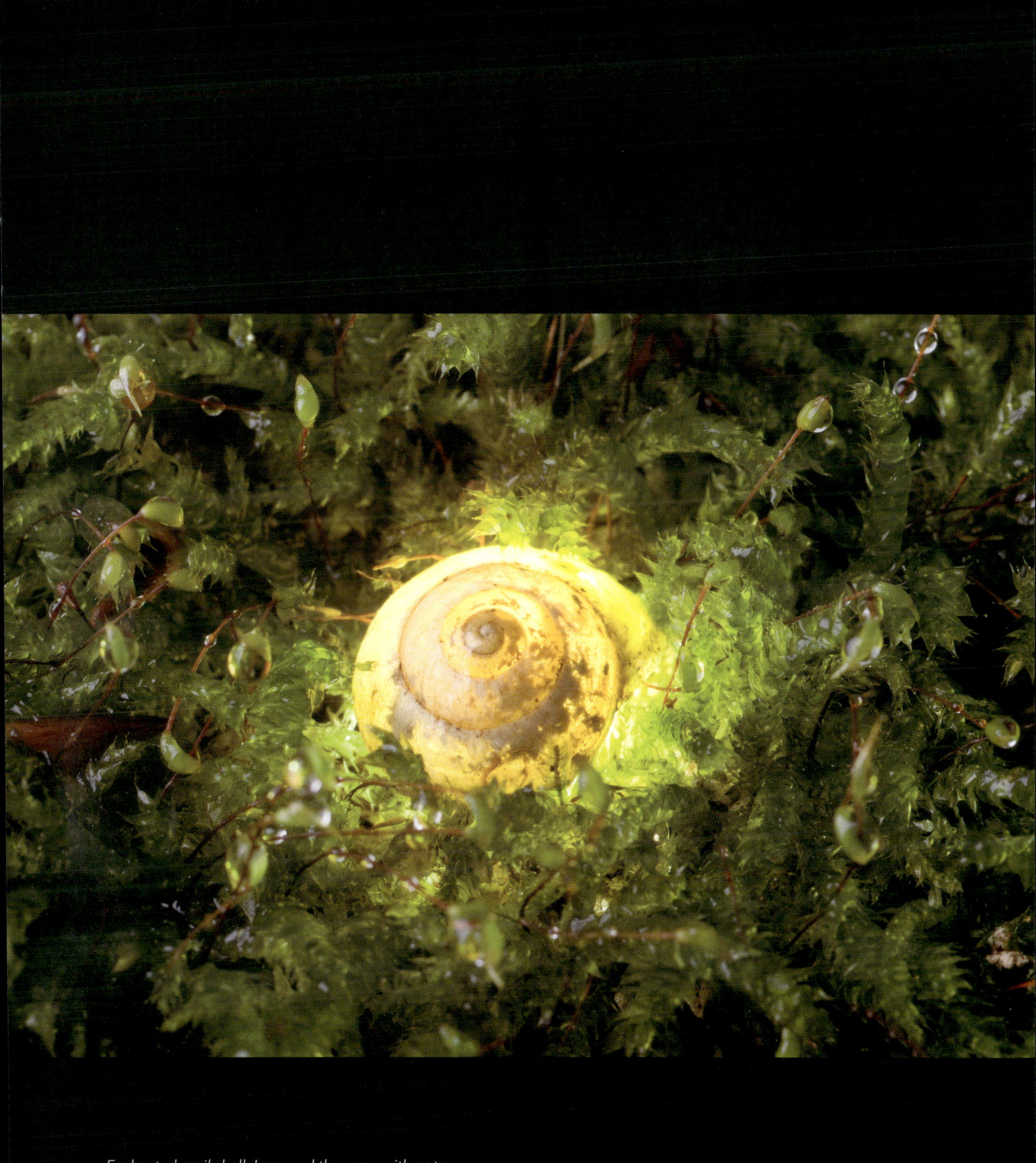

Enchanted snail shell. I sprayed the moss with water
from a spray bottle shortly before taking the picture
to make it look fresh and healthy.
f/16, 2.5 , ISO 100, 60mm, studio flash unit, one flash
head with softbox, LED flashlight

Tabletop Photography

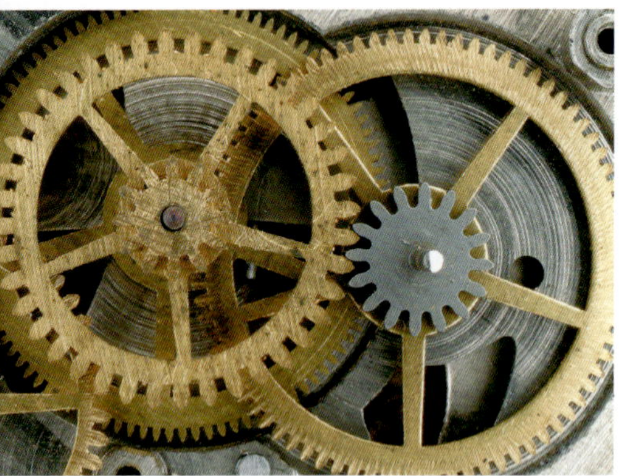

The light from a ring flash effectively eliminates shadows, revealing detail in even the most intricate of subjects. The even light makes tiny signs of wear and tear visible resulting in a clinical appearance.

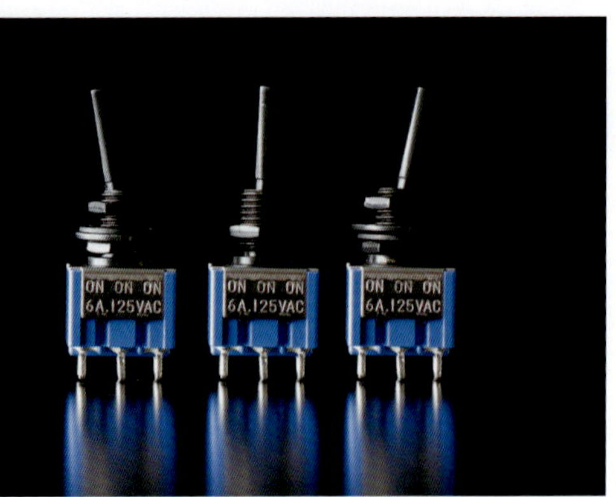

Not all product photos need to be shot on a neutral surface. Here, a semigloss plastic mat provides interesting reflections. This image makes the salient feature of this switch—the three different switch positions—very easy to observe.

The subjects for tabletop photography are also of the small and tiny variety, including electronic components, jewelry, watches, and also detail shots of larger objects. The requirements for documenting these objects are as diverse as the objects themselves. The idea that light makes the picture is an even truer statement with respect to tabletop photos, because the objective of these images is usually not simply to document small objects, but to compose them in a way that is interesting for the viewer. The shape and contours of the subject also plays a large role.

The importance of the lighting requires that photographers pay a good deal of attention to planning the setup of a shoot. It often helps to draw up sketches of the construction illustrating what you want to achieve with your image. The next step, then, is to take a few test shots, which you can use to analyze any potential problems with your lighting, such as unwanted reflections or surface details that don't appear properly illuminated in your subject. With the information in your analysis, you can then make small, targeted adjustments by adding additional sources of light or small mirrors or reflectors to get closer to your ideal result. A small studio lighting unit with a modeling light is a big help, but with a bit of experience two or three manually controlled system flash units that can be outfitted with various light-shaping tools will also do the job nicely.

Your best bet for a lens is something with a focal length of 50mm or 60mm, which approximates the way in which the human eye naturally perceives objects. For more complex lighting setups, you may want to reach for a 105mm lens to allow you to shoot farther away from your subject.

Getting Reflections Under Control

Tabletop photographs often are composed of a variety of different surfaces that sometimes compete with or detract from one another. Working with shiny objects poses some specific challenges when it comes to managing reflections. Completely eliminating these may not always be the best option, however, because considered reflections appearing in the surfaces of some of your subjects may actually improve your image or accentuate certain shapes. You might choose to attach a cross of cardboard strips onto the front of a softbox to create a reflection in a glass or bottle of wine that looks like a win-

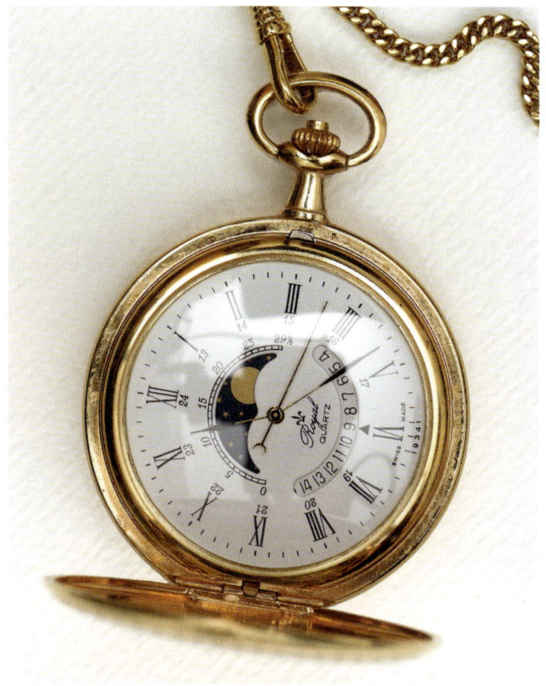

The curved glass of the pocket watch's face reflects both the camera and the room's white ceiling in this photo

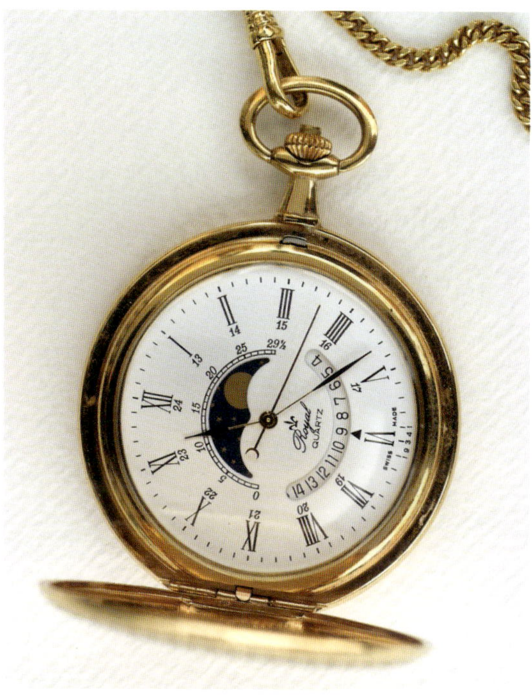

Black cardboard reduces the reflections dramatically. Both images: f/7, 1/200 s, ISO 100, 60mm, repro stand, daylight

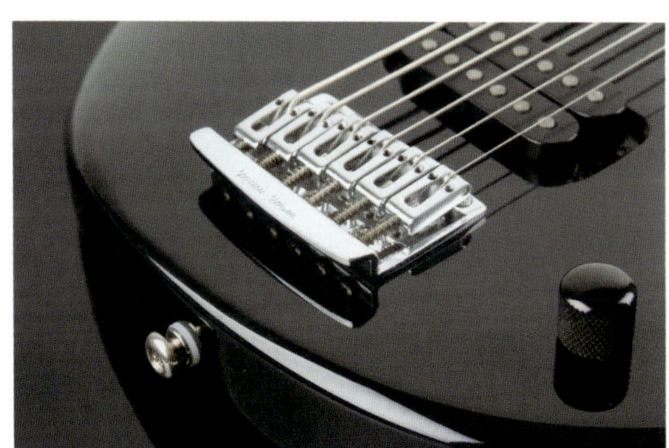

Viewers sense that the guitar has a glossy surface because reflections are integrated into this photo

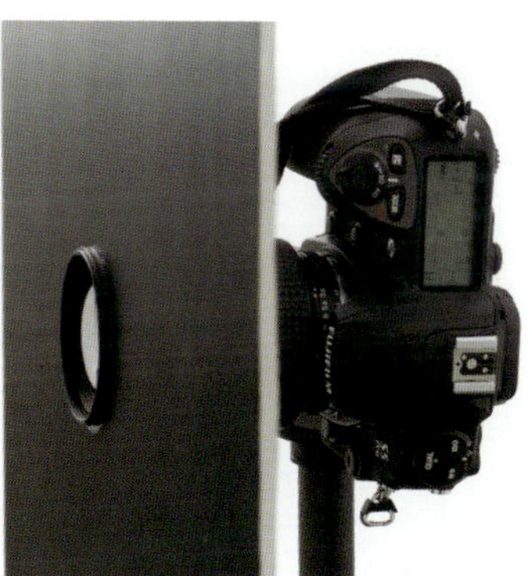

Shooting through a hole in a piece of black cardboard is an effective way to remove reflections from your photos

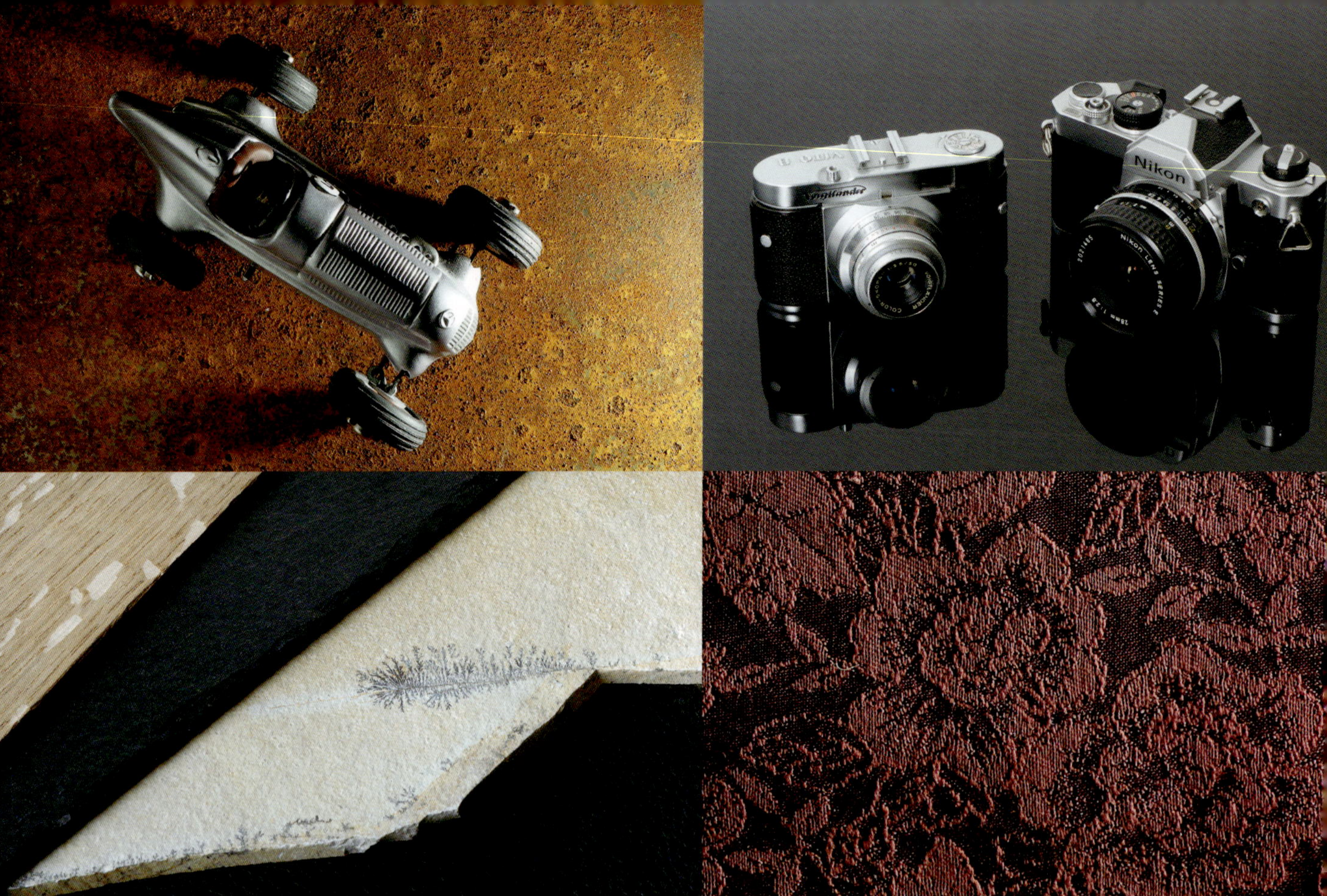

Top left: Model car on rusted sheet metal. The weathered surface contrast markedly with the silver toy car. It also spurs an emotional response to the tin toys of yesteryear.

Top right: Plastic sheets serve well as reflective surface materials, but they scratch relatively easily. Glass sheets with pieces of colored cardboard tucked under them are another option.

Bottom left: Interesting surface materials can be found anywhere: stationery shops, hardware stores, or a glazier's workshop, for example

Bottom right: Side lighting accentuates the textures in surface materials

dow, for example. The cardboard cross-divides the light of the flash into four even areas and the resulting reflection gives the viewer the impression that the photo was shot in a room with windows.

If your goal is to eliminate reflections, one tried-and-true method is pointing your lens through a hole in a black piece of cardboard. Your face and hands will be hidden and won't show up as reflections in your subjects. Similarly, wearing a black sweater will make your torso disappear. Those of you who are up for it can attempt to use a shiny Christmas ornament to try to find and root out any lingering, pesky reflections marring your images.

Surface Materials and Backgrounds

The importance of staging an engaging surface material beneath your tabletop subjects and a background behind them can't be overstated. Over time you can build up a collection of different materials to construct these elements: slabs of stone, various metal surfaces, textured papers, grained synthetic leather, wood veneers, sand, gravel, fabrics, colored cardboard, unusual stationary or wrapping

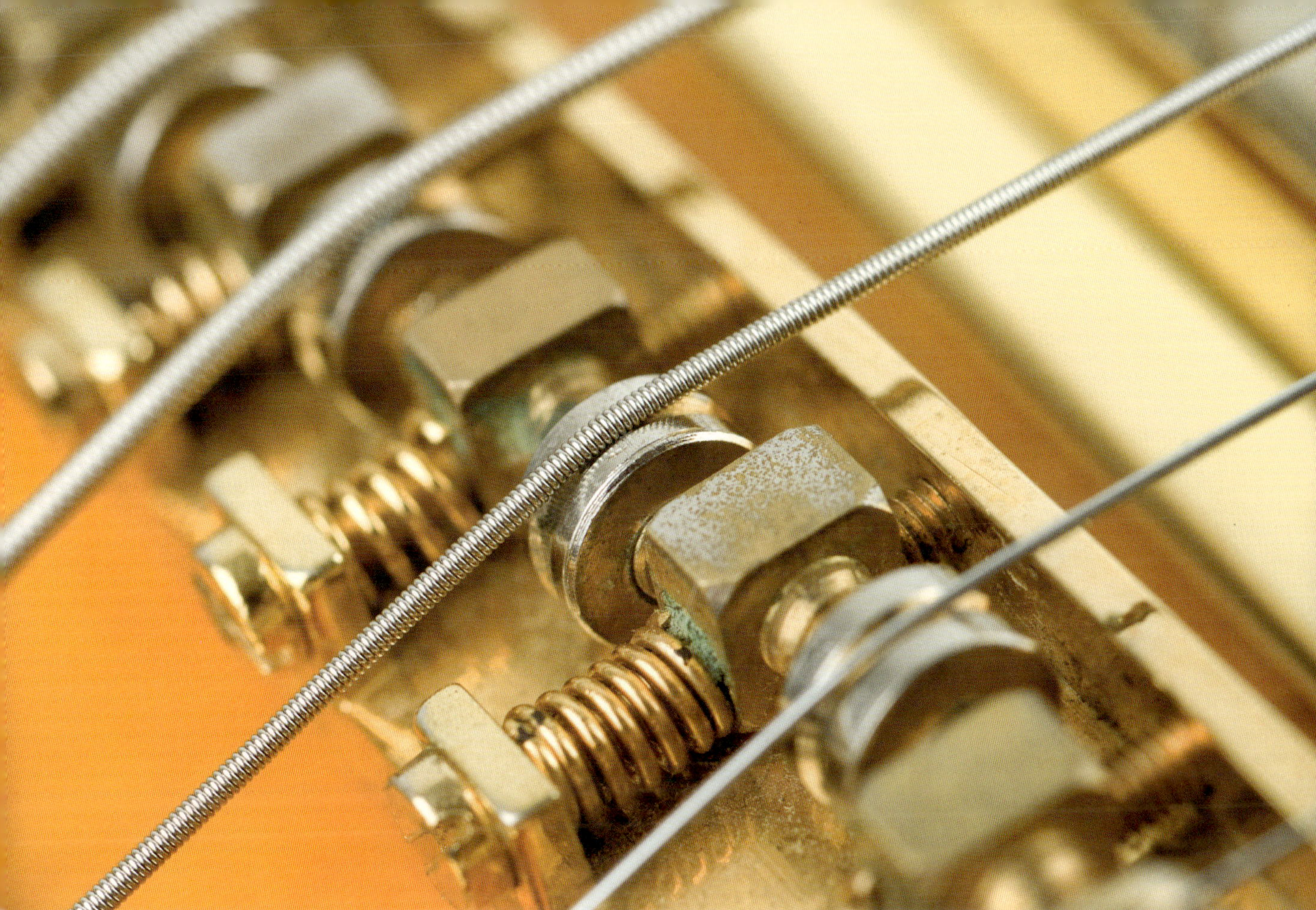

paper, lacquered wood from old furniture showing weathering, metal surfaces with patina—you simply cannot ever have enough of these materials. If the background for your image will appear somewhat blurry in your shot, you can also use prints of other photographs of materials or cloud structures on matte paper. Just be sure that the direction of the lighting in your background image meshes well with the lighting in your current photo.

Highlighting Textures

How the surface textures of the material below and behind your subject render in your photographs is critical to the overall look and feel of the image. You can use lighting tricks to modify how these textures influence your photos. Side lighting is extremely effective for highlighting these textures; soft light often fails to bring out details in the surfaces of your image.

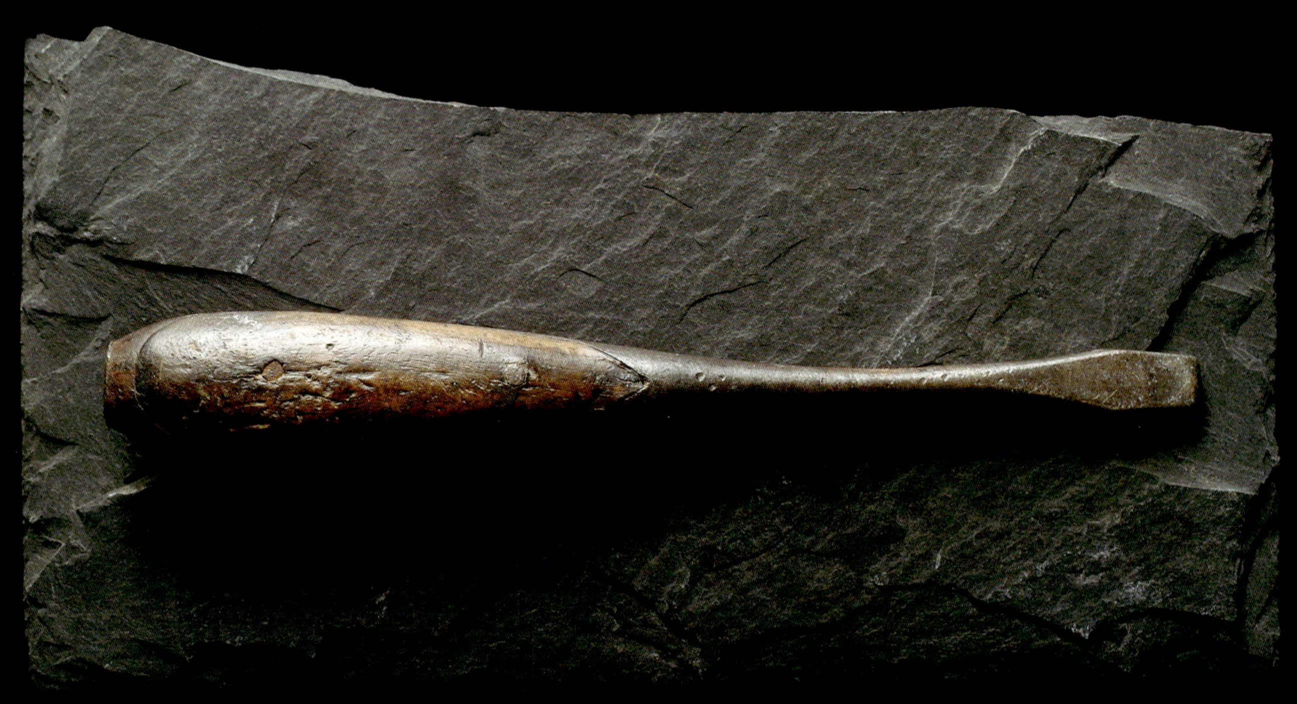

A softbox placed at the same height of the subject
will produce a soft side light that brings out the shape
and surface textures of the subject without creating a
shadow that is problematically dark

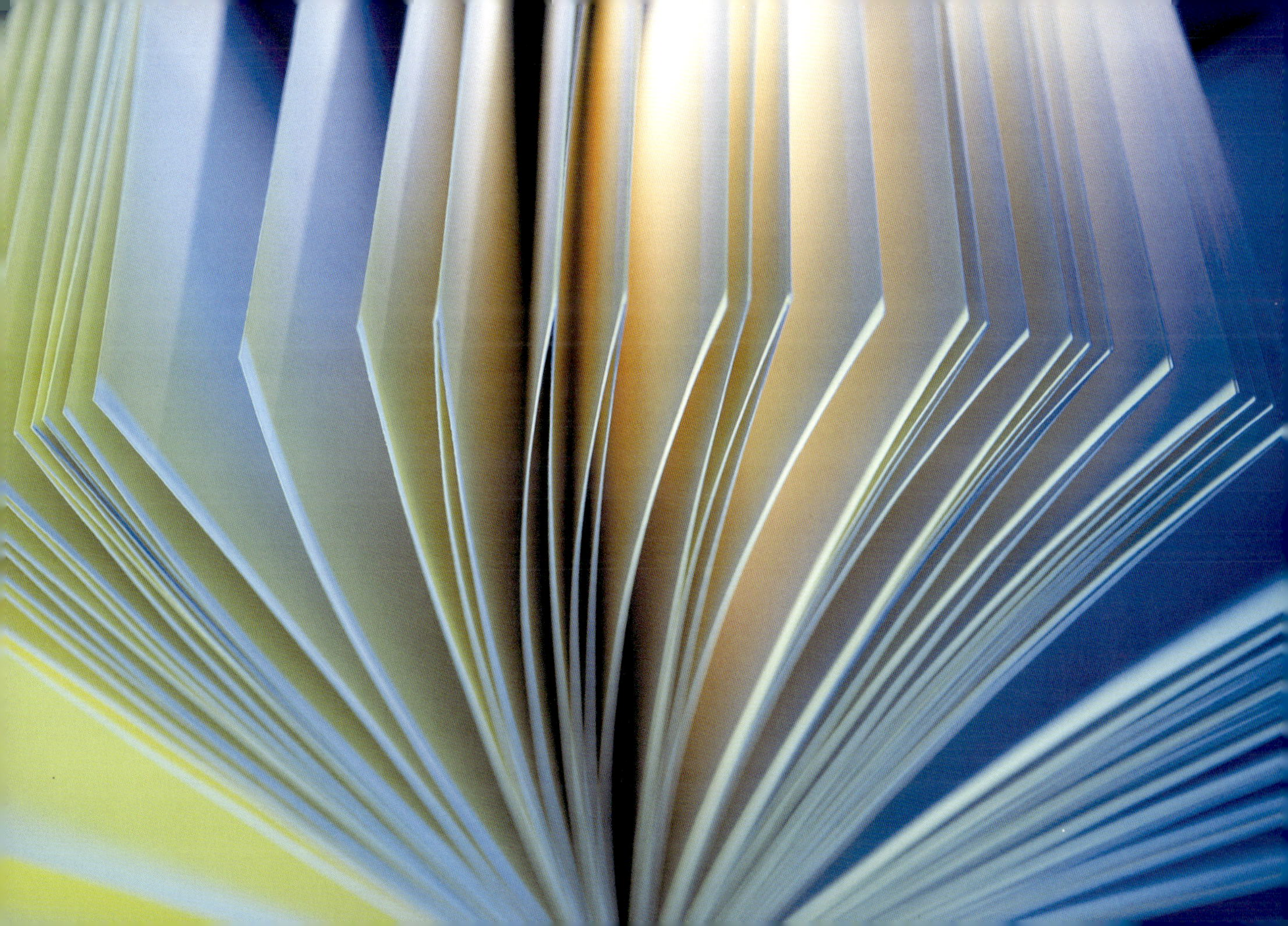

Smoke, Steam, and Fog

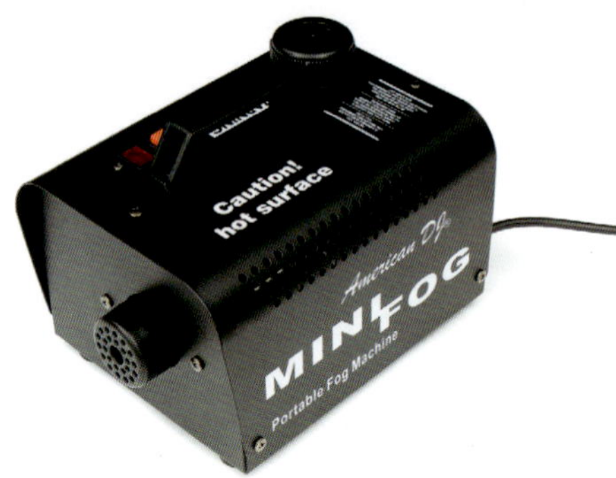

Small fog machines are relatively inexpensive, but they are not the most practical option for macro photography

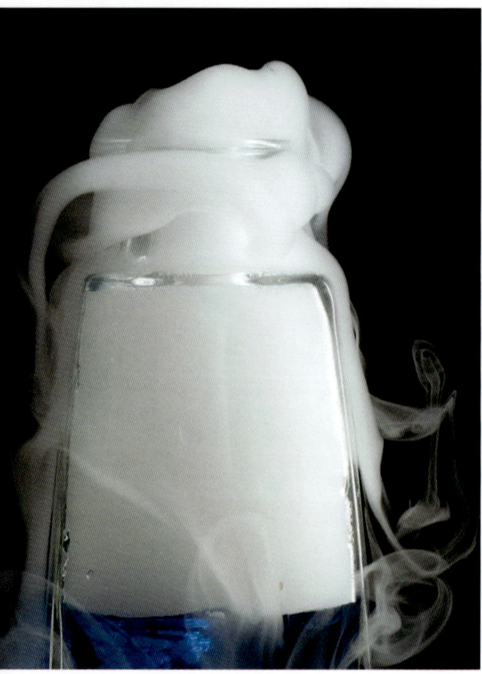

The gas produced from dry ice is heavier than air, so it sinks downward rather than rising up

When I'm shooting tabletop images, I frequently find myself wanting to use smoke, steam, or fog. These substances differ from one another: smoke comprises solid particulate matter that is the residue of combustion, while steam and fog are composed of fine droplets of water. These substances look best when shot against a dark background.

Both continuous lighting and flash are useful when photographing with these elements, but they produce very different results. Light from a flash freezes the motion of gas-like elements in place, so it is useful when you want to depict the bewitching eddies and swirls of the smoke that rises from a candle that has just been blown out, for example. Continuous lighting allows you to emphasize the fluid-like softness of smoke or fog by slowing down the shutter speed.

There are a few tried-and-true tricks for creating smoke and vapor in a tabletop studio:

- *Dry Ice*
  Dry ice produces a velvety, dense fog that is heavier than air, so it sinks to the ground.

- *Fog Machines*
  These devices create intense fog from a special fluid. They tend to put out a large volume of fog, though, making them less than ideal for the generally tight quarters of a tabletop studio.

- *Incense and Tobacco Smoke*
  Smoke from an incense stick or tobacco rises very quickly, creating attractive loops and swirls, making it most ideal for targeted uses in your photos.

- *Hot Potato*
  Placing a piping-hot potato behind a subject and breaking it open just before taking your picture is an effective way to incorporate steam into a shot. To get the maximum effect, you'll want to use a relatively large potato that's been cooked thoroughly—and you'll want to work quickly.

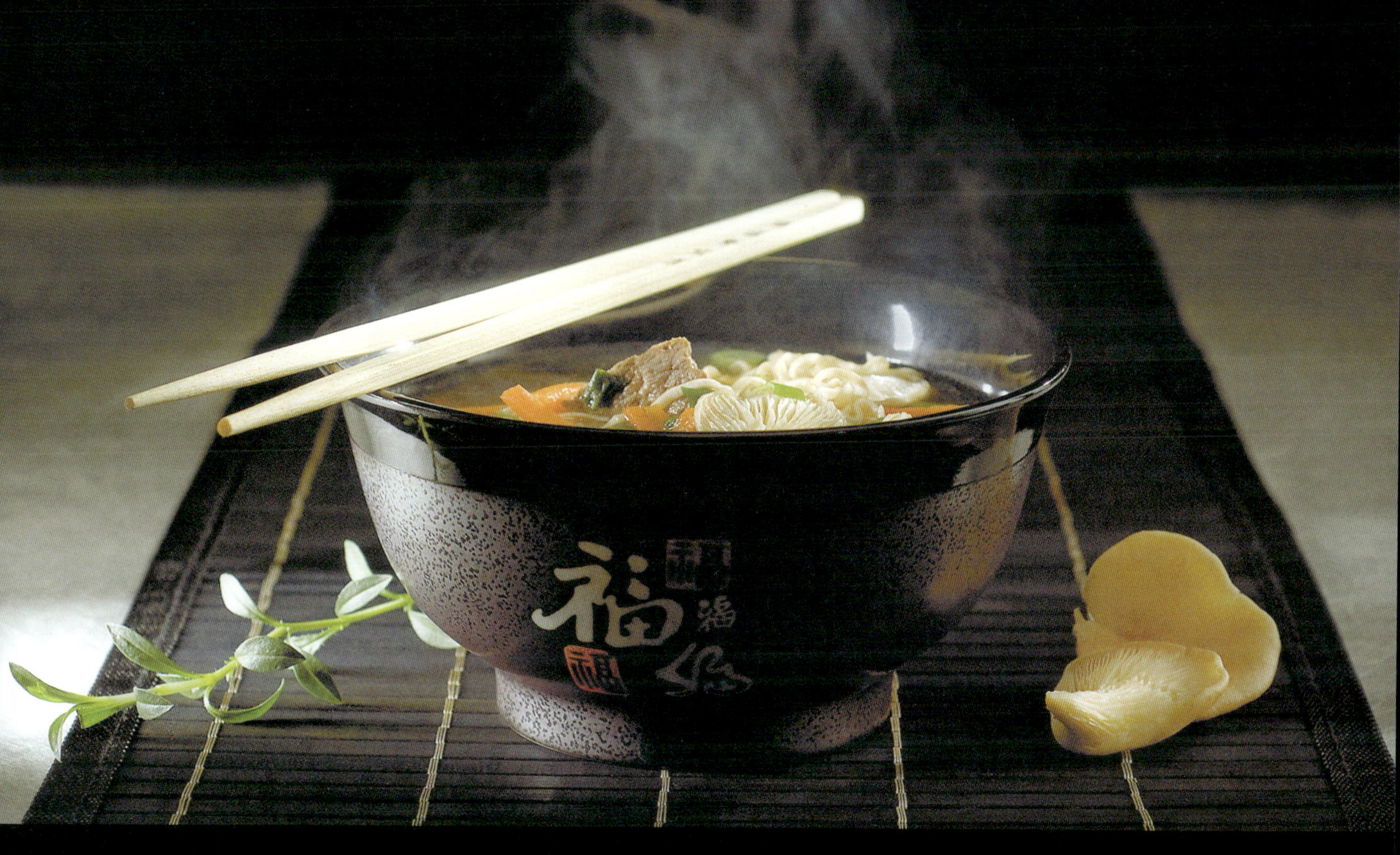

Chinese soup. A hot potato strategically placed behind the bowl was the source of steam for this photo. The broth of the soup was thickened with gelatin to prevent the ingredients from sinking out of sight.
f/6.3, 1/200 s, ISO 200, 60mm, studio flash unit.

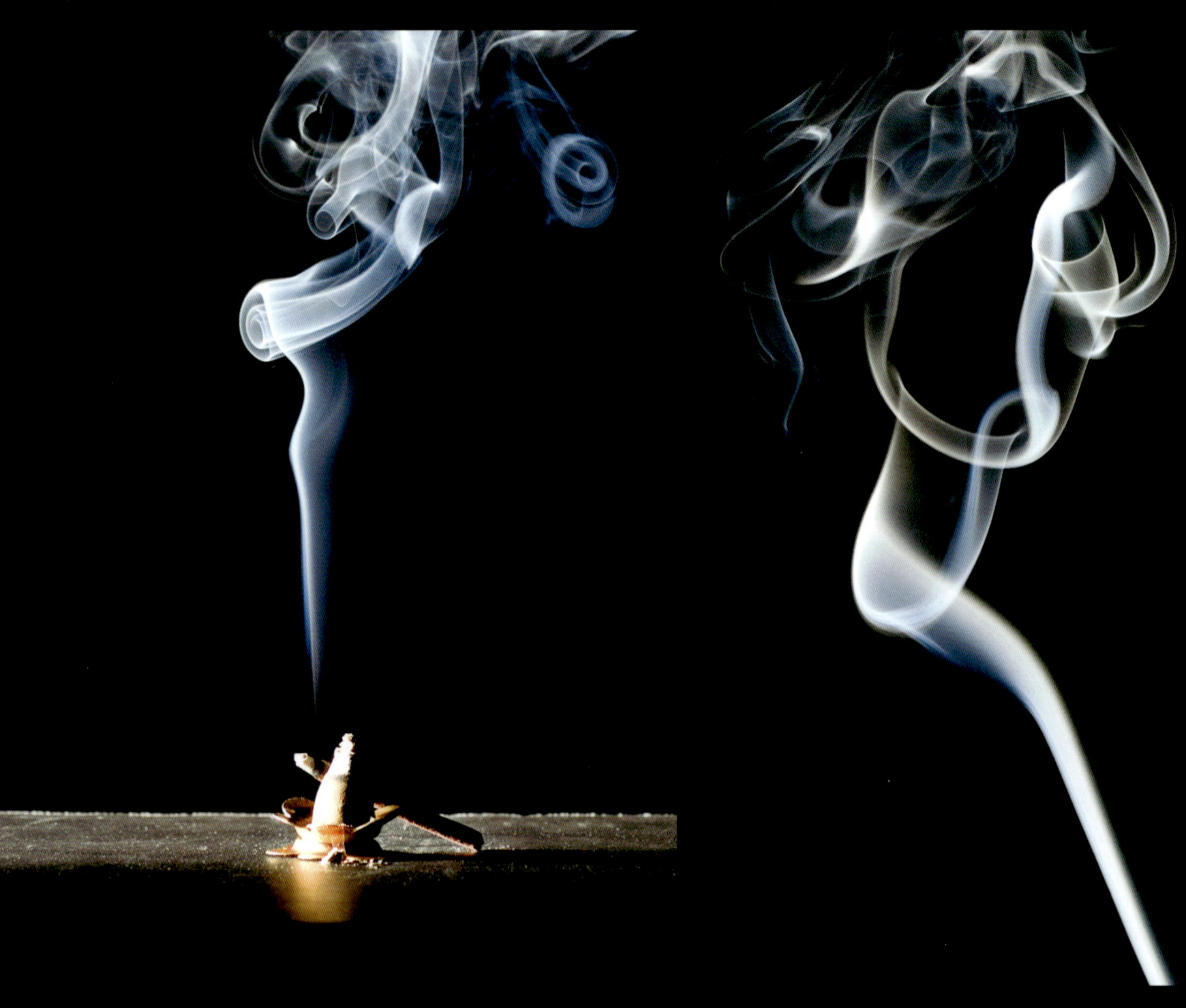

Smoke from an incense stick looks great when lit with harsh side light. The rising heat causes the smoke to eddy and swirl in mesmerizing and ever-changing shapes.

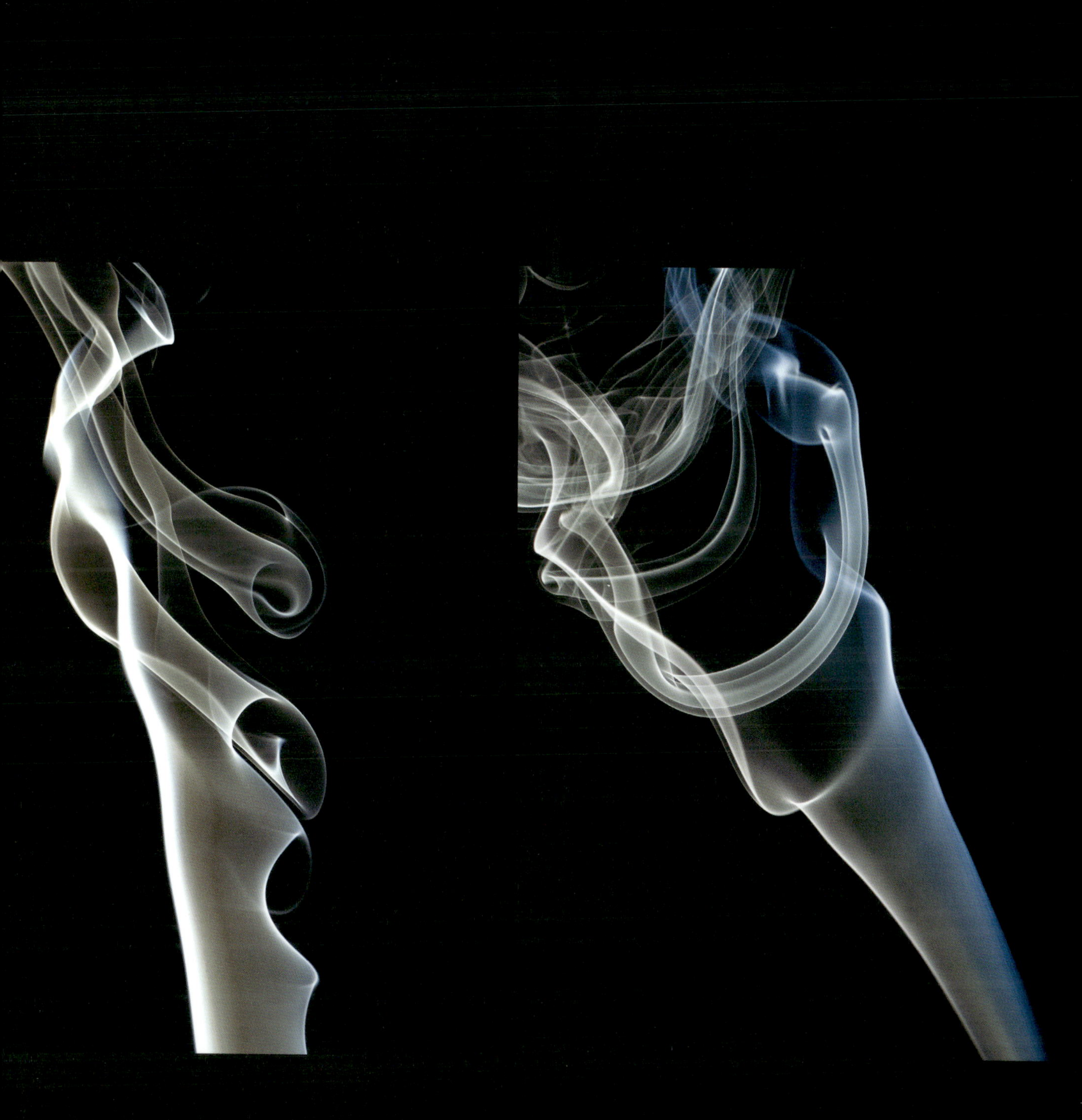

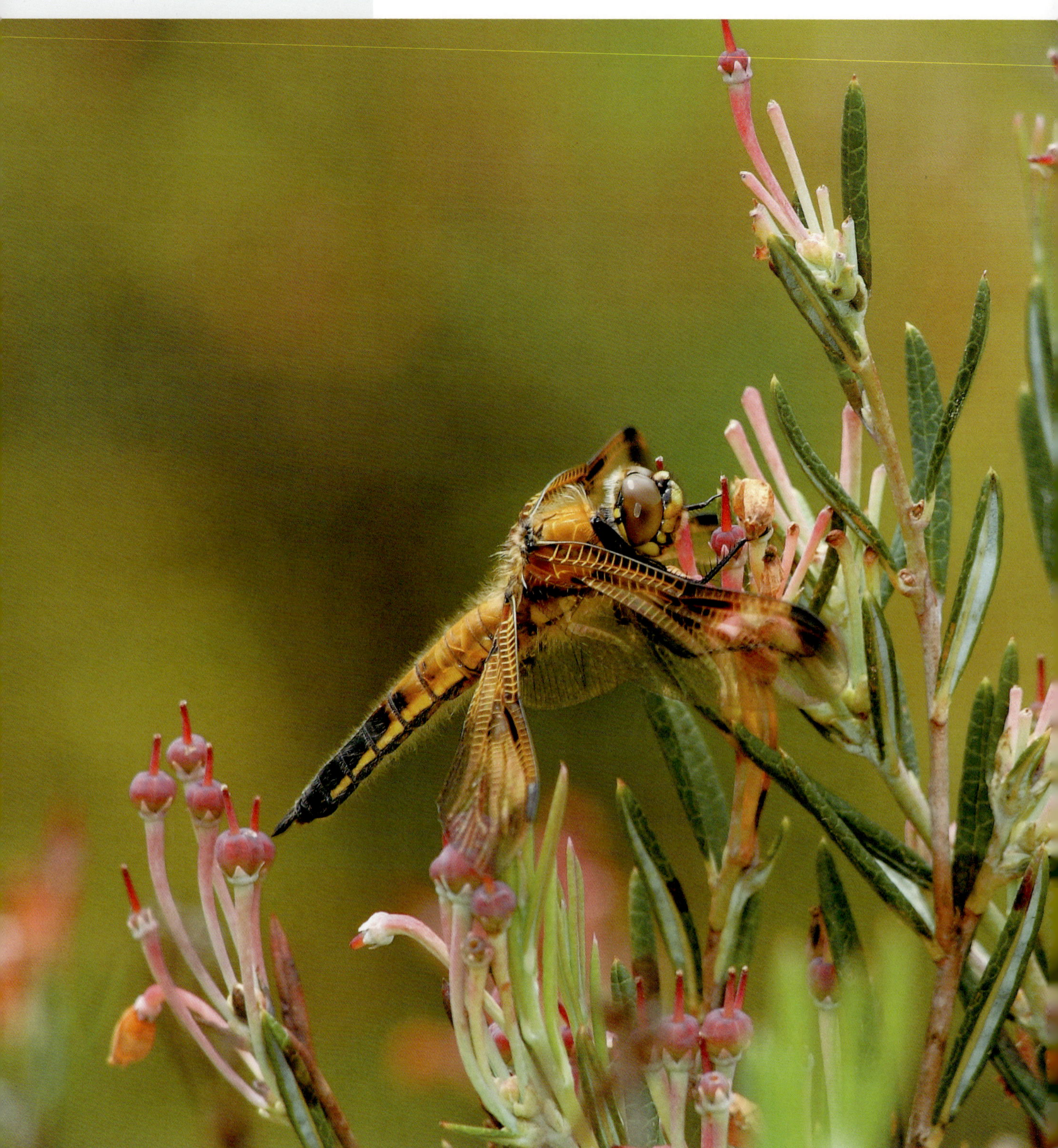

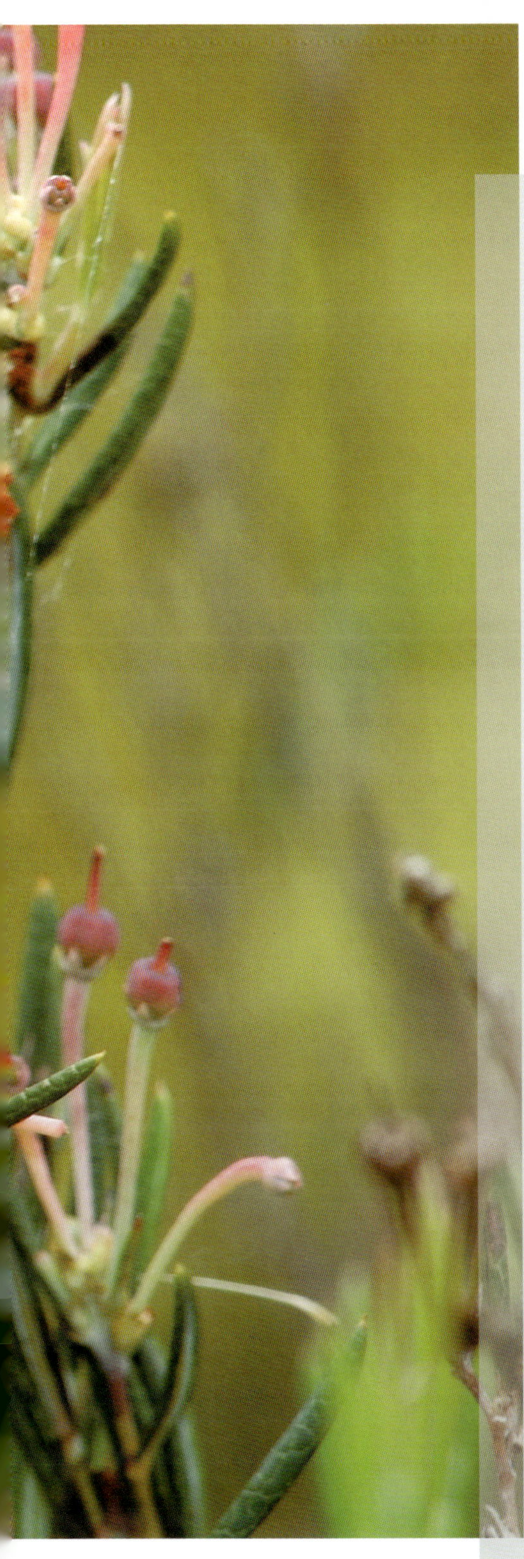

Macro Photography in Nature

Photographing dragonflies is not an easy task. As soon as you catch sight of them, they flit about with breathtaking speed in a whirl of motion. That was my experience on the day I captured this image while shooting at a pond in a botanical garden. I already had a few successful pictures of dragonflies under my belt for the day, and I had just packed up my equipment when I noticed this four-spotted skimmer resting on a rather tall plant. By the time I reassembled my tripod, got my camera out, and attached my 300mm telephoto macro lens, the dragonfly was, of course, long gone.

Fortunately, four-spotted skimmers have a tendency to return to their favored vantage points where they can look over their territory. I noted where it had rested before and focused in advance on that precise location on the plant's stem. A while later, the specimen returned as expected. I made a quick, minor adjustment to the focus, and I was in business.

I also decided to try to use my system flash head for fill lighting for a few subsequent images. As I set it on my camera and programmed it in manual mode to fire at 1/8 of its output, I also compensated the exposure down 1/2 EV. The small reflection in the dragonfly's eye is the only way to tell that flash lighting was used at all.

Four-spotted skimmer
f/9.5, 1/90 s, ISO 160, 300mm, modest fill flash

Backyards and Balconies

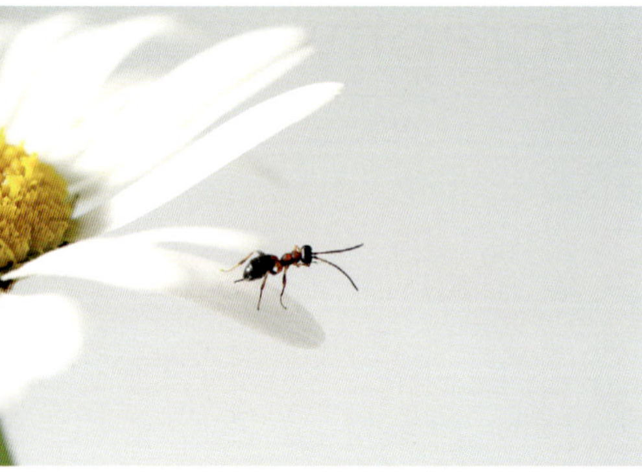

I found this tiny ant posing on a daisy by chance as I was walking through my yard. Fortunately, I was carrying my camera at the time.
f/8, 1/125 s, ISO 100, 50mm

Taking pictures in your own yard is relaxing. Calmness and tranquility are easy to come by, and those are qualities of real value when trying to capture certain macro subjects. For example, you can set up your camera on a tripod and leave it focused on the same place for a few hours. You might pick out a specific blossom, and stand at the ready with your remote shutter release, ready to capture whatever photogenic guest happens to stumble into your image. You can also carry out stress-free experiments with light barriers or small flash units, because you won't have to carry your equipment very far. And if rain starts to fall, it's easy to bring all of your equipment in to safety.

Yards, gardens, and balconies offer a rich variety of subject material for your macro photography practice, too. You can keep track of specific plants throughout the year to be able to photograph them under ideal circumstances when the time comes. You can undertake long-term projects such as taking a series of time-lapse photos of an opening blossom or the various stages of growth of a plant.

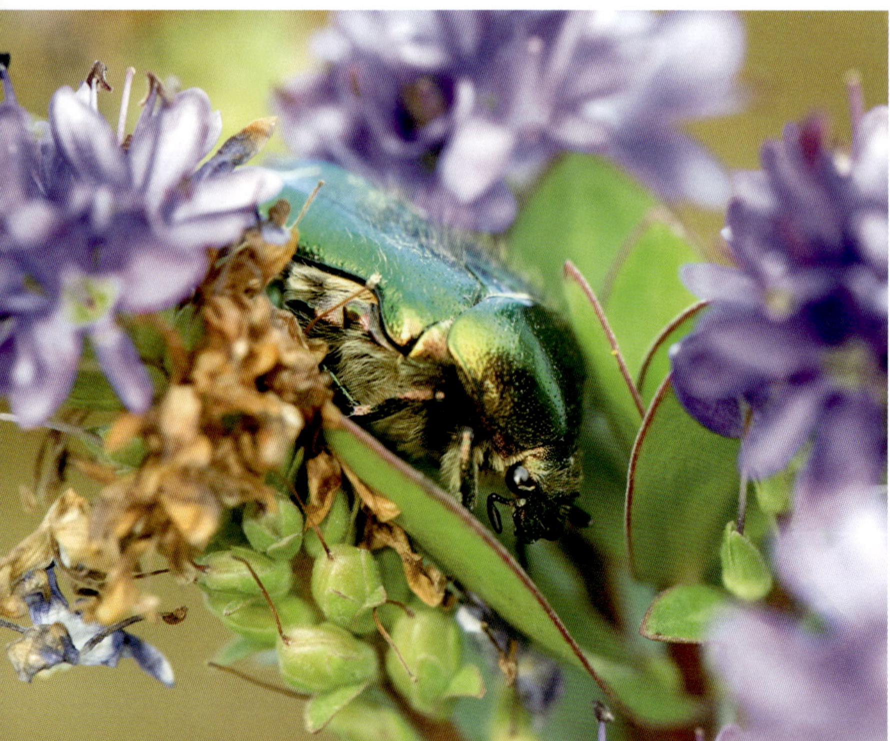

A rose chafer in a window planter. This beetle visited a window planter on our balcony in the evening. Because the day was already growing dark, I set the ISO to 6400 in order to achieve shutter speeds that meant I could shoot handheld.
Nikon D800, f/8, 1/250 s, ISO 6,400, 180 mm

Chaos Yields Opportunity

Letting a part of your yard run wild is an effective way to bring about a wealth of subjects for your macro photography. Floral diversity is your objective here rather than neatly organized plants. But even if you want to keep things relatively organized, choosing the right mix of plants is all it takes to attract a variety of insects and animals to your yard. A few examples follow.

Butterflies

Some examples of plants that butterflies like to feed on include meadowfoam, nettles, wild carrot, boneset, summer lilac, meadow knapweed, or blueweed.

Bees

Globe thistles, deadnettles, poppies, clover, lupin, hollyhocks, foxgloves, delphiniums, sunflowers, and wild roses offer bees pollen and nectar throughout the year. And an herb garden with chives, garlic, lavender, sage, and thyme will please many insects, along with the cook in your life. Don't harvest all of your chives and garlic, though; allow some of the plants to blossom.

General Insects

Building an insect nesting box, or an insect hotel as it's often called, is easy to do on your own. Bundled bamboo shoots, rolled straw mats, or pieces of wood with holes in them make for good base materials, but even wood wool (excelsior) or clay pots filled with bundled twigs will do the job. One particularly popular method is to construct water features made of shallow vessels with a few stones lying in them.

Stones and Moss

A collection of stones overgrown with moss is a subject that you can come back to over and over again as a macro photographer to discover new things. Dry stone walls, or walls built of natural stone without using mortar, have many inviting nooks and crannies for insects and lizards to explore. These walls also serve as fascinating backdrops for macro images, because their geometric patterns offer a nice contrast to the organic shapes of leaves and blossoms.

The Concrete Jungle

Even if you live in the city and don't have a yard of your own, you can still use window planters, a handful of flower seeds, and a dollop of imagination to build a macro photographer's paradise on a balcony or windowsill. All four seasons will offer different subjects for your macro shooting pleasure.

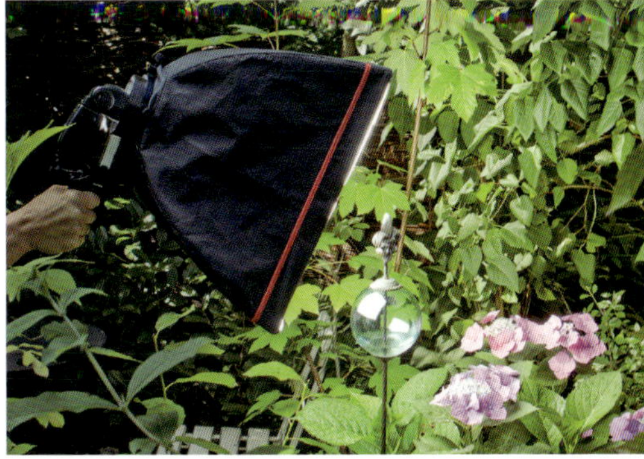

If the lighting in your yard is insufficient, you can easily set up a system flash unit or a small softbox to brighten up your subjects

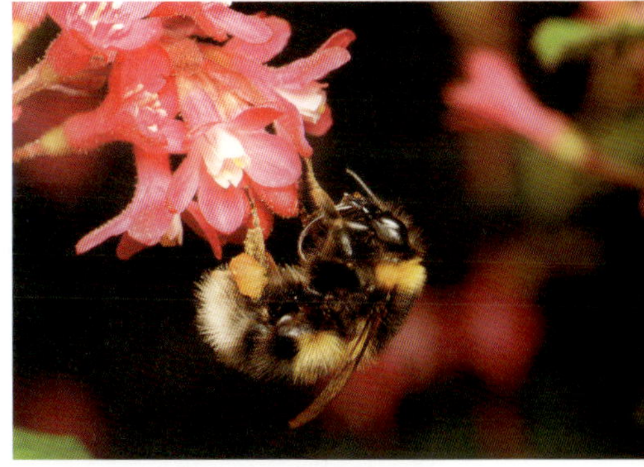

Insects are critical to the pollination process for all sorts of plants. If you reward these little critters with a messy and overgrown part of your yard, you'll be rewarded with a fund of fascinating subjects.
f/8, 1/60 s, ISO 400, 105mm

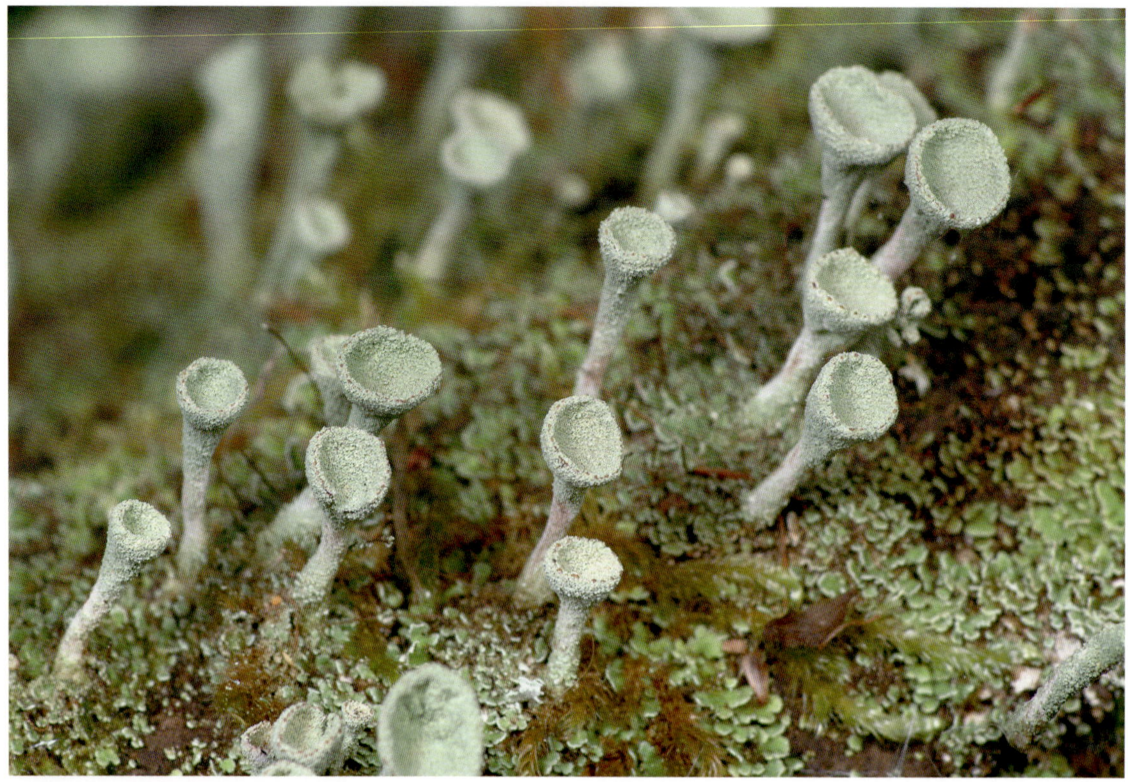

Trumpet moss on an old stone. Even when left to its own devices, nature never ceases to yield new subjects.
f/9.5, 1/125 s, ISO 200, 90mm

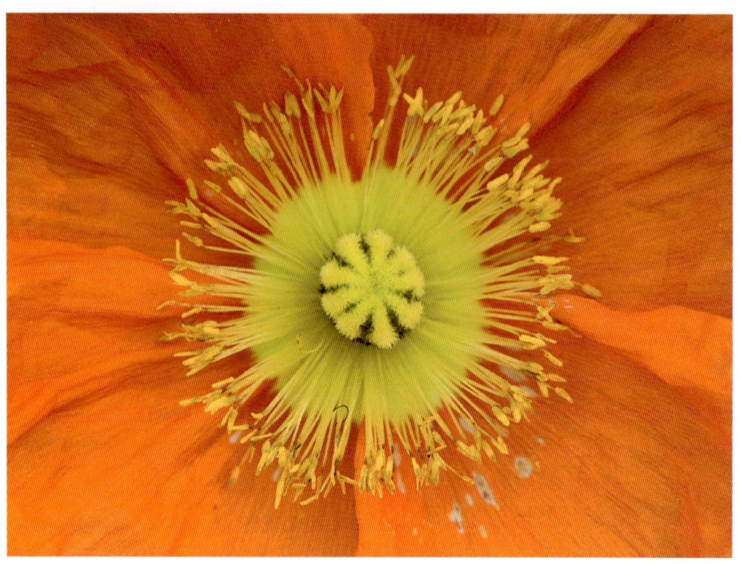

Right: While bugs on an apple tree may be bad news for the farmer, they are a welcome discovery to macro photographers. Both images: f/11, 1/125 s, ISO 400, 50mm, system flash, small attachment softbox

What you seed in spring is what you can photograph in summer. Detail of a poppy blossom.
f/5, 1/500 s, ISO 320, 105mm

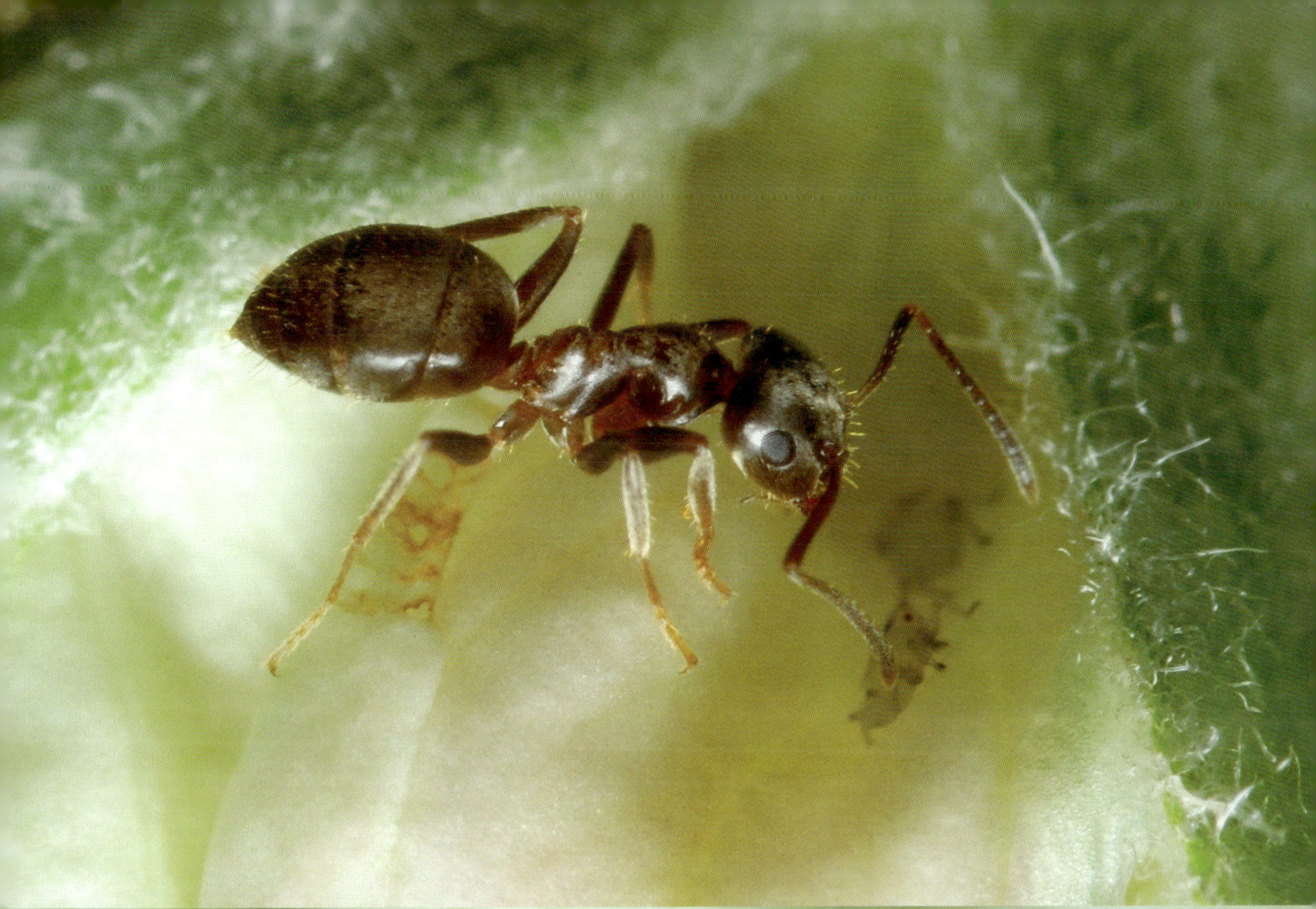

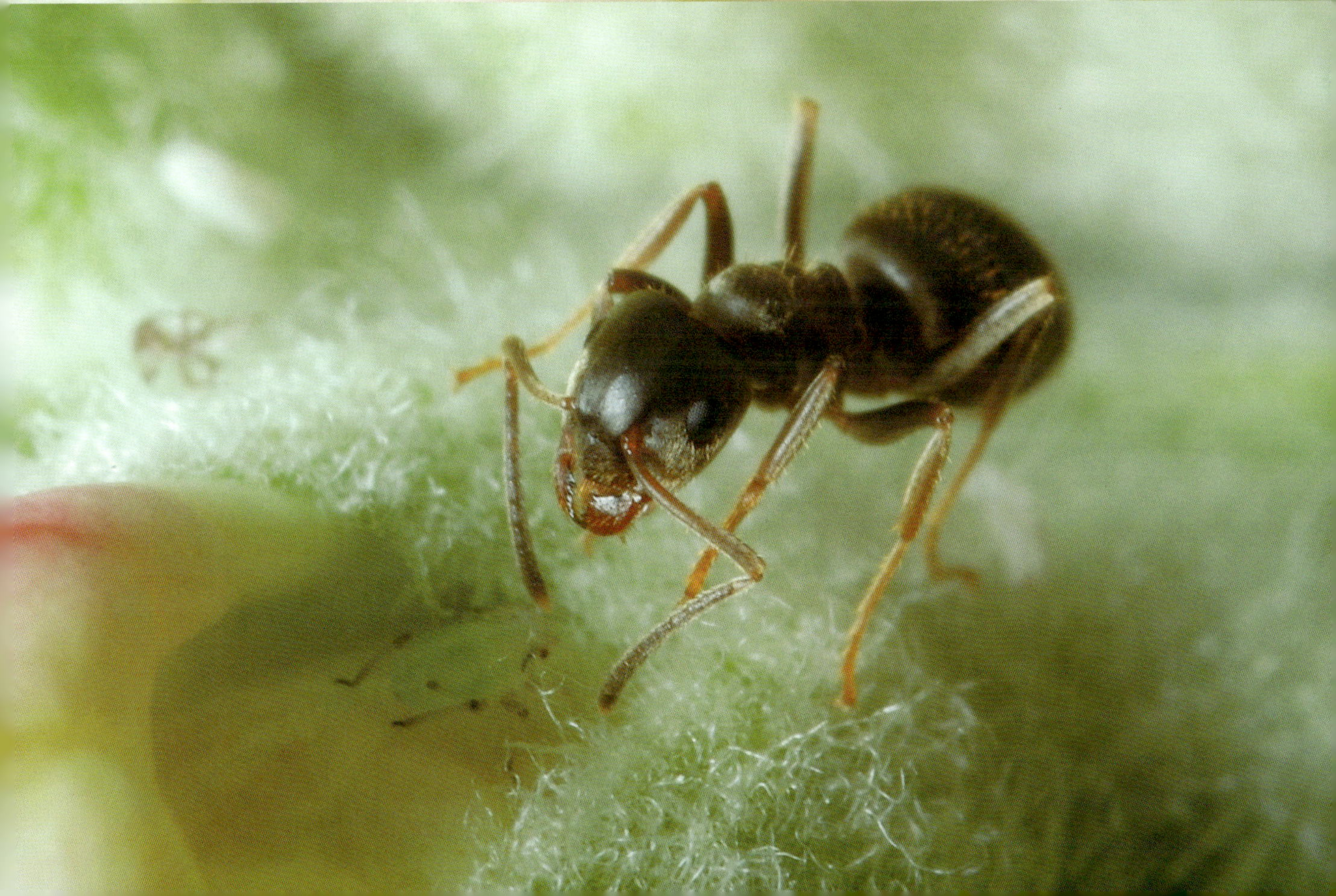

Into the Wild

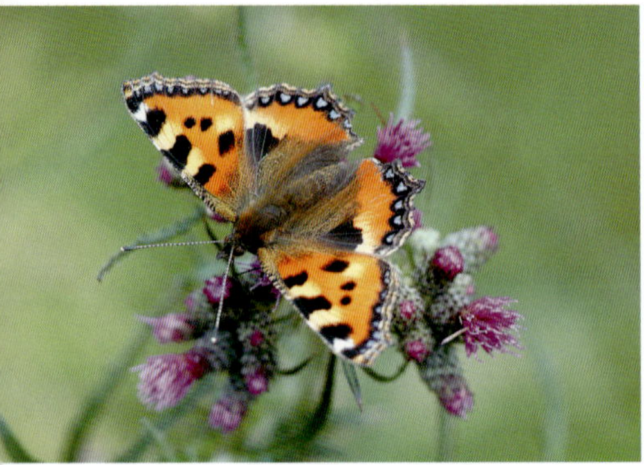

Small tortoiseshell. The transition areas around the edges of forests are not used for agriculture or other human endeavors, which makes them beloved areas for butterflies.
f/4.5, 1/180 s, ISO 200, 210mm

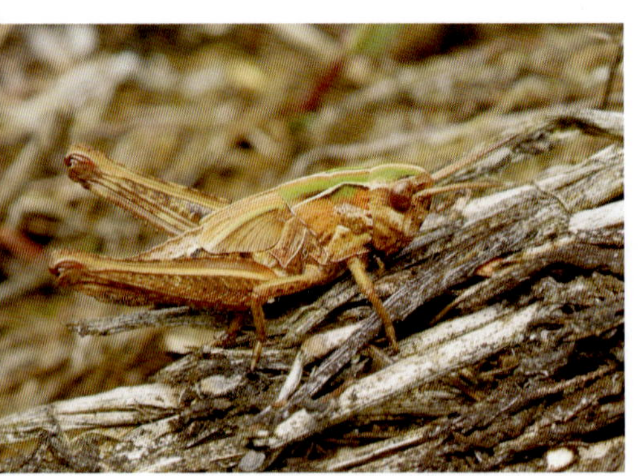

Many creatures rely on camouflage as a means of defense. It often takes a second look to discover subjects like these.
f/9, 1/60 s, ISO 400, 105mm

Spending a day with a camera in a summer meadow bustling with life is paradise on earth for macro photographers. Even small areas of land contain an unimaginable diversity and plethora of subjects to discover. Above ground, brilliant flowers and flying insects are the main attraction.

Constantly on the search for food, bees and butterflies aren't the easiest of subjects to pin down in a macro photograph. Patience is your ally here. Picking a plant to focus on and waiting for guests to arrive is generally a more effective strategy than trying to scramble after airborne targets. You can use your time waiting to tidy up the area around the blossom of your choosing by, for example, repositioning a few distracting blades of grass.

If you scratch below the surface of the earth, however, you'll discover layers of life and an abundance of subterranean residents. Now you've arrived at the realm of beetles, locusts, spiders, caterpillars, snails, and the like. Rustle the dirt gingerly when looking for such creatures because many of them instinctively shy away from vibrations.

Meadows aren't the only mother lode for macro photographers. Forests and fields yield a wealth of opportunities, as well. In general, photographers will find the most success when exploring areas that aren't too disturbed by human development. In other words, if an area has little or no practical use for agricultural or commercial activities, you're more likely to come across a greater density of interesting subjects. Investigate borders and transition areas like the edges of a field or the outer areas of a forest, but also the banks of a stream, steep inclines, and the areas at the edges of glades.

It goes without saying that you should always heed nature conservation regulations that may affect the areas of your exploration. Stay on trails when wandering off them is prohibited. Even though this limits your photographic freedom, you will still find plenty of interesting subjects along the edges of the trail. Using a telephoto lens gives you a bit more flexibility to explore regions removed from the beaten path.

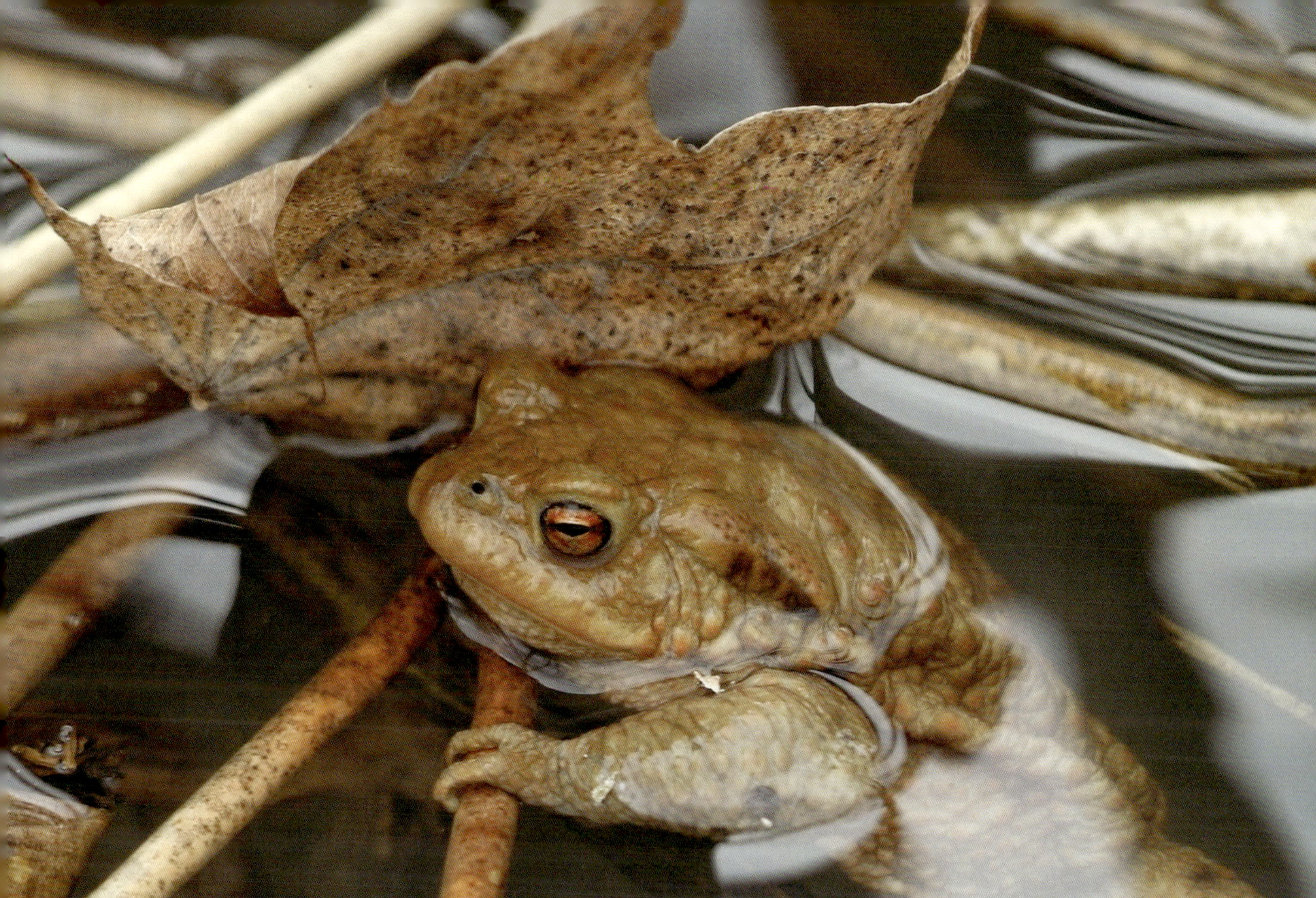

Spring

Spring marks the beginning of the high season for macro photography. The first buds emerge from the frozen earth at long last, and the natural world awakens from its winter slumber. The scenery's dominant color is still brown, but green increasingly emerges and splashes of color dot the landscape. Shoots and blossoms from growing plants make for top-notch macro subjects, the earliest of which are often crocuses and snowdrops. They offer a moving contrast of life with the lingering patches of snow that may surround them. Somewhat later, tulips emerge, and toward the end of spring, the fruit trees bloom, providing an unbelievable variety of subjects in every pastel color imaginable.

Insects accompany the arrival of the first flowers. Bees on the hunt for nourishment from crocuses, checkered lilies, and squill blossoms are early harbingers of spring.

Toad migration is one special vernal event of interest to photographers. Around the beginning of April, female toads head out to return to the location where they themselves hatched. The mass migration is a survival strategy that one can observe in many species across the globe. The more animals that undertake the dangerous

Toad in a forest pond. The toad migration gets under way around the beginning of April. It's an opportunity that should not be missed for macro photographers.

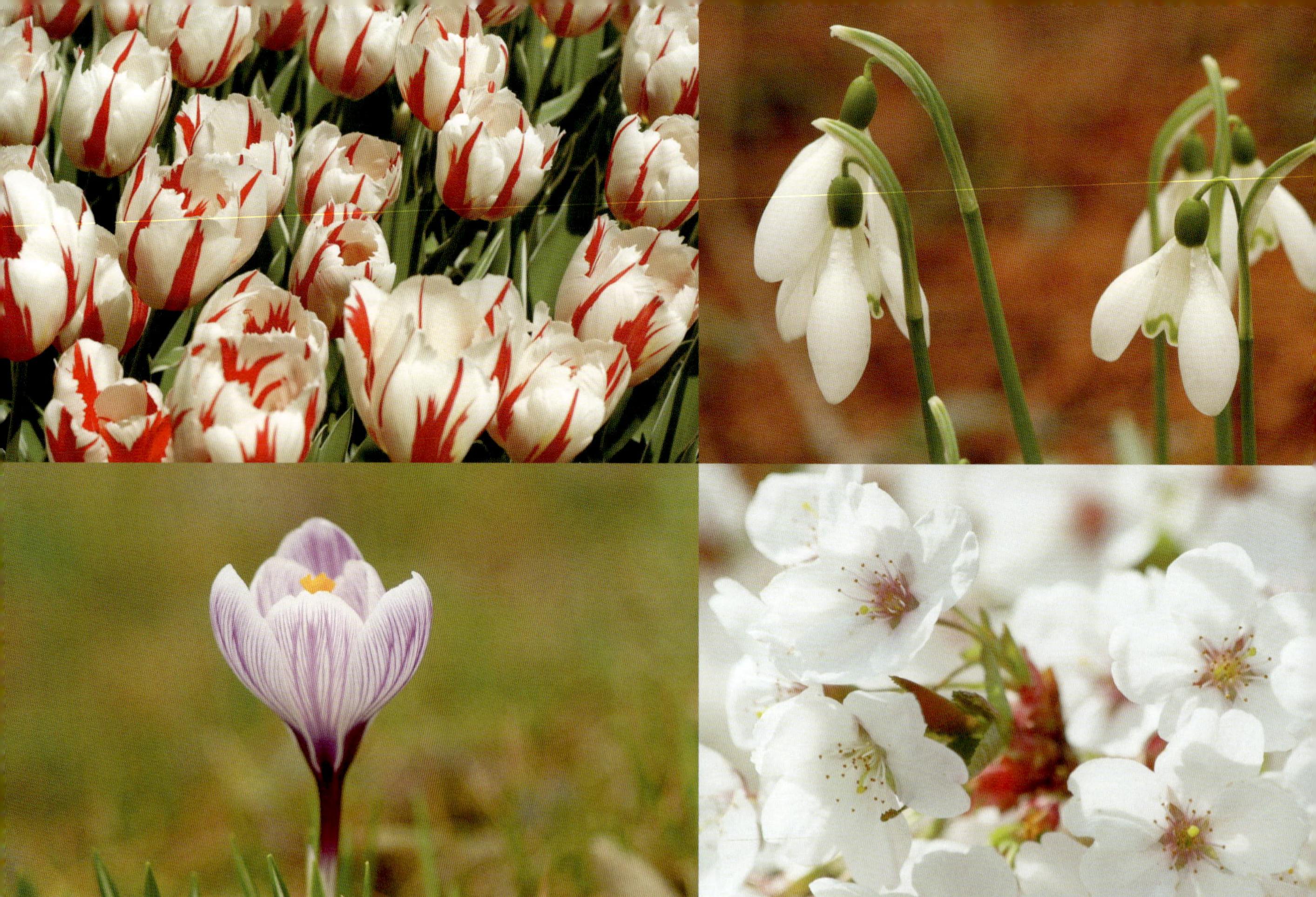

journey at the same time, the more that will successfully reach their destination. Simultaneous migration gives animal species a better chance at preserving their existence in the future.

Summer

Butterflies and dragonflies are two darlings of macro photography, but the summer months offer up a variety of other subjects, too. Dragonflies are most easily found between May and August near ponds and other calm streams and creeks. Many species of dragonflies tend to pick a perch and then return to it frequently to survey their territory. Observing their patterns of movement for a while can give you a good idea of where you should set up your camera to increase the likelihood of getting your desired photo.

A little background knowledge about the habits of butterflies goes a long way in the effort to photograph them. Small tortoiseshells can often be found on stinging nettles, for example, and orange-tip butterflies tend to be attracted to cuckoo flowers. If you wake up early, keep in mind that the time just after sunrise in the early morning is a good time to work, because many insects are less active during

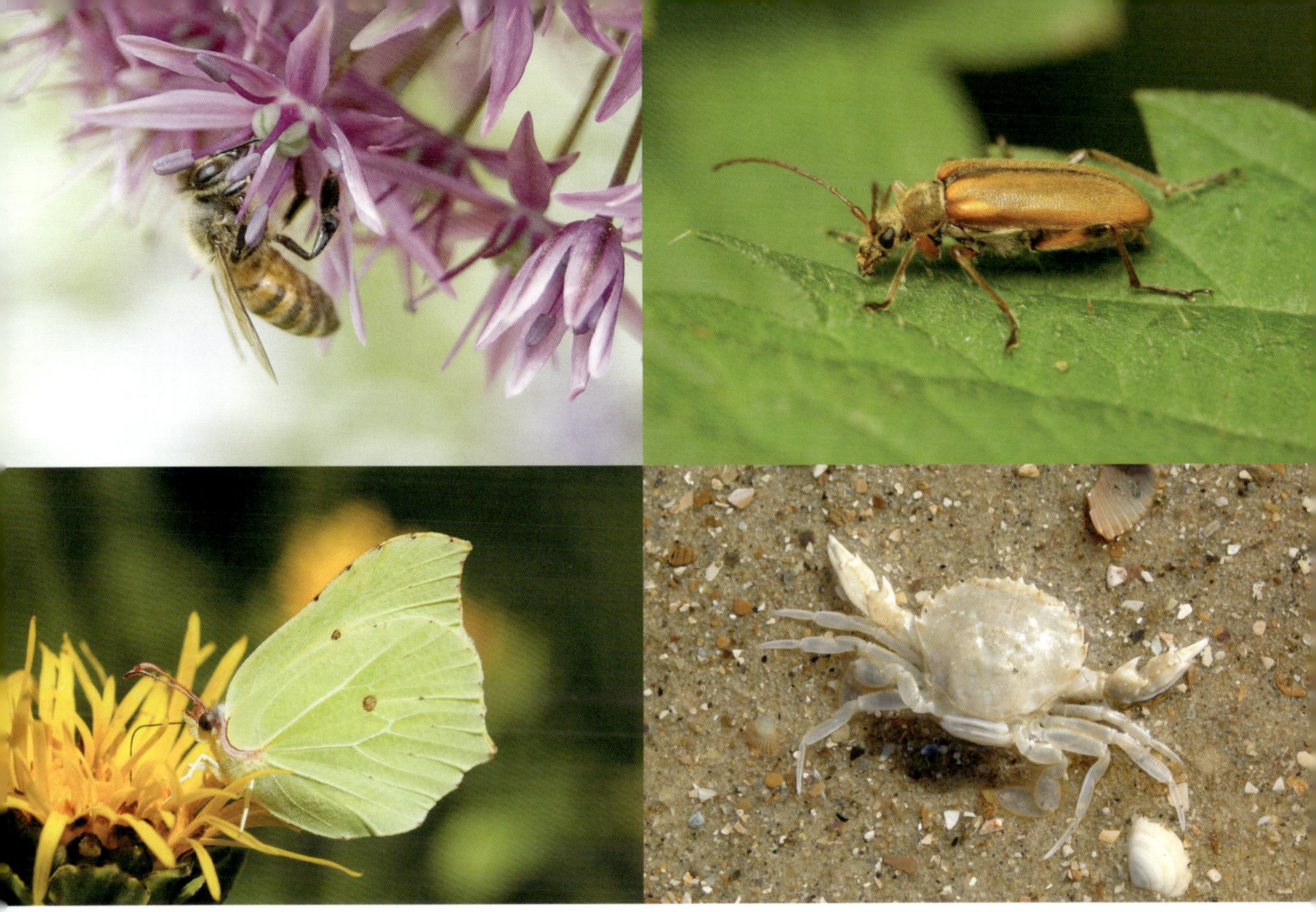

Summer offers a plethora of subjects no matter where you are: a private yard, a forest, a meadow, or a vacation destination

that time and easier to capture in a photo. Sunlight throughout the summer is often quite harsh, so it's wise to carry a reflector with you at all times during this season so you'll be prepared to lighten up problematically dark shadows in your images.

Autumn

The fall months offer up some of their most appealing subjects immediately after a rain shower or in the morning before the dew hasn't yet disappeared for the day. Plants and spiderwebs will be ornamented with droplets of water. Using a detached flash unit is a good way to illuminate these subjects, because the localized light creates an attractive highlight on the surface of the droplets and accentuates their shape.

On such damp days, you may want to bring a waterproof pad, such as a camping mat, with you to protect your knees and clothes from getting dirty or soaked when you need to kneel down for a shot. If rain or dew do not occur naturally, you can always simulate their appearance using a small spray bottle to strategically moisten the subject at hand.

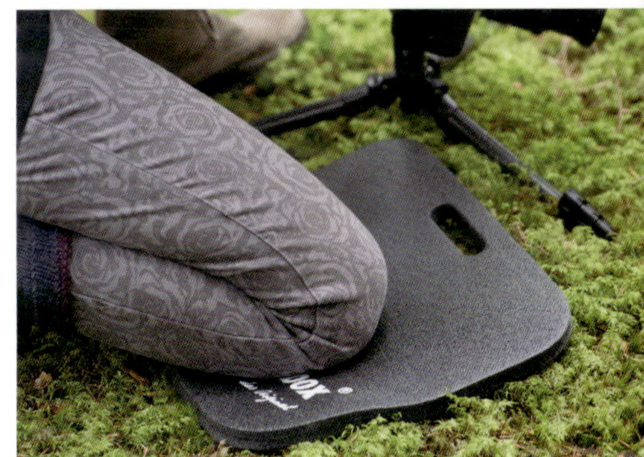

A waterproof pad can protect your clothing from getting dirty or wet

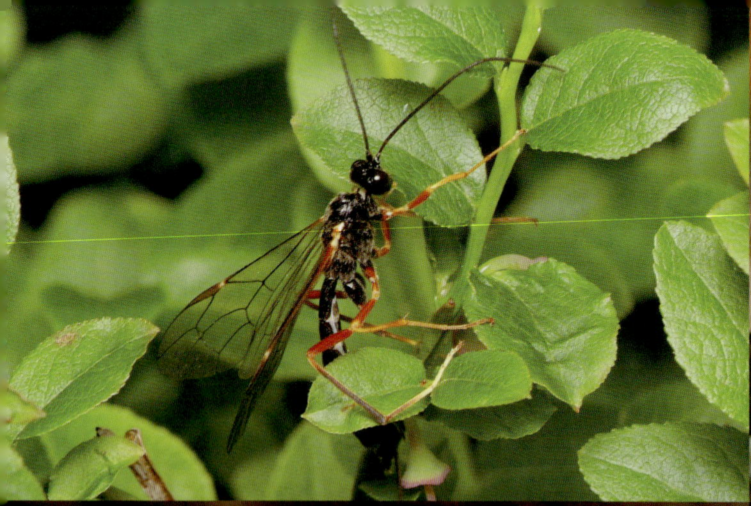

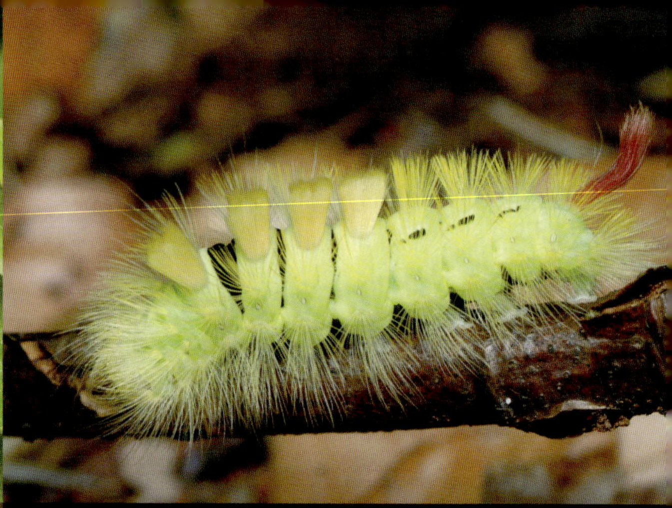

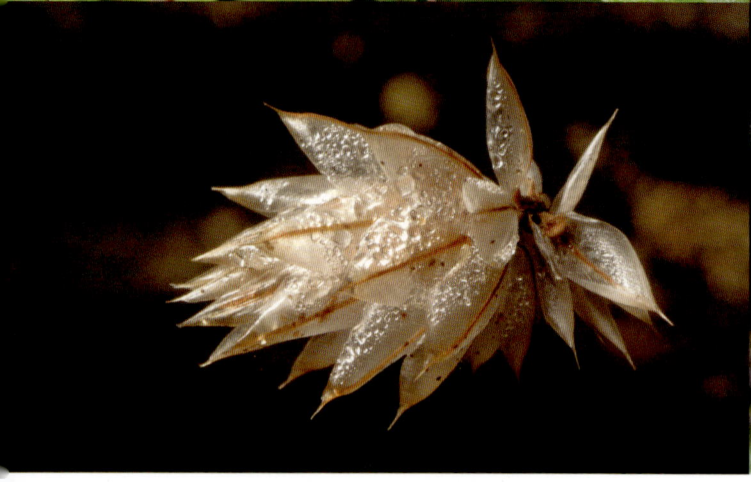

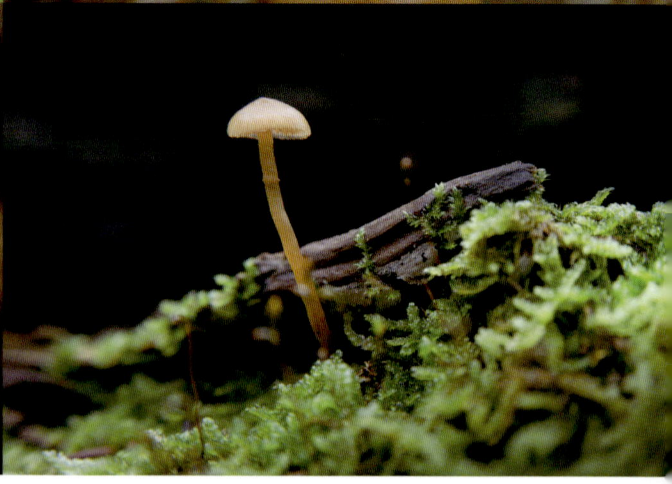

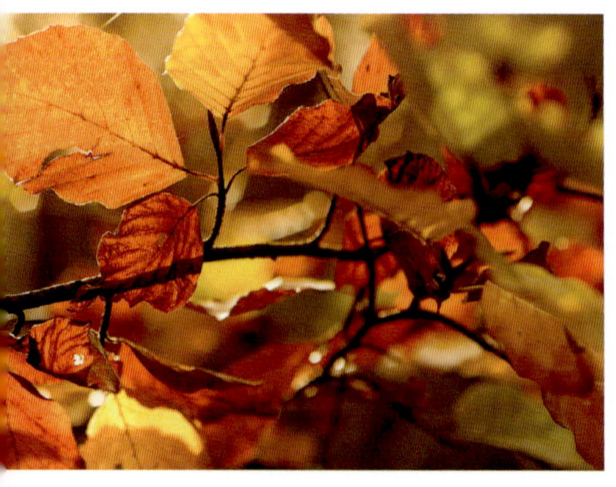

When photographing autumn leaves with backlighting, experiment with your camera's white balance setting. It's often a good trick for making the rich colors of your image even more intense.

Toward the end of autumn, natural changes to available sunlight make things tricky. The days will be getting shorter with winter just around the corner. For photographers with day jobs, this seasonal change means pursuing photographic activities after work may be impractical, so taking pictures on weekends or with artificial lighting may be your only options.

Fall also has a distinct color scheme made up of dark green with red, orange, and gold tones. During this time of year, many plants reveal signs of weathering and age that make for interesting structural photographs. Another delight of autumn is the low sun in the afternoon sky, which creates ample opportunity for unusual and fun lighting circumstances. Fall also marks the arrival of the heralded mushroom season. It's worth budgeting some time for this occurrence, because mushrooms often disappear just as quickly as they arrive. And you'll have to wait another year if you miss the opportunity when it knocks.

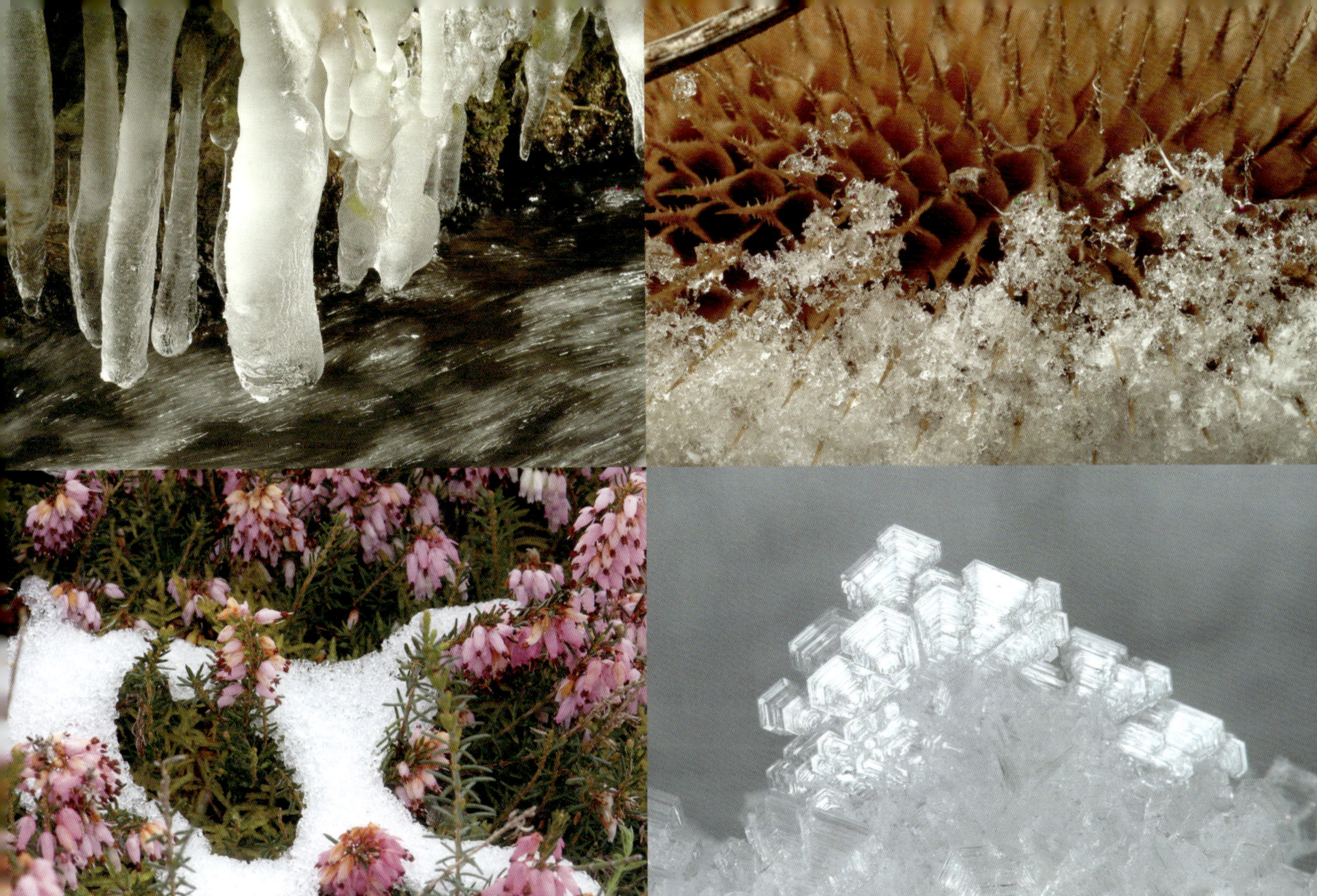

Ice and snow are interesting macro subjects during the winter months, especially when you contrast them with the first blossoms of plants that eventually return to bloom

Winter

Wearing a heavy coat, gloves, a scarf, and a hat doesn't make taking macro pictures any easier. But donning these winter clothes to head out into the cold means you will be rewarded with a wonderland of opportunity. Ice and snow offer an inexhaustible variety of subjects: frozen streams, bizarre ice structures, icicles, freezing fog forming on plants, and individual snowflakes. Frost patterns appearing on windows—once a much beloved subject for macro enthusiasts—are becoming less common nowadays because double-paned glass and other improvements in window quality prevent them from forming. But it's possible to re-create this frost by resting a piece of glass horizontally on a couple of blocks in your yard for the night. If the conditions are right, the rising dampness from the earth will condense and freeze in an attractive frost pattern, which you can photograph in the morning. Side lighting and a dark background are effective for increasing the contrast of these photos.

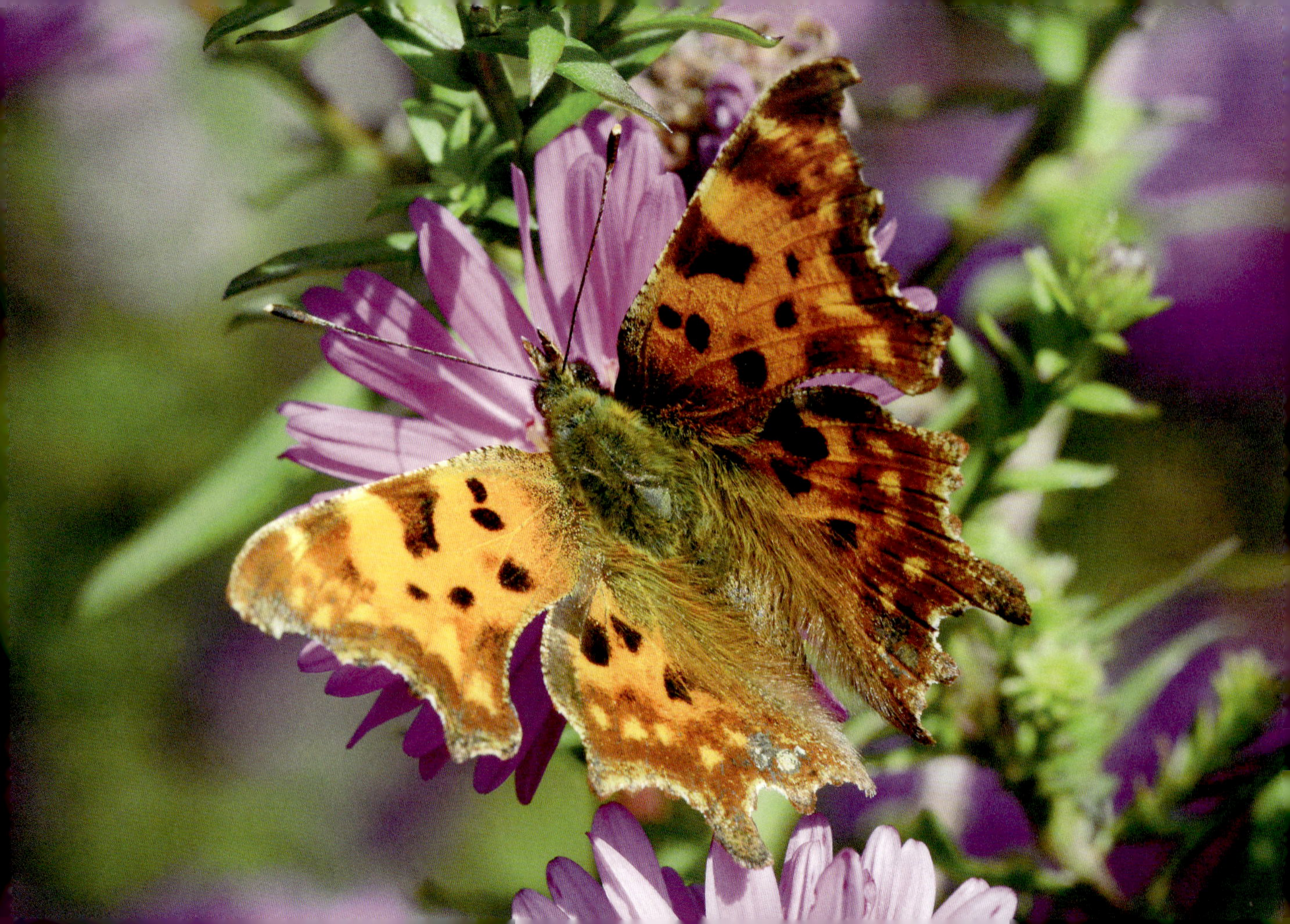

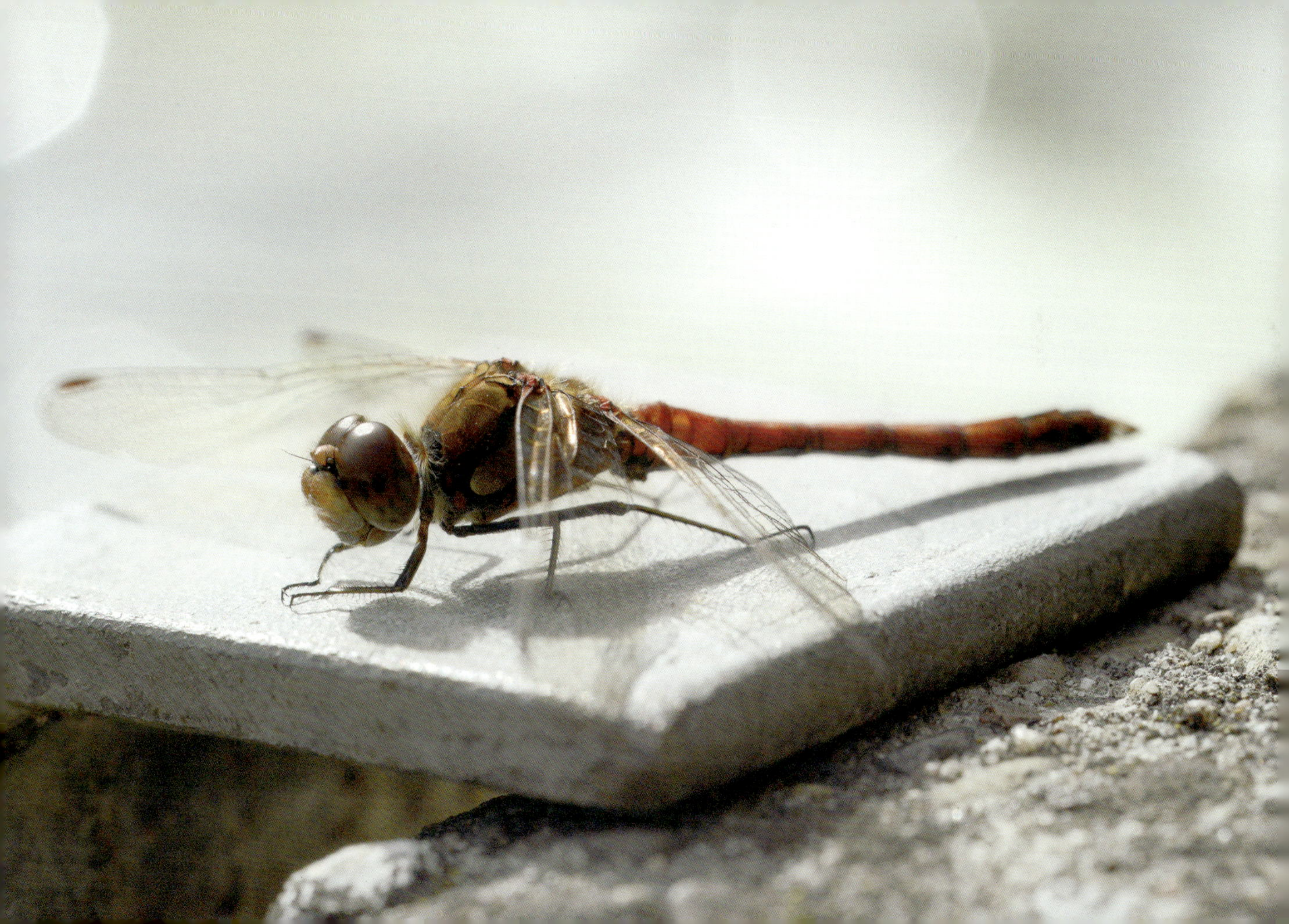

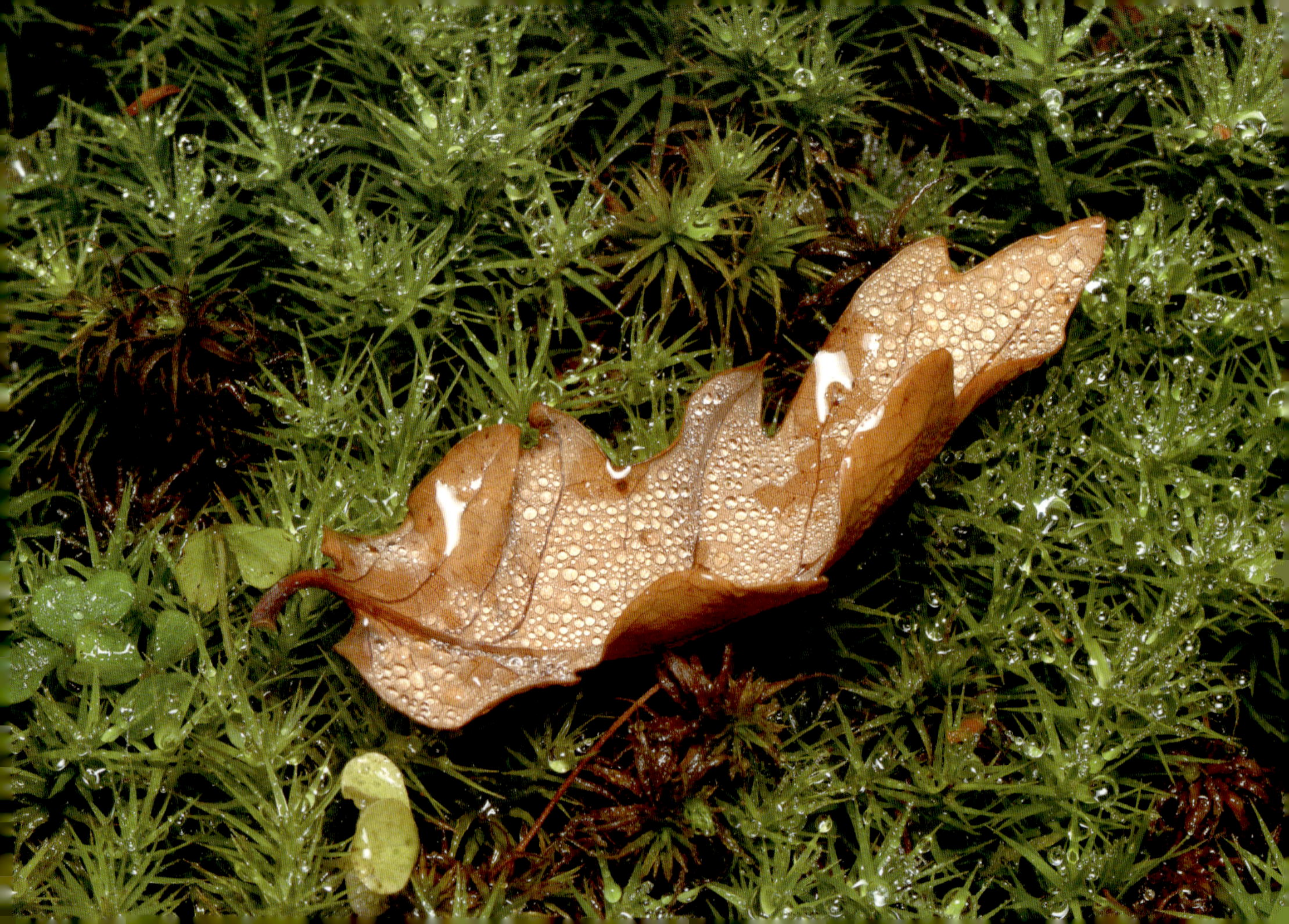

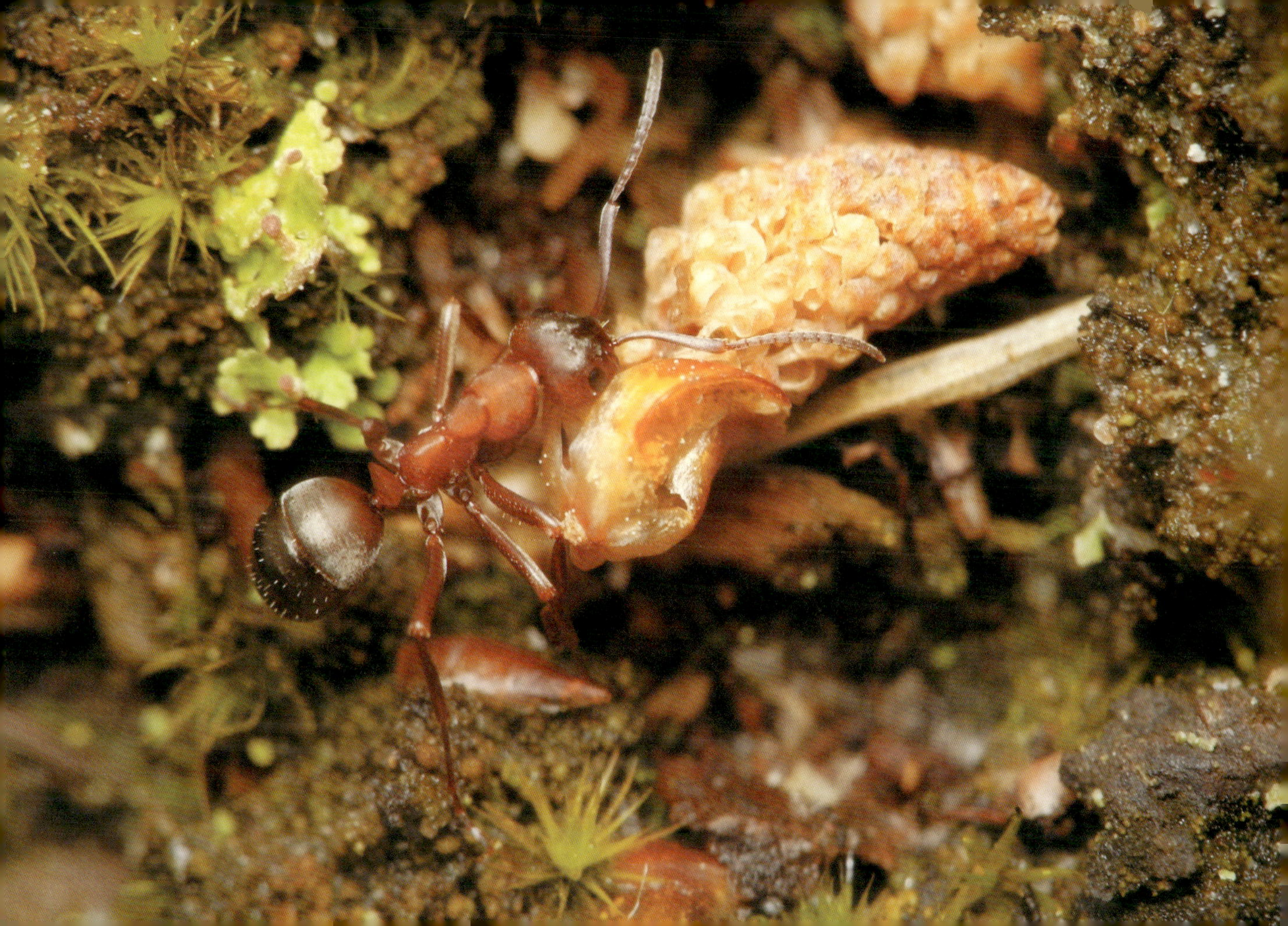

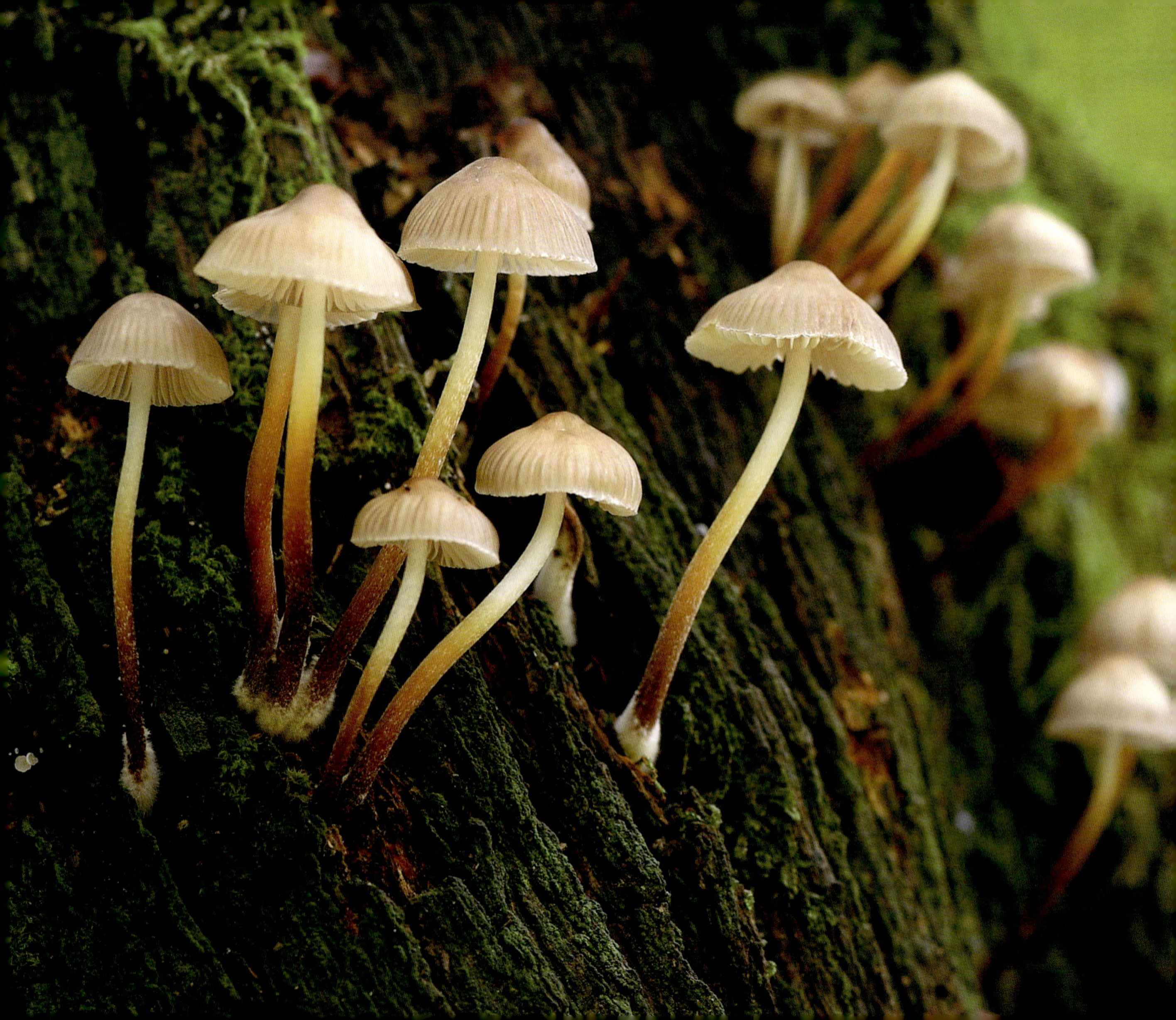

Stefan Dittmann
Fungal Photography

Hardly a day goes by when Stefan Dittmann is not out in the forest hunting for mushrooms. His particular passion is the species he finds in his home of Lower Franconia, in Germany. He goes to great lengths to depict his subjects in their natural environs, and his results are often on display in exhibitions. He mainly relies on the natural light of the forest, with occasional accessory lighting or reflectors when needed.

Microscopy is another of his passions, which he has pursued for more than 15 years. Small crystals in particular are a subject of great interest to him. You can find image galleries and additional information about photographing mushrooms on his website at *www.dittmann4.de.*

Beautiful bonnet mushrooms
*Pentax *ist DS, f/8, 1/10 s, ISO 200, 90mm*
Photo by Stefan Dittman

Photography in the Fungal Kingdom

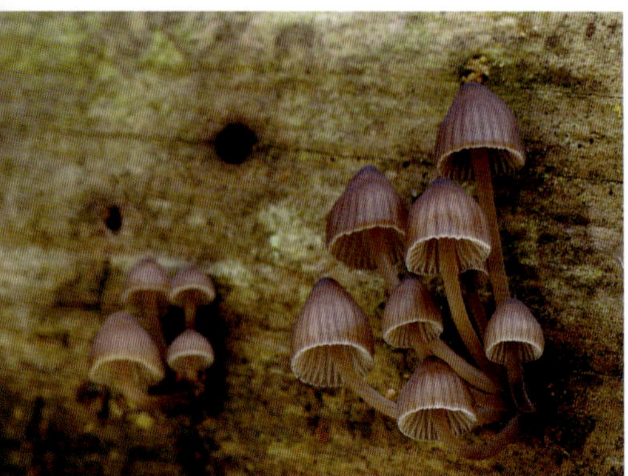

Clustered bonnet mushrooms
Pentax K10D, f/5.6, 1/2 s, ISO 100,
90mm
Photo by Stefan Dittman

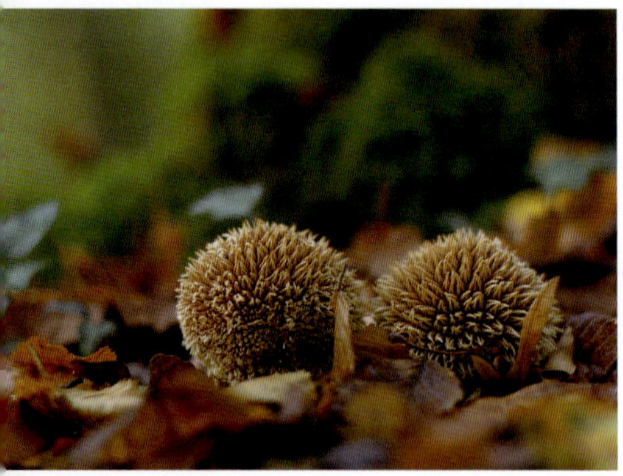

Spiny puffball mushrooms
*Pentax *ist DS, f/4, 1/20 s, ISO 200,*
90mm
Photo by Stefan Dittman

Macro photographers transport viewers into miniature worlds. One of these tiny landscapes is the fungal kingdom. Mushrooms are a good subject for beginning macro photographers because they are motionless for the most part, and their stability means that you can still shoot without problems in a gentle wind. Their immobility also means that slow shutter speeds are not a problem as long as your camera stays steady. And because mushrooms are not miniscule in size, you don't necessarily have to use a macro lens, because you can often shoot full-format images using a normal lens.

The first objective when composing an image of a mushroom is to settle on the best perspective. If you have stumbled across a worthy subject, take it in from every angle and identify the most attractive perspective and angle of view. You should be considering various circumstances, including the position of the sun, where your focal plane should lie, the background elements, and the ground beneath your subject. In general, the lower your camera's position, the better. When possible, it's always advisable to include the gills on the underside of the cap, or lamellae as mushroom experts call them, in your photos. A grand specimen standing atop a tree stump is a golden opportunity for a mushroom photographer on the prowl.

A piece of aluminum foil or light-colored cardboard is an effective tool for illuminating the underside of the cap—and such materials don't weigh much so they're easy to carry. Position the reflector on the ground and to the side of the mushroom to brighten up the gills to make sure they're clear in your pictures.

In cases when your targeted mushroom is growing directly on the forest floor, you will likely need to kneel down, so a picnic cloth is useful for preventing your clothes from getting dirty. It's also advantageous to use a tripod that allows for very low camera positions or a simple beanbag to support your camera. Angle viewfinders and live-view modes are additionally helpful for monitoring your picture's frame and focus. I generally use my camera's two-second self-timer, but remote shutter release systems are just as effective.

Normal lighting conditions in the forest generally offer enough ambient light, obviating the need for artificial light. Pictures of mushrooms shot with flash look anything but natural and shadowing is often a problem. If the ambient light really isn't cutting it, however, try using a flashlight to brighten things up. Try to use a neutral-white

LED bulb rather than a traditional incandescent one, because the neutral light is favorable. And definitely set your white balance appropriately before taking your pictures, or at least shoot RAW files so you can adjust the color temperature after the fact during post-processing.

When shooting with a sturdy stand—a tripod or a beanbag—opt for the lowest possible ISO setting to minimize image noise. Selecting the optimal aperture generally requires a compromise of sorts. On one hand, it's useful to choose a small aperture opening to elongate the depth of field so that your subject will be adequately sharp from at least the front edge of the mushroom cap to its stalk. On the other hand, keeping the aperture wide is desirable for causing the background to soften and blur a bit for a pleasant effect. One way to arrive at the optimal solution is to shoot a bracketing sequence with different aperture settings. Mushrooms aren't going to run away on you; being able to use this option is a clear advantage to other disciplines of macro photography. After you return home, you can inspect the results on your computer monitor and select the photo with the best depth-of-field characteristics.

Some of photography's basic principles hold true with mushroom photography, too, including the golden ratio and working with various depths in your images. When looking for potential subjects, take their surroundings into consideration. A beetle or pinecone in just the right spot can make a masterpiece out of what would otherwise have been a straightforward picture of a mushroom.

It goes without saying that photographers should respect their natural environs, but you'll inevitably come across others who have damaged a specimen by carelessly positioning a tripod on the forest floor or who have ripped out a protected plant species that happened to be in the way. Please be diligent when working amid the natural world.

Anyone who takes pictures of mushrooms is bound to take up the art of identifying species sooner or later. That includes identifying edible sorts, which means some photography treks may result in a tasty snack or two in your backpack. Treat yourself only to the species that you are completely confident about. If you are not entirely sure about a mushroom, take it to an expert for verification or simply don't risk eating it.

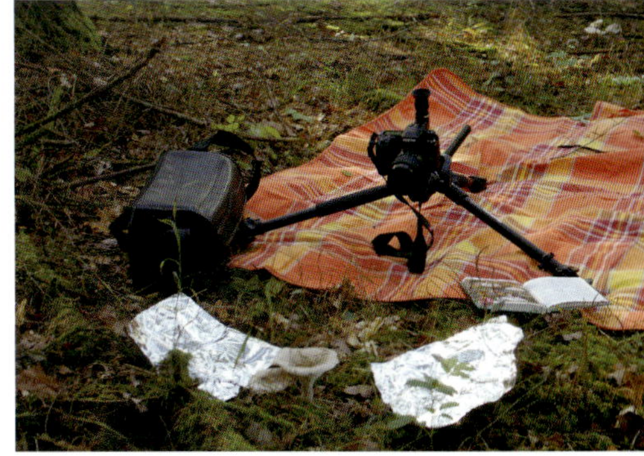

An example shooting setup in the forest

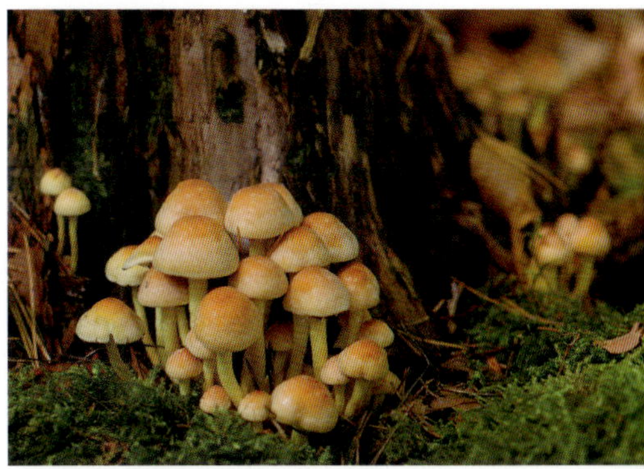

Sulfur tuft mushrooms
*Pentax *ist DS, f/5.6, 1/125 s, ISO 400, 50mm*
Photo by Stefan Dittman

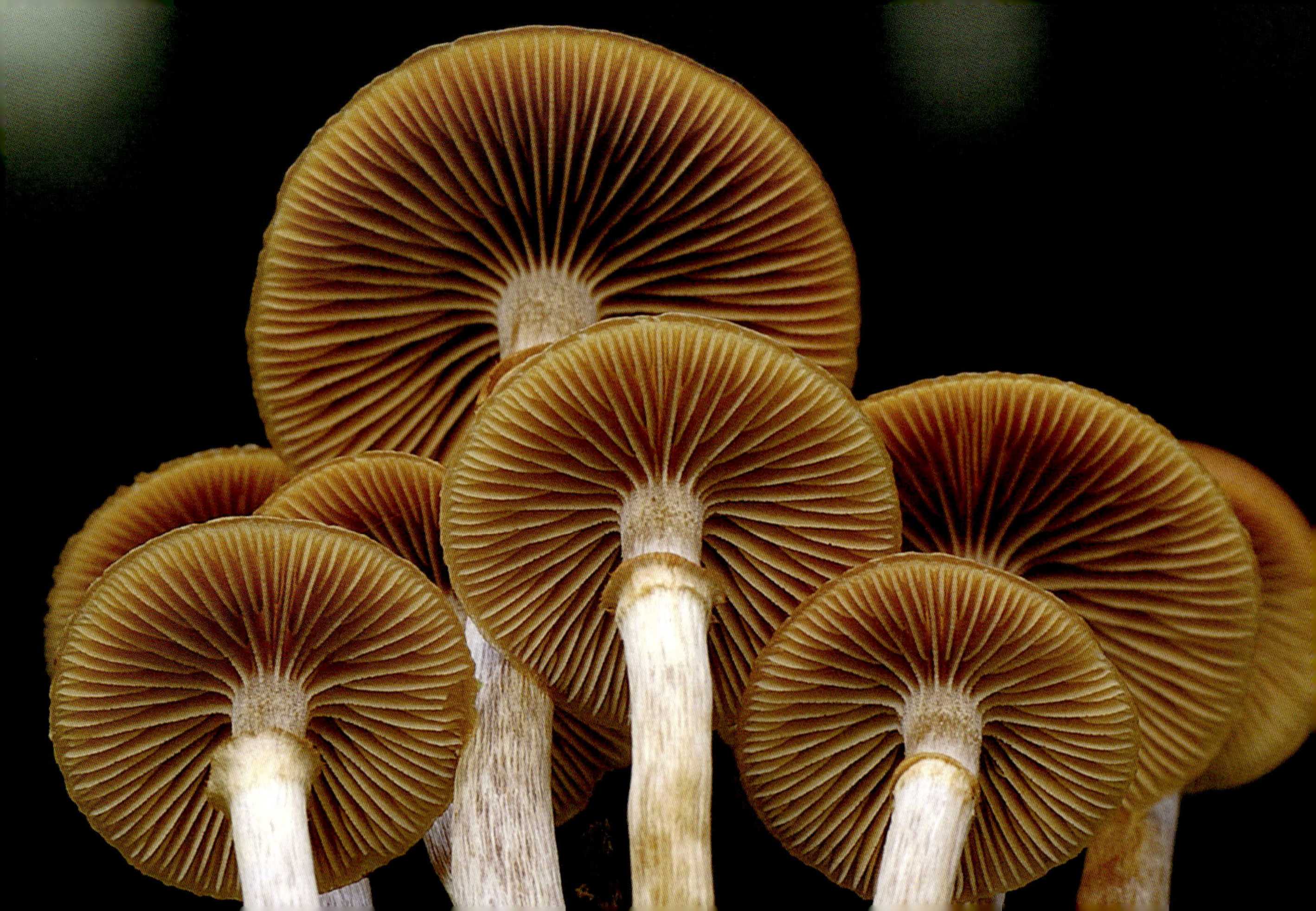

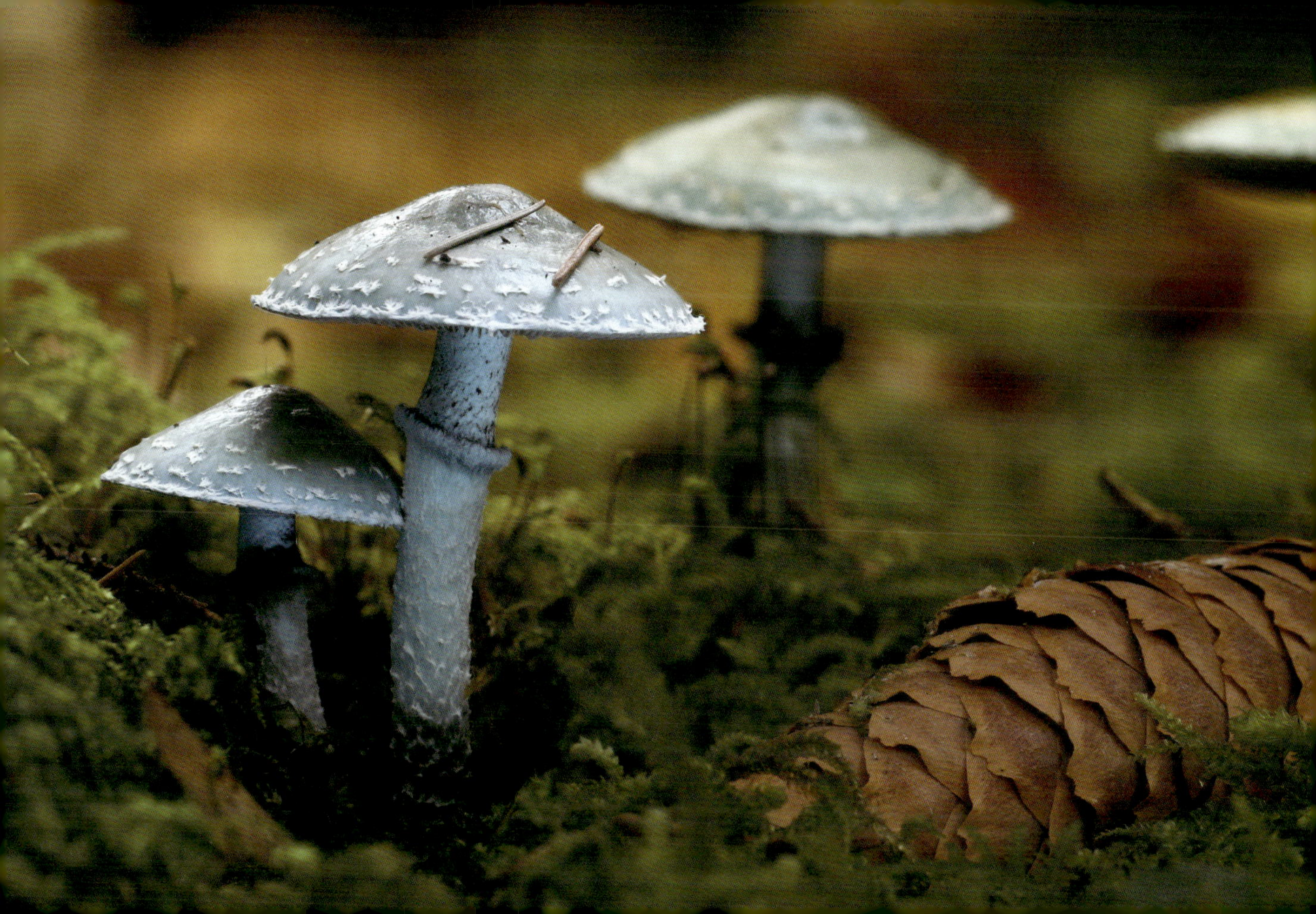

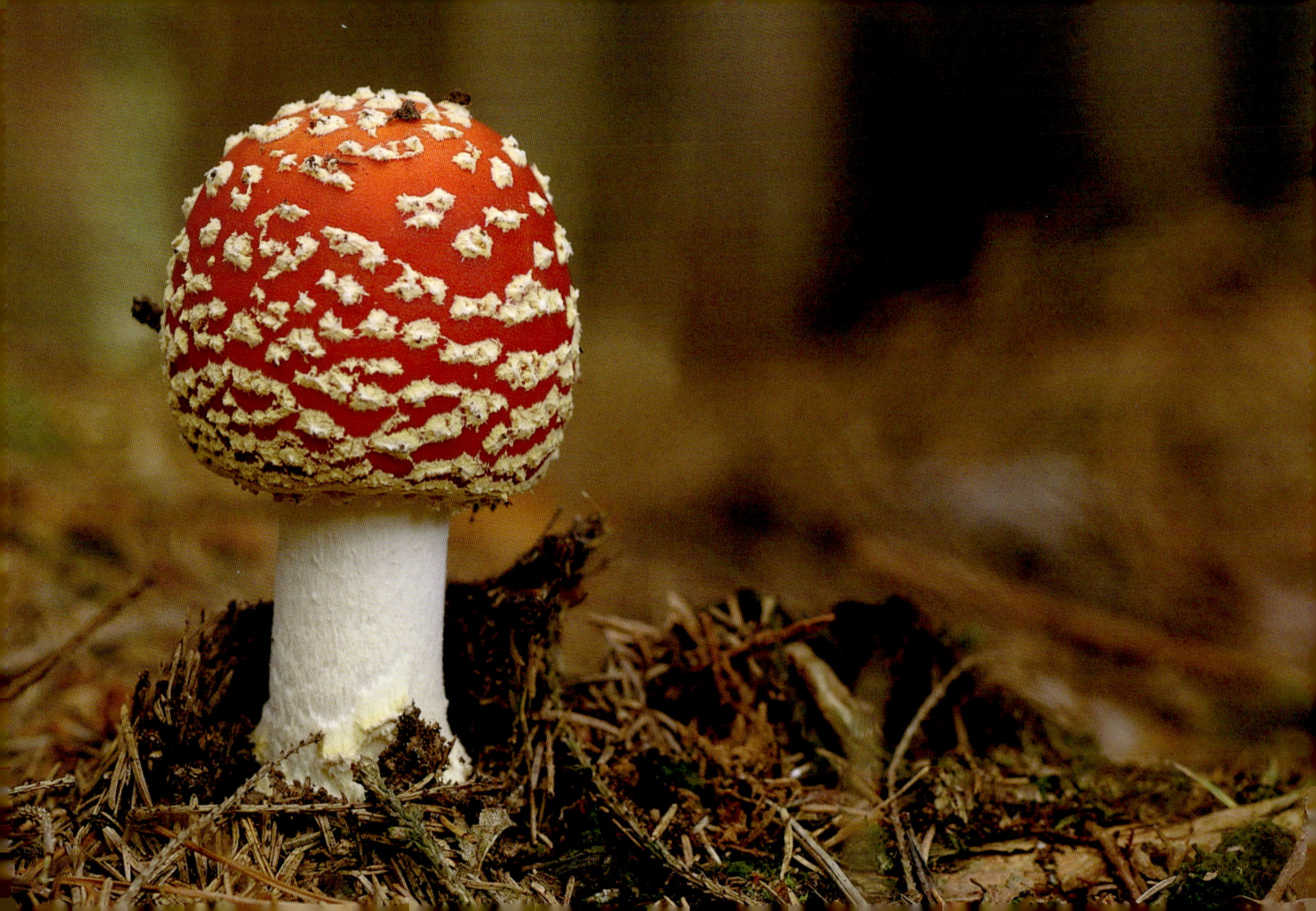

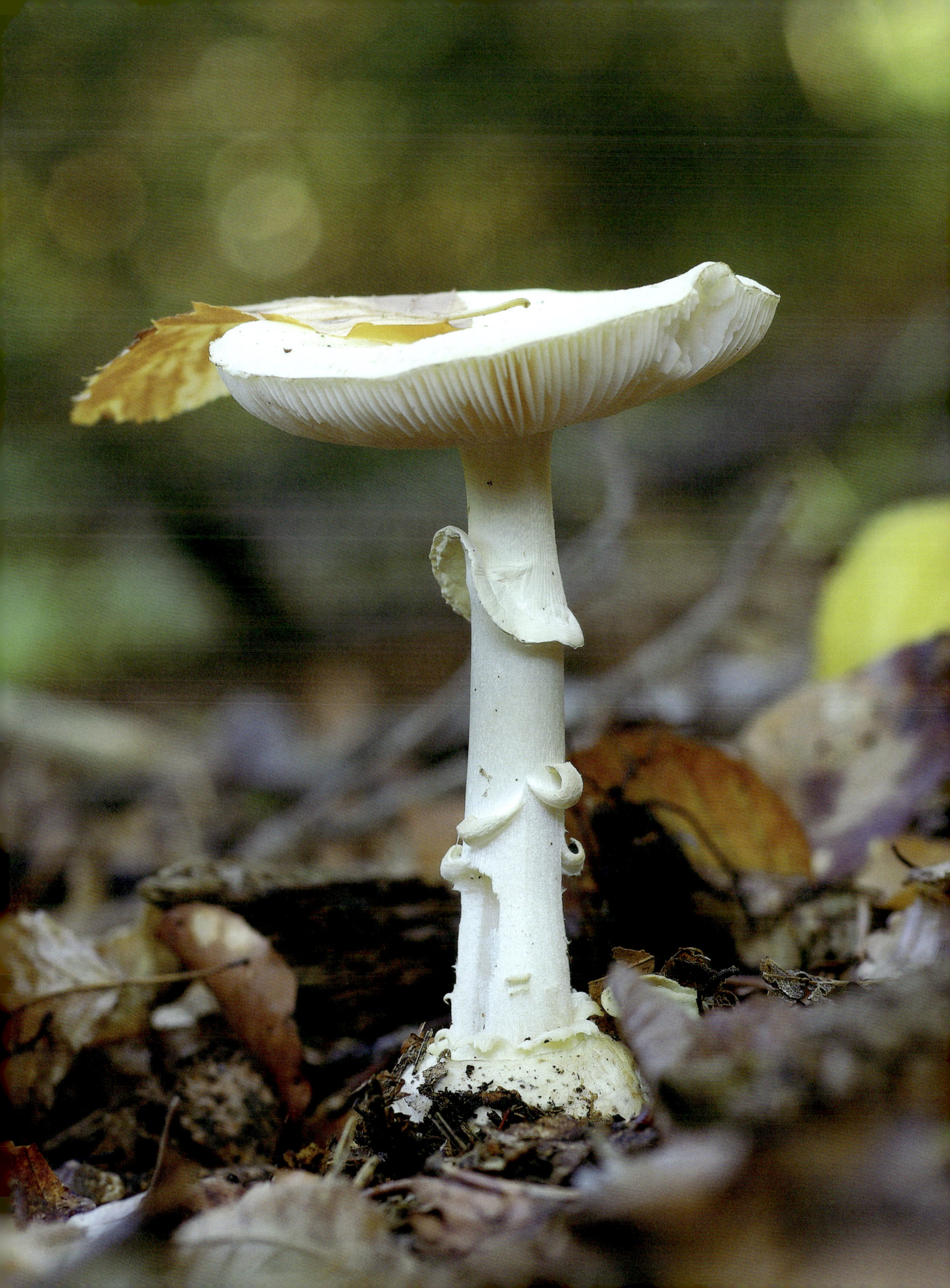

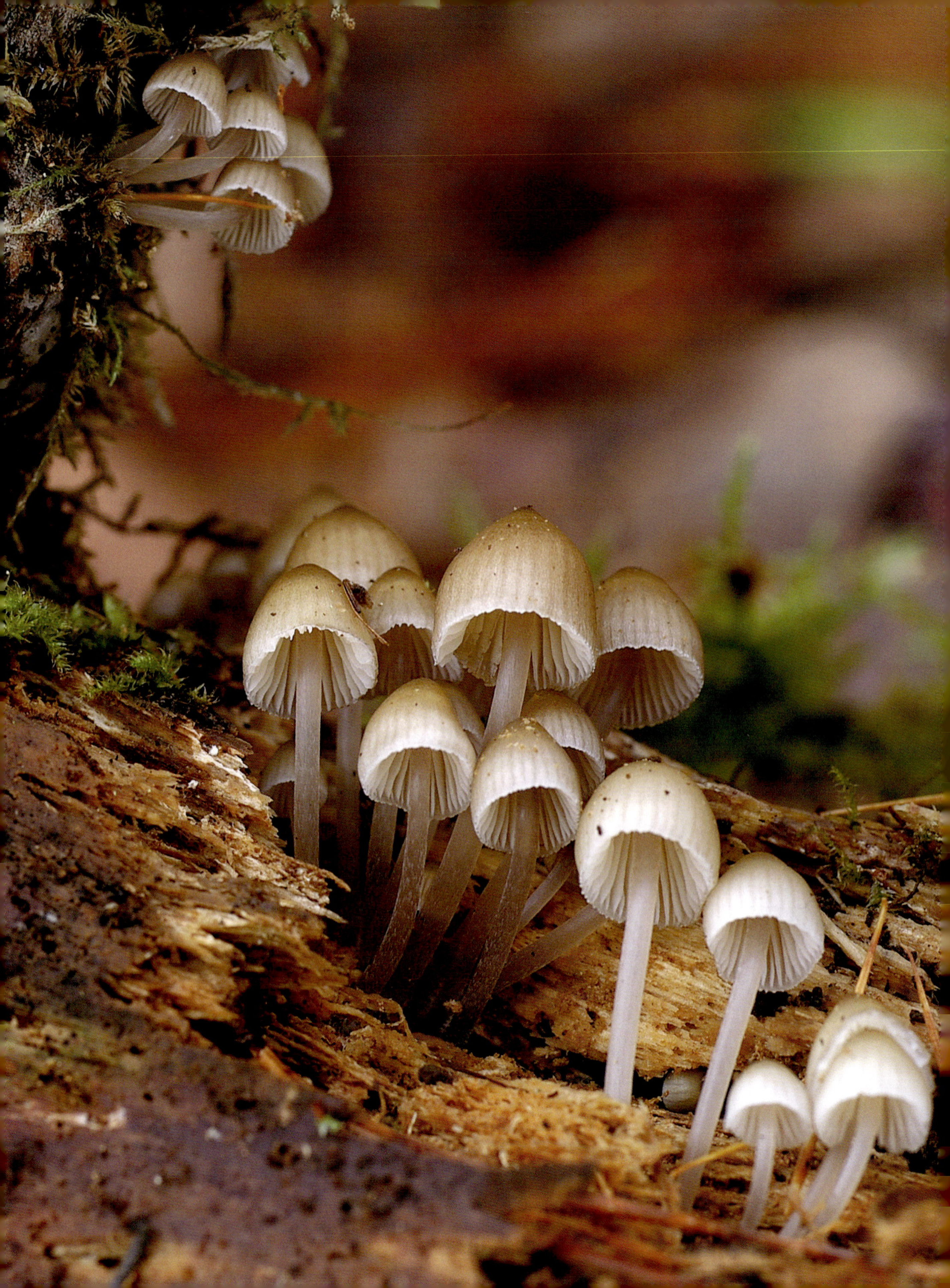

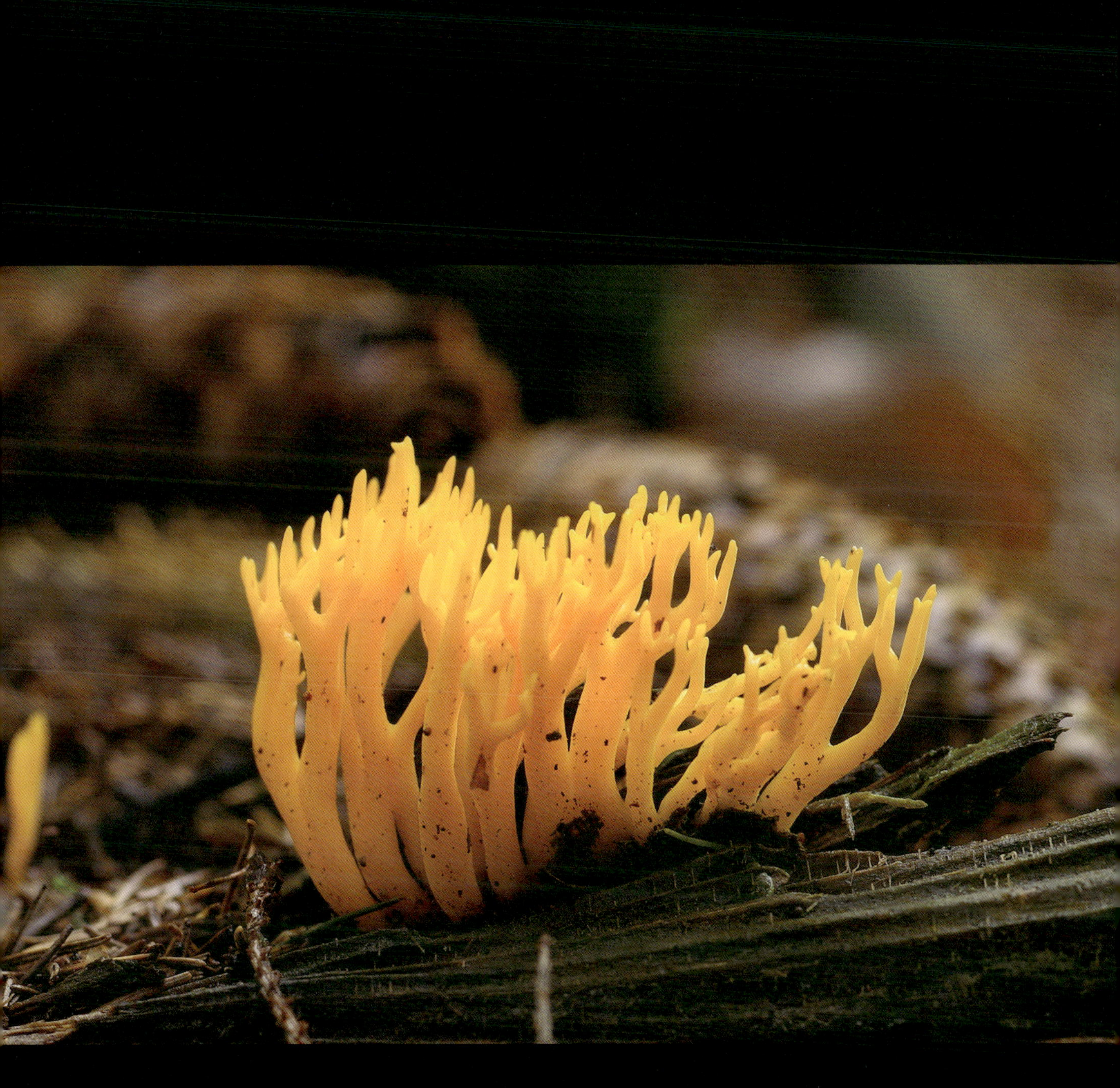

Beautiful bonnet mushrooms
*Pentax *ist DS, f/8, 1/10 s, ISO 200, 90mm*
Photo by Stefan Dittman

Yellow stagshorn mushroom
Pentax K10D, f/5.6, 1/20 s, ISO 200, 90mm
Photo by Stefan Dittman

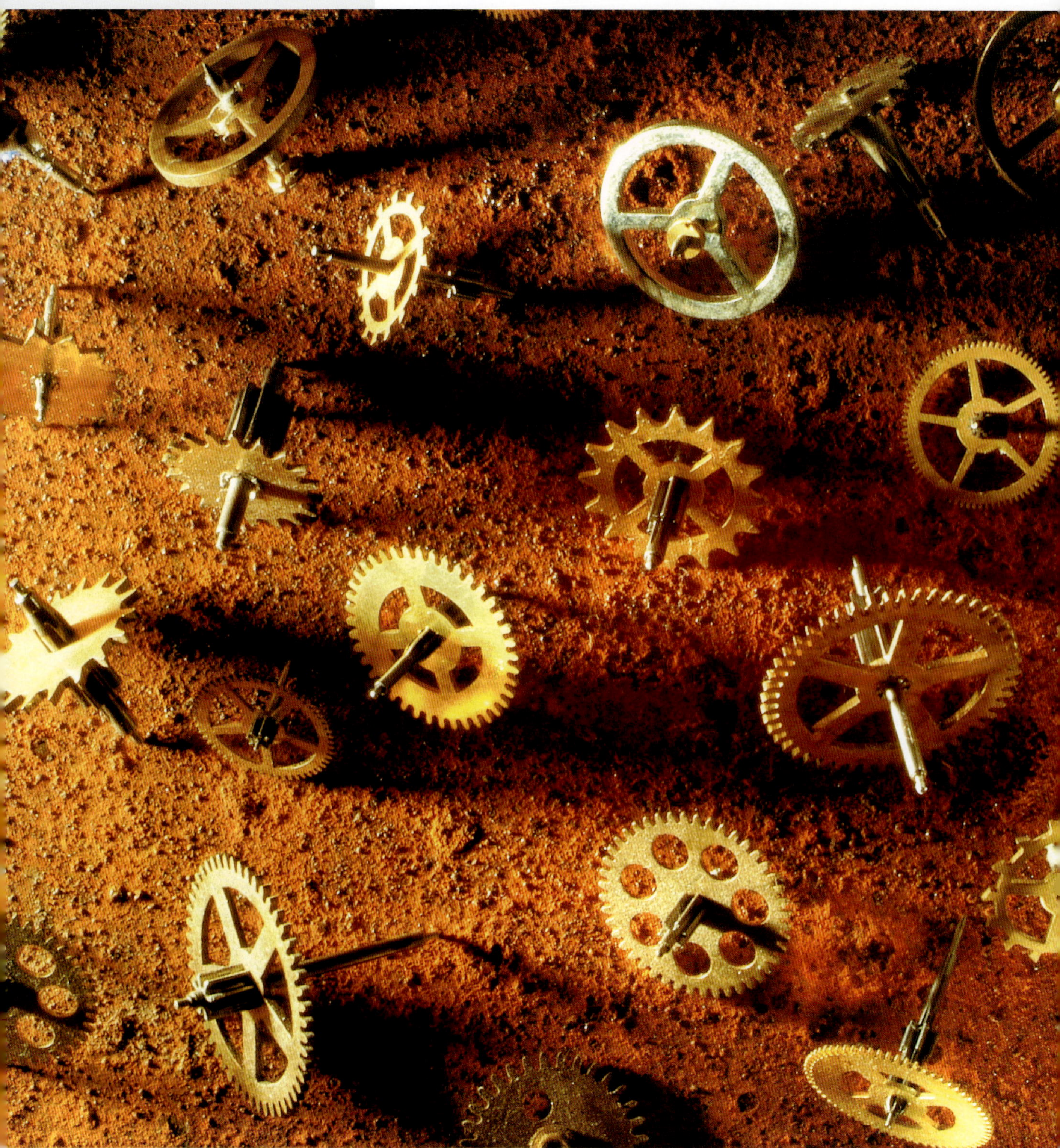

Special Shooting Techniques

Macro photography can involve a great deal more than taking pictures of small objects. The full palates of lighting and shooting techniques available to general photographers are also available in the macro world; they are just applied to smaller dimensions.

A bit of preparation was required to create this image of various gears. The first step was fabricating the surface material. I started with a sheet of iron and used a sponge to coat it in vinegar for a few days. Over time the uniform rust texture developed.

After arranging the rusted sheet with the various gears on a repro stand, I set up two system flash heads on the left side of the tableau at the same height of the subject. This intense side light is responsible for the long shadows. Next I positioned a few small mirrors pointed in different directions on the right side of the gears, so the light from the flash would bounce off in an unpredictable array and create several highlights on the surfaces of the gears and reflections on the rusted iron.

The flash strobes didn't have a modeling light, so it took a few test shots and made adjustments to refine the lighting for the scene.

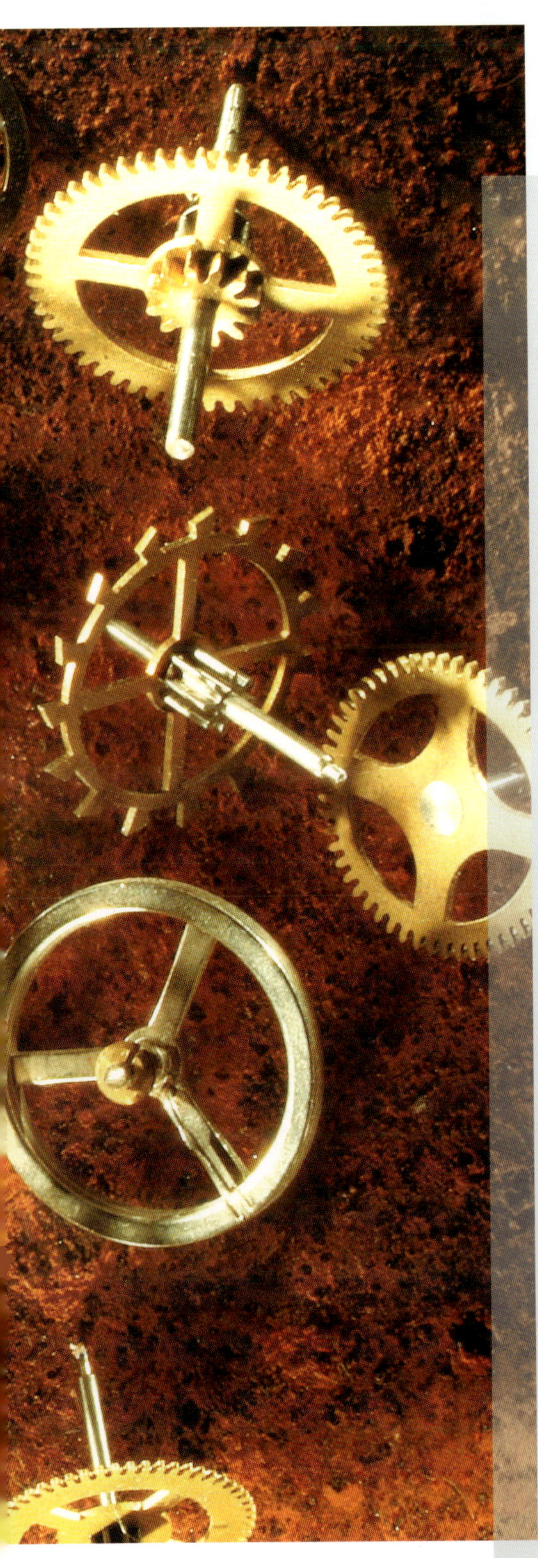

Gears on rusted iron
f/27, 1/125 s, ISO 100, 50mm, two system flash units

Multiple Exposures

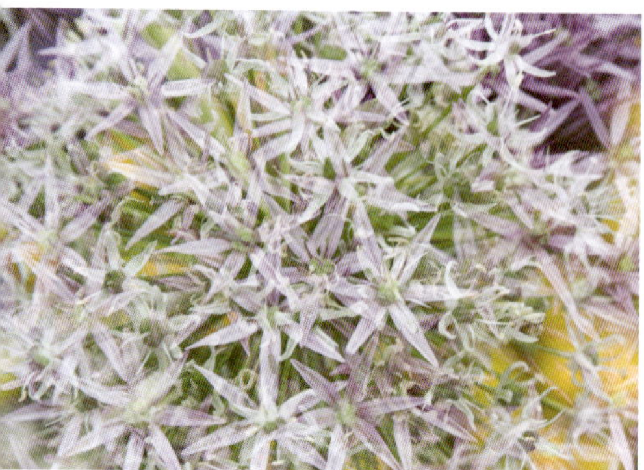

This multiple exposure of flower blossoms features interesting nested patterns

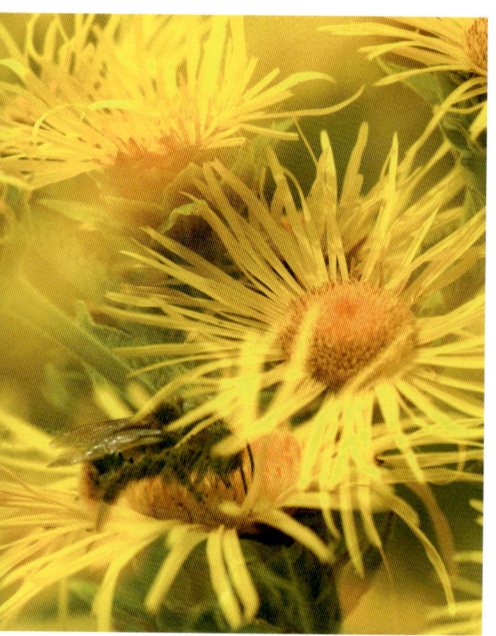

The possibilities are limitless

In order to use this technique, your camera needs to have a dedicated multiple exposure mode. I've used a Fuji S5 Pro for my illustrations here, and it is able to compile up to 10 individual exposures into one final composite image. Comparable models from other manufacturers offer similar functionality.

The process for creating such images is relatively straightforward. First select the multiple exposure mode in your camera's relevant menu. This menu point is also where you often define how many exposures you would like to use. After you expose your first image, the camera will remain in a standby mode until you press the shutter release button again, which will record the second exposure. You have time between shots, in other words, to readjust the focus or find a new subject. Most of the time, however, you will have planned out the individual components of your multiple-exposure image ahead of time.

After the final exposure is recorded, you generally have to press OK before the camera completes the process. Most camera models will remain in multiple exposure mode for only one series of shots, after which they automatically revert to single-exposure mode. If you want to create another multiple-exposure image, you need to reactivate it again from the relevant menu point.

You can mimic this process by creating a montage of several photos in an image editing program, of course. Even though you would have significantly more control over the component images, the unforeseeable chance and luck that is inherently involved in actually exposing multiple images is part of the charm of this technique. Furthermore, it's very difficult to imitate the natural transparency and softness that arise from true multiple-exposure images by using software. When creating a multiple-exposure photo, you're not combining multiple images; instead, the shutter is opening multiple times and allowing more light to reach an already existing image.

Subject in Subject

One variation using the multiple-exposure technique is to switch the subject between capturing the subsequent frames. This method works best when you combine one exposure of a repeating texture such as leaves or blossoms with another exposure that has a sharp contrast, such as a backlit shot of a plant or some other dark object in front of a light background. By combining the images, you effectively fill up the one subject with the texture of the other.

Multiple Focal Planes

Photographers shooting with a tripod can mimic the process of focus stacking directly in their camera by creating multiple exposures using component frames with multiple focal planes. Keep in mind that moving the focal plane forward or backward in an image causes the angle of view to change minimally. Because of this phenomenon, it is best to avoid using individual frames with modestly shifted focal planes, because the sharp areas in the component images won't overlap congruently and you'll end up with some doubled edges. You are better off working with an open aperture and creating component images with significantly divergent focal planes. The resulting image will show varying degrees of blur between the planes of focus.

Blur Effect without Filters

You can also use the multiple-exposure mode to create an interesting blur effect by exposing a blurry image on top of a sharp one. The subject in the frame remains identical, but the first image should be in focus and the second one should not be in focus.

The intensity of the softening effect depends in part on the degree of blur in the component exposures, but also on the number of component exposures used for the multiple exposure. Experimentation is the best way to fine-tune this method.

Manual Multiple Exposures

If your camera doesn't have an integrated multiple exposure mode, then this workaround is for you. Stop down the aperture as far as you can, and select a very slow shutter speed. Release the shutter when you're ready, and immediately swing a piece of black cardboard to block the lens. The camera will still be exposing the frame, but essentially no light will be reaching the sensor. To record the "second" exposure, pull the cardboard from the lens and then immediately return it to block the lens for the remainder of the exposure window.

This method of creating a multiple-exposure image is experimental, because it is impossible to regulate the duration of time in which the light is effectively reaching the sensor.

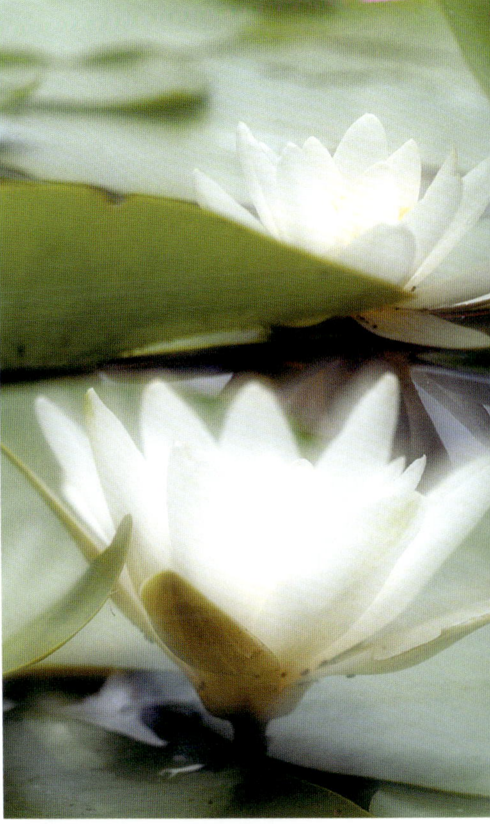

The first exposure for this image was focused on the flower in the foreground; the second exposure, on the flower in the background

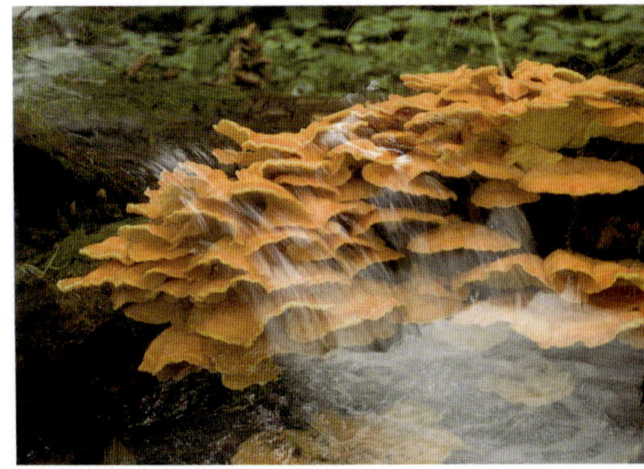

A cascade of mushrooms and water combined in the same image

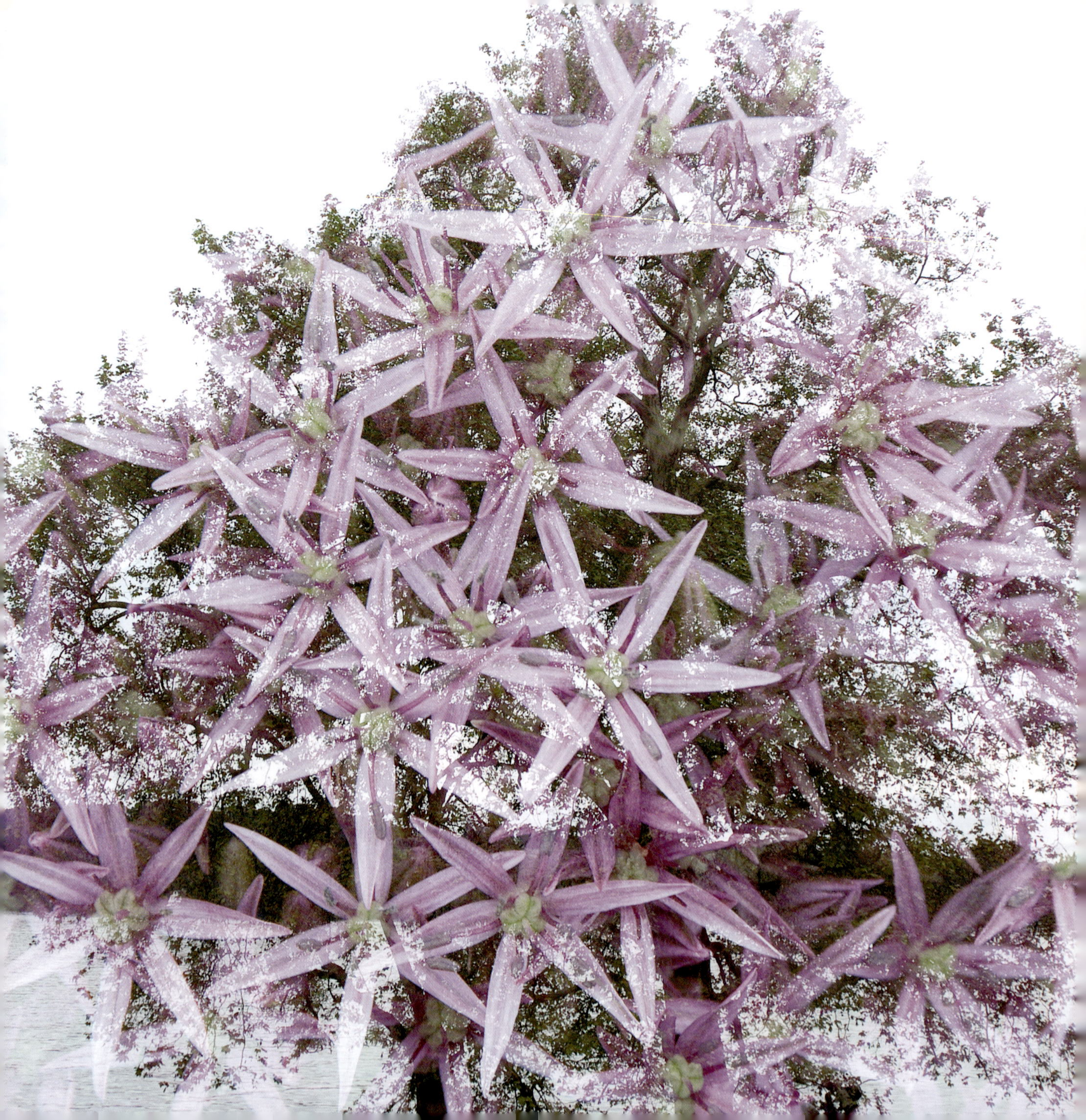

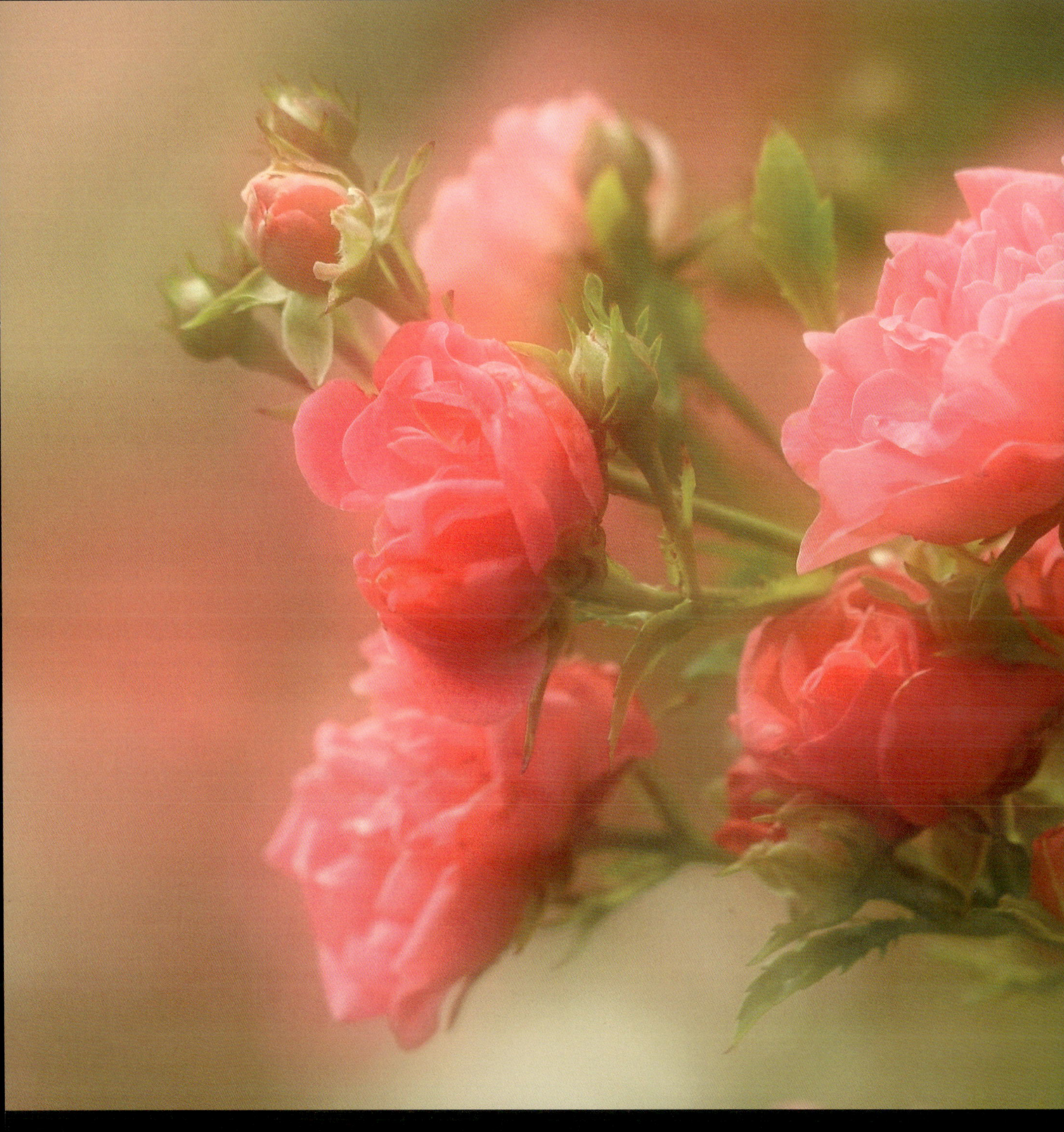

Double exposure created with one sharp exposure and one out-of-focus exposure. Overlaying these two versions of the same subject creates an attractive blur effect without having to use a filter.

Focus Stacking

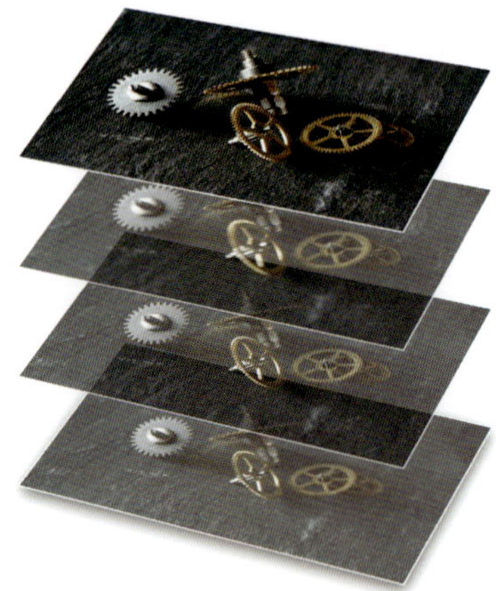

Focus stacking combines multiple component images that each have a slightly shifted focal plane

An inadequately small depth of field is a recurrent problem for macro photographers, and the further you dive into the macro realm, the more of an issue it becomes. The solution of stopping down the aperture quickly reaches its practical limits, leaving only special techniques, such as using shift lenses, to bring an adequate focal range into your macro images.

Focus stacking is one powerful solution. This method involves blending multiple component images with varying focal planes into one final image. In principle, you can manually carry out the entire focus stacking process with two component images in Photoshop or any other comparable image-editing program that uses layers by allowing layer masks to transition into one another. To do this, set the masks up so that only the parts of the exposure that were in focus are visible. It is possible to work manually if you have only two or three component images, but any more than that, and you will run into trouble. An increasing number of component images not only increases the time involved to carry the process out, but it also makes it much more difficult to get different parts of the image to line up congruently, because the camera position changes minimally with each shot.

But let's get started at the beginning.

Preparing the Subject

The amount of thought and time you put into preparing your subject before you even take your first picture is what makes or breaks the final result of the focus stacking process. A high-quality composite result naturally depends on the series of component images that are as perfect as possible.

Dirt and dust on the subject can completely ruin the entire effort. Unfortunately, problematic particles of debris on a tiny subject often aren't visible to the naked eye. When you're getting started with a project, always take a few test images up front to closely evaluate how optimal your subject appears. If you skip this step, you run the risk of stacking not only layers of sharpness, but also dust, which leads to a retouching process that is not justified by the end result.

A blower designed to clean the sensor and a paintbrush are usually the only tools you need to tidy up your subject to avoid this fate.

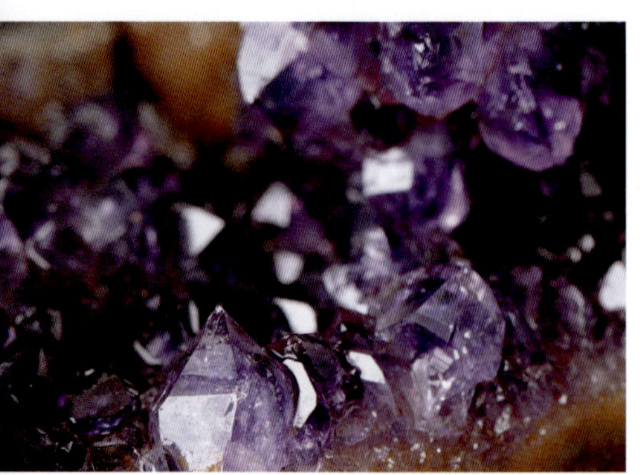

At a magnification level of 1:1 with an aperture stopped down to f/32, the depth of field encompasses only the first few millimeters. Everything else is blurry.

When photographing living objects such as insects or parts of plants, take extra care not to harm your subject while you clean it up.

As long as they're not water soluble like salt crystals, most minerals and geologic specimens can be cleaned with lukewarm water and a fine, soft brush. But even with crystals, you may be working with delicate structures that can't withstand any direct contact, so exercise caution.

Prepping the Camera and Lighting

The next task is to set up your camera and to prepare the lighting. There are multiple ways to create multiple component images with a slightly shifted focal plane position. Simply adjusting the focus with the lens is often a viable option when photographing simple subjects at a modest level of magnification. But affixing the camera to a focusing rail offers photographers much greater precision in controlling the focal plane position for each image.

When photographing rigid objects (a geode, for instance), mounting your camera and the subject's holding device to a common platform is an effective way to prevent them from running into one another. For nonrigid objects like plants, however, it is better to mount the camera and the subject independently, because any time you touch the configuration, you run the risk of causing elements of the subject to move. Along these lines, using a remote shutter release system further minimizes the risk of any unwanted movement from the process.

The lighting needs for a focus-stacking shoot are highly dependent on the nature of the subject at hand, but in most cases you'll want to use a flash. Further lighting control can be exercised using light tents and softboxes to minimize harsh shadows; small pieces of strategically placed black and white cardboard to absorb or reflect light as needed; and small mirrors to direct reflections in targeted ways. In other words, all of the methods and techniques used in tabletop photography are at your disposal.

Shooting

The number of component images you will need to create a composite image that is sharp from front to back depends on the depth of your subject, the level of magnification, and the aperture you're using. As a general rule of thumb, 20 to 30 exposures will produce a good result if you're not shooting with a wide-open aperture. F-stops between f/8 and f/22 are a good starting frame of reference.

Stacking images shot at a magnification of 1:1 will yield results ranging from good to great in quality. Precision becomes more critical the larger the magnification factor becomes. When shooting images

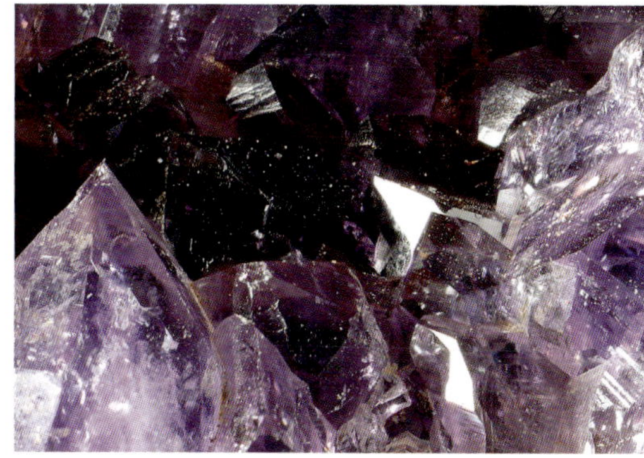

The facets of the geode aren't the only thing on display here—dust particles are also problematically conspicuous. A thorough cleaning of your subject is a critical early step.

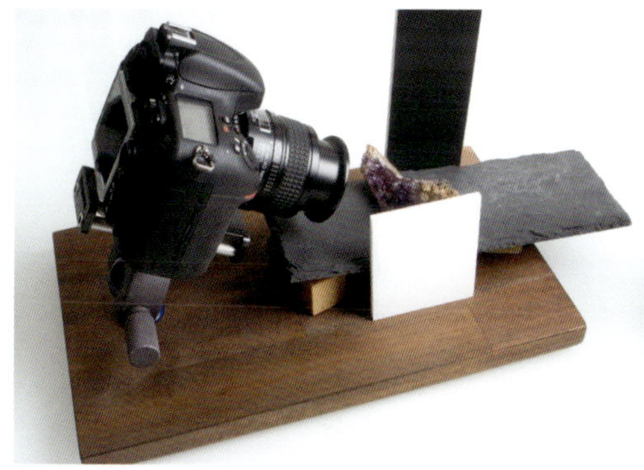

Mounting your entire shooting configuration on a stable piece of wood is an effective way to prevent your camera from colliding with your subject. In this setup, the camera is attached to a ball head mount equipped with a focusing rail. Small pieces of black and white cardboard serve to absorb and reflect light, respectively.

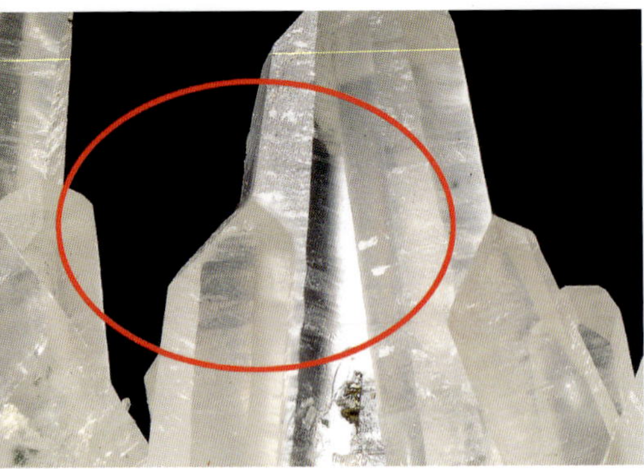

Subjects with elements that are too similar sometimes cause rendering mishaps that have to be manually retouched later.

magnified to multiple times the original subject size, you'll need precise control down to tenths of a millimeter.

As much as we all love modern technology, keep in mind that a successful image depends mostly on effective lighting, a thoughtful camera perspective, and a fitting background. If these fundamental elements aren't in accord, technology won't help you produce a stunning image. So take as much time as you need to configure your shooting setup and to design the lighting. Another practice worth following is to avoid framing your subject too tightly; work with a good 10-percent buffer when creating your component images, and then crop to your desired format after you've stacked the images.

Stacking

There are various applications available for actually stacking your component images. They vary in what they do and how they work, but fortunately they all offer demo versions or are available as freeware, so spend some time testing the different options out with your own images before settling on your favorite.

Photomerge | The simplest option is to use the Photomerge feature integrated into Photoshop and Photoshop Elements. The end results are perfectly adequate for personal use, but they do require a bit more post-processing. *www.adobe.com/de*

Helicon Focus | Although not free, Helicon Focus is a professional-grade solution that produces excellent results. The developer offers a 30-day, fully functional free trial on its website, so you can test it out before committing. Among other functions, Helicon Focus offers 16-bit support and can process RAW files. *www.heliconsoft.com*

Zerene Stacker | This program also requires purchase and can run on Mac OS X, Windows, and Linux platforms. Its developer also offers a 30-day demo version. *www.zerenesystems.com*

Combine Z | A freeware solution, Combine Z runs only on Windows Vista and Windows XP. *www.hadleyweb.pwb.blueyonder.co.uk*

MacroFusion | MacroFusion is an open-source program that runs on Linux. *www.macrofusion.sf.net*

Enfuse | Another open-source option, Enfuse is compatible with Mac OS X, Windows, and Linux. *www.enblend.sourceforge.net*

All of these programs come with minimum requirements for your computer's processing power if you want to obtain results with any sort of promptness. These requirements stem from the need to process large amounts of data. With 40 or more high-resolution images, the bytes add up quickly.

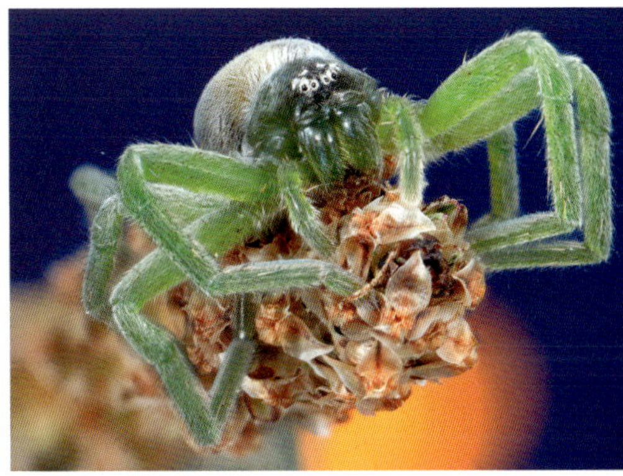

Green huntsman spider
Photo: H. Ch. Steeg

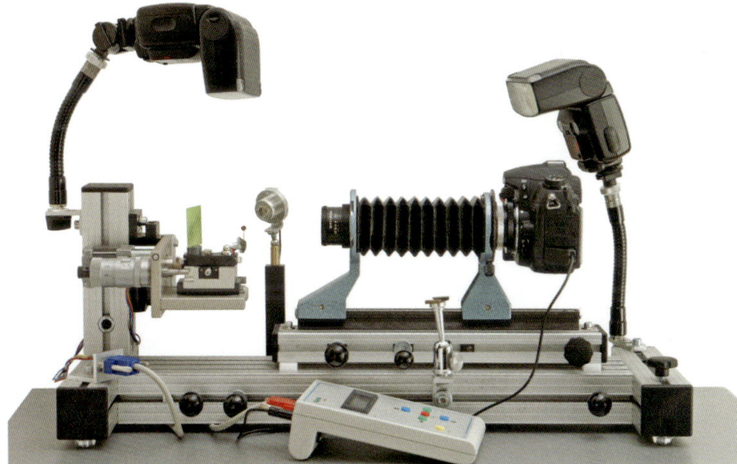

Regulated by a microcontroller, this stepper motor–based system is capable of producing automatic exposure sequences and permits photographers to go well beyond the 1:1 barrier
Photo: H. Ch. Steeg

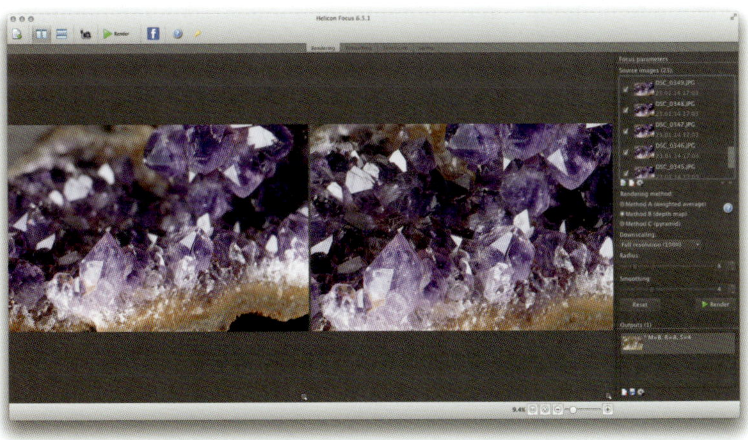

Helicon Focus is a professional stacking application that offers significantly more control variables than Photoshop's Photomerge feature

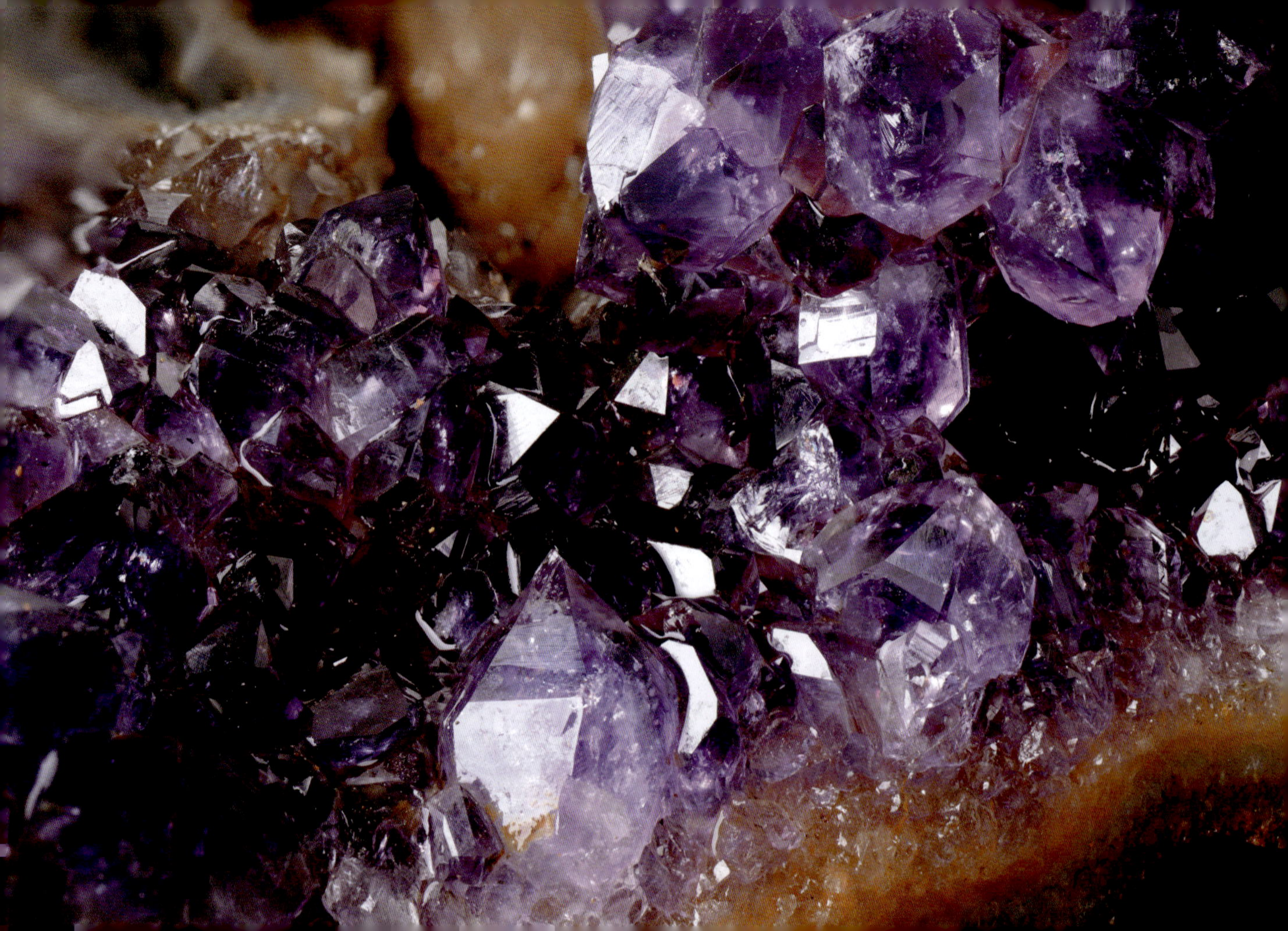

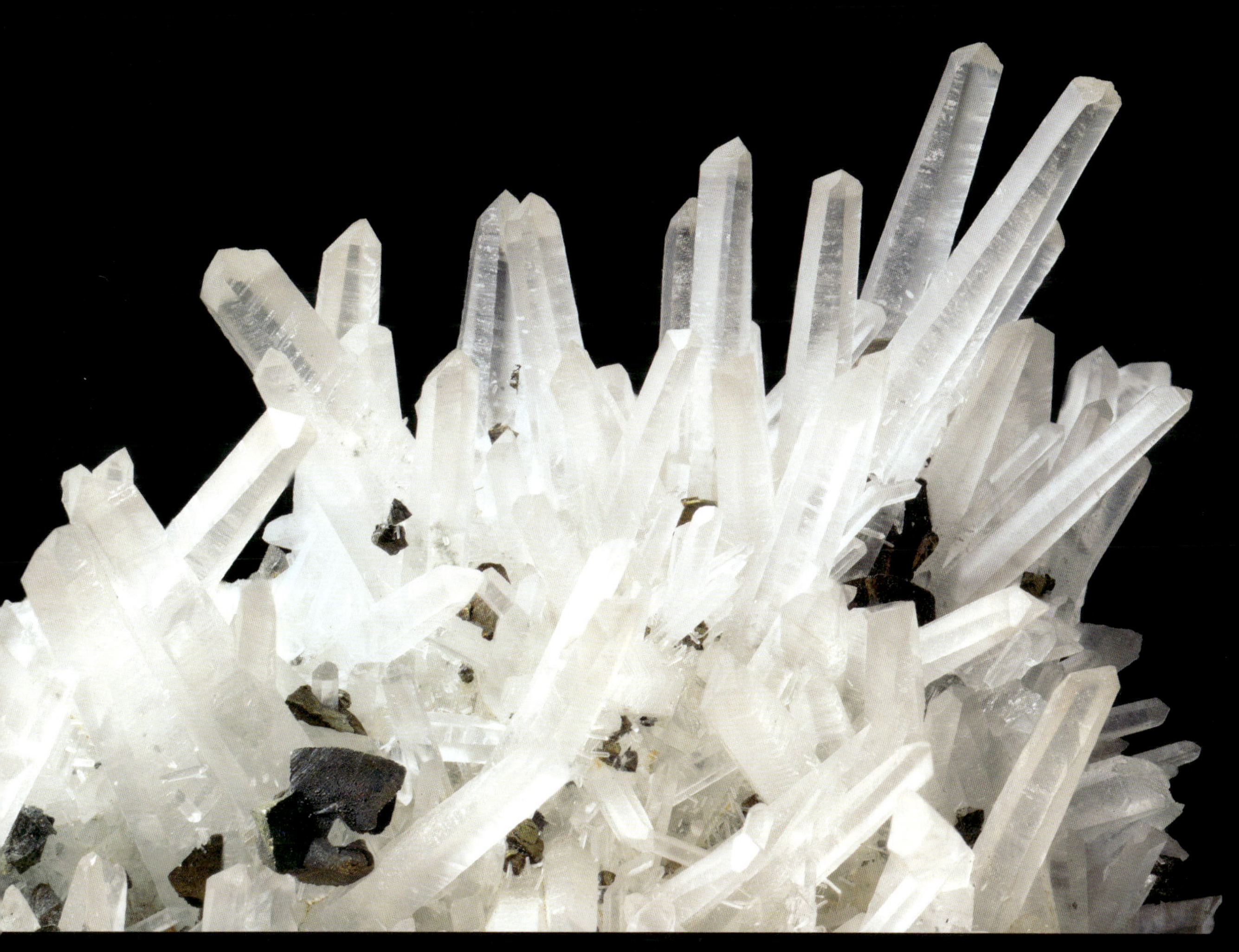

Rock crystal and pyrite
29 images stacked in Helicon Focus
Studio flash unit with a 70cm beautydish and
honeycomb filter

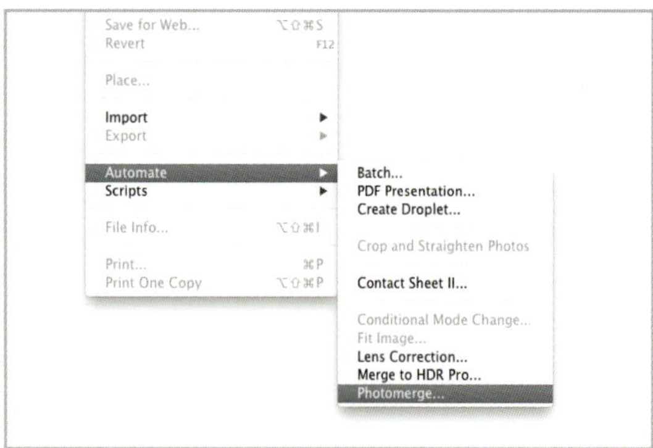

Step 1: Start the stacking process in Photoshop by navigating to File > Automate > Photomerge

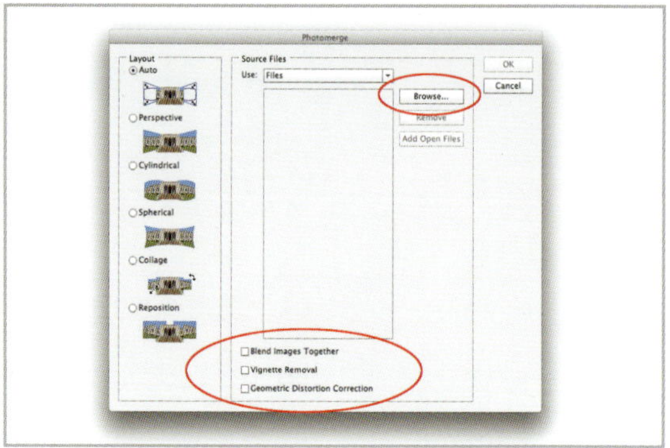

Step 2: Deselect all of the checkboxes, and click the Browse button

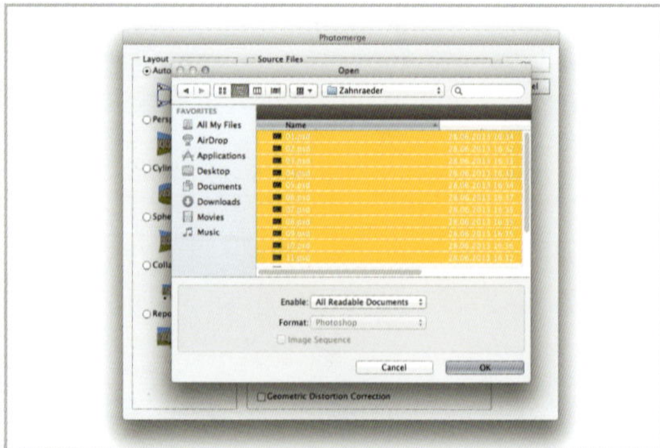

Step 3: The window that pops up lets you select the images that you want to stack. You can also select an entire folder

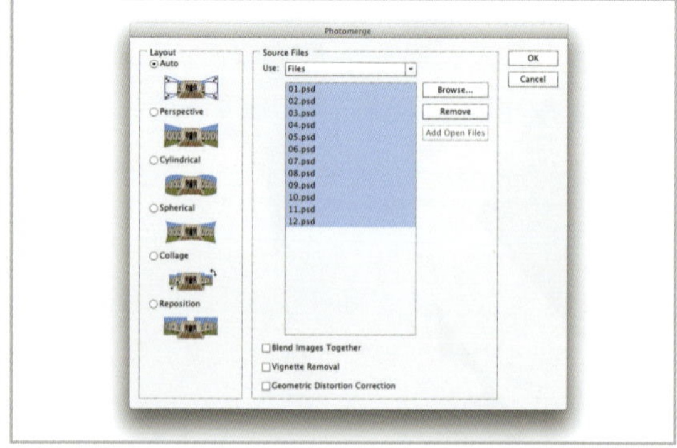

Step 4: Your selected files will now appear in the Photomerge window. Reselect the images that you want to process again, and confirm your selection by clicking the OK button.

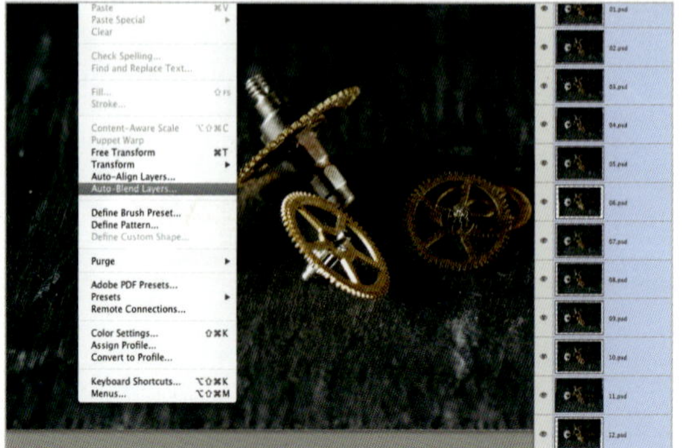

Step 5: The component images will now be aligned with one another and will appear as layers in the layers palette. Now select Edit > Auto-Blend Layers.

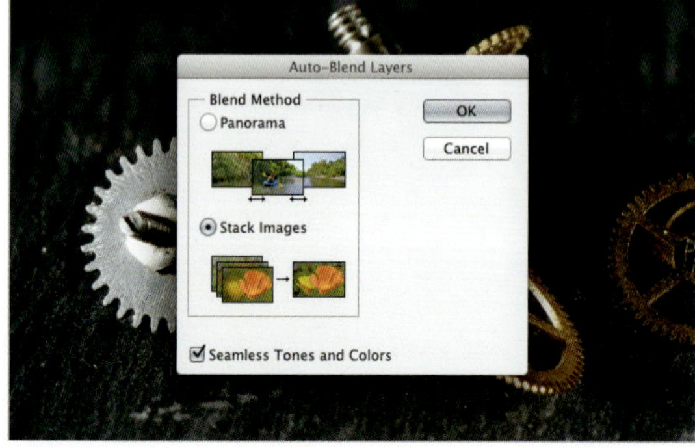

Step 6: Make sure Stacked Images is selected in the next window. And now all of the layers selected in the layers palette will be blended together using layer masks.

Focus Stacking in Photoshop

The Photomerge feature available in Photoshop (starting with version CS4) and Photoshop Elements is a good starting place for anyone interested in learning how to use focus stacking for the first time. This application is not as powerful as Helicon Focus or other specialized stacking applications and the results often require some manual editing, but it is relatively simple to execute; see the step-by-step instructions to follow.

The sharp regions of your component images should ideally overlap as much as possible, because Photomerge automatically aligns—or more often superimposes—them automatically during the initial processing step. But rendering errors are impossible to avoid completely, especially with regular patterns with high contrast, such as the gears, or with glare from reflective surfaces. You can usually edit these errors out with a bit of retouching after you complete the photos you want stacked.

If you discover that you're excited by what you can accomplish with Photomerge, you will likely want to graduate to a full-blown focus-stacking application relatively quickly.

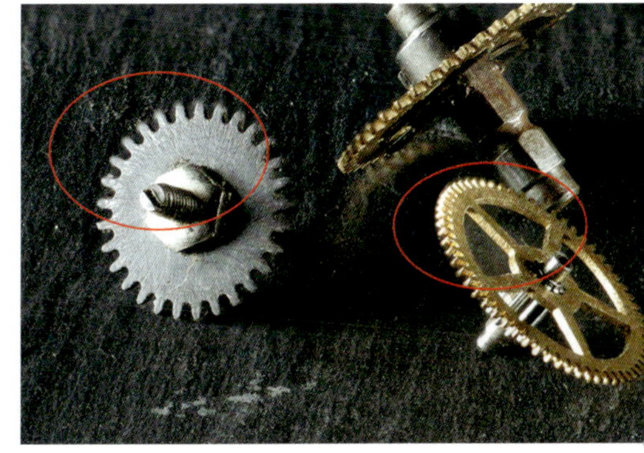

Last but not least, retouching is often necessary to correct rendering errors.

16 component images were sufficient to compile a photo that was sharp from the foreground to just beyond the farthest gear

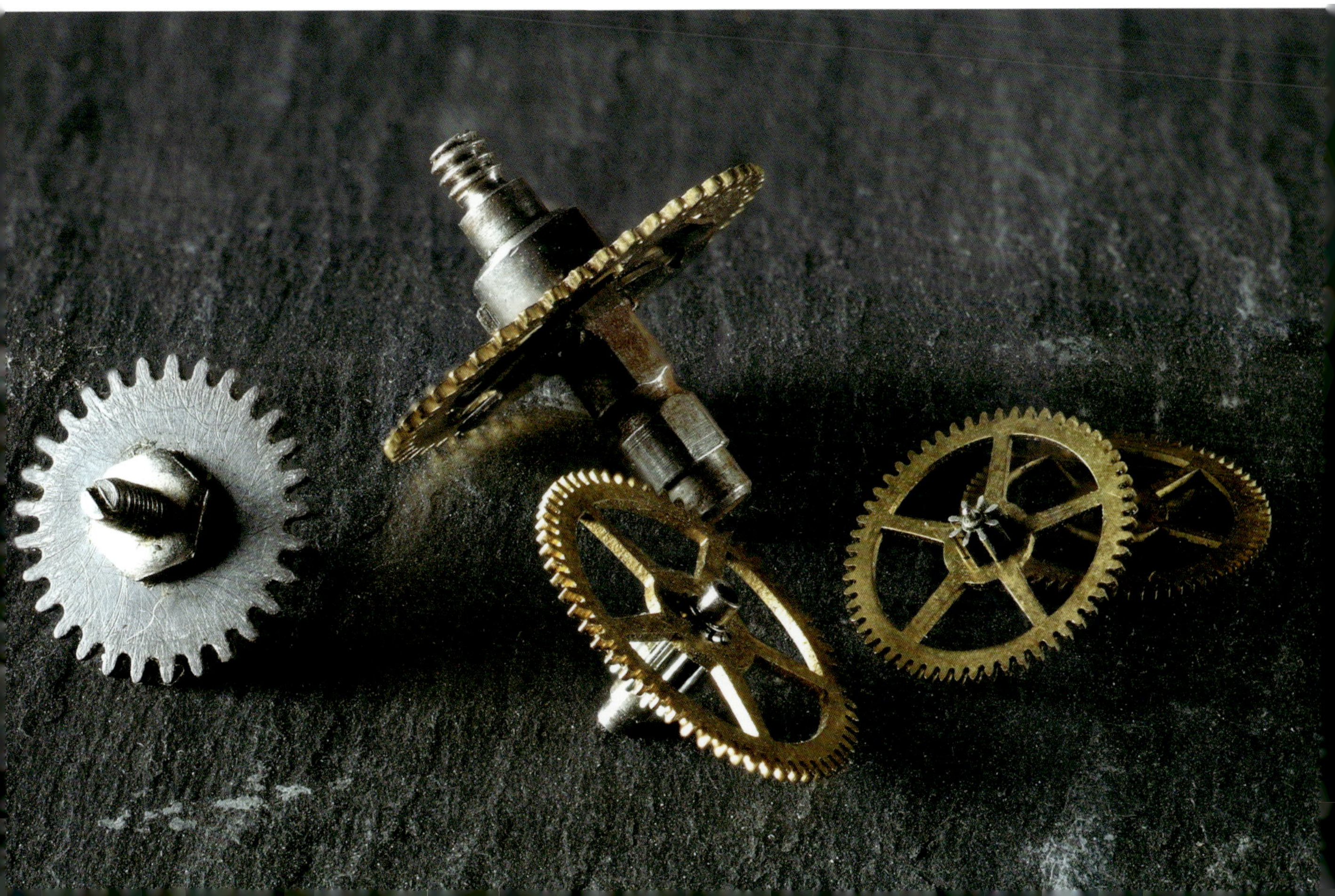

Light Painting

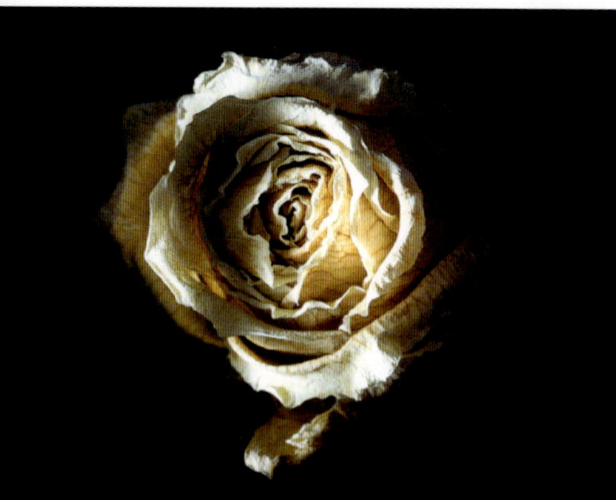

You can even paint miniature subjects, such as this dried rose, with light by using a sufficiently focused beam of light. You'll need a dark room, a narrow aperture, and a slow shutter speed.
f/25, 15 s, ISO 100, 60mm

Painting with light is a diverse technique that can be put to interesting use with macro photographs. For light, you'll need a flashlight with either a traditional incandescent bulb or an LED bulb. You'll also need to winnow the cone of light emitted from these devices into an even more focused area to work with your tiny subjects. Options for focusing the light include various light guides designed specifically for this purpose as well as jury-rigging a similar light funnel out of a hollow aluminum rod (a narrow black straw will also do the job).

A brighter source of light is not necessarily the better choice when you wish to use this method. Brightness is better controlled by elongating the exposure window and "painting" over specific areas more thoroughly. The longer the exposure window, the more time you'll have to paint your masterpiece. A dark room is a necessary prerequisite for this technique because it demands the use of slow shutter speeds.

Simulating the appearance of having used multiple sources of light is no problem, even if you have only one flashlight at your disposal. You'll just need to turn the flashlight off and on accordingly to create your desired lighting effect. Using transluscent, colored sheets as filters for the flashlight provides even more creative opportunities: you can have a full palette of colors at your disposal.

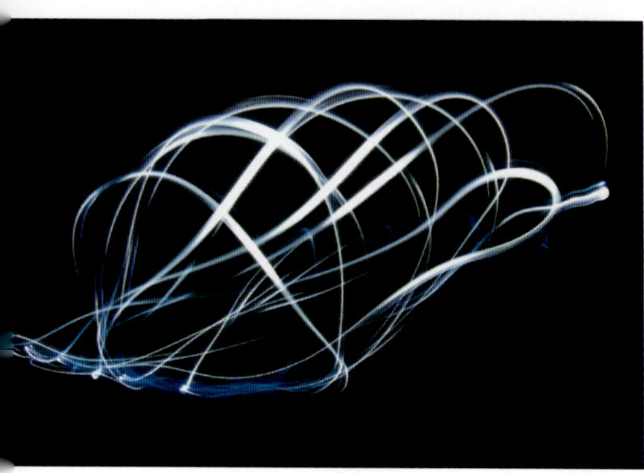

Light painting also readily yields abstract subjects. A single LED lamp dangled from a string over the lens for this image.
f/22, 20 s, ISO 100, 24mm

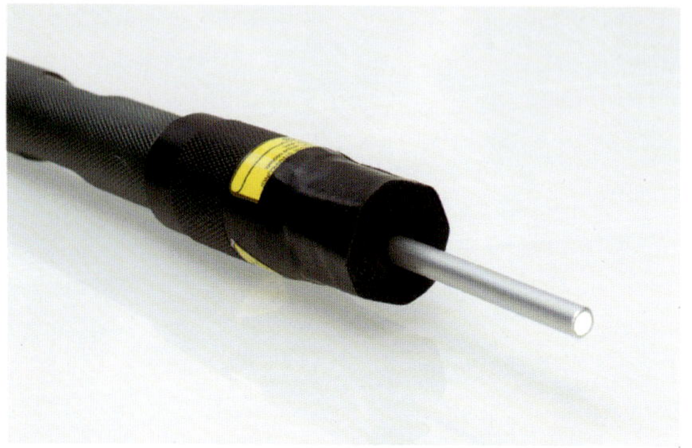

An aluminum straw, a bit of foam rubber, and some adhesive tape are all it takes to significantly focus the beam of light from a flashlight

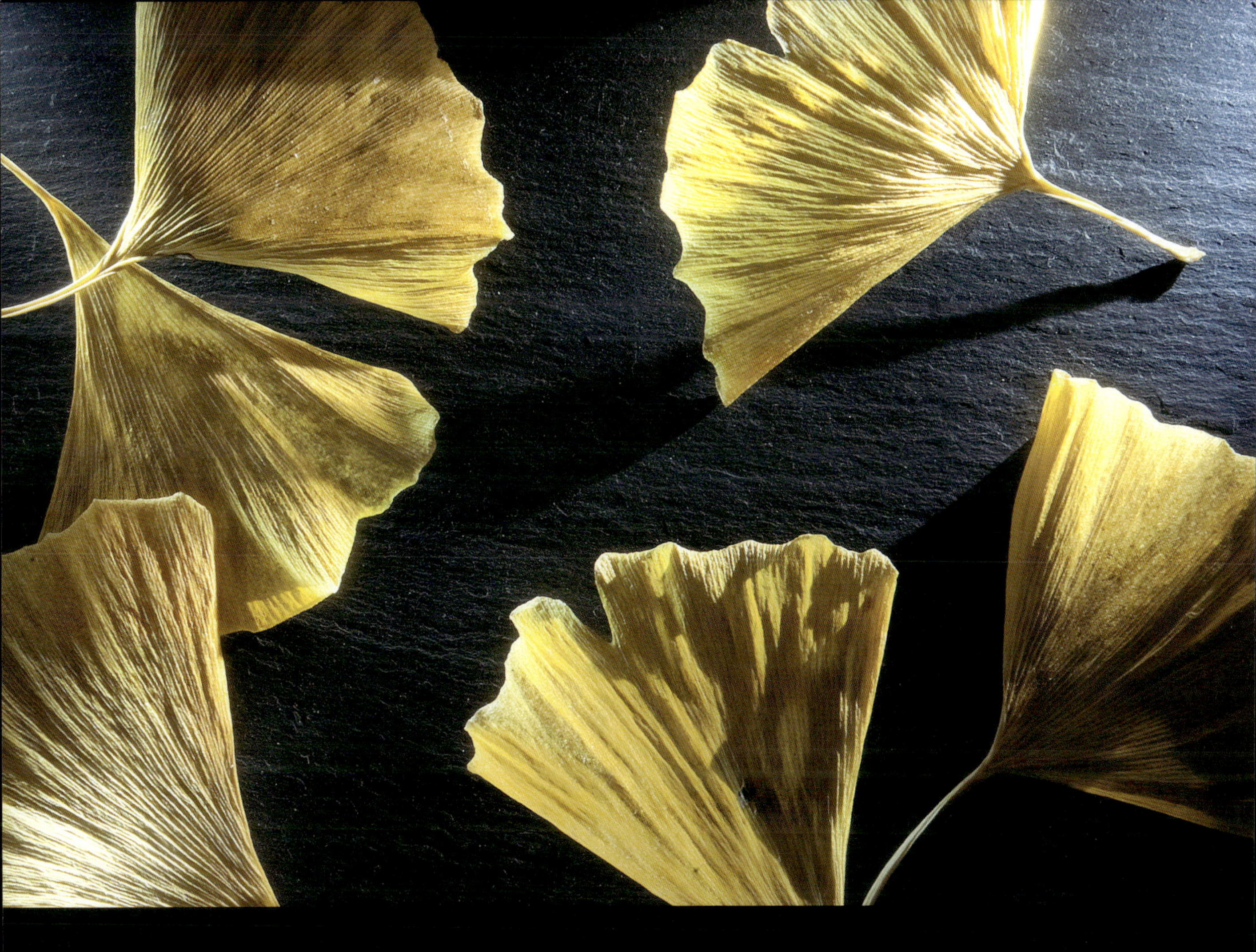

Dried ginkgo leaves. You can create interesting lighting effects even with only one small LED light on hand. The entire scene here was further brightened with a system flash and a softbox.
f/22, 10 s, ISO 100, 70mm

Interval Shooting, Time-Lapse, and Stop-Motion

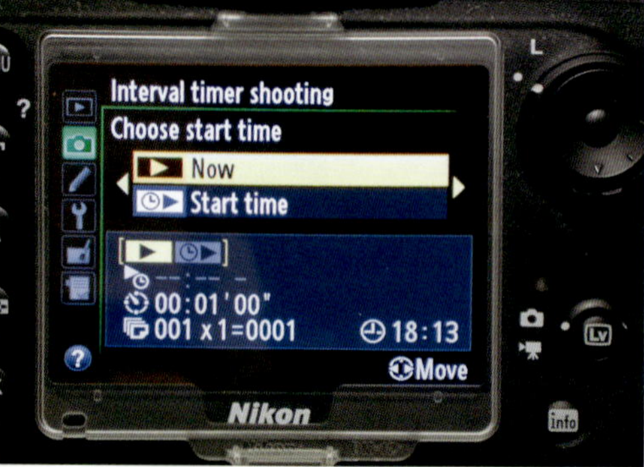

Many cameras feature integrated interval shooting modes, where you can program the starting time, the number of exposures to collect, and the overall duration of the shoot.

Documenting how specific natural elements change over time is a fascinating exercise. The resulting images can be presented as a series of stills or produced into a small motion picture.

Interval Shooting

Shooting consistent images of the same subject at regular intervals of time yields photos that individually freeze specific moments in place but that collectively reveal the continuous development of nature. The period for such an exercise can be relatively short (to capture the blossoming of a flower, for example) or relatively long (to reveal the changing autumn colors or the growth of a plant). This method concisely and concretely displays natural changes to viewers that occur too slowly to be observed in person.

Some cameras feature integrated interval-shooting modes, which makes this process much easier. There are also remote shutter release systems that offer this function. You can also create the individual images manually. If you are relying on the camera to capture the images independently, you will need to leave it turned on for the duration of the project, so make sure it's hooked up to a power source.

In some cases, you may not want to leave your camera set up on location during the intervals between exposures. Setting up an old tripod with a quick-release plate in your desired shooting location is one option for getting around this problem. Leave the tripod, but take your camera between shots.

Even though a compact or bridge camera often produces decent results for standard close-up pictures, DSLRs are practically indispensable when working in the macro range, especially over long periods of time. You need to be able to control the focus range and the focal length precisely to obtain good results. But above all else, don't change your shooting settings if you end up turning your camera off in between shots. In fact, it's advisable to use a bit of tape to fix your zoom and focus rings in place to avoid inadvertent shifts.

Time-Lapse Recordings

The images obtained through interval shooting techniques can be edited into a time-lapse video using the appropriate software. A frame rate of around 24 images per second is required to produce a

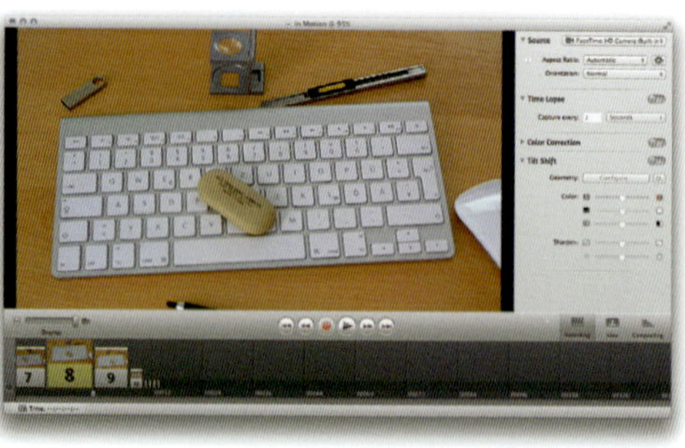

Stop-motion applications such as iStopMotion enable you to produce complete films out of individual still images and to export them in common video formats. You might document the self-propelled journey of pens and other writing utensils across your desk, for example.

smooth, even playback. For a film lasting one minute, that requirement means you would need 60 x 24 component images, or a total of 1,440 pictures. By the same logic, if you were to take one picture of the same plant every day for a year, you'd end up with 365 pictures that could produce a film lasting around 15 seconds.

Stop-Motion

Stop-motion is yet another technique for animating a series of individual still images. In this method, the subject is altered in a small way between each exposure. You might advance a figure by a millimeter or two, for example. After the component images are edited together in an animation application such as iStopMotion, you end up with a short film sequence, in which the figure appears to move by itself across the scene. A bit of practice is needed to get a feel for how many intermediate exposures you need to get your desired playback appearance, so start with brief clips and relatively simple subjects. It's critical to keep your camera position identical from one shot to the next and to use the same lighting. You also will want to use a remote shutter release to keep camera shake at bay. Even relatively modest cameras on today's market far surpass the technical specifications needed to produce HD quality video playback, which means that producing stop-motion films is a great opportunity to dust off an old 3- or 4-megapixel camera hiding in the closet. iStopMotion (*www.boinx.com*) is a popular stop-motion program for Mac OS X; and AnimatorDV (*www.animatordv.com*) is an option for Windows.

Flipbooks

The simplest way of joining individual images into an animation is to create a flipbook. Several providers now offer programs for doing this.

Applications

The uses for time-lapse and stop-motion videos are vast and varied. You might use them to animate a logo composed of individual flower petals. You might also want to post do-it-yourself project instructions or progress videos to your personal website or to YouTube. There's a whole subculture of amateur videographers who create scenes using Lego figures as characters. You can have fun exploring this medium because many of the applications needed to produce video clips are relatively inexpensive or available as freeware.

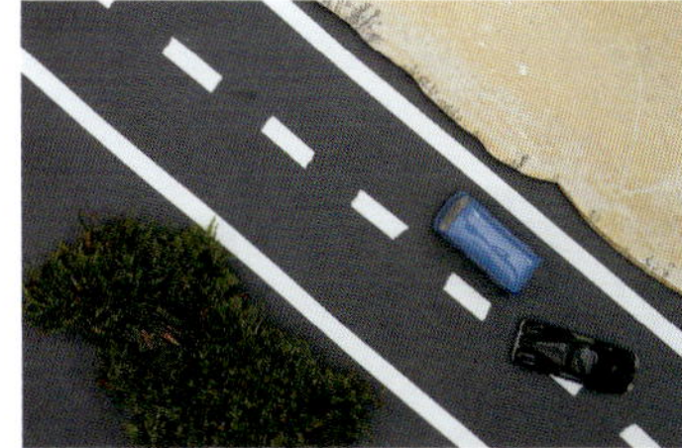
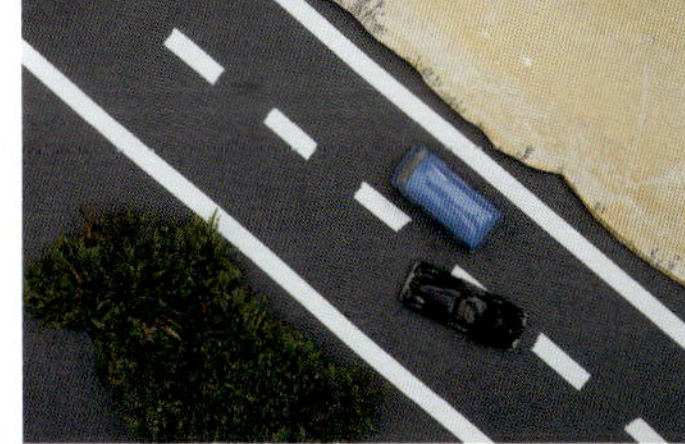
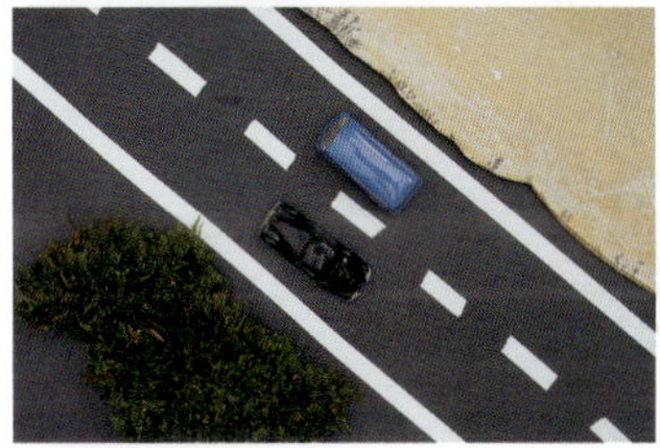
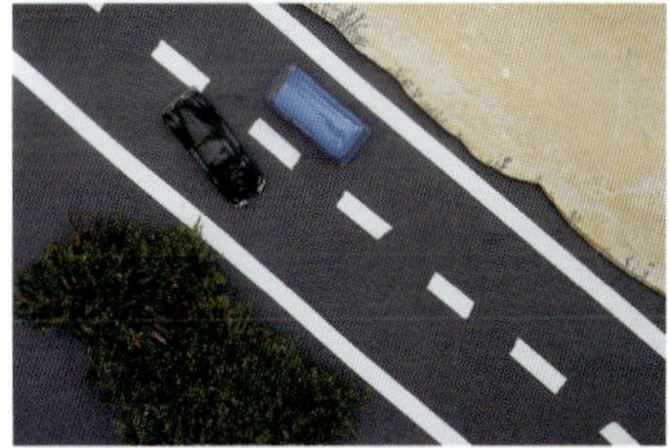
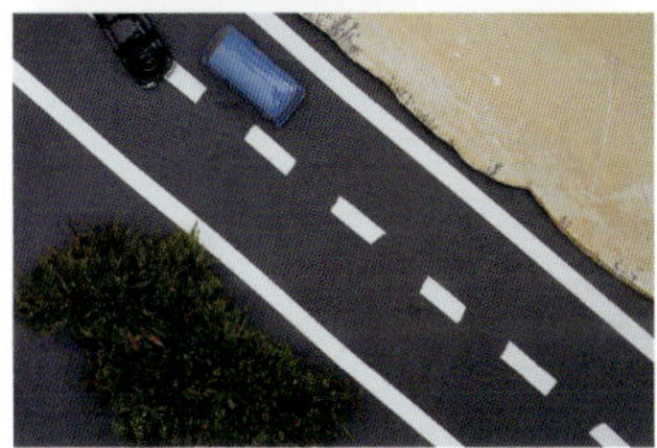

Passing maneuver: small stop-motion animations are relatively easy to produce. Simply move your subjects slightly for each new exposure. Model cars and Lego figures are fun subjects for getting started with this technique.

High-Speed Photography

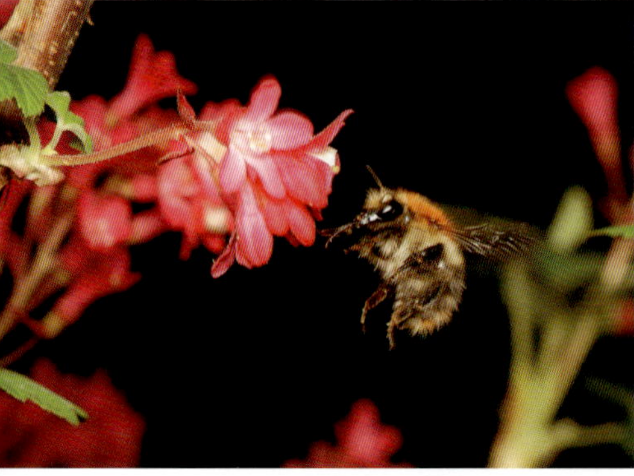

Photographing insects in flight without using special equipment requires a bit of luck. The moments of an insect's final approach to land on a flower or leaf are good opportunities for success.
f/9.5, 1/60 s, ISO 200, 105mm, system flash with small attachment softbox

Nature features not only countless subjects that are too small for the human eye to perceive well, but also subjects that move so quickly that we cannot take them in without the assistance of technology. Flying and jumping insects are prime examples.

Equipment

High-speed photography requires the use of one or more flash units because the quick movements that this type of photography aims to capture are frozen not by the shutter's speed, but by the ultrafast pulse of light from the flash. Depending on the output settings, a flash's duration may be 1/12,000 s or shorter, which is more than sufficient for most high-speed exposures. System flash units are ideal for this because of their compact size, but it's important that their output is capable of being controlled manually.

When photographing objects that are not particularly fast, such as a bee that has landed on a flower or a bug that is just about to take off, it's generally possible to release the shutter by hand with a good degree of success. For quicker subjects—insects in flight, for example—a photoelectric triggering sensor, or light barrier, is for all intents and purposes a requirement.

Insects in Flight

Mounting your camera, flash, and light barrier to a single structure enables you to prepare for capturing images of flying insects by predetermining your image frame and the focus. Although building this configuration is the first step toward creating high-speed images of flying critters, you'll also have to rely on luck when shooting, because the composition of your photographs is largely out of your hands. To have greater control over how flying insects appear in your images requires significantly more preparation. Tighter image frames require higher standards for precision and reaction time.

Drops and Other Falling Objects

Capturing the mesmerizing and fleeting formations of liquids that occur when drops or other objects fall into them is one of the most common subjects for high-speed photography. With a bit of luck and practice you can photograph simple setups of this kind without using a light barrier (see the following pages). But more complex setups,

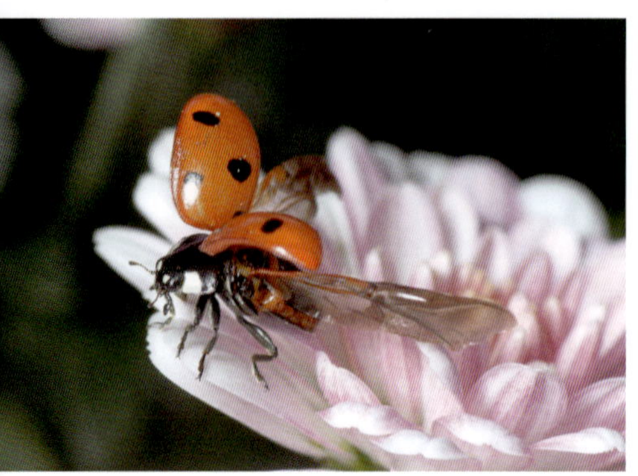

Remote flashes make it possible to freeze even quick movements in place
f/8, 1/125 s, ISO 200, 90mm

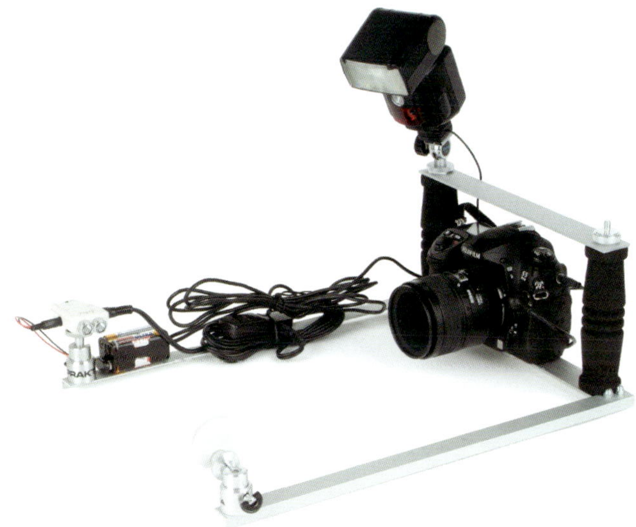

A simple light barrier system mounted to a fitting frame makes it possible to capture fascinating images of flying insects

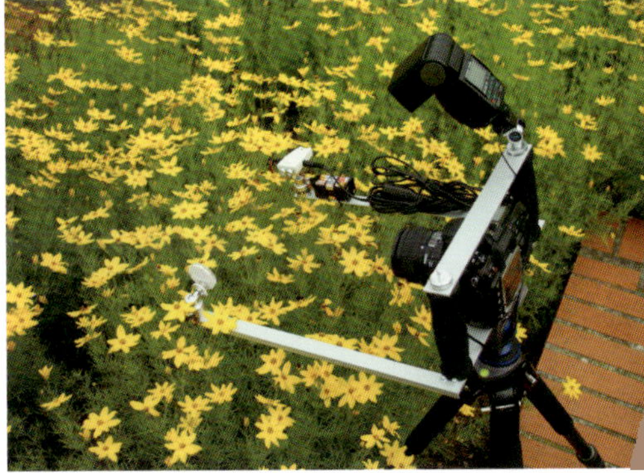

To increase your yield of successful images, mount the frame supporting your light barrier to a tripod and position the entire contraption in a flower garden

such as drops falling on drops, require not only a light barrier, but also a system that allows you to control the size of a drop as well as the exact time and height of its release. If your objective is to capture more straightforward subjects, however, such as a piece of fruit dropping into a glass of water, then small light barriers, such as the Jokie[2] from Eltima, are all it takes. (*www.eltima-electronic.de*)

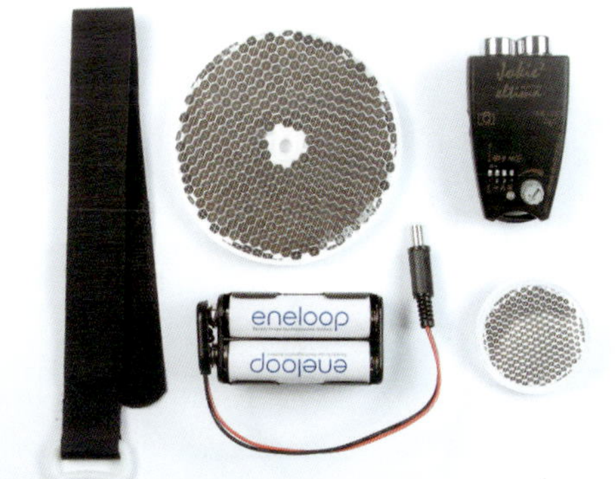

The Jokie[2] from Eltima is a compact, entry-level light barrier system that produces excellent results
Photo: Eltima

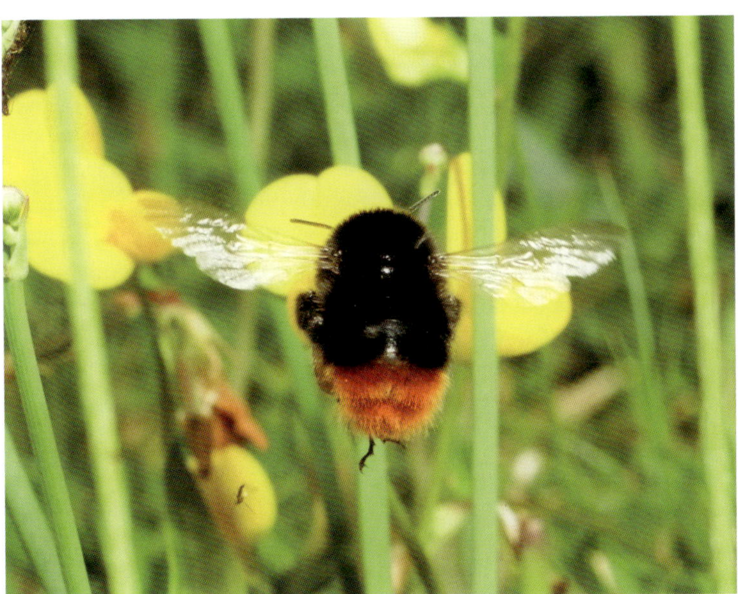

When an insect trips the light barrier, the camera and flash fire automatically. If the insect is moving too quickly, however, it can easily escape the depth of field, so not every shot is a winner.

High-Speed Studio Photography without Light Barriers

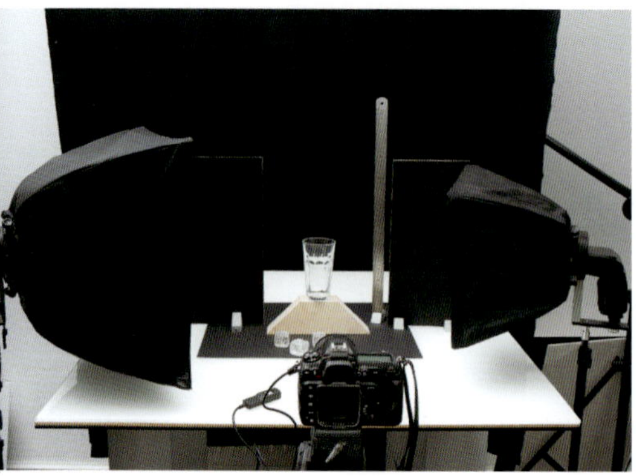

The shooting configuration for photographing an ice cube falling into a glass of water. The most important thing is to use system flash heads, which have the extremely brief pulse durations necessary for freezing movements in place.

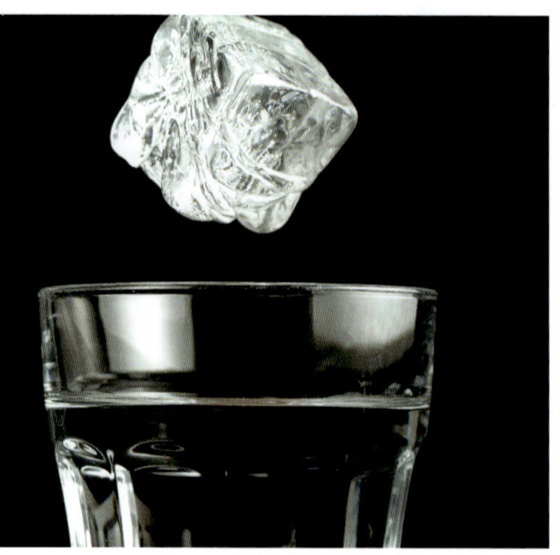

A bit early. The ice cube didn't have time to strike the surface of the water. I altered the height from which I dropped it for the next attempt.

Light barriers are not the only way to freeze fleeting motions in place photographically. But pursuing alternate methods requires a greater reliance on luck, and it is effectively impossible to replicate your results. In the following paragraphs, I explain the steps of this method using the example of an ice cube dropping into a glass of water.

Preparations

High-speed photo shoots require lots of preparation—there's no way around it. This particular project requires the collection of a variety of items to have on hand before starting to photograph anything: an ice cube made from acrylic glass, a water glass, a pitcher of water for refilling, a bucket and cloth, paper towels for cleaning up water spots, a replacement glass in the event that the first one took a tumble and broke, and a ruler with a holding device to standardize the height at which the ice cube was dropped.

For photographic equipment, you will need two system flash units with softboxes (around 30cm x 30cm), pieces of black cardboard for shielding the light from the flashes, a shooting table, and, of course, a camera and a tripod. Using a pane of glass with the necessary mounts is also advisable to protect your camera from having water splashed on it.

The Setup

The setup for this shot is effectively identical to the configuration for producing a classic black background. Use a black, absorptive fabric for the backdrop that is sufficiently far away from the subject so it won't receive light from the flash. Use two pieces of black cardboard to further shield the light from the flashes. The flash units themselves should be set at the same height as the glass of water and directed toward the subject at about a 35° angle. Take a few dry test shots to fine-tune the ideal angle for the lighting. Shooting should be done in manual mode.

With an aperture of f/9.5, the entire glass was in focus from front to back. You will want to use the max flash sync speed, which for my example was 1/125 s. When you get all of the reflections of light off the glass to look how you want them to by tweaking the angle of the flash heads, you are ready to get started with the actual photography.

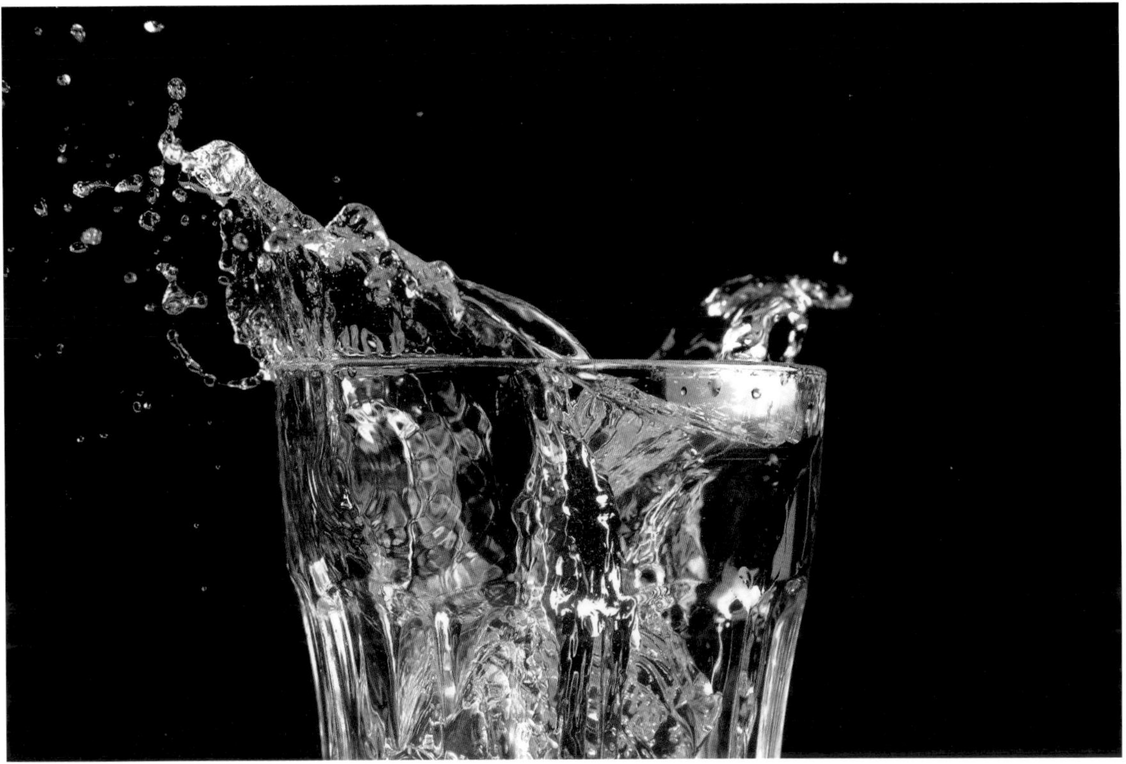

Bull's eye! The ice cube landed in the glass and created an attractive wave that stayed within the depth of field f/9.5, 1/125 s, ISO 200, 60mm, two system flash units with small soft-boxes

And Launch!

Now you can pour water into the glass and get started with the first drop. The ruler positioned near the glass serves as a reference for the drop height of your ice cube or other object.

Because we're not using a light barrier, the trick, of course, is to release the shutter manually using a remote trigger system right as the object lands in the glass. A premature exposure can be corrected either by lowering the drop height for your next attempt or delaying the moment at which you release the shutter. After a few attempts you'll get the hang of it. If the moving elements in your images are still showing some blur, you can reduce the power output for the flash units to make the duration of their pulse even shorter. Doing so will also require that you widen the aperture a bit or increase the ISO speed to compensate for the diminished lighting.

Each exposure that is timed correctly will look different, owing to the highly variable and unpredictable spray pattern of the water. In most cases, an ideal splash is one that sprays laterally and remains within the depth of field so the droplets stay sharp. Even photographers who use a light barrier are powerless to influence the way the water appears at the critical moment.

High Dynamic Range—HDR

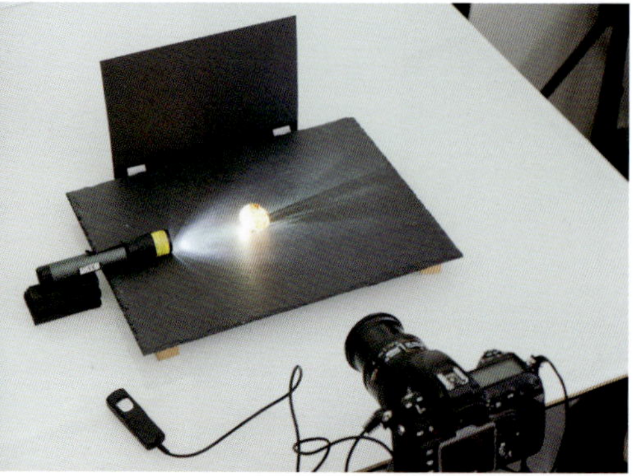

The light from the LED flashlight is intensely directed at the subject, but it's so bright that the highlights get blown out resulting in a loss of image detail

High-quality digital cameras are generally capable of capturing a dynamic range of around 8 to 10 exposure values, which is usually sufficient for normal pictures shot with relatively soft light. But it is a recurrent problem that a subject's dynamic range surpasses what a camera is able to capture in a single exposure. When shooting in direct sunlight, for example, images will contain both dark shadows and very bright areas, and photographers often have to live with compromises. Bright artificial lighting can also produce the same problematic situations.

One possible way of dealing with this problem is combining multiple exposures—each exhibiting a different dynamic range—into a single, composite image. If you're photographing a moving subject, then you won't be able to create a series of images shot at different shutter speeds to create an HDR image. But you can start with one RAW file to develop a few identical images with shifted exposures.

The example picture used to illustrate this process features a Chinese lantern flower (*Physalis*), which lacks the gift of mobility, so I accordingly decided to shoot a series of images with slightly different exposure settings. One reason for this decision is that Photoshop is capable of compositing HDR pictures from RAW files.

The problem with the *Physalis* in our example stems from trying to create an attractive reflection of light on the nearly black surface material. The intensity of light required to achieve this pattern of light grossly overexposes the edges of the subject nearest to the light source (an LED flashlight). Exposing the brightest areas of the lantern blossom properly causes the shadows to lose all their detail. Settling for a compromise and basing the exposure on a midtone results in both clipped shadows and blown-out highlights. Neither one of these options was acceptable, so I decided to capture four images at different exposure levels and then combined them into a single HDR photo.

Component Images

A sturdy tripod and a remote trigger system minimize the risk of inadvertently shifting your camera between each exposure. And a black piece of cardboard positioned behind your subject will create an even, dark background for each shot. Ideally your camera will feature an exposure bracketing mode, so you'll only need to touch

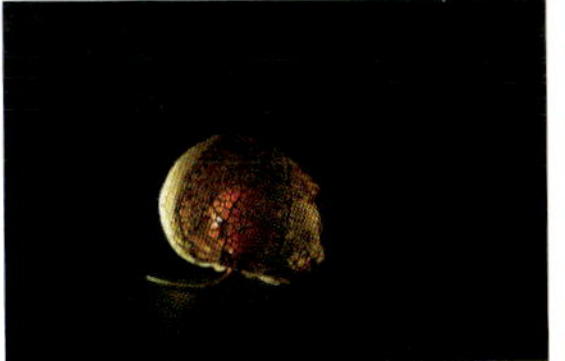 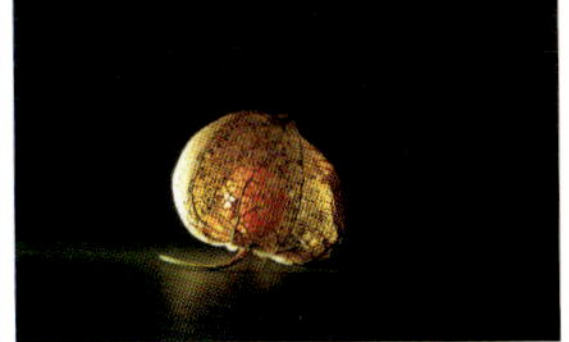 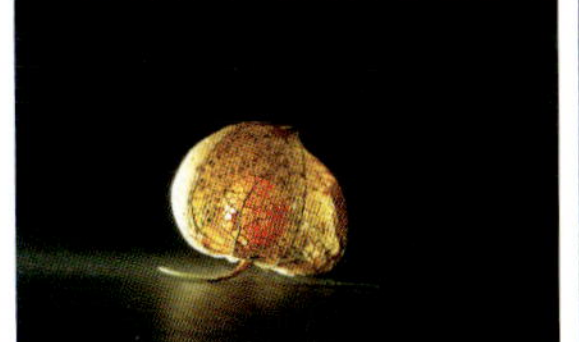 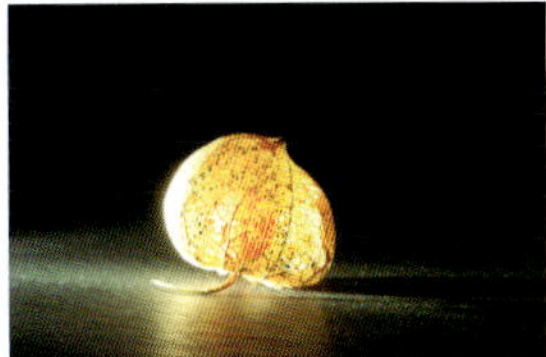

f/14, 1/60 s, ISO 400, 105mm   *f/14, 1/40 s, ISO 400, 105mm*   *f/14, 1/15 s, ISO 400, 105mm*   *f/14, 1/6 s, ISO 400, 105mm*

your camera one time. Having to touch your camera between each exposure dramatically increases the likelihood of altering the lens's perspective.

Compiling

When it's time to merge your component images into one, open Photoshop and navigate to *File > Automate > Merge to HDR Pro*. Then select the component images or an entire folder that you wish to use in the first window that opens.

After confirming your selection, a new window will open offering a variety of controls and options. At this point, you still have the opportunity to select or deselect individual component images in the film strip to influence the final appearance of your composite.

Select *Remove Ghosts* if you shot your component images manually. And under the Presets menu, select *Photorealistic* to create a result that looks natural and evenly blended throughout. All of the other sliders and settings tend to produce stylized or surreal results.

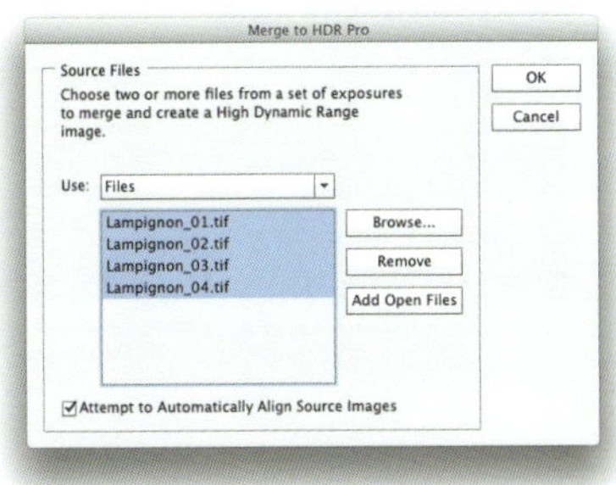

You can select the component images after clicking Merge to HDR Pro

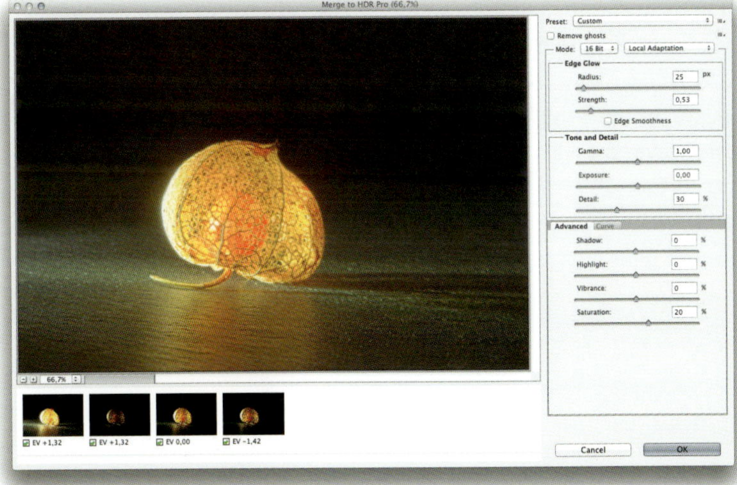

Photoshop's integrated HDR function offers a variety of sliders to influence the appearance of the result, but they are largely geared to produce stylized effects. The default settings offer a good starting point that can be edited later if you're looking only to extend the range of tonal values and nothing else. The Remove Ghosts feature is useful if you have any slight variation in the component images.

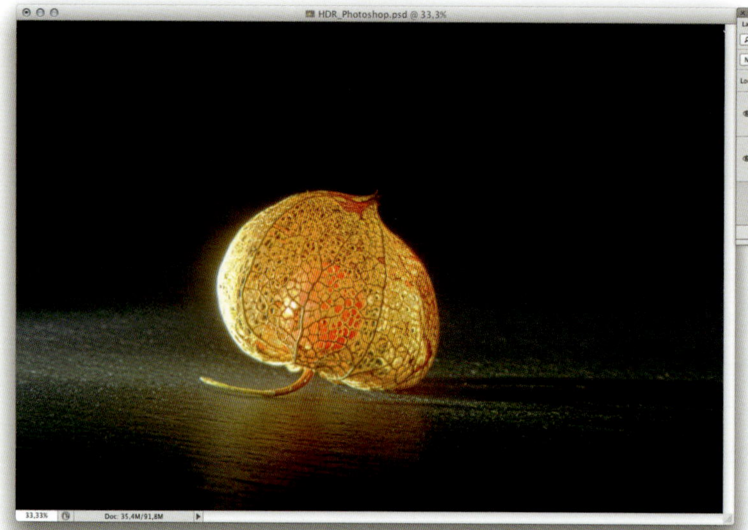

I blended the darkest exposure over the HDR image using a layer mask in an effort to further darken the front edge of the lantern flower

After confirming your settings, Photoshop renders the HDR image and opens it as a new file. At this point in the process, I typically retouch a few rendering artifacts resulting from dust or scratches and the like. The composite image will feature an evenly mapped distribution of tones over the entire tonal range—but no further. Aside from influencing the HDR process through your selection of the component images or via the sliders already mentioned, Photoshop does not offer options for further specifying what areas of which component images to emphasize.

For my image of the lantern flower, I wanted the foreground to be nearly as dark as it appeared in one of the darker component images, but I wanted the areas around the *Physalis* to exhibit the range of contrast from all of the component images. I also wanted some light to illuminate the surface below the blossom's stem.

As a way of fine-tuning the appearance of my HDR image, I added several of the component images as layers to the rendered picture. Using layer masks, it was then simple to create gradients to accentuate certain parts of specific component images to achieve the exact look I wanted.

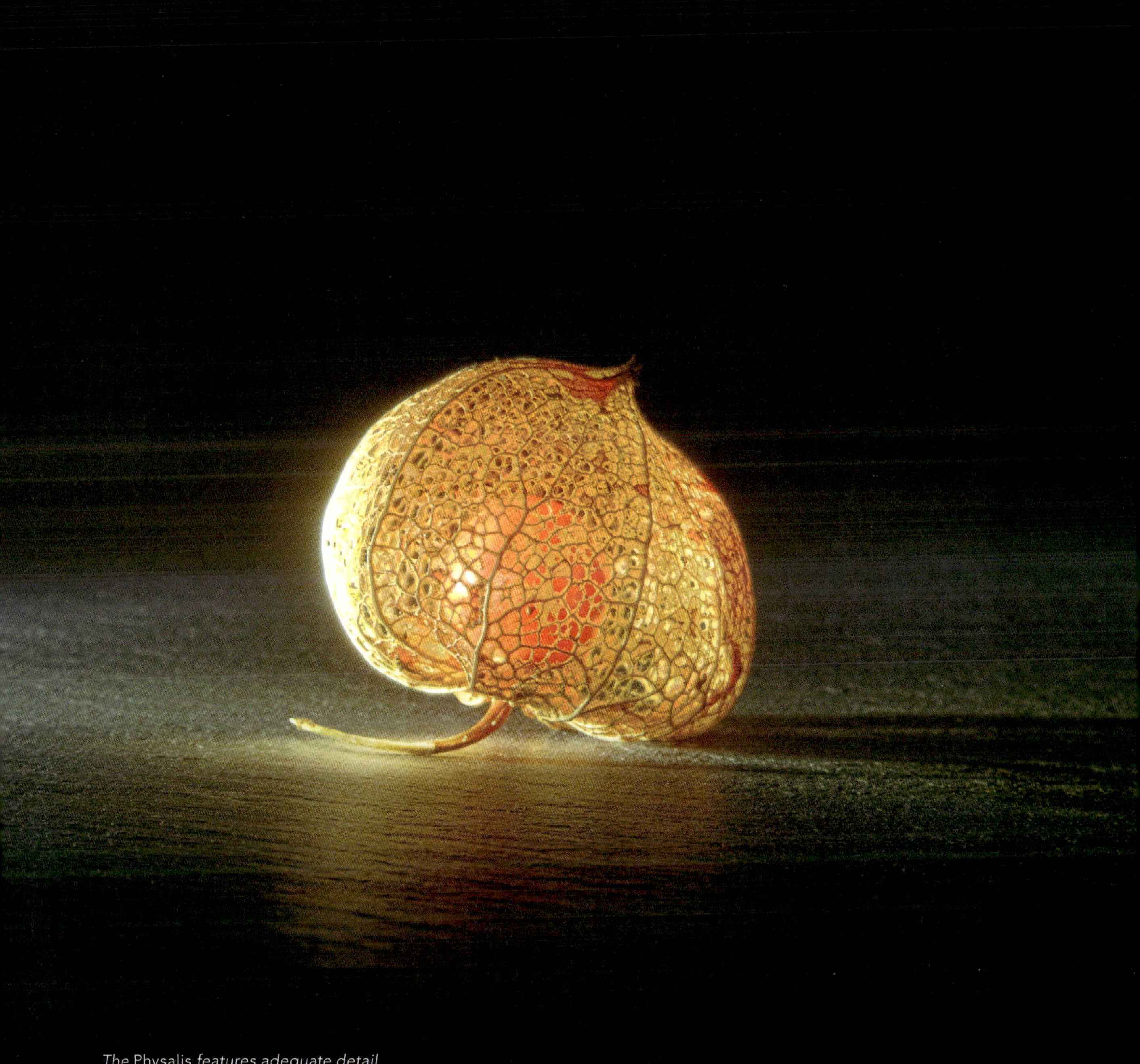

The Physalis features adequate detail
throughout while neither the highlights nor shadows are clipped

Macro Panoramas

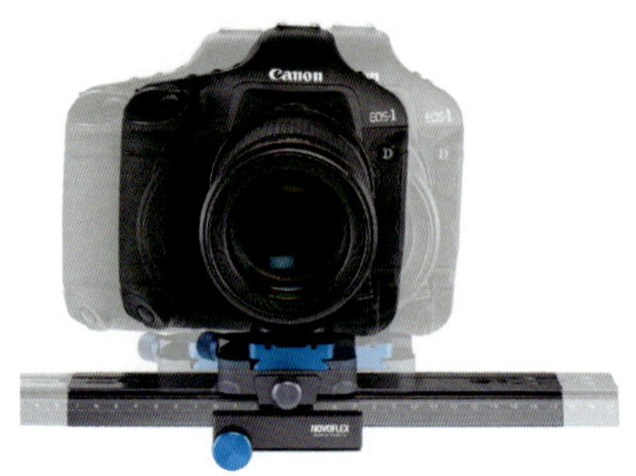

*One-dimension of movement using
a focusing rail
Photo: Novoflex*

Panoramic photos are typically used to capture the sweeping beauty of landscapes and architectural subjects, but there are also instances when it makes sense to combine a few individual macro images to create a high-resolution, larger-than-usual composite image. You might, for example, want to create a zoomable image of plants that allows viewers to explore the tiniest of details, or you may need to prep a large-format image for printing (several square meters). Even if it's possible to capture a subject in a single frame, a multishot approach may be the best option for subjects that are particularly broad or tall.

The process for creating a panoramic image is similar to that of focus stacking, but in this case, rather than shifting the camera's focal plane forward and backward to capture component images, the camera's perspective is shifted horizontally or vertically or rotated around a center point.

Single-Plane Panoramas

Panoramas of relatively simple subjects can be created by mounting a camera to a focusing rail and then shifting it horizontally. Similarly, simple vertical shifts can be created using the height setting of a tripod. These methods are practical when working on location out in the wild.

When in the studio, however, you're better off attaching your camera to a repro stand that allows you to shift the camera forward and backward (y-axis) as well as up and down (z-axis). Also using an additional focusing rail allows you to move the camera left and right (x-axis). This setup makes it possible for you to manipulate your camera precisely to any point in space within the full range of your equipment. Adjust the position of the camera along the z-axis to ensure that it is at the desired distance from the subject, and move it along the x-axis to cover the full breadth of your subject. The camera should stay at the origin along the y-axis, unless you plan to create multiple series of exposures.

Before you're ready to start capturing images, position your camera at the starting position, so the viewfinder image reflects what you want to see for your first image. Then slide the camera through the entire range of movement (along the x-axis) while inspecting to see if the focus is at the right spot throughout and to ensure that the camera's end point is exactly where you want it.

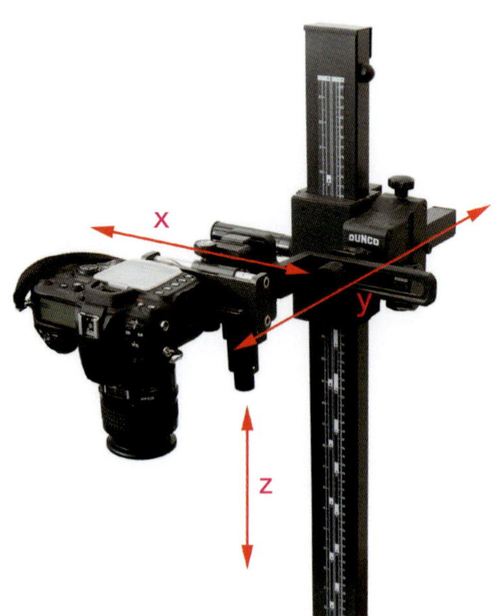

*Three dimensions of movement using
a repro stand in combination with a
focusing rail*

Lighting and Exposure Metering

Even and consistent lighting throughout the entire process of capturing your component images is essential for a decent-looking final panorama. If you're using a system flash unit, position it far enough away from your subject so that the pulse of light has enough room to diffuse. You can alternately use a softbox or a similar device for softening the light accordingly.

Natural lighting introduces some uncontrollable variables into the process, but try to work at a time when the lighting is fairly constant, such as when the sun is hidden behind a solid layer of clouds.

An easy way to manage the exposure settings when creating panoramas is to first shoot an overview image of your entire subject using the aperture-priority mode (A). Once you obtain a satisfactory exposure, switch into manual mode while retaining the identical settings so that they will remain fixed for each individual image you take. If you try to shoot the entire series in aperture priority, the metering process may cause the camera to choose a different shutter speed if a darker element of the subject were to enter the frame, for example.

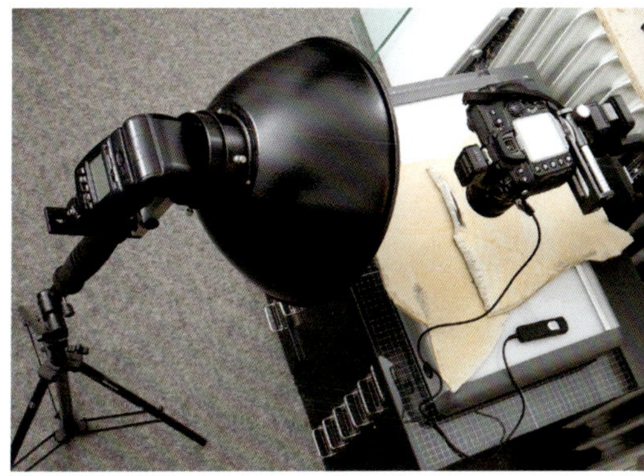

The setup for shooting a panoramic photo of a feather: a repro stand with focusing rail and a system flash unit with a beauty dish attachment

Shooting

Take the first picture and then slide the camera along the focusing rails parallel to the subject. Repeat the process while trying to get 30- to 40-percent overlap from one shot to the next.

Stitching

JPEG or TIFF image files can be processed directly, but RAW files will need to be developed before they can be stitched together. The best way to develop a few RAW files to combine into a panorama is to start with the lightest image of the series and then use the *Previous conversion* option from the general settings menu in Adobe Camera Raw to develop the subsequent photos. Go ahead and save all the developed files in the same folder to make things easier in the next steps.

After you have the source files prepped, open Photoshop and navigate to *File > Automate > Photomerge* to bring up the relevant window. From here, select the *Collage* and *Blend images together* options, and choose the images you'd like to use. After a few moments you will have the panorama prepared as a PSD file with layers and layer masks, ready for any final corrections or edits you think are necessary.

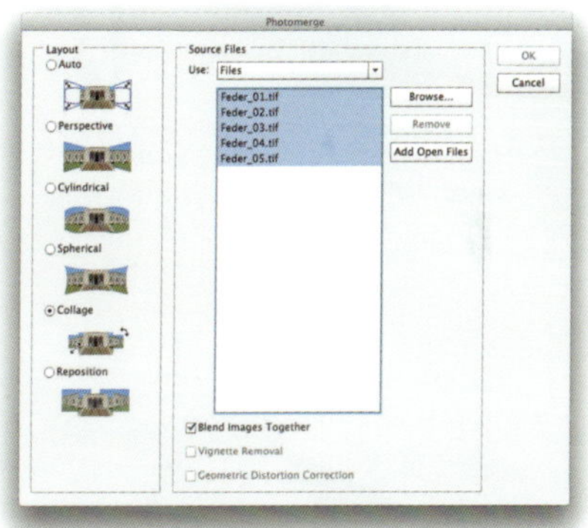

In the Photomerge window, select Col- lage *and* Blend images together

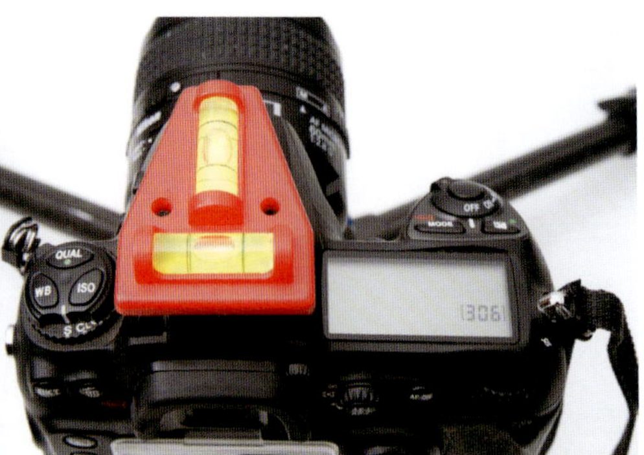

A bit of craftiness is all it takes to mount a simple bubble level from a hardware store to a hot shoe mount

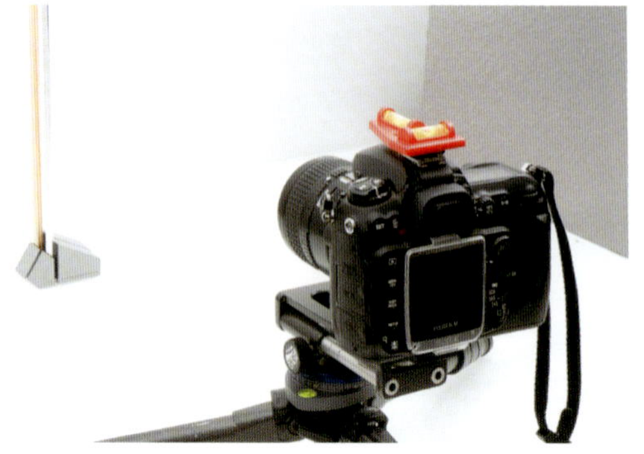

The exact pivot point can be determined by shifting the camera's position using the focusing rail

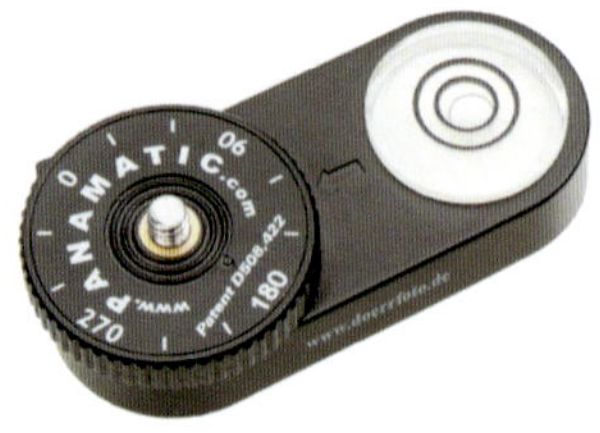

Out-of-the-box solutions like the Panamatic camera indexer and level aren't as precise as the full-blown method using focusing rails, but they produce decent results for your first forays into panoramic macros

Rotation

Rather than shifting the camera along the x-axis, another option is rotating the camera around a center point up to 360° to create a series of images for a panorama. There are two main challenges with this method: finding the ideal center point for the rotation and finding a subject worth documenting in this manner.

As has been discussed, the depth of field when photographing macro subjects is often miniscule. This fact makes it difficult to find locations where relevant subject elements remain within the depth of field while rotating a camera by 180° or more. Accordingly, rotational panoramas are most practical when you're not photographing with a large magnification factor—perhaps when creating an overview shot of a meadow, flowerbed, or group of mushrooms.

Determining the Pivot Point

It takes a small experiment to determine the proper pivot point for your camera-lens combination (which is technically the center of the *entrance pupil* as opposed to the *nodal point* as it is often and confusingly called). First mount your camera to a focusing rail and a panorama plate, and align it horizontally using a bubble level.

Next, position two vertical sticks in front of your camera so that the one in front completely hides the one behind it when you look through the camera's viewfinder. Rotating the camera to the right or left generally causes the rear stick to become visible.

Now use the focusing rail to slide the camera back as far as it takes so that rear stick remains completely congruent from the perspective of the camera as it is rotated to the left and right. The more precise you are in this step of preparations, the better your results will be when you stitch the component images together later. Beginners and photographers working with simple subjects can get away with using a panorama adapter mount with an integrated bubble level.

Shooting

The actual images can be shot relatively quickly. Your component images should feature approximately 30-percent overlap with the preceding exposure, as was the case with single-plane panoramas featuring a lateral shift in perspective. Again, the more precise you are in each individual step, the better the final results will be.

Stitching

Once again Photoshop's Photomerge feature is the device for stitching the individual images into a panorama. This time, select the *Auto* and *Blend images together* options when selecting your photos,

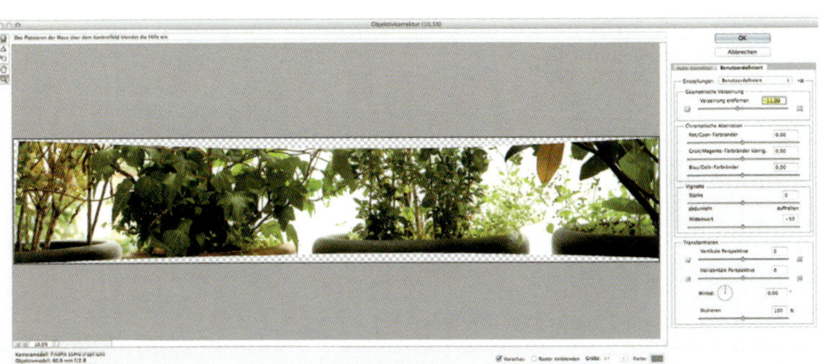

The Lens correction *filter largely takes care of the inevitable distortions that occur when stitching together a rotational panorama*

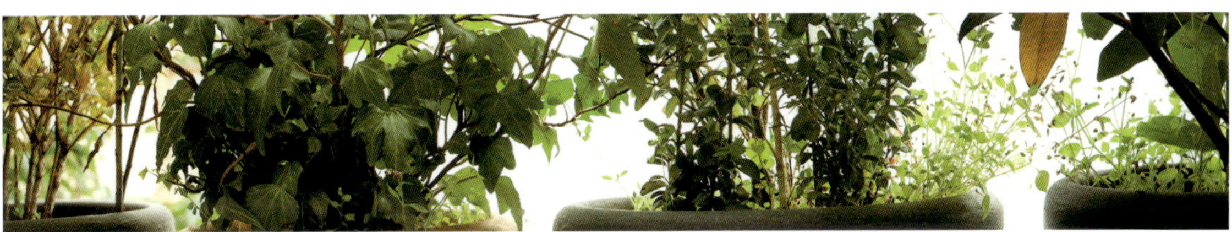

The final panorama: flowerpots on the balcony. Panorama made from eight component images, each shot at f/14, 1/15 s, ISO 100, 60mm, daylight, image size: 14,080 x 2,460 pixels

and the result will be a panoramic image that appears significantly compressed in the middle, resulting from the cylindrical projection of the individual images.

You have a couple options for dealing with this distortion easily. The first is the *Lens correction* feature in Photoshop. Another method is simply to crop the evidence of the distortion from the image without correcting it at all.

Manufacturers will sometimes provide basic panorama stitching programs with the purchase of compact or bridge cameras, and these bare-bones programs tend to do a very good job. Some manufacturers have even started integrating panorama functionality directly into the camera's software, so users need only select the relevant mode with no further effort needed.

The art of compositing images is complex—and well beyond the scope of this book. If you're interested in learning more, I heartily recommend *Photographic Multishot Techniques* by Juergen and Rainer Gulbins, published by Rocky Nook.

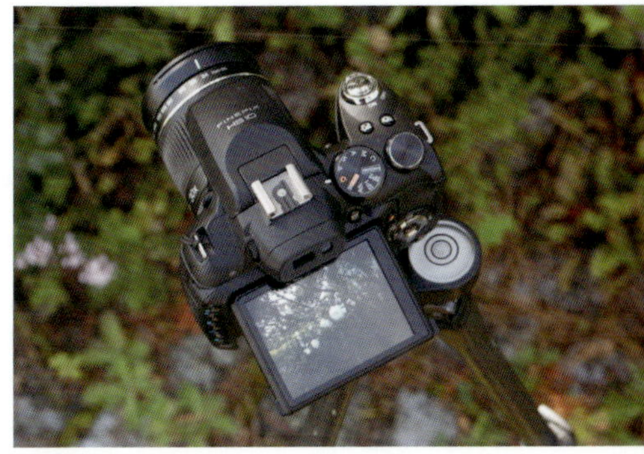

Precisely leveling your camera will noticeably improve the quality of your final image—whether shooting with a panorama plate and a focusing rail or a simple rotating plate

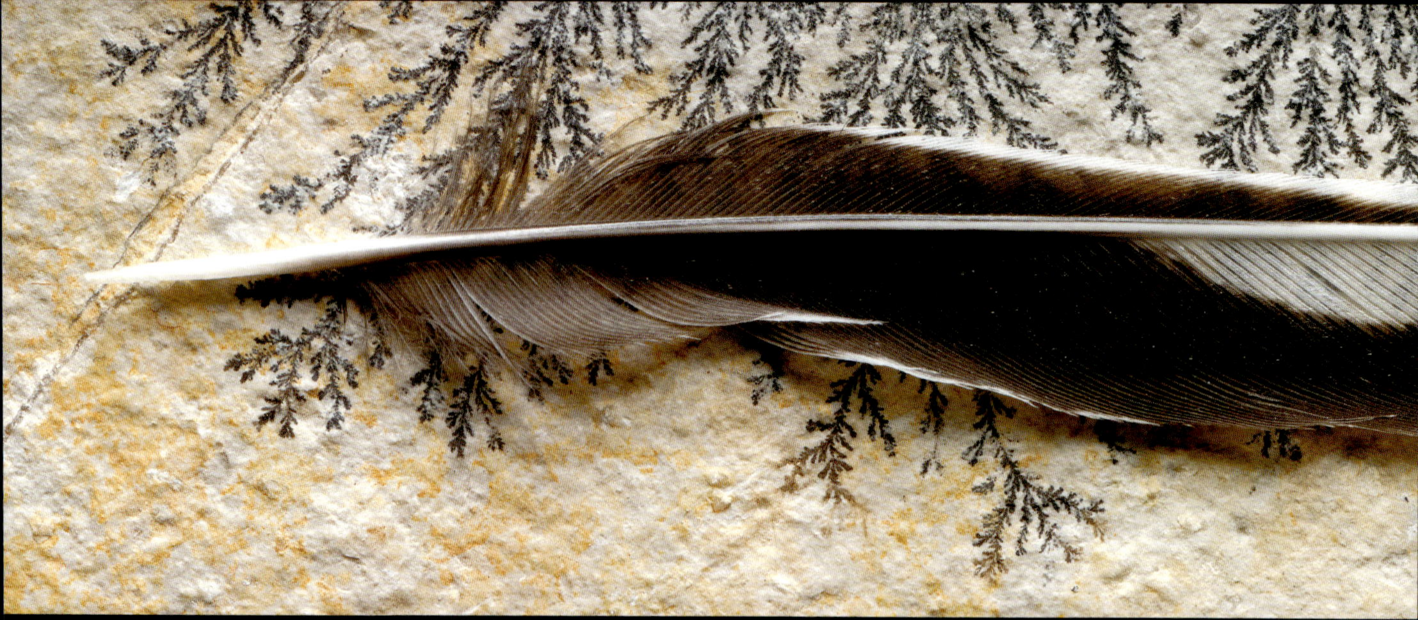

Feather on limestone with dendrites. Panorama made from five component images, each shot at f/22, 1/200 s, ISO 100, 60mm, system flash with a beautydish attachment, image size: 9,015 x 1,816 pixels

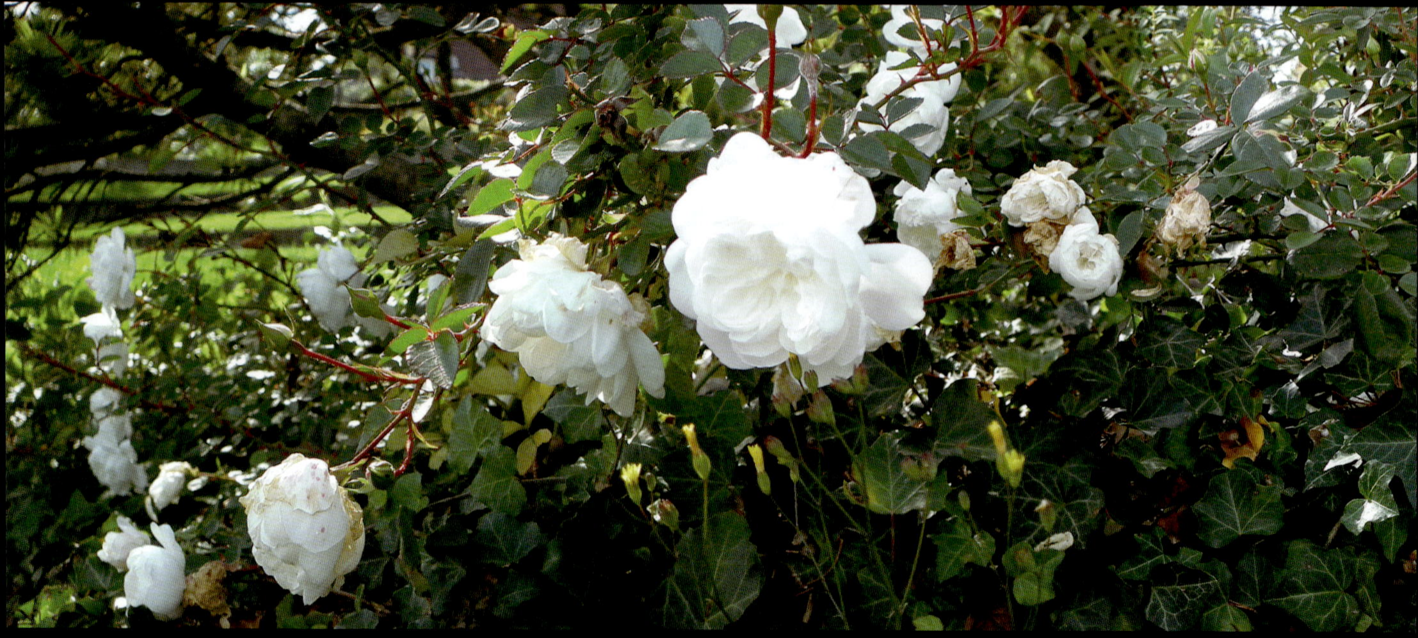

Roses and ivy in a city park. Panorama made from eight component images, each shot with a Fuji HS10 at f/4, 1/250 s, ISO 100, 7.6mm, daylight, image size: 10,4000 x 2,350 pixels

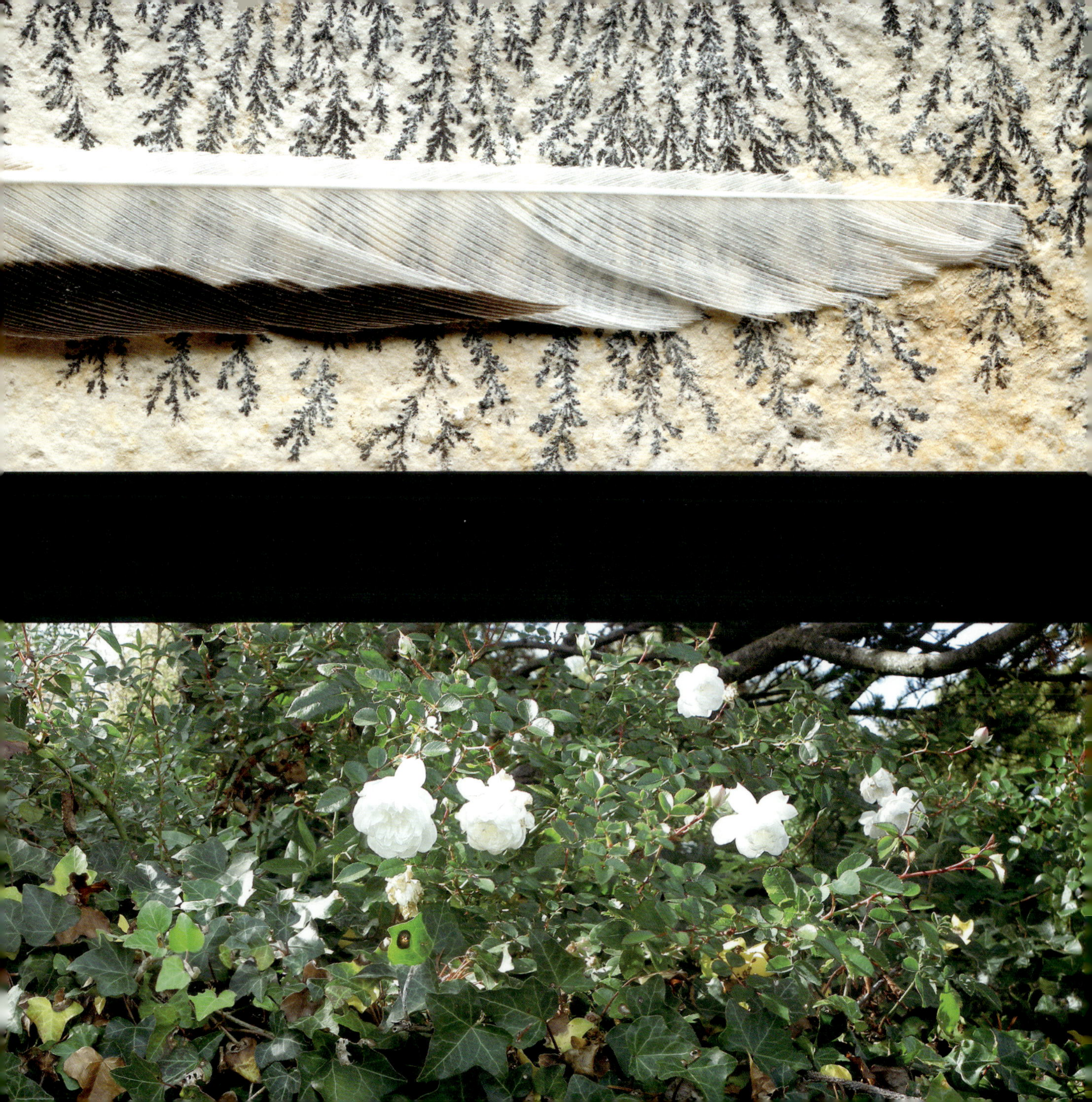

Creative Experiments

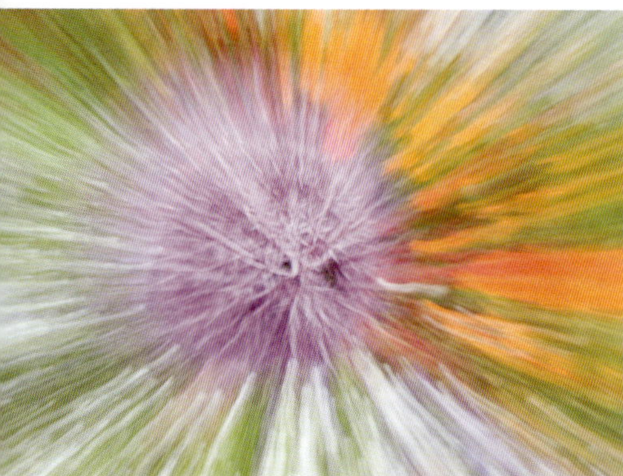

The zoom effect is created by adjusting the focal length during the exposure window

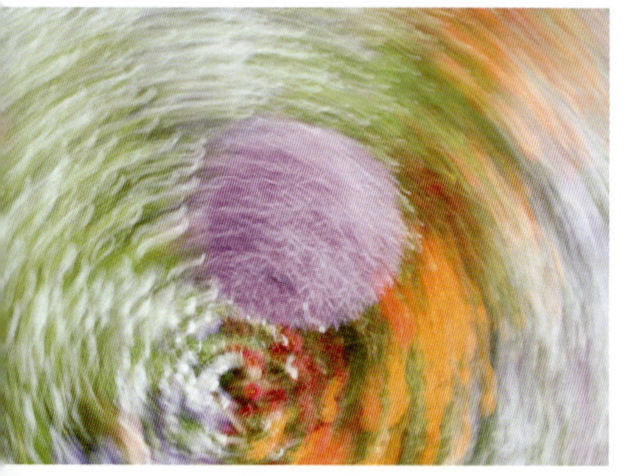

Rotating the camera around its optical axis during the exposure window results in swirls of color

Macro photography offers no shortage of opportunities to explore nontraditional exposure techniques to create interesting effects or to defamiliarize everyday objects. Potential subjects for creative treatments are everywhere you look, but intense colors and striking shapes are particularly rewarding.

Zooming

This effect will be familiar to many readers. It first gained popularity in the seventies with the advent of relatively affordable zoom lenses. The technique is carried out by mounting your camera to a tripod and then altering the focal length setting during the exposure window. Slower shutter speeds are required to execute an even adjustment and to obtain worthwhile results. A good starting point is 1/8 s, but you may find yourself using even slower shutter speeds, especially if you also incorporate other camera movements such as panning while zooming.

Rotating

In principle, this method is comparable to zooming during the exposure window, but instead of altering the focal length, the photographer rotates the camera around the lens's optical axis. The resulting image will feature circular patterns of color that at times take on a tunnel-like appearance. Rotating the camera around the optical axis by hand is no precise science, so the center point of the resulting circles is often not positioned in the center of the image area. If you're looking for a bit more control over the critical movement, consider using a tripod and a lens with a tripod collar that facilitates rotational movements.

Panning

Brief or prolonged movements of the camera in horizontal, vertical, or diagonal directions during the exposure window results in visual textures that resemble the effect of a modern artist's brushstrokes. You can modulate how soft or defined the streaks of color in your images appear by deciding whether to establish a sharp focus of your subject before starting the exposure. Changing the speed of your movement, using slower shutter speeds, or waiting to start the panning motion until after the shutter has been released, are other

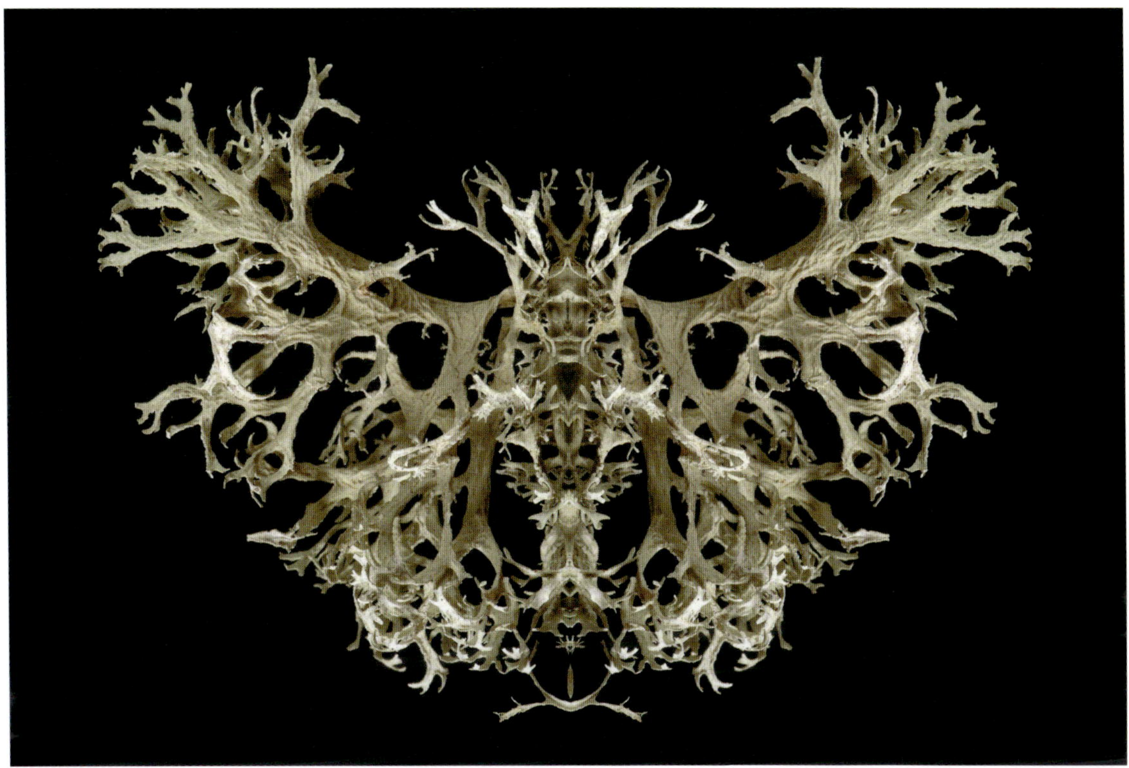

Mirroring subjects creates interesting and often bizarre formations. When I look at this piece of moss reflected over a vertical axis, I see a shaman wearing a bird costume.
f/13, 1/125 s, ISO 200, 105mm, studio flash unit

methods to influence the look and feel of your resulting image. Practice is the best way to refine your panning technique and get a feel for the types of subjects that yield interesting results when photographed with panning. In sunny weather, you may need to stop the aperture down completely or attach a grey filter to the lens in order to use this method and its requisite slow shutter speeds. An overexposure of around 1.0 EV is generally favorable for producing heighted color intensity.

Mirroring

Symmetry can be found all across the natural world, from human faces to plant structures to animal bodies, to name a few. This naturally occurring phenomenon may explain why it is so fascinating to mirror or reflect subjects to create new and unusual formations. Macro pictures that feature truncated images are particularly strong candidates for this treatment because it's more likely that viewers won't immediately identify the method used to create the effect or be able to solve the magician's trick. You can create astounding objects, animals, plants, ghosts, and mythical creatures simply by duplicating an image, mirroring it over its vertical axis, and then setting the two versions side by side.

Shallow Focus

The general practice when shooting macro photos is to stop the aperture down as much as possible to maximize the depth of field. Working with a wide-open aperture, however, is not without its own charms. Subtle details and textures disappear almost completely and the image comes alive based on how shapes and colors are organized. Image composition becomes a much more important factor when using this method in comparison to conventional macro techniques. The most attractive results are usually obtained by positioning the focal plane at the subject's closest edge. A simple background that is adequately far away from the subject rounds out the general look and feel of these types of pictures.

Overexposing

Deliberately overexposing subjects by a few stops is yet another creative macro technique—especially when shooting colorful flowers. When used with a wide-open aperture, this technique produces delightful transitions between colors, enveloping the subject in a warm light and giving the photograph qualities more reminiscent of a watercolor painting.

The front-most edge of the mushroom cap is in focus here, but everything else is swimming in blur, creating a soft, fairytale-like quality f/4.5, 1/50 s, ISO 2000, zoom lens at 78mm, daylight

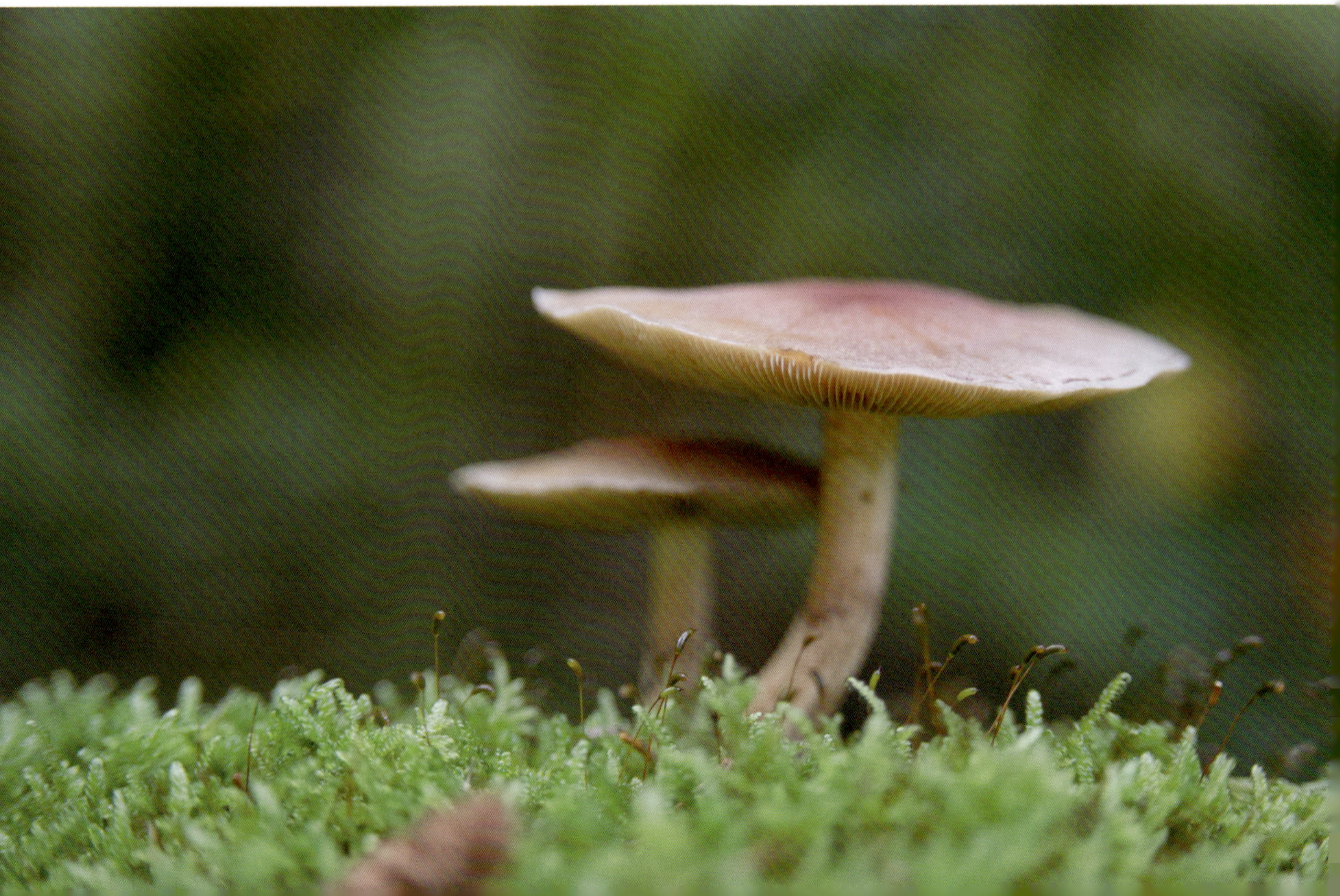

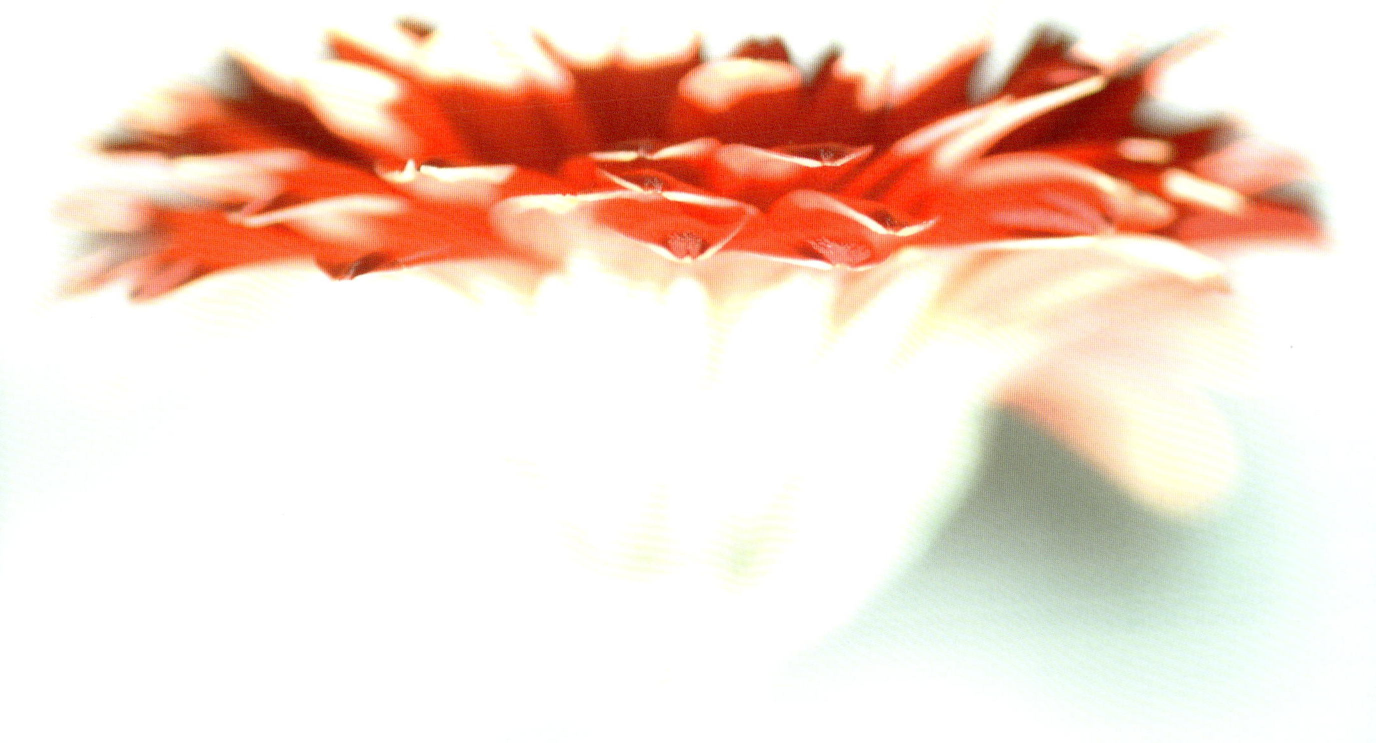

This photo of a gerbera blossom makes use of a very tight range of focus and deliberate overexposure f/3.3, 1/60 s, ISO 200, 50mm, daylight

You'll get the best results with this technique if you use a DSLR with a high-quality lens that has a large maximum aperture. Having a camera capable of capturing a wide range of tonal values is also important in order to avoid clipping in the highlights.

Intense colors in your main subject and a bright background further complement the look produced by this technique. In ideal cases, your images will feature an almost creamy transition between the subject and the overexposed, intensely bright areas of the image. This technique is often used in food photography, where photographers like to overexpose backdrops with additional lighting with the goal of giving viewers enough room to let their imaginations run wild. You can further improve the composition of your image by strategically placing objects in areas beyond the depth of field so that they appear as nothing more than vague swaths of color. Take a look in any modern cookbook, and you will find creative ideas for how to style and shoot a variety of objects from the natural world.

Infrared Macro Photography

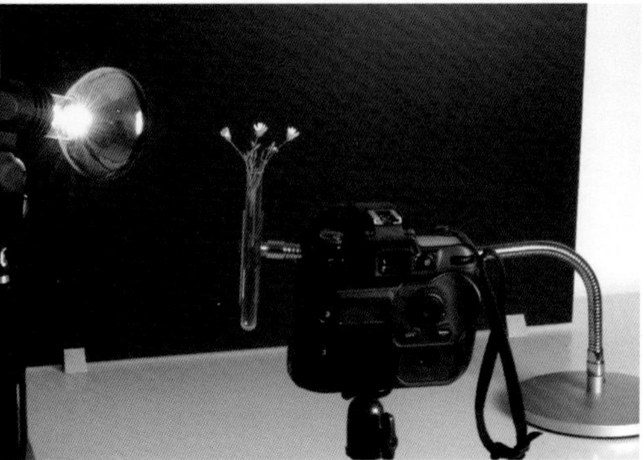

Infrared macro photography general-ly requires the use of a sturdy tripod, because shutter speeds often have to slow down to a few seconds when using cameras that are not specially modified for this type of work. In addition to natural sunlight, you can also use infrared lamps for lighting.

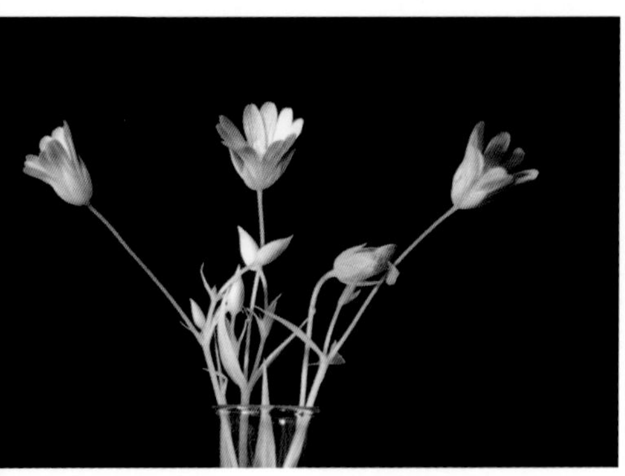

The result here shows flowers illuminated with a range of light that normally is not perceptible to the human eye
Fuji S3 Pro, infrared filter 740nm, f/8, 25 s, ISO 400, 50mm

Infrared (IR) photography has become significantly easier in the digital era of photography. In theory, the only tools required to shoot IR macros is an area filter to remove the spectrum of visible light and a tripod. The IR radiation capable of being used for photography is also called *near IR radiation*, and its wavelength is directly next to the red area of visible light, starting at around 780 nanometers. The human eye is not capable of perceiving this light.

Camera and Filters

In theory, all digital cameras are capable of sensing IR light, but many manufacturers include an IR cut filter directly in front of the image sensor to prevent IR radiation from causing color distortions to the range of visible light. So the picture is not as rosy as it initially sounds. It's fairly easy to determine whether your camera is capable of capturing IR radiation by carrying out this little experiment: take a picture with a relatively slow shutter speed of a standard remote control. If the diode on the remote control shows up as a bright point in your image, you can safely assume that your camera is equipped to shoot IR images.

If your camera seems up to the task, you'll need a filter, such as an IR filter No. 87, to filter out light with wavelengths shorter than 740 nanometers (effectively removing visible light). Attaching an IR filter requires filter threads on your lens, of course, or the relevant adapter mount. That may be required if using a compact or bridge camera.

Plants of all kinds make fantastic subjects when shooting IR im-ages, because the color green is particularly effective at reflecting IR light, meaning it appears nearly white in the exposed photo. If plants are set against a blue, cloudless sky, all the better, because such a background will appear nearly black in the final image, and this dramatic color contrast emphasizes the detail in the botanical structures. Shooting IR images often requires exposure windows last-ing several seconds, so a tripod and a remote shutter release system are indispensable for avoiding troublesome vibrations.

If you're hesitant to spend a lot of money on an expensive IR filter, you can hold an unexposed, developed (e.g., black) section of slide film in front of your lens. This method will work for getting started, but the results will be significantly worse than using a proper IR filter.

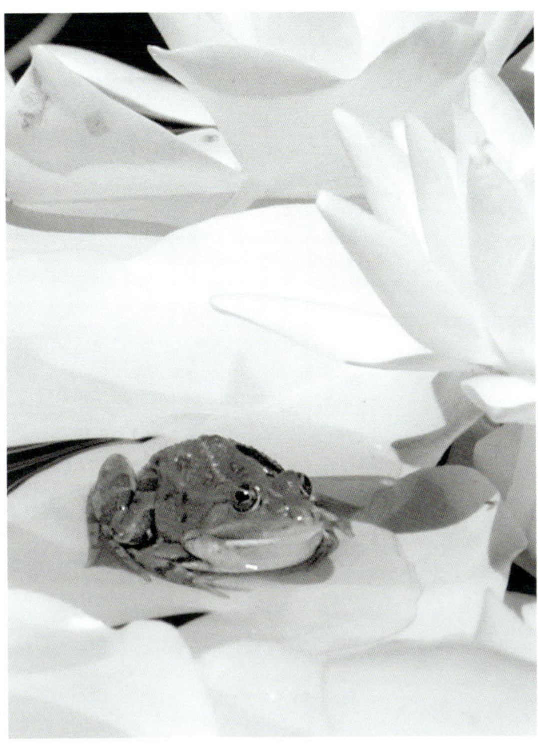

This green frog sitting on a lily pad lost his camouflage when photographed with infrared light
Nikon D70s, infrared filter 740nm, f/8, 1.3 s, ISO 200, 105mm

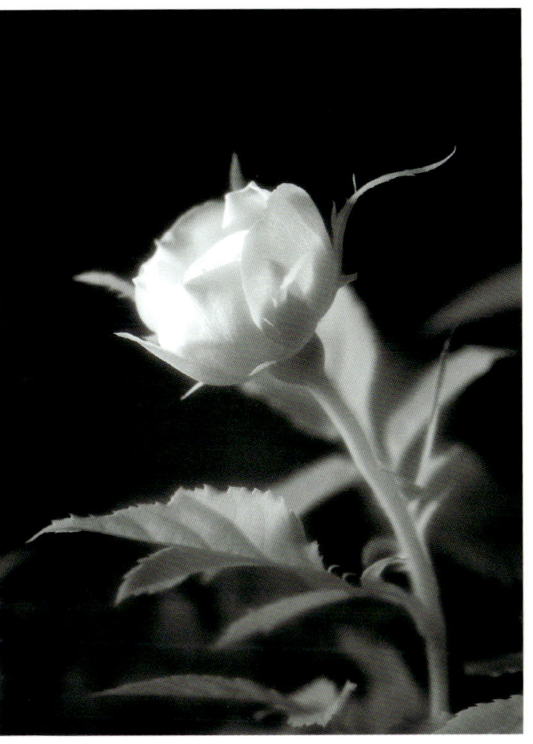

Infrared rose
Fuji S3 Pro, infrared filter 740nm, f/4, 30 s, ISO 200, 105mm

Infrared Macro Studio Photography

One of the usual requirements for IR photography is an abundance of sunlight—the more, the better. Even the slightest of movements during an exposure can cause a macro image to blur significantly, however, which poses a problem for photographers of the miniscule. Fortunately, IR lamps are readily available on the market, making it possible to shoot in the studio environment where the wind won't blow. When working indoors with these lamps, use black cardboard to shield your backdrop from receiving too much light.

Camera Conversion

Exposing with shutter speeds fast enough to enable you to shoot handheld is a possibility, but it will require that the IR cut filter be removed from your camera's sensor. Some specialized camera equipment companies offer this service. More information is available at sites such as *www.lifepixel.com*.

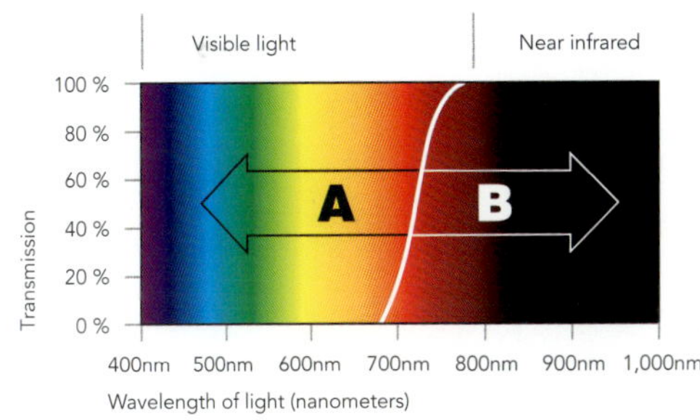

An infrared filter blocks a majority of light from the visible spectrum (A) and allows only electromagnetic radiation in the near infrared range and higher (B)

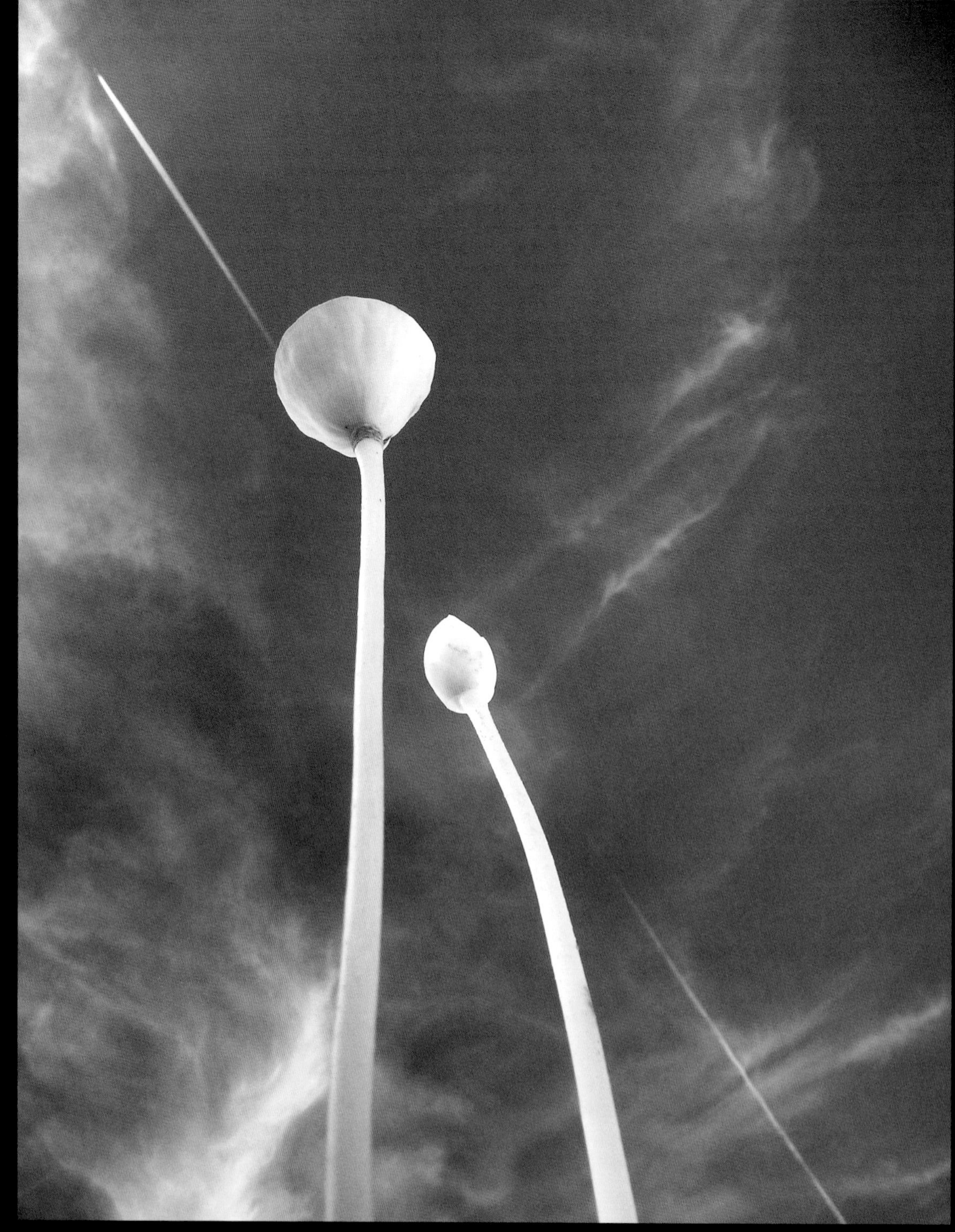

The unusual perspective of this photo makes the stems
of these lilies seem like futuristic structures. The air-
plane coincidentally passing through the background is
the icing on the cake.
Nikon E 5400, converted for infrared capture, f/3.1,
1/200 s, ISO 50, 5.8mm

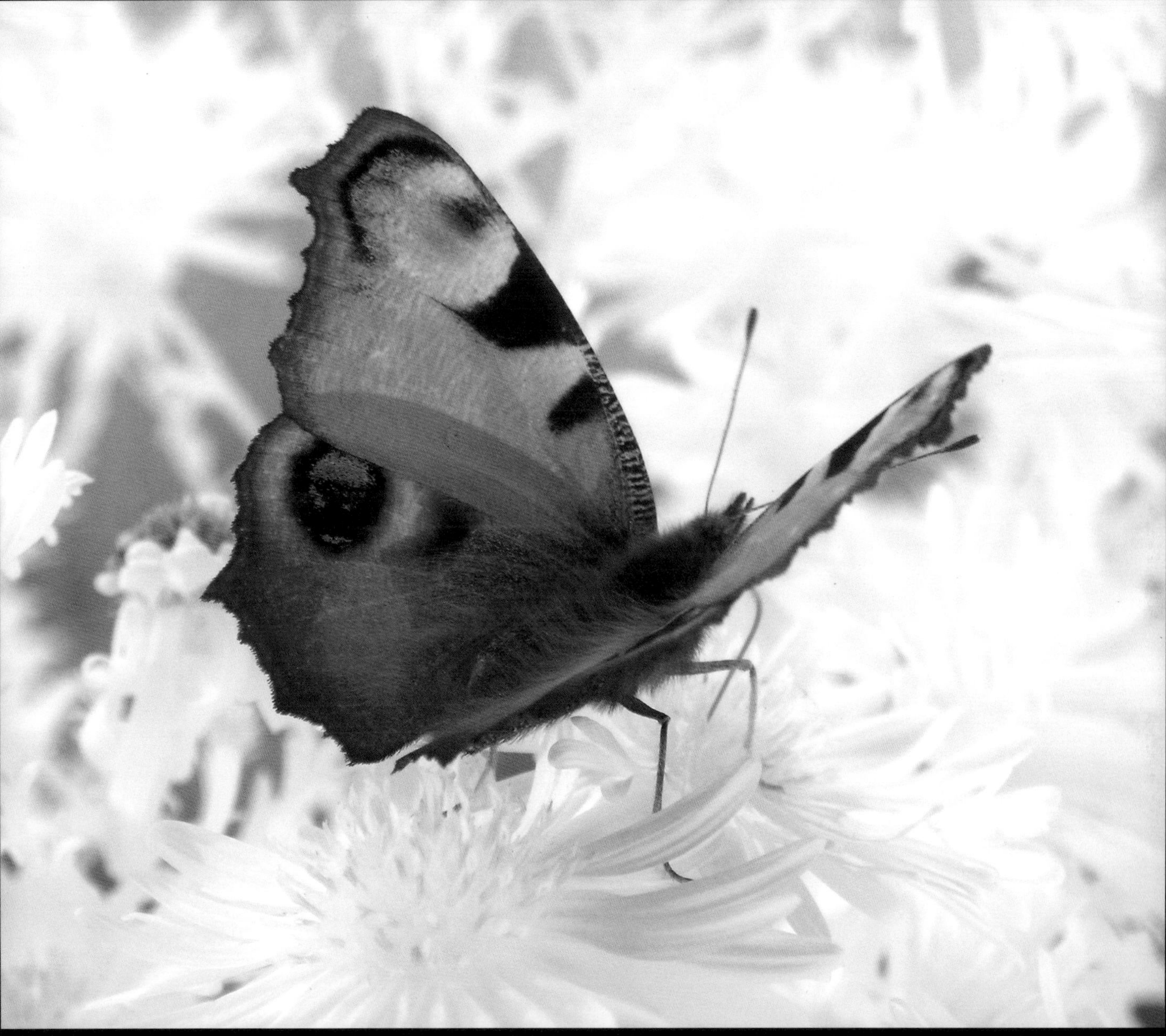

Infrared peacock butterfly. Shooting infrared images handheld requires a camera whose IR cut filter has been removed. Nikon E540, converted for infrared capture, f/5.2, 1/100 s, ISO 50, 24mm

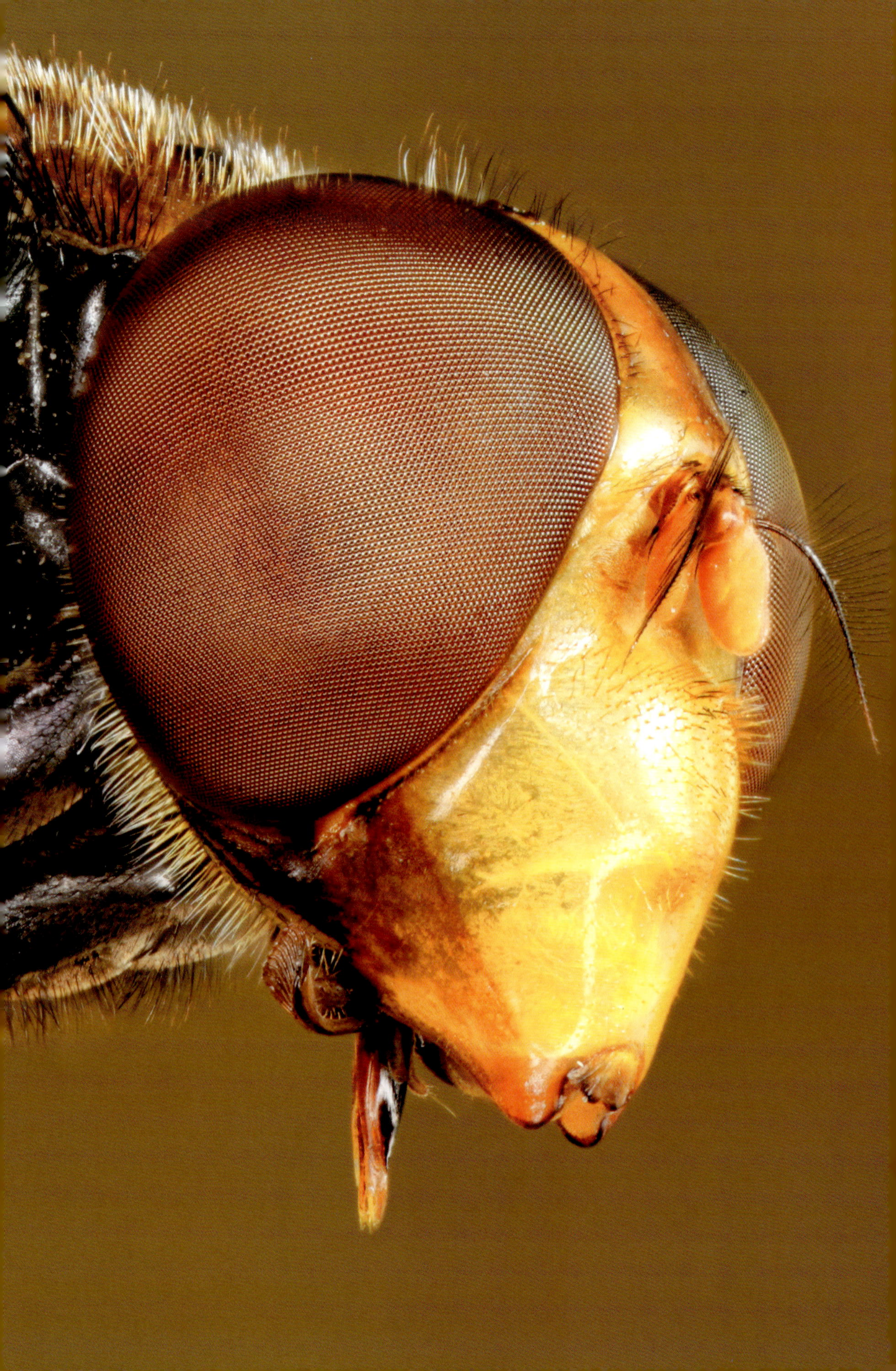

Jan Metzler
Focus Stacking

Photographer Jan Metzler (born 1969) has intensively honed his craft as a macro photographer for many years and has accordingly come up against the limits of depth of field more than a few times. Using the technique of focus stacking, however, he has jumped well beyond the boundaries of conventional macro imaging to reveal the smallest of nature's treasures in stunning detail to viewers across the world.

Jan's technique requires the use of a sophisticated lighting system, special magnifying lenses, reverse mount adapters, and an X-Y table capable of precisely controlling positioning down to fractions of a millimeter.

Additional photos from Jan Metzler as well as a variety of information on the subject of focus stacking can be found at *www.focus-stacking.de*.

Pellucid hoverfly
Canon EOS 50D, 28 component images, f/6.3, 5 s, ISO 200, Canon MP-E 65mm 1:2.8 1–5x Macro
Photo by Jan Metzler

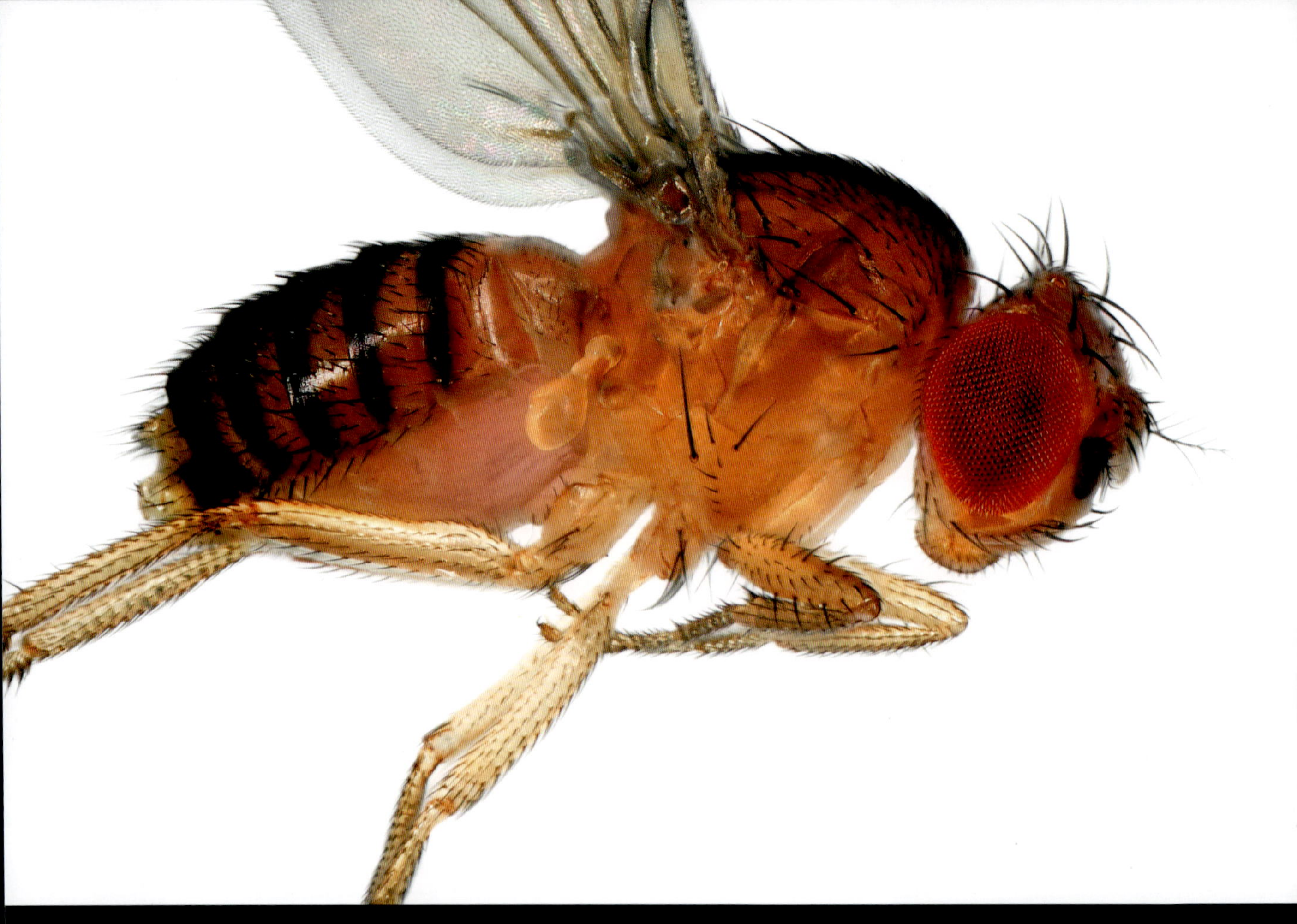

Fruit fly on a light table
Canon EOS 50D, 27 component
images, f/5,1/8 s, ISO 200, MP-E 65mm
Photo by Jan Metzler

Pellucid hoverfly in a light tent
Canon EOS 50D, 99 component
images, f/5, 1/8 s, ISO 200, MP-E 65mm
Photo by Jan Metzler

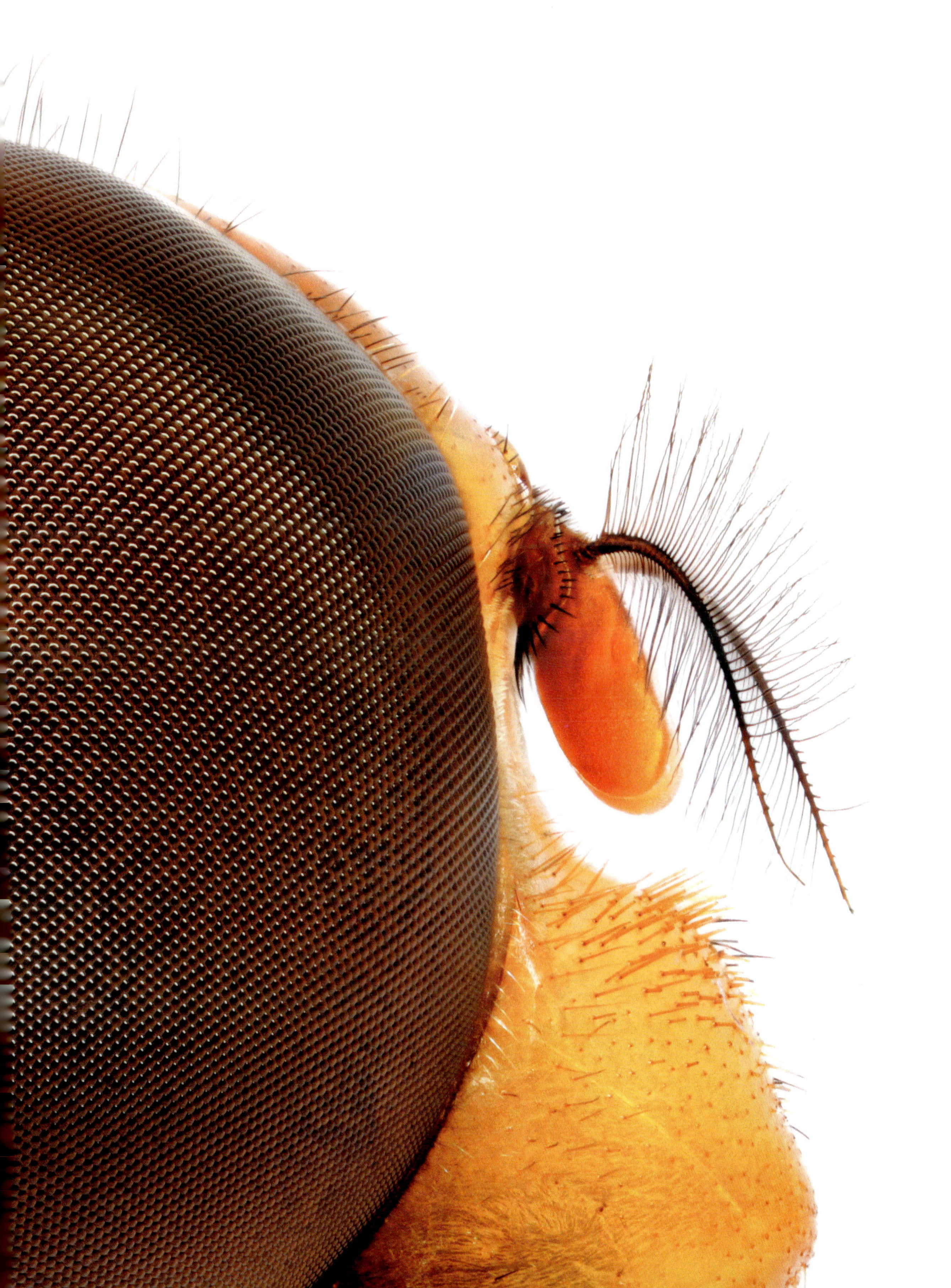

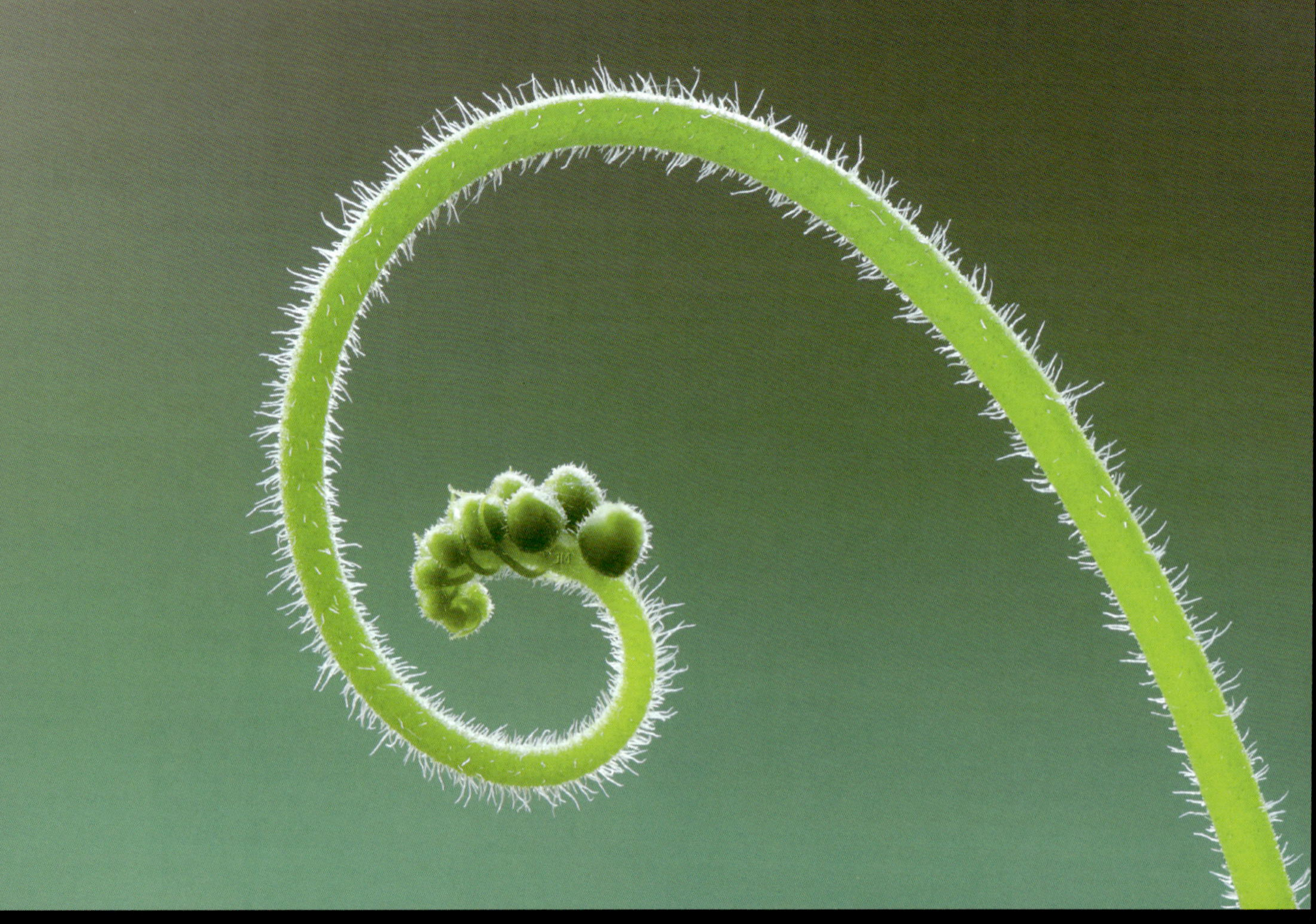

On the cusp of blossoming near the
windowsill. The attractive green in the
background is simply the natural appearance of the yard.
Canon EOS 50D, 9 component images,
f/3.5, 1/5 s, ISO 200, 100mm
Photo by Jan Metzler

An aphid snacking on a daisy
Canon EOS 50D, 28 component images,
f/6.3, 1/160 s, ISO 100, MP-E 65mm
Photo by Jan Metzler

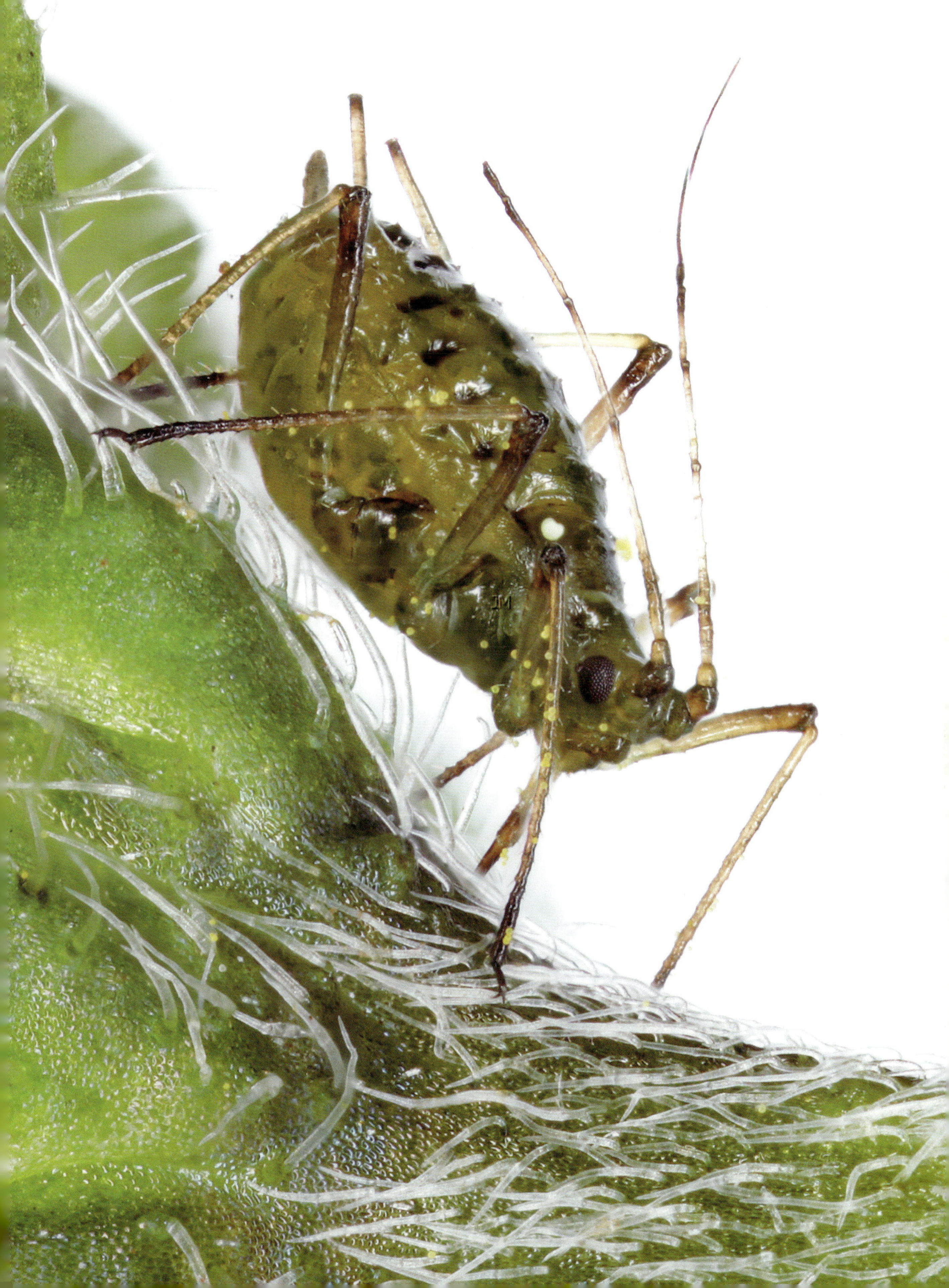

Advanced Focus Stacking

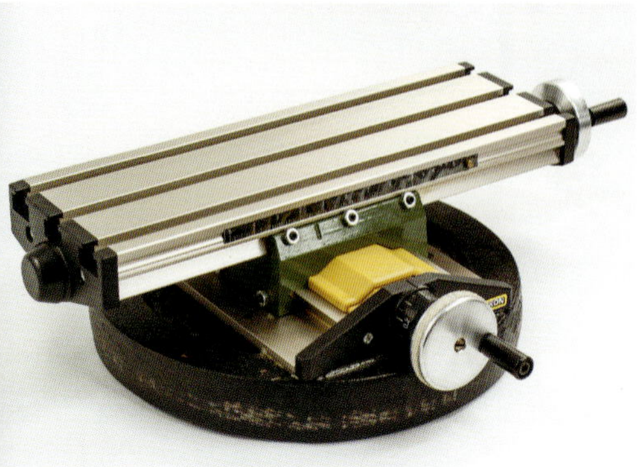

Professional focus stacking requires the use of a precision X-Y table

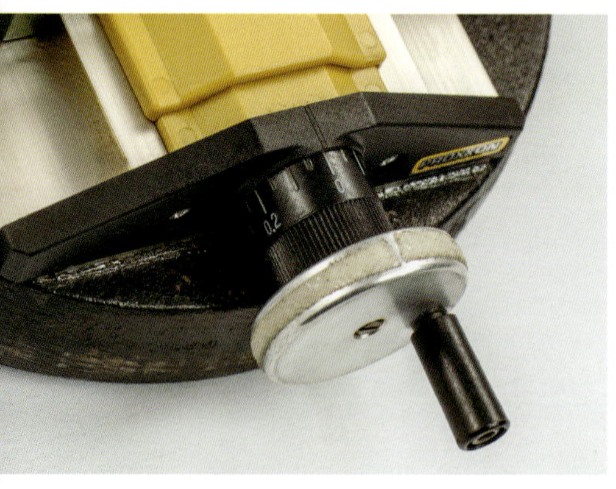

Each hash mark equates to a shift of exactly 0.05mm

Hobbyists who are already well versed in the methods of focus stacking may wish to engage with an advanced process for reaching levels of magnification well beyond 1:1. When shooting component images up to the 1:1 magnification threshold, conventional macro focusing rails are sufficiently precise to adjust the position of the focal plane by the necessary 1mm or 2mm increments required to manage the narrow depth of field. More powerful magnification levels, however, shrink the depth of field even more, necessitating the need for a device capable of allowing you to precisely and comfortably adjust the distance between the camera and the subject by increments less than 1mm.

The manufacturing industry uses devices called *X-Y tables* that make it possible to adjust the positioning of objects with exceptional accuracy. You can use these devices with extreme precision to capture the component images necessary for powerful focus stacking applications. This advanced technique differs from the traditional approach: rather than moving the camera in relation to the subject, you are moving the subject while the camera remains stationary.

Not having to move the camera is a plus because you can set it up and leave it undisturbed throughout the entire process. Moving the heavy combination of a DSLR and its lens on a macro focusing rail typically results in potentially problematic reverberations—especially at high levels of magnification. These vibrations are readily visible in the camera's live view, and they require that you wait for three or four seconds before taking each picture for the movement to subside. Using a precision X-Y table eliminates this issue because it enables you to move the subject while the camera system remains still.

I mount my X-Y table to a heavy base plate to keep the shooting surface stable and minimize the risk of things shifting as a result of small bumps or moments of carelessness. The entire setup is fairly heavy, but that means it is also relatively immune to inadvertent shifts caused by manipulating the tuning dial, which has to be turned frequently while shooting.

Additional Equipment

Magnification levels greater than 1:1 can be attained by using standard macro lenses in combination with one or more extension tubes as well as with bellows lenses. Other options include mounting a variety of lenses in reverse (using the proper mount) or using lens attachment options capable of being affixed to the front of a camera lens.

Tweezers of various sizes and shapes are useful tools when it comes to positioning your subject with delicate accuracy. Brushes or a small blower designed to clean debris off of an image sensor are also useful tools for removing loose dust and other dirt particles that tend to be found on dead insects.

Even with more than adequate lighting, it's important to use a stable tripod and a remote shutter release system (whether wired or wireless) to produce images free from blur. Avail yourself of the mirror lockup feature that your camera likely has if you plan to use the viewfinder rather than the live view to monitor your shooting. Doing so will prevent small, troublesome vibrations that occur when the mirror swings out of way for the sensor to receive light.

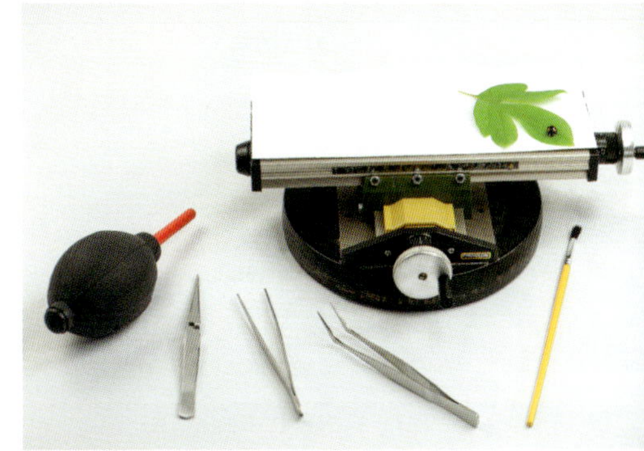

Tweezers, brushes, and blowers are handy for making tiny adjustments to your subject's position and for getting rid of troublesome dust particles

Execution

I used a ladybug (*Coccinellidae*) that I found lifeless on my balcony as a sample subject to illustrate my method on these pages. I opted for a magnification factor of 3:1—comfortably attainable using an extreme macro lens—to depict the subject with sufficient size while also being able to include some area around it. I set the camera's exposure settings to f/5, 1/10 s, and ISO 200. At this aperture setting, the depth of field was very narrow, meaning that each image for the stack needed to be separated by approximately 0.1mm. In other words, the subject needed to be moved 0.1mm closer to the camera for each subsequent shot.

Setting insects on organic surfaces such as an individual leaf tends to make the subjects appear more dynamic, as opposed to a clinical specimen on a white surface. After positioning the subject on the X-Y table and programming my desired camera settings, I adjusted the camera to find the position for the first exposure in the stack. A setup featuring a ball head atop a tripod with a macro focusing rail makes achieving this critical positioning much easier.

Now you can fine-tune the lighting. The chitinous exoskeleton of many insects causes bright reflections that can look unattractive in the final image, so experiment with different positions for the lighting to figure out what works best. I used a ring light for this shot and eventually found the best angle to avoid too much glare on the insect's face. Reflections can be pesky and difficult—sometimes impossible—to eliminate, but relying on the live view on your camera's monitor is an effective way to gauge what works best.

Once you're satisfied with your lighting, it's time to start collecting images for the stack. As already mentioned, start with exposing

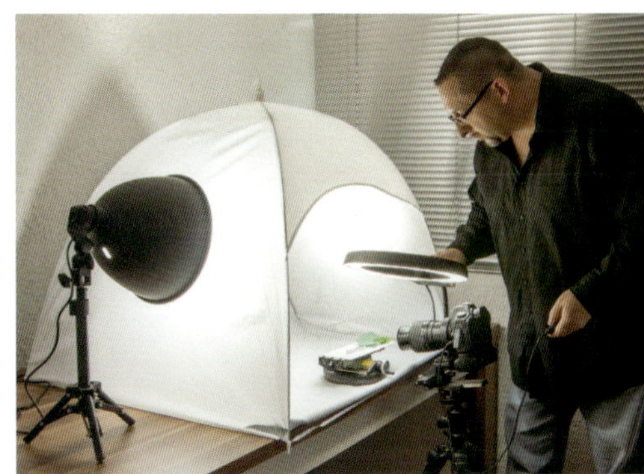

Lighting is provided by special daylight lamps and a light tent

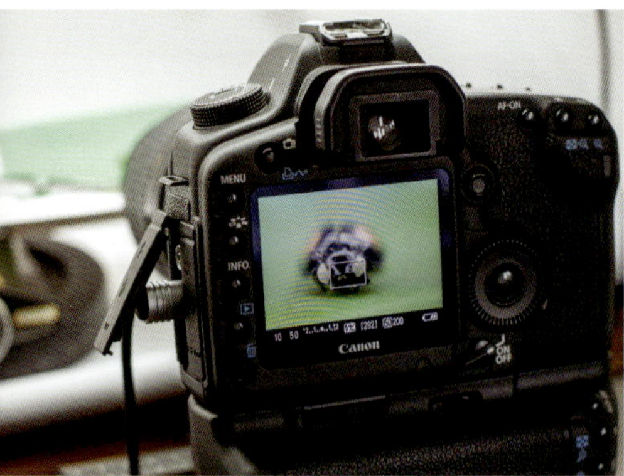

Keep a close eye on the sharpness and the lighting by regularly inspecting your camera's display

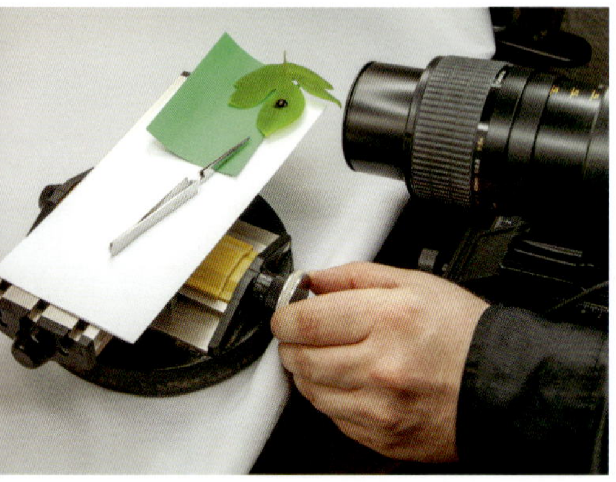

Bumps and vibrations should be avoided at all costs while shooting your series of images

an image at the closest point of your subject while using a remote shutter release system…*click*.

Don't change anything on your camera for any of the subsequent images in the series. All of the images in your stack should be shot with the identical exposure settings. Before taking the next photo, turn the X-Y table's front dial counterclockwise to shift the table surface 0.1mm toward the camera. Each graduated mark on this professional-grade cross slide amounts to 0.05mm, so a shift of 0.1mm is equal to one short and one long hash mark on the dial's scale. After making the barely noticeable adjustment, shoot the second frame for the stack…*click*. I repeated these steps until I reached the middle of the subject. The bug's back half is not important—nor is it even visible—for the frontal perspective I used.

Turn the dial counterclockwise again for what amounts to a 0.1mm shift, and take the next picture…*click*. A total of 43 images was shot for my example; this stack of photos covered the foremost detail of the ladybug's face to its midsection (when viewed from the front). This series of images accordingly provided a complete depth of field with a length of 4.3mm.

Consider how using alternate exposure settings would alter the requirements for collecting the component images of a stack: shooting with a magnification of 1:1 at f/8 means that the depth of field for a single image is approximately 1mm (with a full-frame sensor)! At the same f-stop (f/8), but now at a magnification of 3:1, you'd have about 0.24mm to work with as your depth of field. The f-stop I used (f/5) offered me a depth of field approx. 0.15mm in length, but because the focus of the individual component images needed to overlap somewhat, I went with shifts of 0.1mm between each shot so the stacking software had enough data to produce a seamlessly sharp final image from front to back.

The above-mentioned depth-of-field measurements for specific shooting settings are based on using a full-frame sensor, and they are approximate values. If you're using a sensor of a different size or a different f-stop or level of magnification, experiment a little to figure out the length of your depth of field and how much the subject needs to shift between each image. The next step in the process is to allow a focus stacking program to compile all of the images with their miniscule depths of focus into a composite or stacked image exhibiting continuous sharpness from front to back.

Tips and Tricks for Focus Stacking

Shooting dozens of component images for a stack is practical only with stationary or inanimate objects. It's extremely difficult to use the focus stacking method with living insects, for example, because they are constantly active in some way. They might move a leg or parts of their mouth, or they might simply lower an antenna by a millimeter or two for a brief second. In many cases you won't be able to detect these movements with the naked eye; you may even be convinced that they are remaining perfectly still. But that's not the case! These micro movements will become visible in your component images and they have the potential to ruin an entire stack.

Spiders resting on a stone wall or some other motionless object represent a rare exception. But even spiders that appear to be completely still on a leaf or in a web will respond to the slightest bit of moving air. Even if a weatherman would call the conditions calm and windless, that spider will detect movements and respond in ways capable of rendering an entire stack of photos useless.

Here's my tip: When photographing living insects that are sitting still or spiders in the wild, choose an aperture that offers a longer depth of field so you have the chance to create a calm deck comprising maybe 4 or 5 component images. Sure, collecting 12 or 20 exposures would offer more detailed resolution in the end, but that won't matter if motion blur compromises the quality of the stacked image.

Are More Images Better?

This question can't be answered generally, because it depends on a number of variables such as the magnification factor, the f-stop, the subject's dimensions, and the subject's surface qualities (e.g., whether it has fine hairs or is shiny and smooth). Subjects with hairs and objects with delicate textures require finer adjustments or more closely spaced component images with a wide aperture.

Using a larger magnification (e.g., 3:1 instead of 1:1) means more component images are required (assuming the f-stop is constant), because the depth of field increasingly flattens out at higher levels of magnification. For similar reasons, wider apertures (i.e., smaller f-stops) necessitate a larger number of component images than narrower apertures. And last but not least, the required number of component images is highly dependent on the depth of your subject or the depth of the area you wish to remain sharp.

It's important for the depths of field of the component images to overlap somewhat; otherwise the stacking software will have problems rendering the images. Without sufficient overlap between subsequent images, unsightly gaps and blurry streaks will show up in the final result. When shooting a series for a focus stack, it's also important to use the lens's optimal aperture, where the benefits of stopping down to achieve a larger depth of field are balanced against the drawbacks of increased diffraction blur at smaller apertures.

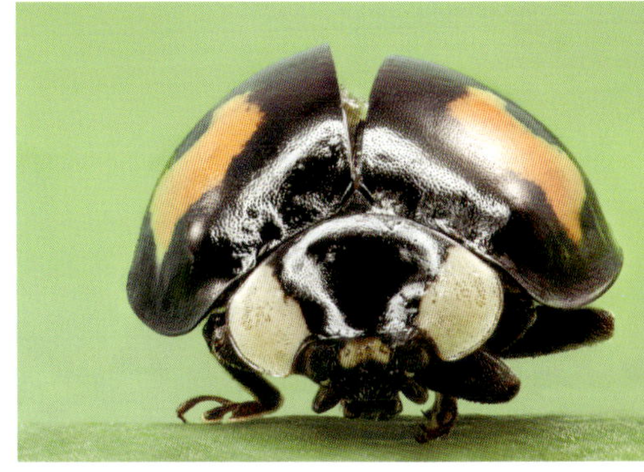

This is how the final image looks after some retouching work with an editing program
Photo by Jan Metzler

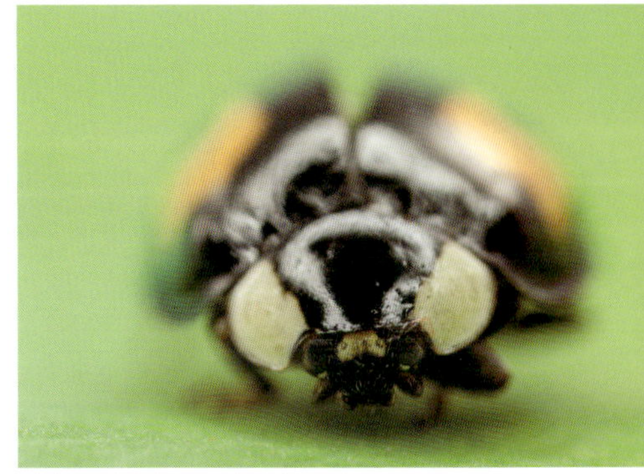

This is the first image of the stack—focused on the foremost element of the subject
Photo by Jan Metzler

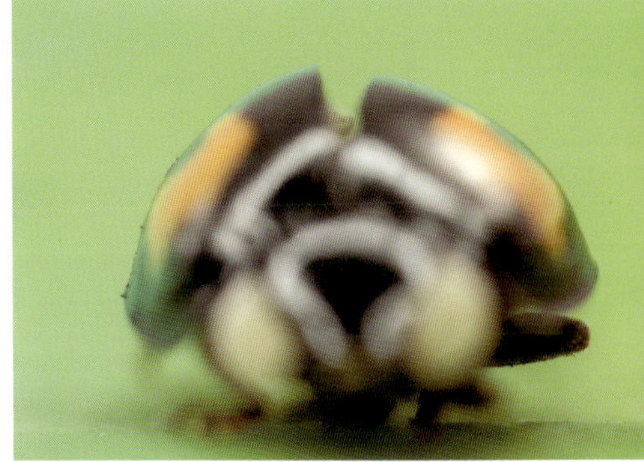

And this is the last image of the stack—focused on the subject's middle
Photo by Jan Metzler

Editing Is Essential

In comparison to "standard" photography, focus stacking requires a significantly greater post-processing effort. A small speck on the sensor may result in a single blemish in an individual frame, but when a dozen or more photos are stacked, the speck creates a problematic streak running through the entire stack and seriously compromises the final image. For example, creating a stacked picture of a dead insect found on your windowsill will likely necessitate a great deal of retouching with the clone stamp tool in the image editing program of your choice to tidy up deposits of dust and other blemishes on the body and various facets of the critter. Various forms of fungal decay that are barely perceptible to the human eye but that are very conspicuous under magnification may also need to be cleaned up. In fact, potential subjects that may have been resting lifeless on the windowsill for too long are simply beyond the point of use for these types of images.

After this retouching process is complete, stacked images can be further refined through various standard editing practices, such as removing noise, sharpening, tone mapping, color correction, white balance adjustment, filter effects, and so on.

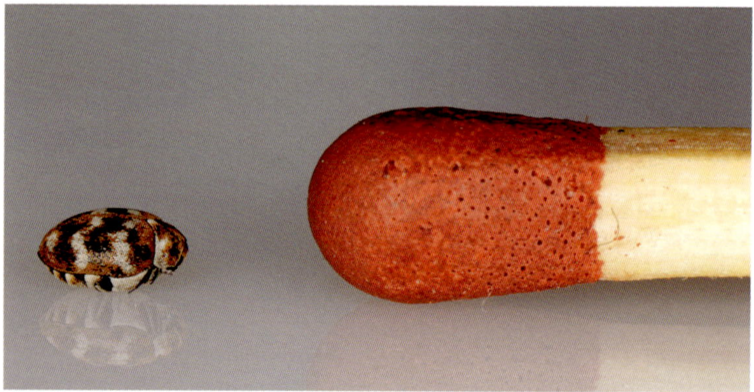

Varied carpet beetle, with a match head
for scale
Canon EOS 50D, 21 component images,
f/6.3, 1/60 s, ISO 100, MP-E 65mm
Photo by Jan Metzler

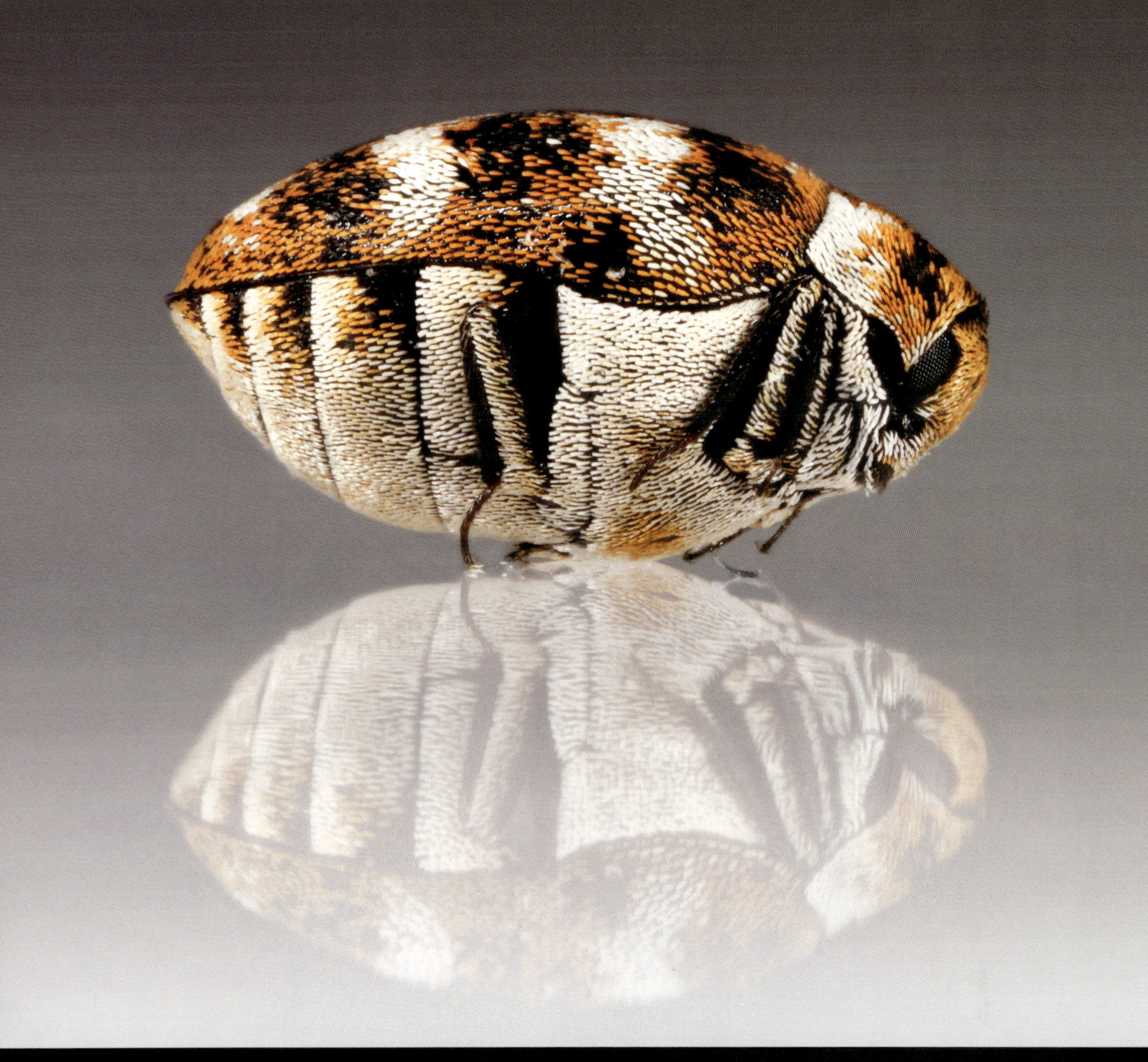

Varied carpet beetle
Canon EOS 50D, 21 component

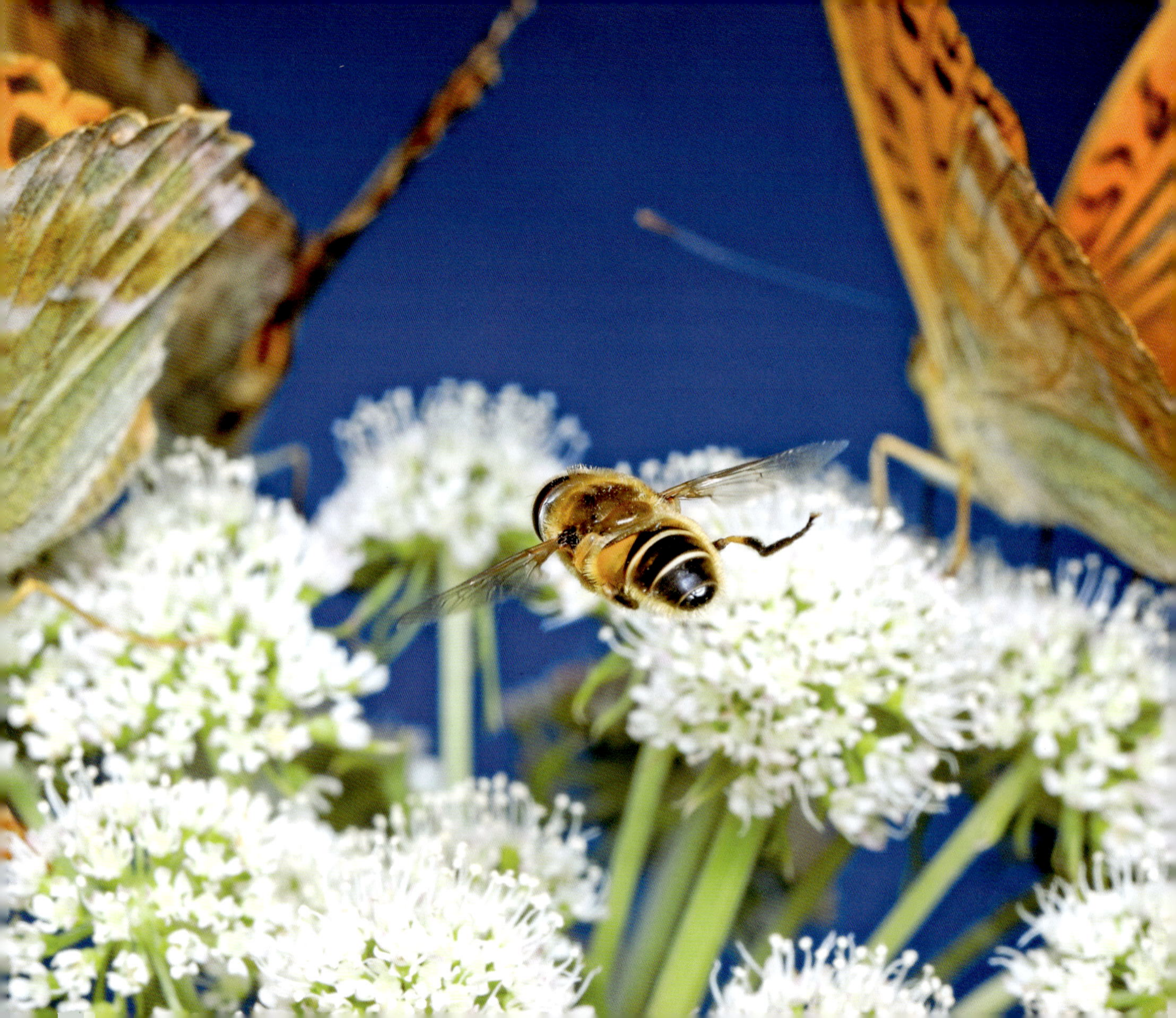

Hans Christian Steeg
High-Speed Photography

From an early age, nature photography fascinated Hans Christian Steeg—macro photography in particular. He's a physicist who works in electronics development for a company that supplies the auto industry with equipment. His work background complements his interest in the specialized branches of macro photography including, for example, high-speed photography.

A range of equipment for high-speed shooting is not readily available on the photography market, which means he engineers and builds his own tools for the job—such as special light barriers and custom brackets and mounts designed to support these structures—largely on his own.

In 2014 dpunkt published his book, Highspeed, which explores the art and practice of high-speed imaging.

Hoverfly
Nikon D80, Componon-S 4/80
Photo by Hans Christian Steeg

Caught in Flight: A Q&A with Hans Christian Steeg About High-Speed Photography

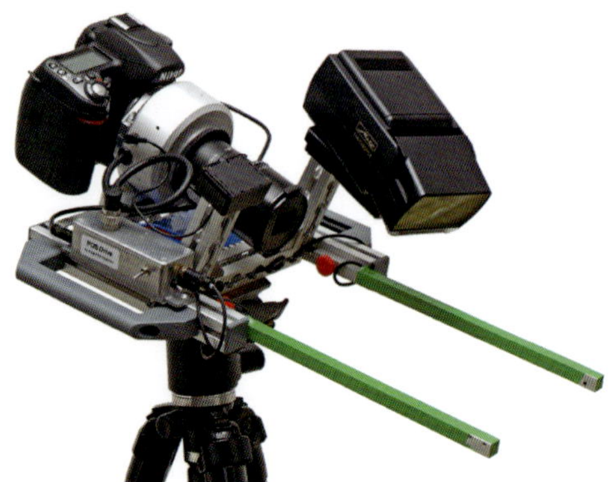

A portable system for photographing flying insects. A fast external central leaf shutter system replaces the slower internal focal-plane shutter, which dramatically improves the reaction time to within two milliseconds of when the light barrier is tripped. A special electronic system controls this external shutter as well as the light barrier. A Componon-S 4/80 or an Apo-Rodagon 4/80 serve well as a lens. Lighting is provided by two Metz 40 MZ-3i units that operate at 1/64 to 1/256 of their max output depending on the subject. The system accordingly allows for shutter speeds of around 1/20,000 s to 1/50,000 s.

How far can you go into the realm of macro photography when working with light barriers?

The answer to this question depends directly on the ability of the light barrier to detect objects as well as how precisely the system can detect objects. A reflective light beam detector is sensitive enough to react to objects around 1mm in size. Because of the divergence of the light beam, however, this level of sensitivity is not uniform across the entire detection area, and the detection performance also depends on the diameter of the reflector, which typically falls in the 20mm to 40mm range. A through-beam sensor, which is superior at concentrating its detection beam, will generally offer better results.

Laser light barriers are also suitable for working with tiny subjects in the macro range because their narrow, parallel detection beams precisely locate and respond to miniscule subjects.

What circumstances are best for maximizing the chance of capturing an insect in flight?

Your chances are best wherever the density of flying bugs is greatest. A summer meadow with blooming varieties of the celery family, for example, will attract interesting insects. On most days, your barrier will trip in half-minute intervals if you position your system over an attractive blossom.

What opportunities exist for composing your photographs?

Aside from taking care of the basics, such as sharpness and exposure, your control over composition is effectively limited to the background design for your scene. When shooting with a stationary light barrier system, for instance, you can style and position various natural elements or pieces of cardboard behind your key detection area. In contrast, you're basically stuck with whatever is naturally present for your background with portable light barrier systems that you would use on location. And you have utterly no control over how photogenic your subject will appear within the frame—it's up to chance whether you find your results satisfying or not.

What percentage of your photos are successful?

The rate of success, or yield, of high-speed photography is determined by your system's latency. A light barrier itself is generally fast enough to detect any intruding object, but cameras are significantly less quick to react. Shutter lags are often long enough to allow the subject plenty of time to scurry away before the flash finally discharges. A quick central leaf shutter will generally increase your rate of success. The yield is impossible to estimate for portable light barriers—success with these devices relies on chance as much as the prowess of the photographer.

Is there a long learning curve when getting started with light barriers? Or will I start producing attractive pictures right away?
You will get results immediately simply by positioning your light barrier setup in an area offering a plethora of subjects. Whether the results will be good, however, is not within the photographer's sphere of influence. You can only do your best to operate your system correctly. Practicing with your equipment extensively before heading out into the field is highly recommended to ward off user error and any preventable complications later on.

How fast do insects fly?
That's a tough question to answer, because insect speed is difficult to measure. A bee weighed down with pollen can barely travel faster than 0.5 m/s. In unencumbered, straight flight they can reach 8 m/s. Dragonflies and skipper butterflies can travel at speeds up to two or three times as fast as that and are among the fastest of the insect world.

What's the best way to approach subjects?
If you want to photograph an insect that isn't buzzing around a blossom and is more or less isolated by itself in flight, then you'll need to stalk it with a portable light barrier system. The more you try this method, the more discoveries you'll make. Some beetles and shield bugs, for example, are sluggish to react to stimulus and are difficult to coax into flight. Exercise patience, though, or they'll take to the air as soon as you take your eyes off them. In contrast, other bugs, like grasshoppers, are rather jumpy, as their name implies. Setting up shop near the exit of a wasp's nest is a good way to ensure that one of its residents will trip your light barrier regularly, but for obvious reasons, don't disturb the wasps too much.

Aside from the extreme examples, the patterns of behavior in the insect world are diverse and varied. For the most part, bugs are erratic and unpredictable with their movements, which means that luck will always play a principal role in capturing the images you seek.

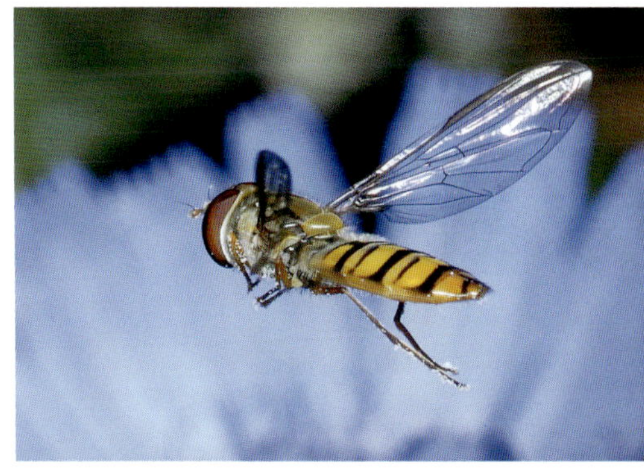

Hoverfly
Nikon D80, Componon-S 4/80
Photo by Hans Christian Steeg

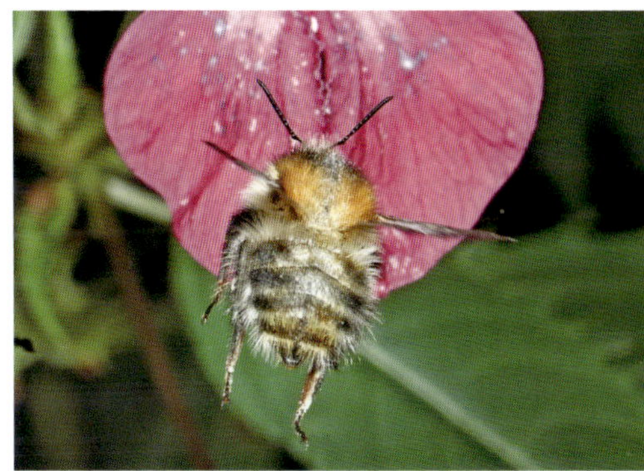

Wild bee on Indian balsam
Nikon D80, Componon-S 4/80
Photo by Hans Christian Steeg

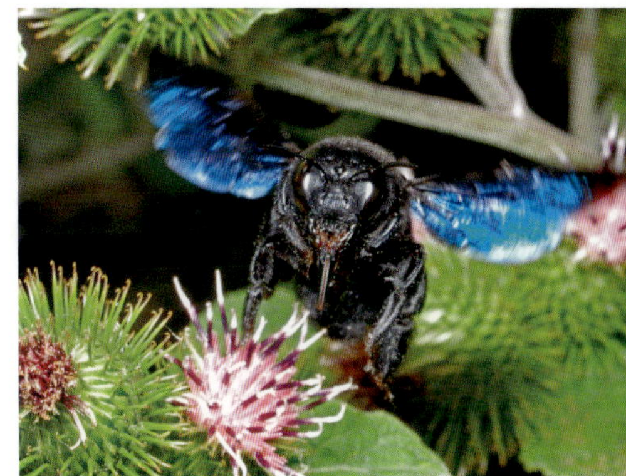

Carpenter bee collecting pollen
Nikon D80, Componon-S 4/80
Photo by Hans Christian Steeg

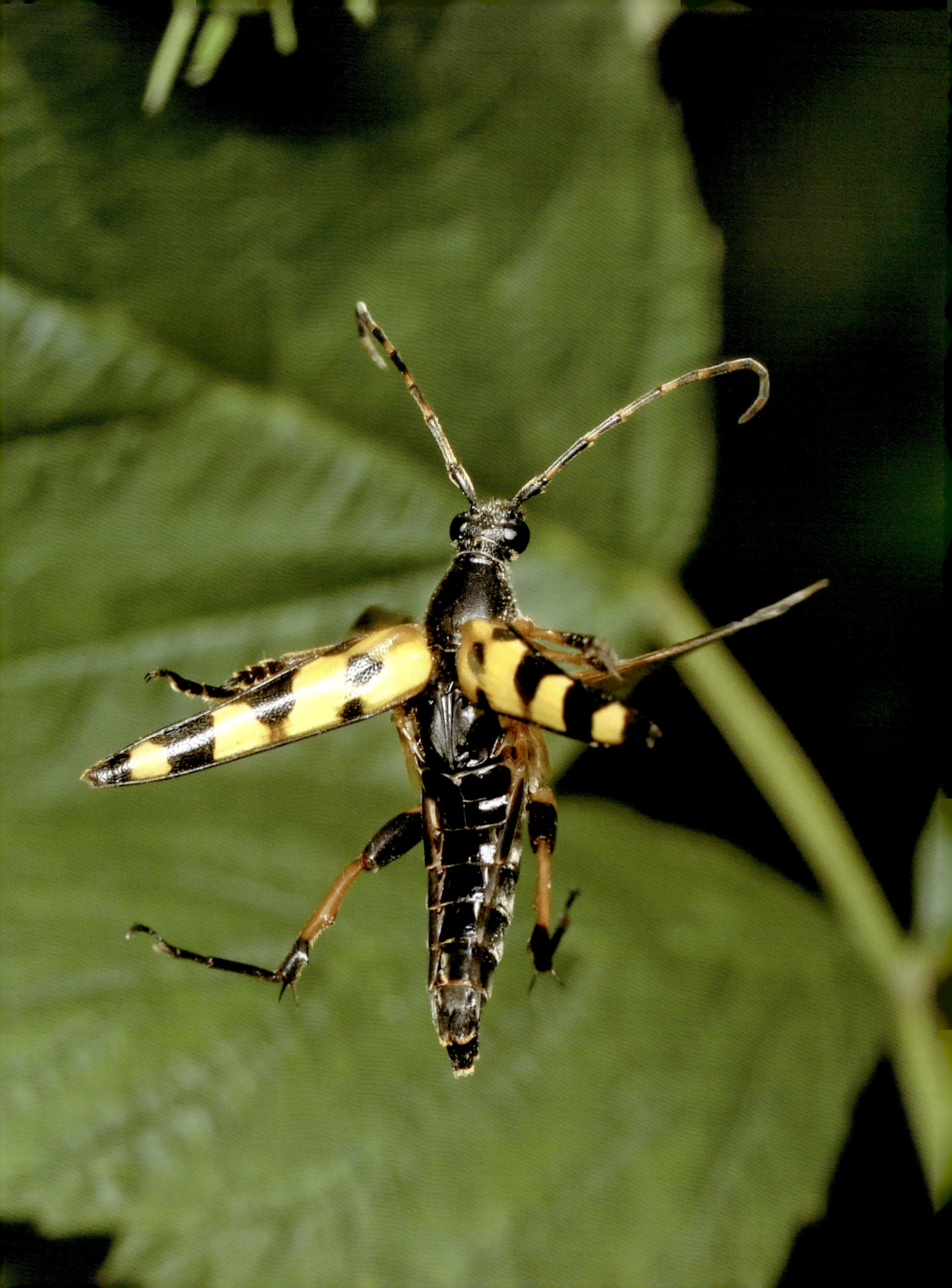

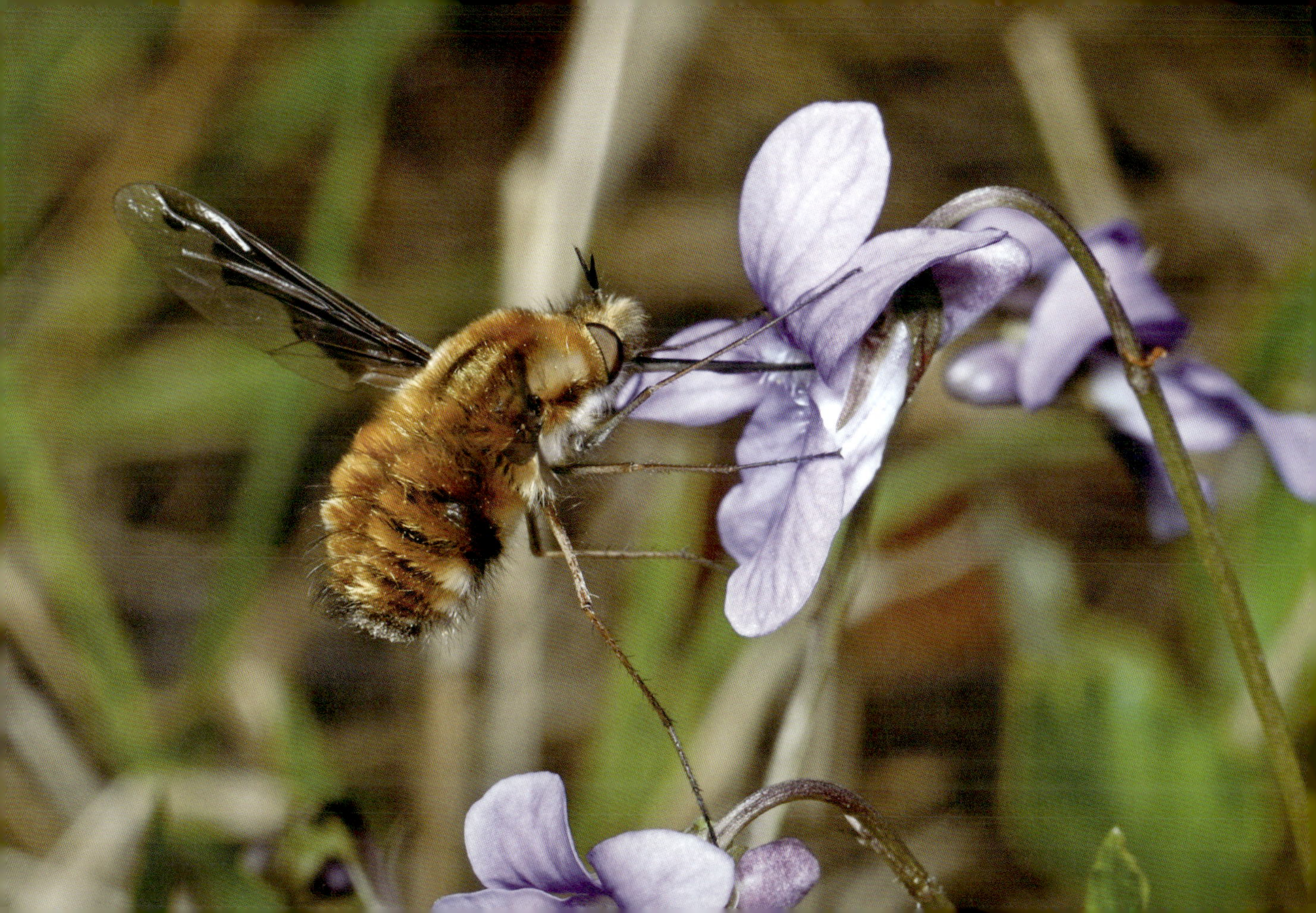

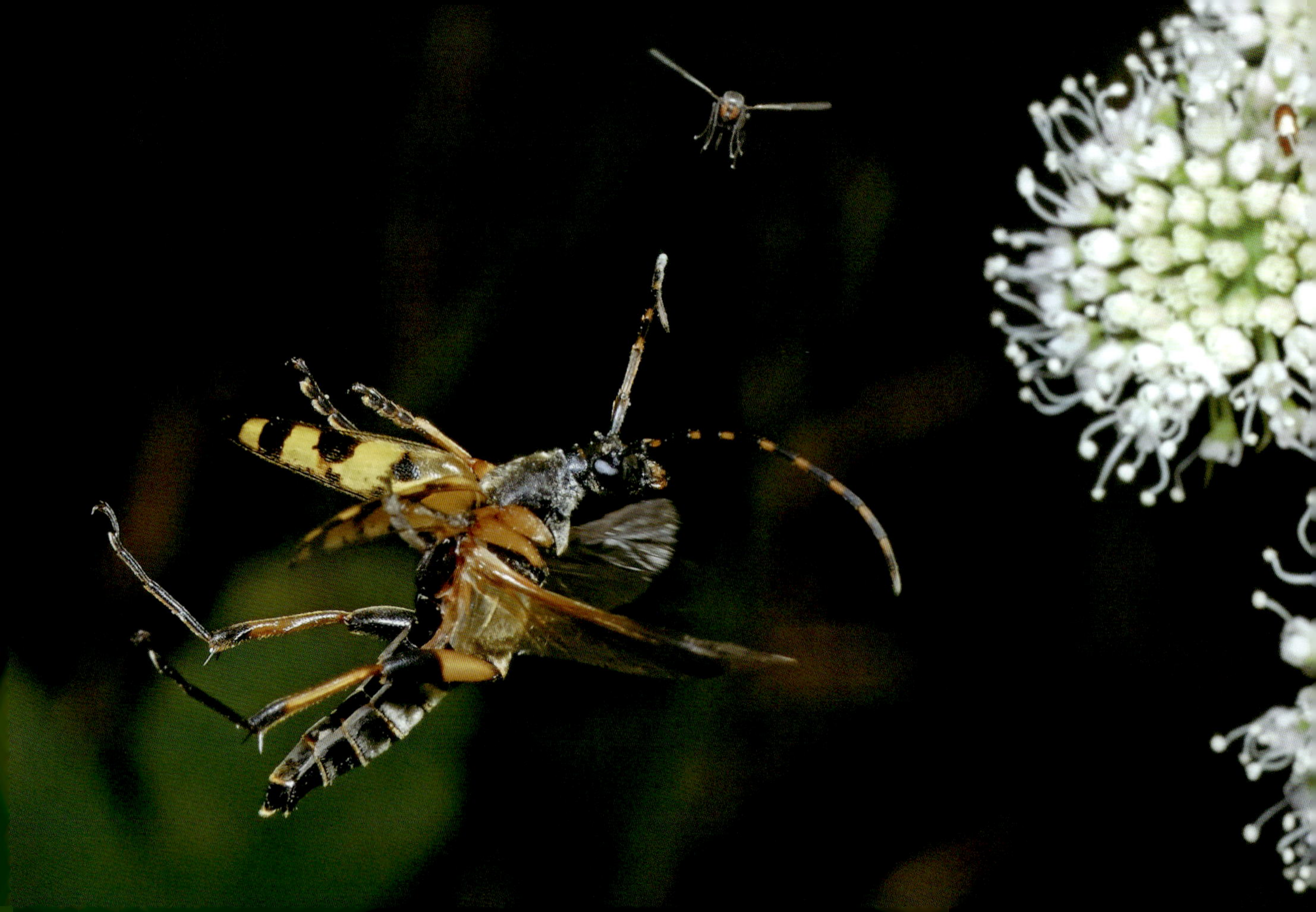

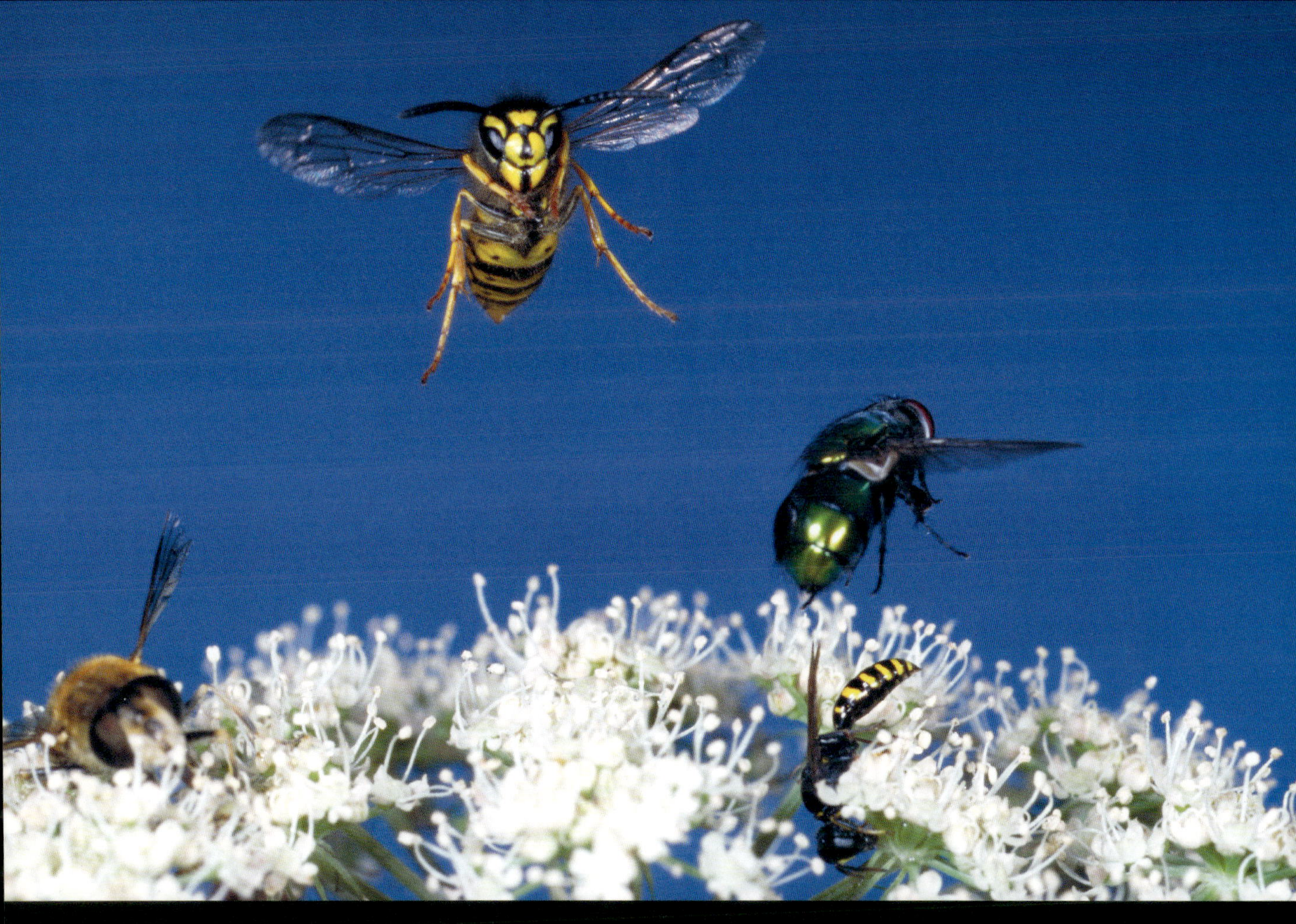

Common wasps
Nikon D4S, Photar 5.6/120, scan from slide
Photo by Hans Christian Steeg

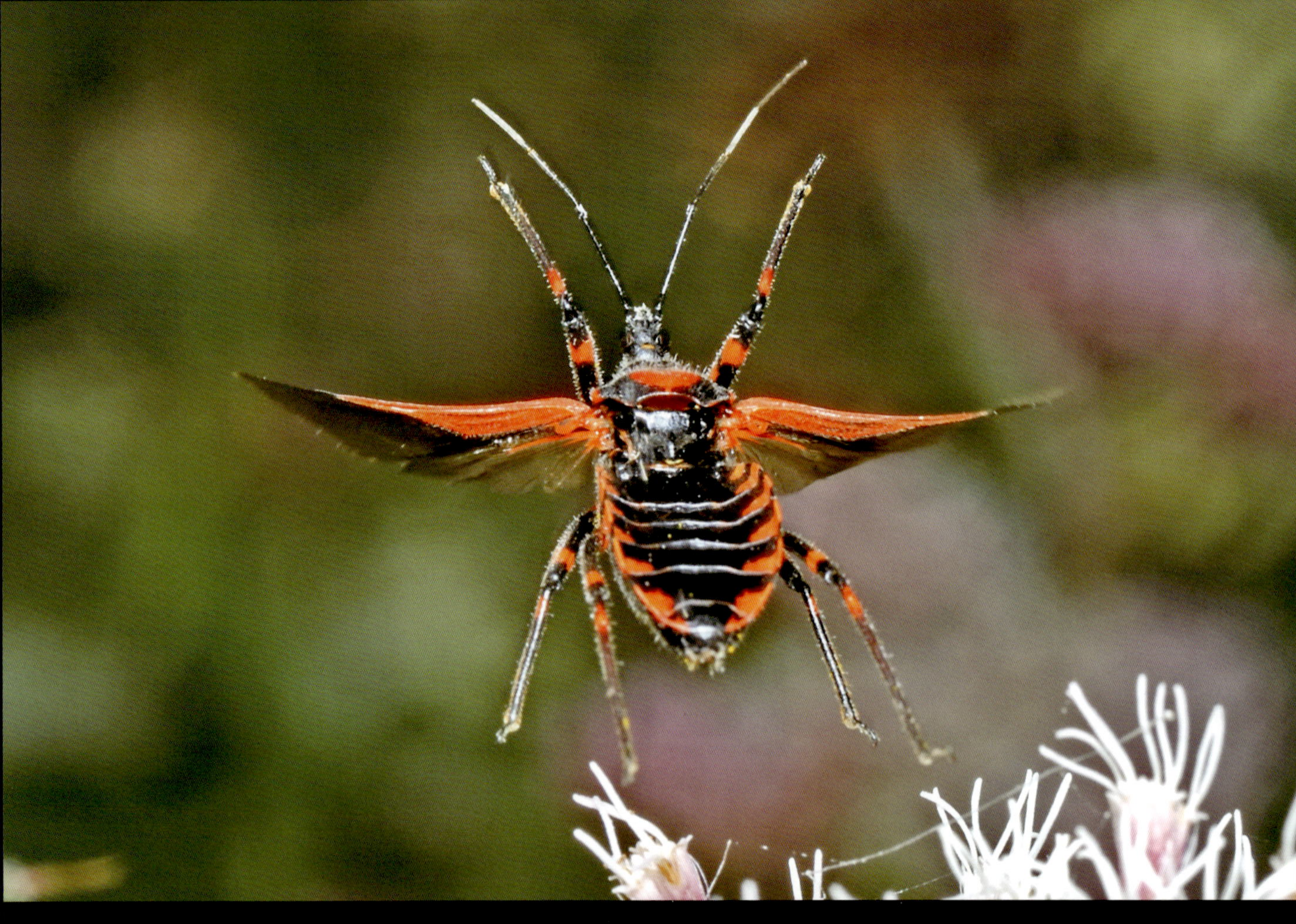

Red assassin bug (Slovenia)
Nikon D80, Componon-S 4/80
Photo by Hans Christian Steeg

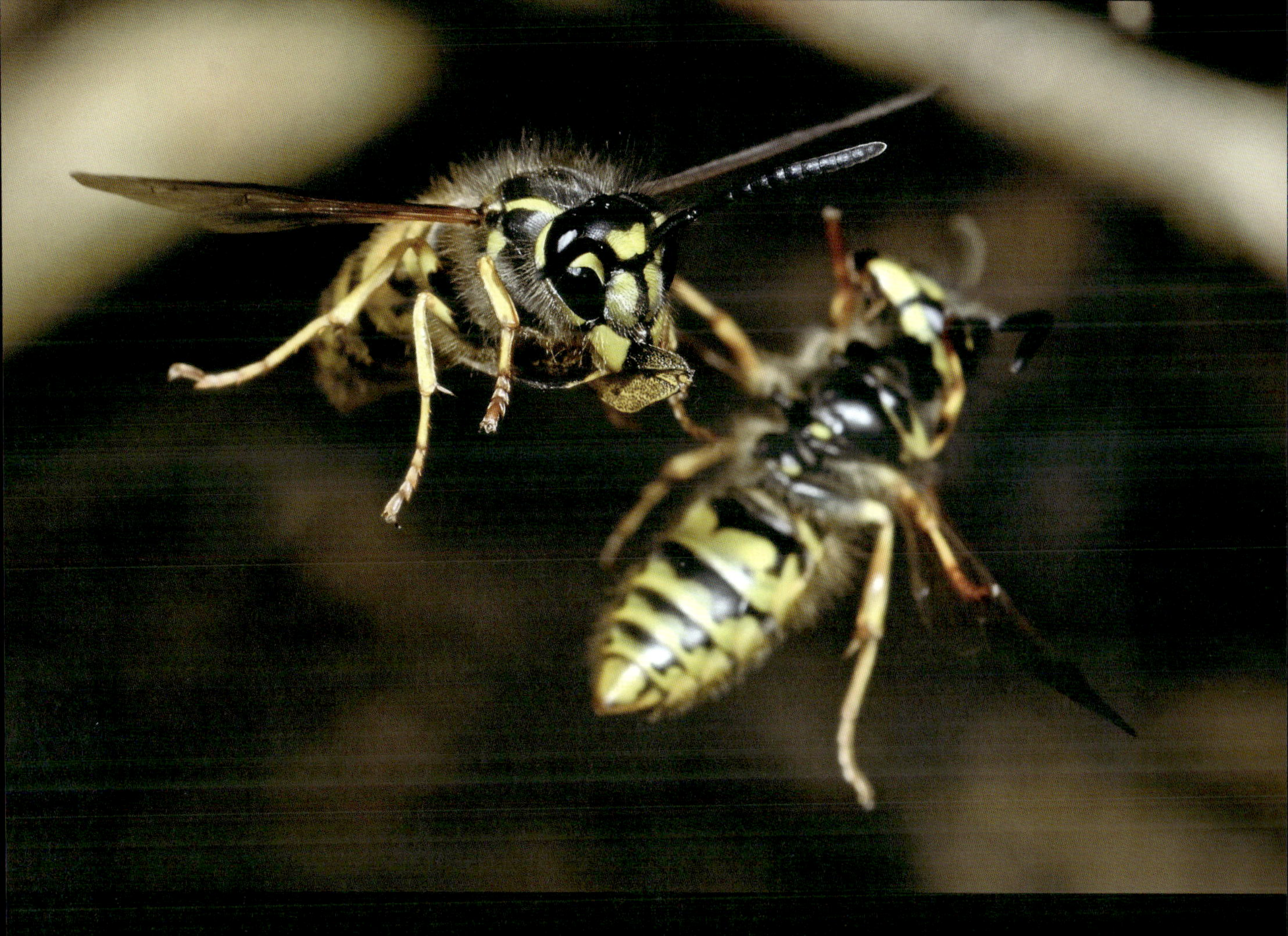

Midflight collision
Nikon D7000, Photar 5.6/80
Photo by Hans Christian Steeg

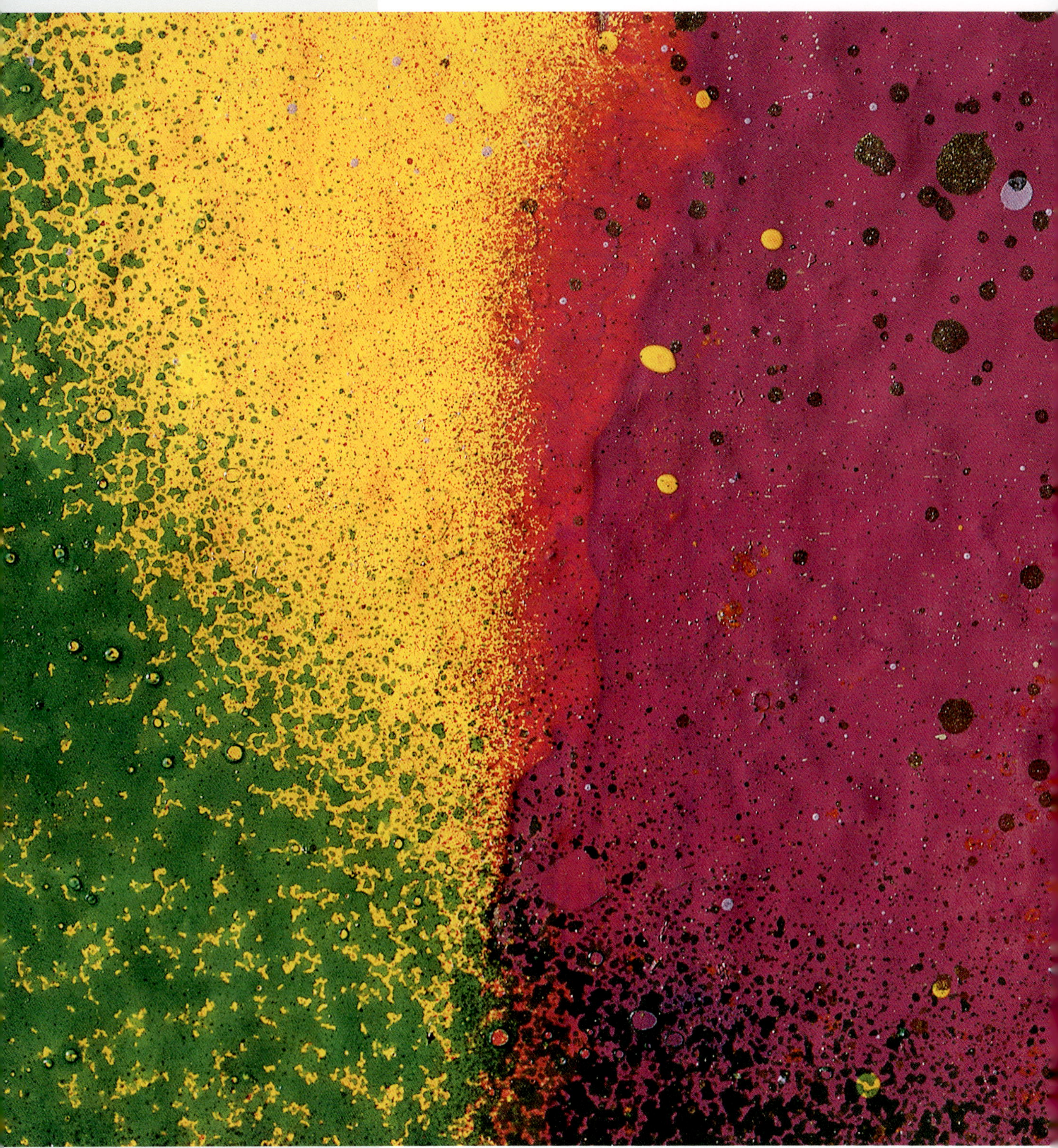

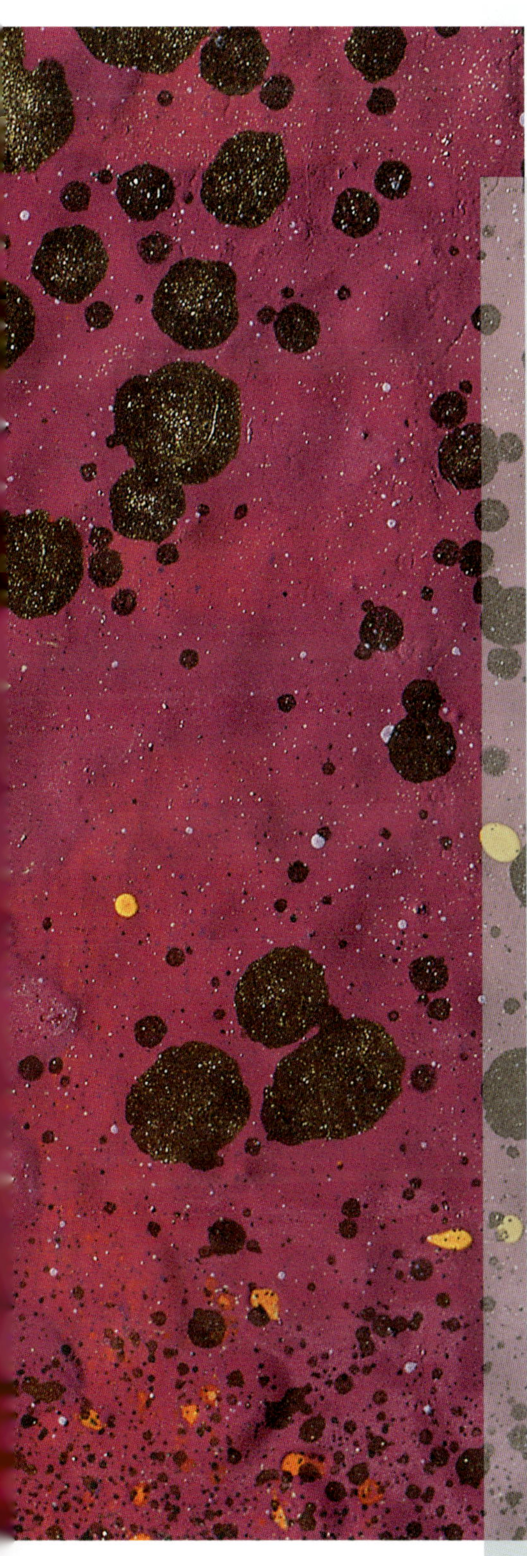

Searching for Subjects

People tend to always associate the same subjects with macro photography: objects from the botanical, etymological, and perhaps technological kingdoms. People also tend to understand the purpose of macro imaging to be relatively limited in scope: revealing familiar objects from the natural world in larger-than-life pictures. But there is an amazingly complex world of abstract beauty hidden in the ordinary world around us.

I shot the image on the left—along with many others like it—in a park in my hometown, where a gallery of graffiti art is always on display. Large, vertical sheets of concrete provide a canvas for revolving artists to display their work. The installations are fascinating to take in from a normal perspective, but zeroing in on individual details reveals an incredible wealth of shapes and colors that result from repeatedly painting or spraying over previous murals. Accordingly, these photographs don't reveal the work of an individual artist; they document unintentionally collaborative creations that have been in development for weeks, months, and even years. The closer you get to these paintings photographically, the more opportunities you discover for images of singular beauty comprising overlapping textures, blending colors, and random shapes. These macro images represent a frozen moment of a constantly changing canvas.

Graffiti detail
f/8, 1/250 s, ISO 200, 50mm

Discovering, Searching for, and Collecting Subjects

Subjects for macro photography can be found anywhere. Some you will discover simply by walking around with open eyes; others you have to search for in specific circumstances, and some are dependent on the time of year or the time of day. Materials are critical to macro photography—perhaps more so than any other photographic discipline.

Discovering Subjects

If your goal is to explore the mini cosmos around you and to document your discoveries, then all it takes to find an abundance of subjects is to keep your eyes peeled. You'll quickly develop a sense

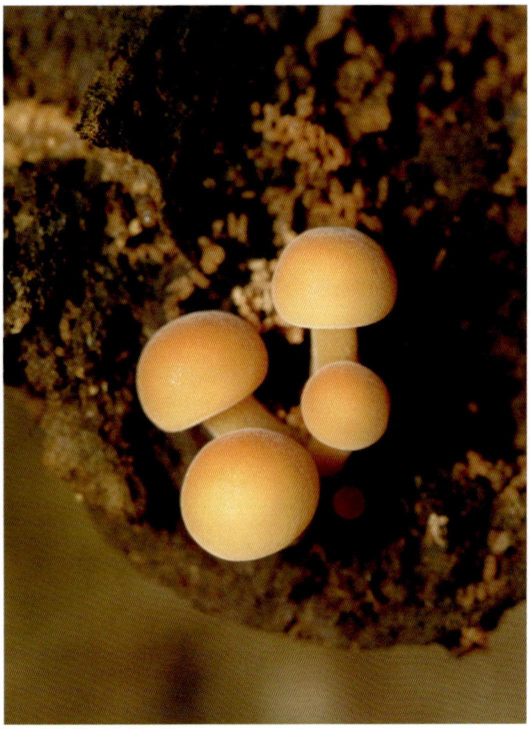

Autumn is mushroom season. Fungi love moisture and warmth, so a day or two after a rainstorm is an ideal time to search for them.
f/5.6, 1/250 s, ISO 640, 180mm

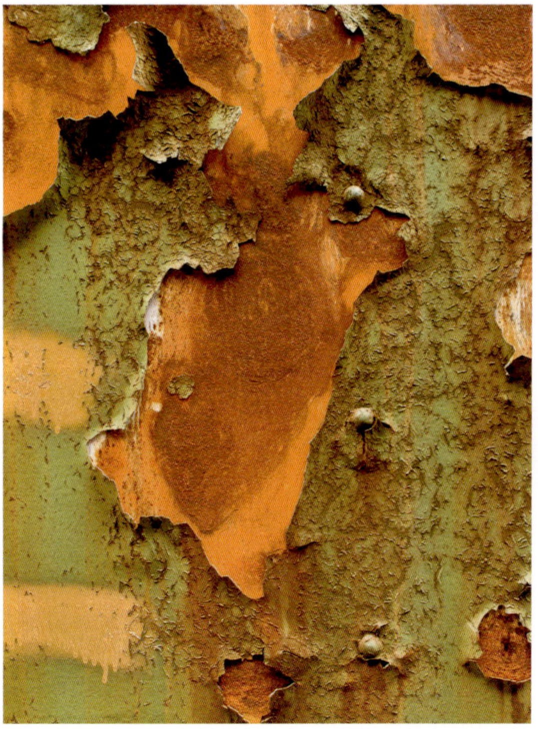

Rust is ubiquitous. Locations betraying telltale signs of wear and tear on a large scale will also offer up compelling subjects well-suited for close-up and macro photographs.
f/4.1, 1/100 s, ISO 100, 12.2mm

of where to look, which stones to overturn, and which fences to climb in the quest for interesting subjects. The promise of a rewarding location is often evident in the larger characteristics of the scene. A flower-strewn meadow bathed in sunlight offers a range of not only floral subjects but also all the insect life inherent to it. Areas where the passage of time is clearly evident are similarly rich with possibilities. If decay is present on a large scale, then you can count on signs of wasting away to be present in small ways, too. Abandoned train stations, junkyards, and industrial wastelands are teeming with subjects representing all stages of ruin. In a best-case scenario, the natural world will have started to return to these areas, offering contrasts of rusty industrial metals with budding plants, such as dandelions pushing up through cracks in asphalt, mushrooms sprouting on rotting balconies, and so on. Even those who are not on the hunt for specific subjects will have no shortage of subjects to choose from—nature provides.

Searching for Subjects

Things get a little more complicated when you have specific inclinations for what you want to photograph. This fact is doubly true when specific species of plants and animals are what you have in mind. Finding these subjects requires a bit of background knowledge for the flora and fauna in question to ensure that you will position yourself to be in the right place at the right time with your camera. Consulting reference material is a good starting point to find out when certain species blossom, migrate, or mate. This research will minimize your reliance on chance to bring you to your subject, and it also helps you plan for what equipment to bring. Advance learning, in other words, may help you decide to leave an additional lens or piece of lighting equipment at home, freeing up some space in your gear bag.

Collecting Subjects

Yet another interesting exercise for cultivating subjects for studies in macro photography is collecting materials from sites that can later be styled and staged in a studio at home. This method comes with the benefit of being able to work in a highly controlled environment with sufficient lighting to create reproducible lighting and high-quality results without having to worry about external influences. I recommend taking the time to clean your collected materials on-site as much as possible, so that once you return home, you can focus your energy and excitement right away on capturing shots.

Collecting various materials suitable for use as backgrounds or decoration is also a worthwhile endeavor. Having a store of stones,

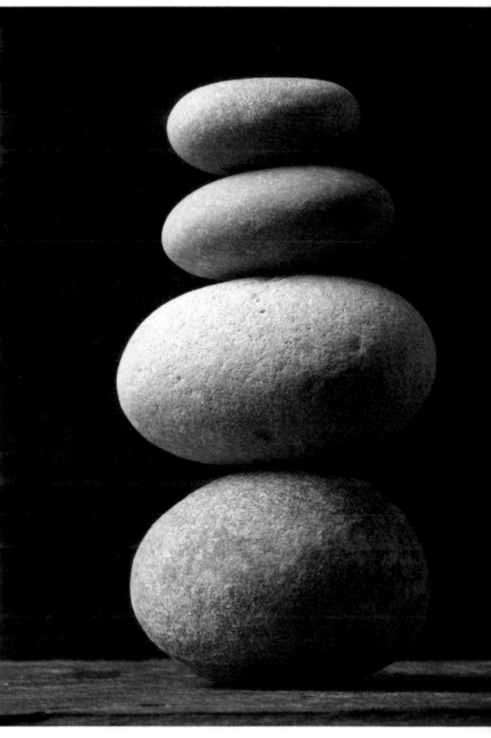

The look and feel of this photo is established largely through side lighting. I brought the stones home with me after visiting Lake Constance.

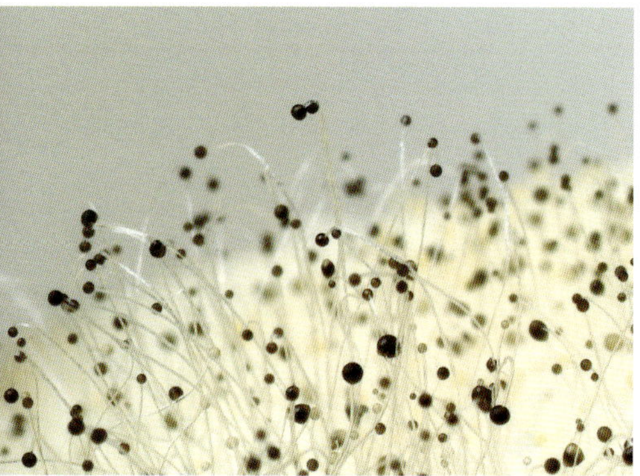

Mold on a piece of cheese

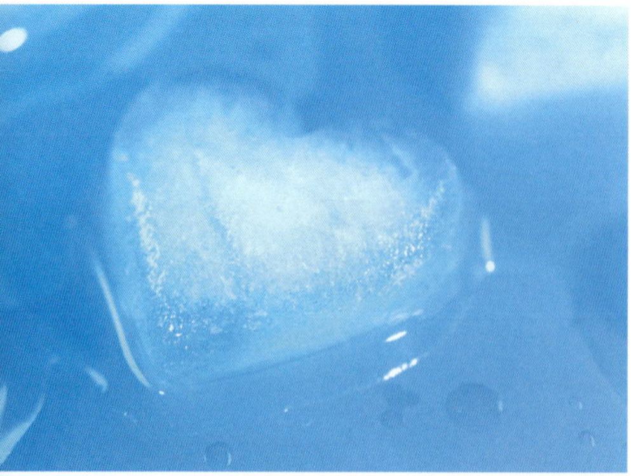

Ice cubes can be made in a variety of interesting and unusual shapes

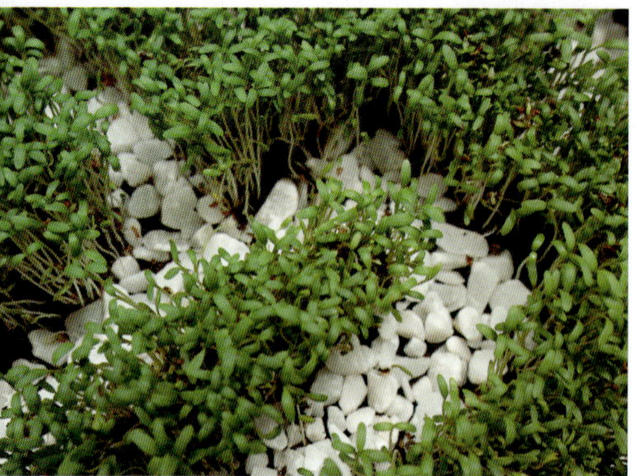

Cress sprouts within a few days and grows very quickly—here in the shape of a labyrinth

dried grasses, weathered wood, and other interestingly shaped objects improves your ability to compose and arrange studio images dramatically.

Creating Subjects

If you can't find what you're looking for, creating subjects on your own is always a possibility. You might, for example, grow a culture of mold on a bowl of yogurt or you might create ice cubes in various shapes. Your yard is also a rich place to grow subjects to fuel your macro ambitions. A bag of wildflower seeds will yield a trove of floral subjects in addition to inviting curious insects into your domain. Even planters on the balcony or hanging from a window are more than enough to grow a garden of subjects. Plants are fascinating and rewarding specimens throughout all the stages of their growth.

Gifting Subjects

Spontaneously gifting someone a bouquet of flowers is not only a kind gesture, it's also a welcome opportunity to take some pictures. Assembling the best images from the shoot into a collage and having it printed in a large format is a lovely way to remember the occasion as well as to have something to cherish long after the flowers have wilted.

Documenting Subjects

Macro photography can also play a role in documenting memorable experiences like an unforgettable summer vacation. You might, for example, endeavor to create a "digital herbarium" cataloging all of the plants in the location of your destination. This type of project may offer a more rewarding memento than usual snapshots of beaches and tourist sites. The Internet offers a wealth of information about the flora and fauna of specific regions in the world, as do nature conservancy organizations and bookshops. Using these resources to prepare for your trip may prove to be a gratifying way to gain an entirely different perspective of your destination.

Opposite: Flower seeds are fascinating in their own right. Of course, with a bit of patience, they also grow into attractive photographic subjects.

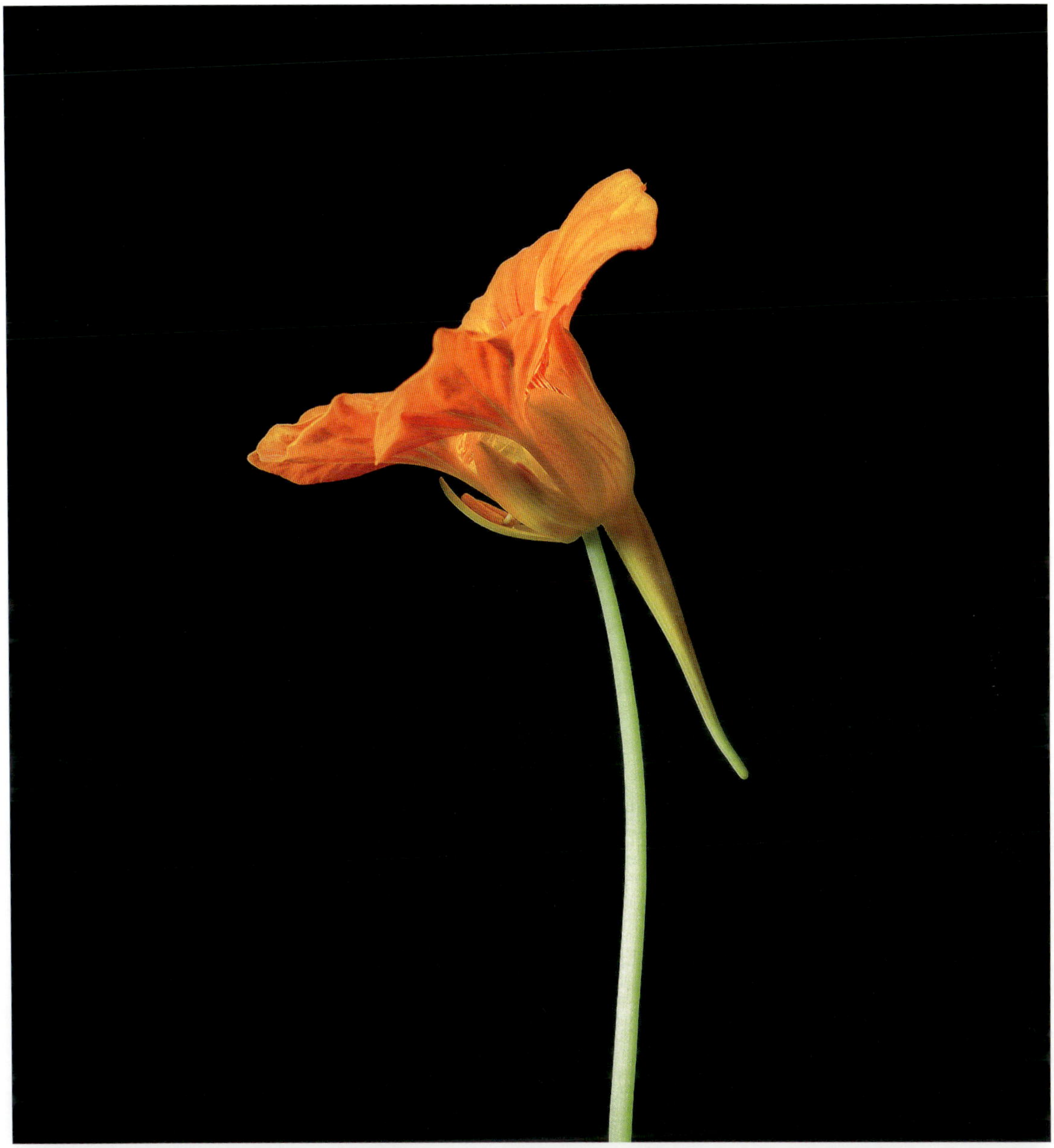

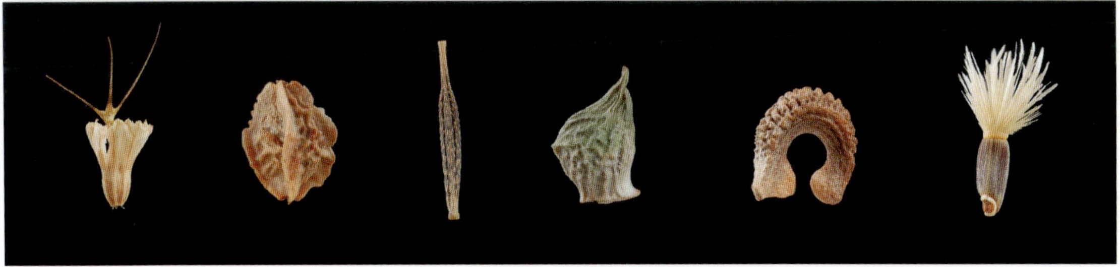

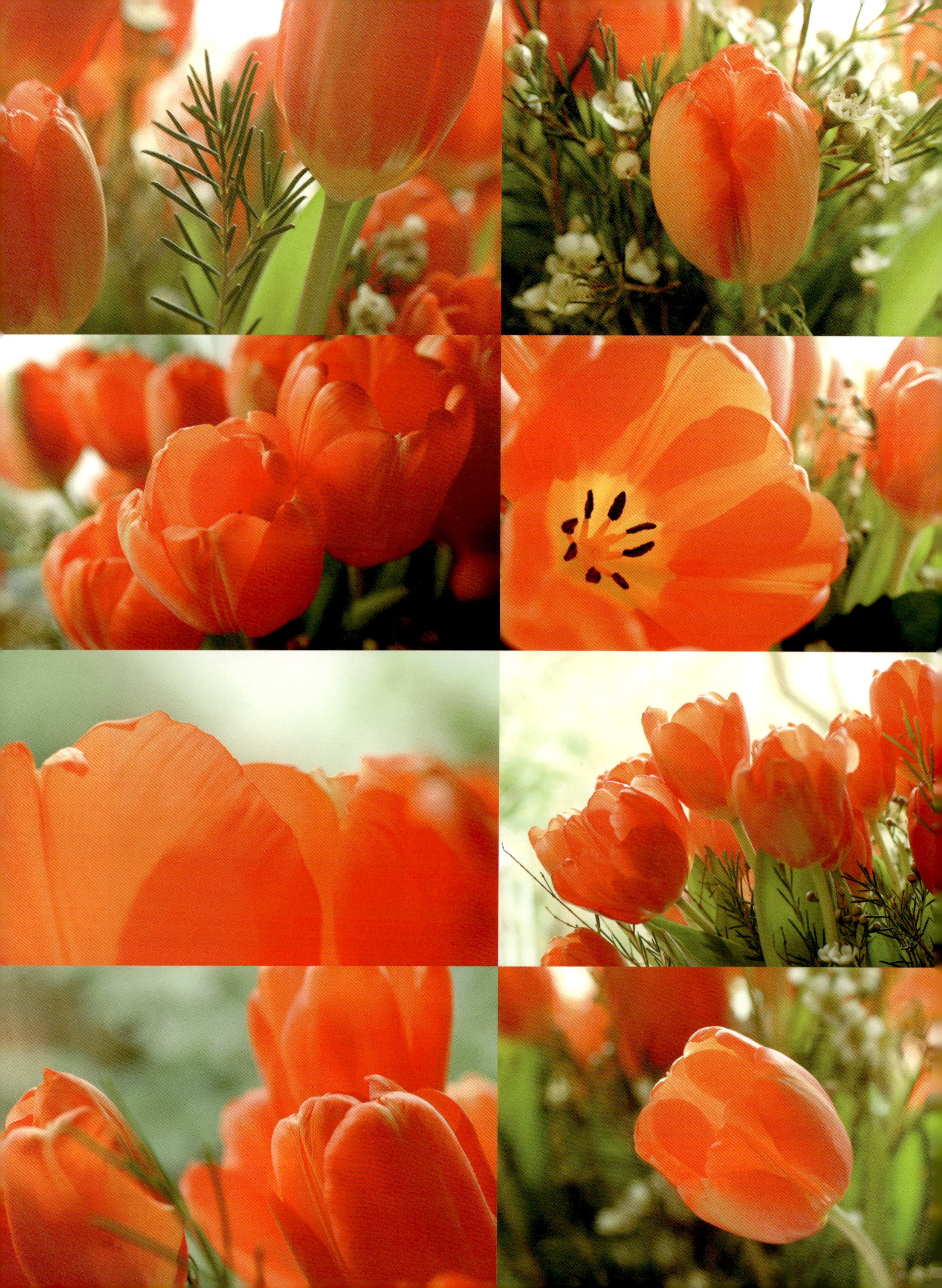

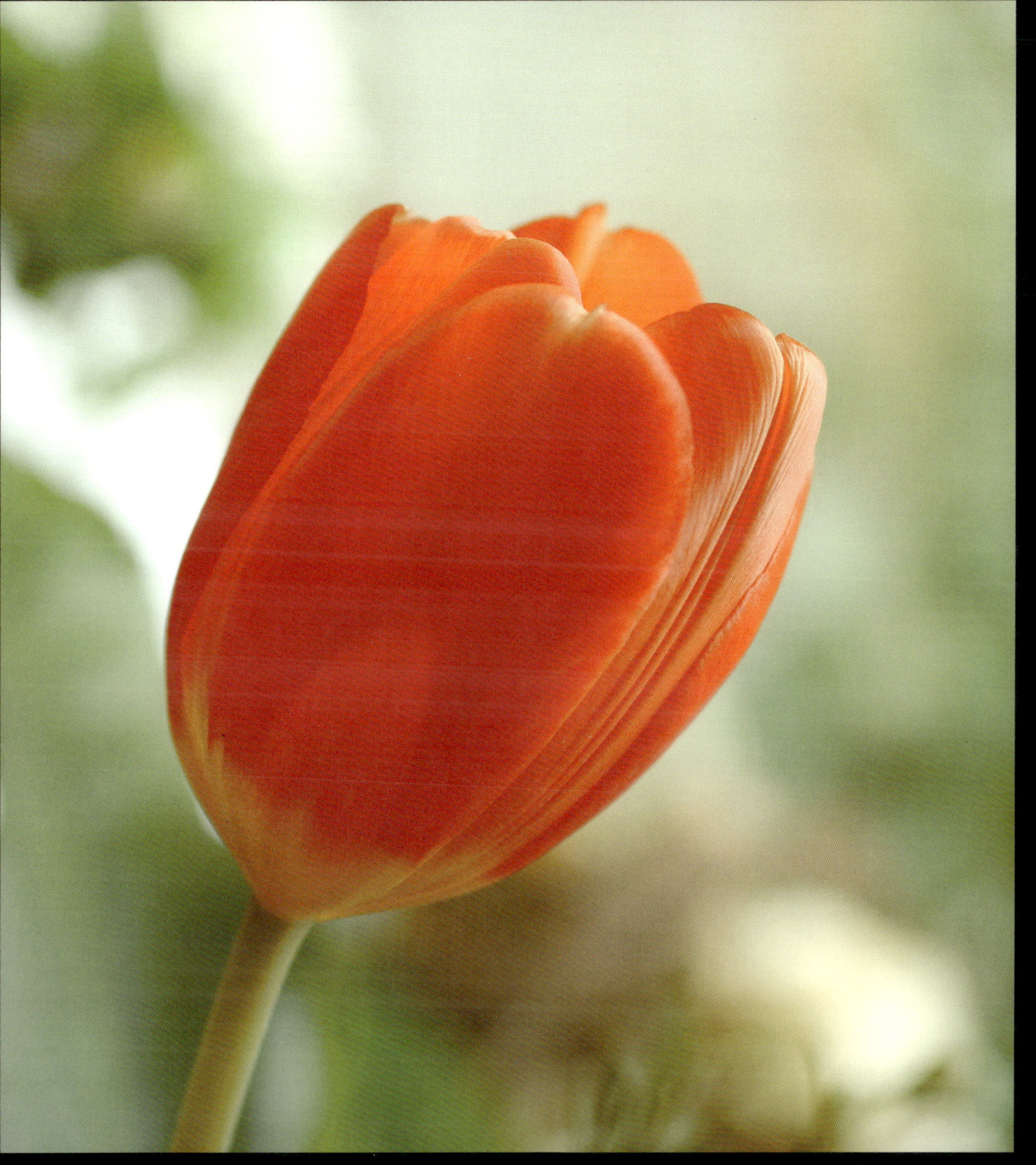

Flower bouquets are all too happy to sit for a
lengthy macro photo shoot. Using a wide aperture
produced attractive bokeh. The images were shot
with a 50mm macro and a 20mm wide-angle lens.

Variations on a Theme

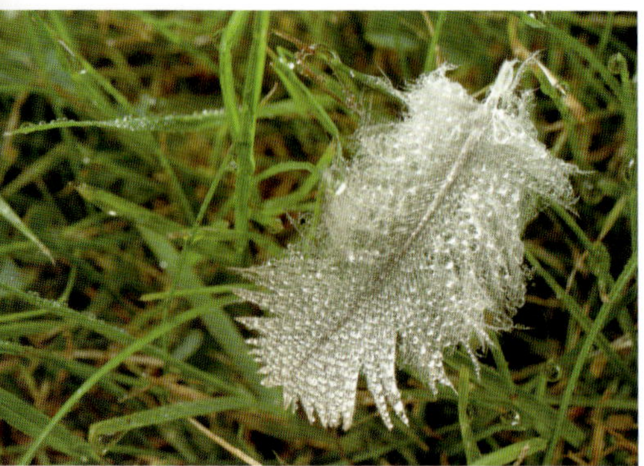

*Found still life
f/13, 1/125 s, ISO 100, 50mm, system
flash with softbox*

*Right page, top: Abstract detail of
parrot feathers
f/8, 1/60 s, ISO 160, 105mm, studio
flash with softbox*

*Right page, below:
Detail of a feather duster
f/16, 1/125 s, ISO 100, 160mm, studio
flash with softbox*

Eventually a day will come when you think to yourself, "I've already photographed everything there is to photograph. It's time for me to hang up my camera and try something else." For most of us, this feeling comes up now and again throughout our lives. There's no value in trying to avoid feeling this way; the trick is to engage with this lack of motivation creatively.

One way to generate ideas that often lead to unexpected images is to settle on a specific theme and to shoot a series of images that connect to it. For example, you may decide to shoot a series documenting the life cycle of a native butterfly from the larval stage to an emerged butterfly, including depictions of favored plants for feeding and its habitat. Alternatively, you can settle on a single subject, such as feathers. At first, bird feathers probably come to mind. But as you start engaging with the theme, more and more possibilities arise until you have a nearly inexhaustible fund of ideas. Feathers can be found in a variety of contexts ranging from the utilitarian (bedding and quill pens) to the spiritual (Native American ceremonies) to the fashionable (boas and hats). You can photograph the same subject under various circumstances: staged in a studio; as a clinical, documentary photograph; as an abstract image; and much more.

The theme doesn't need to be a concrete object, either. Abstract concepts such as "blue" or "soft" work well too, giving you an endless range of possibilities. Temporal subjects such as the mutability of nature also make for rich photographic series. For instance, you may document the full life cycle of a flower from the seed up through blossoming, pollination, the growth of fruit, ending with the withered plant.

Yet another exercise is to document a meadow from a variety of perspectives, first starting with an overview shot and then zeroing in on an individual plant, specific details about that plant, and finally all the way into the extreme macro perspective. A systematic plan, in other words, is an effective way to counter photographer's block. Accepting some creative constraints is a productive way to force yourself to generate new ideas that you likely wouldn't otherwise have considered. And these ideas can in turn be used with a range of subjects.

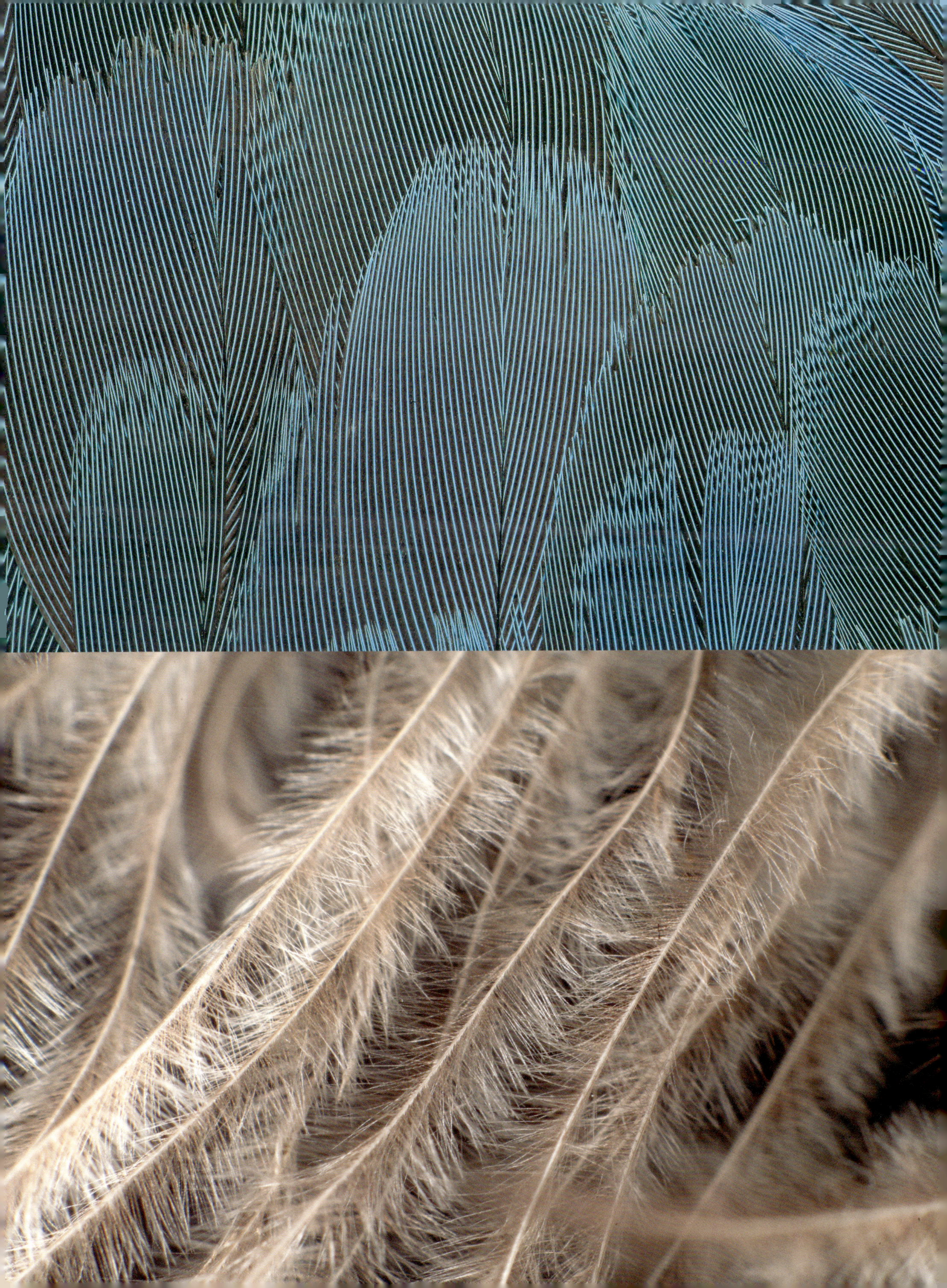

Abstract Subjects

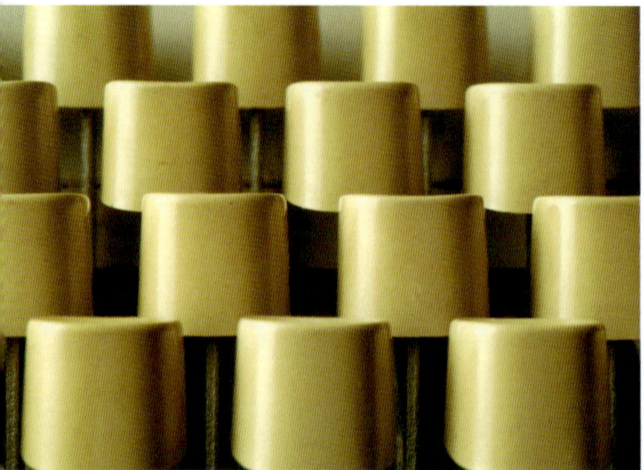

Keys of a 1960s typewriter
f/22, 1/125 s, ISO 100, 60mm, studio
flash with softbox

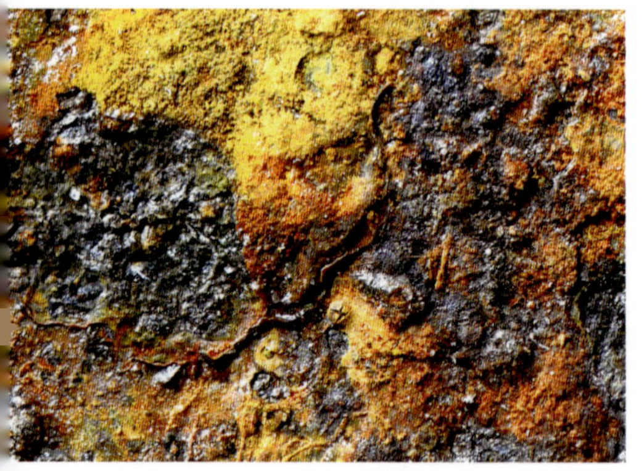

Rusted metal surface
f/8, 0.6 s, ISO 100, 60mm macro lens
with 31mm extension tube, mirror
lockup, desk lamp for lighting

Abstract photographs at the macro level are particularly fun because viewers often aren't able to identify what the subject actually is at first glance. These images effectively become mini visual puzzles, forcing viewers to look at familiar objects from an unfamiliar vantage.

When shooting relatively flat subjects with magnification levels up to 1:2, it's relatively easy to position the camera parallel to the subject, producing sharpness across the subject's entire body. A repro stand is likely needed if you're aiming to move even further into the macro perspective. Taking abstract macro levels at magnification greater than 2:1 generally requires a bellows lens with a focusing rail and the requisite stands.

Faithful color reproduction is usually not a pressing concern with abstract photography, so lighting plays something of a secondary role. Ring flash units and LED ring lamps offer even lighting, but they also tend to flatten out subjects. In contrast, side lighting is a powerful choice if you want to accentuate surface textures in your subjects. A simple desk lamp will do the job as will a system flash. Furthermore, you can create interesting lighting effects with hand-held flashlights with adjustable light beams and small LED lamps.

Use of continuous lighting can cause shutter speeds to slow down significantly, making the risk of camera shake a more pressing concern, especially at high levels of magnification. Activating the mirror lockup mode, or at least using a remote trigger system, are effective ways of circumventing this problem.

Subjects that lend themselves to abstract macro treatments can be found anywhere: around the house, in your office, in nature, inside a piece of electronics, or even on the surface of everyday objects. A magnifying glass is a helpful tool for scouting potential subjects, even though you'll discover many subjects just by looking around casually. The power of magnification unlocks the fascinating beauty and details around us, and the closer you can view ordinary subjects, the more discoveries you'll make. What may seem to the naked eye like a uniform, sealed surface will appear more like a craggy landscape or an abstract painting when viewed up close.

If you have children in your family, show them a few of your successfully defamiliarizing images, and encourage them to guess what they're looking at.

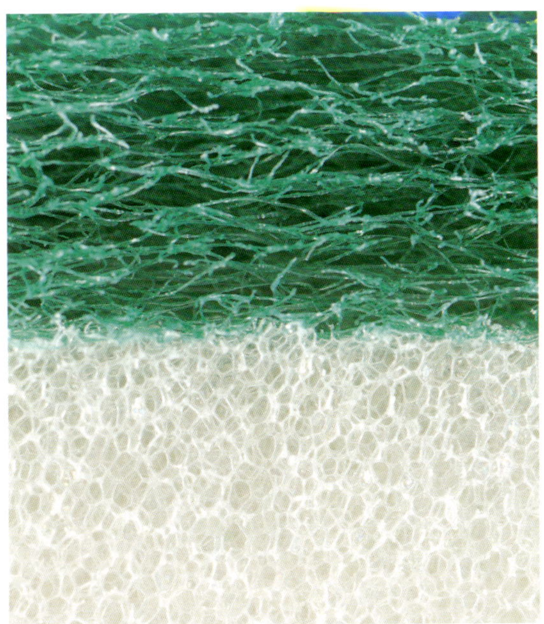

Detail of a sponge. Interesting subjects can be found anywhere, including the kitchen.
f/18, 1/200 s, ISO 100, 60mm, studio flash with beauty dish and honeycomb filter

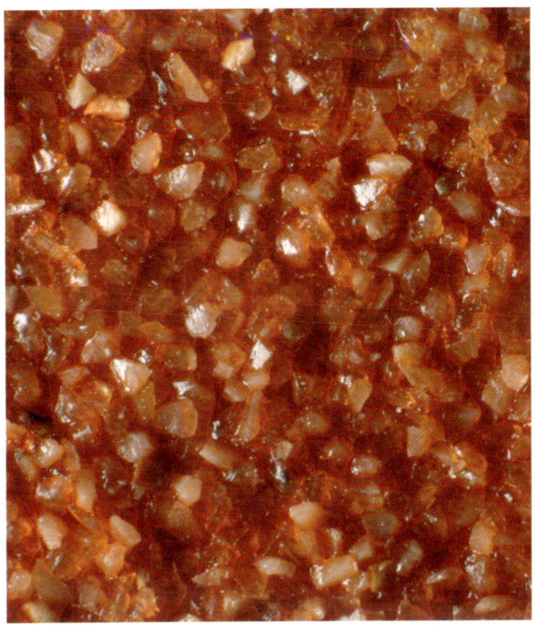

Hobby workshops offer plenty of subjects, too: 60-grit sandpaper

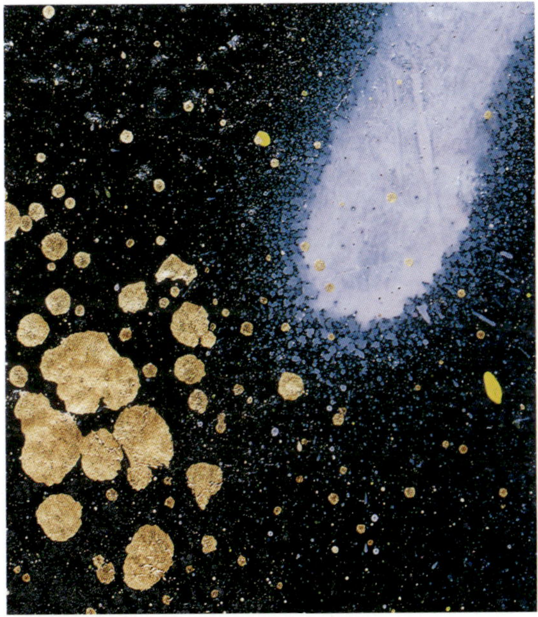

Graffiti detail
f/8, 1/250 s, ISO 200, 50mm, daylight

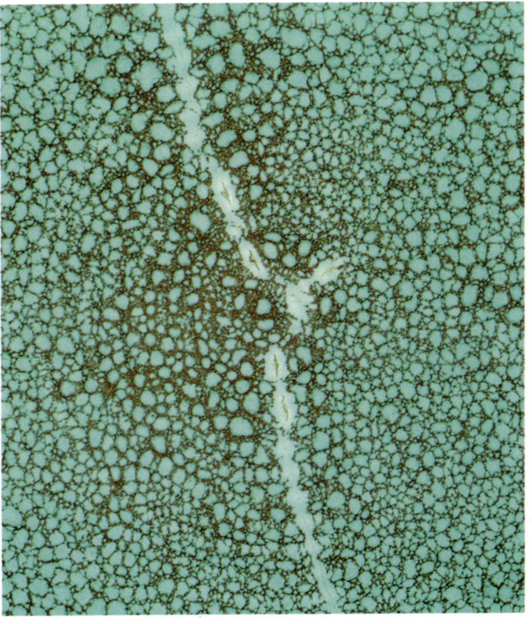

Detail of ceramic glaze
f/9.5, 1/15 s, ISO 200, 50mm, tripod, daylight

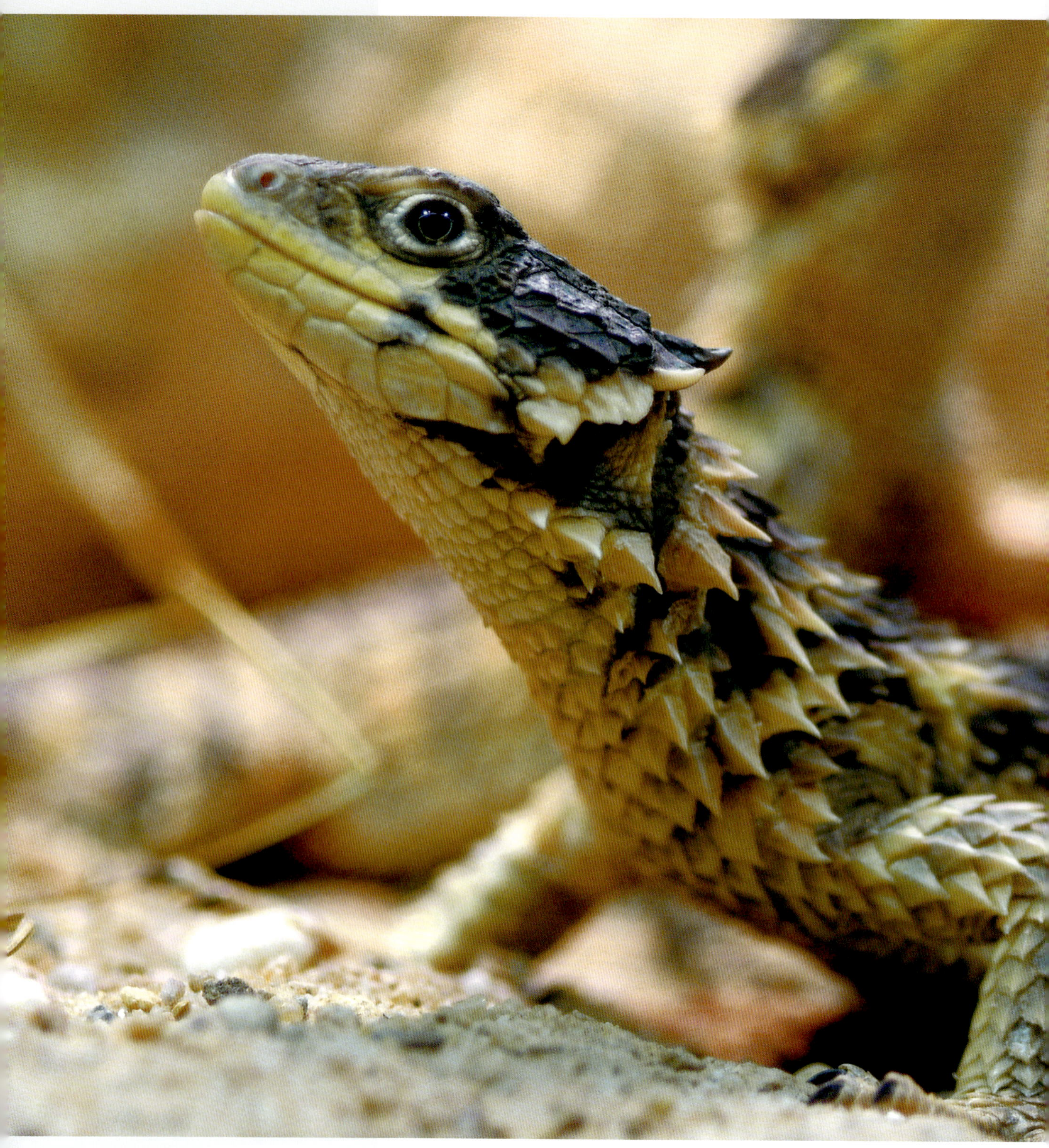

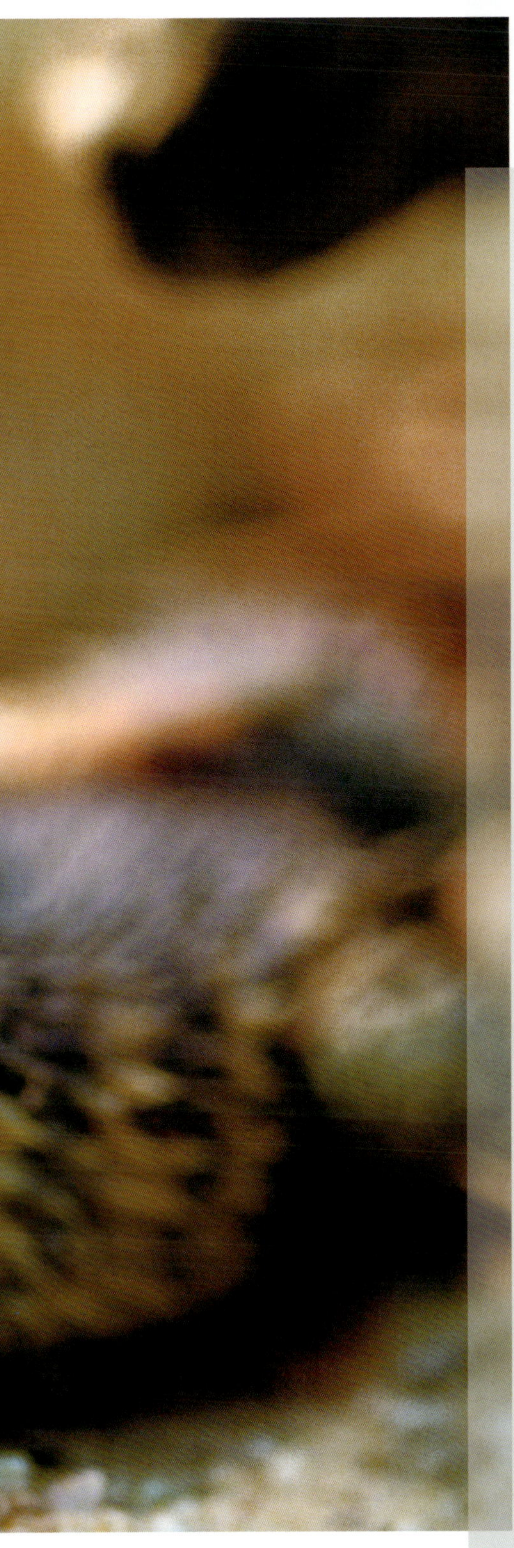

A Day at the Zoo

Even though you can find stunning macro subjects in the orbits of your everyday life, sometimes the urge to take pictures of exotic plants and animals is over-powering. In these instances, a trip to a zoo, aquarium, botanical garden, butterfly garden, or an insectarium is a practical way to gain quick access to rare orchids, poisonous spiders, exotic lizards, and iridescent fish.

These locations are not always public places, so they come with some rules that photographers should heed, especially regarding the use of photographs shot on private grounds. In most cases, personal use of images is unrestricted, but organizations often insist on being identified and credited when such photos are used in commercial publications, such as books and newspapers.

Institutions often post photography guidelines on their websites, but if you can't find the answers to your questions there, don't hesitate to reach out to some-one during your visit to ask a few amicable questions. In my experience, striking up such a conversation tends to open doors. You might learn some interest-ing information that otherwise would have remained unknown, such as when rare plants blossom or when specific animals tend to be active. These details will be welcome to most photographers, and they can play a pivotal role in discovering uncommon subjects.

Lizard at the zoo. Having to negotiate complicated mixed lighting is often unavoidable when taking pictures in a terrarium. For this image, I had to deal with warming lamps and various other forms of artificial sources of light. In these cases, finding a compromise is the only thing to do.
f/4, 1/90 s, ISO 400, 105mm
Location: Wilhelma, Stuttgart, Germany

Zoos

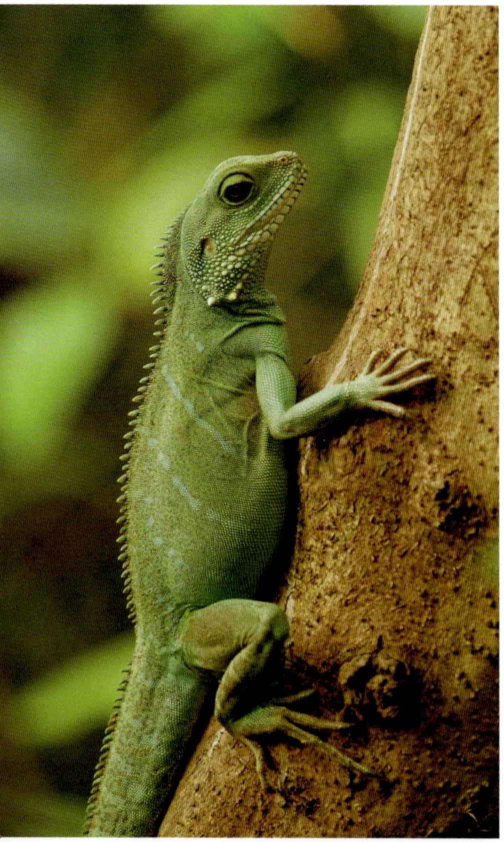

The relatively snug viewing areas at zoo exhibits make it difficult to compose photographs of animals with attractive backgrounds. One recourse for this challenge is using a telephoto lens and a wider aperture to reduce the background to a pleasant blur. Fuji S3 Pro, f/4, 1/200 s, ISO 400, 300mm

There may be no other location on earth that offers up such a concentration of fascinating subjects for photography as a zoo, where you can find polar bears and penguins alongside tigers and a plethora of tiny subjects to boot. The abundance of subject matter generally makes it impossible to shoot everything in a single day. There are a few things to keep in mind in order to produce the best possible results when taking pictures in a zoo.

Not being able to freely walk around your subject in search of the optimal camera perspective is a major constraint. In all but the rarest cases, zoo exhibits offer only a small area for visitors to crane their necks for better views, which makes it difficult to capture the inhabitants with their best face forward. Working with a telephoto lens and a wide aperture offers some relief, in that you can reduce distracting elements behind subjects, such as the bars of a cage behind a bird, into an unrecognizable blur that doesn't detract from the quality of the image.

Even though animals are unable to flee as they would be able to in the wild, patience is still a virtue when working in zoos. If a specimen won't come out from behind a leaf for a clear shot, don't sweat it: move on to your next subject and return later in the day. With a bit of luck, the critter will have overcome its shyness and be ready for its moment in front of the lens.

A busy weekend day at the zoo is not an ideal time for a photographer trudging around with an unwieldy assortment of gear to go about his or her business. Instead, you might try to arrive shortly after the gates open in the morning on a weekday when crowds will be smaller. Zoos often post schedules for special events that happen on the grounds as well as interesting events that happen throughout every day. These scheduling details can be helpful when planning out the sequence of your work. For example, if you note that the sea lions are being fed at a particular time—and likely to draw a crowd at that time—you might plan to make use of the relative calm in the aquarium to concentrate on the subjects you intend to photograph there. On the other hand, these advertised special events are also often occasions that offer up unusual subjects that may attract your attention as a photographer—the blossoming of an exotic plant or the offspring of a rare animal species.

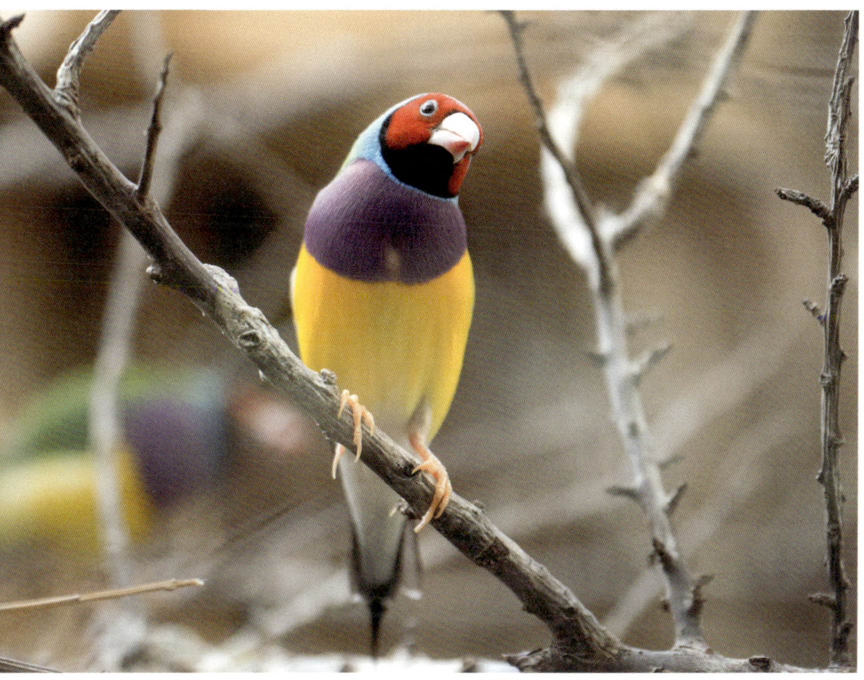

Positioning the camera up close to the cage or glass of an animal's enclosure eliminates the appearance of the grating or reflections from pictures
f/4, 1/200 s, ISO 2000, 180mm
Location: Wilhelma, Stuttgart, Germany

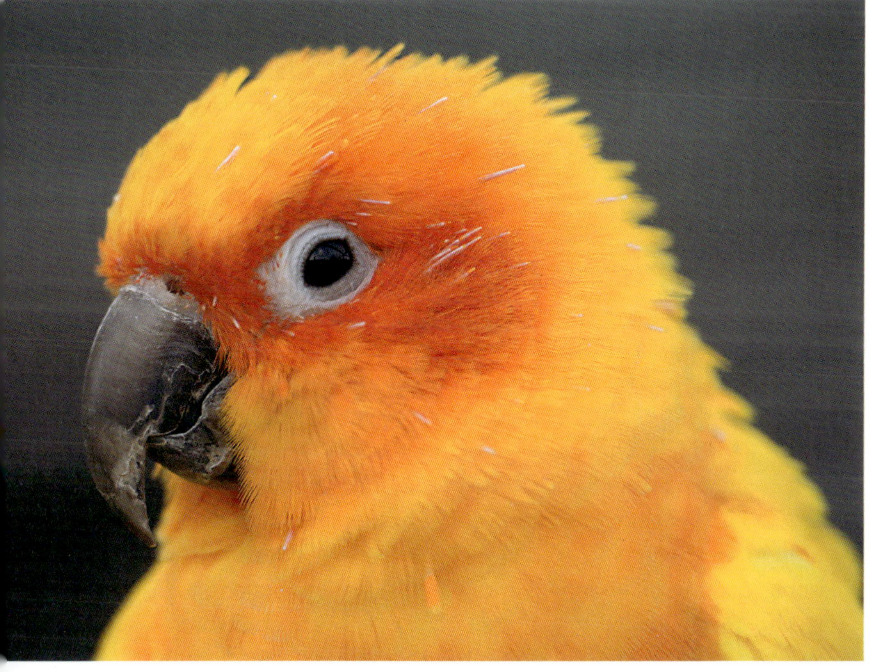

Lenses with long focal lengths or telephoto conversion lenses are essential for capturing portraits of small birds
f/5, 1/800 s, ISO 1250, 180mm, 2x teleconverter
Location: Wilhelma, Stuttgart, Germany

Botanical Gardens

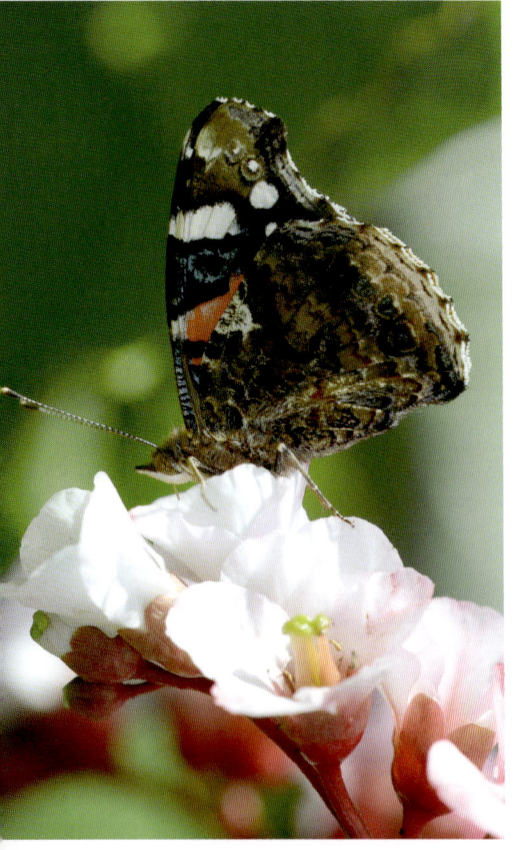

Painted lady butterfly. Flowers and blossoms are the main attraction at botanical gardens—for photographers and butterflies alike.
Nikon D800, f/8, 1/1,000 s, ISO 1000, 180mm
Location: Botanical Gardens of Tübingen, Germany

Botanical gardens are among my favorite locations to take photographs. They offer not only a wealth of subjects from the plant and animal realms, but also the peace and quiet to engage with these specimens thoughtfully—especially on weekdays. Spring and summer are predictably the main time when these gardens erupt in a sea of blossoms for visitors to enjoy. And that's true not just for visitors of the human kind: butterflies, dragonflies, and other little critters know that this occasion is worth treasuring, too. Accordingly, a visit to a botanical garden is also a fantastic opportunity to photograph insects.

This profusion of subject matter makes living with a few restrictions as a photographer an acceptable trade-off. Setting up a tripod in the middle of a flowerbed is understandably frowned upon, so bring along a lens in the telemacro range to be able to still get appreciably close to your subjects. Focal lengths ranging from 150mm to 300mm are ideal both for taking pictures of shy insects as well as for documenting details in plants positioned at the back of a flower bed.

Botanical gardens offer up a ton of information about the subjects likely to catch your eye, at least those of the plant kingdom. And conversations with gardeners or other visitors are also likely to yield interesting and useful details.

Outdoor Habitats

Botanical gardens are usually arranged into various habitats and climate zones that feature representative plants from these regions. On a single afternoon you may pay a visit to an alpine garden; shady creeks with gently curved ferns; a local farmer's garden; small ponds with frogs, newts, and dragonflies; bamboo forests; beds of tulips; and much more. The wetland regions that resemble small landscapes are particularly photogenic, but even the habitats that at first may seem less stunning offer no shortage of subject material ranging from moss and lichen to interesting stones to details of plants. With the right macro treatment, even small and otherwise nondescript blossoms can take on an otherworldly beauty that has nothing to hide, even in comparison to glamorous and oft-coveted orchids.

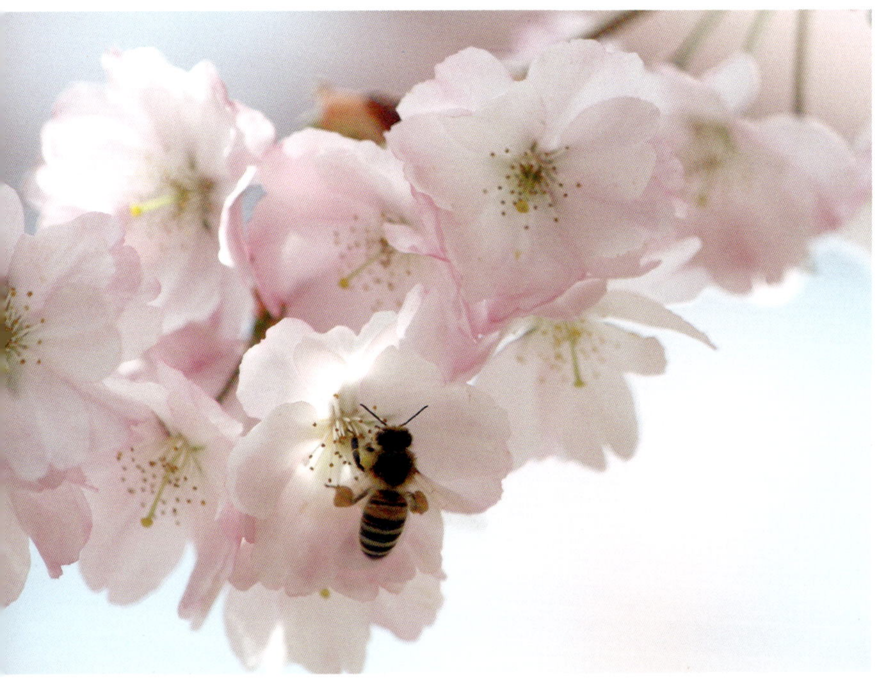

Vernal cherry blossoms bathe every-thing in a sea of soft pink. Here the light-blue sky in the background cre-ates a thoroughly pastel composi-tion contrasted by the solitary bee.
f/5.6, 1/1,500 s, ISO 400, 300mm
Location: Botanical Gardens of Tübingen, Germany

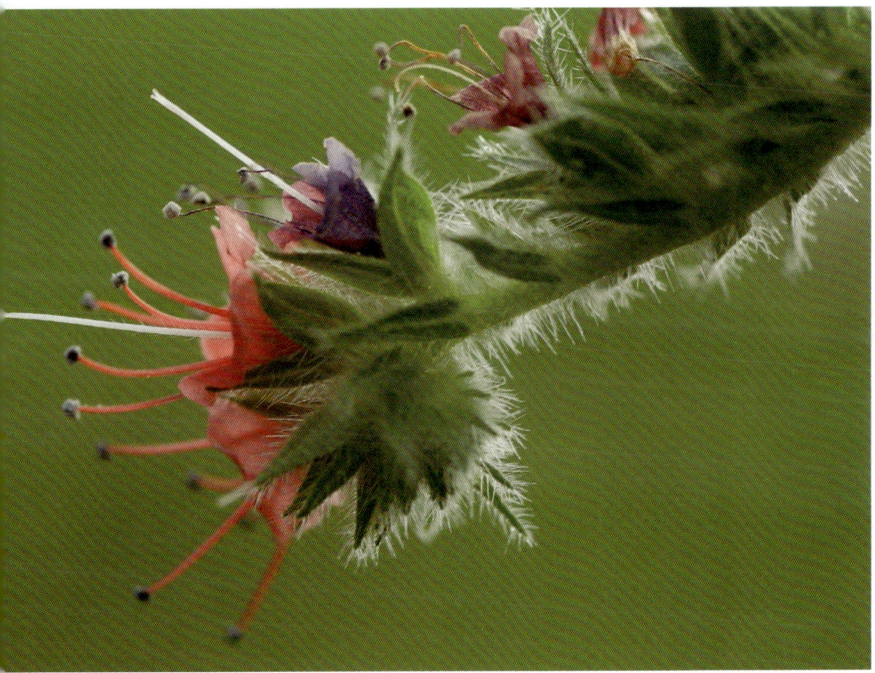

Detail of a blossom. Gentle back-lighting highlights the plant's deli-cate fuzz and the distant background elements offer a nearly even green surface for a backdrop.
f/9.5, 1/750 s, ISO 800, 150mm
Location: Botanical Gardens of Tübingen, Germany

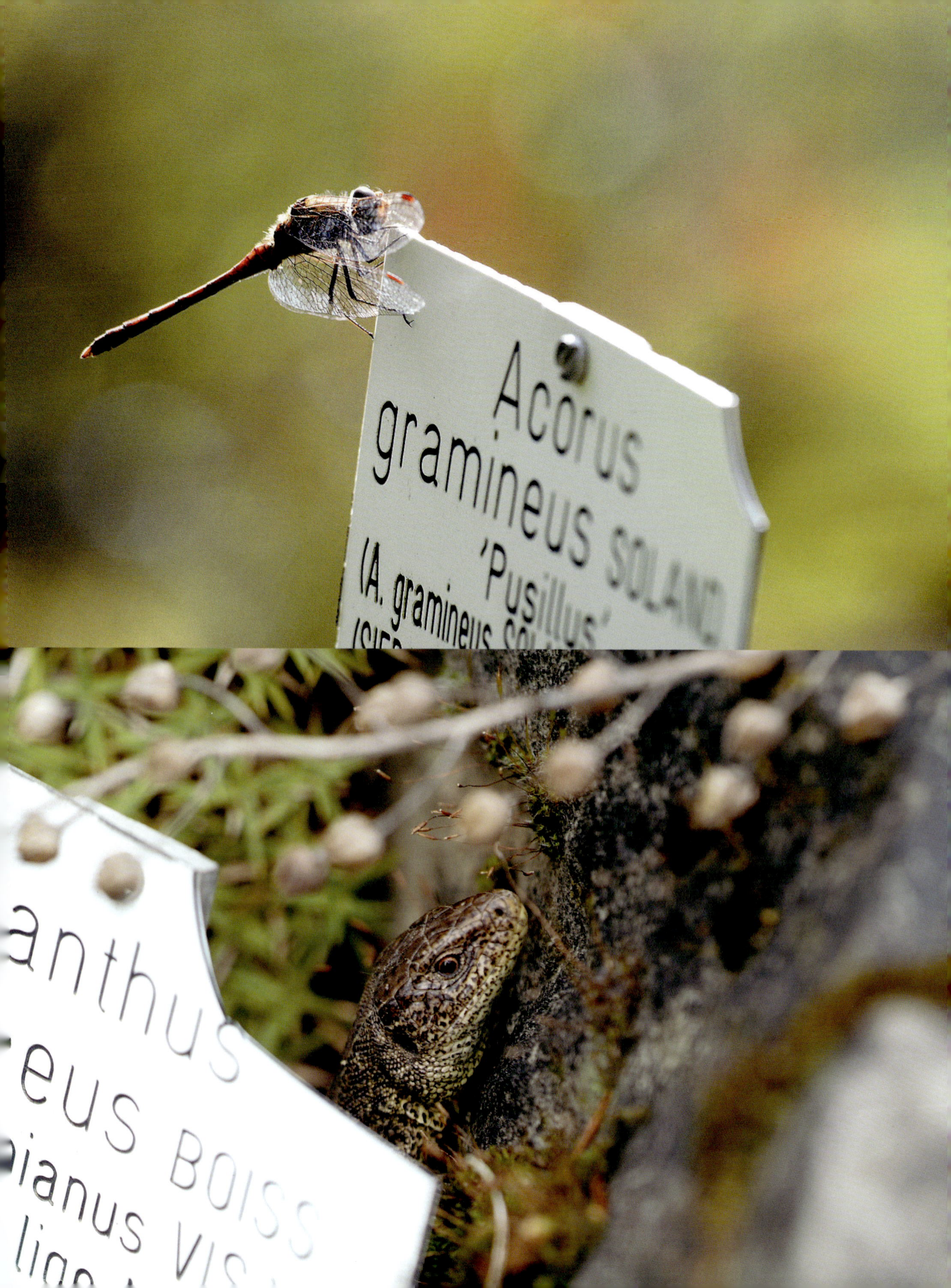
Acorus
gramineus SOLAND
'Pusillus'
(A. gramineus Sol.

anthus
eus BOISS
nianus VIS

Greenhouses

In addition to their outdoor exhibits, many botanical gardens feature greenhouses containing various tropical and subtropical plants as well as notable species from desert climates. Telephoto lenses pull their weight in these settings by making it possible to reach far away subjects. Fortunately, shooting at longer focal lengths from a tripod is more of a possibility when inside a greenhouse, because wind is less likely to rustle a subject during an exposure. Bridge cameras with image stabilization and a good zoom range also do quite well in these circumstances.

Taking pictures in a greenhouse with their often tropical conditions comes with its challenges. As soon as you step inside the warmth, the air's humidity immediately causes your lens and display to fog up. There are a few ways of circumventing this problem. Some greenhouses will feature a warm-air blower specifically designed for drying condensation formed on cameras and eyeglasses. Alternatively, you can use a microfiber cloth to wipe your equipment down manually. If this is your plan, I suggest using a skylight filter or another type of protective filter on your lens to minimize the risk of scratching your expensive front lens element.

If you don't have any recourse for the condensation, you'll simply have to wait for your equipment to acclimate to the conditions. The process may take up to 15 or 20 minutes, but you can use the time to scout potential subjects and plan your first images.

The Cold Months

Nature offers plenty of exciting macro subjects, even when the thermometer drops during fall and winter: bizarre, arresting seed capsules; frost-bedecked spider webs; iced-over ponds, and much more.

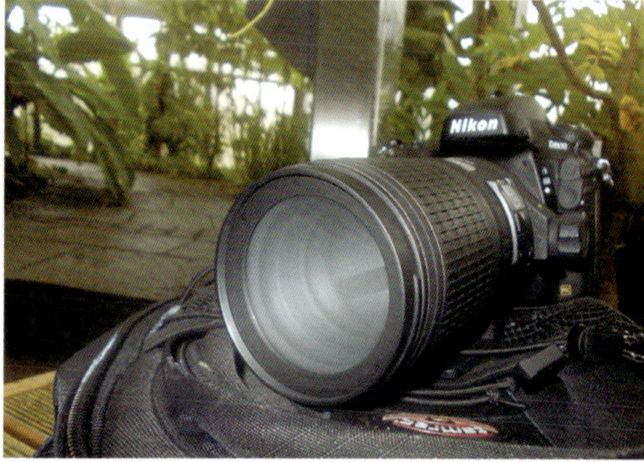

The tropical conditions in some greenhouses can quickly cause a lens to fog up. A microfiber cloth is one way of managing condensation...

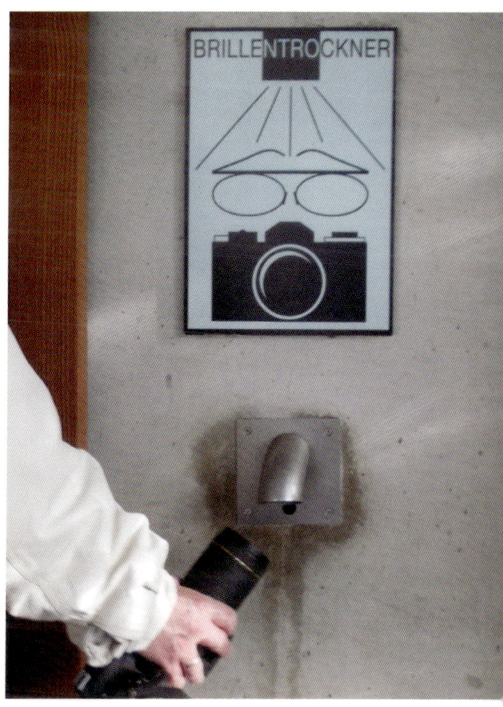

...or blow dryers specifically intended to dry eyeglasses and camera lenses are another option.
Location: Wilhelma, Stuttgart, Germany

Animals sometimes steal the show even if plants are the real stars of a botanical garden

Left page, top: Meadowhawk dragonfly illuminated with evening backlighting
f/6.3, 1/2500 s, ISO 2000, 180mm

Left page, bottom: Sand lizard
f/4, 1/250 s, ISO 400, 150mm
Location for both images: Botanical Gardens of Tübingen, Germany

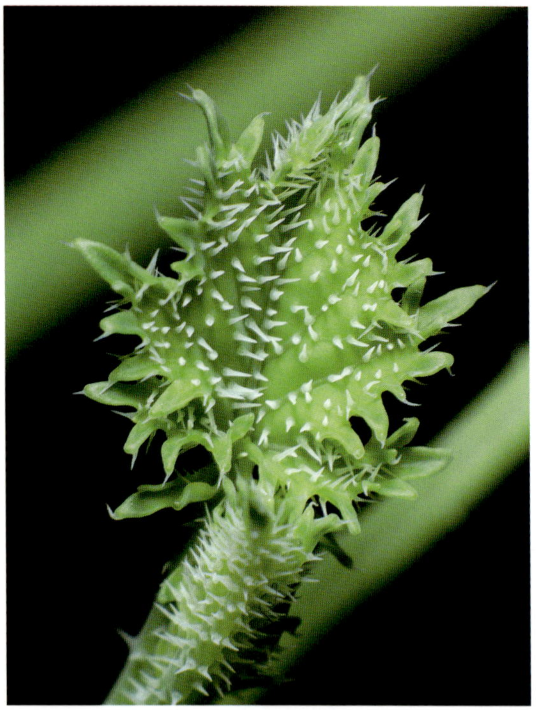

*Working without flash in greenhous-
es is often impossible, especially
during the darker months. A softbox
helps to keep light from the flash
head sufficiently soft.
f/8, 1/125 s, ISO 160, 50mm, system
flash with softbox attachment
Location: Botanical Gardens of
Tübingen, Germany*

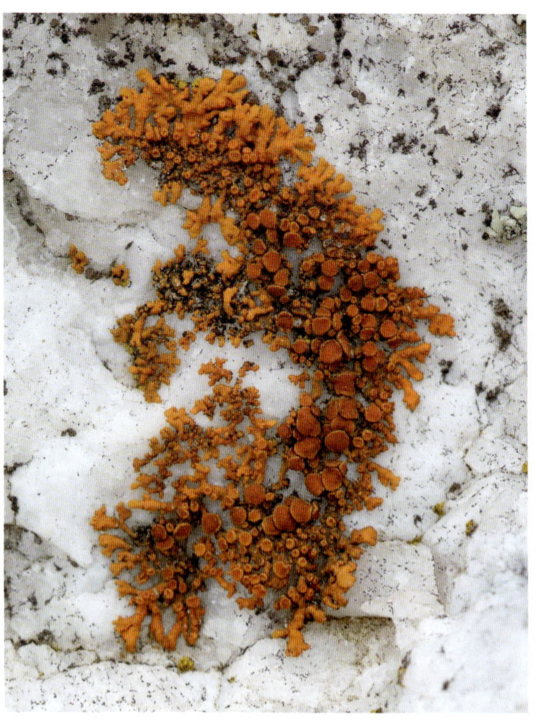

*Lichen on quartz. It's not always easy
to find a standpoint for photographing
lichen that brings all of the elements
of the image onto a single plane.
f/6.7, 1/180 s, ISO 400, 105mm
Location: Botanical Gardens of
Tübingen, Germany*

Dewdrops often linger on outdoor subjects during the early morn-
ings of the cooler months. Early risers have a great opportunity to
discover unconventional subjects by examining how these drops of
moisture decorate the natural world. Interesting highlights can be
created in the dewdrops to underscore their spherical shape by using a detached flash with a softbox attachment.

Moss and lichen are typically easier to find during winter months,
and they often create a desirable contrast of color with the otherwise brown or grey ground. You may need to use a detached system
flash head to produce lighting conditions enabling a depth of field
sufficient for bringing these subjects, which aren't always neatly positioned on a defined plane, into focus. A softbox renders attractive,
diffuse light.

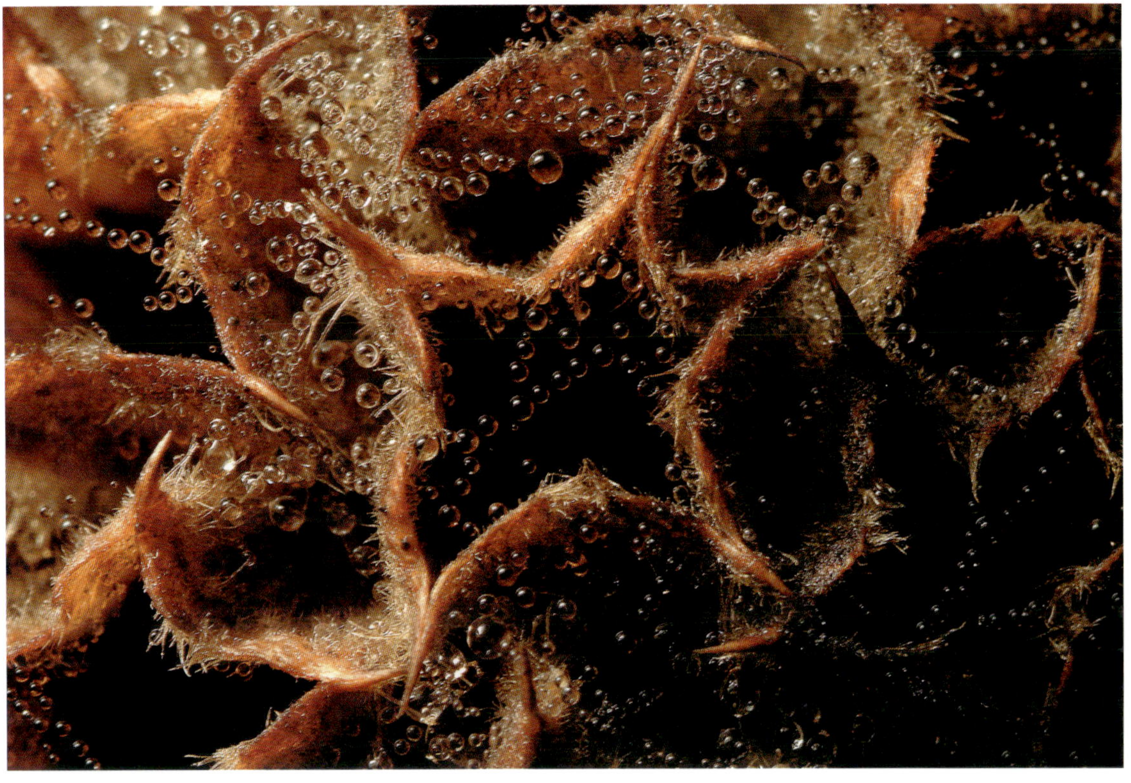

Botanical gardens offer many photogenic subjects even during the doldrums of fall and winter. I use a small softbox with a system flash to create reflections in the water drops and to accentuate their dimensionality.
f/11, 1/60 s, ISO 200, 50mm, system flash with softbox attachment
Location: Botanical Gardens of Tübingen, Germany

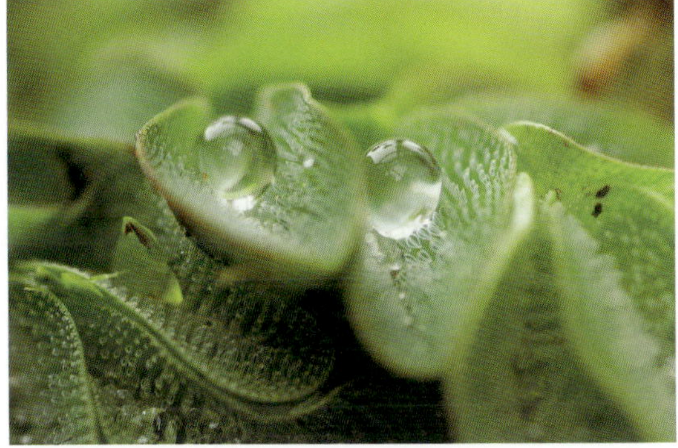

Picture within a picture: The droplets reflect the greenhouse's ceiling. Even with a high ISO value and an open aperture, the shutter speed was still limited to 1/125 s.
f/4, 1/125 s, ISO 1600, 105mm
Location: Botanical Gardens of Tübingen, Germany

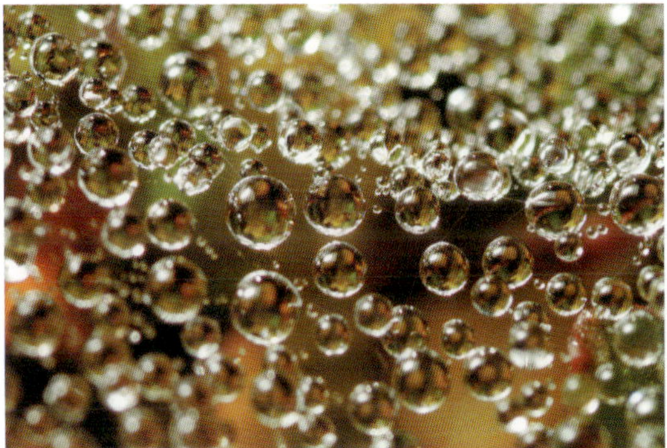

Reflected highlights cause these dewdrops on a spider's web to look like a pearl necklace
f/10, 1/60 s, ISO 200, 50mm, system flash with softbox attachment
Location: Botanical Gardens of Tübingen, Germany

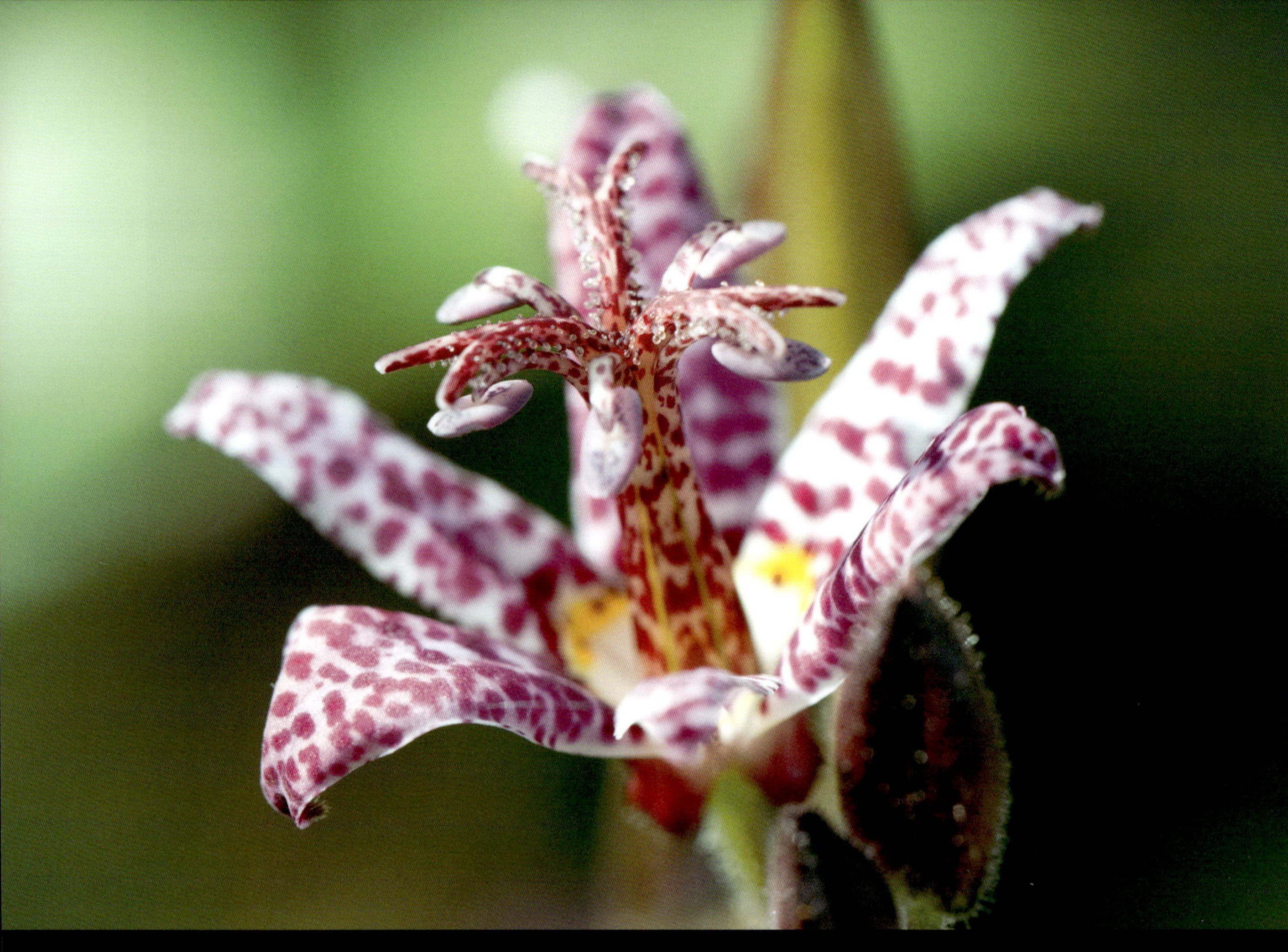

I shot this image out in the open on a windy day.
A high ISO setting allowed me to capture a sharp
image despite the wind.
f/8, 1/2,000 s, ISO 2500, 180mm
Location: Botanical Gardens of Tübingen, Germany

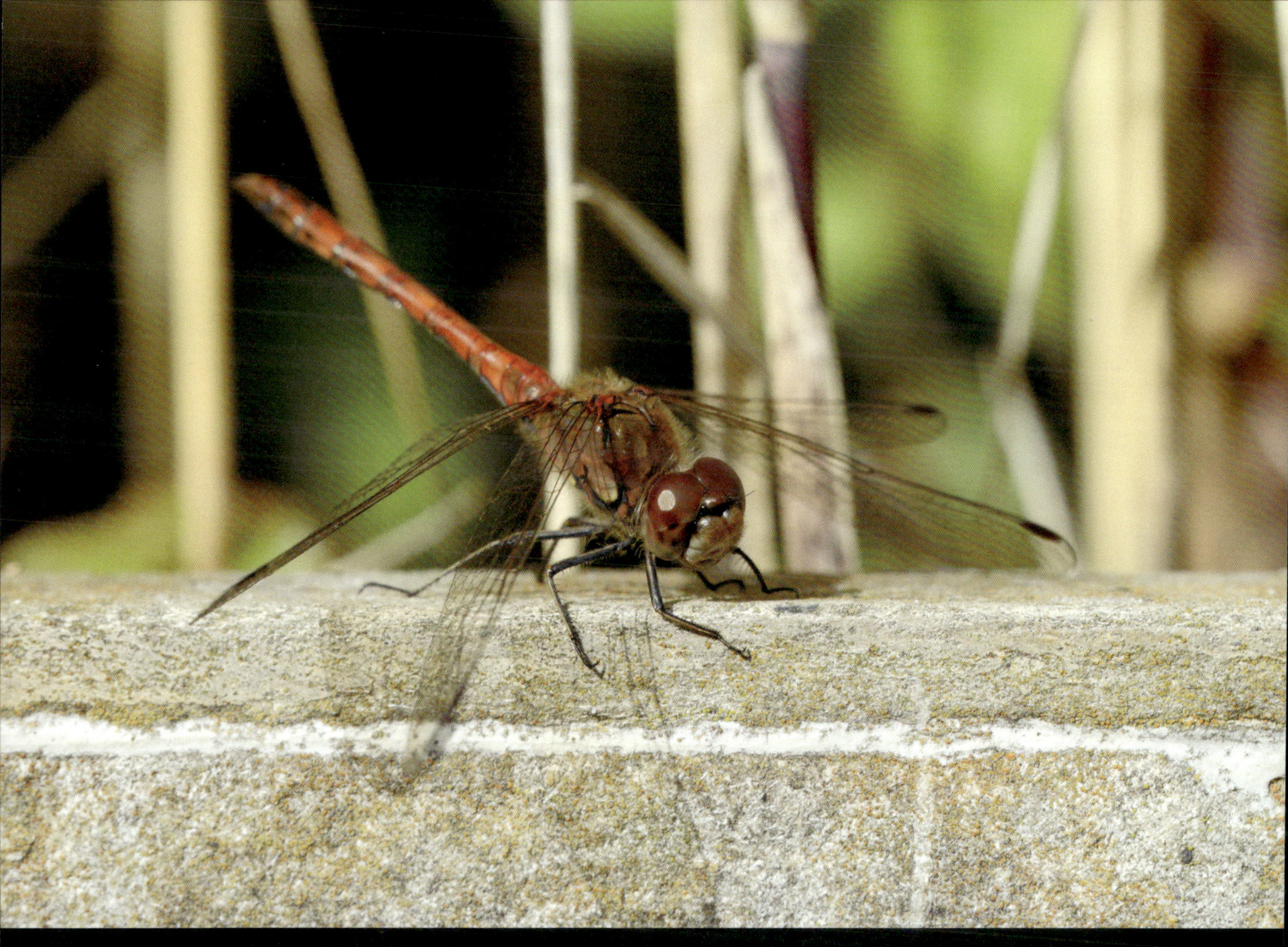

Meadowhawk dragonfly. Dragonflies like to sit atop a perch so they can keep an eye on their hunting grounds.
f/11, 1/1,000 s, ISO 1000, 180mm
Location: Botanical Gardens of Tübingen, Germany

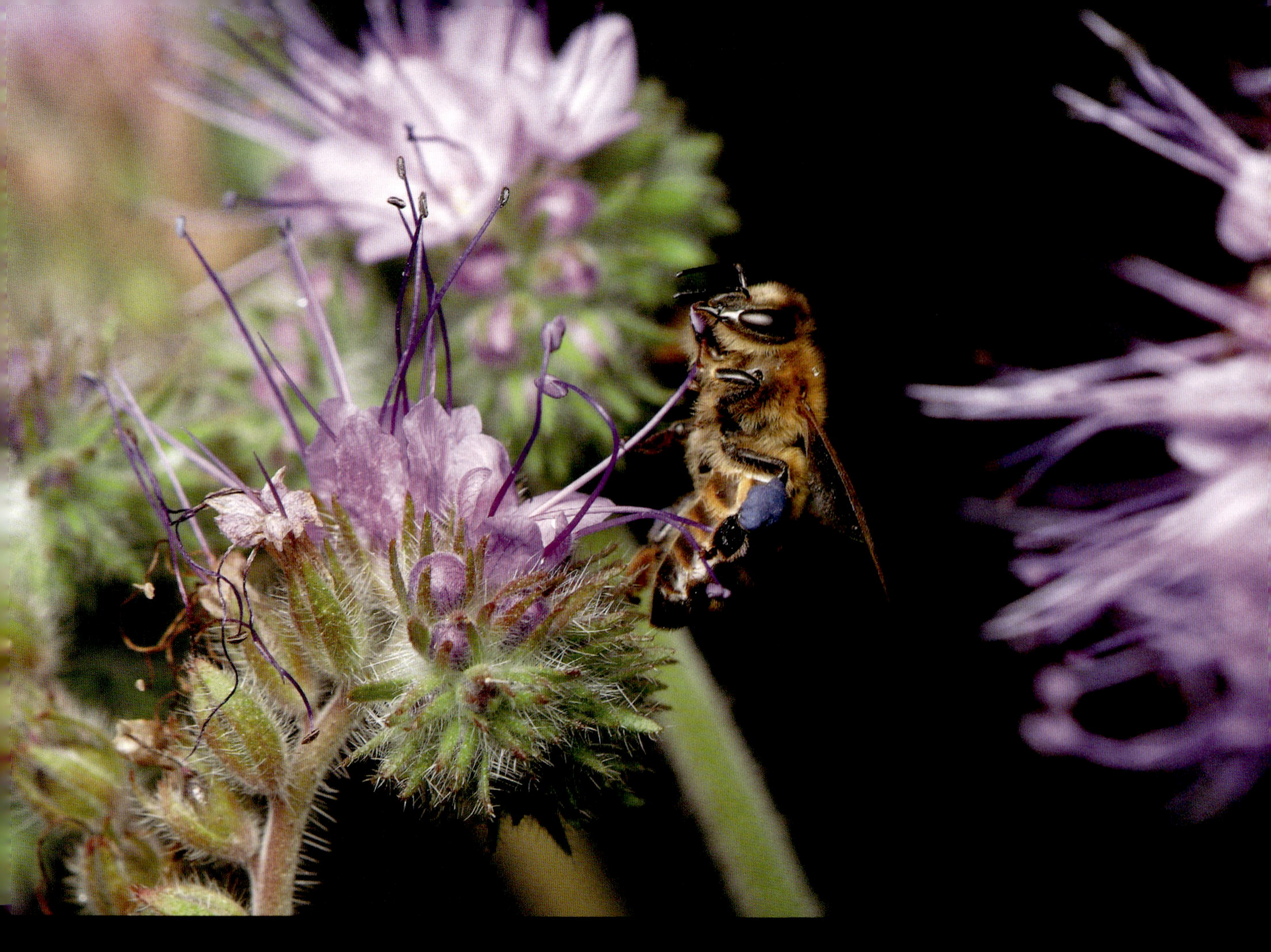

A bee in search of food
f/8, 1/60 s, ISO 160, 150mm, fill flash with a softbox
Location: Botanical Gardens of Tübingen, Germany

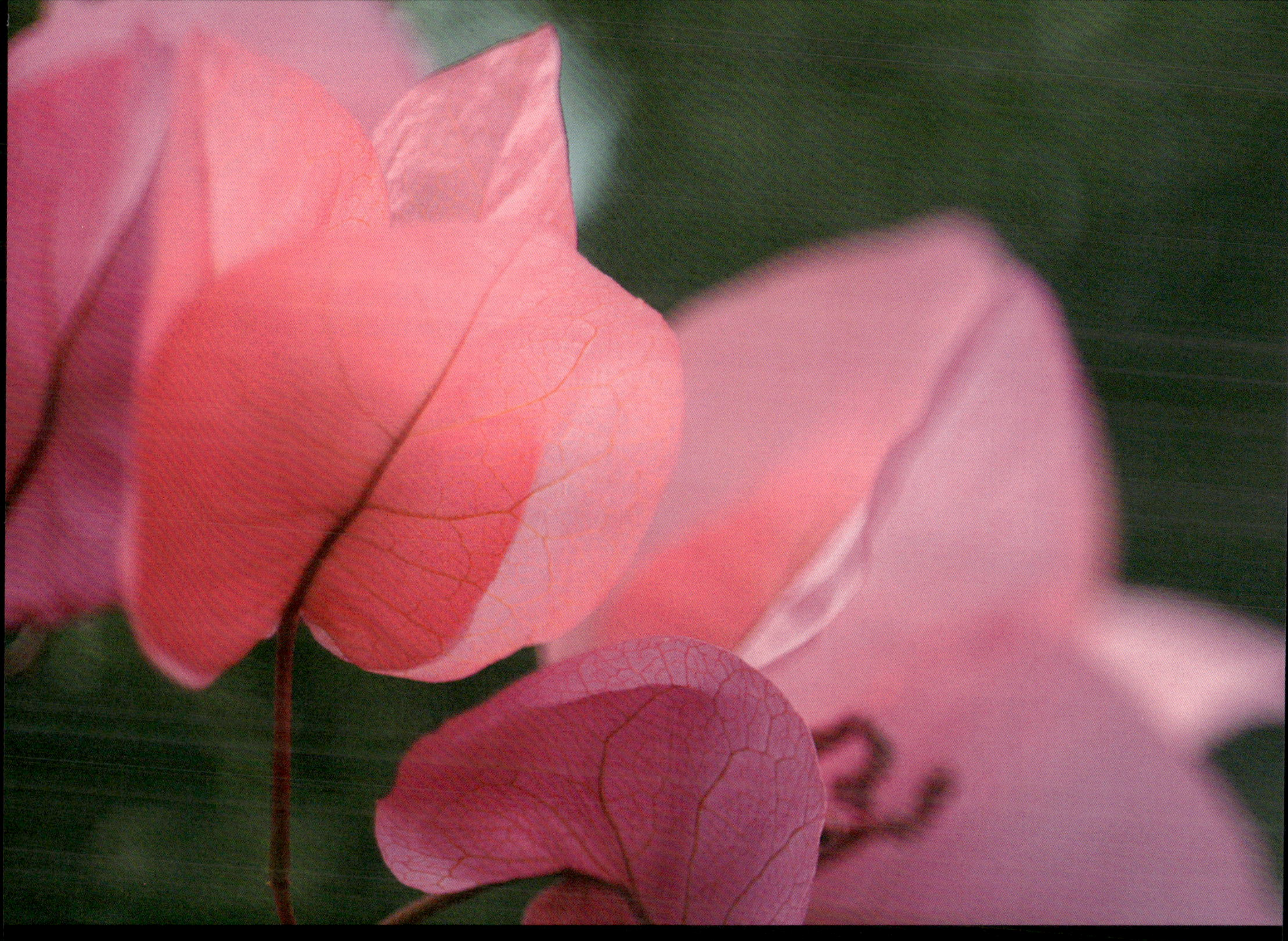

The colorful petals of a bougainvillea
f/5.6, 1/90 s, ISO 200, 50mm
Location: Botanical Gardens of Tübingen, Germany

Butterfly Gardens

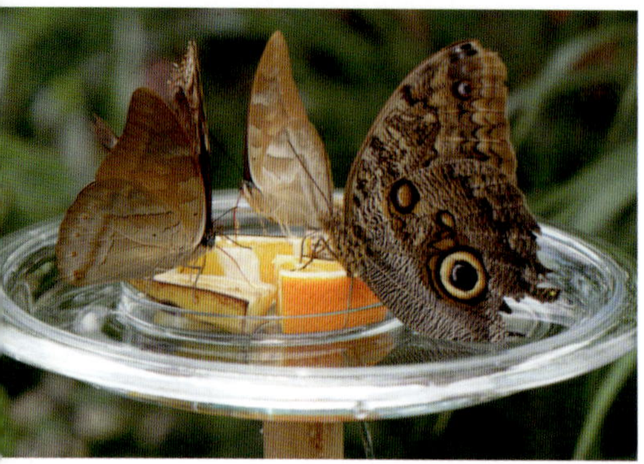

Owl butterflies. Feeding butterflies usually remain very still, but they aren't the most compelling subjects for a photo.
f/5.6, 1/500 s, ISO 1600, 150mm
Location: Isle of Mainau, Germany

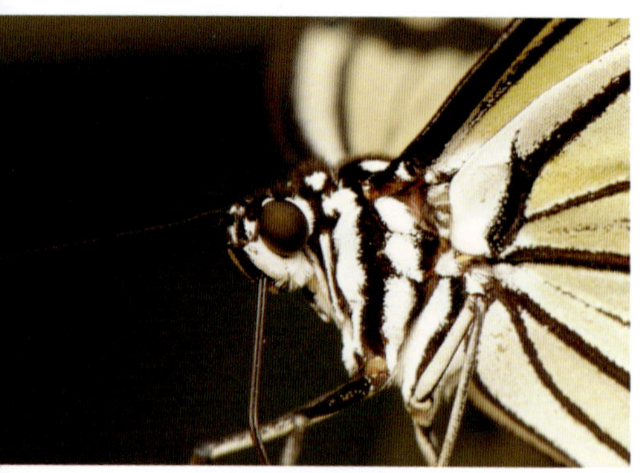

Paper kite butterfly. You can use the opportunity to create a few interesting portraits by altering the perspective of your shot and eliminating the food from the image.
f/8, 1/60 s, ISO 400, 105mm
Location: Isle of Mainau, Germany

Butterfly exhibits are a paradise for macro photographers regardless of the season. They afford the chance to interact with exotic butterflies from around the world without much effort at all. These gardens typically require that you stay on marked paths, which makes lenses with focal lengths of 105mm and longer practical for getting close enough to subjects without encroaching on their flight zone. Wild butterflies typically are more likely to flee when approached than the specimens you come across in such gardens.

The lighting conditions in butterfly gardens are generally comparable to those found in greenhouses, which means you may have trouble shooting handheld. I recommend starting with an ISO of 800 and going up from there, as necessary. Most modern DSLRs can handle sensitivity levels in that range without a problem; bridge cameras, in contrast, may start to run into trouble at that point, resulting in a loss of image quality. Butterflies tend to be rather docile creatures, especially when resting on a surface, so even compact and bridge cameras with image stabilizers and a strong zoom lens will be more than adequate for capturing excellent images in these environs.

Monopods equipped with a ball head mount are more practical for use in butterfly exhibits than tripods. They make it easier to follow butterflies from plant to plant without having to set up a tripod again for each new location. The feeding sites typically located throughout butterfly gardens represent ideal opportunities for creating up-close-and-personal portraits of these magnificent creatures. You can generally work with normal ISO settings, the mirror lockup mode activated, and a remote trigger system if you wish. Feeding butterflies are typically so focused on their food that they tend not to move around much, giving you the chance to capture excellent portraits or detail shots of colorful wings. I usually treat 1/30 s as the maximum shutter speed, though, because speeds any faster than that come with attendant risks of ruinous motion blur.

Shooting Perspective

In most cases you will be trying to photograph a butterfly with its wings completely closed or completely open—in part owing to the way that these animals prefer to hold their bodies. If your subject's wings are entirely closed, you can shoot with a relatively wide aperture and still keep most of the key areas sharp while allowing the

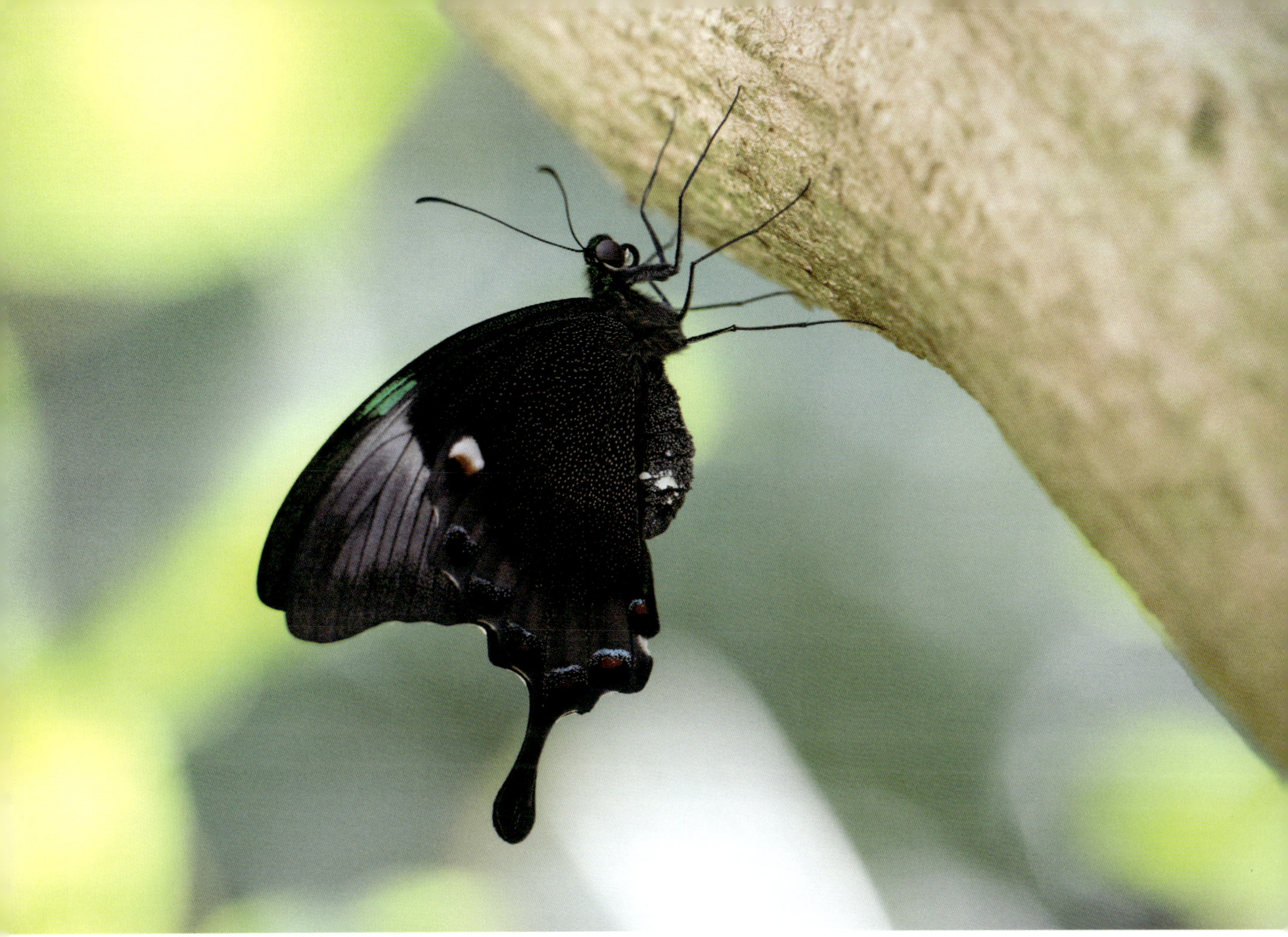

Swallowtail. Using a wide aperture caused the background to soften into blurry swaths of color—but with the added expense the tips of the wings also lost some of their sharpness.
f/5.6, 1/400 s, ISO 3200, 180mm
Location: Wilhelma, Stuttgart, Germany

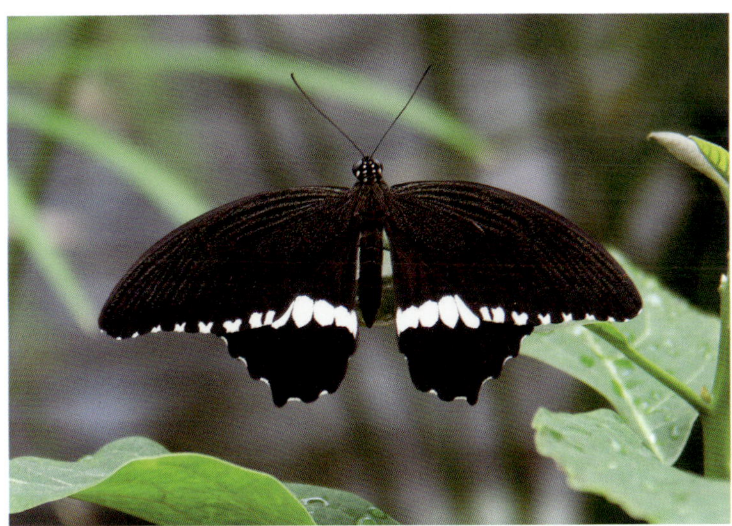

Common Mormon. Background details are much more prominent in butterfly pictures shot from above; the smaller sensor of the bridge camera used to take this picture was also a factor here.
f/3.5, 1/60 s, ISO 100, 50mm
Location: Isle of Mainau, Germany

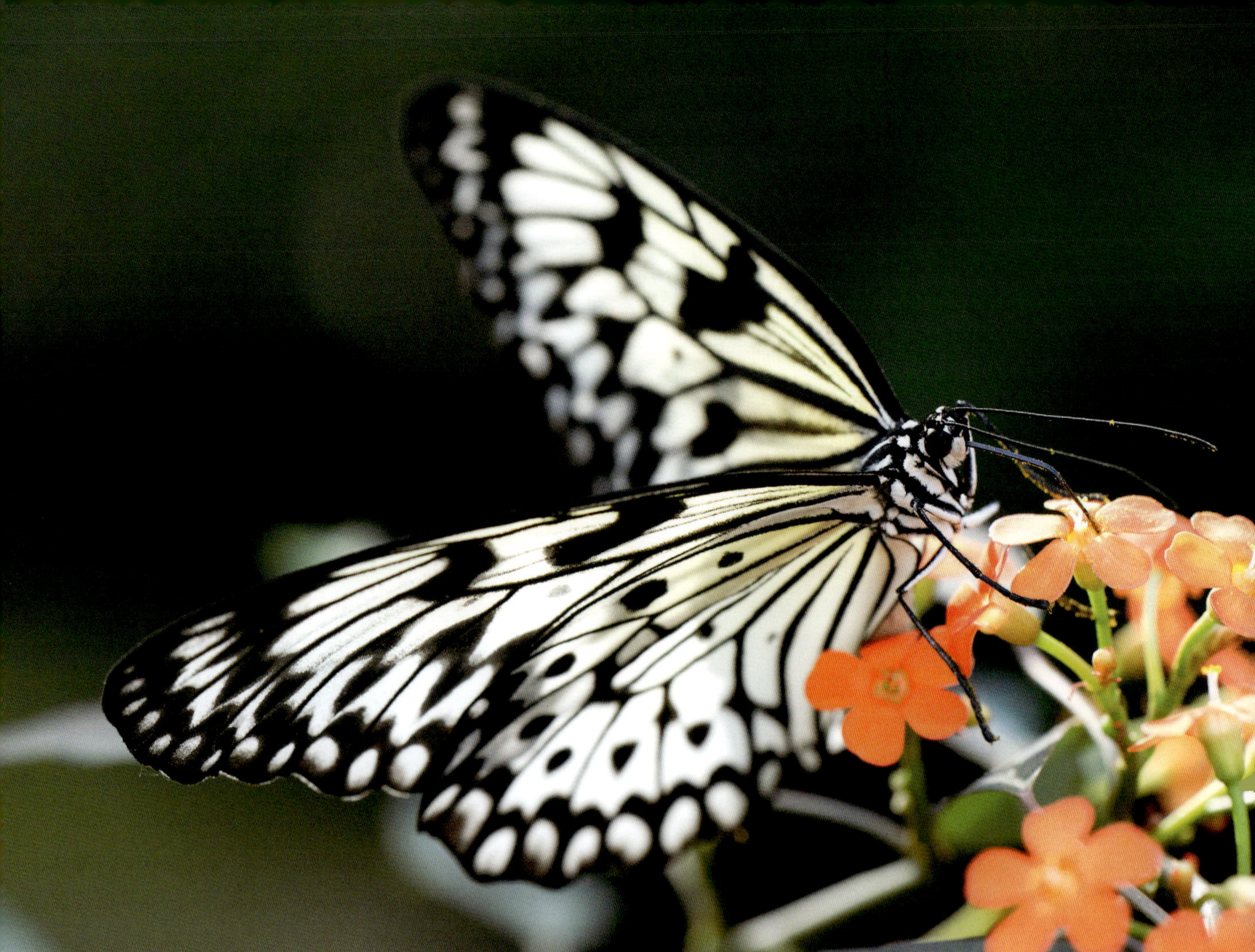

Paper kite butterfly. Shooting hand-held requires the use of high ISO values.
f/7.1, 1/400 s, ISO 4000, 180mm
Location: Wilhelma, Stuttgart, Germany

background to melt into a blur. Open wings typically demand that you stop down a bit to keep them sufficiently in focus. More times than not when a butterfly's wings are open, you'll want to position your camera above it, pointing down. This configuration makes the background (which in this situation would actually be the surface on which the critter is resting) a more important feature of the image. Photographers would do well to consider this when planning the composition of their images.

To Flash or Not to Flash?

A flash is a practical way to deal with the less-than-ideal lighting you'll come across in most butterfly exhibits. When using artificial lighting, however, make sure that you avoid situations where the foreground is adequately lit, but the background fades to near or total darkness due to being far enough away to not receive enough light.

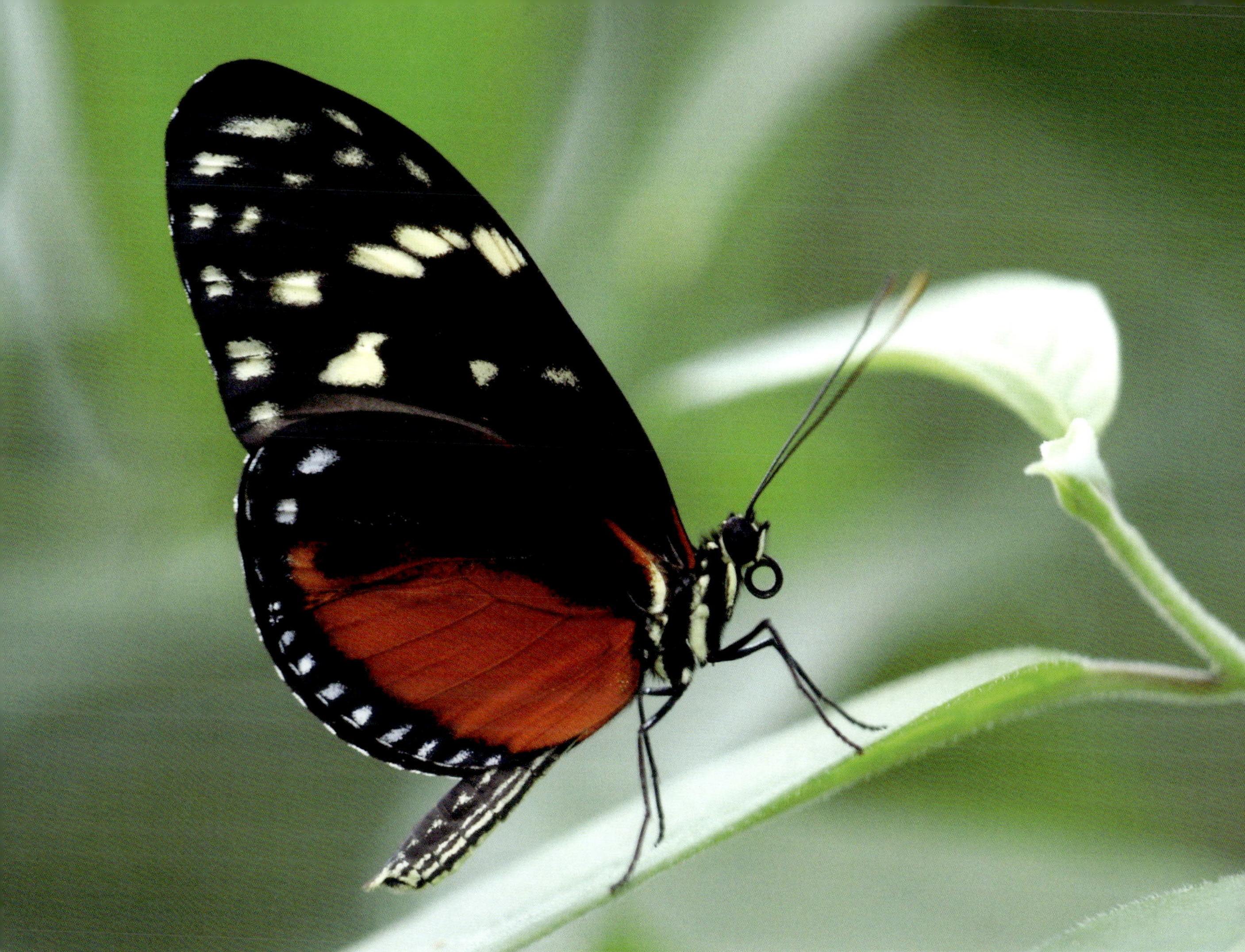

Passion butterfly. With a bit of patience, butterflies can be a very rewarding subject.
f/3.3, 1/180 s, ISO 1600, 180mm
Location: Isle of Mainau, Germany

Harsh, distracting shadows and unwanted reflections off shiny leaves are other perils of flash photography that you'll need to consider.

If you decide to go the route of using a flash despite these challenges, consider using a softbox and positioning your flash away from your camera. And definitely inquire in advance whether flash photography is permitted at all within the gardens. I find pictures taken in nature more attractive, because the background tends to fit in with the composition more organically.

Aquaria and Terraria

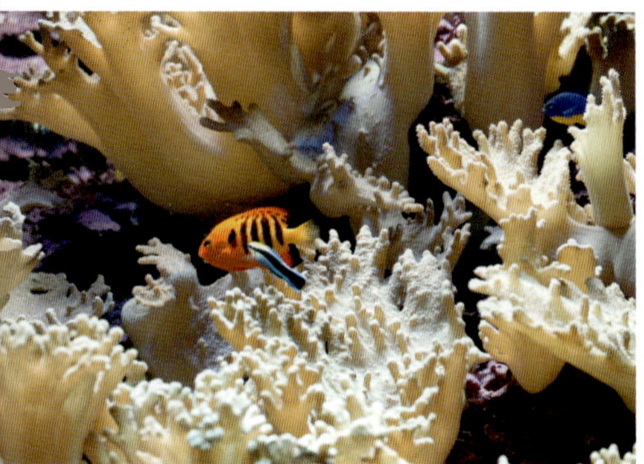

Using a telephoto lens at somewhat of a remove makes it easier to avoid reflections and distortions when taking overview images of small aquarium tanks
f/6.3, 1/125 s, ISO 6400, 180mm
Location: Wilhelma, Stuttgart, Germany

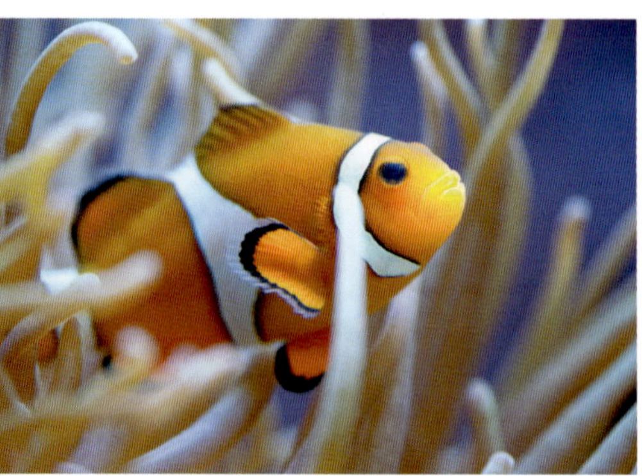

No trip to an aquarium is complete without a photo of a clownfish
f/4.5, 1/200 s, ISO 6400, 180mm
Location: Wilhelma, Stuttgart, Germany

Zoo aquaria and terraria are exhibits of special significance to macro and close-up photographers: the creatures housed in these areas are generally of a relatively small size, making them appealing subjects.

Photographing animals living in small tanks requires adequate preparation, though, because there are significant technical challenges to producing brilliant images. But let's start with the good news. The types of subjects in aquaria and terraria of interest to macro photographers generally live in tanks with a much smaller depth than the larger residents of the sea. Smaller depths mean you can use shorter focal lengths to good effect. Don't leave your telephoto lens at home, though, because longer focal lengths also have their advantages.

What makes telephoto lenses practical brings us to one of the main challenges of photographing animals living in tanks. The glass walls that contain these animals are very thick, in part to withstand the significant pressure from the water on one side, and in part to withstand any potential impacts from viewers who may bump an object against them. The thickness of the glass directly leads to losses in image quality, because the light not only has to travel through water from the subject to the lens, but also gets distorted somewhat by the glass. The surface of the glass also tends to get dirty—on the inside of the glass, dirt and grime naturally build up, and on the spectator side, fingerprints and surface scratches are everywhere. These imperfections will be readily visible in your images if you try to shoot at an angle. Accordingly, your best bet is to work with the shortest distance possible for the light to have to travel. In concrete terms, this means shooting directly through the glass and waiting until your subject moves to assume a fortuitous position in order to optimize your image quality.

It's better to capture overview images of small tanks using a telephoto lens from some distance rather than a wide-angle lens from close range, because the light emitted from all areas of the tank will pass through the glass pane in nearly a straight path with the telephoto lens.

Minimizing Reflections

Reflections are yet another of the challenges photographers face when trying to photograph objects on the other side of thick glass,

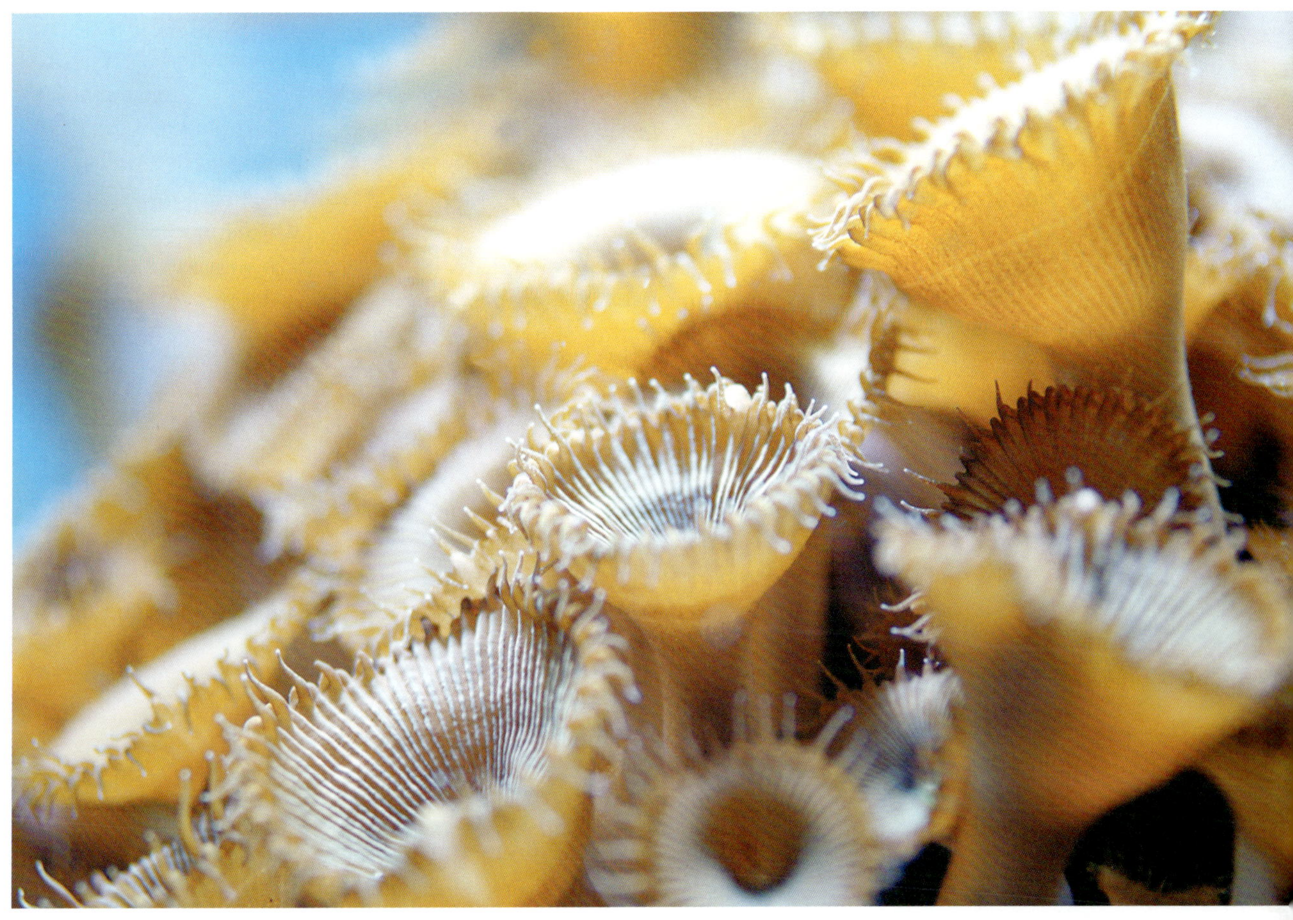

Aquatic plants are relatively easy to photograph. The poor lighting conditions in aquaria typically require that photographers use a high ISO setting to be able to shoot handheld.
f/3.5, 1/25 s, ISO 400, 50mm
Location: Wilhelma, Stuttgart, Germany

which often is the case in zoos. There are a few ways to circumvent this problem, including using the beloved polarizer filter. This method is not fully adequate on its own, however, because polarizers have their most significant effect when shooting at an angle with respect to the glass, and as just discussed, doing so means you'll end up contending with distortions on account of the glass's thickness.

Another option—one that generally offers better results—is to reach for that telephoto lens and to set up your shot at a slightly larger shooting distance. Wearing dark clothes will minimize the likelihood that your visage will show up on the glass. Alternatively, you can equip your camera with a lens hood and position your camera directly on the aquarium glass. With the lens so close to the glass, all of the scratches and blemishes on the surface of the glass will be outside of the depth of field, minimizing their effect on the picture at hand.

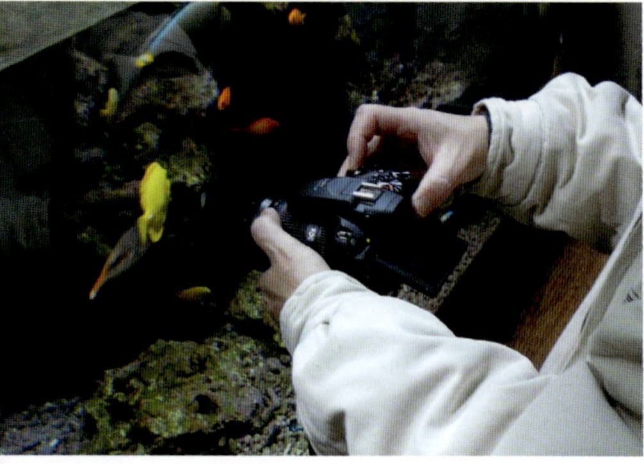

One way to minimize the appearance of reflections when photographing subjects behind glass walls is to use a rubber lens hood and position your camera directly up against the glass Location: Wilhelma, Stuttgart, Germany

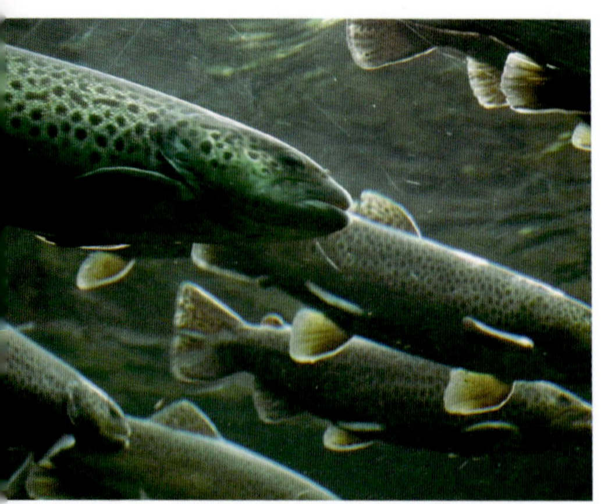

Rainbow trout. Shooting at a sharp angle with respect to aquarium glass heightens the visibility of surface scratches. And the refraction of the glass produces color fringing at the bright edges in the scene.
Bridge camera, f/3.6, 1/20 s, ISO 800, 24mm
Location: Wilhelma, Stuttgart, Germany

Lighting Conditions

The lighting found in aquarium and terrarium exhibits at zoos is often not conducive to easy photography. In general, the tanks themselves feature lighting that doesn't mesh well with the lighting in the visitor areas. Terrariums often feature heating lamps because reptiles love to warm themselves. All of these diverse sources of light result in a complicated mixed lighting situation over which photographers have no influence. Shooting RAW images is your one recourse to balance out the resulting color casts afterward while editing your images.

Flash photography is often either discouraged or prohibited outright to prevent undue stress on the animals. But using flash is inadvisable for other reasons too: it introduces yet another type of lighting to the scene, further complicating the mixed lighting situation. It also inevitably produces uncontrollable reflections on the tank's glass walls. These constraints effectively force photographers to bump up the ISO setting in order to work with fast shutter speeds and a stopped down lens. Photographers using contemporary DSLRs and other cameras with great image noise performance are definitely at an advantage here. You can certainly use the slower shutter speeds made available by using a tripod and/or image stabilizers for some subjects, but aquarium residents in particular aren't likely to stay still long enough for this method to be practical.

Reptiles and insects are another story, though. You can often shoot at ISO 100 while using a tripod and long exposure windows because these creatures often stand still as a stone for long stretches of time. The thick glass walls are still an issue to contend with, and the enclosures for some poisonous animals also sometimes feature a type of netting to sound an alarm in the case of an emergency. These constraints make finding the ideal shooting position complicated.

Contrasts

Photographers in aquaria and terraria also have to contend with broad ranges of brightness in the images they want to capture. An animal sitting near a lamp, for example, or the jellyfish passing by a point source of light pictured on the next page are two situations that can result in overexposed areas. You will also encounter high-contrast situations when taking over-under images in aquaria where a part of your subject is above water while the other part is below. The contrast of brightness in the two image areas is often so bright that there's no way around having to brighten or darken the respective areas while editing your images afterward.

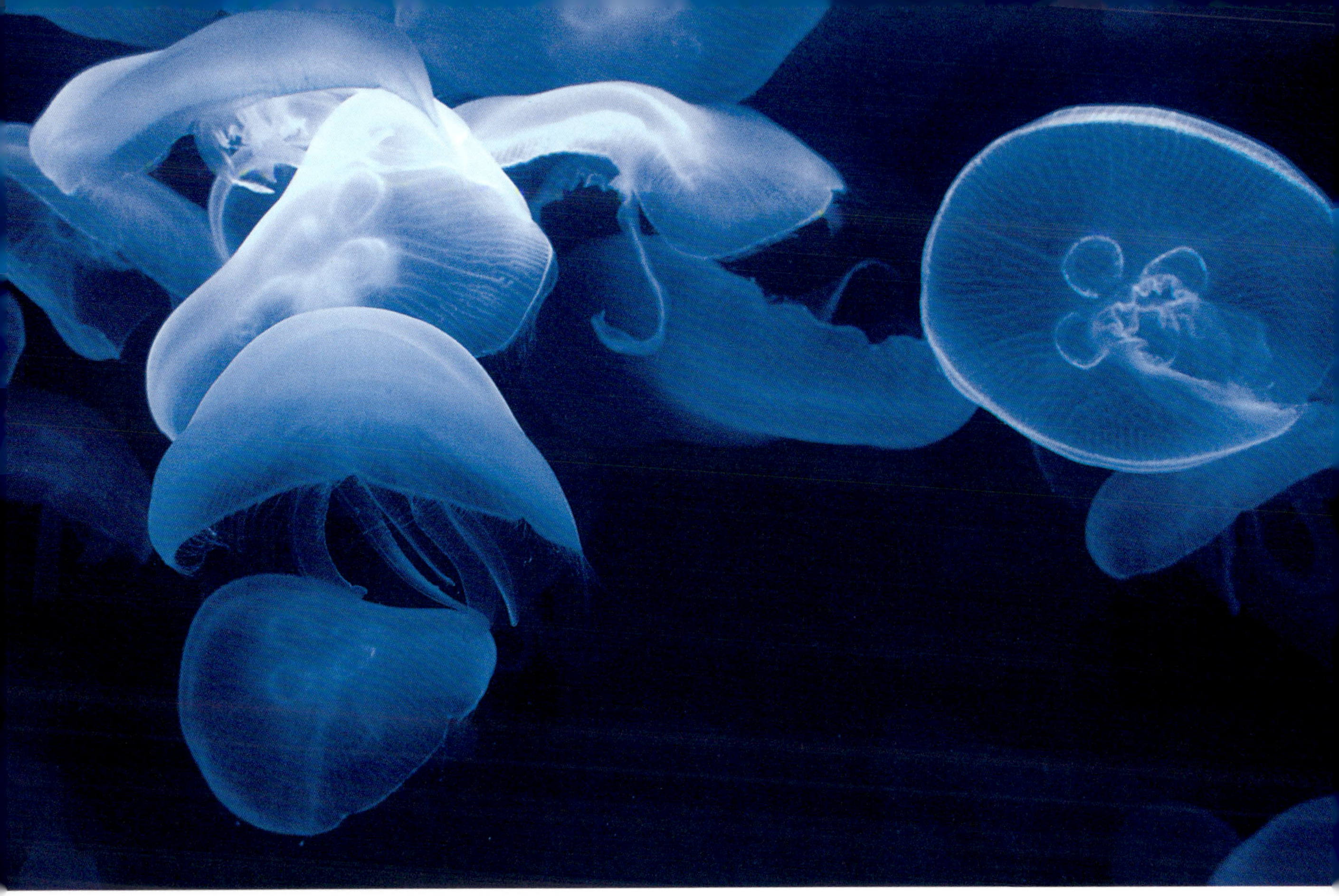

*Jellyfish are particularly photogenic when illuminated by a point source of light
so they contrast sharply with a dark background
f/7.1, 1/80 s, ISO 6400, 24mm
Location: Wilhelma, Stuttgart, Germany*

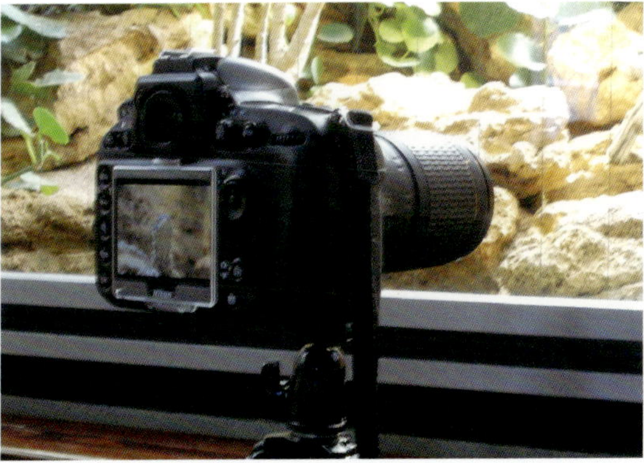

*Reptile inhabitants of terraria are generally amenable to
being photographed with slower shutter speeds and a
tripod
Location: Wilhelma, Stuttgart, Germany*

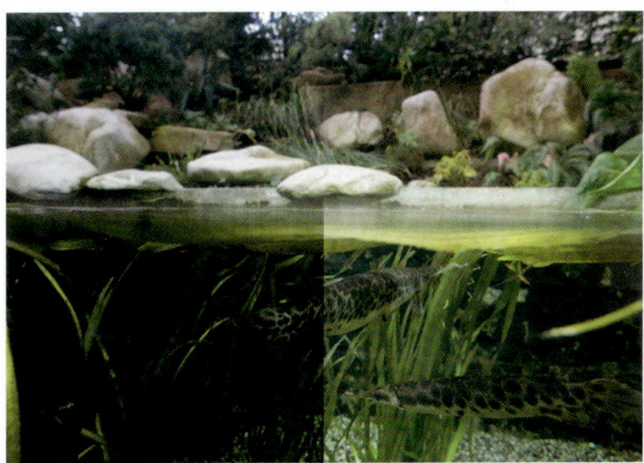

*An over-under image from an aquarium. The underwater
region of the photo needed to be significantly brightened. The left half reveals the original image, and the
right half shows the result of brightening up the underwater area.
Location: Wilhelma, Stuttgart, Germany*

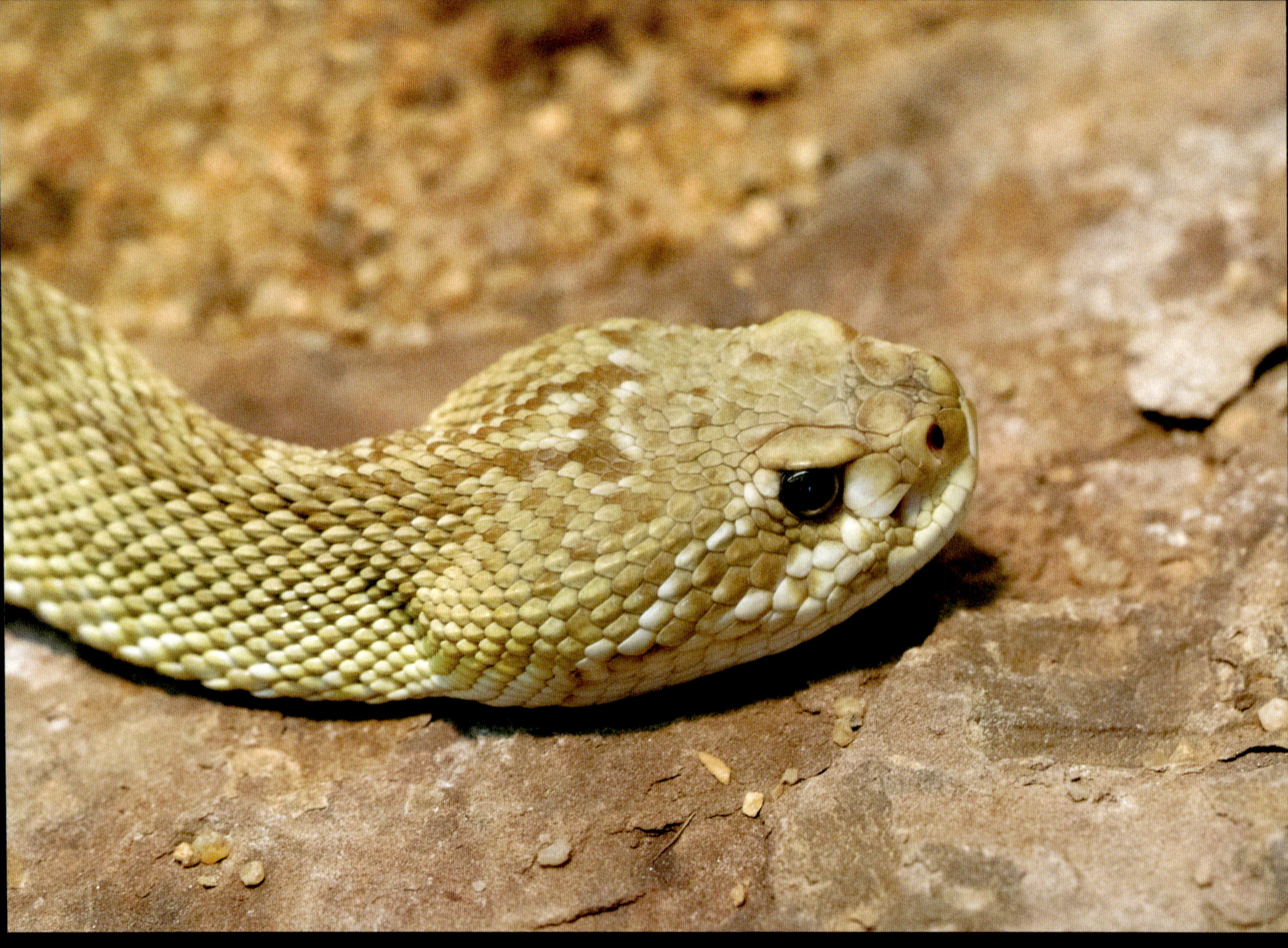

Terraria offer the chance to approach rattlesnakes and other deadly creatures without assuming any risk. Some tanks for these dangerous animals feature embedded alarm wires for the safety of human visitors. Adopting a camera position extremely close to the glass is a way to ensure that these wires fall well outside of the depth of field for your images.
f/8, 1/60 s, ISO 3200, 105mm, tripod

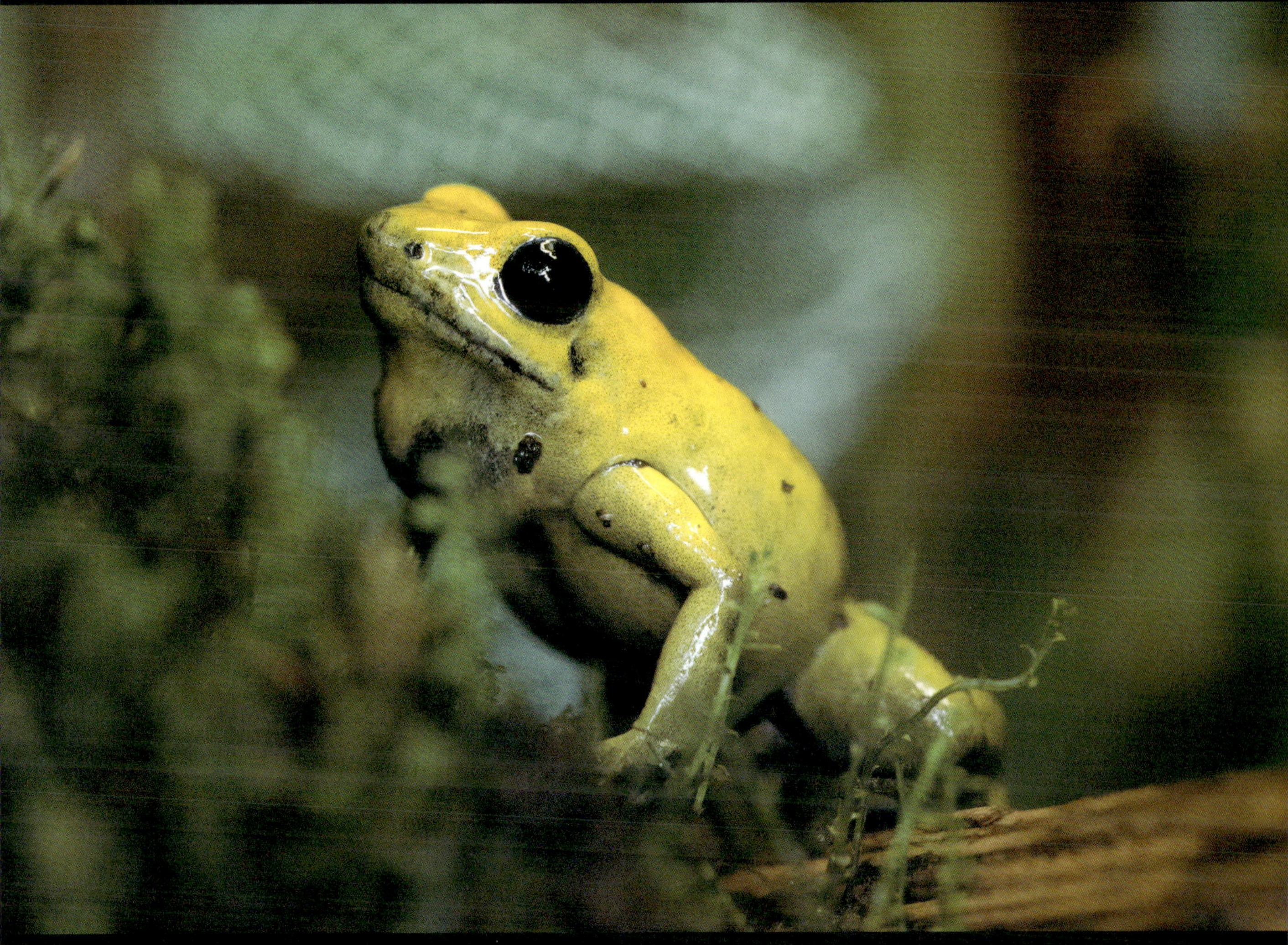

Yellow poison dart frog. A telephoto macro lens is the right choice for getting closer to small animals hiding near the back of their enclosures.
f/7.1, 1/250 s, ISO 4000, 180mm
Location for both images: Wilhelma, Stuttgart, Germany

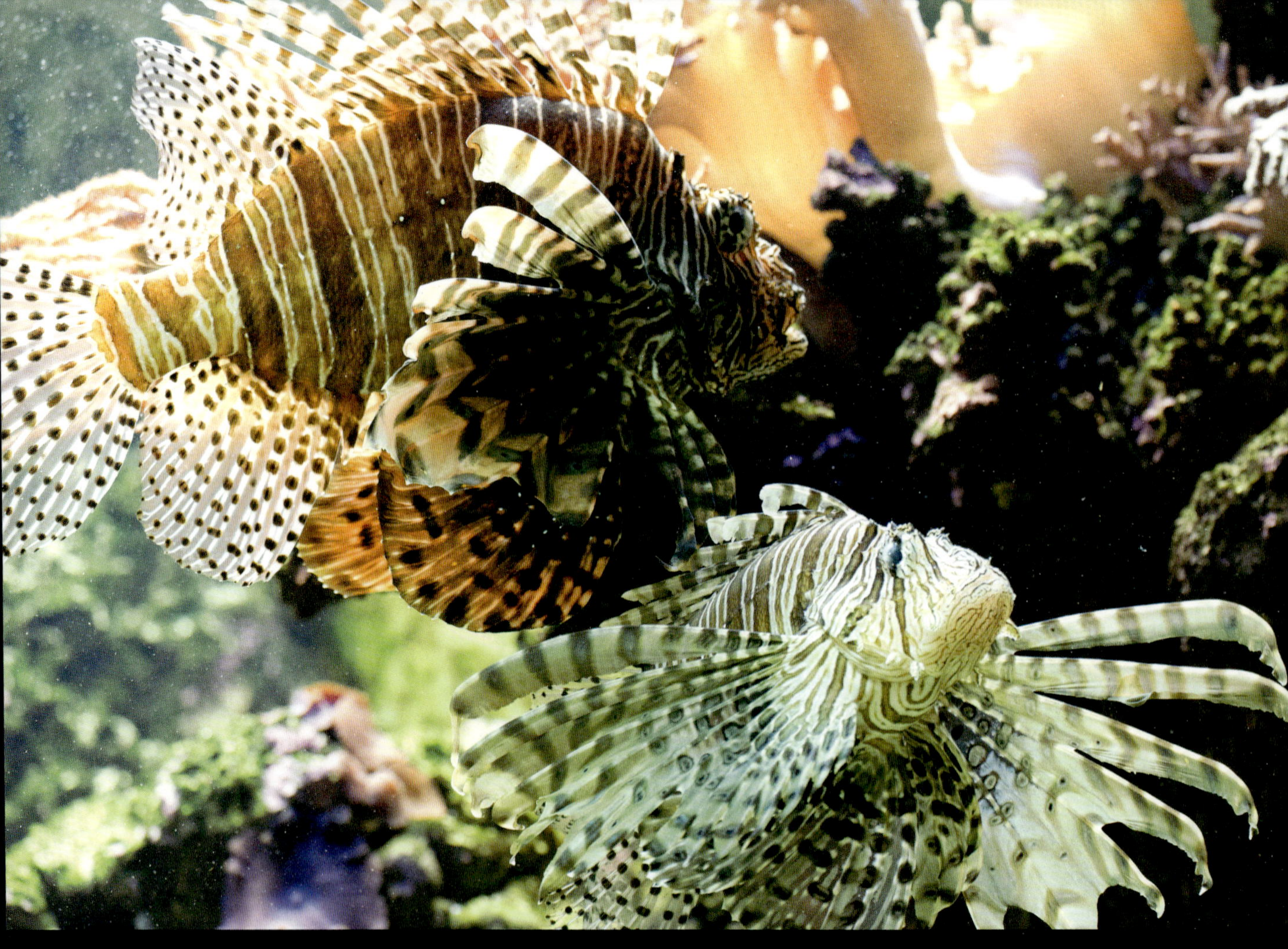

Two lionfish. A tripod is an effective tool for realizing images of slowly swimming subjects. You'll likely still need to use a high ISO setting to prevent motion blur.
f/6.3, 1/60 s, ISO 6400, 180mm
Location: Wilhelma, Stuttgart, Germany

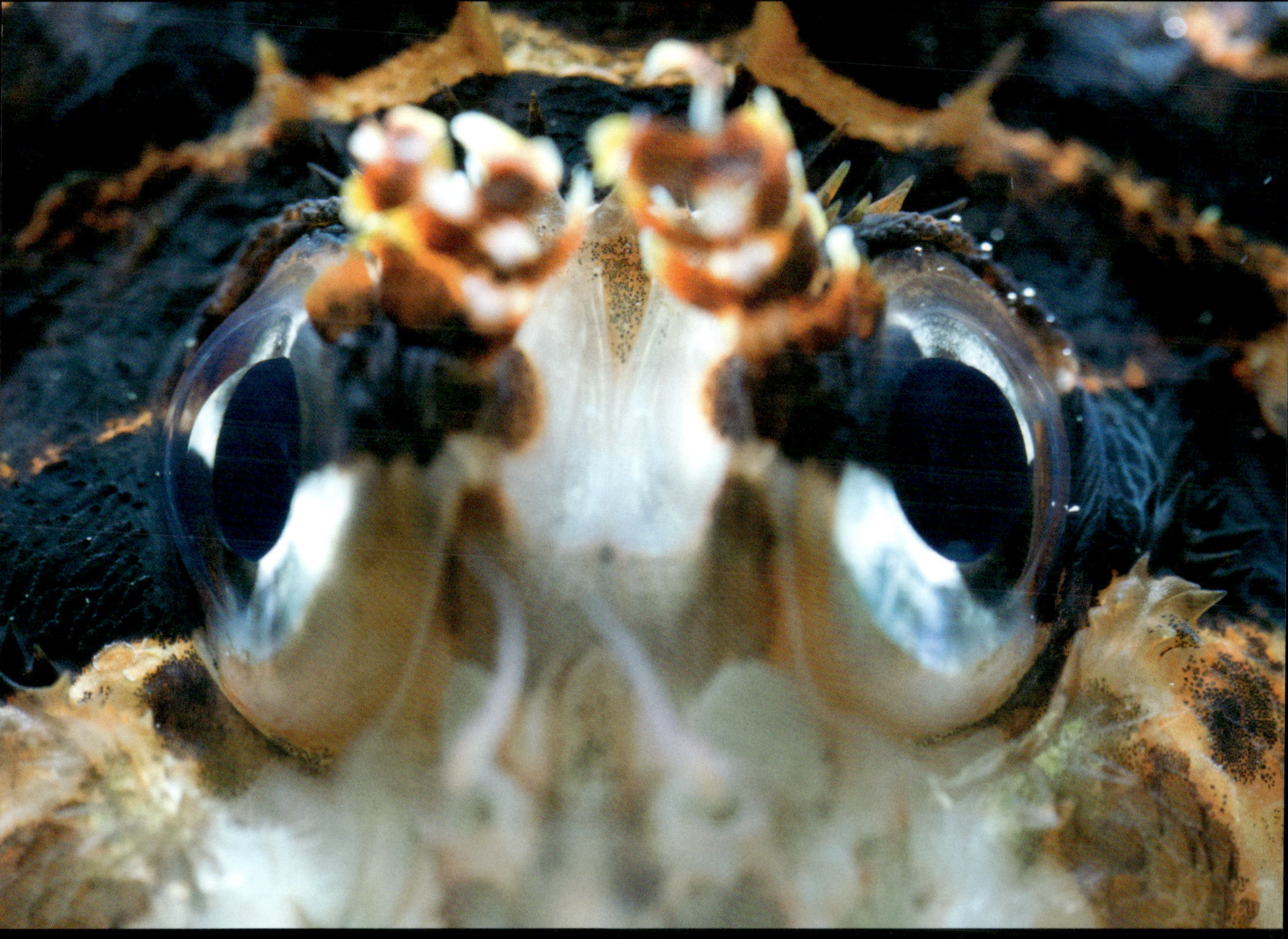

Who's watching whom? Adequately supporting your-self against a railing or something similar often gives you enough stability to capture successful detail images even when shooting handheld.
f/6.3, 1/100 s, ISO 6400, 180mm
Location: Wilhelma, Stuttgart, Germany

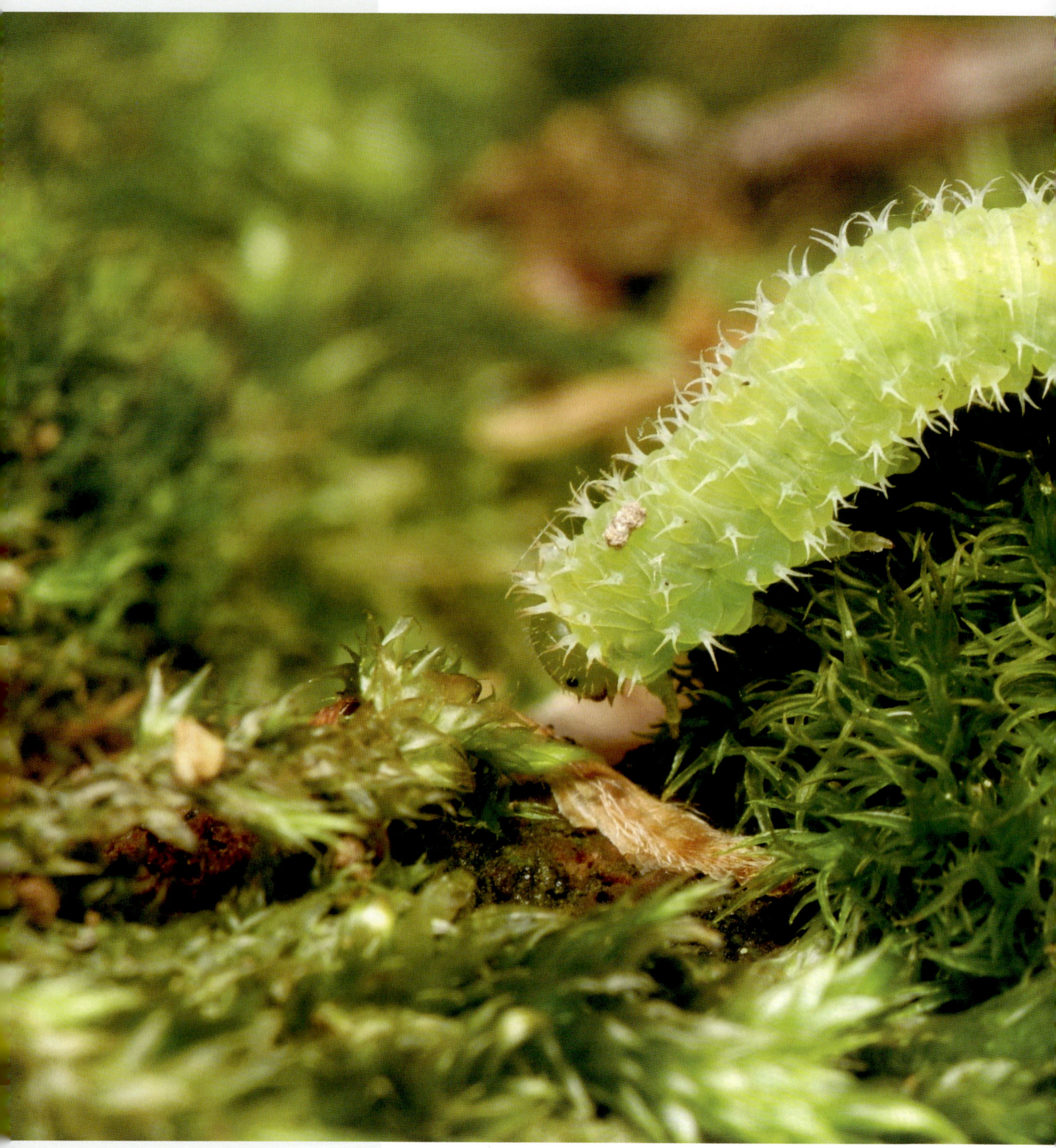

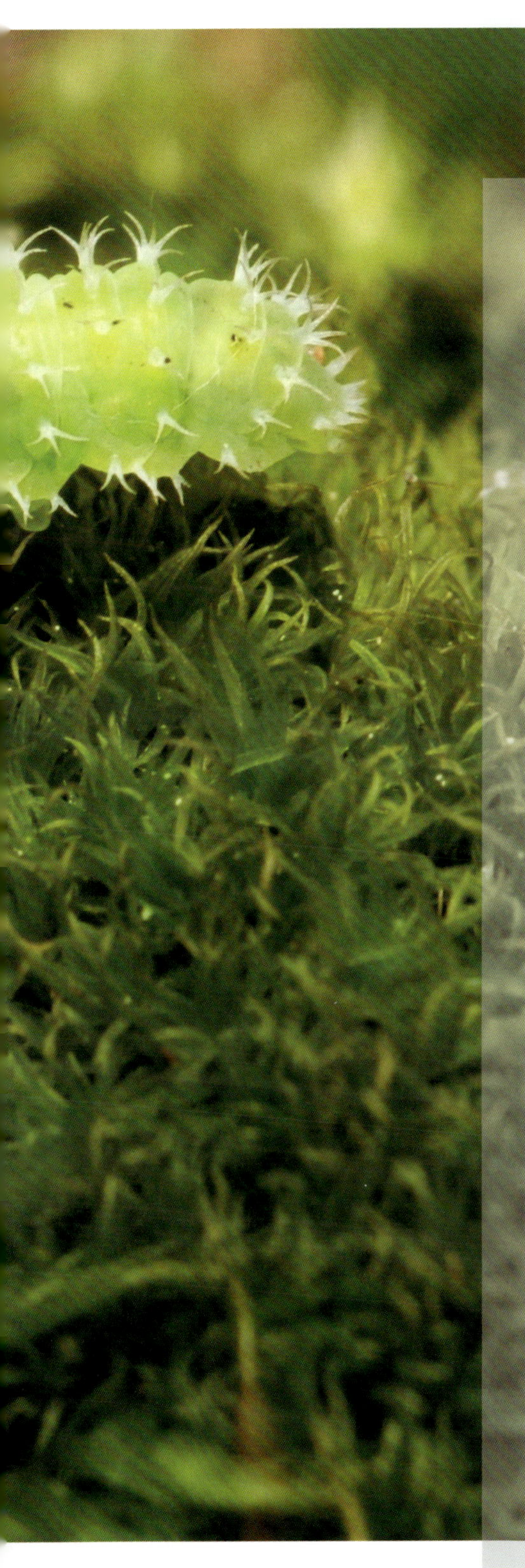

Image Editing

In what circumstances is it appropriate to alter an image? How much digital alteration is fair game? These questions are debated ad infinitum in Internet forums, and the opinions on the matter are usually diametrically opposed.

A few years ago, I was riding my bicycle through Hoge Veluwe National Park in the Netherlands when a rain shower caught me off guard. Fortunately, I was able to find some shelter under the canopy of a small oak grove where I waited for the rain to cease. As I was waiting, I discovered a small grub, which I later learned was the larva of a sawfly. I shot a few images with different exposure settings and then continued on my journey after the rain stopped. It wasn't until I returned home and inspected my photos on my computer monitor that I discovered the best of the pictures I had taken of the caterpillar was also imperfect in that I had inadvertently truncated the subject at the right image border. Faced with this situation, I decided to use the right part of the bed of moss from another photo to rescue the image.

My intention of editing my photo in this manner was not to misrepresent reality in any way. There actually was moss to the right of the larva, so I tend to think of this type of edit as entirely justifiable.

You have to decide for yourself where your threshold is for justifiable image editing. Photography competitions usually spell out clear guidelines for what is permissible and what is not, so if you intend to submit your work to these contests, it's important to play by the rules.

Sawfly larva on moss
f/13, 1/60 s, ISO 200, 50mm, system flash with softbox

Post-processing Photos

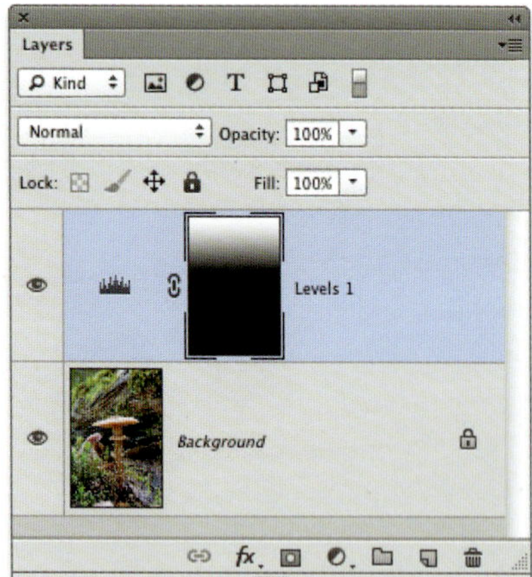

Adjustment layers with layer masks allow photographers to partially adjust the Levels of an image. Edits to the image apply in areas where the mask is white but don't apply where the mask is black. The effect of the edits gradually tapers between these two extremes.

The photograph you intend to take and the image that comes out of the camera are not always one and the same; image editing offers ways to bring the latter closer to the former. The extent of the post-processing needed depends entirely on the quality of the baseline image. In general, you should always strive to use photographic methods to obtain the best image possible. But some circumstances render perfection impossible, so Photoshop and other comparable image-editing programs belong in a photographer's bag of tricks just as much as a camera or a lens does.

A full tutorial of the capabilities and processes of digital image editing is beyond the scope of this book, and I have no intention of providing the world with yet another discussion about using Lightroom for RAW conversion. What you'll find next are a few step-by-step guides for image-editing practices that I use in my daily work.

Adjusting Levels

Taking pictures in a forest comes with a specific set of challenges. One of them concerns the behavior of light: images shot beneath the trees often have brighter upper regions and darker lower regions. In most cases, a reflector used during the exposure can reflect enough light on the lower areas to easily fill the shadows. But there are always times when you won't have a reflector on hand, which leaves post-processing as a viable option for correcting this undesirable distribution of light.

The example photo used to illustrate this process has a further complication: the mushroom cap casts a shadow over the underside of the cap, meaning either the gills will appear too dark, or the top of the mushroom cap will appear too bright depending how you decide to expose the scene.

The easiest way to correct this problem is to make a partial adjustment to the image Levels. To do this, open Photoshop and navigate to *Layer > New Adjustment Layer > Levels*. This adjustment layer appears above the background layer and is automatically provided with a layer mask—the layer mask simply has to be activated. Now select the Gradient tool and set the foreground to black, and apply a gradient with black at the bottom and white at the top. The corrective measure you apply now will only affect the unmasked areas of the image, or in other words, the bright areas of the layer mask.

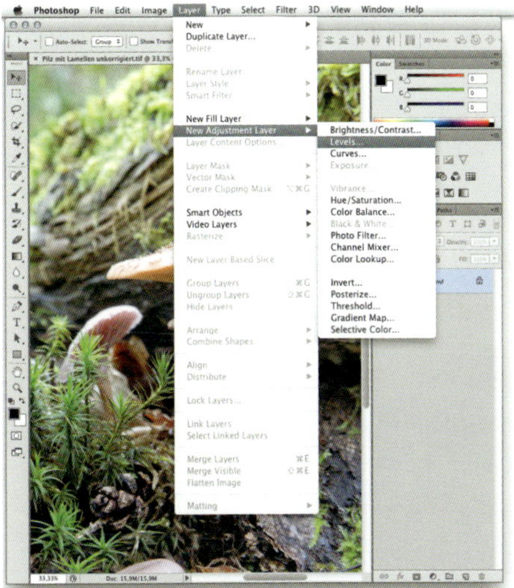

The first step is creating a new adjustment layer by selecting Levels

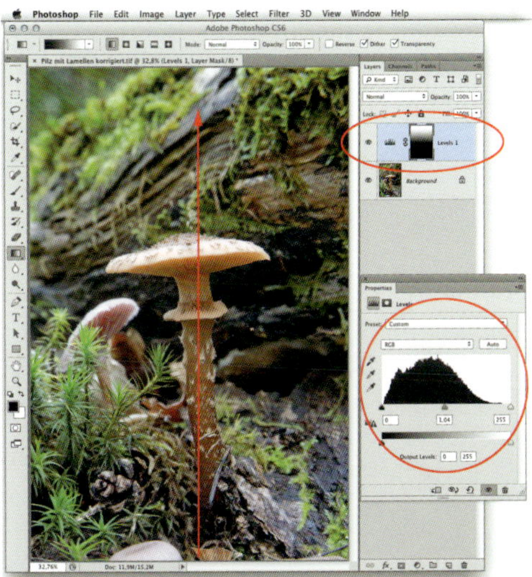

Then apply a gradient from black to white for the layer mask of the adjustment layer. At this point you can finally make your adjustments to the Levels.

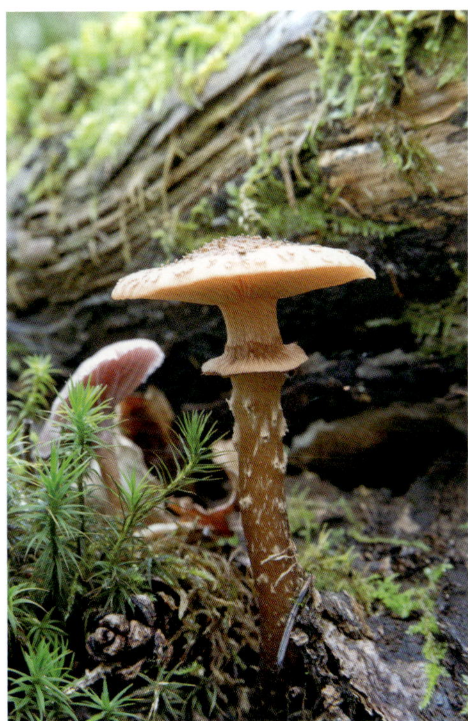

The upper third of the original image is too bright, requiring that the histogram levels be tweaked accordingly. To do this, I shifted the middle tones to the right, or toward the highlights.

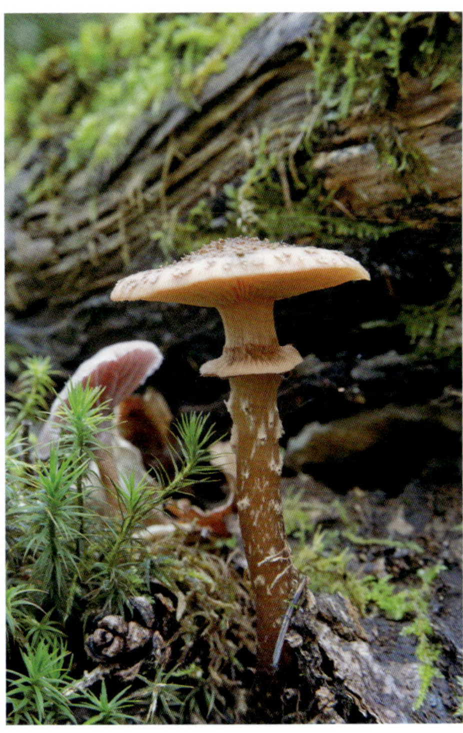

The photo appears much more balanced after editing the image

The gradient ensures that there is a seamless transition between the corrected and the uncorrected parts of the image.

You can also opt to use the brush or the airbrush tools to paint on the layer mask manually, giving you even more control over how and where the corrective measures are applied. In addition to this partial adjustment of the Levels, other adjustment layer options include Curves, Selective Color Correction, Black & White Conversion, Channel Mixer, and others.

Add Noise

A photographer's goal when capturing an image is generally to minimize the appearance of image noise as much as possible. But there are cases when adding noise is desirable, such as when you need to apply a new background to a subject or extend the existing background of a subject. It can be difficult to make the texture of the new areas of the background seamlessly match the rest of the image, particularly when solid colors and gradients are in play. It's also difficult to match the micro textures of the image when softening individual elements or overlaying cloned areas with the stamp tool. This challenge can be overcome with the Add Noise feature in Photoshop.

The image of the fly on the leaf was shot at a relatively high ISO, so image noise is readily visible in the original image. In order to extend the background organically, it's necessary to replicate the appearance of the image noise in the areas being added to the frame. I opted to use the narrow strip near the top of the image border as the basis for extending the background, because there wasn't much room to work with the stamp tool. This method meant that the shades of green would exhibit seamless transitions.

Next I copied, pasted, resized, and softened the target area (as described in greater detail in the image captions), and then finally applied the Add Noise filter. Adjusting the Amount value allows you to mimic the noise appearance in the original image, so the final result features a homogenous transition area. You can further modulate the appearance of the noise by selecting the Uniform or Gaussian options. The Monochromatic feature is useful when excessive color noise becomes distracting, such as in the grey tones of a shadow on a white ground. The last step was to uncover the tip of the leaf that was covered by the added image area. To do this, I used a layer mask and the Brush tool with a soft edge.

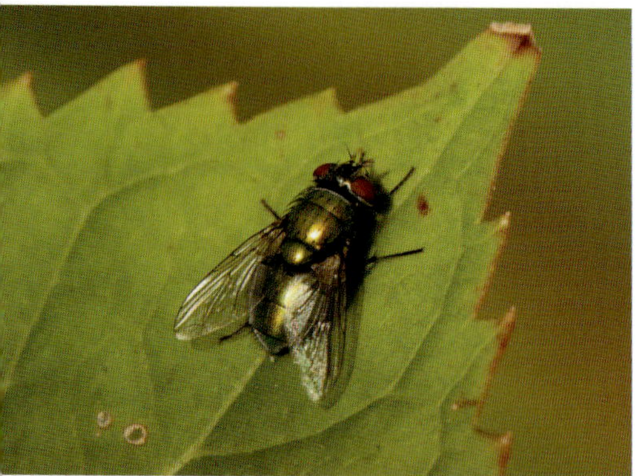

The upper edge of this leaf serving as a resting place for a fly is unattractively close to the upper border of the image

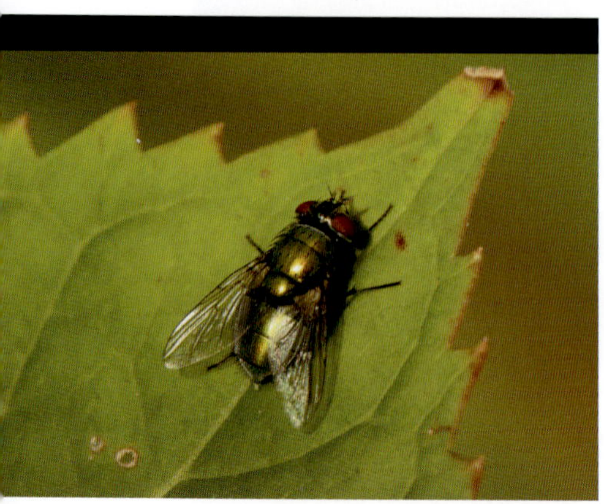

The first step is adding a bit of space for the extended background. The color of this added background area is irrelevant at this point.

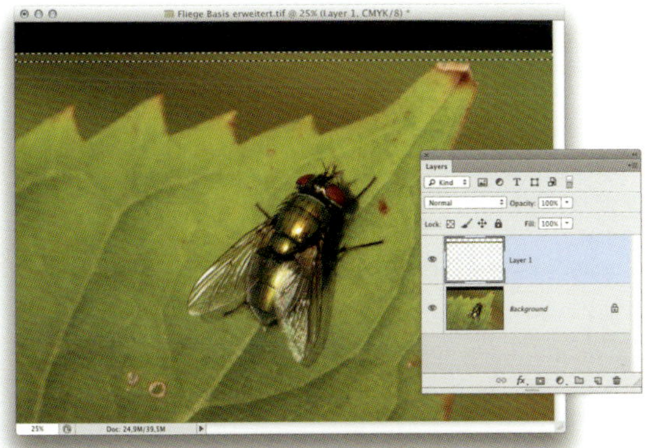

I copied a narrow strip near the top of the image to serve as the basis for my new background area. I then pasted it as a new layer.

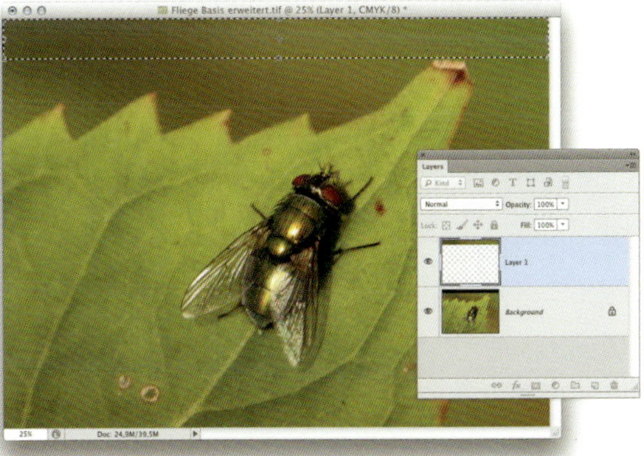

Now the new area can be deliberately stretched to cover the added image area, as well as to overlap with a small portion of the original image

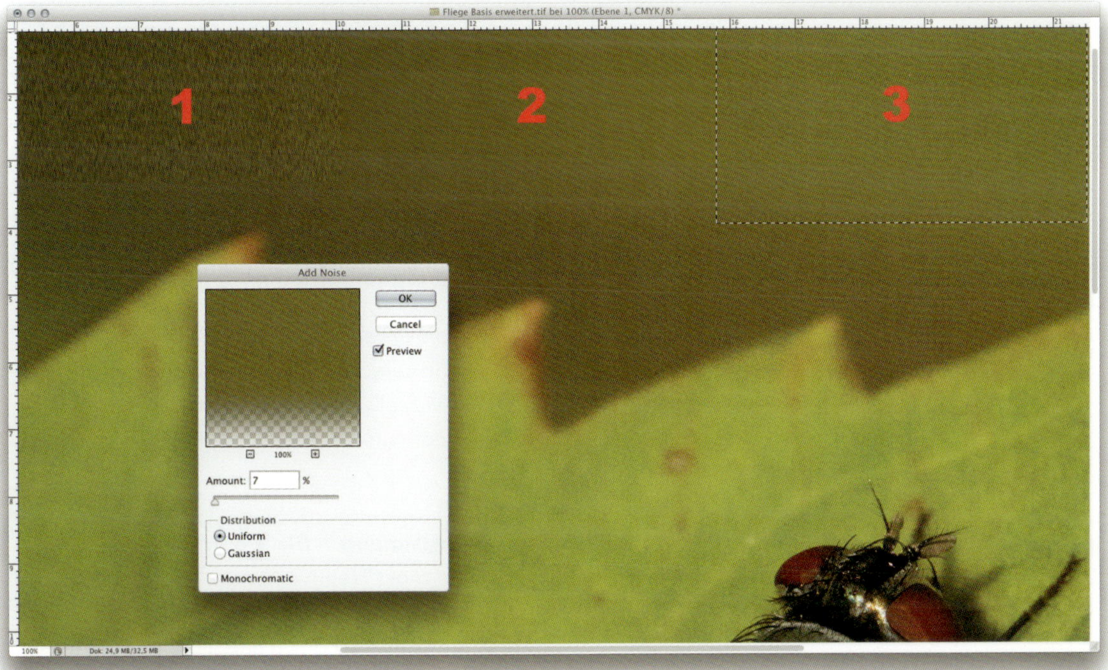

This process creates a striated texture (1) that can be smoothed out by applying "Gaussian Blur" (2). This softening, however, wipes out all of the texture from the image area in question, which is where the Add Noise function comes into play (3). By using an Amount of 7 and selecting the Uniform option, Photoshop generates noise comparable to what was present in the original picture. Softening the edge of the new background area results in a seamless transition with the original image.

Black & White Conversion

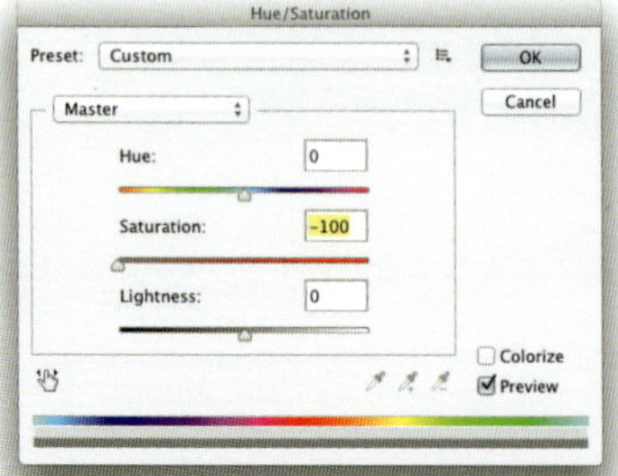

There generally aren't many situations when a black-and-white macro image is needed, but you may occasionally want to supply an image for a newspaper or create a flier at a copy shop. Photoshop offers many ways of converting color images to black and white.

Converting to Greyscale | *Image > Mode > Greyscale*
The simplest way to create a black-and-white image is to convert the picture to greyscale. The result is a good basis for adjusting the Levels.

Desaturation | *Image > Adjustments > Desaturate* or
Image > Adjustments > Hue/Saturation
The resulting image will be relatively dark, but it can be adequately brightened by adjusting the Levels.

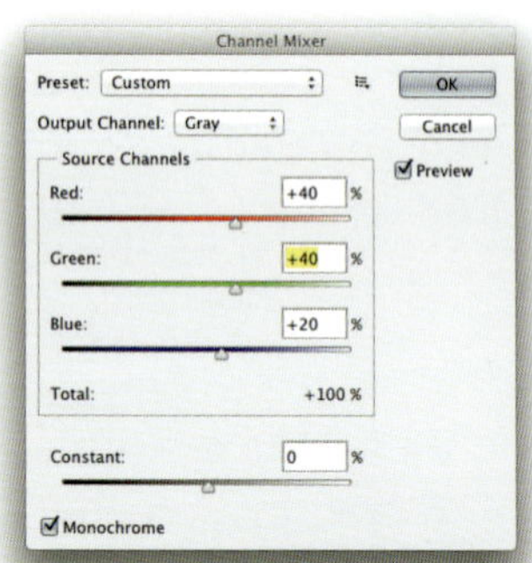

LAB | *Image > Mode > Lab Color*
To create a greyscale image, open the Channels palette after switching the image mode to LAB and remove the *a* and *b* channels. Or use the clipboard to copy the Lightness channel into a new file.

Channel Mixer | *Image > Adjustment > Channel Mixer*
With the Monochrome option selected, you can modulate each of the three RGB channels individually to control the extent to which each channel is used in the conversion process. Adjusting the sliders influences the entire image.

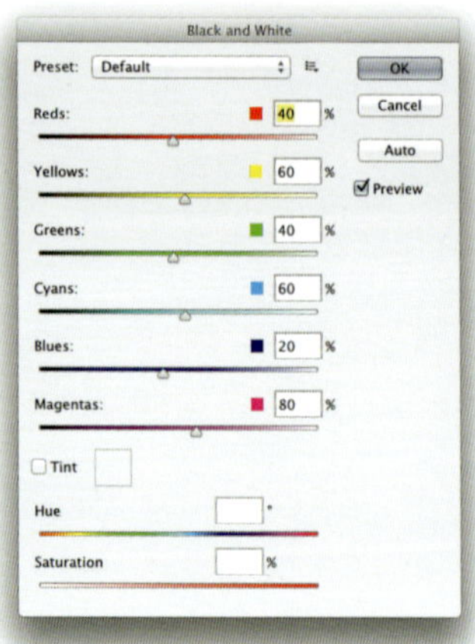

Black & White | *Image > Adjustments > Black & White*
This method offers users the most creative control over the conversion process. Photoshop offers six color sliders to influence the way that different color areas are converted. You can amplify or diminish specific colors to boost contrast, for example.

With the exception of the methods that explicitly convert the image into greyscale or LAB, these techniques will leave images converted to black and white in RGB mode. To prep an image for print, you'll still need to convert it to greyscale.

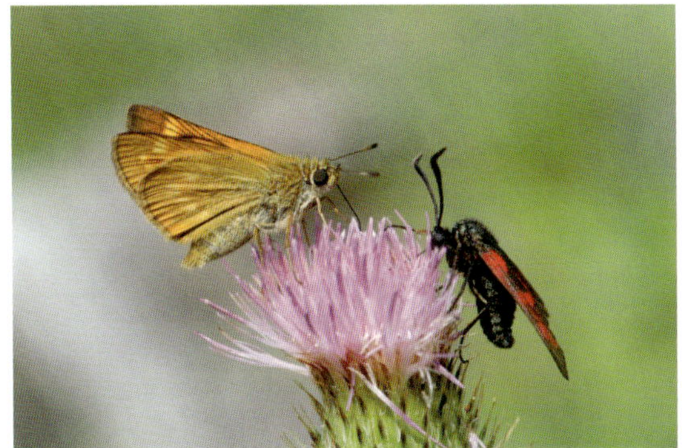

The image should be in RGB mode

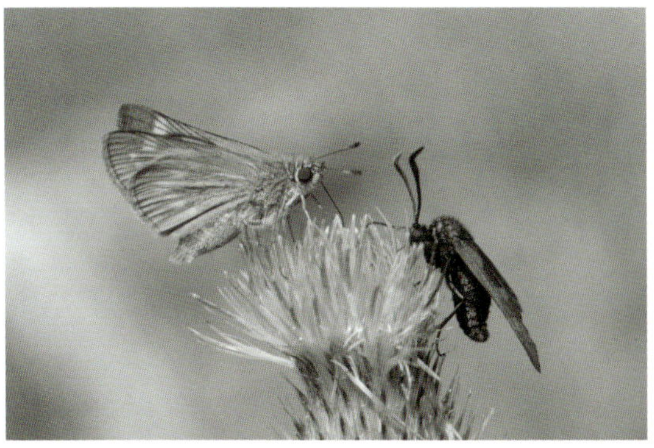

Simply converting the image to greyscale generally does not produce the best results immediately. Adjusting the tonal levels is often required to enhance the converted image.

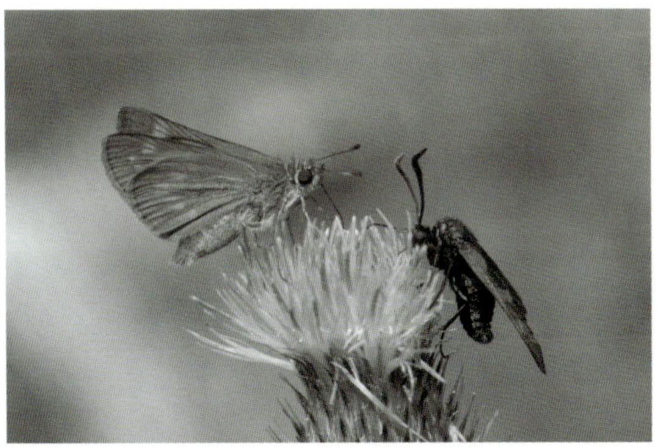

Using the Desaturate or Hue/Saturation tools often produce a black-and-white image on the darker side. Post-conversion editing is also recommended if you go this route.

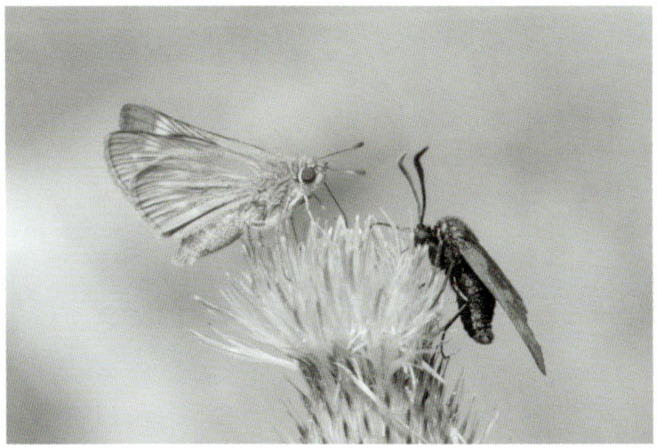

In contrast, converting the image by isolating the Lightness channel after converting the image to LAB mode offers more subtle treatment of the tonal values but an overall image that is too light

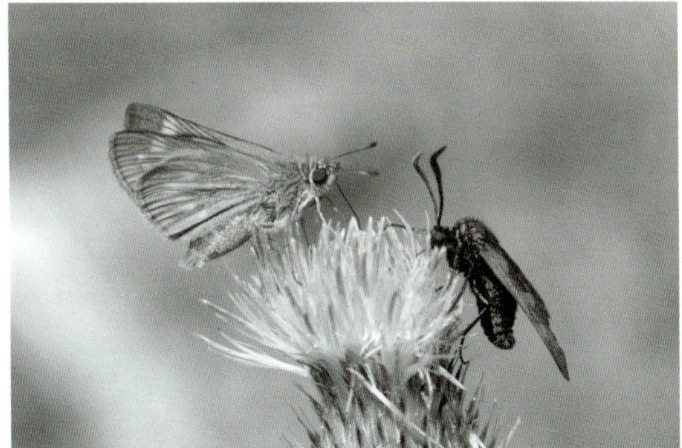

The Channel Mixer offers users a good degree of control over the conversion results, but extreme settings tend to produce grainy images

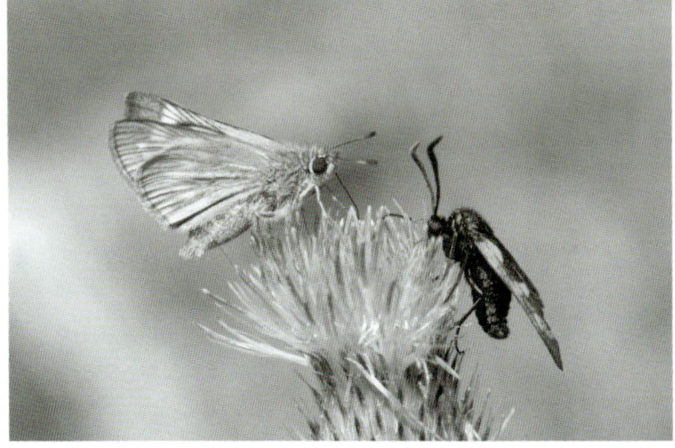

And the Image > Adjustments > Black & White method offers photographers the most influence over the conversion results, including the ability to modulate specific areas of color to increase contrast

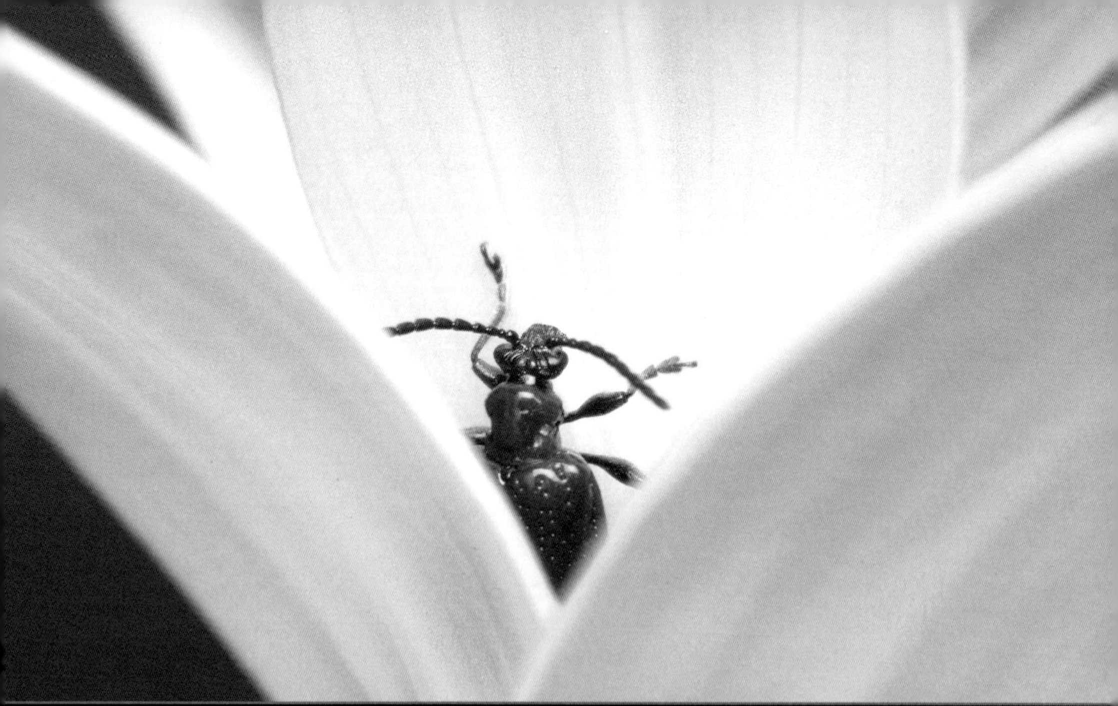

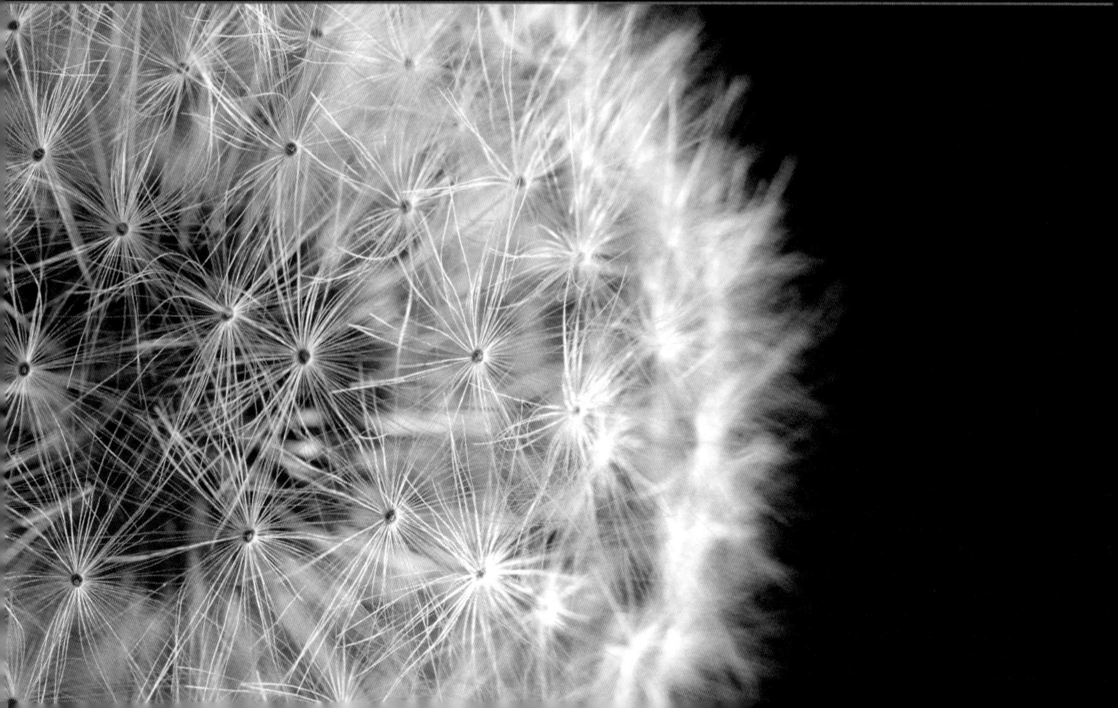

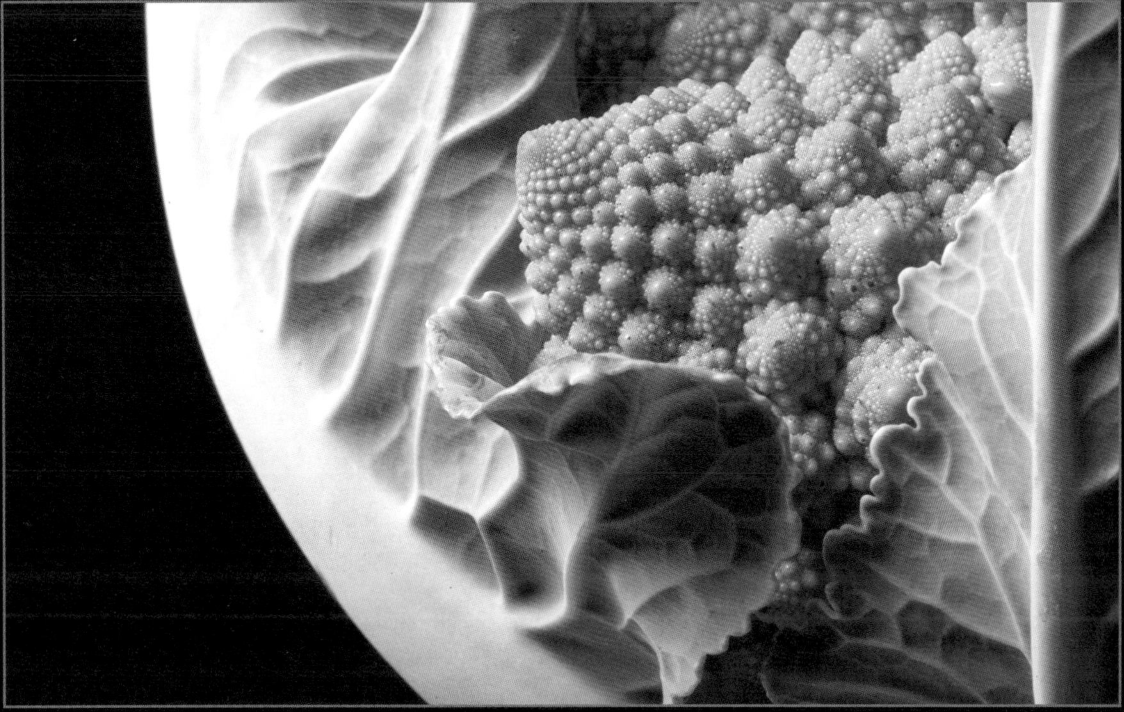

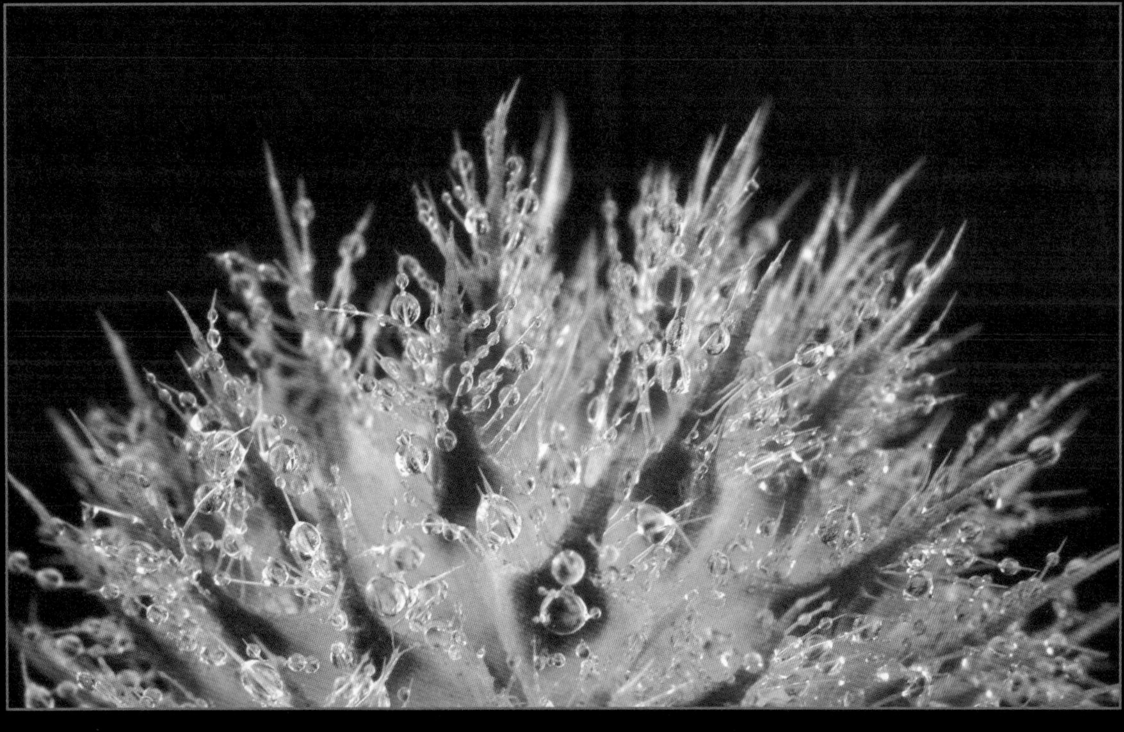

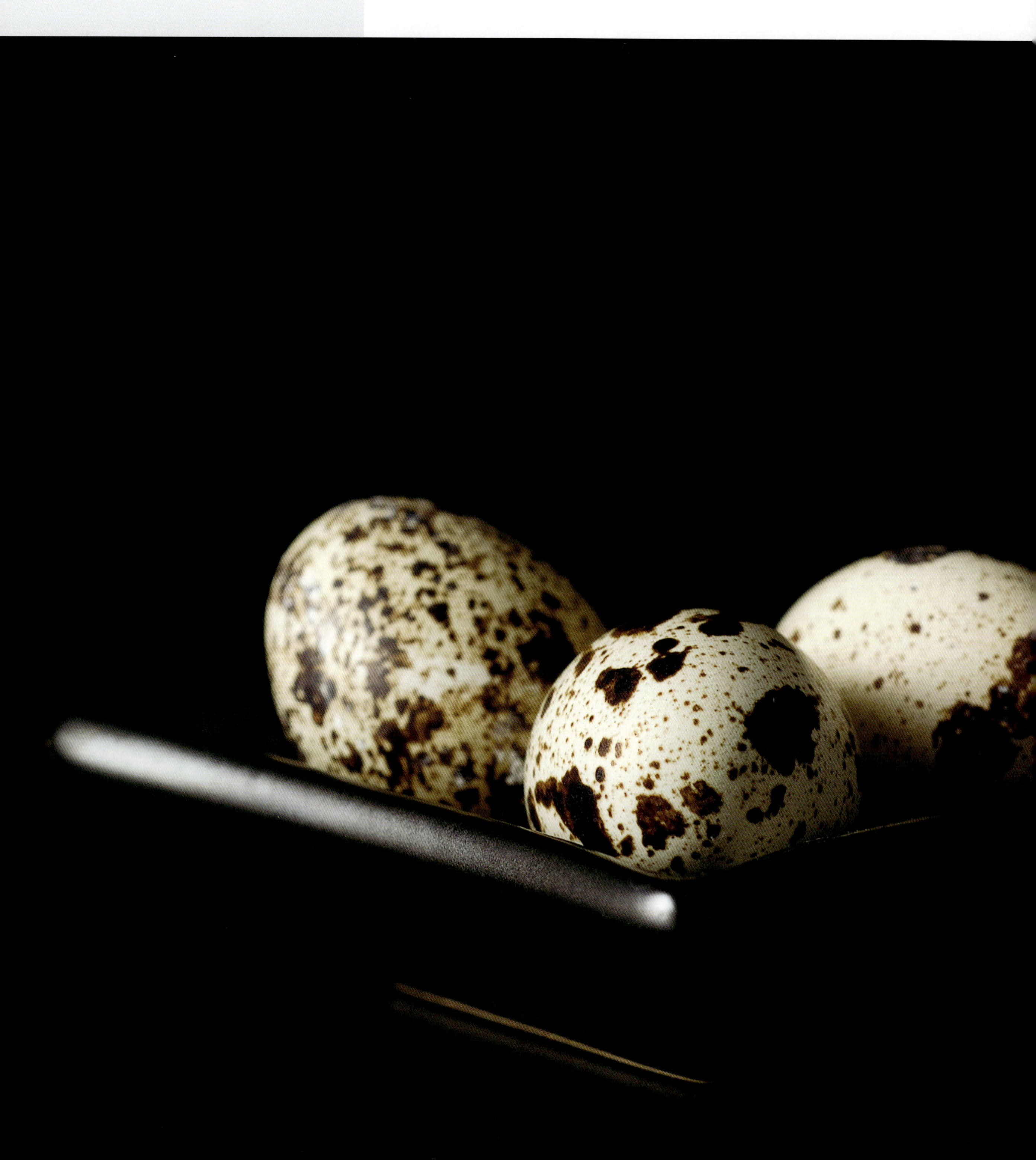

Working with Light

Light is the key to photography—and macro photography is no exception. Here's a small experiment you can conduct if you'd like a concrete demonstration of how different lighting situations can alter the appearance of a scene. Take a simple subject, such as the quail eggs used here, which are about 3cm in length, and take a series of photographs after dark using nothing but a desk lamp in an otherwise unlit room. Shift the position of the lamp for each exposure. You'll quickly see how shadows change and how reflections form and then disappear depending on how close or far the light source is from the subject. You can also explore the effect of using a reflector, such as a simple sheet of copy paper, or using indirect flash by reflecting the light off a white wall.

Quail eggs in a ceramic bowl
f/8, 1/200 s, ISO 100, 60mm, studio flash unit with softbox

Exposure Metering

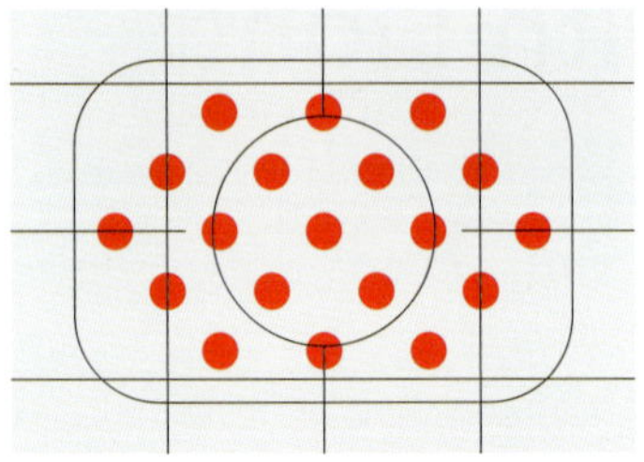

Multi or matrix metering methods collect and weigh light data from across the image area when calculating an exposure value. These systems also factor in the shooting distance and the subject's coloration into the metering equation.

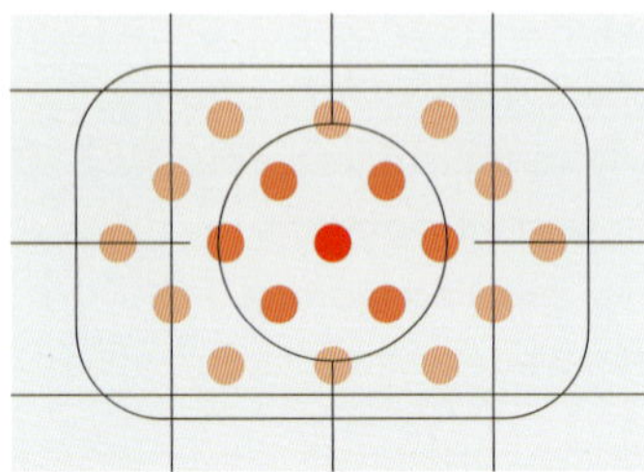

Center-weighted metering places an emphasis on the light data collected from the middle of the image area over the data from the surrounding image regions

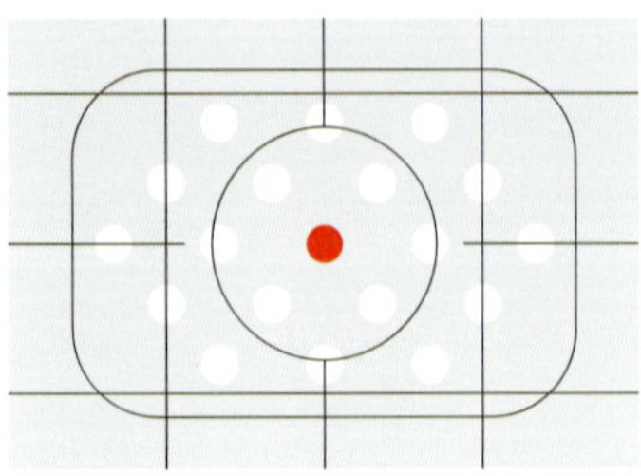

Spot metering uses the grey value for a specific metering field corresponding to the most important image element to calculate the exposure value

Nowadays we typically rely on values produced by internal metering systems and never think twice about them. In most cases, automatic metering systems produce outstanding results, thanks largely to the ever-improving technology that camera manufacturers are able to produce. But photographers will always come up against situations that supersede what automatic metering systems are capable of managing. When this is the case, you need to be ready to intervene to get the results you want.

In general terms, a camera's integrated metering system simply measures the quantity of light reflected off of the subject and offers appropriate combinations of shutter speed and aperture given the current ISO setting. An average reflectance of 18 percent is the baseline for these calculations. The process becomes more sophisticated only in that some exposure metering techniques weigh the values metered by specific fields differently. Accordingly, obtaining a proper exposure for an image depends on three variables: how reflective the subject is, the exposure metering method, and the intentions of the photographer.

Multi or Matrix Metering

This metering method calculates one average light value for an image based on data collected by metering fields distributed across the entire image area. These systems generally weigh data from key parts of the image more heavily, and they also take the shooting distance into account. This method usually produces nicely balanced exposures for relatively uncomplicated subjects.

Center-Weighted Metering

As the name implies, center-weighted metering methods prioritize the metering data collected from the center of the image area over that collected from the surrounding regions. This method is most useful when your main subject is located in the center of your image.

Spot Metering

Spot metering bases the exposure on an even more specific source of light data: a single selected metering field. Imagine that you wanted to take a picture of a full moon in the night sky (the moon is not exactly a macro subject, but it illustrates the value of spot meter-

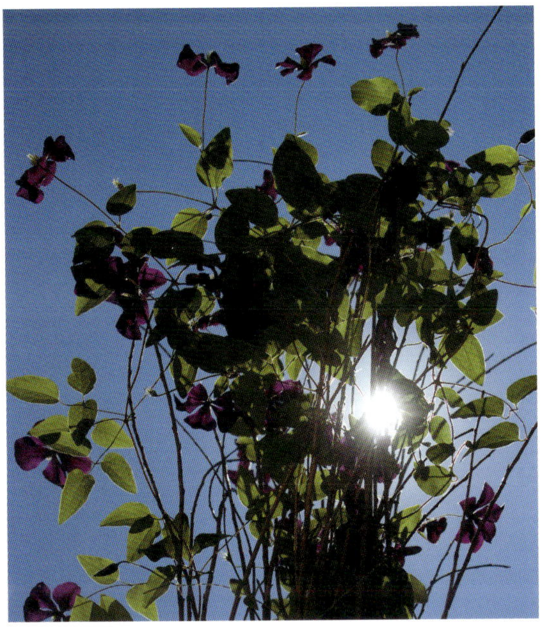

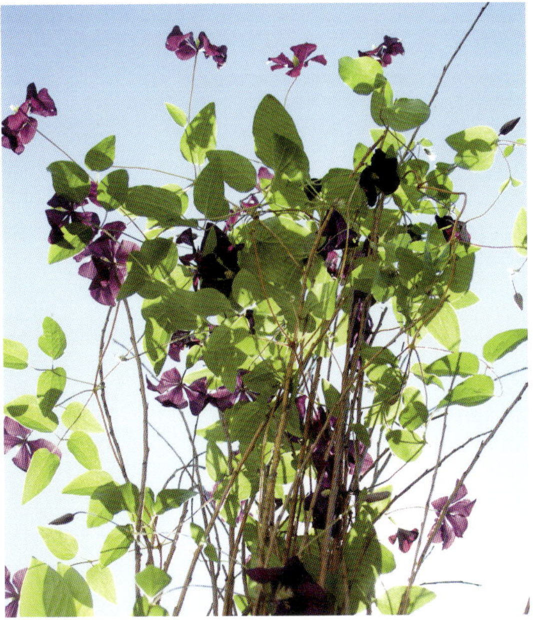

The standard metering method is insufficient here, producing an image that is too dark due to the intense backlighting. The direct sunlight shining through the branches is the critical factor.
f/4, 1/2,500 s, ISO 100, 28mm, multi metering

Spot metering based on the leaves improved the situation and when combined with a slight shift to the camera's position to hide the sun behind the leaves we end up with a properly exposed result
f/4, 1/1,250 s, ISO 100, 28mm, spot metering

ing clearly). If you were to use matrix or center-weighted metering, the surface of Earth's satellite would be dramatically overexposed in your image, because both metering methods would take portions of the surrounding night sky into account when calculating a light value. Alternatively, using spot metering to base the exposure on the moon itself would produce an image that would more delicately reveal the details of light and shadow in the moon's surface.

Exposure Compensation

Automatic metering systems are not equipped to handle some specific lighting situations, such as subjects that feature particularly bright or dark areas as well as low-key or high-key scenes. Exposure compensation offers a way to adjust the exposure manually to handle these situations more effectively. Most cameras enable photographers to adjust the exposure in increments of 1/3 EV. Some cameras display the effective exposure compensation in decimal form, so the display may read + or – 0.3, 0.7, or 1.0, whereby 0.3 actually represents a compensation of 0.333… and 0.7 corresponds to 0.666…. Compensating the exposure by +1.0 EV is theoretically tantamount to increasing the exposure by one stop by opening the aperture one

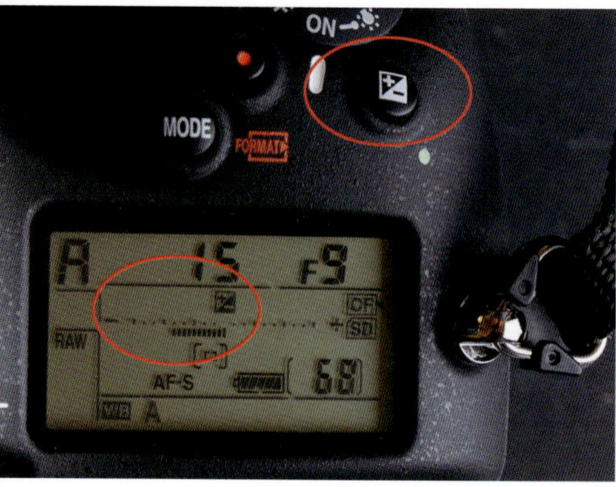

The exposure compensation feature allows you to fine-tune the exposure setting in 1/3 EV steps. The effective compensation amount is usually indicated on the camera's display.

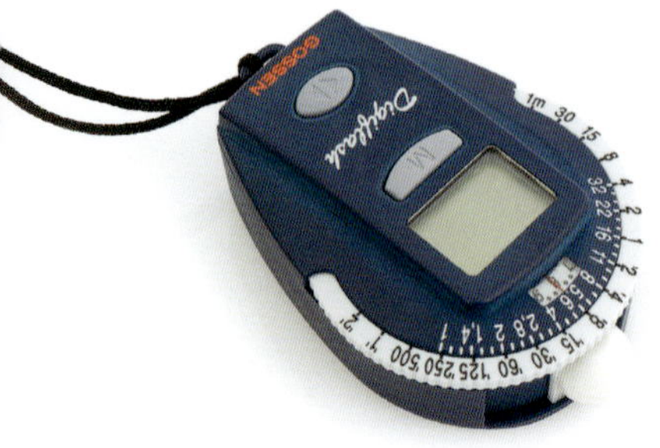

External lighting exposure meters are a huge help in the studio, especially with relatively complex lighting setups

stop (e.g., switching from f/8 to f/5.6) or increasing the shutter speed (e.g., from 1/500 to 1/250 s).

If aperture priority mode (A/Av) is activated to maintain a fixed aperture setting, the camera will effect an exposure compensation adjustment by increasing or decreasing the shutter speed. Consider the following example and the noteworthy potential implications: You're shooting a quickly moving subject at ISO 100, with an aperture of f/8 and a shutter speed of 1/1,000 s. Increasing the exposure compensation two stops (+2.0 EV) will force the camera to expose with a shutter speed of 1/250 s, which may pose motion blur problems.

Increasing the sensitivity to allow for the desired aperture and the appropriate shutter speed would be a more effective approach in this situation. Sticking with f/8 and 1/1,000 s would require an ISO setting of 400 rather than 100 to maintain the same effective exposure. A reference table for making adjustments of this kind can be found in "The Basics in Numbers" section in chapter 1.

As an alternative to using a camera's exposure composition setting, you can always switch your camera's exposure mode to manual and then increase or decrease the aperture and shutter speed settings as desired. This method produces the same effective result, although it may be slightly less efficient in practice.

There is no way to measure how much exposure compensation is needed for a given image (if there were, there would be no need for this feature in the first place), so trial and error is called for in figuring out how to handle certain situations. If you're not confident about how much to compensate, you can always shoot a series of images at different settings. With time, you'll develop a good feel for the types of adjustments that are necessary for specific lighting situations.

RAW Images as an Alternative

Saving RAW files for your images is one way to get around needing to fine-tune the exposure settings while shooting. Be aware, however, that retroactively adjusting the exposure settings of a RAW file tends to result in a loss of image quality to some extent. Compared to JPEGs, however, this loss is quite manageable. Adjustments of +/– 1 to 2 EV are no problem. When in doubt while shooting, err on the side of slightly underexposing your images because it's much easier to brighten shadows than it is to reconstruct blown-out highlights.

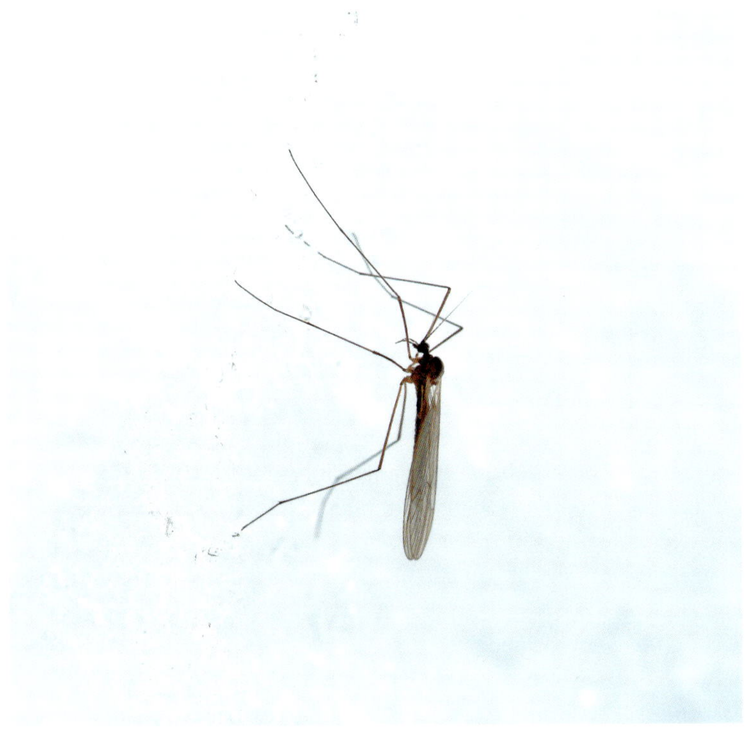

In the Studio

Small flash exposure meters are a useful tool for photographers who often shoot with multiple sources of light and flash in the studio. But they tend not to be practical beyond the close-up range. You likely won't have enough room between your subject and your camera to use these devices properly when shooting macro images with a magnification greater than 1:1. At this range, using trial and error to produce test shots is your only recourse for getting closer to your desired exposure.

Using continuous studio lighting equipment typically obviates this problem, allowing you to rely on the camera's internal metering system. Unfortunately, many extension tubes and bellows lenses don't support a camera's metering functionality, so here again, you're left either using an external meter or relying on trial and error.

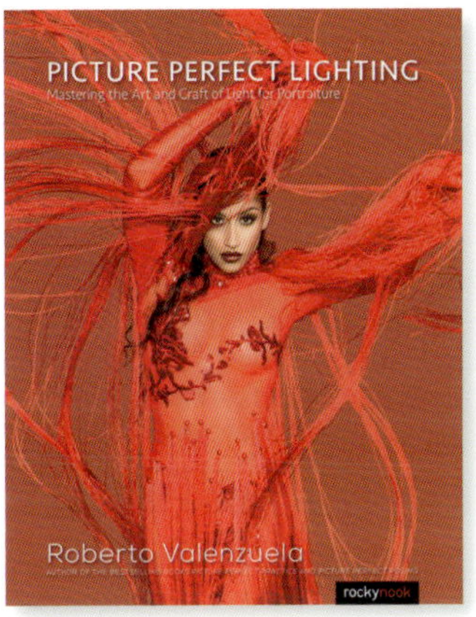

Book recommendation:
Anyone interested in further reading about light should check out Roberto Valenzuela's book, Picture Perfect Lighting, *also from Rocky Nook*

Lighting on the Go

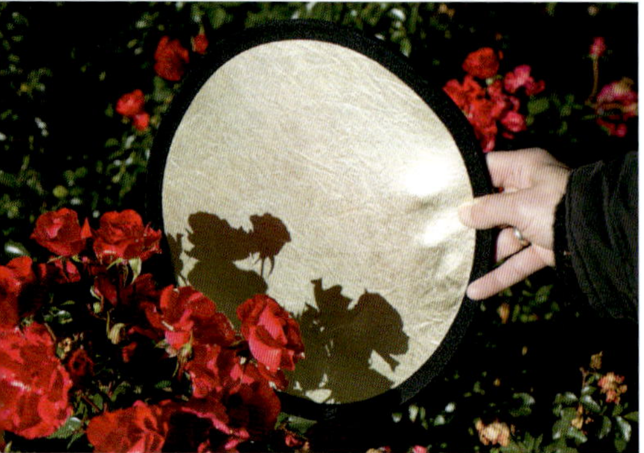

Small, foldable reflectors have a place in any equipment bag. The brighter the ambient light, the more powerful these tools become.

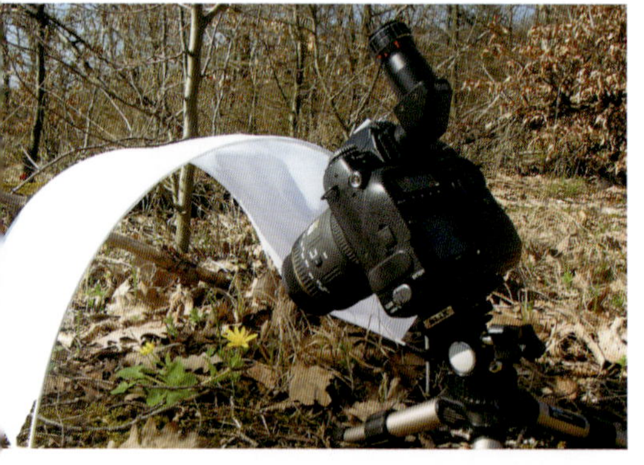

A small light tent, which you can easily build out of a sheet of white nylon from a kite and a couple fiberglass stakes, filters light, rendering a softer illumination

Lighting can be something of a challenge when shooting outdoors. You will frequently come across situations in which the light is insufficient for the task at hand, does not support the look you want, or may be too soft or coming from the wrong direction.

Reflectors and Diffusors

A reflector is the simplest way to direct light to a targeted part of your image. The photography market offers foldable reflectors in a range of sizes, and one with a diameter of 25cm is a good choice for macro purposes. Most models have a silver surface on one side and gold on the other, but you can also find some with white on one side and grey on the other. The latter type doubles as a grey card when setting the white balance.

Reflectors are also relatively easy to make on your own out of rescue blankets from first aid kits, the inner foil packaging of a coffee container, or a piece of aluminum foil. If using a rescue blanket or a piece of aluminum foil, crumple it up first and then unfold it to increase its scattering effect. In a pinch, you can also use a white piece of copy paper or even a white T-shirt.

Mirrors have practical utility in their ability to function as a second (or third) source of light. They can be used to reflect sharp, focused lighting at targeted areas of the subject. You can find plastic mirror-like options on the market, so you won't have to worry about glass breaking in your equipment bag.

Diffusors have the opposite effect of reflectors: they filter light and make it softer. These tools are also available in photography shops, but they, too, can be crafted on your own with relative ease—by using the white nylon of a kite, for example. Translucent films found in stationery stores also do the job. For smaller subjects, you can even get away with using a CD jewel case that's been roughed up with some sandpaper.

LED Lamps

The range of LED lamps that are practical for bringing with you on photo excursions is broad and varied: flashlights, area lights, ring lights, and even sharply focused gooseneck lights. They won't allow you to use shutter speeds as fast as you might be able to with flash units, but they do allow you to preview your lighting before taking any pictures, which can be a real advantage, especially for newer photographers who might still be getting a feel for lighting techniques. If faithful color reproduction is of concern to you, look for LEDs that are specifically designed for photographic use. They generally have a light temperature of approximately 5,000 K, and will prevent color casts from appearing in your images.

LED lights tend to produce rather harsh light. Because they often feature multiple small bulbs, they tend to lead to an unwieldy number of reflections on the subject. Using a diffusor or an indirect angle is accordingly required in some situations, which, unfortunately, leads to a decrease in effective light output. Small LEDs marketed as keychains come in handy for certain effect lighting treatments.

Internal Flash

Another option for creating some fill light—one that doesn't require additional equipment—is to rely on your camera's built-in flash. Many cameras offer the ability for photographers to manually control the integrated flash's output. When using a TTL automatic flash mode, you can generally tweak the flash output for your purposes by using the relevant button and dial. The results produced by this method sometimes have an artificial feel since it creates harsh shadows due to the fact that the light is always coming from the direction of the viewer. In other words, you'll want to use the integrated flash infrequently. Further complications arise when the tight shooting distance means that the camera's lens actually shadows some of the light from the flash from reaching the subject.

System Flash Units with Softbox Attachments or Reflectors

Direct flash lighting casts harsh shadows and tends to make subjects look busy. Softboxes are a great way to soften a flash's output to eliminate this problem. Because macro subjects are small, a small softbox attached to a system flash head works nicely. Something approximately 18cm by 28cm in size works very well to bathe subjects in an even light. I built the attachment on this page myself using some black foam and a piece of material from a diffusor, which I purchased in a photography shop. You can, of course, purchase finished options if you'd prefer, but chapter 12 has instructions for crafting a simple reflector.

System Flash Units with Professional Light Shaping Tools

Divorcing your flash from your camera gives you some extra flexibility as a macro photographer. You can position your lighting to suit your needs for each individual shot. With this method, a softbox of around 30cm by 30cm is plenty large for most macro subjects while

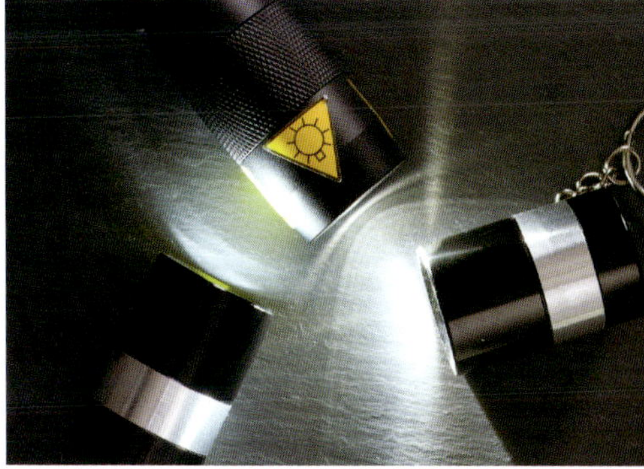

Small LED lights make it possible to easily create interesting lighting effects that would be more difficult to simulate with flash lighting

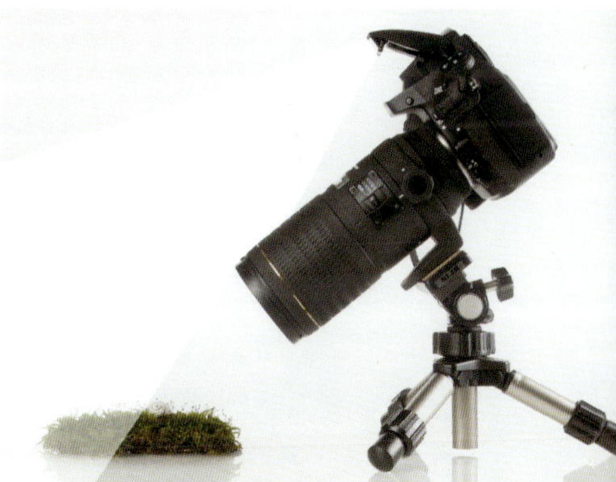

A macro lens can sometimes block direct light from a camera's built-in flash from reaching the subject

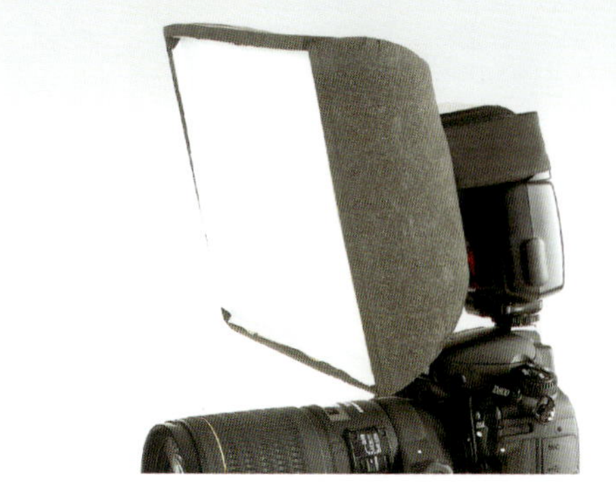

A self-made softbox attachment for a system flash head

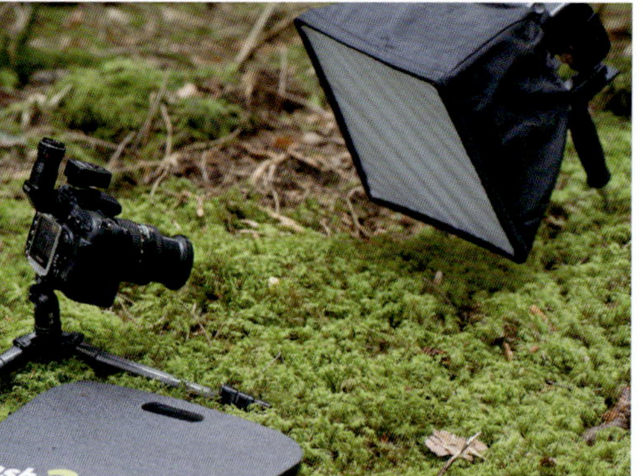

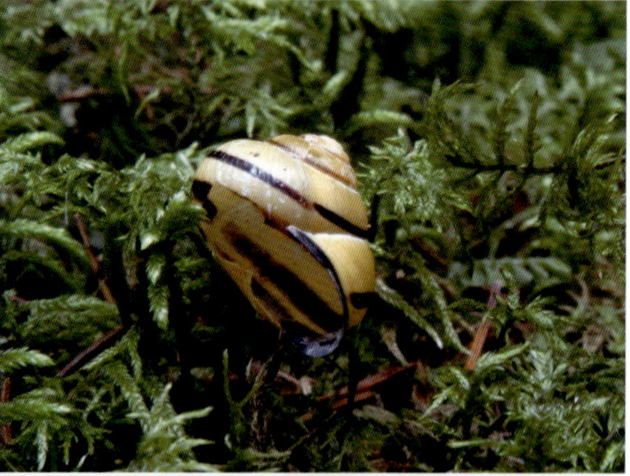

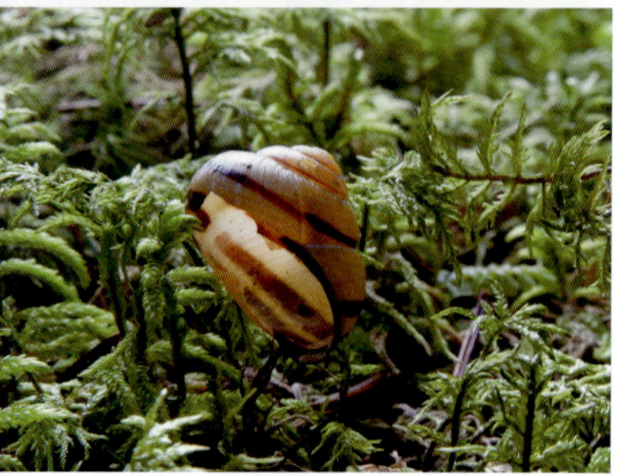

Top: The combination of a system flash unit and a 30 x 30cm softbox produces very even light for photographing small objects without any harsh shadows

Middle: Snail shell in ambient daylight

Bottom: Snail shell with soft backlighting from the softbox

still retaining the benefit of being easily transportable. Softboxes of this size can be equipped with a handle so they can be held in front of, over, or next to your subject. A stake equipped with tripod threads is another option for supporting professional light-shaping tools. Shots near the surface of the ground are much easier with this type of device, because it's relatively simple to to fix an adapter, flash, and softbox in soft soil.

With this type of setup, flashes are generally controlled via infrared or radio control. In most instances, you'll want to adjust the flash settings manually, because you'll need to compensate for the loss of light of one or two stops that results from using a softbox to filter the output.

On the Go with the Nikon Wireless Close-Up Speedlite System R1C1

The ideal lighting situation for many macro photographers is a sophisticated system that mounts directly onto the camera. Nikon approximates this ideal closely with the R1C1 wireless close-up speedlite system that is compatible with Nikon Creative Lighting System functionality. The kit comprises two flash heads with a guide number of 10 that mount to a ring. The ring attaches to the filter threads of the camera lens. The mounting ring can work with lenses featuring thread diameters up to 70mm. It can also support more than two flashes if you're interested in increased power.

The flash units are Nikon SB-R200s, and the controlling unit is an SU-800. This setup further allows you to work with one or more additional flash units, such as an SB-800 and/or an SB-900 programmed in different groups. This level of control comes close to what you can achieve in the studio, giving you tons of flexibility to compose and realize a wide range of images. You can create richly atmospheric images by modulating the direction of the flashes on the mounting ring or by separating one of them for effect lighting. For example, you might position one of the speedlites in the grass behind your subject while the second one illuminates the main subject.

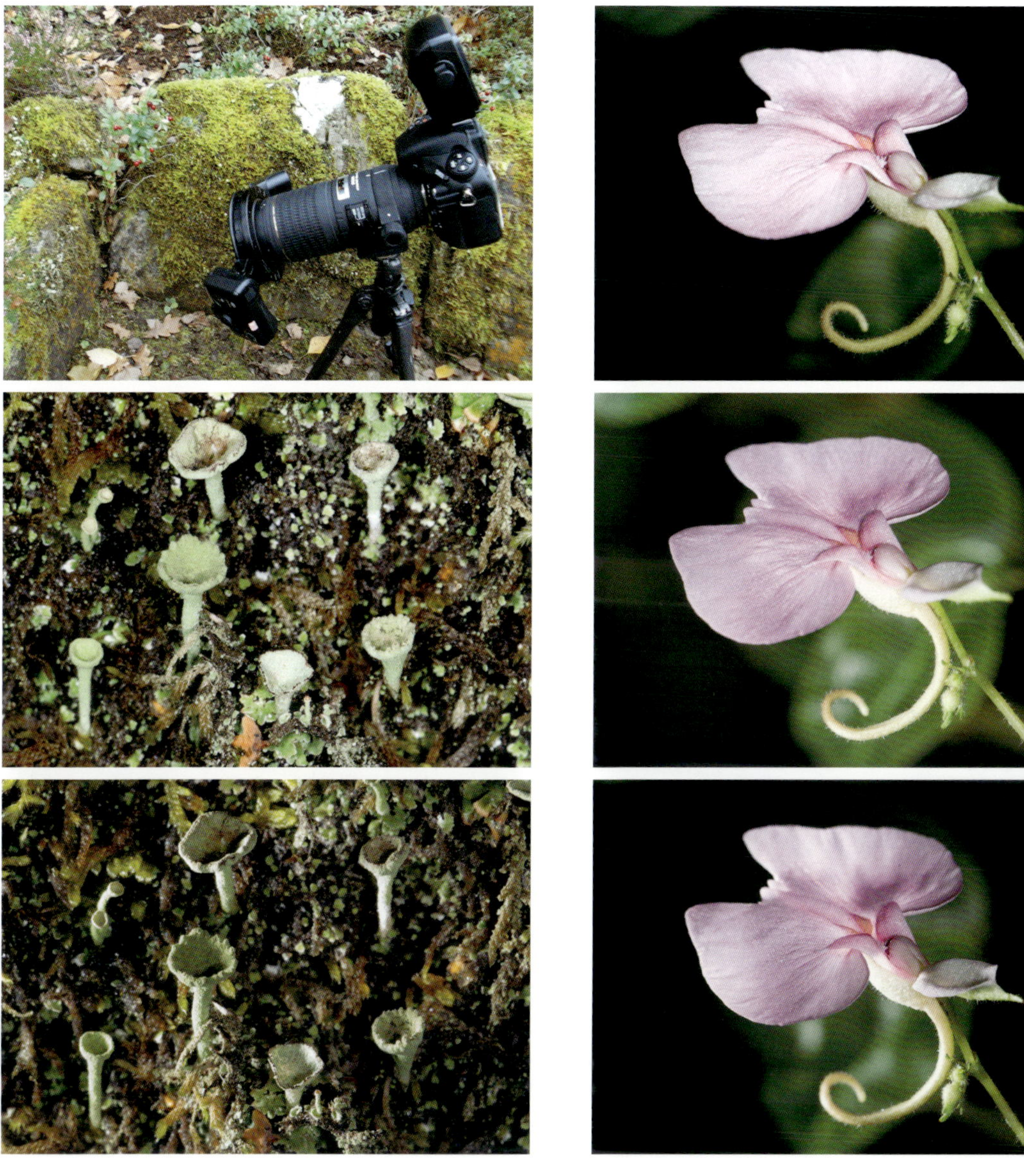

Top: Lighting produced by the Nikon R1C1 wireless close-up speedlite system comprising SB-R200 flashes with an SU-800 controlling unit for managing multiple units

Middle: Used in the standard twin flash arrangement, this macro lighting kit produces nearly shadow-free images

Bottom: The SB-R200 slave flashes can alternatively be set up apart from the camera, allowing for a range of creative lighting options, such as using side light, for example

Locations: Botanical Gardens of Tübingen, Germany

Top: For this shot, I positioned both of the SB-R200 flashes from the Nikon R1C1 kit on the mounting ring and pointed them directly at the flower—one from the left and one from the right. The result is somewhat flat.

Middle: I moved the two SB-R200s here so one was positioned on the upper right part of the mounting ring and the other was on the lower left. I directed one of the heads to flash the subject and the other to flash the background.

Bottom: For my final shot, I left one SB-R200 attached to the top mounting ring and directed it downward toward the subject. I removed the other flash from the ring and positioned it near the ground, pointing up at the flower. The result here is much more three-dimensional.

A Comparison of Portable Lighting Options

Silver Reflector

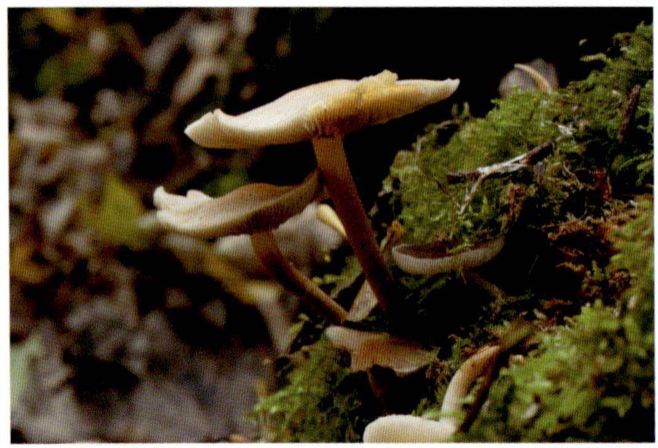

The gills and the stems of these mushrooms are dark, but they're still visible. Only a modest bit of extra light is needed.

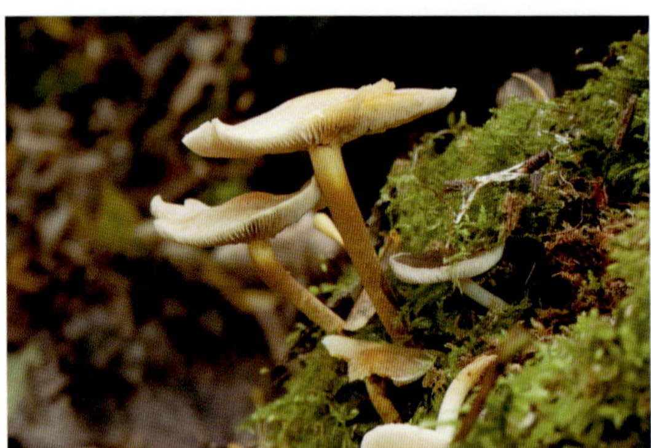

A reflector brightens the underside of the subject while leaving the background evenly lit. The gold color of the reflective surface produces a warmer color of light than a silver or white reflector would have. Reflectors are of minimal use on cloudy days and near the forest floor because there is significantly less light to reflect. Small reflectors can be easily built at home using aluminum foil or any other reflective material.

LED Light Painting

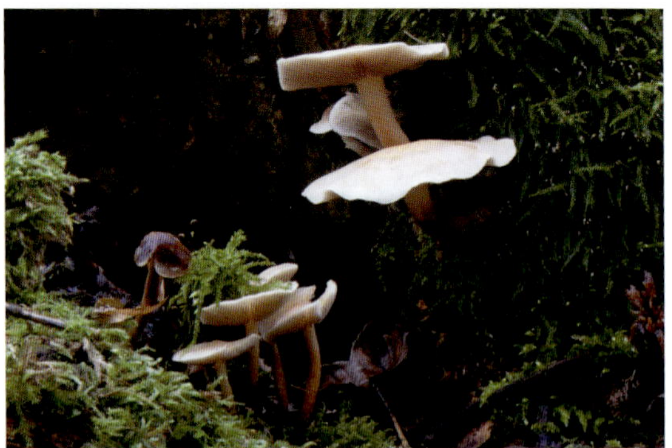

Using a light painting technique with a flashlight is an effective way to brighten targeted areas within an image

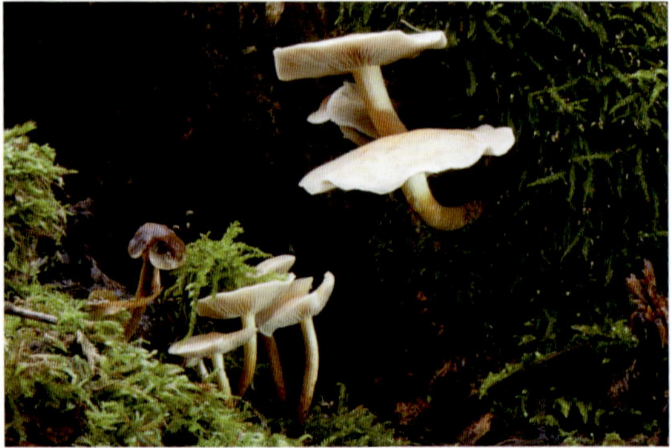

LED flashlights can be used to brighten up specific image areas, such as the mushrooms in this scene. Depending on the LEDs used, the results can skew toward looking artificial, but photographers can modulate the quality of light by using various films and filters in front of the flashlight. Light painting techniques always come with the risk of problematic shadows, so keep an eye on them while you're working. The smaller mushrooms on the left look good here, but the shadow affecting the larger group on the right is distracting. Light painting requires the use of a tripod, because it takes a little while to adequately paint your targeted image areas. An LED panel light would have allowed for a shorter exposure window, but it would have been impossible to target the light as precisely as with a flashlight.

Internal Flash

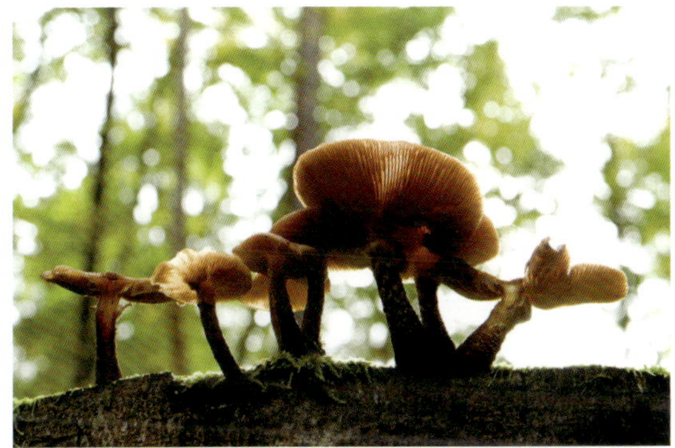

In this scene, intense backlighting causes the denser parts of these mushrooms to appear nearly black, while the thin translucent areas are bright with transmitted light

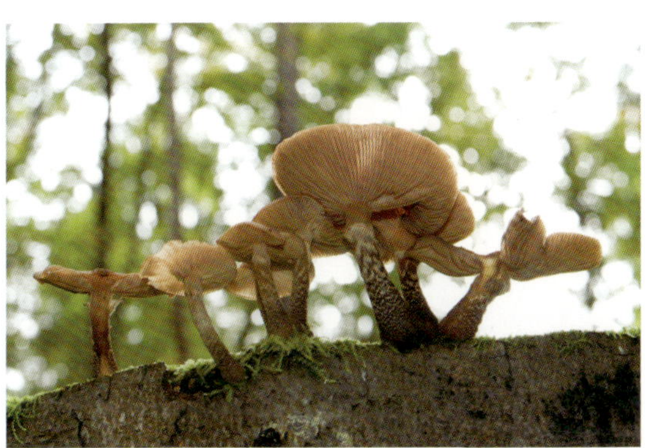

Using the internal flash (in this case, manually set to 1/20 of its output) to produce fill lighting prevents dark subject areas from receding into obscurity. Even though the flash succeeds at brightening these dark areas, it creates a somewhat unnatural feel to the scene because point sources of light produce such harsh shadows and lighting qualities that don't organically mesh with the ambient conditions of the scene. A built-in flash does have a huge advantage, though: it's impossible to forget it at home, and it doesn't require any extra gear in your bag.

System Flash with Softbox

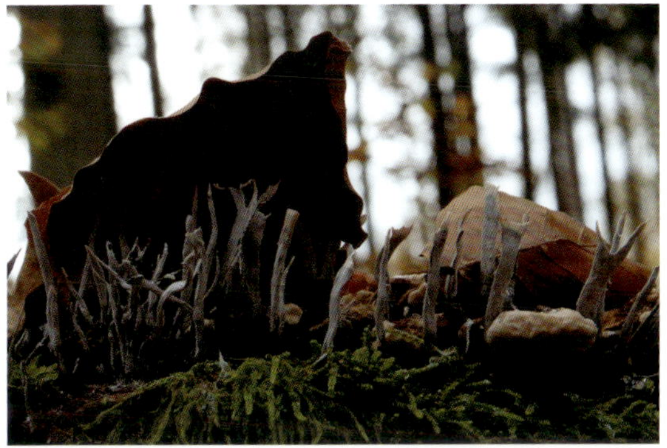

Even dismal cloudy days can produce backlighting situations that cause parts of a subject to appear too dark

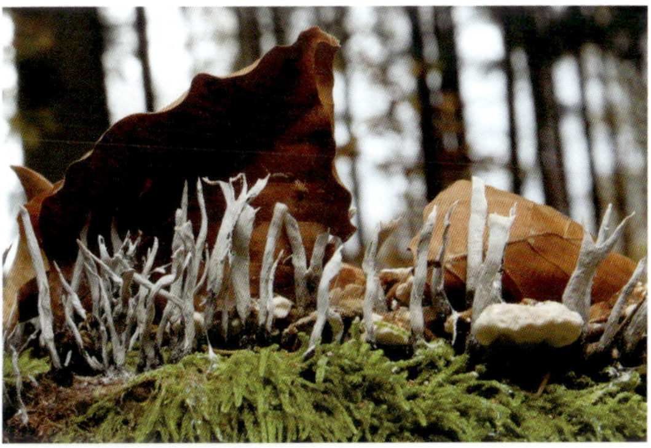

System flashes modified with softboxes are especially useful for creating soft, even fill lighting. For this picture, I used a remote trigger to fire a flash head set to 1/8 of its output. The flash was modified using a 30cm x 30cm softbox, which was positioned about 1 meter from the subject. Having the freedom to position your light source independent from your camera frees you up to experiment with a wide range of lighting options.

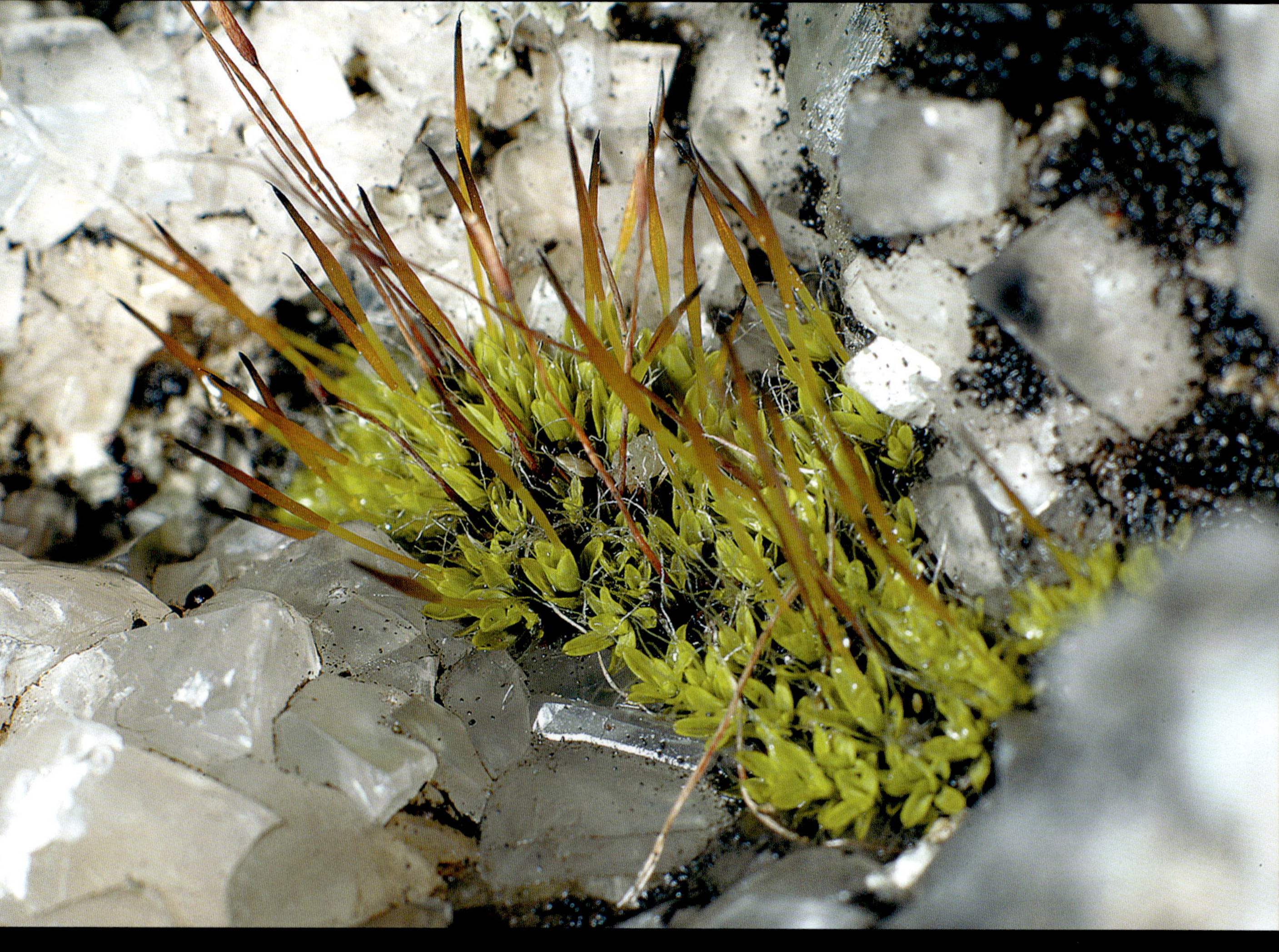

With subjects as inaccessible as this bit of moss growing in a crevice, artificial light is often the only way to capture a satisfying result. Here a softbox with an edge length of 30cm allowed for an image with nearly no shadows.

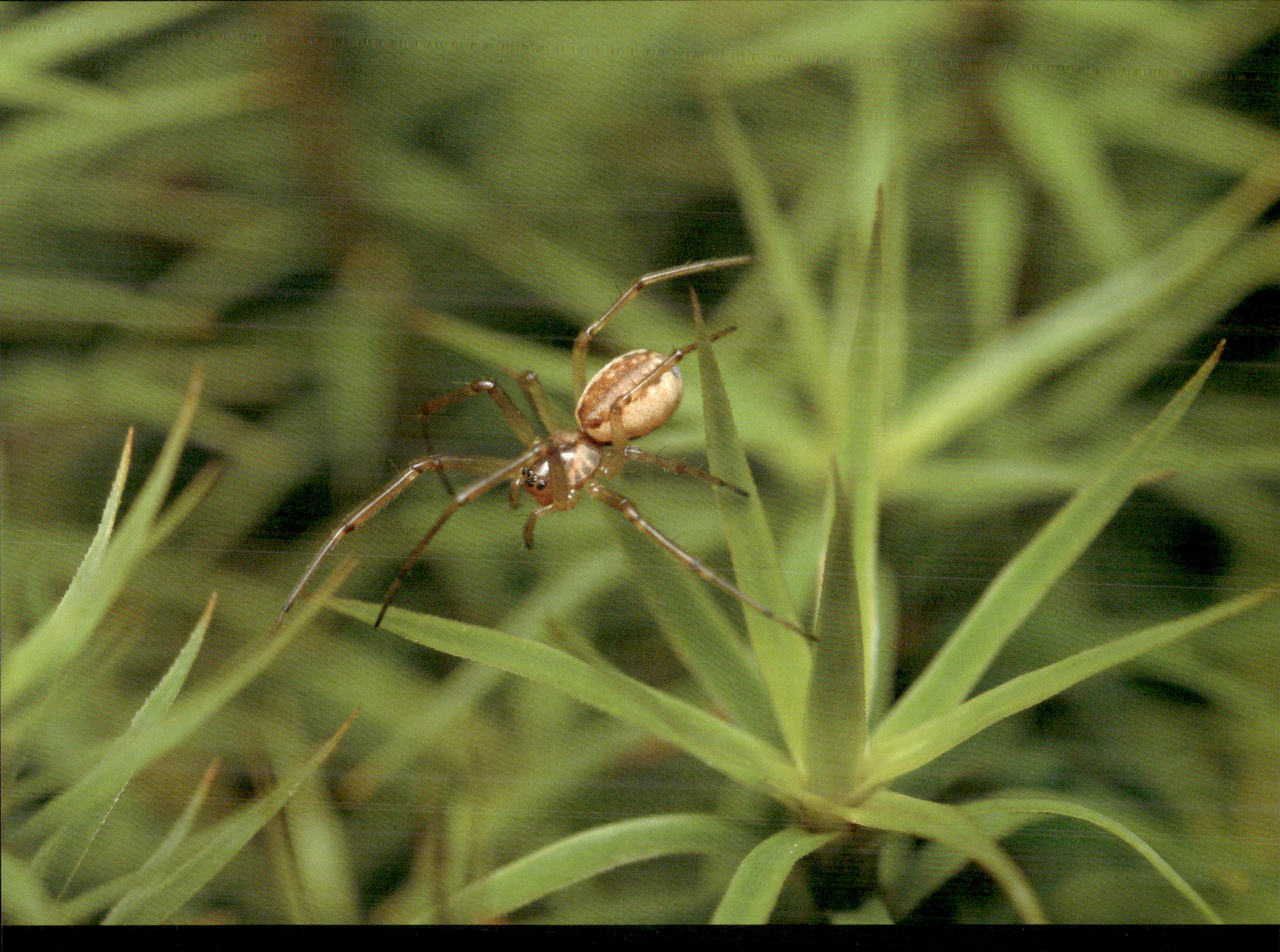

A spider, just a few millimeters in length, balances
artfully on the tips of neighboring plants. The large
lighting area of a softbox attached to a system flash
also succeeded in brightening up the background

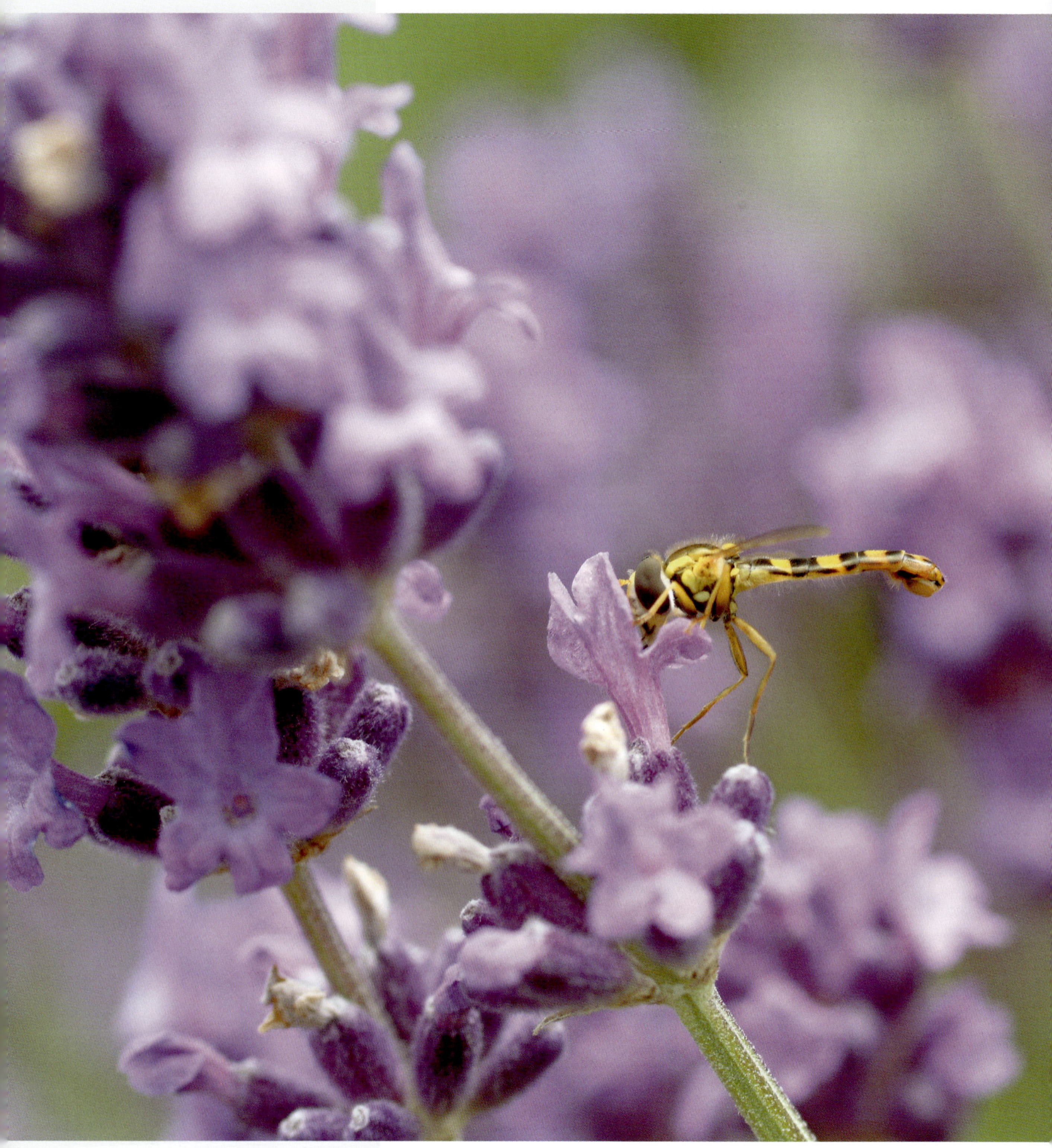

Composition

Subjects don't always need to fill up the entire image area. In many cases, their surroundings are a critical component of the scene.

This image of a small hoverfly in the middle of a lavender field works for a variety of reasons. The color contrast between the various purple tones of the lavender blossoms and the black-and-yellow pattern of the insect is striking, for starters. Another key effect arises from the horizontal orientation of the bug's body within a scene otherwise dominated by diagonals. What makes this particular image so successful in my eyes is that it suggests the incredible bounty of nature by depicting a tiny insect amid a sea of sustenance. It's a symbol for the land of milk and honey.

Image composition depends not only on the formal aspects of dominant lines and colors, but also on the overall message of the photograph. As a photographer, you can compose with many types of thematic contrasts, such as "big and small" or "singular and plural."

Hoverfly in a lavender field
f/6.7, 1/180 s, ISO 400, 50mm

Image Design

Why is it that photographs never exactly match the way we see reality with our eyes? After viewing an image, we often ask ourselves, "Were the shadows really that dark? Where did the rich ambiance of the scene go?"

Our subconscious is responsible for the discrepancy between our natural perception and the capabilities of a camera, lens, and sensor. The brain is hardwired with an image-editing software that makes current computer editing applications seem quaint. Our natural sensory system automatically filters out irrelevant details and stores information about the mood of the scene, the quality of light, and even details such as smell and wind and so on. Dark shadows are brightened; contrasts are modulated; colors are intensified. Put another way, our memory stores an idealized version of reality.

A camera is not capable of mimicking this process. Instead, it captures the appearance of how things actually are within the limits of its technical specifications. It is the photographer's job to depict reality in a way that speaks to the emotional side of our subconscious. We have a number of tools and methods at our disposal for achieving this goal, starting with selecting the format and orientation of the image. They also include the styling of critical image details, the inclusion or exclusion of background elements, and everything up to the choosing or influencing the lighting of a scene.

Choosing the Right Format

Deciding on the format for a macro image largely depends on the subject at hand. The goal of most macro photographers is to depict their subject as large as possible, which means evaluating alternative formats may be an afterthought. I recommend always considering an alternate format as soon as you identify your initial instincts. It's often not until you take the time to view your subject from all sides before you realize the opportunity of shooting a portrait-oriented image instead of a landscape one. You can always reject your alternative consideration later.

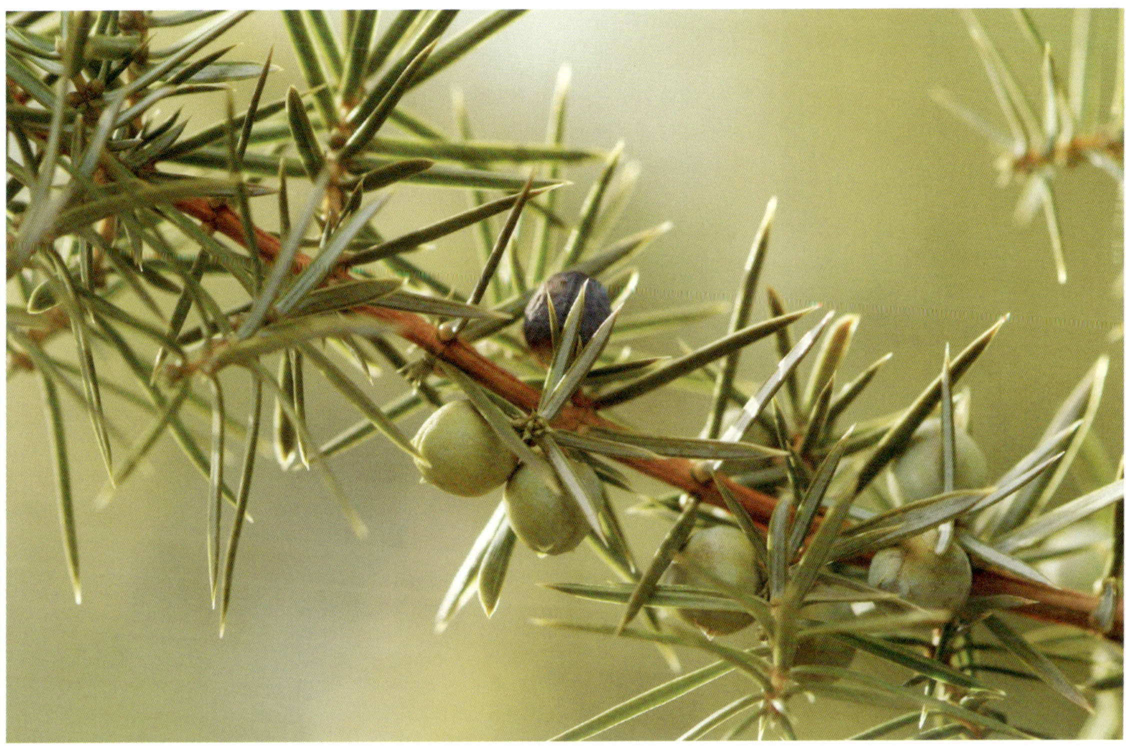

The landscape format approximates our natural perception. It also is well suited for being displayed on monitors, televisions, and projectors.

Landscape Format

Landscape orientation is in many ways the default, because of how cameras are constructed. The entire ergonomics of a camera are based on shooting in landscape format, largely because this format more closely resembles humans' natural, broad field of vision. Holding a camera for a landscape-oriented shot is generally less likely to result in camera shake, too. For all intents and purposes, landscape orientation is the default option: it emphasizes the breadth of the subject and produces a calm and steady feel. For these same reasons, however, it also can come across as somewhat boring, so it is particularly important to consider perspective, dominant lines, and other design possibilities when shooting in landscape.

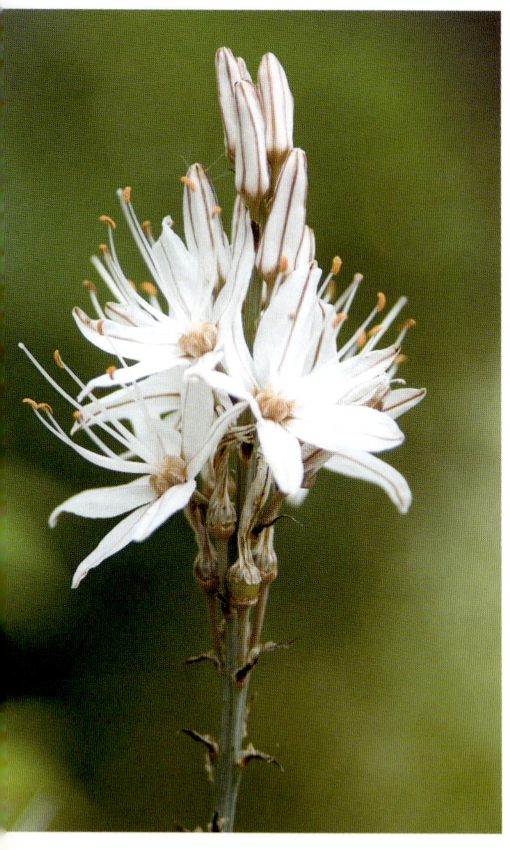

Portrait formats accentuate the upward growth of plants

Portrait Format

Portrait orientations generally bring more tension into a picture; in essence, they are upward moving and dynamic, making them a particularly suitable format for plants. Adopting a low, upward-looking perspective can underscore the effects of a portrait format. The converging verticals phenomenon that is such a big issue with architectural photography comes into play here, but it is less of a concern with photographs of nature.

Presentation media are generally designed for a landscape format, which means, unfortunately, that portrait-oriented images usually appear smaller on monitors and such.

Square Format

In the time since most medium-format film cameras have been put into retirement, the square format has fallen by the wayside. Digital cameras are not set up to capture square image areas, which makes it more difficult to compose with this format in mind while shooting. In general, you'll need to settle on cropping during post-processing to produce the desired format.

Square images don't offer viewers immediate clues about how to read the content of an image, which is both a challenge and an opportunity for photographers to organize the subject matter of an image thoughtfully and purposefully within the square frame. Square

Extreme horizontal formats with aspect ratios of 2:1 or greater are effective in situations where you need or want to leave distracting elements above or below your subject out of the picture

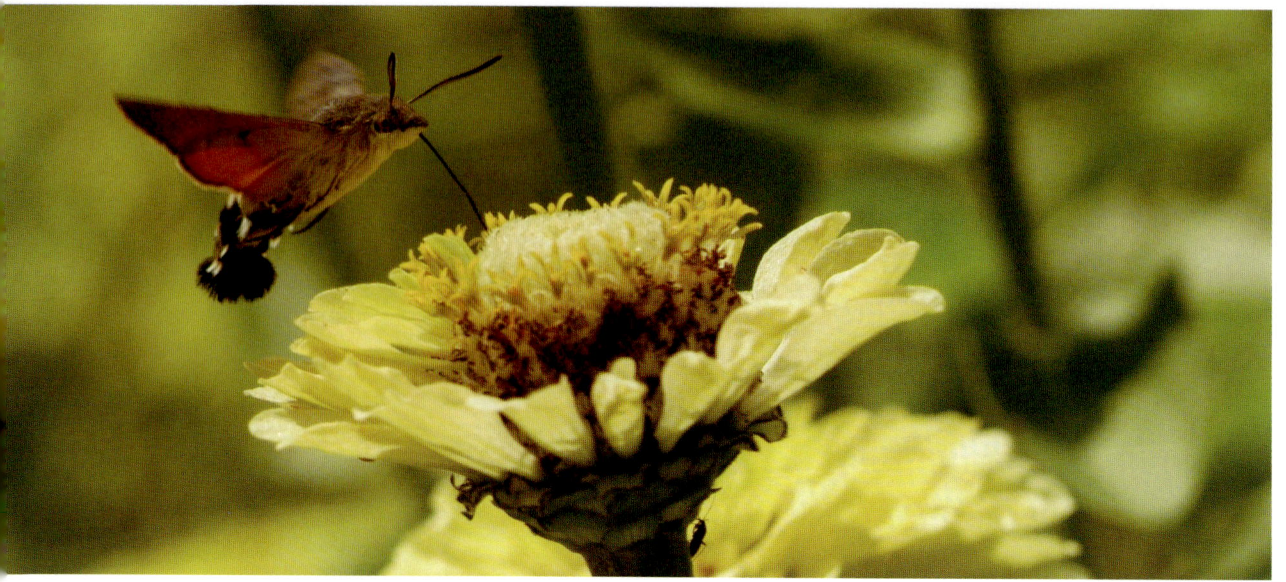

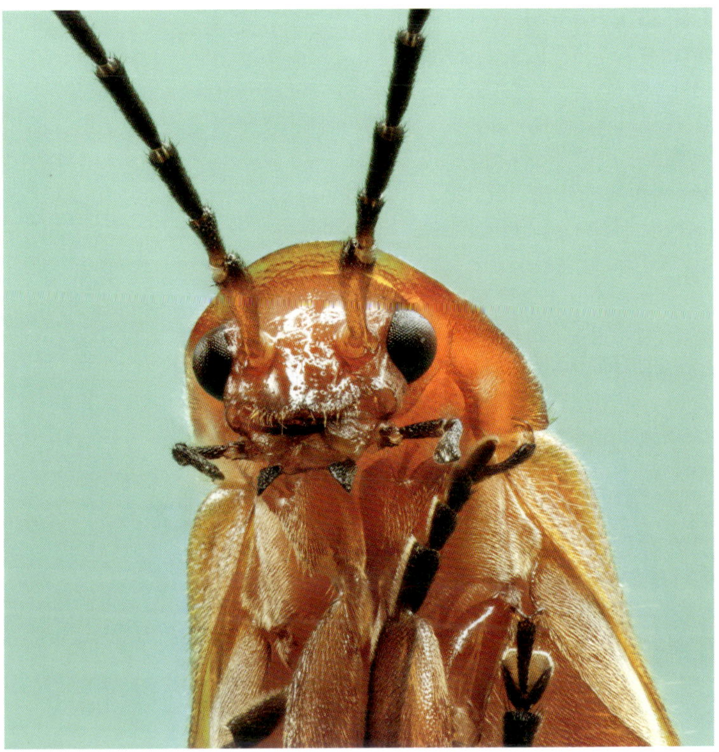

Red soldier beetle. A square format works very well for sober, documentary images—especially for portraits of animals.
Focus stacking
Photo: Jan Metzler

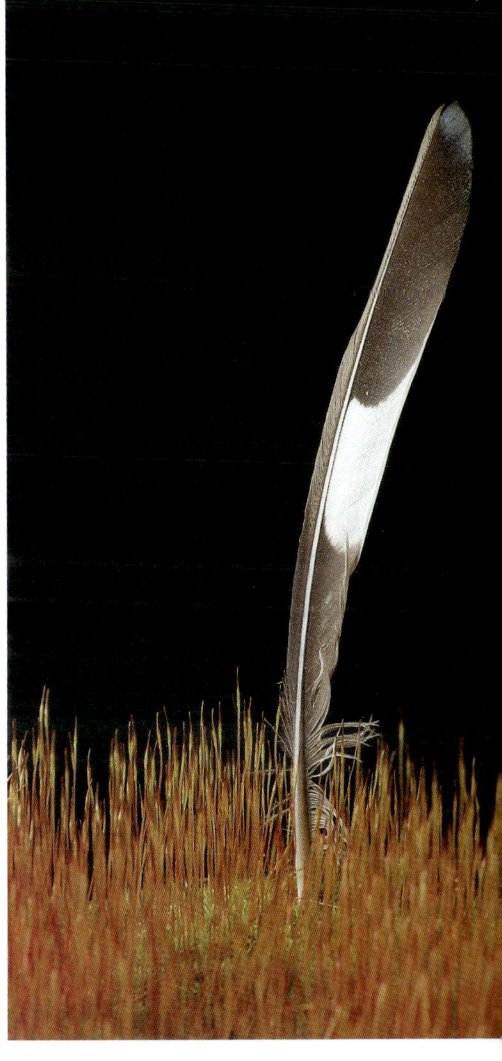

Extreme portrait formats have the charm of being highly unusual, but they aren't used in macro settings all that often. They have the disadvantage of being difficult to display digitally.

images offer a neutral, documentary perspective, and they work well for insect portraits because the orientation influences the viewer's attention to focus intensely on the main subject.

Extreme Formats

Adopting extreme landscape or portrait formats often produces highly engaging results, but they require the right subjects to be successful—and finding them is not always easy. Outside image regions often are reduced to nondescript areas of color when working with a wide-open aperture. These formats are especially useful, however, when you need to eliminate distracting elements that detract from the composition of your image. For more information about a unique method for shooting in extreme formats, see the section on macro panoramas in chapter 6.

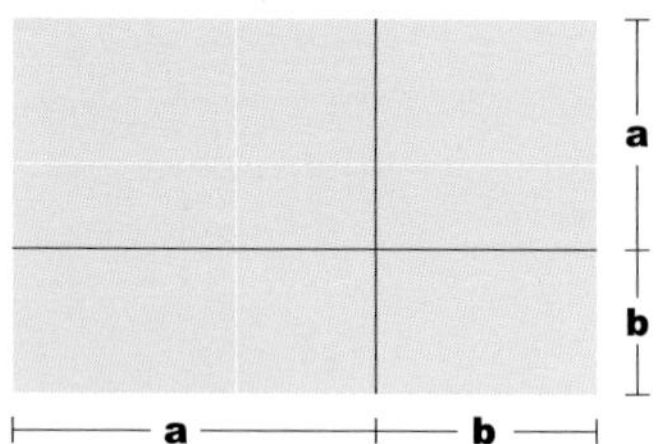

Image division according to the golden ratio: a is to b as the sum of a and b is to a

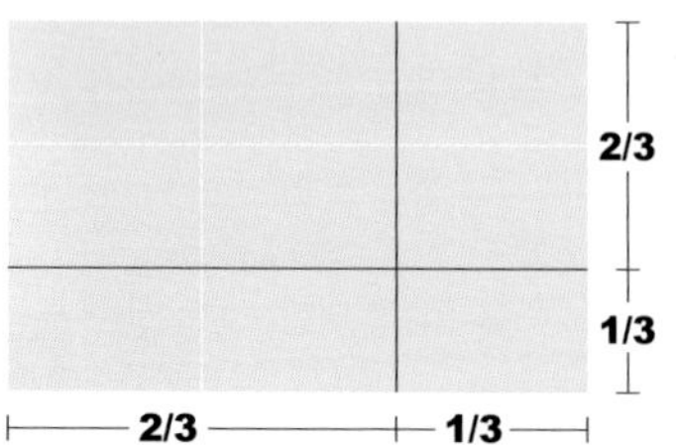

Image division according to the rule of thirds, showing a relationship of 1/3 to 2/3

Using a square as a visual memory aid can be useful for finding a line that is close to the golden ratio with the aspect ratios of most modern digital cameras

The visual center of an image is slightly above the true, mathematical center line

Image Composition

The more time you spend studying the theory of image design, the more you'll discover that you probably already follow a number of the recommended guidelines. On one hand, this automatic behavior is good, because it means you've learned and internalized key concepts; on the other hand, it may indicate that you are stuck in a predictable design framework and that you tend to produce images similar to each other, even if they are attractively composed. Image design guidelines should never be taken as hard-and-fast rules—going against the grain is sometimes the best way to capture outstanding photographs.

The Golden Ratio

Composing images according to the golden ratio means bringing certain dimensions of an image—in our case, dimensions pertaining to the width and height of an image—into a harmonious relationship characterized by the following: *the ratio of the length of "a" with respect to the length of "b" is equal to the ratio of the total length of "a" plus "b" with respect to the length of "a."* A golden rectangle is one in which the ratio of the long and short side lengths exemplify the golden ratio.

The theory behind the golden ratio comes from the world of nature, where it manifests itself in a variety of ways, including the leaves of ivy and dog rose. It also shows up in the proportions of the human body. It is no wonder that we tend to find objects and images exemplifying the golden ratio harmonic and aesthetically pleasing.

The Rule of Thirds

Another framework for composing images, which is slightly easier to imagine and implement in practice than the golden ratio, is the rule of thirds. For this method, the image area is divided into three evenly spaced rows and three such columns. The result is a grid comprising nine equally sized rectangles that each individually feature the same aspect ratio as the entire image area. Just as with the golden ratio, these lines and their intersections offer a framework along which to orient key image details. The guidelines for the rule of thirds are slightly closer to the outer edges of the image area, which invites more tension into the scene.

The Guidance of a Square

One special quality of a golden rectangle is that another golden rectangle automatically forms if you lop off a square whose dimensions are equal to the shorter dimension of the original rectangle. While looking through the viewfinder, you can use this information

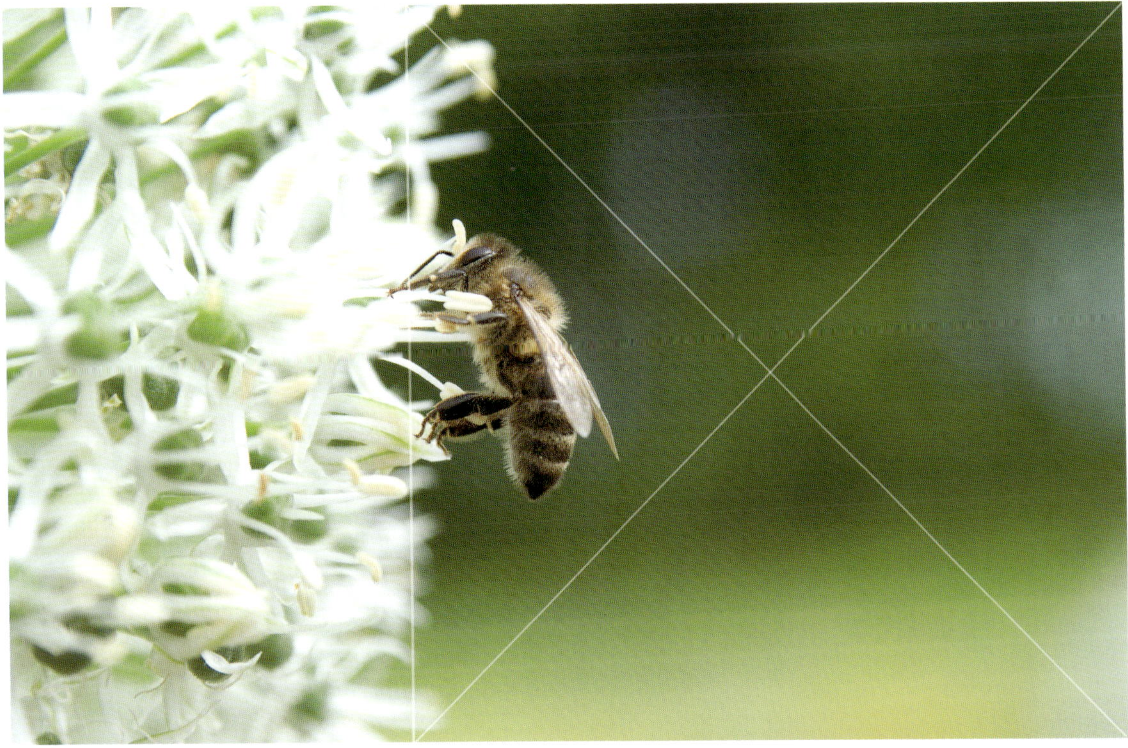

A vertical division approximating the golden ratio. It's not difficult to tell that the right portion of this image closely resembles a square. The bee here is roughly in the center of the image vertically, because it would have been pushed too close to the image border otherwise.

This photo's composition relies heavily on the rule of thirds. The mushroom cap is positioned exactly on one of the intersection points and the sloping moss also passes through two such points. The mushroom's stalk aligns with the left vertical line and the clump of moss in the background off to the right ends at the right vertical line.

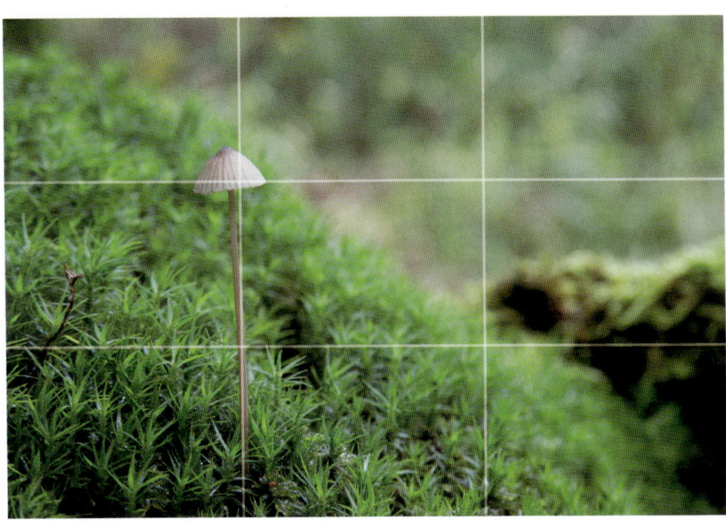

to imagine a square formed with the left or right edge of the image area and an equal length of the top and bottom edges. The missing vertical fourth side of the square would divide the image area roughly at the golden ratio.

For aspect ratios different from the golden rectangle, such as the 2:3 ratio that many popular digital cameras exhibit, the missing vertical edge of the square more closely approximates the rule of thirds rather than the golden ratio.

The Visual Center

For optical reasons, the visual center of an image is not the same as the absolute center point of the image height: it is slightly above this line to avoid the viewer from perceiving that the subject is sliding downward. There is no exact rule to follow here—you'll want to evaluate each subject on a case-by-case basis. This principle of optical compensation for the vertical center also comes up when creating photo mounts and frames.

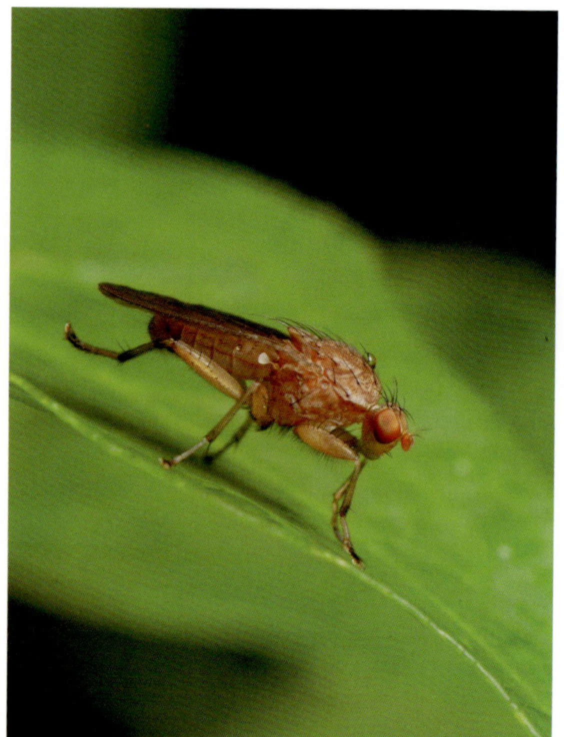

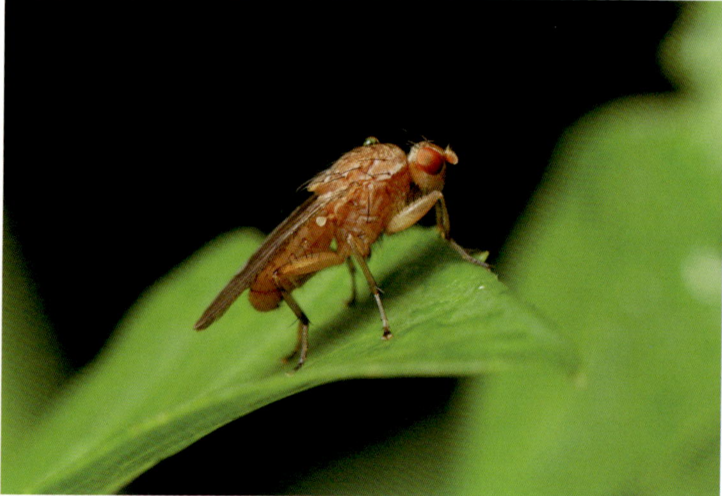

Above: The edges of the leaf open in a funnel-like shape toward the subject. The main element of the image, the fly, is positioned slightly above the middle line.

Left: The sharpness and the lighting work well here, but the dominant lines make the image feel as though it's tipping over to the right

Dominant Lines

The prominent contours in an image influence what viewers pay attention to, but they also affect the overall character of a photograph. Their effect is always based in part on the image format in which they are featured. For example, horizontal lines within a landscape-oriented image offer stability and breadth, but when positioned in the upper two-thirds of a portrait-oriented image, horizontal lines tend to interrupt the overall upward motion of the picture. If they are featured in the lowest third of a portrait image, they offer a basis on top of which the upward motion is founded.

Diagonal lines often support the perspective used for an image, but they also function to throw an image out of optical balance and give it the feeling of tipping to one side. Prominent diagonals bring energy and movement in a specific direction to an image. The effects of diagonal lines can be felt even when visible lines are actually present. Our subconscious instinctively draws imaginary diagonal lines between certain depicted objects, such as elements that appear offset or staggered, or even color accents in opposed corners of a frame.

Parallel lines bring stability and order to an image. The more parallel lines, the more structured the image will feel—all the way up to an extreme case of stability created by multiple sets of parallel lines forming a regular grid.

Bowed or curved lines offer softness and fluidity of movement to a picture, but they can also create tension and energy depending on where they are featured and how they are used in relation to the other primary contours of an image. In all instances, however, curved lines bring movement into play.

Intentional Disruptions

One compositional technique for attracting viewer attention to a specific part of an image is to disrupt prevailing patterns with nonconforming elements, such as prominent lines that run against the prevailing movement, but also any sort of object that stands out because of its shape or color. One example that many readers will be familiar with is a carton of eggs with one brown egg surrounded by white ones. The same effect can be created by using one broken egg or one egg with a feather on top of it (aligned, of course, at a diagonal to the prevailing lines of the carton), and any number of other similar techniques.

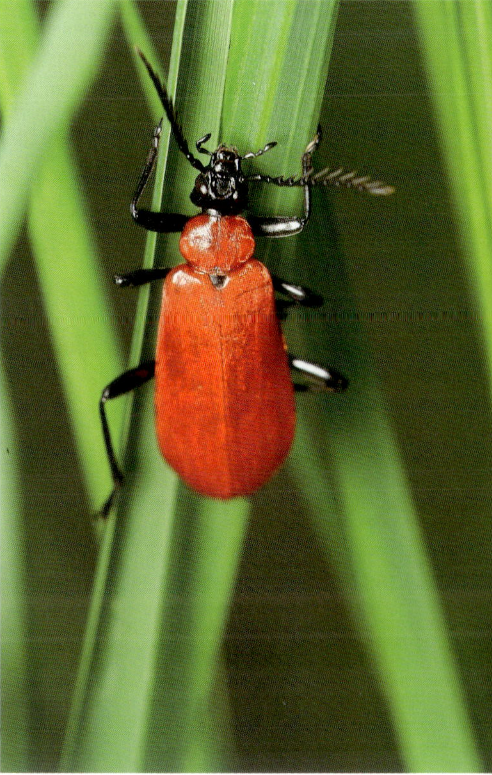

The main contours of this image complement the image format and underscore the movement of the picture: the beetle isn't sitting still on the stalk; it's moving upward

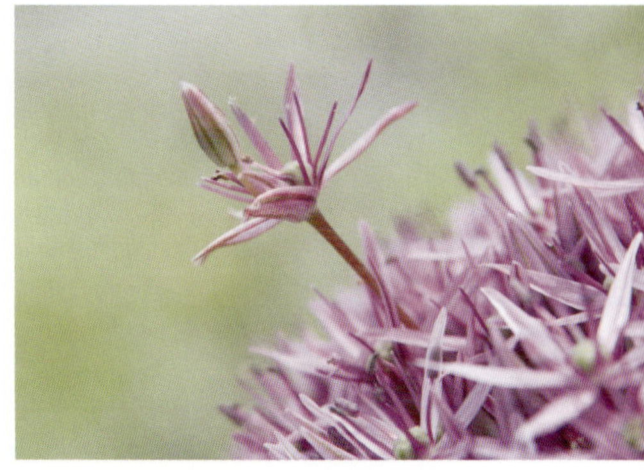

Our eyes automatically follow the prominent lines in an image. The viewers' attention stays focused on the small blossom that sticks out and disrupts the gently curved diagonal.

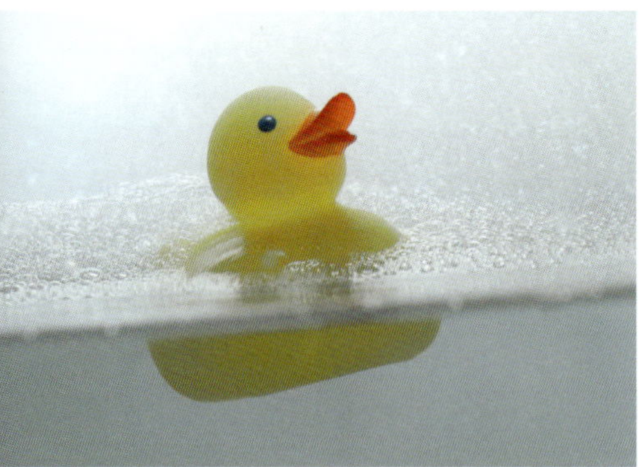

An unconventional camera perspective can turn an otherwise common object into an engaging subject

Choosing a Suitable Perspective

A human's eyes are located at roughly 160cm to 170cm above the ground, depending on one's height. This fact naturally influences how we see things and how we photograph them. In most cases, small objects are shot from above, large objects from below, and everything else is roughly shot from eye level. You can exploit these expectations as a photographer to produce creative results.

Altering Standpoint

Choosing an unexpected perspective can elevate unexceptional objects into fascinating curiosities. And the power of an unusual perspective is not limited to everyday items—it also holds true for macro subjects. With the right perspective, small objects can turn into massive buildings, and a complete landscape can be fashioned out of moss, a stone, and a few leaves. Shifting the camera's position is all that it takes to achieve these effects.

Images of insects shot at eye level are engrossing because they seem to be from the perspective of a another member of the species and accordingly have a very authentic appearance. Images of plants and mushrooms shot from a worm's-eye view have a charm of their own. The ultralow camera position combined with a wide-angle lens produce unconventional but attention-grabbing pictures.

Articulated or folding camera monitors make it much easier to capture images at ground level. If your camera's display is fixed, you can always resort to using an angle viewfinder. Yet another very convenient option is the remote control systems that feature live-view displays, such as the smartphone apps discussed earlier in this book.

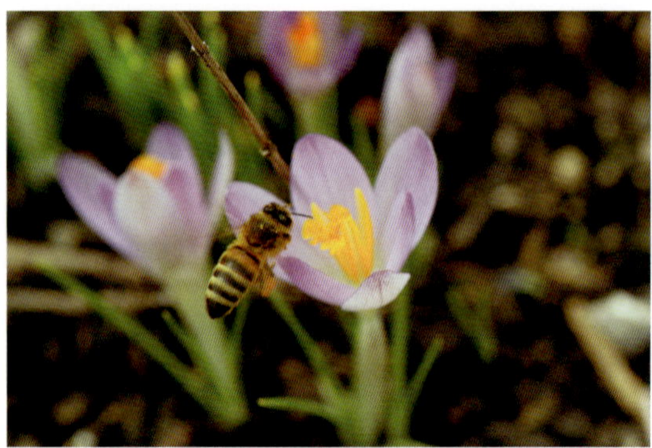

Insects shot from above look the same as when they are viewed from a normal perspective

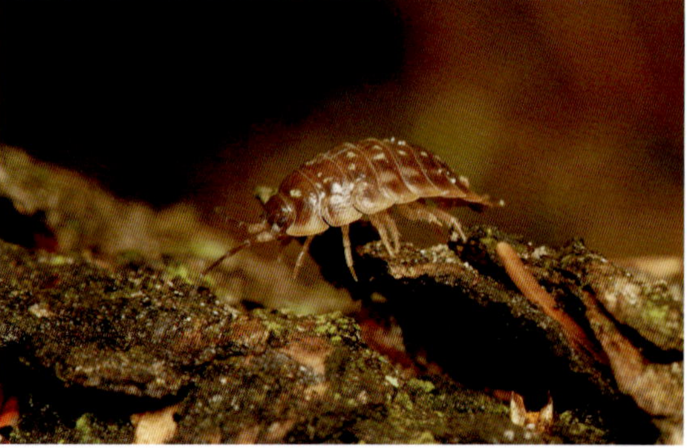

When shot at the same level of the subject, the perspective feels as though it belongs to one of the subject's counterparts and as though it belongs to the same world as the subject

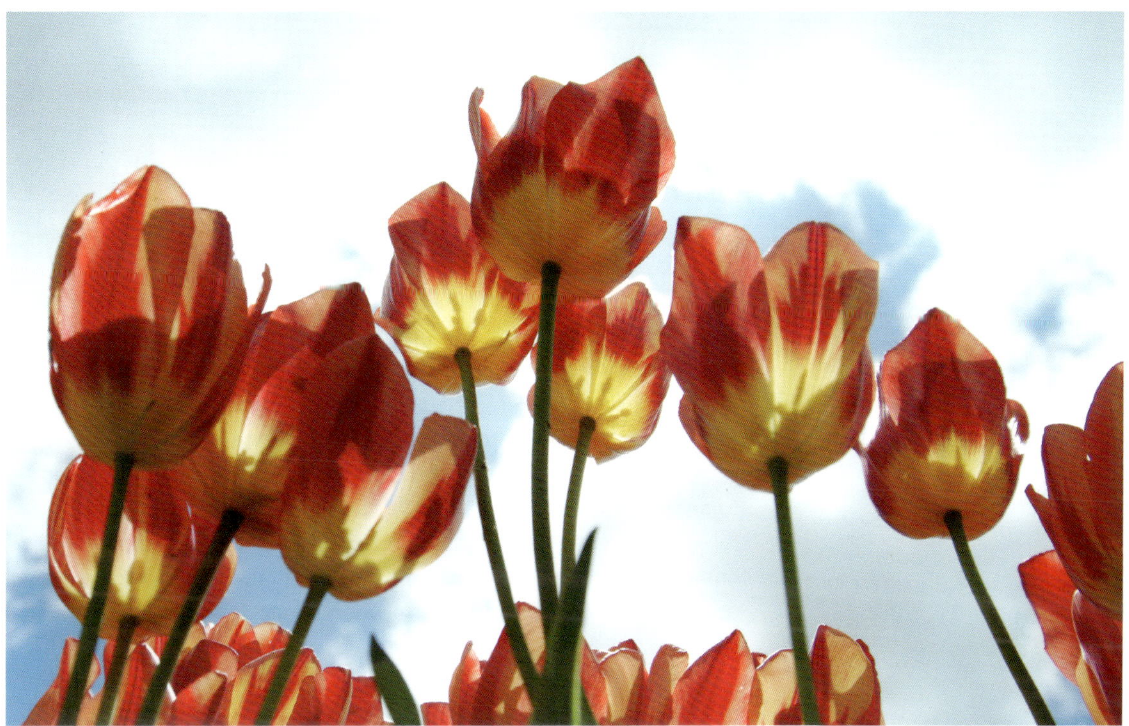

If the physical circumstances are too tight to realize a worm's-eye-view perspective, then a compact camera with a good minimum focusing distance set to a wide-angle focal length may be an effective workaround.

Some subjects allow you to remove them from their natural location and reposition them in an area that is easier to photograph from your desired perspective. After the shot you can return the item to its original position. Alternatively, you might be able to dig up a bit of earth in front of your subject to make it possible to shoot from a lower position. Take special care not to hurt or damage your subject when using these options.

Almost all subjects will be backlit to some degree when shot from below, so you'll likely want to use a small additional reflector to brighten up the underside of your subject.

Subjects shot from a worm's-eye view appear properly imposing. When capturing images from this perspective it helps tremendously to use an angle viewfinder if your camera doesn't feature an articulated display screen.

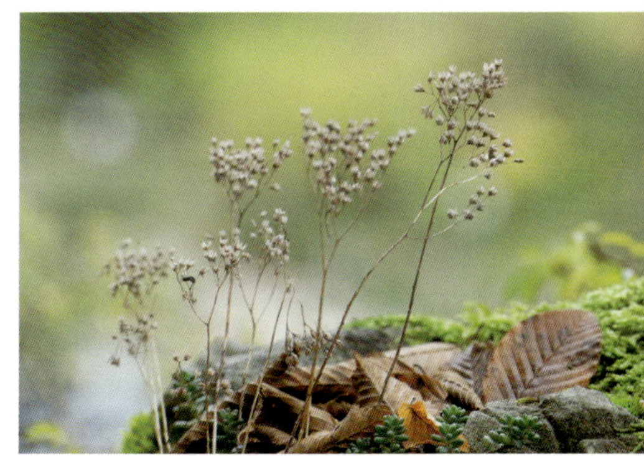

A small patch of grass and some moss amount to a full landscape when shot from the right perspective

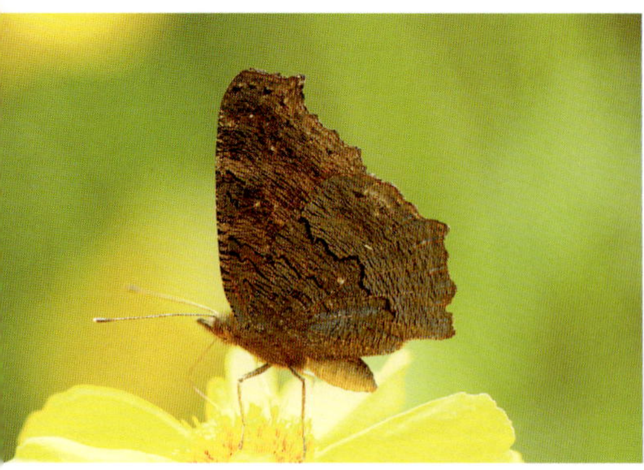

This butterfly stands out dramatically from the background because of the intense contrasts of color and sharpness

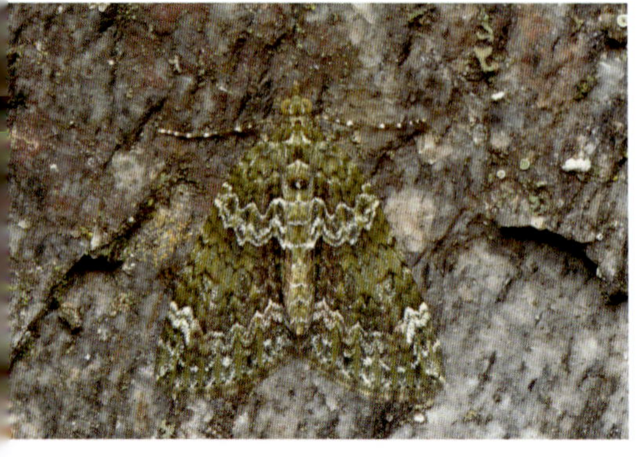

Deliberately emphasizing contrasts here would have been a mistake because the main detail of interest in this image is how well the moth blends in with its surroundings

Creating Contrasts

Contrasts establish tension in photographs, and they allow photographers to give added optical or emotional emphasis to specific subjects. There are many different ways to create contrasts between the main subject and its background, and they can be combined for varied and even more dramatic effect.

Contrasts of color and brightness are the two most conspicuous methods for drawing a distinction between two areas of an image. Sharpness contrast, or situations when the main subject is depicted sharply but the background is more or less blurry, comes into play most often when there is a significant distance between the subject and the background elements. An open aperture will allow the background to effectively melt into a seemingly flat surface.

Contrasts of shape also have the power to bring life and tension to an image. This type of contrast forms when objects exhibiting different formal qualities—such as angular and round or stretched and compressed objects—are near to one another. Images can also rely on emotional contrasts that form when juxtaposing elements are, for example, hard and soft, rigid and fluid, or fresh and dried.

Some images rely on contrasts to establish and communicate the key features of their content. For example, when stationary objects that appear sharp in an image contrast with blurry objects that are obviously in motion, the contrast conveys the speed involved.

The options available for designing macro images while working in the studio are many, but when on location in nature, the primary options for improving a simple snapshot into a composed photograph are the camera's position and aperture. An altered camera position can create an entirely different image, even if the shooting settings are kept constant. A larger distance between the subject and the background will make the background appear softer and blurrier even if the aperture remains constant; or a small shift of the camera's perspective may cause a blossoming meadow to take up most of the background rather than a dismal stone wall.

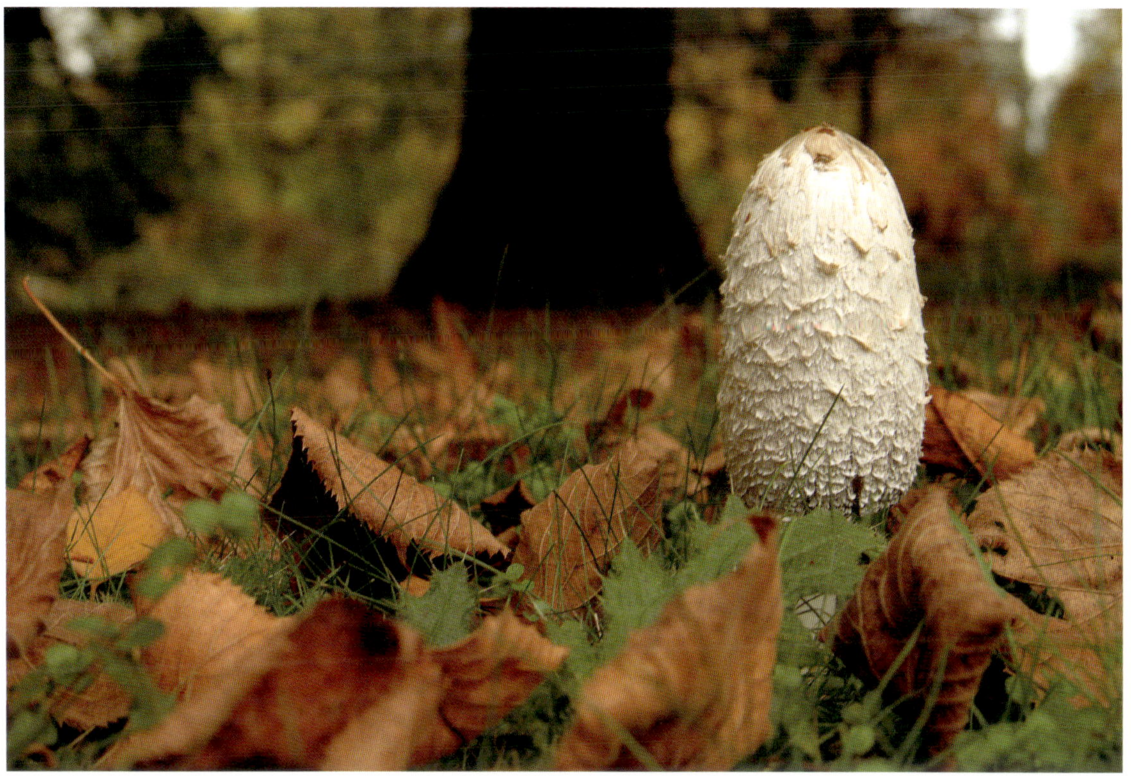

Mushroom in a city park. The light-colored mushroom stands out from the darker background. The different levels of sharpness in the image also create a sense of spatial depth.

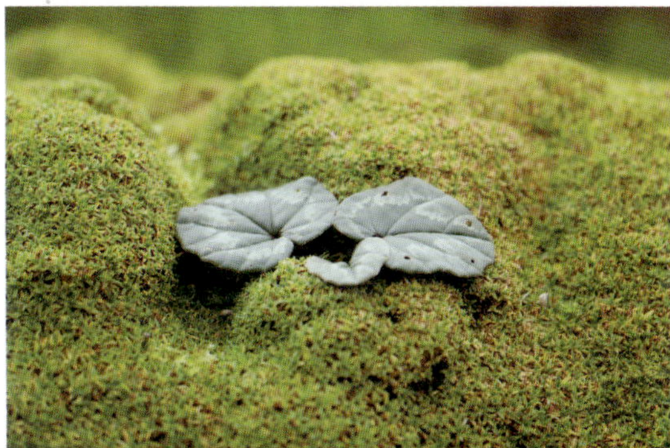

*Even though the colors of the subject and its background are relatively similar, a dramatic contrast arises on account of different textures and shapes of the plants
Location: Botanical Gardens of Tübingen, Germany*

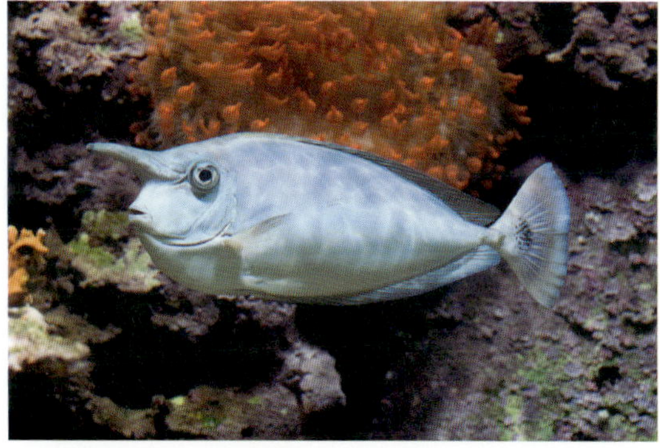

*A sought-after composition often requires patience. I had to wait here for a while for this fish to swim into position.
Location: Wilhelma, Stuttgart, Germany*

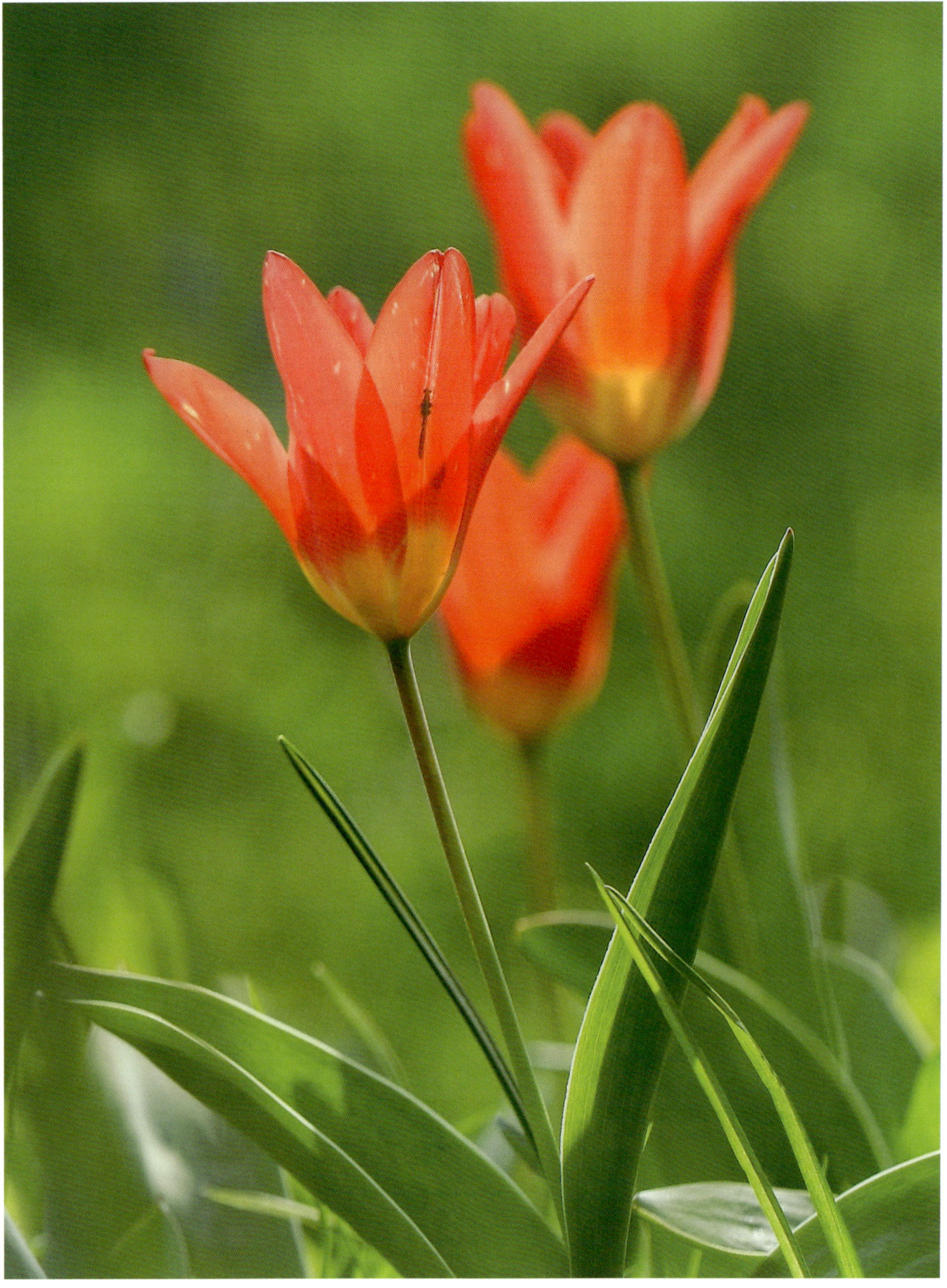

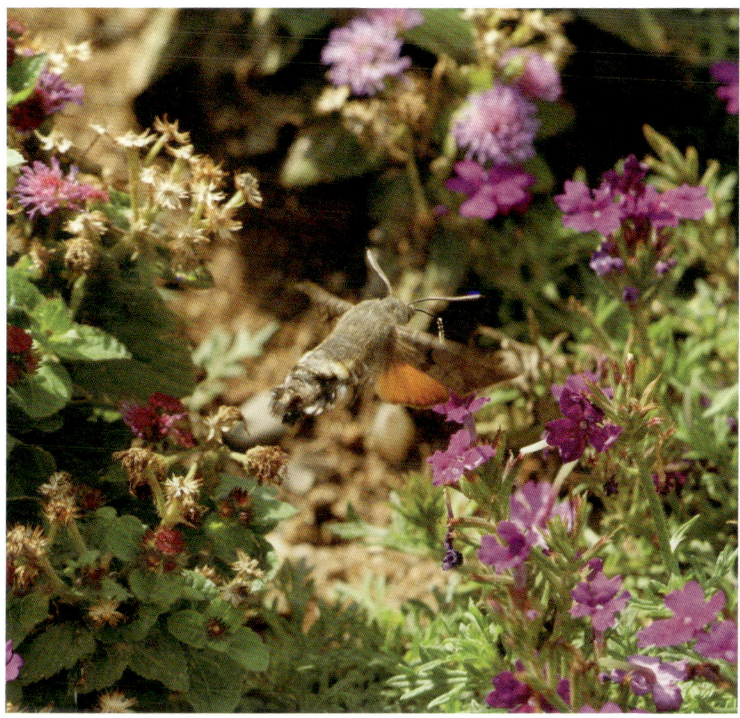

From this perspective, the humming-bird hawk-moth is barely visible. Too many other objects are located on the focal plane, and the whole scene is much too busy—not to mention that the color of the moth is very similar to the ground.
f/8, 1/1,000 s, ISO 800, 150mm
Location: Botanical Gardens of Tübingen, Germany

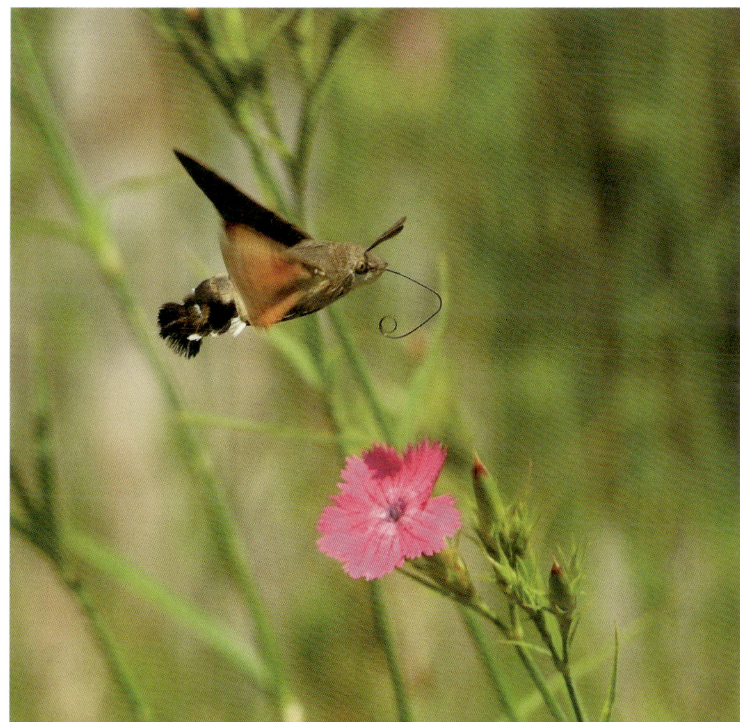

An entirely different result despite using the same focal length, aperture, and shutter speed. The change in perspective yields a much more effective photo. The moth's entire body and the blossom are located within the depth of field, while the background is sufficiently far away to be reduced to blur.
f/8, 1/1,000 s, ISO 800, 150mm
Location: Botanical Gardens of Tübingen, Germany

Left page: Red and green are complementary colors, so the color contrast here is optimal for separating the subject from its background. And the wide-open aperture creates a pleasing effect of graduated sharpness for the blossoms.
f/5.6, 1/350 s, ISO 400, 150mm

Creative Camera Angles

Sometimes all it takes is a small step to the side to create an entirely different picture of the same subject. These images of a clematis vine from my balcony demonstrate this. All three pictures were taken within a few minutes of one another on a fall evening with the sun low in the sky—the light was effectively the same for each shot. The first picture (below) reveals the vine in a warm evening light. Here, the plant stands out in an appealing way against a shadowy background.

The second photo (opposite page, top) resulted from shooting on the other side of the plant and using a lower perspective. From this angle, the evening sky became the backdrop. In backlit situations like this one, it's necessary to overexpose significantly to retain enough detail in the leaves so the vine doesn't become a black silhouette. The sky effectively turns white as a side effect of this adjustment, but the sharp contrast continues to allow the vine to stand out against its background.

Returning to eye level offered yet another entirely different image (opposite page, bottom). From this angle, the dark facade of a neighbor's house functions as the backdrop. I moved my shooting position a bit to the left, which made the house take up the entire

A clematis vine with the evening sun positioned behind the photographer. The warm glow from the low-lying sun nicely highlights the vine against a shaded background.

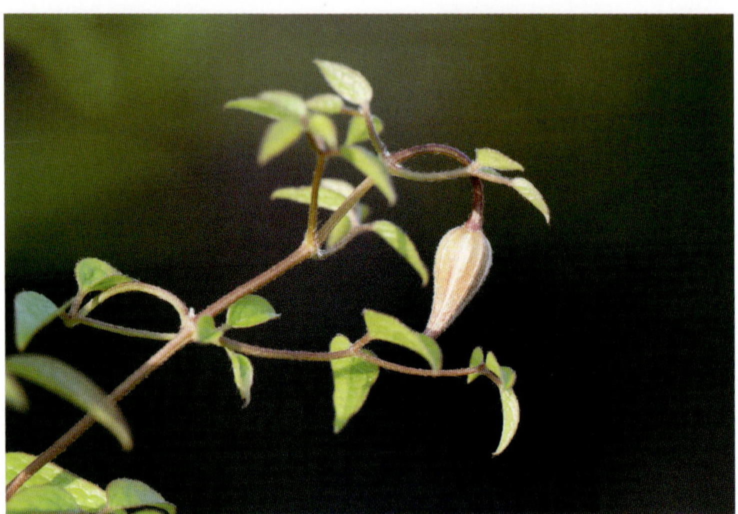

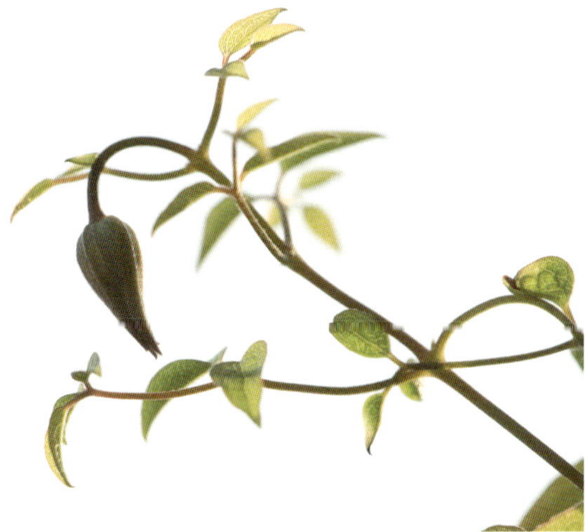

Shooting from below the vine with the evening sky as the backdrop creates a backlit situation that infuses the leaves and highlights their subtle textures

background and caused the clematis tendril to be fully bathed in light. The pronounced backlighting resulting from this configuration turned the delicate hairs surrounding the bud and the stem into a glowing aura.

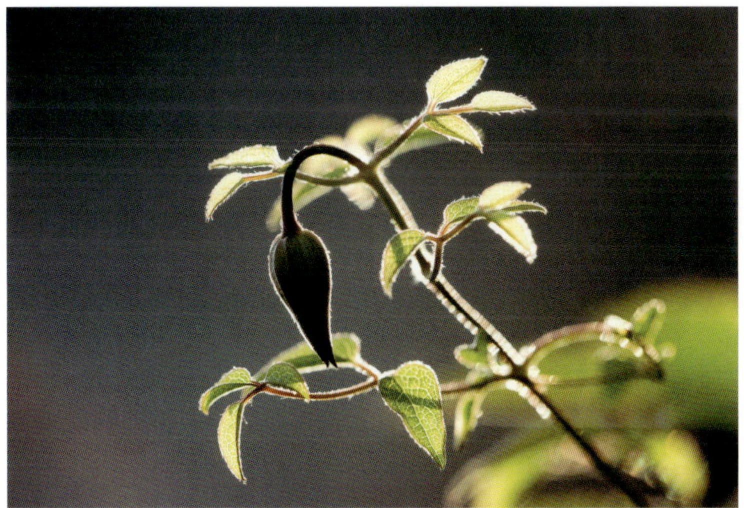

From this perspective, the dark facade of a neighboring house moved into the background, and the subject became sharply backlit, causing the subject's colors to glow and the fine hairlike structures on the bud and stem to turn into a luminous halo

Setting the Scene with Light

Shooting on location in nature means you will encounter a wide range of qualities of light. In most cases, a few tools and tricks will enable you to shape and alter ambient light to your desired ends, whether it's boosting contrast or softening shadows. Mastering these techniques makes it possible to influence the shape and color intensity of your subject to fulfill your specific intentions for an image.

Harsh Light

Direct light emitted from a point source produces brilliant colors, but it also results in dark, harsh shadows and intense contrasts that can make an image seem overly busy. The following solutions are effective at managing circumstances with this type of light:

- Using flash to brighten the shadows
- Placing a reflector
- Positioning a diffuser between the light source and the subject

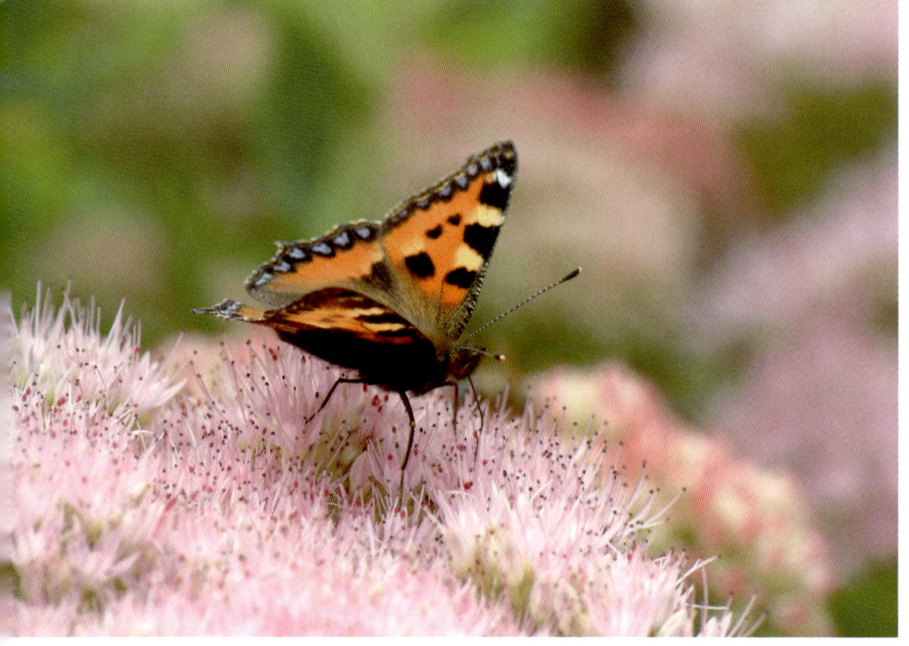

Small tortoiseshell butterfly.
An overcast sky produces soft light
and nearly shadow-free images.
f/5.6, 1/180 s, ISO 400, 90mm

Soft Light

Overcast skies offer soft light that results in images featuring minimal shadows and pastel-like colors. If the lighting is too diffuse for your purposes, then you can use flash or another point source of light to achieve more contrast.

Glancing Light

During the hours early in the morning or late in the evening just before the blue hour, the low-lying sun produces warm, atmospheric light. Glancing light may not strike your subject in the right place, however, and there are a few options for managing this situation. The most direct solution—albeit one that is not often possible—is to move your subject to a location where this type of light better serves your purposes. Alternative options include:

- Altering your standpoint
- Waiting until the light is in the right place
- Deflecting the light with a mirror

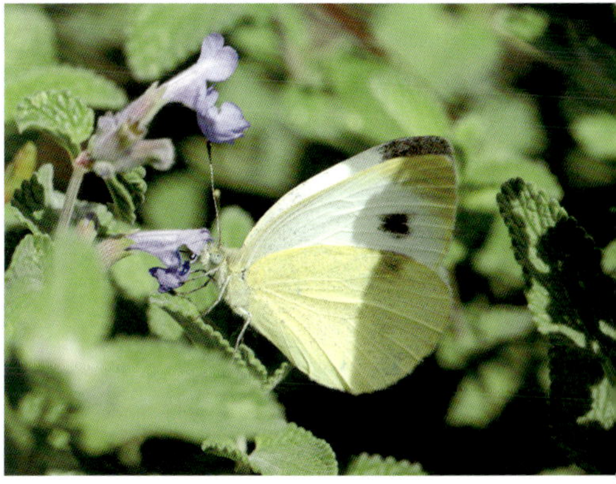

Cabbage butterfly. Direct sunlight creates harsh shadows that often compromise an image's composition. f/11, 1/1,500 s, ISO 1000, 180mm

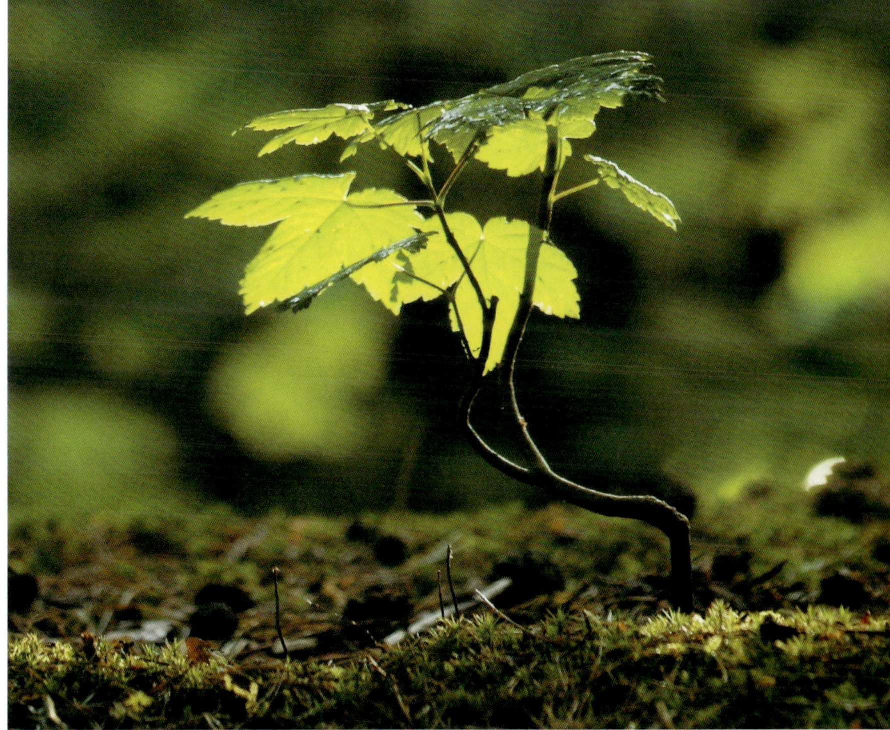

Side light produced from the evening sun low in the sky creates a richly atmospheric look f/3.5, 1/500 s, ISO 800, 150mm

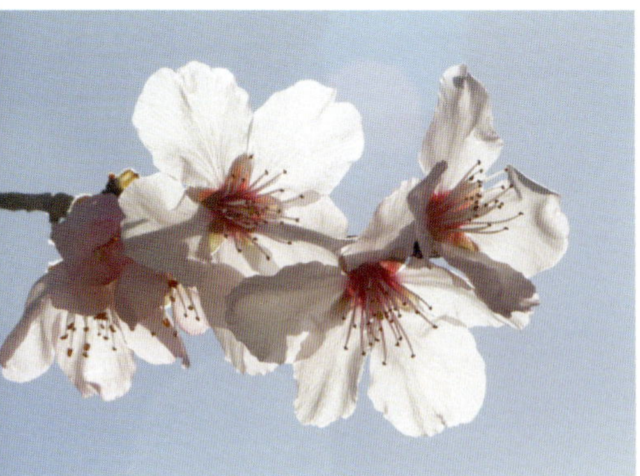

Backlight can emphasize hidden details in subjects featuring translucent material

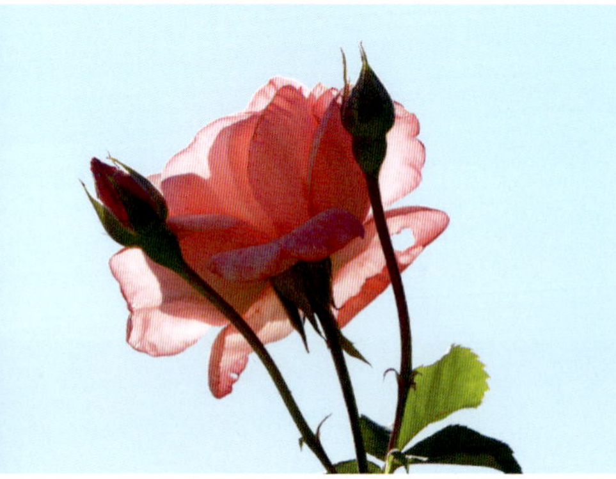

Backlit objects mostly composed of opaque material often require brightening; otherwise they'll appear as silhouettes

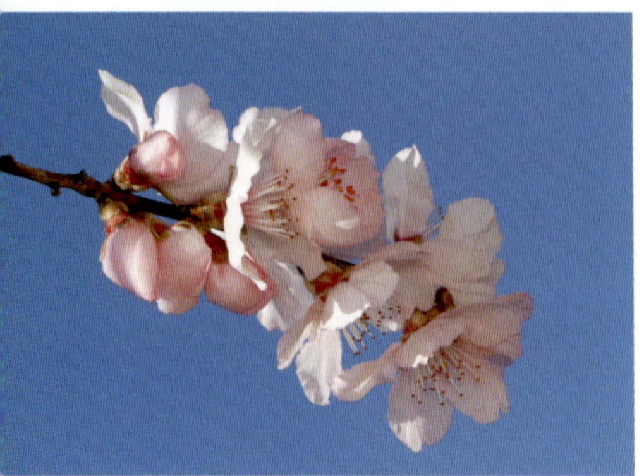

Side light emphasizes the three-dimensional shape of a subject

Backlight

Backlight situations can be varied, and how you ultimately handle them will depend on the subject you're photographing. When shooting delicate, translucent objects, such as flower petals, you can exploit backlight to reveal structures and details in the flower that might otherwise be hidden to viewers. Opaque objects, however, often require some form of brightening to prevent them from appearing as dark silhouettes in your image.

A sunset offers light that can be used attractively as backlight—in part because the sunlight is much less intense in the late evening, which means blooming is less of a concern. Backlight offered by the setting sun has an enchanting quality, especially when it turns the delicate hairlike structures on plants into a glowing aura. Options for managing backlight include:

- Using a reflector to brighten the foreground
- Using fill flash
- Altering your standpoint

Side Light

Lighting directed from the side of a subject tends to emphasize its physical shape. Minor adjustments to your shooting position or to the orientation of the subject itself can result in dramatic changes to its appearance.

In situations when side light is too harsh, you can brighten up the subject's opposite side easily with a reflector. Use silver or white reflectors for a clear, neutral light, or use gold reflectors for a warmer appearance. The reflectors striped with silver and gold that are often used in the realm of portrait photography are also very useful for macro purposes.

Light from Below

When light illuminates a subject from below, it is often referred to as theater lighting. This situation doesn't come up all that frequently in nature, but creating this effect with a flash can produce delightful results in the right circumstances. Subjects take on a surreal and dramatic appearance in this light. As an alternative to a flash, a large mirror can also be used to reflect ambient lighting upward. Theater lighting has its strongest effect when the image areas surrounding the subject are sufficiently dark.

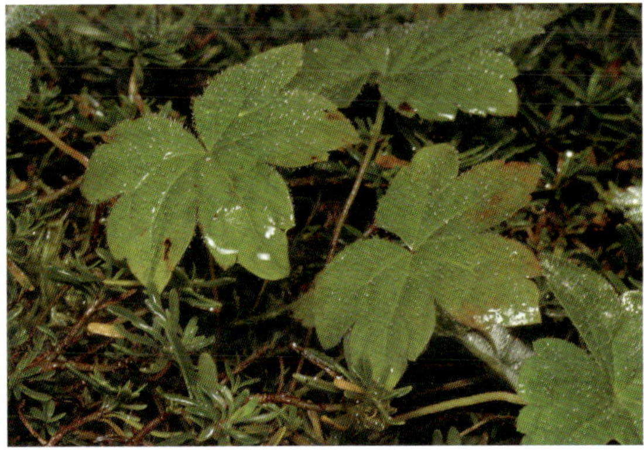

The quality of natural light can be influenced and altered, but using flash lighting is not always the best solution, as can be seen from this image

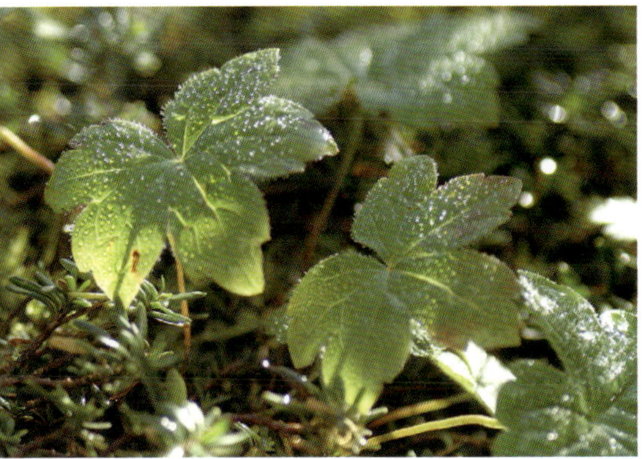

Sometimes a little patience is all it takes to manage difficult lighting situations. The light here improved significantly once the sun emerged from behind a rain cloud.

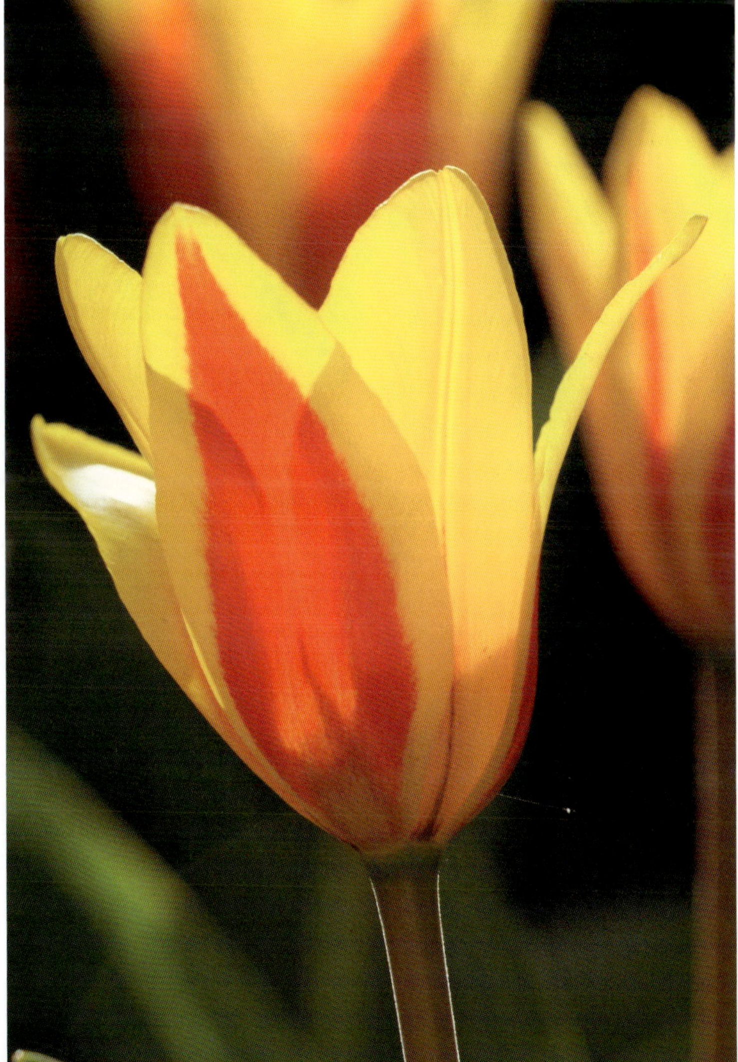

Backlight from above caused the colors of this tulip to stand out intensely. The sunlight also created a nice highlight on the outside edges of the flower's stem that sets the subject apart from the background. Lighting like this can often be found in the late afternoon, just before the sun sinks into a source of glancing light. This image was shot in the middle of April around 7 p.m.

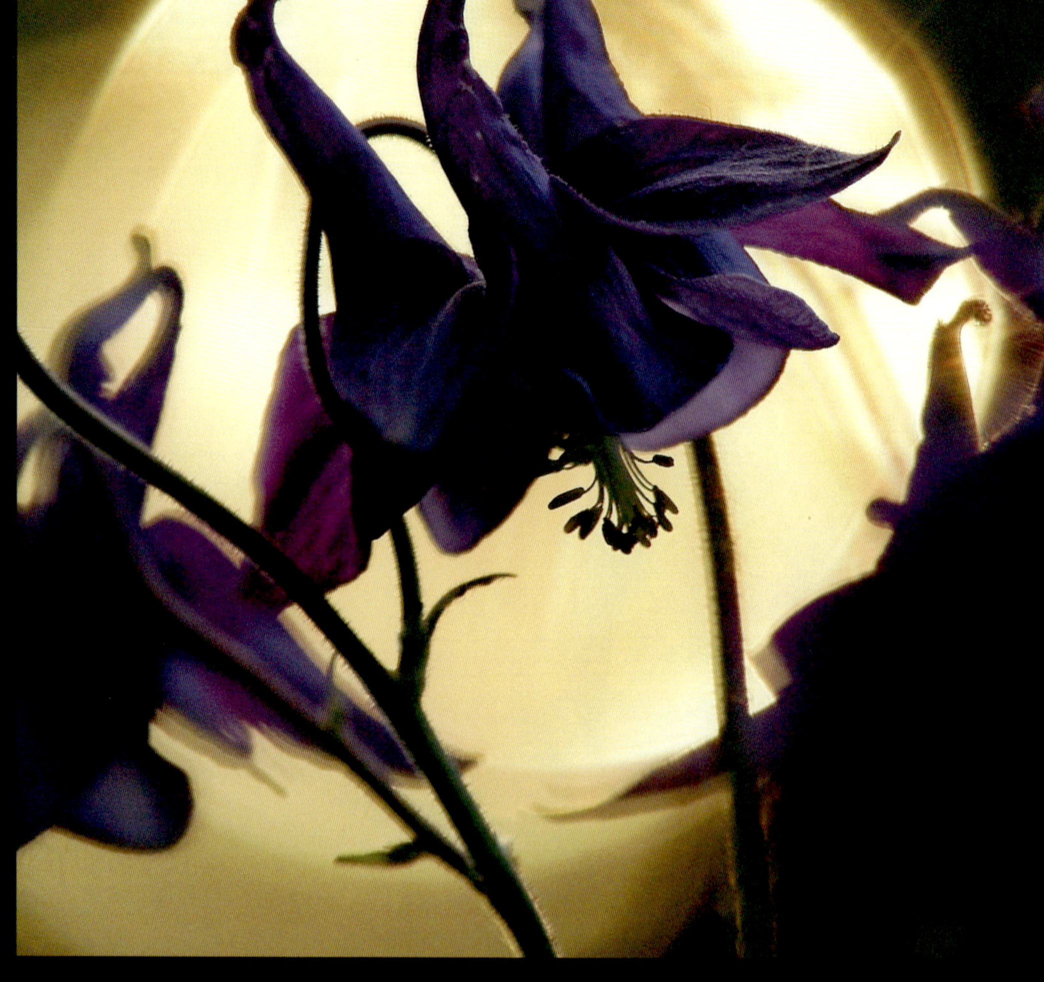

I opened the aperture all the way and increased the ISO
setting to 1600 so I could photograph these flowers during
the evening. I isolated the subject from an otherwise uniform
grey-brown background by positioning a flashlight about
1 meter behind the flowers.
f/3.2, 1/1,000 s, ISO 1600, 150mm

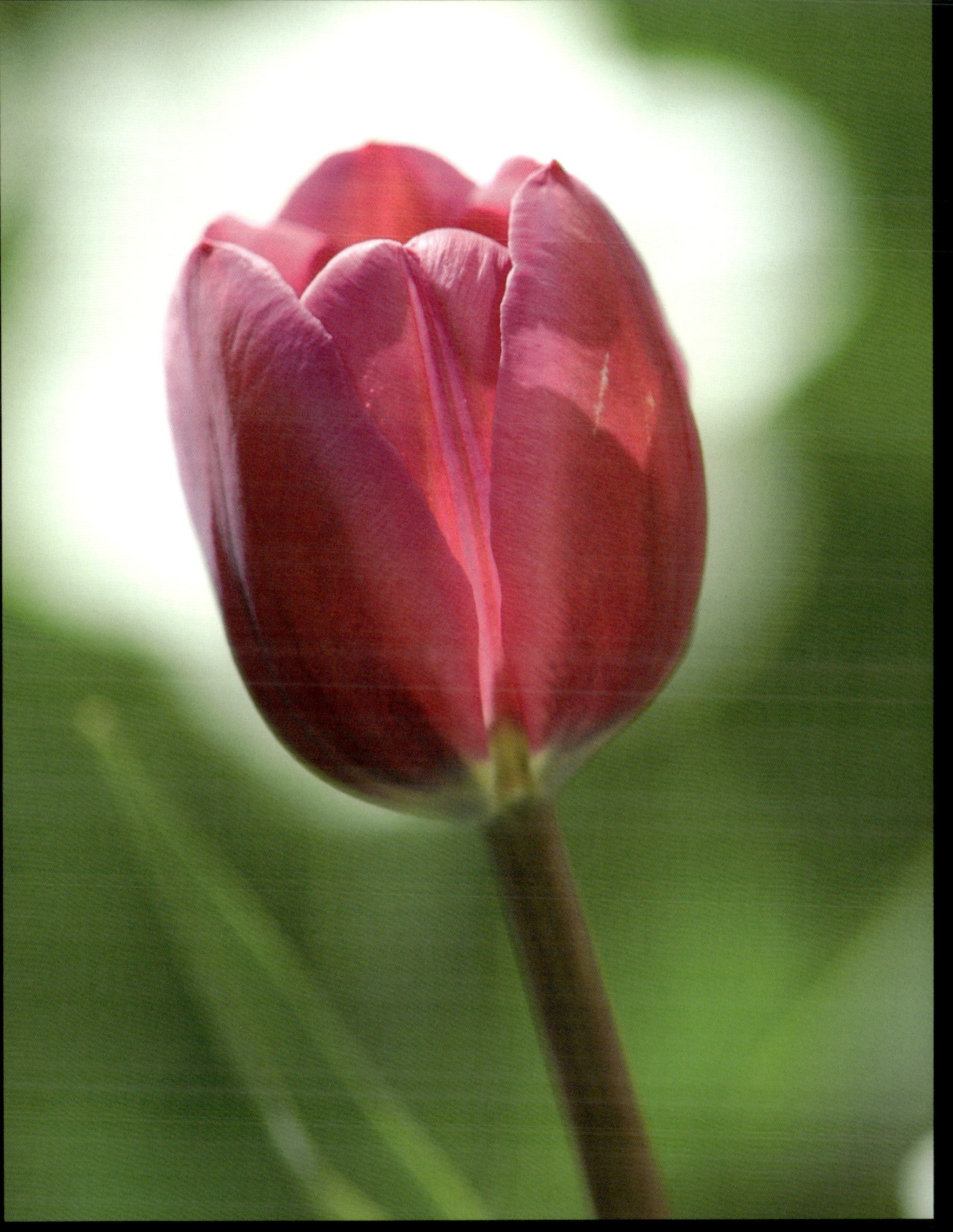

Using a telephoto lens reduced the background to a relatively small area, and a wide aperture produced the desired effect of blur. I aligned my shot so that a daffodil far in the background resulted in the attractive aura surrounding the subject.
f/4, 1/1,500 s, ISO 400, 300mm

Focus as a Design Tool

Along with lighting, depth of field is one of the key limitations for macro photographers. Depending on the magnification, it can drop down to millimeters or even tenths of a millimeter. One mistake that beginning macro photographers often make is paying too much attention to the positioning of the subject itself and not enough attention to its background with regard to how it figures into the overall composition. Not attending to the background thoughtfully may result in images where the subject doesn't pop out sufficiently or where too many distracting details clutter the image area. Pay attention to all of the elements within your image, and pay special attention to the extent to which each of these elements is located within the depth of field.

Positioning the Focal Plane

When working with a wide-open aperture, the focal plane effectively represents the entire functional depth of field. When photographing insects and other small animals, it's important to position the focal plane on the subject's eyes. Any photo with a subject's eyes out of focus will be interpreted as a mistake.

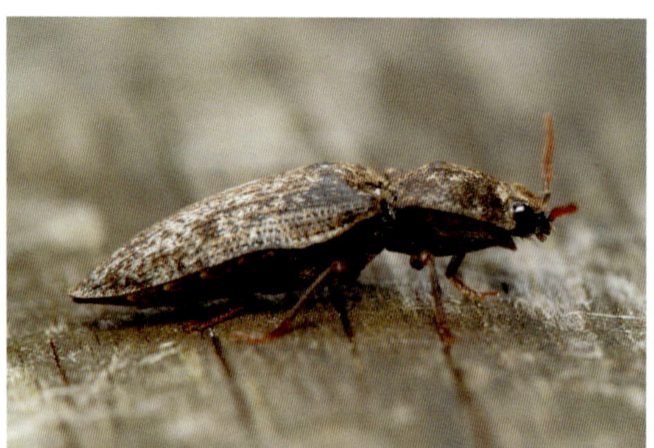

Beetle on a tree trunk. The focal plane is positioned exactly on the subject's eye, with even the closest parts of the shell already blurred. The surface of the wood clearly shows the very narrow depth of field.
f/8, 1/60 s, ISO 400, 150mm

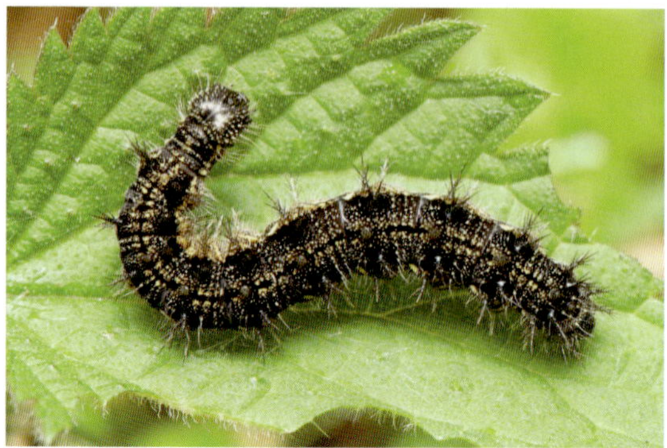

Caterpillar on a nettle leaf. Here the focal plane is positioned precisely on the subject's back. The blur in some areas, such as the spines pointed upward, is barely noticeable.
f/9.5, 1/60 s, ISO 400, 105mm

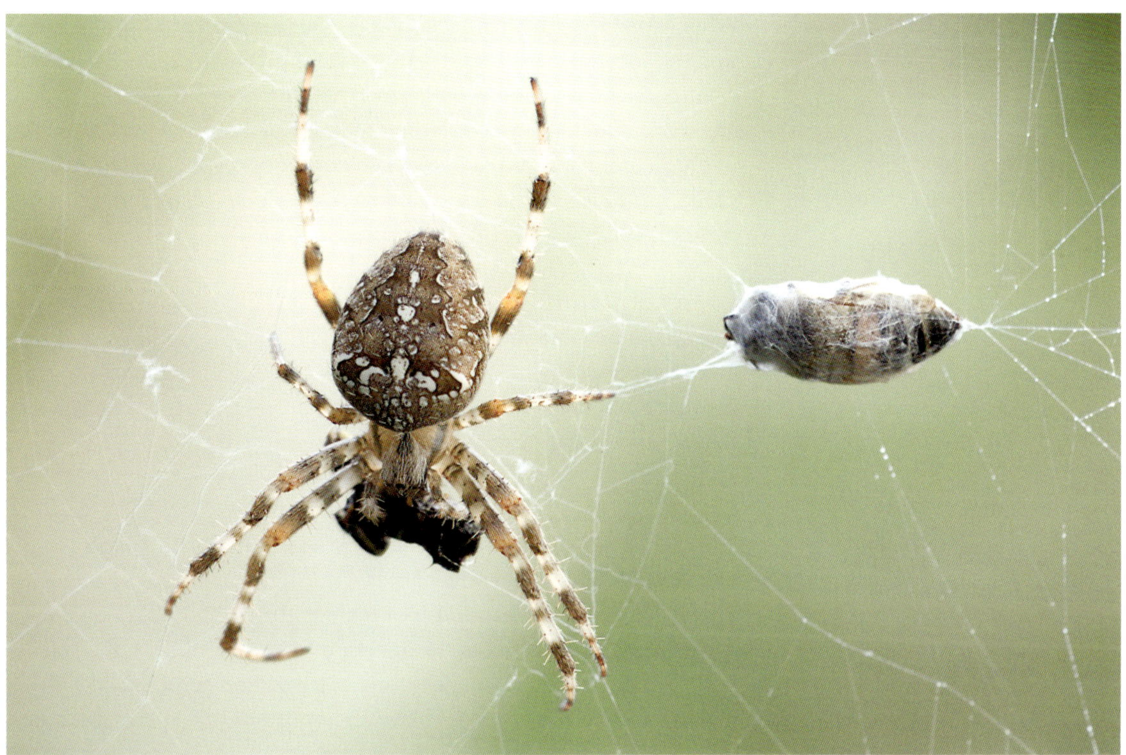

Spider with prey. The subject stands out dramatically from the background, thanks to the right shooting position and the use of a wide-open aperture with a DSLR.
f/5.6, 1/250 s, ISO 640, 180mm

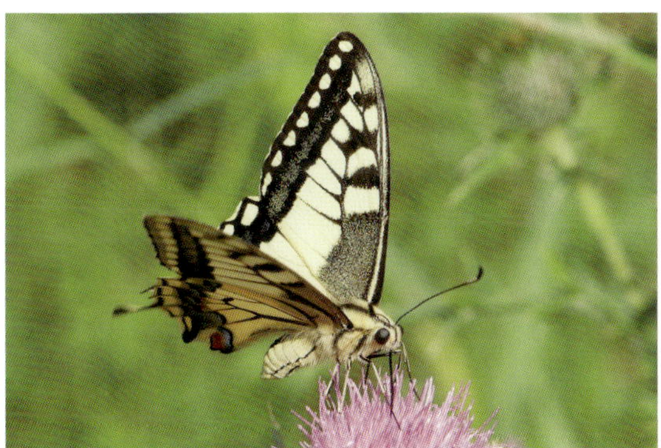

Swallowtail butterfly. Sometimes you have to live with compromises. For this shot, f/8 wasn't sufficient to capture the entirety of the butterfly in focus, and it would have been preferable to have the background be even more blurry.
f/8, 1/250 s, ISO 400, 150mm

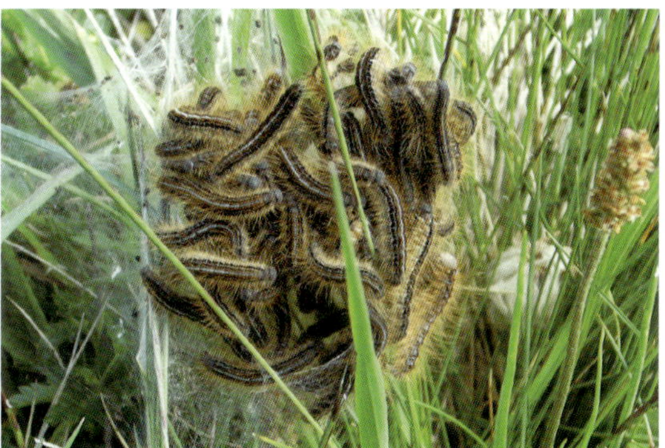

Caterpillars by the wayside. Compact digital cameras come in handy when you need as large a depth of field as possible because they have such small image sensors.
Panasonic FX3, f/4.1, 1/100 s, ISO 100, 12.2mm
Photo: Karl-Heinz Frey

When working with abstract subjects, the question of where to position the focal plane is less straightforward. In these cases, determine what part of the image should carry the added significance of appearing sharp. Once you've settled on that, you may want to use the rule of thirds or the golden ratio to finish composing your image. In some cases, it may be valuable to sacrifice some depth of field for the purpose of realizing a specific intention.

Layers of Depth

Composing an image to feature layers with varying degrees of sharpness profoundly increases its spatial depth. Objects aligned along a diagonal and sequences of repeating identical or nearly identical elements tend to underscore this effect.

Bokeh

The properties of a lens determine the aesthetics of an image's blur, or its bokeh. The look and feel of the transition areas between what appears sharp and what does not technically is determined by the number and orientation of the aperture blades along with the selected f-stop. In more compositional terms, the positioning of specific elements within the image area plays an important role in the appearance of blur. Other factors including the source and intensity of the lighting also come into play. For example, you can influence the quality of an image's blur by lighting the background in a certain way or using as diffuse light as possible to alter the atmosphere of the scene.

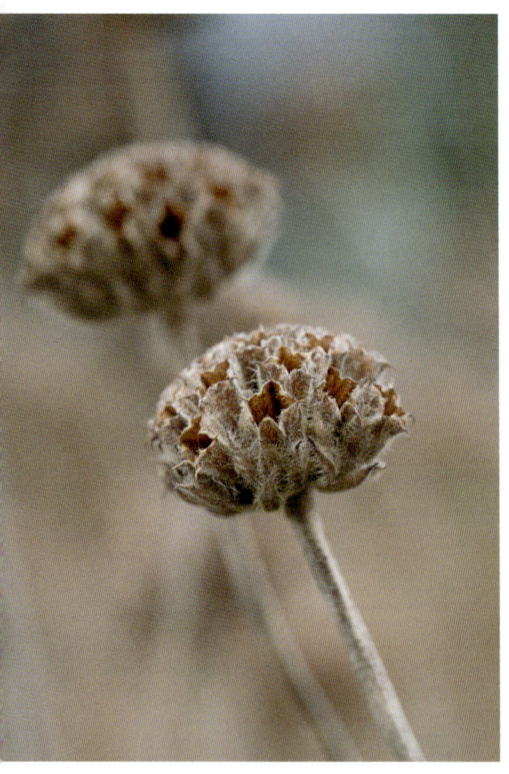

The increasing level of blur as you move farther into the picture creates a profound sense of spatial depth f/7.1, 1/100 s, ISO 2000, 180mm

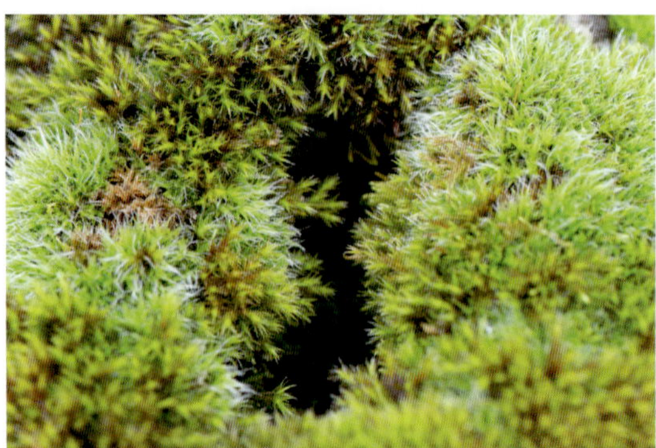

Bed of moss at f/9. The focus is positioned in the top third of the image on one of the overhanging bits of the moss. The blurry foreground establishes spatial depth.

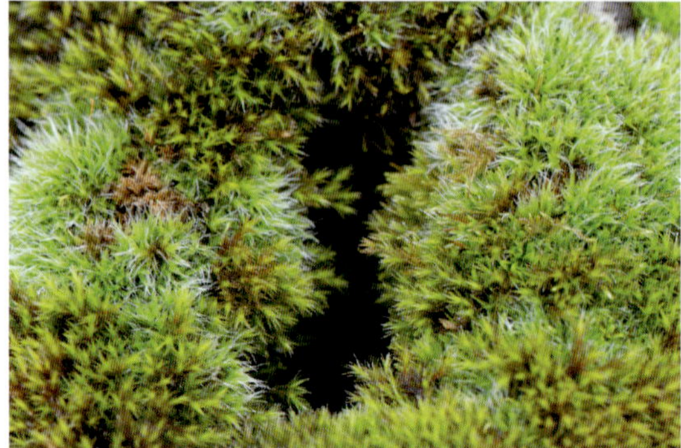

Bed of moss at f/14. The focus is positioned in the lower third of the image somewhere between the pieces of moss. This version feels less cohesive compositionally, even though more of the subject falls within the depth of field.

There are many creative opportunities when working with a wide aperture and the extremely tight depth of field it produces. Here the image comprises different regions of increasing blur. The foremost blossoms are more or less sharp, the ones immediately behind them are already a bit blurry, and the ones near the back are completely out of focus.
f/4, 1/30 s, ISO 200, 150mm

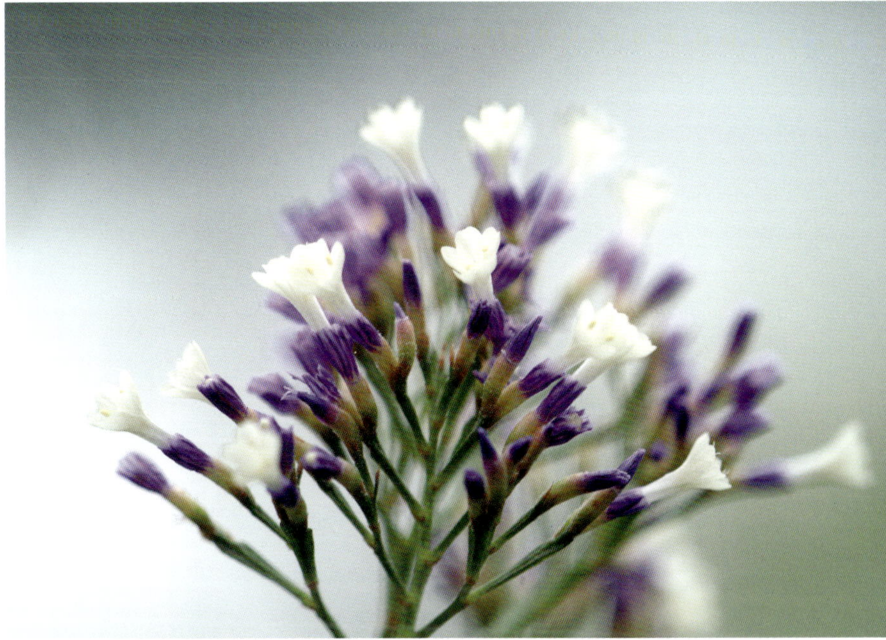

Dive even deeper into the macro realm, and the depth of field for an open aperture shrinks to mere millimeters. Blur can be used creatively in these settings, too. This image relies on a limited palette of colors and blur to produce a subtly expressive atmosphere. The look and feel of blur is known as bokeh.
f/5.6, 1/1,250 s, ISO 160, 150mm

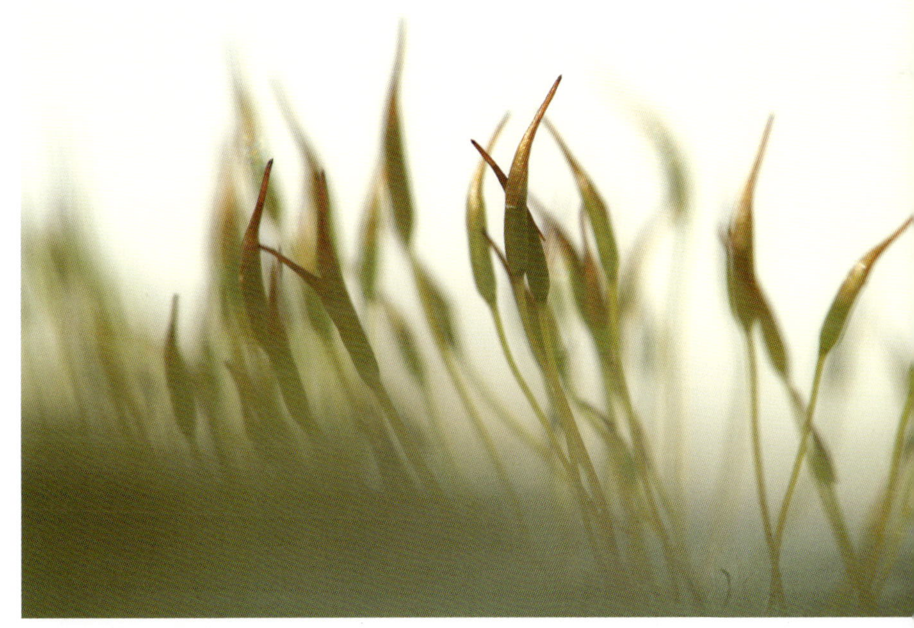

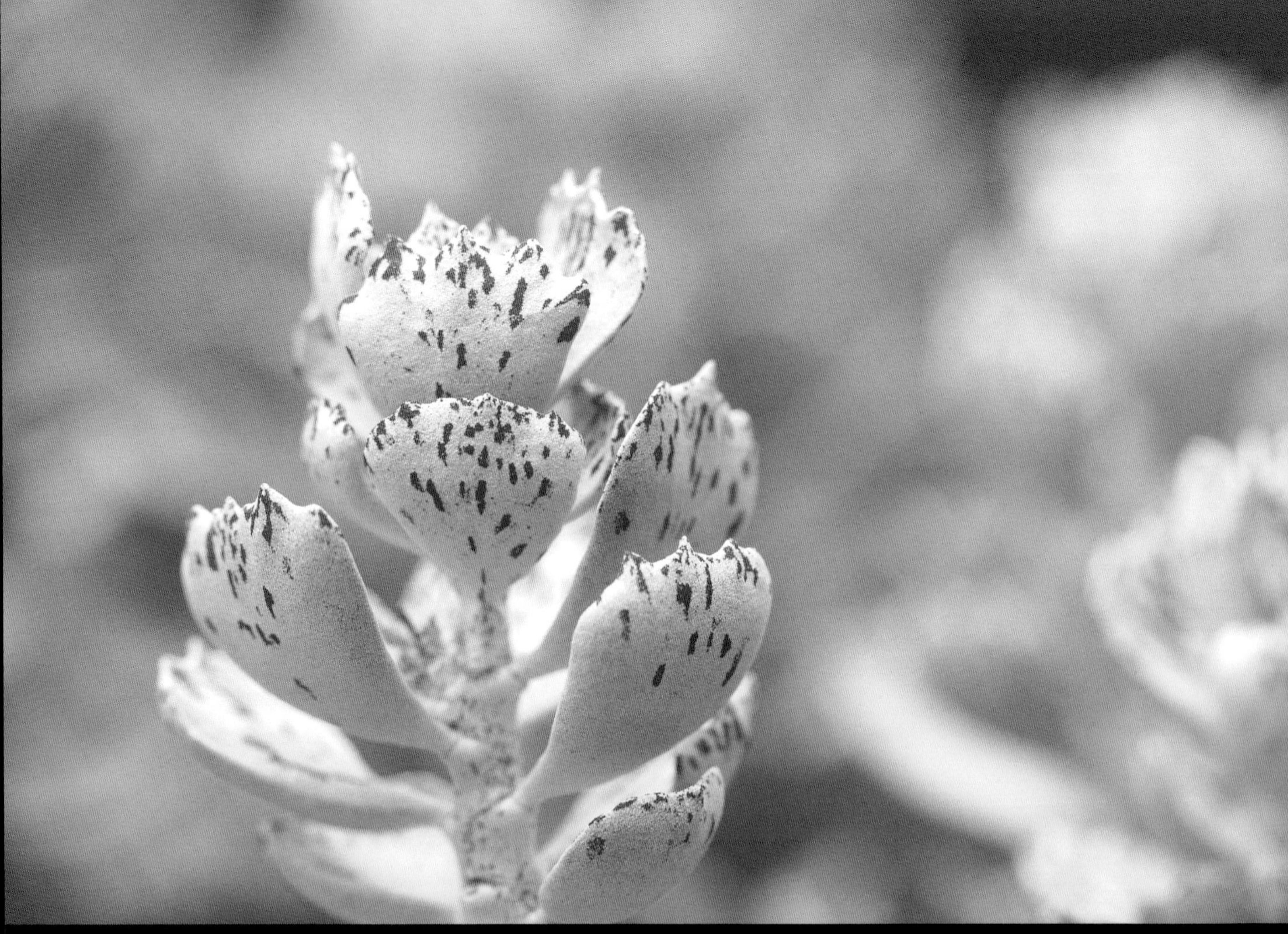

This image resembles a pastel drawing, thanks to a
nearly monochrome color palette and the abundance
of blur resulting from the background being so far
away from the subject
f/7, 1/200 s, ISO 2000, 180mm
Location: Botanical Gardens of Tübingen, Germany

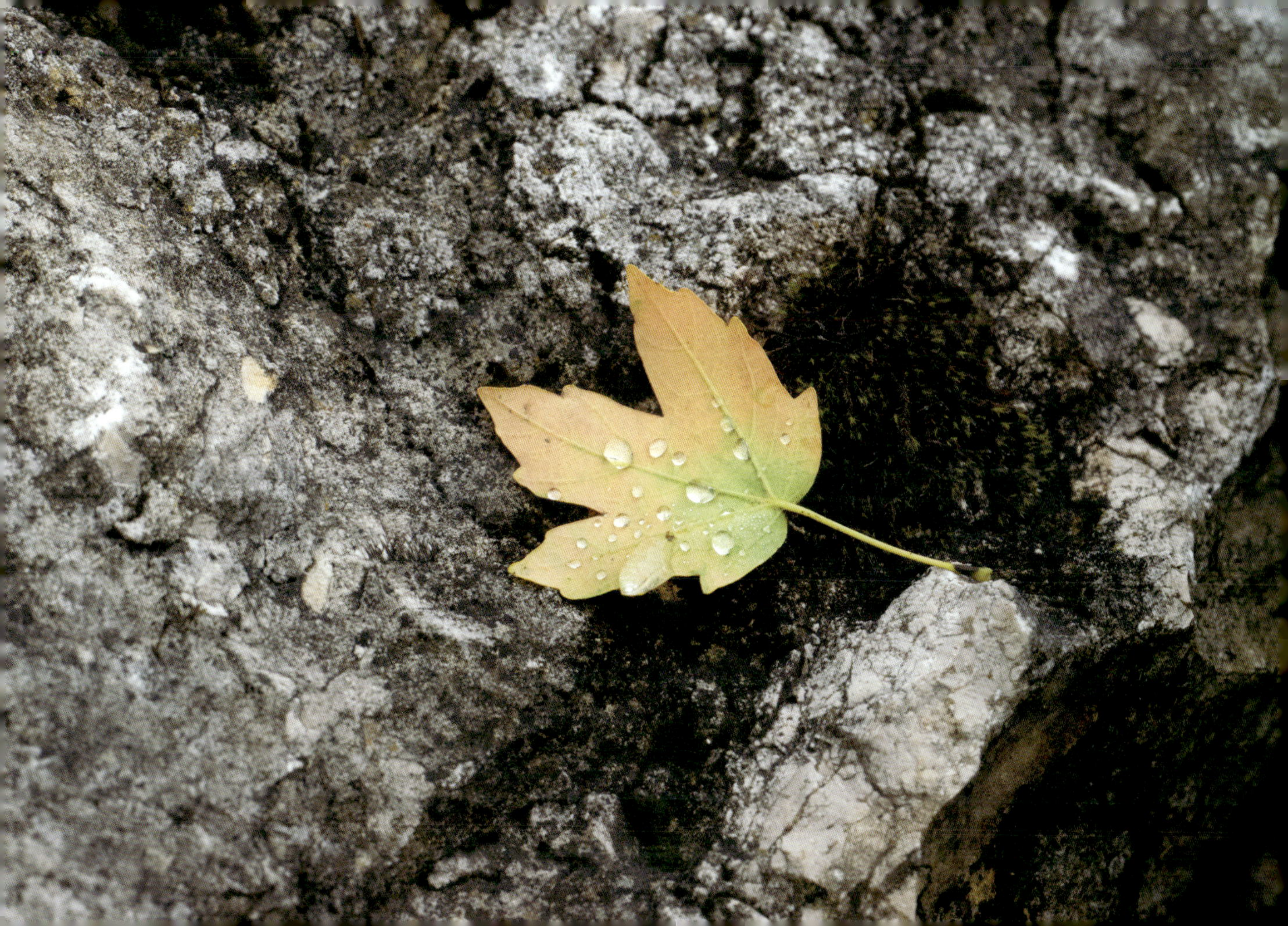

Accents of Color

Color contrasts can be used to stress specific elements within an image. To use this method, align your shot so that the subject appears in front of a background color, offering as much contrast as possible. You'll often have to alter your shooting position to bring a desirable background color into the right place. Animals that are prone to fleeing from photographers in search of an optimal angle of view may not be the best subjects for this technique, but plants won't put up any resistance to a protracted search for the ideal perspective.

The orange of this mosquito forms a pronounced contrast of color with the green of the leaf it is resting on
f/9.5, 1/60 s, ISO 200, 105mm, system flash unit with softbox

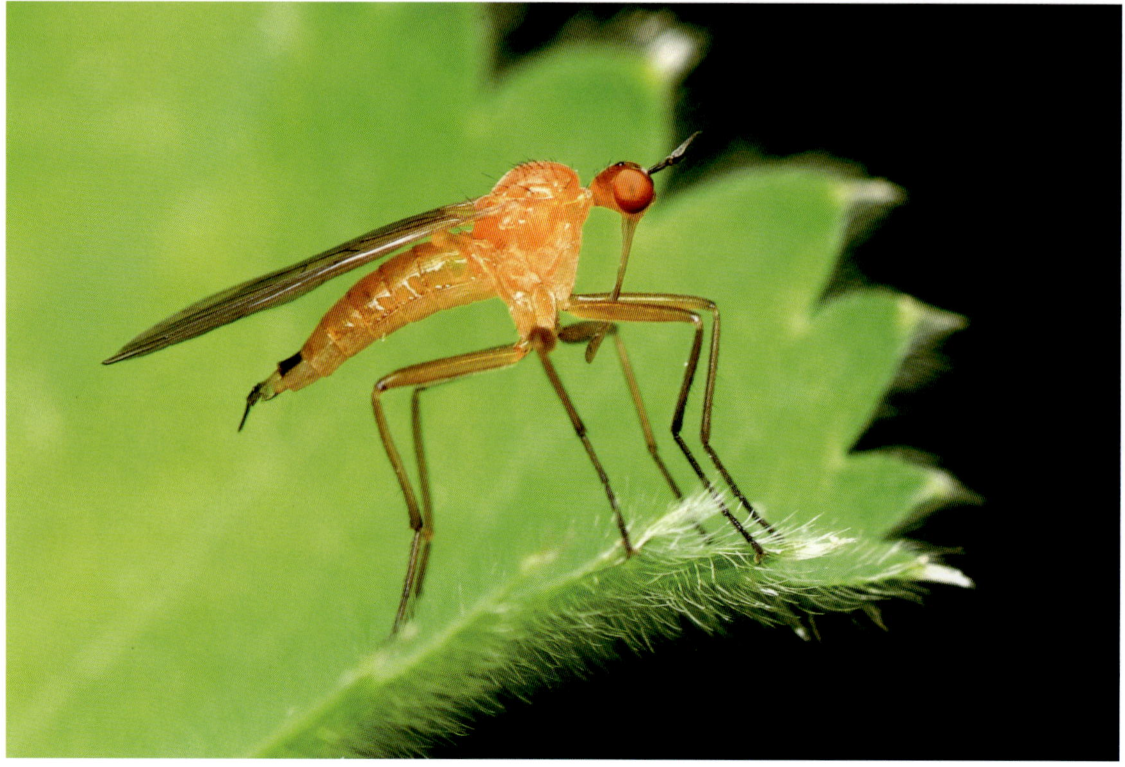

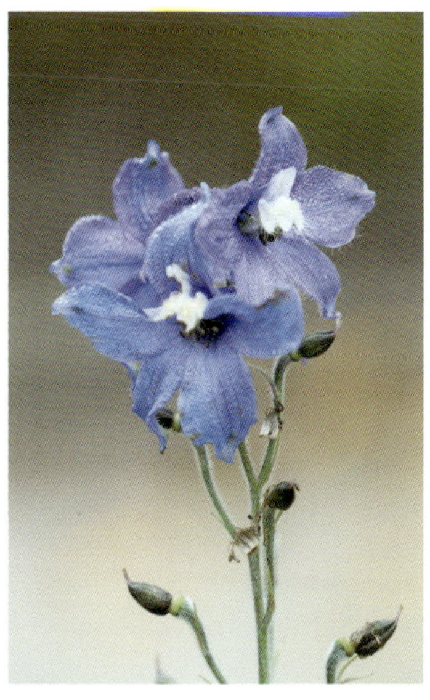 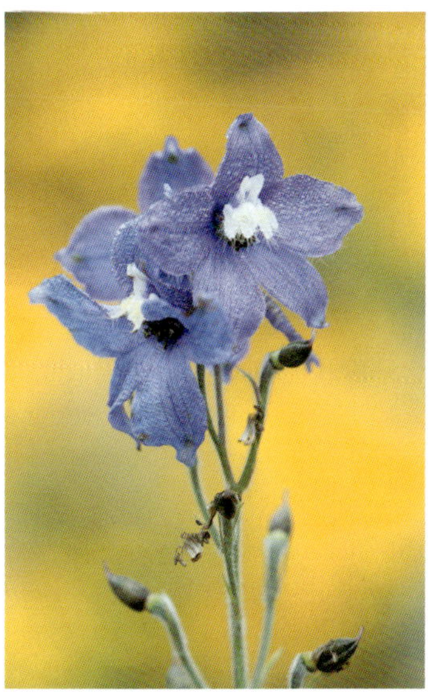

A minor adjustment to your shoot-ing perspective is often all it takes to compose an image with a vastly improved background that offers a beneficial contrast of color. Case in point: A simple turn of the camera replaced a rather dreary sidewalk (left) with a bed of yellow flowers (right) for the backdrop of this image.

Red on green. Color contrast causes these intense flowers to stand out sharply against a flat background obscured in blur. The composition depended on the use of a wide aperture and the substantial distance between the subject and its background.
f/2.8,1/60 s, ISO 400, 150mm

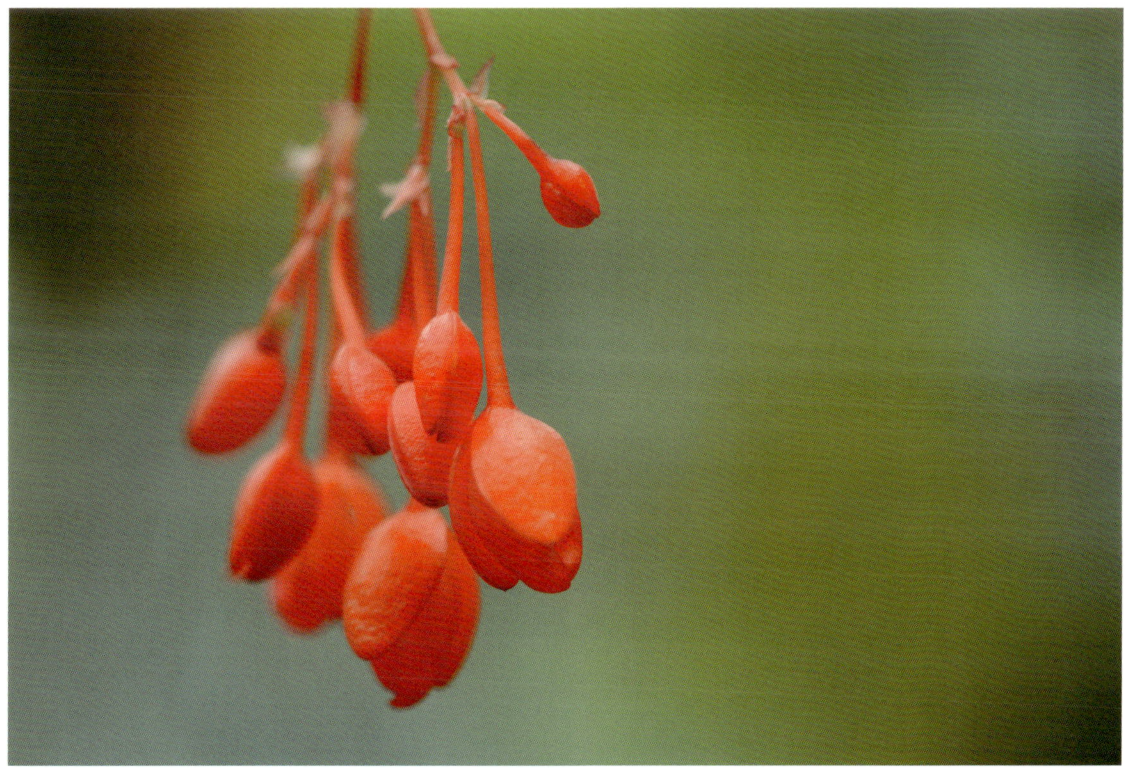

Limiting Colors

More is not always better when it comes to colors. Deliberately limiting or reducing the range of colors in an image often produces enchanting results. Note that this compositional technique is different from desaturating the colors of an image—here I'm suggesting you limit an entire image to one dominating color, the saturation of which can remain high. As with black-and-white photography, this technique increases the attention on the shapes and forms of an image, making thoughtful composition and careful attention to prominent lines of the utmost importance. An open aperture is often a useful tool when employing this technique for producing soft tones of color that flow into one another. Images with a limited palette are particularly effective at conveying and intensifying moods.

Chinese bitter orange. A wide aperture melted the background into a flat surface with subtle nuances of color.
f/7, 1/1,000 s, ISO 1000, 180mm Location: Botanical Gardens of Tübingen, Germany

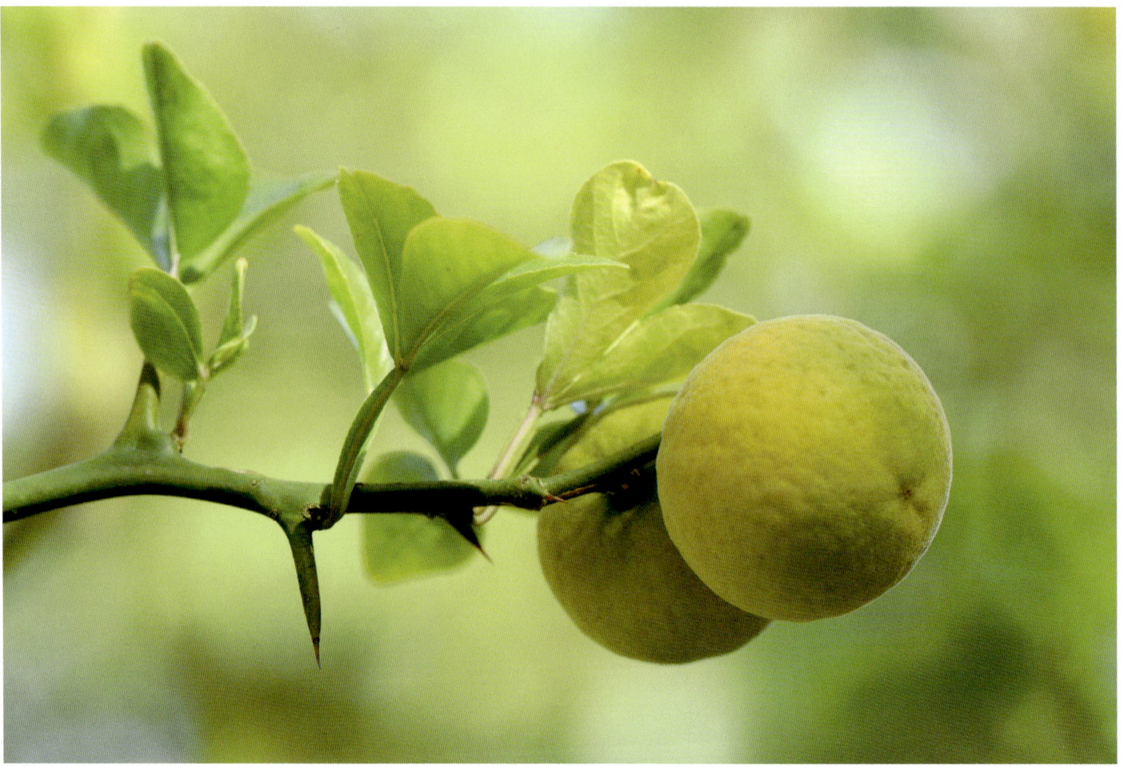

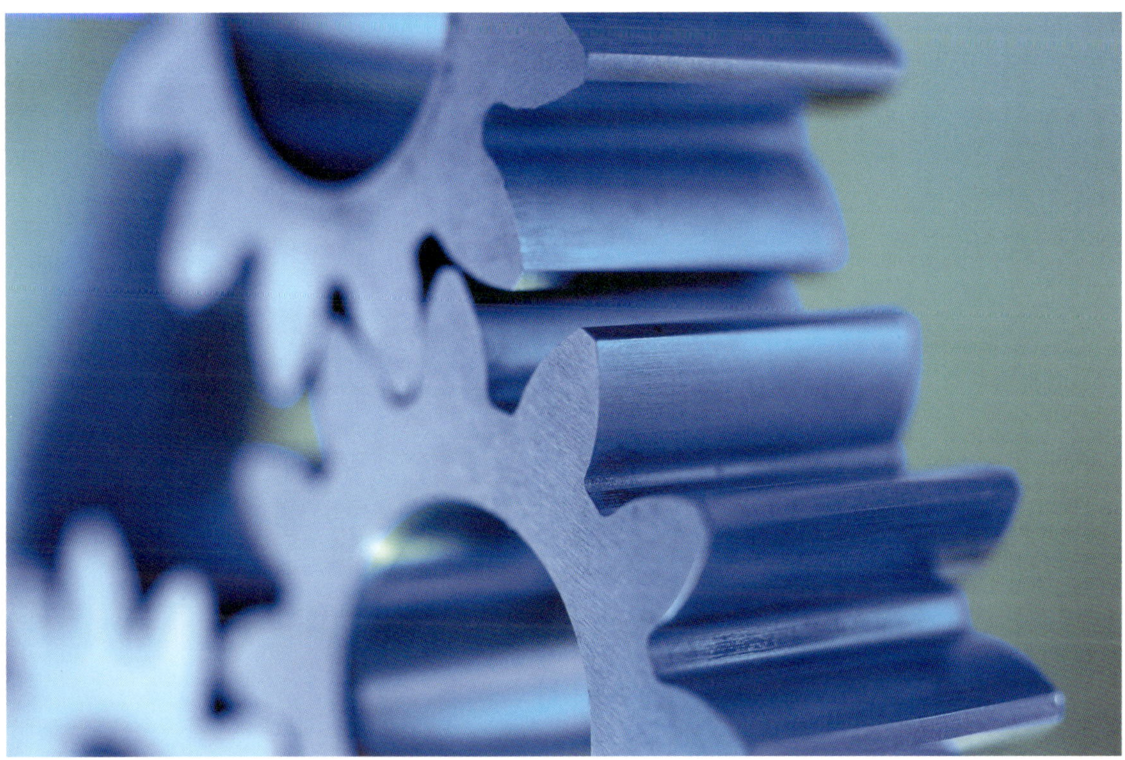

Gears. Fluorescent lamps filtered through transparent blue material provided light for this image, and the background was made up of colored cardboard. Continuous lighting is helpful when working with colored light because you can inspect the appearance in real time through the camera's viewfinder.
f/8, 1/200 s, ISO 100, 50mm

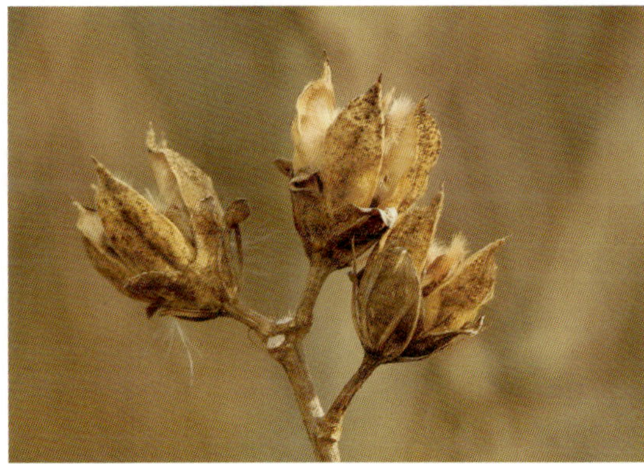

The autumnal feeling of this image arises not only from the subject but also from the color palette
f/6.7, 1/60 s, ISO 200, 150mm

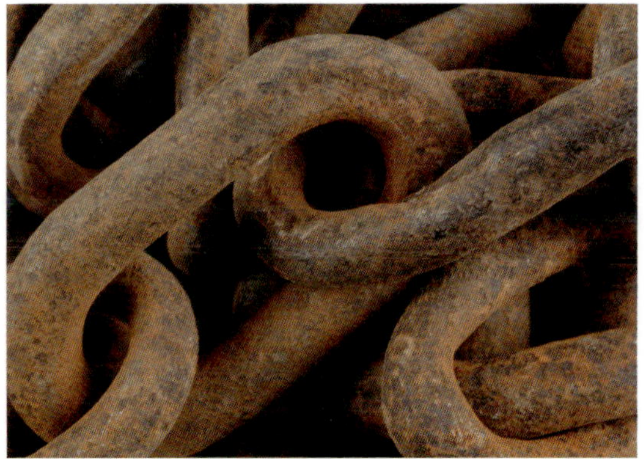

Rusty metal chains. Two studio flash units with softboxes provided the necessary intensity of light to be able to achieve a large depth of field and an even illumination.
f/22, 1/200 s, ISO 100, 60mm

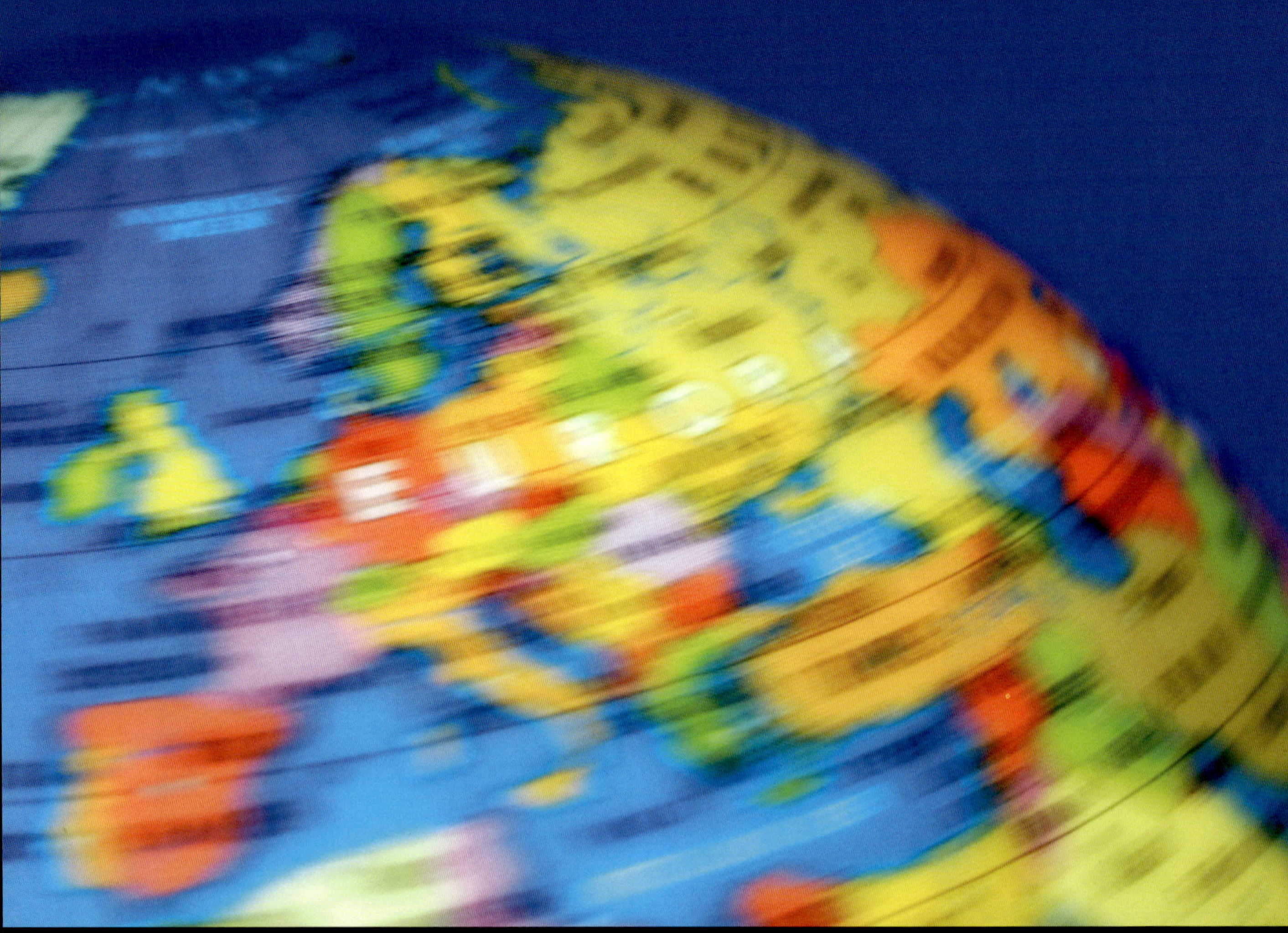

Not all close-up and macro images need to be in focus. Motion blur is a key feature of this image and its intentions. Sustained lighting is essential for these types of pictures, because the pulse from a flash would freeze the movements in place.
f/13, 1/20 s, ISO 200, 50mm

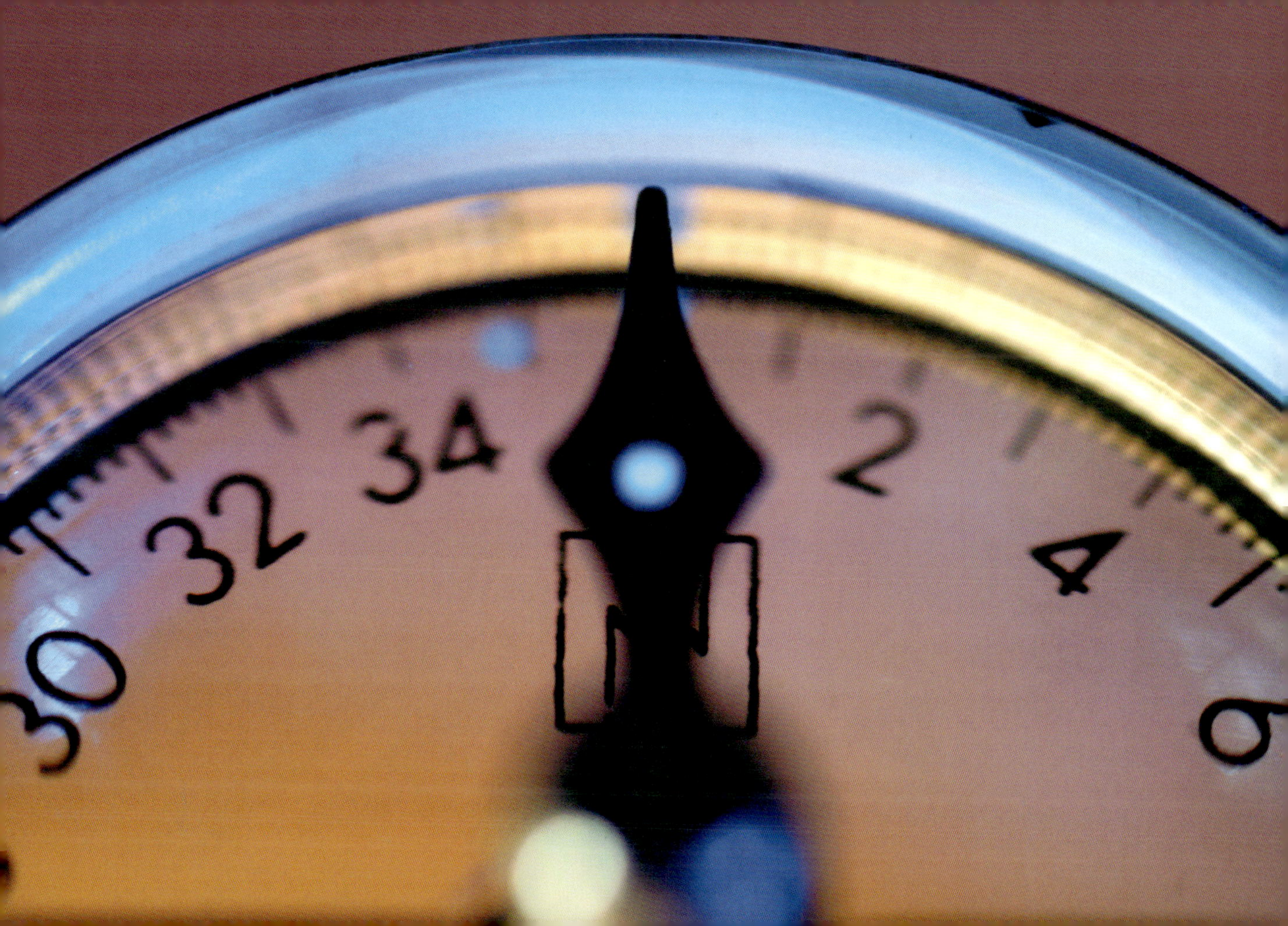
30
32
34
2
4
6

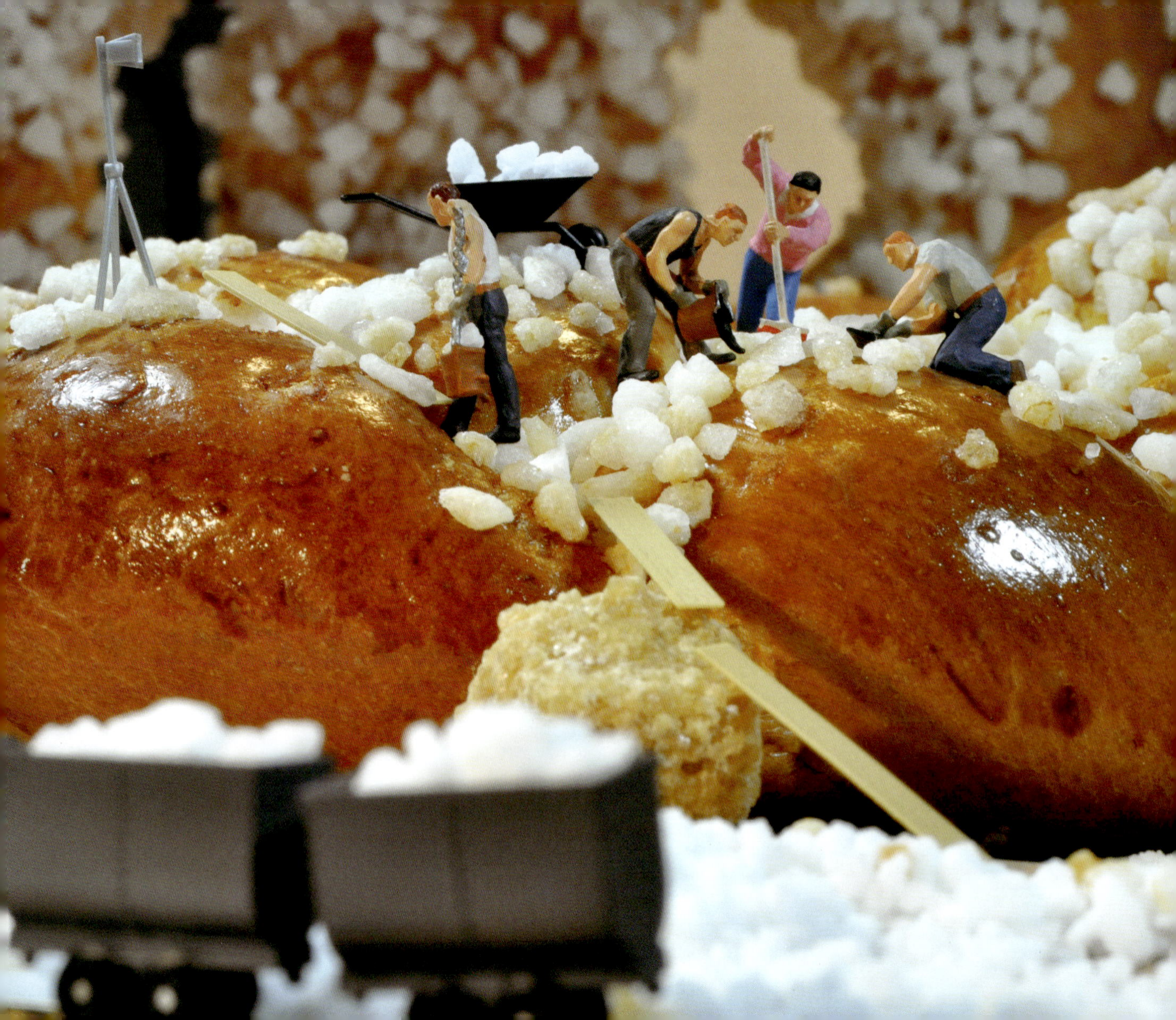

Tips from the Pros

Bernd Schloemer
Miniature Street Art

Bernd Schloemer first started taking pictures of miniature worlds many years ago at the request of a friend, who commissioned him to photograph installations of figurines before their sale. The first shoot involved figurines positioned in a box of hollowed-out bread rolls. After one such shoot, a few figurines were left over, and Bernd decided to have a little fun by arranging them into a scene on the top of a desk, where he improvised a mini photo studio using a desk lamp for lighting. And so a project was born, first featuring images in and around Cologne, Germany, which is where the Colognies project got its name. It has since expanded worldwide. A favor for a friend blossomed into a full-fledged passion. Aside from having fun with his photography, Bernd hopes that his photographic ideas spur viewers to smile, and to think about his creations. In addition to his book and several calendars devoted to his art, you can find many other pictures on his website at *www.colognies.de* and on Facebook.

The Colognies Project

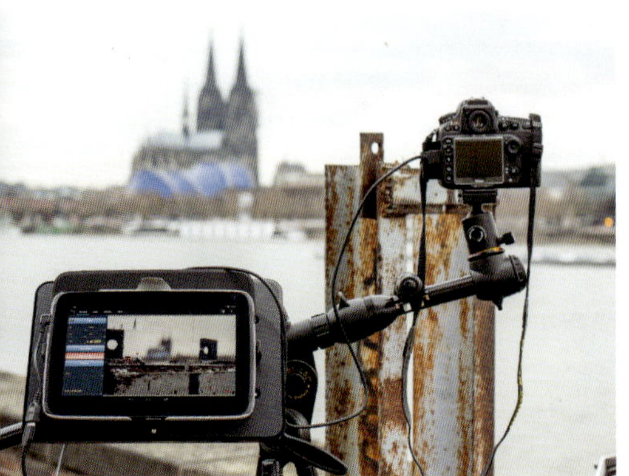

The making of The Beer Drinker on the Rhine
*Canon EOS 5D Mark II, f/ 4.5, 1/80 s,
ISO 1000, 50mm
Photo by Bernd Schloemer*

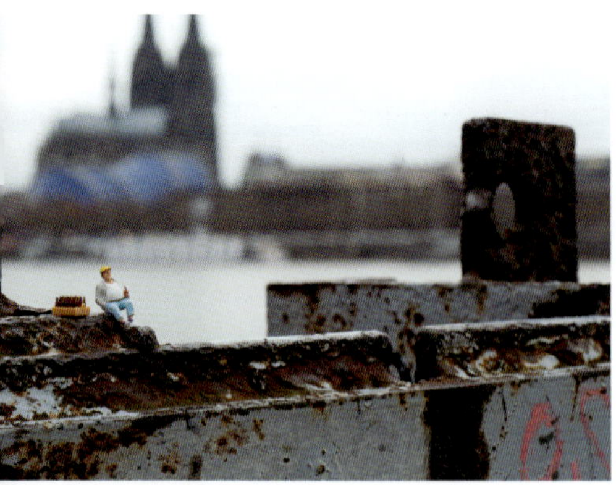

The Beer Drinker on the Rhine
*Nikon D800, f/20, 2.5 s, ISO 100,
60mm
Photo by Bernd Schloemer*

Classification and Themes

The photos of the Colognies project defy categorization to some extent. "Staged miniature street art" is perhaps the most accurate description. The main goal is to create pictures featuring figurines, which are about 20mm tall, in urban environments so that they convey a certain message. The content and purpose of these pictures ranges from comic scenes that aim to make viewers chuckle to more serious themes that cause viewers to reflect. The particular allure of this work is using the magnified perspective of a macro lens to make viewers conscious of commonplace objects such as a cigarette butt or an aluminum can. A nearly endless potential for creativity exists in staging small human figurines sharply in the foreground with objects (and sometimes real people) in the background cast in blur.

Setup and Gear

The figurines in my photos are commercially available, usually for professional and hobbyist modeling needs. They can be built and painted for any imaginable situation and they come in a variety of sizes, which further opens up creative possibilities for staging them in context with different backgrounds and found objects.

For each shoot, I capture two perspectives: a close-up shot and an overview shot. For the macro image, which is more important to me, I use a macro lens with an intermediate focal length (60mm) and shoot from a variety of perspectives. I use a 24mm wide-angle lens to establish the overview perspective. Using a relatively short focal length with the macro lens has the added benefit that passersby tend to realize that you are shooting very close to your set, and they keep a respectful distance. Using a longer focal length would inevitably mean that more figurines would suffer tragic fates as a result of inattentive pedestrians. Other techniques common to the macro world, such as HDR and image stacking are not out of the question for my work. Ghosting issues are a concern, however, because many of my shots feature people moving in the background; I tend not to use these methods when that's the case.

The Macro Shot

I usually position my camera at ground level to capture the macro image—in part because the angle of view is interesting but also because the figurines are so small. For some shots, every millimeter lower that I can get the camera counts. Lying on the ground and using the viewfinder or the live view mode on the camera is anything but comfortable in these situations, and after a rainfall it's especially unpleasant. Rolling out a picnic blanket in a highly trafficked pedestrian area is also not practical, and is sure to garner some pitying stares from passersby. For me, the best solution is to use a tablet device with an application that enables me to remotely control the camera while inspecting the live view. A tablet's screen is so much larger than the viewfinder or display on a camera, so it's easier to evaluate sharpness and depth of field compared to using the depth-of-field preview function on the camera itself. I can quickly and easily figure out what sorts of adjustments to make to the scene to get my desired result.

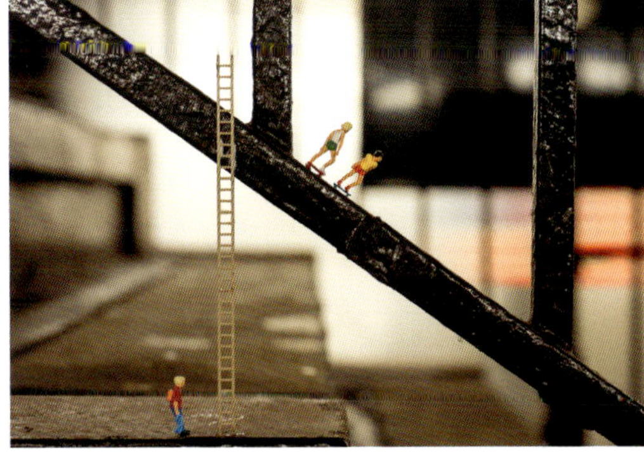

Skaters in the Subway
Nikon D800, f/2.8, 1/30 s, ISO 12800,
60mm
Photo by Bernd Schloemer

The Overview Shot

The purpose of the overview images is to show viewers the relationship of size between the subjects and their real-world surroundings. Depending on how and where my makeshift set is constructed, I try to use standard photographic techniques, such as HDR, as well as common compositional guidelines, such as the golden ratio, to realize the establishing shot. Circumstances sometimes dictate that using such photographic methods are impractical or impossible, however. It's always a challenge for me to find places that allow for an interesting macro image, but also offer the potential for creating an engaging overview photo.

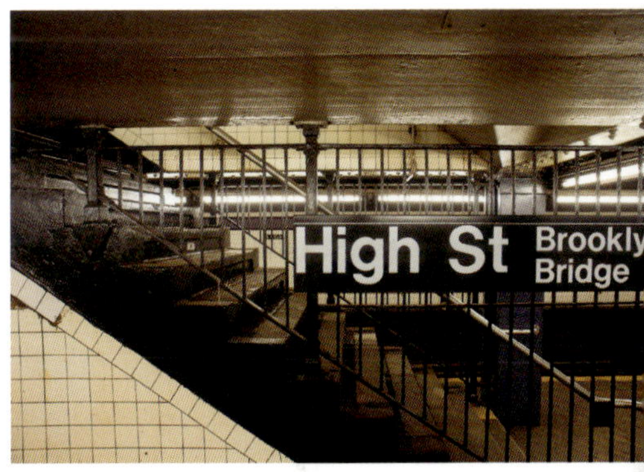

Overview of Skaters in the Subway
Nikon D800, f/2.8, 1/13 s, ISO 12800,
20mm
Photo by Bernd Schloemer

As a rule, I shoot all pictures in the RAW format so I can later use image-editing software to make modest adjustments to exposure and the like without losing image quality. I don't generally edit anything more than tweaking the exposure minimally or possibly removing a fleck of dust from the subject.

Most photographers work with a certain standard of quality in mind, and most are never entirely satisfied with their results—I'm no different. Aside from producing technically sound images, I also make it a point of pride to come up with photographic ideas that charm viewers and spark positive associations with my images. I typically generate my best ideas when engaged in routine everyday activities as opposed to when I'm intensely thinking about what might make an interesting picture. Once I settle on a general concept, I set about finding or crafting the figurines necessary for the scene. Then it's a matter of finding a suitable location. Lighting is a key variable

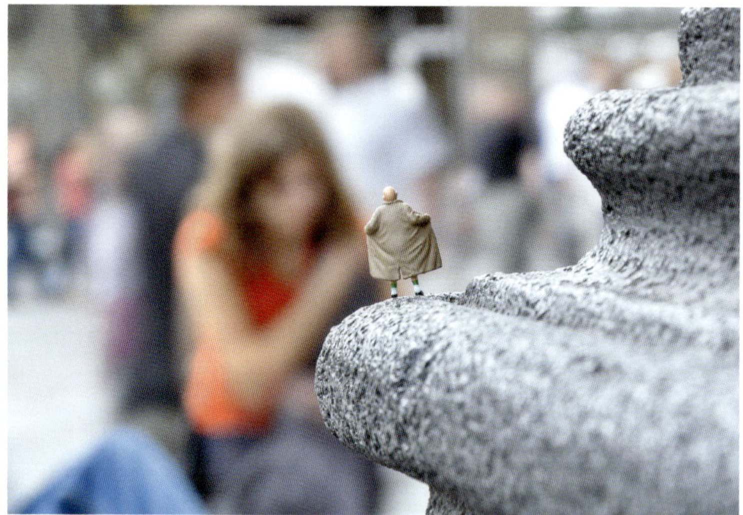

Small Exhibitionist at a Cathedral
Nikon D5000, f/7.1, 1/5 s, ISO 200,
20mm
Photo by Bernd Schloemer

that often influences where and at what time of day I shoot, because generally I rely on ambient light for my work. With any luck, these steps will produce the result I intended.

As is the case with life, however, spontaneity often offers better rewards than the most deliberate and careful of planning. I usually carry a handful of figurines in my equipment bag to position and photograph when I happen upon a potential scene. It never fails that some of these pictures end up being my favorites, while the carefully planned ones end up as rejects.

Experiences

Time and again interesting interactions and situations arise while I'm shooting because passersby fail to notice the tiny subjects that I work with at first glance. Comments such as, "Hey, look, now they're even taking pictures of trash on the street!" come up frequently.

I also have the chance to witness herd instincts in action—especially when I'm working at landmarks and monuments. These locations often feature interesting surface materials such as old stone slabs that I frequently try to use. No one pays me or the landmark any mind while my mini scene is staged, as long as my camera stays out of view. But as soon as I pull my camera out, people tend to stop and wonder what's going on. The onlookers, many of whom are probably not local, will eventually reach for their camera or phone and start snapping pictures of their own, assuming: "Well, if someone else is using that equipment to take pictures of this landmark, there must be something to it, and I should, too."

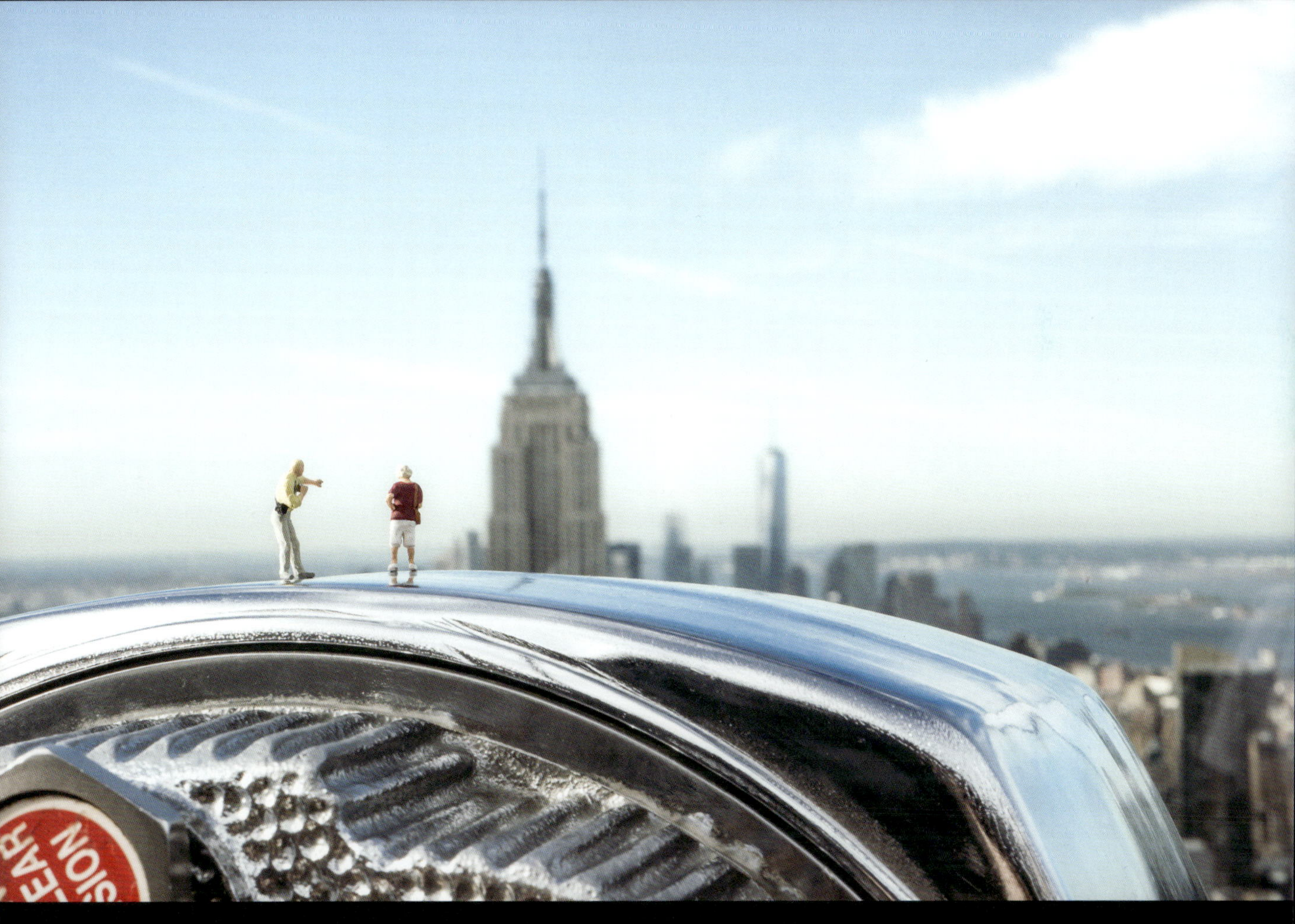

That Way to the Empire State Building
Nikon D5000, f/16, 1/640 s, ISO 400, 60mm
Photo by Bernd Schloemer

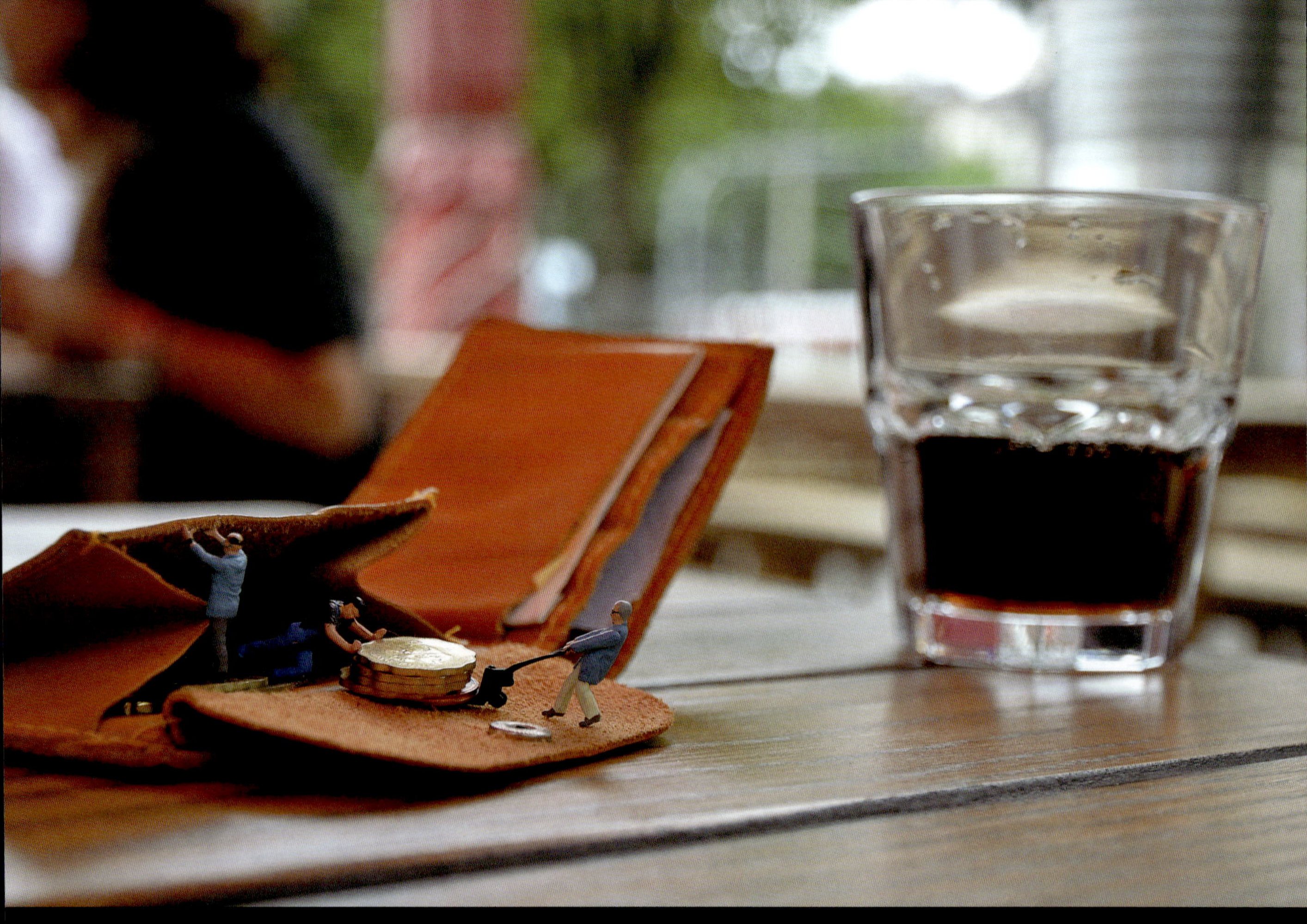

Wallet Thieves
Nikon D5000, f/4.8, 1/25 s, ISO 100, 60mm
Photo by Bernd Schloemer

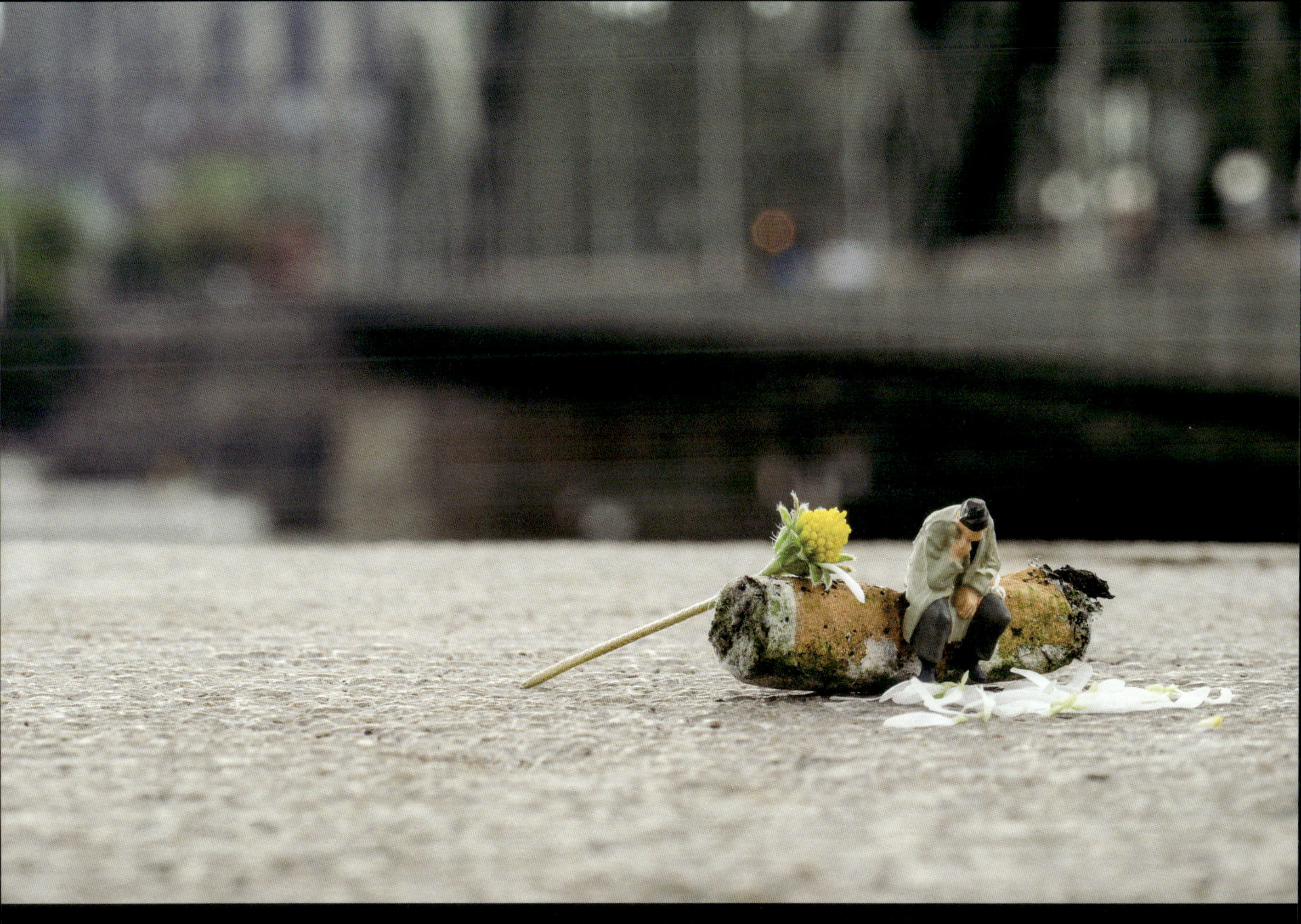

She Loves Me Not. *On a bridge over the Rhine.*
Nikon D5000, f/22, 1 s, ISO 100, 60mm
Photo by Bernd Schloemer

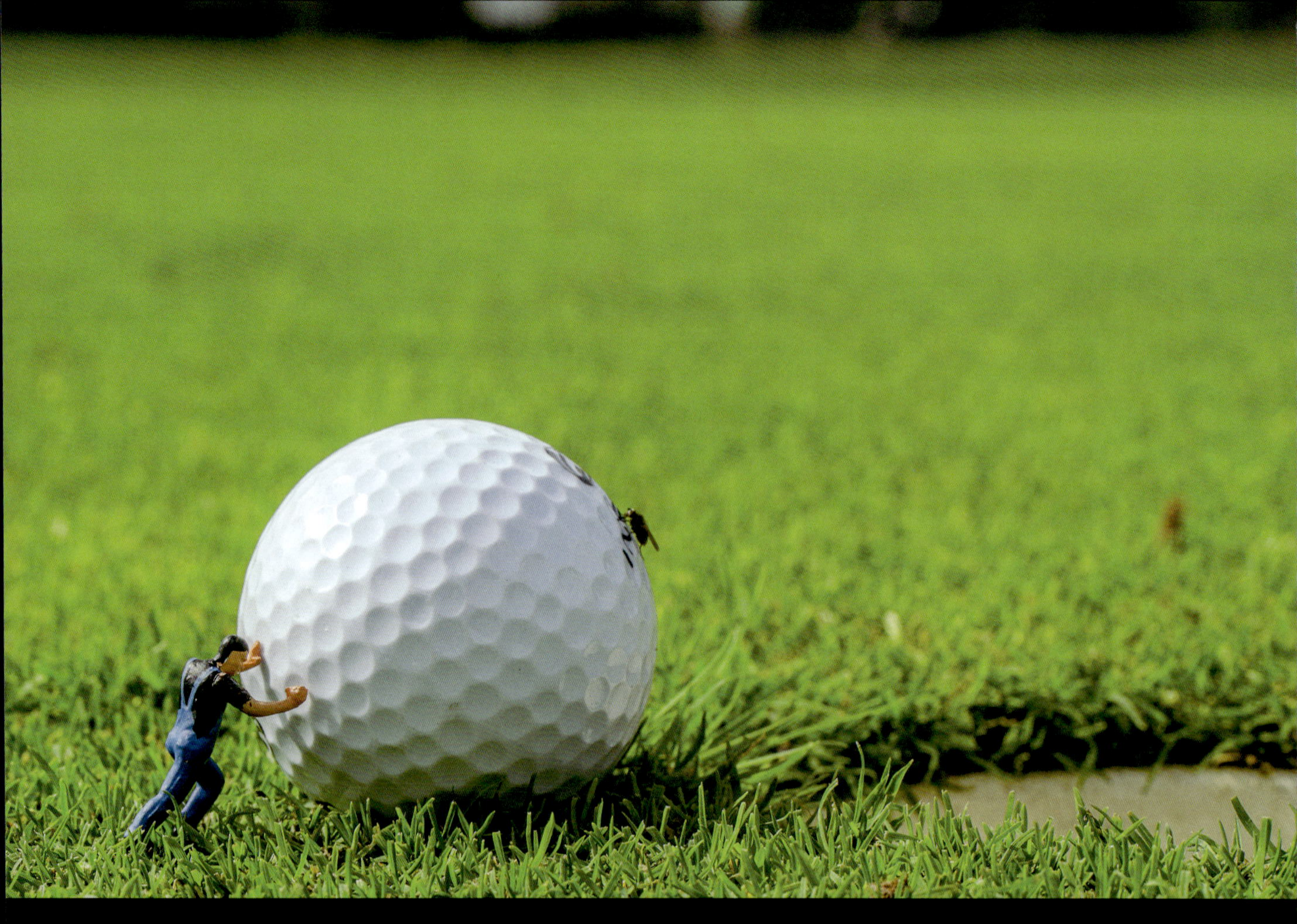

Golf Assistant
Nikon D5000, f/22, 1/250 s, ISO 200, 60mm
Photo by Bernd Schloemer

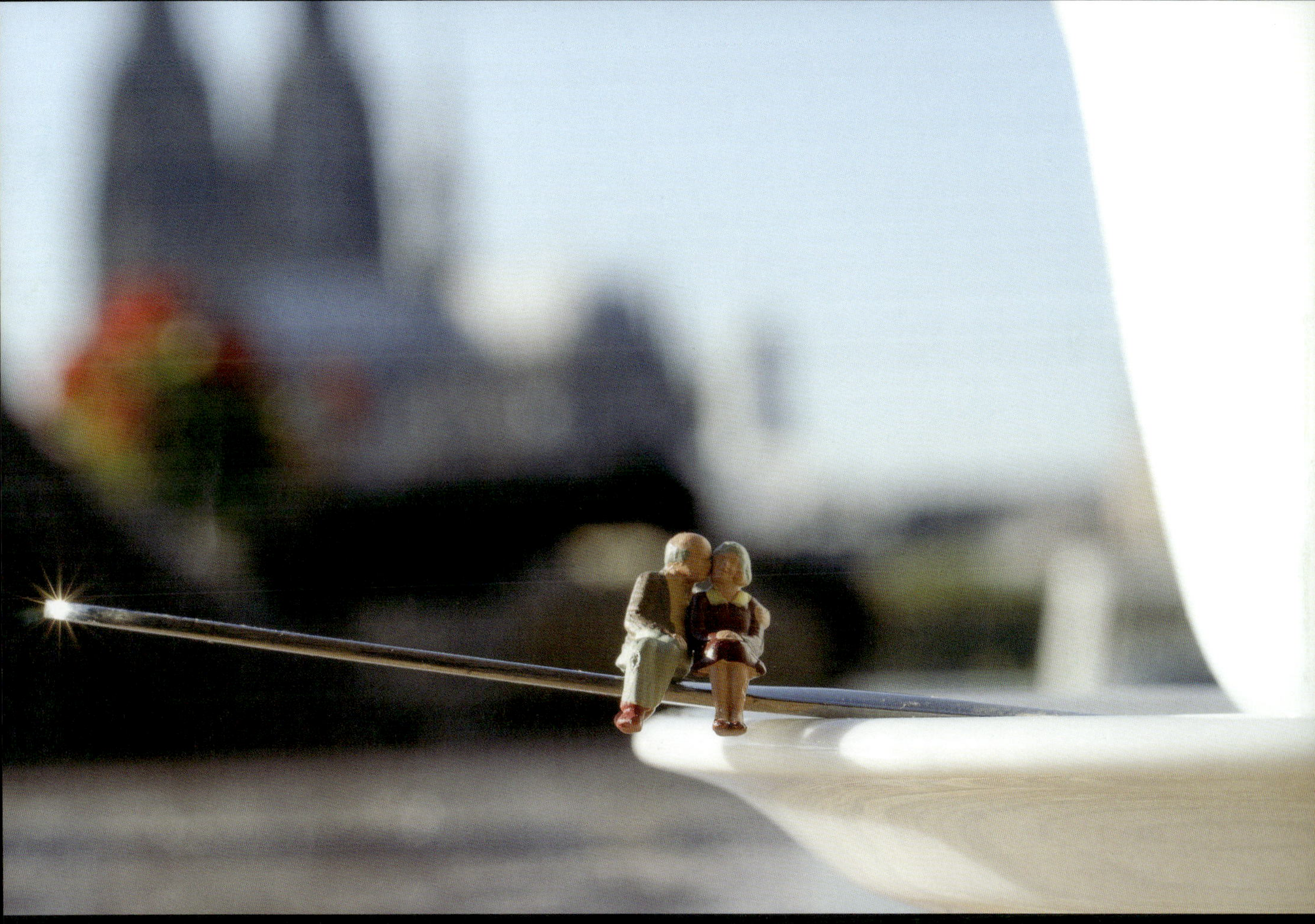

Lovers on a Saucer
Nikon D800, f/29, 1/30 s, ISO 200, 60mm
Photo by Bernd Schloemer

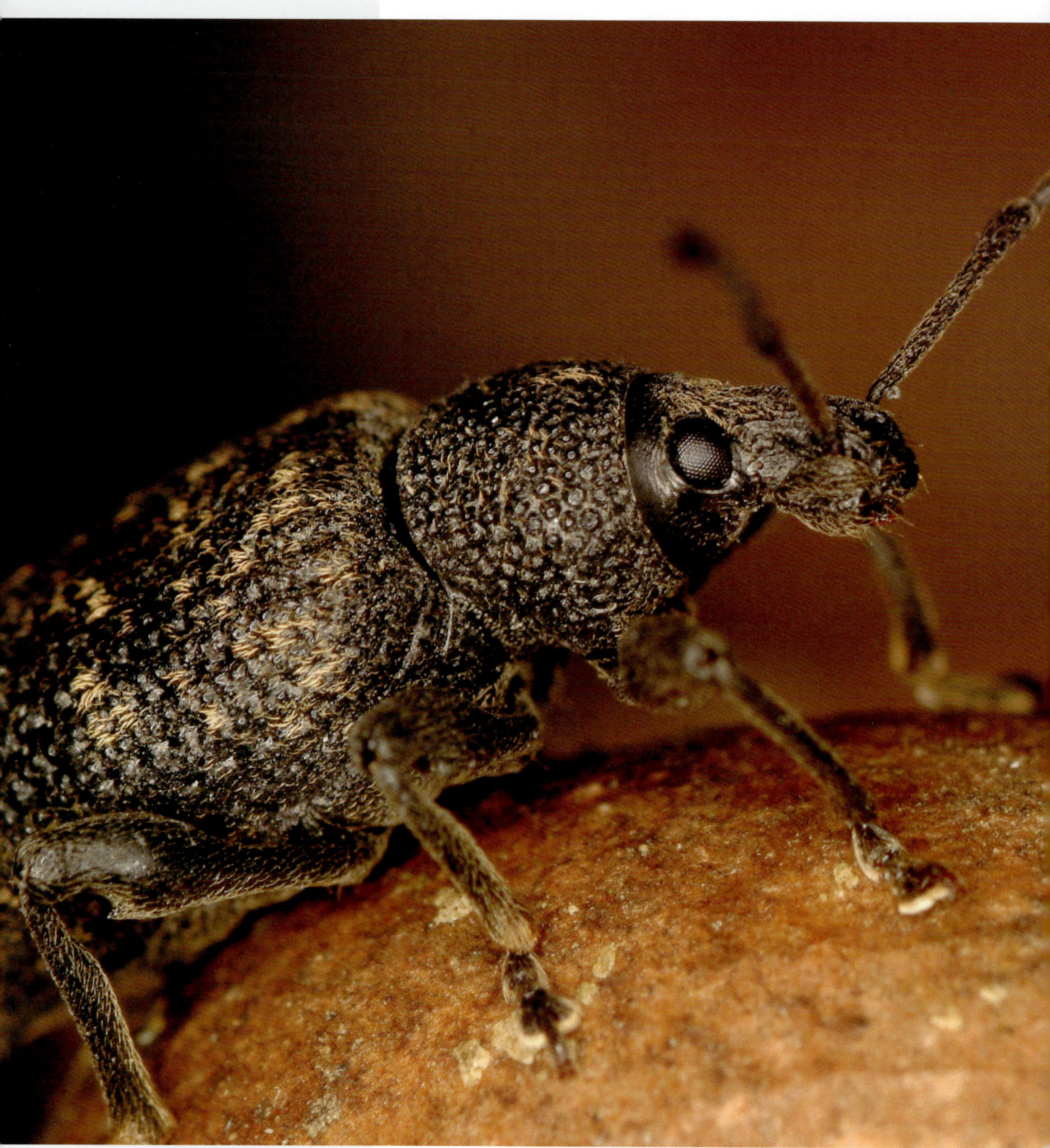

Do It Yourself

Designing and building custom photo equipment has long been a popular trend. The advantages of undertaking do-it-yourself projects are obvious. With a little (or sometimes a decent) amount of time and some craftiness, you can build a range of useful tools for macro photography, from simple devices including small light-shaping tools such as reflector cards for a system flash, to more complex projects such as the linear guide for macro panoramas discussed on the following pages. In many cases, homemade results can hold their own with their professional counterparts, and sometimes custom solutions are the only way to complete a certain task if the right tools or devices aren't readily available for sale.

Anyone who has spent time shooting macro photos has experience with needing improvised solutions to handle particular lighting or support issues. Most photographers will agree that coming up with makeshift solutions to do the job is a satisfying and rewarding activity.

In this spirit, I wish you all the best in your own do-it-yourself endeavors.

Weevil
f/9.5, 1/60 s, ISO 200, 105mm

Using a Macro Lens as a Microscope

Macro lenses are very fast fixed-focal length devices that serve exceptionally well as the basis for a makeshift homemade microscope. In theory, the lens itself needs only to be paired with an ocular, or eyepiece. Depending on the power of the eyepiece used and the focal length of the lens, you can reach levels of magnification well beyond what you can usually attain when the same lens is attached to a camera (often greater than 1:1).

Macro lenses can also be fashioned into reflected-light microscopes with the right eyepiece adapters. A piece of wood makes up the base of the microscope stand pictured here. The leg of a piece of furniture, which has a diameter of 25mm, is screwed into it, and a Novoflex Universal Clamp (max jaw opening 26mm) is attached to that. The Sigma lens used here has a focal length of 150mm. Paired with a 25mm eyepiece, it offers a 6-fold magnification and with a 10mm eyepiece, a 15-fold magnification.

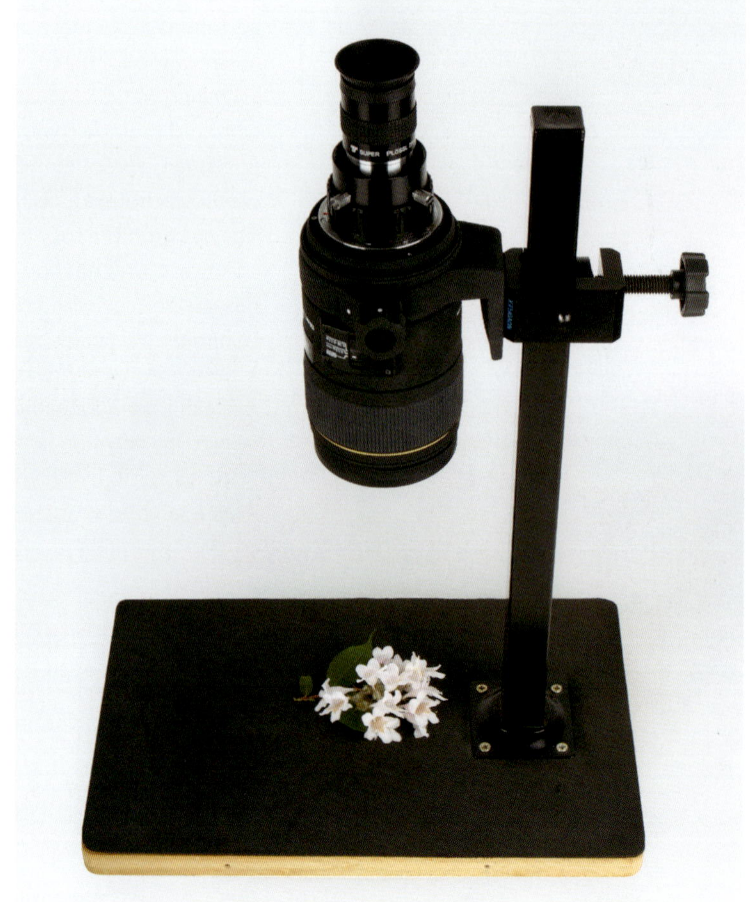

You can calculate the exact level of magnification by dividing the focal length of the lens by the focal length of the eyepiece. For example: a telephoto lens with a focal length of 300mm paired with a 25mm eyepiece would produce a 12-fold magnification (300/25 = 12). Using the same lens with a 10mm eyepiece would get you a 30-fold magnification. If you're using a zoom lens, you can calculate your range of attainable magnification levels by using the maximum and minimum focal lengths for the formula.

The following equipment is needed to outfit a macro lens to function as a microscope: a modified lens cover, a T2 adapter ring that attaches to an eyepiece mount, and the eyepiece itself. You probably have a lens cover somewhere at home, and the other two items can be purchased from specialized retailers who sell telescopes and parts, such as *http://agenaastro.com*.

The lens cap serves as the connecting device between the lens and the eyepiece, which means that it has to be prepared with an opening to fit the T2 threads attached to the eyepiece mount. Use a metal bit to drill a hole in the lens cap to roughly fit the right size. Then use a round metal file to continue increasing the diameter of the hole so that the T2 threads just fit into the opening. Next, with the eyepiece adapter snugly in place, use some superglue to secure the eyepiece mount to the lens cap.

Attach the lens cap—now with the eyepiece mount—to the lens, and insert the eyepiece itself. Set the lens's focus to infinity, and adjust the eyepiece so that your subject comes into sharp focus. Once you've found this position, use the clamping screws on the eyepiece mount to secure the eyepiece in place. In most instances, that is all it takes. However, if you can't produce a sharp image, you'll need to modify your eyepiece so you can slide it closer to the lens. Use a hacksaw to trim off a couple millimeters of the eyepiece's sleeve, and try again.

The resulting microscope has a so-called *direct-vision prism*, which means that the image produced will be laterally reversed and upside down. This will be confusing at first, but you will adjust to it fairly quickly.

Microscopes fashioned out of lenses with focal lengths up to 50mm can generally be held pretty well by hand, which means they can be taken out on excursions to inspect wild plants and insects in greater detail. Handheld microscopes also come in handy when cleaning the image sensor of a DSLR.

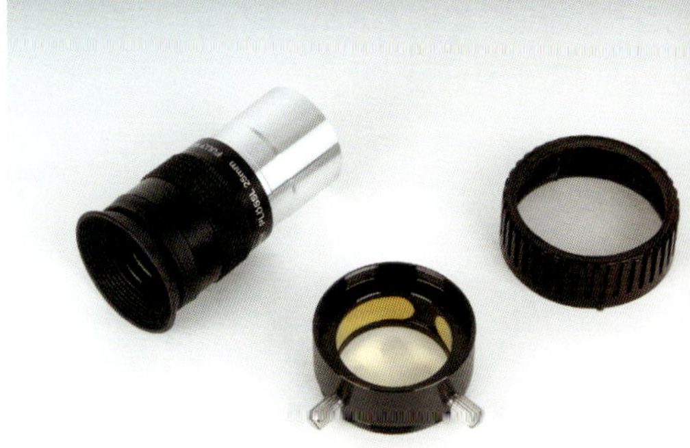

The individual components of the adapter: an eyepiece designed for a telescope, a T2 adapter attached to the eyepiece mount, and a modified lens cap

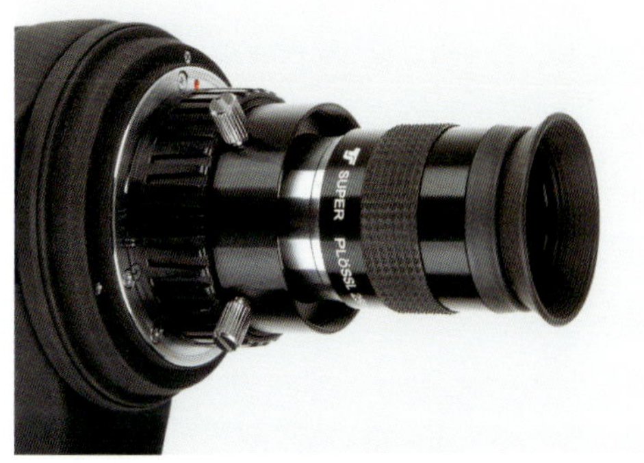

The assembled adapter simply attaches to the lens's bayonet mount to convert a macro lens into a compact microscope with an astoundingly powerful magnification

Guide Rails for Macro Panoramas

Standard focusing rails available for purchase from photography equipment retailers generally have a sliding distance of around 110mm to 140mm, but many macro panoramas require more length than that. One option is to resort to pivoting, but this method results in a loss of sharpness because elements in the image end up being different distances from the camera.

A more effective solution is to craft an elongated guide rail of adequate length on your own. A manual tile cutter makes a great basis for this do-it-yourself project. Any hardware store will carry one, or you may even have one collecting dust in your basement. You'll find models ranging in length anywhere from 40cm to 60cm, but all of them have some basic traits in common: a carriage made of aluminum that travels perfectly straight on two metal rods. These elements are exactly what we need.

The conversion is relatively simple and requires only a couple of tools. In general steps, the process involves first removing the tile cutter's main lever, which is used to score and break the tiles, and then modifying the carriage in order to be able to attach a focusing rail and a ball head mount to it. Aside from the tile cutter, you'll need a quarter-inch screw with a length of 20mm and a washer with a diameter of 25mm. In my example, a focusing rail is used, but you can also dispense with this device and attach the ball mount head

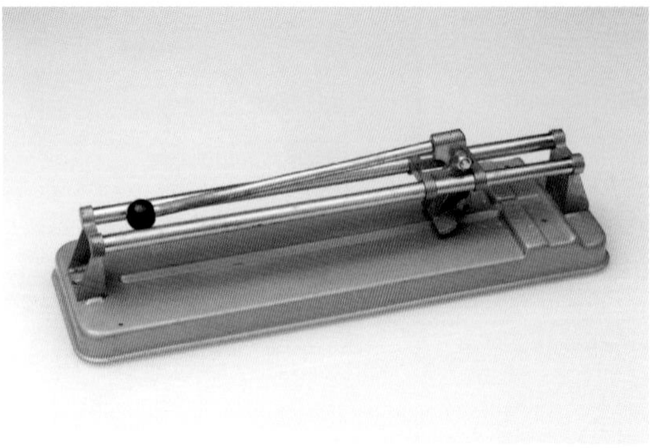

The foundation of this project is a simple tile cutter, readily available in any hardware store. The one I adapted had been stored unused in my basement since our last renovation project.

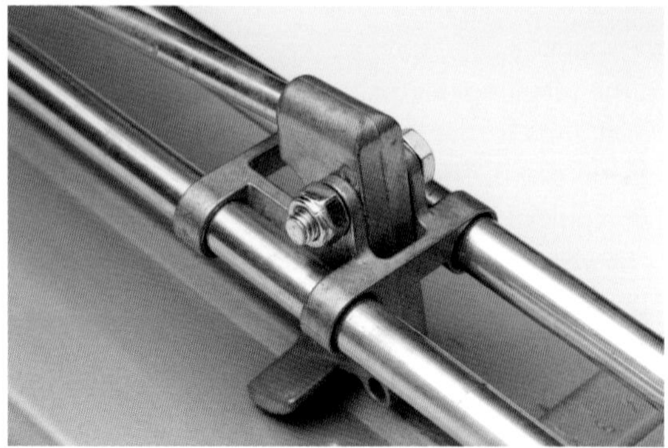

The first step is to remove the lever from the device, because it has no use for our purposes. Simply detach the arm after removing the screw.

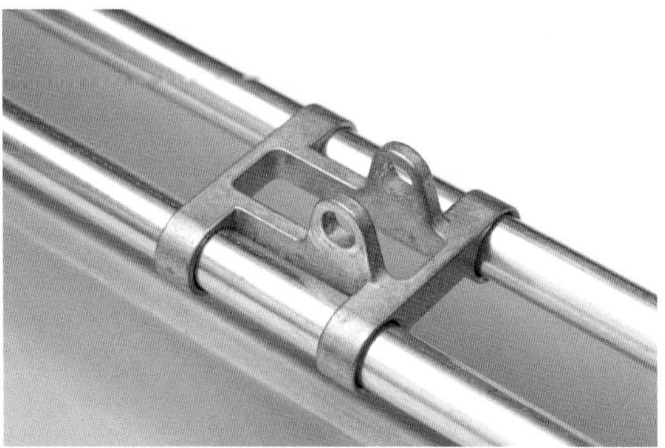

The carriage runs on two metal rods. For smoother movement, you can polish the rails with steel wool (00 or 000).

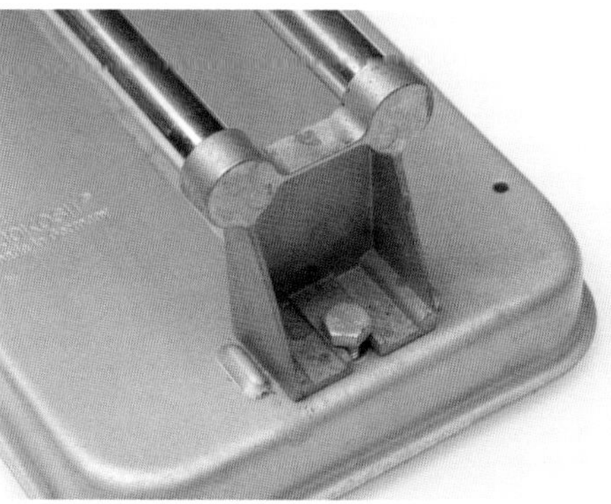

One of the two lateral supports needs to be removed so that the carriage can be slid off the rails entirely

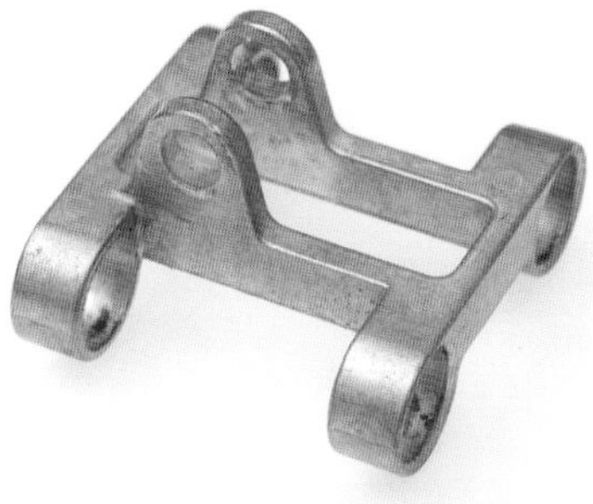

Next, the flanges with holes in them that used to support the lever construction need to be sawed off using a hacksaw. This step is best done with the carriage secured in a vise.

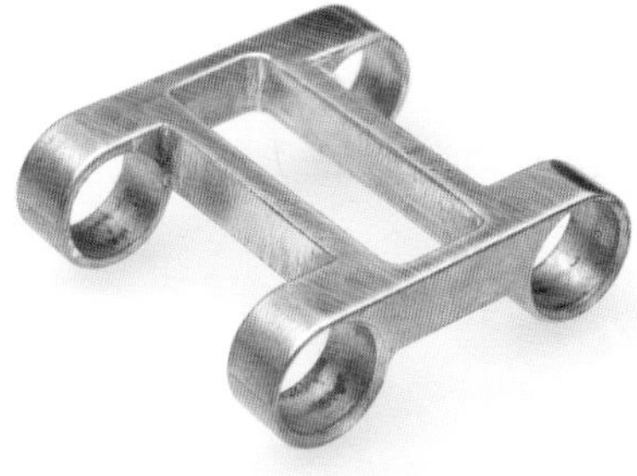

The saw marks should then be filed, sanded, and deburred to produce a smooth surface. You can also polish the inside of the bores on which the carriage slides.

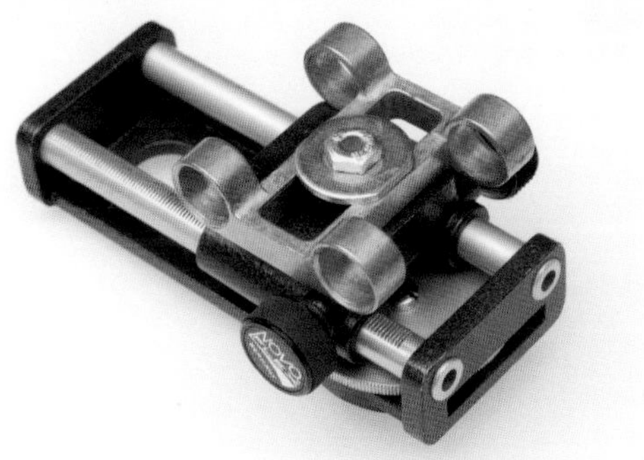

Now the carriage can be fastened to a focusing rail using a quarter-inch screw and the appropriate washer

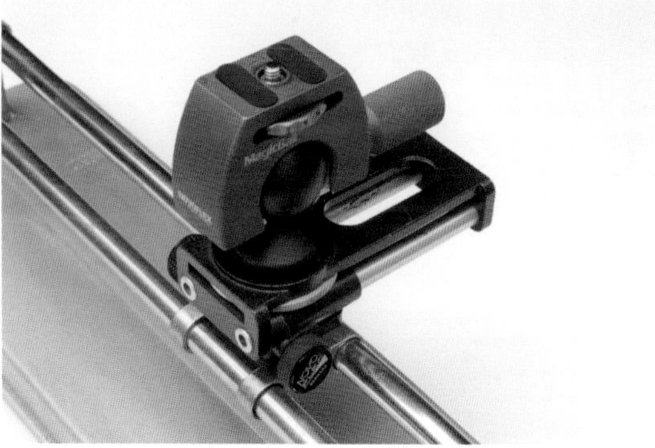

A ball head mount from a photography shop completes the conversion of a tile cutter to a homemade linear guide and makes it possible to tilt the camera as needed. You can also decide to do without the focusing rail and mount the ball head directly to the carriage.

directly to the carriage on the rails, which will give your camera a slightly lower perspective.

This setup allows you to move your camera laterally for a greater distance than would be possible using a standard macro focusing rail. Shifting the camera 360mm, for example, at a magnification of 1:1, would allow for a panorama that was 16 times as wide as an APS-C sensor. For a camera with a resolution of 12 megapixels, in other words, the panorama would be 48,000 pixels wide. Because the carriage of a tile cutter has a small degree of play on the rails, it's wise to stop down the aperture as much as possible to keep the depth of field relatively large.

View online auction websites if you're looking for a readymade option that offers even more accuracy and precision. Searching for the term "linear guide" will turn up a number of options including precision linear guide rails, trapezoidal spindles, and ball-bearing slides that are typically used for CNC applications. These devices will render any remaining concerns about precision moot, and provide the level of control needed for extreme macro shots and focus stacking projects.

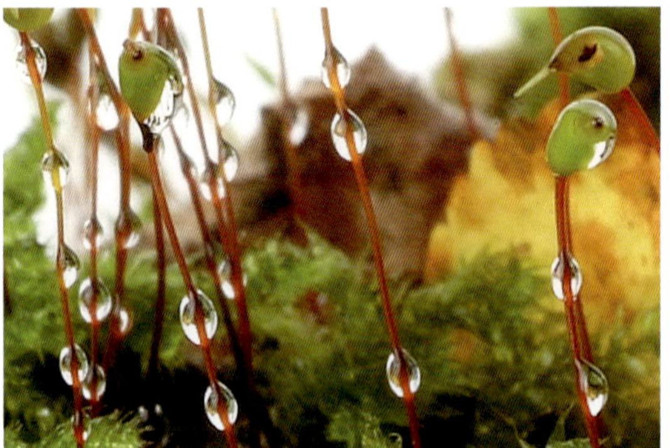
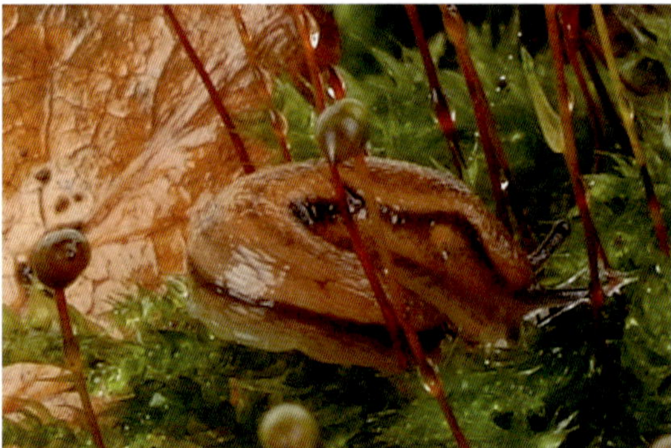

Try to find where these details are located within the macro panorama below

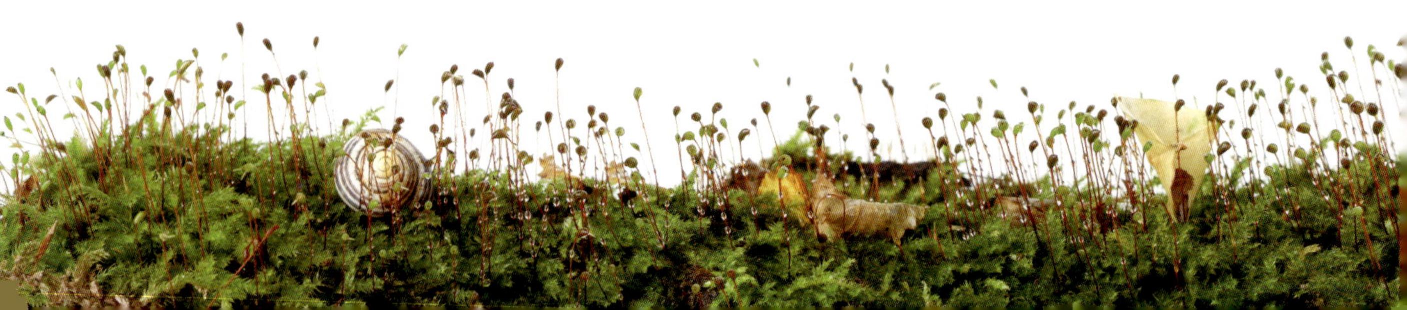

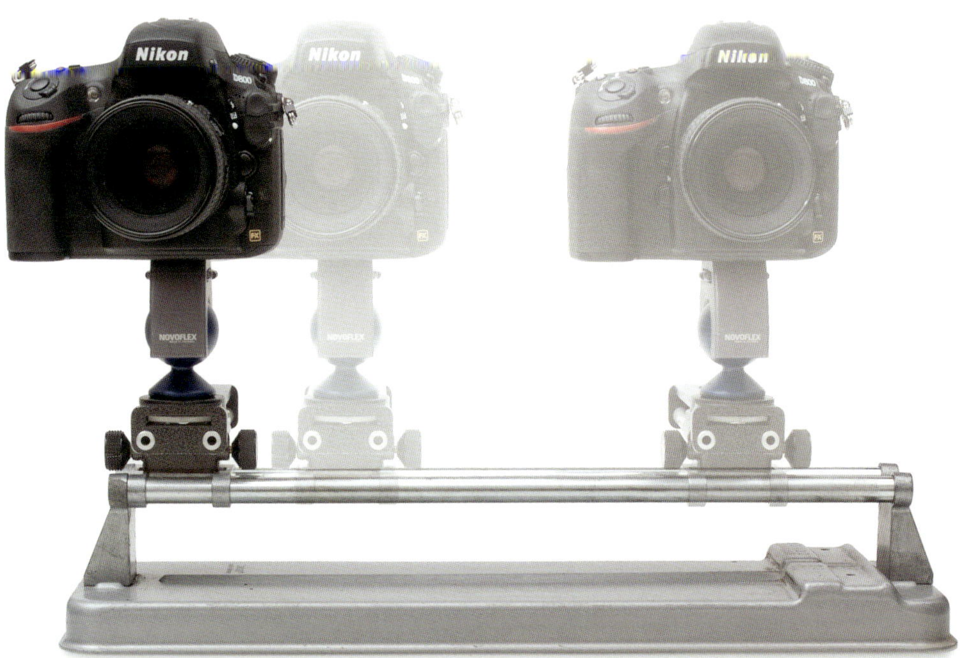

A tile cutter converted into a linear guide rail, offering approximately 36mm of movement. The broad baseplate also makes the device relatively secure.

Below: Moss-covered branch. The full image is 19,160 x 3,093 pixels, or approximately 60 megapixels. The light for the scene was produced by two 400 Ws studio flash units, one at full power and the other at half— each equipped with a softbox. And a Fuji S5 Pro with a resolution of 12 megapixels recorded the shots. The component images were blended into a panorama using Photoshop's Photomerge function.
Macro panorama comprising 13 component images, each at f/29, 1/200 s, ISO 100, 60mm

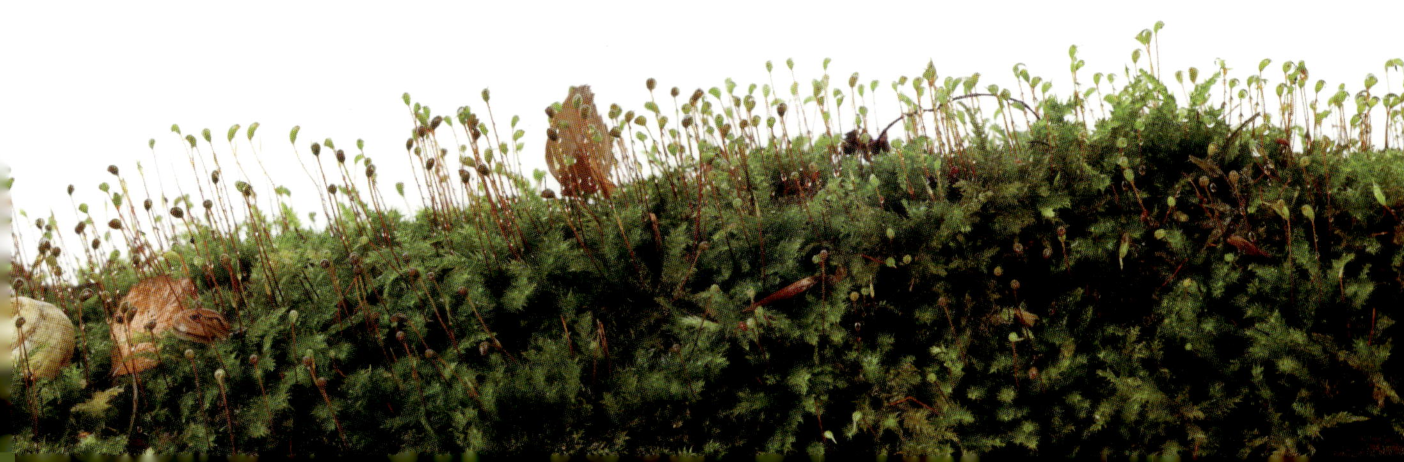

Beanbag Camera Stands

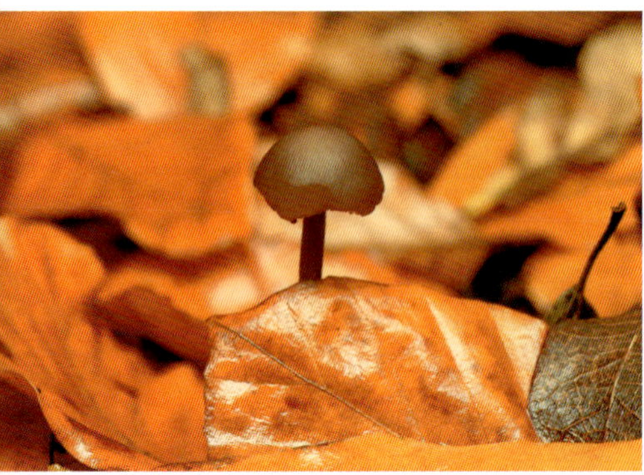

Tripods are often too tall for capturing up-close images of subjects at ground level, such as this small mushroom popping through autumn leaves. Beanbags come in handy for just such situations.
f/9.5, 1/60 s, ISO 200, 50mm

Shooting at ground level is sometimes difficult when using a tripod because they don't always allow for ultralow shooting perspectives. Beanbag camera stands insert themselves nicely into these situations. They dampen vibrations very well, and they protect the underside of the camera and lens from potential damages.

To assemble a beanbag that is 20cm by 16cm, you need two leather scraps that are 22cm by 18cm, a strong 16cm zipper, and potentially a needle for a sewing machine capable of sewing with leather, depending on the toughness of the material. First, sew the zipper along the shorter dimension of the pieces of leather. The seam should be 1cm from the edge, and the zipper should be sewn into the inside (or the unfinished) side of the leather pieces. Now position the two pieces of leather so that the finished sides are against one another, and sew the other three sides of the rectangle closed, again 1cm from the edges. Now you have a sack. Next, turn the sack inside out and fill it up with dried beans, lentils, or Styrofoam beads. I recommend treating the leather with a conditioning cream or spray to make it more resistant to moisture.

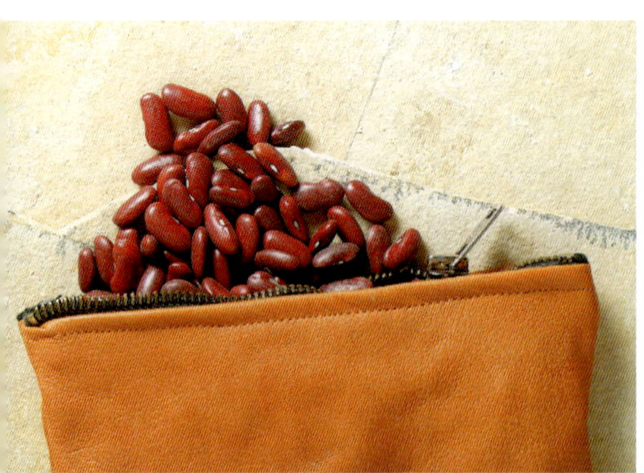

A beanbag can be filled with any normal dried bean. If weight needs to be kept to a minimum, you can also use small Styrofoam beads.

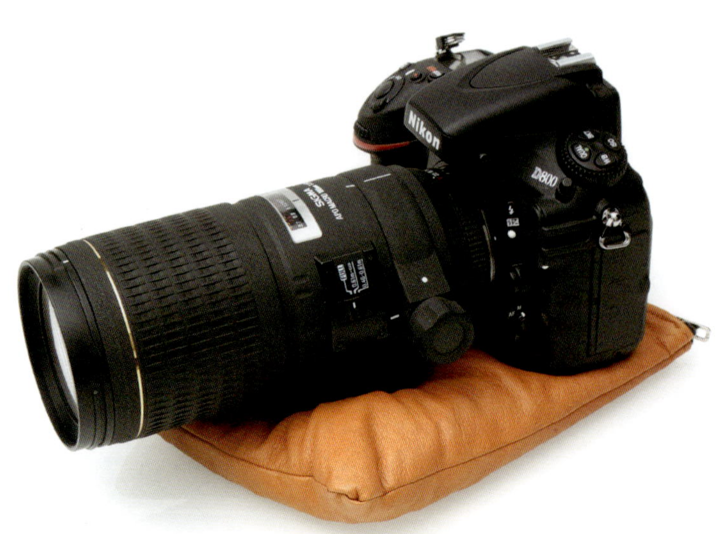

System Flash Reflectors

Making a reflector for a system flash unit is a quick project. Start with a rectangular piece of cardstock trimmed to the dimensions shown in the illustration below. Then use the dull side of a knife to score along the dotted lines to make folding easier. Use a wide rubber band to affix the reflector to your flash, and—finished! With the reflector attached, the light from the flash strikes a larger surface, resulting in softer light that can better be targeted at your subject by angling the flash head. Use a gold, silver, or colored piece of cardstock if you wish to create light of a specific color.

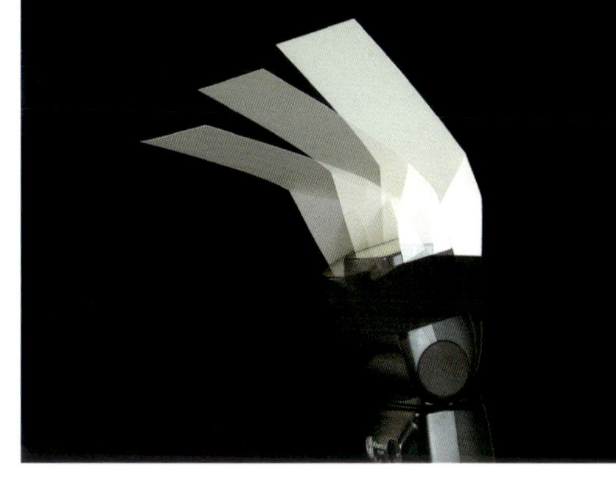

The cardboard reflector pivots with the flash head, enabling soft light from above (even with short focal lengths and tiny shooting distances)

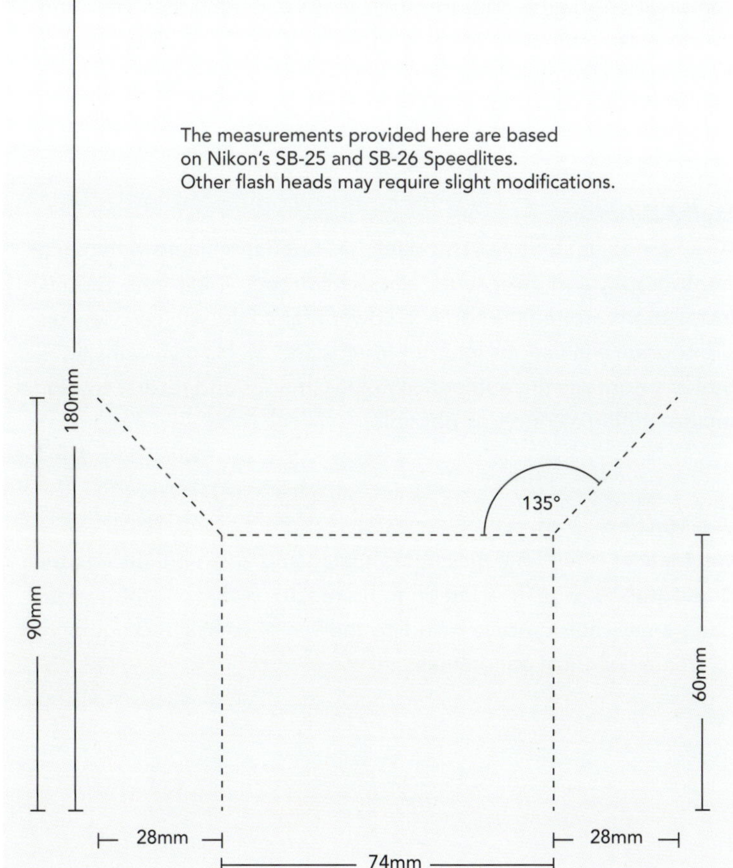

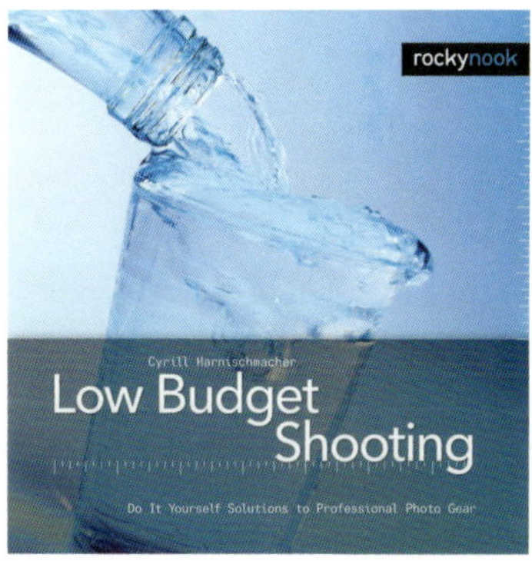

You can find additional projects with step-by-step instructions in my book Low Budget Shooting: Do It Yourself Solutions to Professional Photo Gear *available as an e-book from Rocky Nook: www.rockynook.com*

Acknowledgments

Thanks once again to all of the guest authors for their contributions, and to everyone else who made this book possible. First and foremost, thanks to my family who patiently put up with me and who also, from time to time, served as subjects and models for example photos. I'm also grateful to the Botanical Gardens of Tübingen and to the Wilhelma in Stuttgart, where a number of the photos in this book were taken.

dpunkt.verlag

Based in Heidelberg, Germany, dpunkt.verlag publishes trade books for creative photographers and professional image editors. Its catalog features a wealth of resources about technology, techniques, and composition so ambitious photographers can hone their craft and take better pictures. In addition to the technical side of photography, their books also offer lessons on how to find subjects, where to look for inspiration, and how to see the world with a photographer's eye.

www.dpunkt.de

Stefan Dittmann

As an autodidact, Stefan Dittmann has been fascinated with macro photography and microscopy since childhood. Aside from various installations around his home in Lower Franconia, you can view his photography in various Internet forums and on his own website. Stefan prioritizes the authenticity of his images and resorts to digital image editing as rarely as possible.

www.dittmann4.de

Jan Metzler

Jan Metzler is full-time master craftsman and an ambitious amateur photographer who, in addition to his macro work, concentrates on panoramic photography, including the use of specialized equipment to create spherical panoramas.

www.focus-stacking.de

Hans Christian Steeg

From an early age, nature photography has fascinated Hans Christian Steeg—macro photography in particular. Hans Christian is a physicist who works in electronics development for a company that supplies the auto industry with equipment. His work background complements his interest in specialized branches of macro photography, including, for example, high-speed photography, which he discusses in this book.

www.natur-foto-technik.de

Bernd Schloemer

For many years, street photography has been a primary fascination for Bernd Schloemer. His Colognies project represents his interpretation of this genre. He aims to make viewers both smile at and reflect on his work. Aside from his work as a photographer, he works as a SAP consultant.

www.colognies.de

Botanical Gardens of the University of Tübingen

Information about the Botanical Gardens of Tübingen, including its current program of events, hours of operation, and more can be found at:

www.uni-tuebingen.de/einrichtungen/
zentrale-einrichtungen/botanischer-garten.html

Wilhelma

Aside from information useful for planning a visit—including Wilhelma's history, hours, and programming—you can also read about conservation efforts, individual animal and plant species, and much more at the garden's website:

www.wilhelma.de

On my personal websites, you'll find information about additional publications and the flash2softbox adapter that I developed.

www.lowbudgetshooting.de | www.flash2softbox.de

Index

E

F

G

H

I